Contents

Introduction	4

Discover	6
Top 20	12
Itineraries	22
London Today	30
Eating	40
Drinking	54
Shopping	62

Explore	70
Getting Started	72
South Bank & Bankside	78
Westminster & St James's	100
South Kensington & Chelsea	122
Oxford Street, Marylebone & Mayfair	140
Soho & Leicester Square	162
Covent Garden & the Strand	178
Bloomsbury & King's Cross	192
The City	210
North London	238
East London	254
South London	278
West London	294

Experience	306
Events	308
Film	320
LGBT	328
Nightlife	336
Performing Arts	352

Understand	372
History	374
Architecture	386

Plan	394
Accommodation	396
Getting Around	404
Resources A-Z	410
Further Reference	419
Index	422

Introduction

'It is difficult to speak adequately or justly of London,' wrote Henry James in the 1880s, when the British capital was the most populous and powerful city in the world. 'It is not a pleasant place; it is not agreeable, or cheerful, or easy, or exempt from reproach. It is only magnificent.'

Much has changed since then, but this city's scale and multiplicity still defy description. Despite the collapse of the empire that it once governed, London remains one of only a handful of truly global cities, with more than 300 languages spoken by its nine million inhabitants. Every year, 20 million visitors come to see streets and landmarks dating from Roman times to the present day that have survived fires, bombs, town planners and property developers. And, increasingly, they're being tempted beyond London's bustling core to explore the city's ever-more vibrant suburbs.

Londoners love to complain about the Tube, the traffic and (yes) the tourists, but we know there's nowhere else quite like our city. With its buzzing street life, its hives of government and finance, its world-famous museums and increasingly world-class restaurants, its distinctive neighbourhoods and inimitable pubs, the Big Smoke is so vast, diverse and fast-changing that even long-term residents will never manage to see or do all that it offers. So, whether you're here for a day or a lifetime, let this book guide you to the best of our limitless city.

London

timeout.com / london

302

237

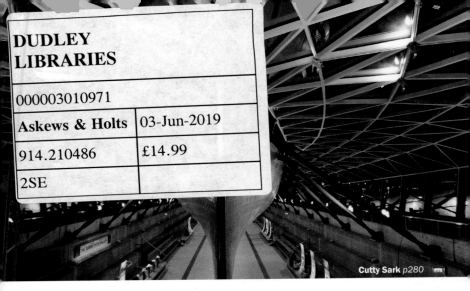

Cutty Sark *p280*

ABOUT THE GUIDE

This is one of a series of Time Out guidebooks to cities across the globe. Written by local experts, our guides are thoroughly researched and meticulously updated. They aim to be inspiring, irreverent, well-informed and trustworthy.

Time Out London is divided into five sections: Discover, Explore, Experience, Understand and Plan.

Discover introduces the city and provides inspiration for your visit.

Explore is the main sightseeing section of the guide and includes detailed listings and reviews for sights and museums; restaurants ❿; pubs and bars ❿; and shops ❿, all organised by area with corresponding street maps for the key areas. To help navigation, each area of London has been assigned its own colour.

Experience covers the cultural life of the city in depth, including festivals, film, LGBT, music, nightlife, theatre and more.

Understand provides in-depth background information that places London in its historical and architectural context.

Plan offers practical visitor information, including accommodation options and details of public transport.

Hearts

We use hearts ❤ to pick out venues, sights and experiences in the city that we particularly recommend. The very best of these are featured in the Top 20 (*see p12*) and receive extended coverage in the guide.

Maps

A detachable fold-out map can be found on the inside back cover. There are also two overview maps (Greater London on *pp8-9*; Central London by area on *pp10-11)* and individual street maps for each of the key areas of the city. The venues featured in the guide have been given a grid reference so that you can find them easily on the maps and on the ground.

Prices

All our **restaurant listings** are marked with a pound symbol category from budget to blow-out (£-££££), indicating the price you should expect to pay for an average three-course meal for two (or the equivalent in a café or sharing plates venue) with drinks and service: £ = under £60; ££ = £60-£100; £££ = £100-£140; ££££ = over £140.

A similar system is used in our **Accommodation** chapter based on the hotel's standard prices for one night in a double room: **Budget** = under £130; **Moderate** = £130-£250; **Expensive** = £250-£350; **Luxury** = over £350.

Discover

Top 20	12
Itineraries	22
London Today	30
Eating	40
Drinking	54
Shopping	62

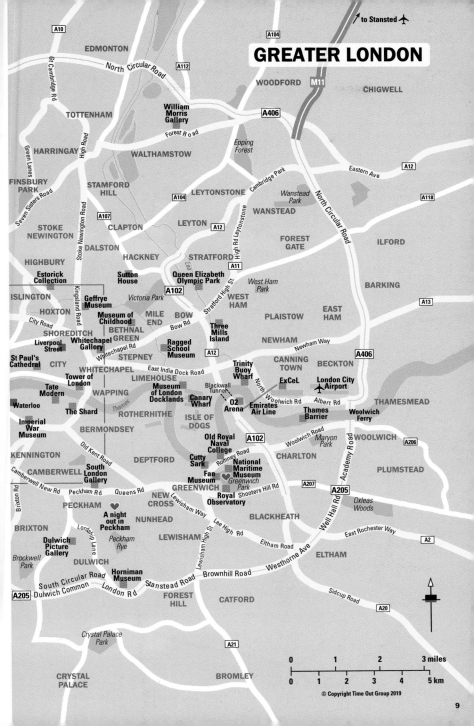

GREATER LONDON

↗ to Stansted ✈

A10
EDMONTON
North Circular Road
A112
A104
WOODFORD M11 CHIGWELL

Gt. Cambridge Rd
TOTTENHAM
William
Morris
Gallery
A406
Forest Road
Epping
Forest
HARRINGAY
High Road
WALTHAMSTOW
Cambridge Park
Eastern Ave A12
FINSBURY
PARK
Green Lanes
STAMFORD
HILL
A104
LEYTONSTONE
Wanstead
Park
A118
Seven Sisters Road
A107
CLAPTON
LEYTON
A12
WANSTEAD
High Rd Leytonstone
FOREST
GATE
ILFORD
STOKE
NEWINGTON
Stoke Newington Road
DALSTON
HACKNEY
STRATFORD
A11
West Ham
Park
BARKING
A13
HIGHBURY
Estorick
Collection
Sutton
House
Queen Elizabeth
Olympic Park
Stratford High St
WEST
HAM
ISLINGTON
Geffrye
Museum
Kingsland Road
Victoria Park
A102
PLAISTOW
EAST
HAM
HOXTON
Museum of
Childhood
MILE
END
BOW
NEWHAM
Newham Way
City Road
SHOREDITCH
BETHNAL
GREEN
Bow Rd
Three
Mills
Island
A406
Liverpool
Street
Whitechapel
Gallery
Ragged
School
Museum
A12
CANNING
TOWN
BECKTON
St Paul's
Cathedral
CITY
Whitechapel Rd
STEPNEY
WHITECHAPEL
East India Dock Road
Trinity
Buoy
Wharf
ExCeL
London City
Airport
Tower of
London
LIMEHOUSE
Museum
of London
Docklands
Blackwall
Tunnel
THAMESMEAD
Tate
Modern
WAPPING
Canary
Wharf
O2
Arena
Emirates
Air Line
Woolwich Rd
Albert Rd
Thames
Barrier
Woolwich
Ferry
Waterloo
Thames
ROTHERHITHE
ISLE OF
DOGS
Imperial
War
Museum
The Shard
BERMONDSEY
Old Kent Road
Old Royal
Naval
College
A102
Woolwich Road
Maryon
Park
WOOLWICH
A206
KENNINGTON
DEPTFORD
Cutty
Sark
Romney Road
National
Maritime
Museum
CHARLTON
Academy Road
PLUMSTEAD
CAMBERWELL
South
London
Gallery
Fan
Museum
Greenwich
Park
Camberwell New Rd
Peckham Rd
Queens Rd
GREENWICH
Royal
Observatory
Shooters Hill Rd
A207
A205
Oxleas
Woods
Brixton Rd
NEW
CROSS
Lewisham Way
East Rochester Way
A2
PECKHAM
A night
out in
Peckham
NUNHEAD
Lordship Lane
LEWISHAM
Lee High Rd
BLACKHEATH
Well Hall Rd
BRIXTON
Dulwich
Picture
Gallery
Peckham
Rye
Lewisham High St
Eltham Road
Westhorne Ave
ELTHAM
Brockwell
Park
DULWICH
Horniman
Museum
Brownhill Road
A205
Dulwich Common
South Circular Road
London Rd
Stanstead Road
FOREST
HILL
CATFORD
Sidcup Road
A20
Crystal Palace
Park
A21
CRYSTAL
PALACE
BROMLEY

0   1   2   3 miles
0   1   2   3   4   5 km

© Copyright Time Out Group 2019

9

SOUTH BANK & BANKSIDE
pp78-99

WESTMINSTER & ST JAMES'S
pp100-121

SOUTH KENSINGTON & CHELSEA
pp122-139

OXFORD STREET, MARYLEBONE & MAYFAIR
pp140-161

SOHO & LEICESTER SQUARE
pp162-177

COVENT GARDEN & THE STRAND
pp178-191

BLOOMSBURY & KING'S CROSS
pp192-209

THE CITY
pp210-237

NORTH LONDON
pp238-253

EAST LONDON
pp254-277

SOUTH LONDON
pp278-293

WEST LONDON
pp294-305

Adelaide Road

NORTH LONDON

Primrose Hill

PRIMROSE HILL

Camden Road
Camden
Camden Rd
Camden College Street
Camden High Street
St Pancras Way
Royal College St

St John's Wood

ZSL London Zoo

Regent's Canal

Mornington Crescent

SOMERS TOWN

Eversholt Street

Wellington Road

Prince Albert Road

Regent's Park

Albany Street

Hampstead Road

Euston

ST JOHN'S WOOD

Lord's Cricket Ground

St John's Wood Road

Park Road

Queen Mary's Gardens

Regent's Park

Euston Road
Euston Square
Warren Street
Gower St
Gt Portland Street

Edgware Road

Marylebone

Baker Street

Portland Place

Goodge Street
Tottenham Court Road

FITZROVIA

Edgware Rd

Marylebone Road

PADDINGTON

Paddington

Praed Street

Edgware Road

Sussex Gardens

Wigmore Street

Marble Arch

Oxford Street

Bond St

Regent Street

Oxford Circus

♥ Liberty

Leicester Sq

SOHO

Lancaster Gate

Bayswater Road

Marble Arch

Park Lane

OXFORD STREET, MARYLEBONE & MAYFAIR

Piccadilly Cir

Haymarket

Piccadilly

Pall Mall

Kensington Palace

Kensington Gardens

The Round Pond

The Long Water

Hyde Park

The Serpentine

Green Park

Green Park

St James's Park

WESTMINSTER & ST JAMES'S

Wellington Arch

Buckingham Palace

St James's Park

Hyde Park Corner

Knightsbridge

Brompton Road

KNIGHTSBRIDGE

Knightsbridge

Harrods

Belgrave Sq

Buckingham Palace Gardens

Grosvenor Pl

Buckingham Palace Road

Victoria St

Victoria

Westminster Cathedral

Kensington Road

KENSINGTON

High Street Kensington

WEST LONDON

Gloucester Road

Science Museum

Natural History Museum

Victoria & Albert Museum

Pont St

Sloane Street

BELGRAVIA

Eaton Sq

Vauxhall Bridge Rd

Belgrave Road

Cromwell Road

Gloucester Road

South Kensington

BROMPTON

Sloane Square

Pimlico

Earl's Court

EARL'S COURT

Old Brompton Rd

SOUTH KENSINGTON & CHELSEA

King's Road

Royal Hospital Rd

Chelsea Bridge Rd

PIMLICO

Grosvenor Road

WEST BROMPTON

Redcliffe Gdns

Fulham Road

Oakley Rd

Chelsea Physic Garden

Chelsea Embankment

Chelsea Bridge

Finborough Road

Edith Rd

Cheyne Walk

Albert Bridge

Thames

Nine Elms Lane

Brompton Cemetery

FULHAM

Fulham Broadway

BATTERSEA

Battersea Park

Queenstown Rd

NINE ELMS

Top 20

From street food to historic sights, we count down the capital's finest

01 Victoria & Albert Museum
02 Street food
03 Houses of Parliament
04 The Shard
05 British Museum
06 Shakespeare's Globe
07 St Paul's Cathedral
08 Afternoon tea
09 National Theatre
10 Tower of London
11 Notting Hill Carnival
12 Royal Botanic Gardens, Kew
13 Westminster Abbey
14 Maritime Greenwich
15 Redchurch Street
16 Tate Britain
17 Liberty
18 St James's Park
19 A night out in Peckham
20 London Transport Museum

01

Victoria & Albert Museum *p128*

Stroll into the V&A's main entrance – that grand hall with its dramatic glass chandelier – and the scale of this museum of art and design, with its combination of stately historical context and cutting-edge modern design, is already apparent. The nearby Science Museum (*see p127*) and Natural History Museum (*see p126*) are fabulous too – but the V&A is unforgettable.

02

Street food *p48*

You can barely swing a tote bag without hitting an artisanal street food stall or provenance-first farmers' market in London these days. They're everywhere, which is great news for foodies on a budget. Take your pick from fish tacos to tea-brined chicken strips to Kim-Kardashian-inspired koftas.

03

Houses of Parliament *p107*

The Palace of Westminster is characterised by neo-Gothic buttresses, towers and arches. It contains 1,000 rooms, 11 courtyards, eight bars and six restaurants, for use by staff, MPs, lords and their guests. Members of the public are welcome too. Book a tour to get a sense of how Parliament functions. You can even have afternoon tea at the end of your tour in a room beside the Thames.

04

The Shard *p94*

In the last decade, skyscrapers have been sprouting beanstalk-like all over the capital (*see p233*). Some have striking architecture (the Gherkin); some have great public spaces (Sky Garden) and most offer expansive views, but the Shard is the undisputed kingpin: it's so tall you almost feel you're on a different plane to the ant city below.

05

British Museum *p198*

This is one of the world's greatest museums, a compendium of key artefacts from most of the significant cultures of the world, from Egyptian mummies and the Rosetta Stone to monumental Mesopotamian sculpture and even an Easter Island head. Entry is free, so you can head back as often as you wish.

06

Shakespeare's Globe *p363*

London's West End is a powerhouse of international theatre, but the best bargain is undoubtedly seeing one of Shakespeare's plays authentically staged at the Globe. It costs only £5 if you're prepared to stand as a 'groundling'. If you can't get a ticket, then visit the exhibition and tour the reconstructed theatre instead (*see p88*).

07

St Paul's Cathedral *p224*

As architectural masterpieces go, St Paul's is at the frou-frou end of things, with its frothy Baroque exterior. But the grandeur of the interior is quite breathtaking – and no less so for Sir Christopher Wren's audacity in giving the authorities precisely the cathedral they didn't want.

08

Afternoon tea *p45*

Rolling up to a grand hotel for a meal that consists largely of cake is one of our most indulgent British traditions. Whether you're looking for something outlandish, or the kind of spread that wouldn't be out of place in Buckingham Palace, London has a tea table with your name on it.

09

National Theatre *p360*

The National Theatre remains the country's leading drama showcase, mixing Shakespeare and the classics with exciting new writing and big-budget productions. Don't miss the chance to see UK theatre at its very best in a building that's a masterpiece of 20th-century architecture.

10

Tower of London *p234*

Who doesn't love a castle? The building of this one was started by William the Conqueror in 1078; since then the Tower of London has witnessed many of the key events in London's history and it's a fabulous showcase for the Crown Jewels, as well as home to the traditionally dressed 'Beefeaters' (Yeoman Warders).

11

Notting Hill Carnival *p299*

Two million people stream into Notting Hill for Europe's largest street party. Massive mobile sound systems dominate the streets with whatever bass-heavy party music is currently hip, but there's plenty of tradition from the Caribbean too: calypso music and a spectacular costumed parade.

12

Royal Botanic Gardens, Kew *p292*

Its origins reach back to 1759, when royal plant collector Queen Caroline began developing a garden. Today, the huge and lovely grounds are dotted with Victorian greenhouses, alfresco sculptures and wonderful plants.

13

Westminster Abbey *p108*

The Abbey is Gothic grandeur at its most splendid. It has hosted 16 royal weddings and every coronation since 1066, and it is the final resting place for many of the great and the good of British history. Don't miss the Queen's Diamond Jubilee Galleries and the exquisite Abbey gardens.

14

Maritime Greenwich *p282*

The grand colonnades of Wren's Old Royal Naval College draw you into historic Greenwich Park, a fine introduction to London's most expansive UNESCO World Heritage Site. It combines the National Maritime Museum, the Queen's House art gallery, the gorgeous *Cutty Sark* sailing ship and, yes, the Prime Meridian.

15

Redchurch Street *p265*

In the heart of Shoreditch, this road – once decidedly rough – is now London's most fashion-forward street, packed with beautiful shop after beautiful shop. Design-concept-shop-cum-cute-café? Here's Modern Society. Low-key, cool homewares store? There's Labour & Wait. It all makes for a great afternoon mooch.

16

Tate Britain *p113*

Since its dramatic extension opened in 2016, Tate Modern (*see p89*) has been hogging all the limelight. But, we find ourselves drawn back to the original Tate: lovely premises, blockbuster shows every bit as good as those at its bombastic younger rival and the entire chronological span of British art since 1545 to walk through. It's not so busy, either.

17

Liberty *p155*

The capital is blessed with many brilliant department stores, from gloriously gaudy Harrods (*see p135*) to trailblazing Selfridges (*see p146*), but none is lovelier or more London than Liberty. Its jumbled rooms are charmingly old-fashioned but full of cutting-edge international fashion and beauty brands.

18

St James's Park *p117*

One of the city's joys is its chain of incredibly central parks: you can walk from Kensington Gardens and Hyde Park through Green Park to St James's barely touching the tarmac. The last is our favourite. Why? It's the prettiest, with lovely lakes for waterfowl, and has a delicious view of Buckingham Palace.

19

A night out in Peckham *p342*

To experience the city's most inclusive, innovative and thriving night scene, head south on the Overground to Peckham, where some of the capital's most exciting bars, clubs and arts venues are clustered: sip Campari on the roof of a car park; eat barbecue treats in a ticket office; play retro arcade games in a bar and then dance the night away in a record shop.

20

London Transport Museum *p183*

We love the Museum of London (*see p227*), but for kids – and, more importantly, kids at heart – the thrill of climbing on and off the classic trains and buses at the Transport Museum never fades. That the museum offers a fine social history of the capital, told through its vital infrastructure, is merely a bonus.

WIMBLEDON
LAWN TENNIS
MUSEUM

EXPERIENCE
WIMBLEDON
—

Take your chance to
see The Championships'
trophies on a
Tour of Wimbledon

BOOK YOUR TICKETS
wimbledon.com/museum
020 8946 6131

Please note tours do not run during The Championships

Itineraries

Explore London's storied past in the daytime – enjoy the city's stellar present at night

ESSENTIAL WEEKEND

Budget £200-£250 per person
Getting around walking, Tube and Overground trains

▶ *Budgets include transport, meals and admission prices, but not accommodation and shopping.*

DAY 1

Trafalgar Square

Morning

Today is a whistlestop walking tour of historic London. Get to Westminster tube station and start the day in Parliament Square, a UNESCO World Heritage Site, to admire the **Houses of Parliament** (*see p107*) and **Westminster Abbey** (*see p108*). You could spend the rest of the morning on an excellent guided tour of either building, but to pack in as much as possible, saunter north along Whitehall and then on to Horse Guards Parade to watch the Household Cavalry perform the daily **Changing the Guard** ceremony at 11am. (*see p311*; it's an hour earlier on Sunday). After the ceremonials, head through the parade ground into **St James's Park** (*see p117*) to see the pelicans and admire **Buckingham Palace** (*see p114*) at the end of the lake. A stroll along the Union Jack-lined Mall will take you through Admiralty Arch to **Trafalgar Square** (*see p104*). The centre of London is an impressive sight. Far beneath Nelson on his column, the Fourth Plinth showcases large-scale contemporary art and sculpture that's always worth a look. The masterpieces of the **National Gallery** (*see p105*) – an encyclopaedia of Western art – are on the pedestrianised northern side of the square; the **National Portrait Gallery** (*see p105*) is just beyond.

Changing the Guard

Afternoon

Just behind St Martin-in-the-Fields, **Barrafina**, the **Tandoor Chop House** and **Terroirs** are all good choices for lunch (*see p185*). Rejuvenated? Great. Catch a heritage Routemaster bus (*see p76*) from the Strand to **St Paul's Cathedral** (*see p224*), Wren's architectural masterpiece in the heart of the City. Walk east, past 21th-century skyscrapers and 17th-century churches to Fenchurch Street, where, if you've booked in advance, you can zoom up to the top of the Walkie Talkie for unbeatable City views from the **Sky Garden** (*see p236*). Cross over the Thames at London Bridge for a late-afternoon snack at **Borough Market** (*see p93*), a cornucopia of produce and street food, before strolling west along the **South Bank** (*see p82*). This walk is modern London's biggest tourist cliché, but it's also great fun. En route, take in some art at **Tate Modern** (*see p89*) – it's free and open until 6pm.

Evening

Stay on the South Bank as the sun goes down. You could spend your evening enjoying a play at either the **National Theatre** (*see p360*) or **Shakespeare's Globe** (*see p363*), a film at **BFI Southbank** (*see p323*), or a concert at the **Southbank Centre** (*see p82*). And for sustenance, drink in the views from **Skylon** or the **Oxo Tower Restaurant** (for both, *see p86*).

Olivier Theatre, National Theatre

Royal Opera House

Bussey Building

DAY 2

Morning

We're not quite done with culture: are you ready for one of the world's finest museums? You betcha – arrive as close to 10am as you can to miss most of the crowds. The **British Museum** (*see p198*) is so full of treasures, you may not know where to begin: try turning left out of the middle of the covered courtyard for the extraordinary monumental antiquities, including the Parthenon Marbles. A morning will never be enough to do the museum justice, but that's all we're giving you today.

Afternoon

Wander south out of the museum to Covent Garden, where there are plenty of restaurants, bars and shops; for our picks, *see p180*. You could take a post-lunch stroll to the **Royal Opera House** (*see p184*) or the **London Transport Museum** (*see p183*), before catching the Tube to Piccadilly Circus. You could flex your credit card in the shops of Regent Street and Oxford Street (including Instagram-friendly department store **Liberty**; *see p155*), but we've got a big night planned, so stroll west to **Fortnum & Mason** to fortify yourself with an indulgent afternoon tea (*see p45*).

Evening

If you're interested in how London has been changing, it's time to introduce yourself to **Peckham** (*see p342*), and from here it shouldn't take more than 40 minutes to get there. Head to Green Park tube station for the Jubilee line east to Canada Water, then hop on the Overground for Clapham Junction getting off at Peckham Rye station. Eat dinner at **Artusi** (*see p287*); watch the sun set over the city at **Frank's Cafe** (summer only; *see p288*), before dancing the night away at the **Bussey Building** (*see p339*).

BUDGET BREAK

For the pound-conscious visitor
Budget £50-£70 per person
Getting around Tube, walking

Good news, pound-stretchers! London, although expensive in most terms, is incredibly cheap for culture. Almost all of the key museums are free to enter, only charging to see their temporary exhibitions. The British Museum, both Tates and all three South Kensington museums are just the start, with many smaller collections (including the Soane, Wallace, Grant and Horniman) also eschewing an admission price. So you can have an extremely satisfying day in London for only as much as you pay for transport and food. To ensure your transport costs are as low as possible, get an Oyster card, or use the same contactless debit/credit card for all your journeys (*see p405*).

Morning

Start at South Ken tube station, which is a short walk from one of London's – indeed, the world's – finest museums. The **Victoria & Albert Museum** (*see p128*) combines a palatial Victorian setting with collections that are a fascinating global history of art and design. Don't miss the stunning double-height Cast Courts or the Photography Gallery (opened in 2018), and we can never resist a cup of tea in the delightfully tiled Arts and Crafts style tea rooms – an affordable treat at £6-£8, including a cake. Morning effectively filled with culture, walk ten minutes north, past the Royal Albert Hall and the Albert Memorial, into **Kensington Gardens** (*see p132*), the lovelier half of expansive Hyde Park.

Victoria & Albert Museum

Albert Memorial *p124*

Afternoon

Mr Moneybags might be tempted to see **Kensington Palace** (*see p133*), but not us skinflints. Head instead to whatever's on at the **Serpentine Gallery** (*see p133*). Afterwards, grab a sandwich and a drink outside the Lido Café, then continue east towards Hyde Park Corner. Jump on the Piccadilly Line to Holborn, then change to the Central Line and get off at Liverpool Street to explore **Spitalfields** and **Brick Lane** (for both, *see p258*). Pick up a cheap snack from the **Brick Lane Beigel Bake** (*see p259*) before mingling with the hipsters on **Redchurch Street** (*see p265*) and Shoreditch High Street. If it's a Sunday continue north to **Columbia Road** to get end-of-the-day bargains at the flower market (*see p270*).

Spitalfields Market

Street performer in Chinatown

Evening

Decisions, decisions. You could stay in the East End for the evening, perhaps heading to **Dinerama** in Shoreditch for a plethora of affordable street food in a party atmosphere (*see p48*), or check out the artsy going-ons at the **Village Underground** (*see p348*). Alternatively, head back into the centre for a night out in Soho, London's go-to place for great cheap eats (*see p164* and *p167*). Take a stroll to soak up the night-time street life, but rather than bust the budget boozing, why not finish the evening with a film at the **Prince Charles** (*see p323*)? There might be a triple-bill all-nighter – after which, the Night Tube runs through Piccadilly Circus station, and the fare is still part of your capped travel for the day, even after midnight...

FAMILY DAY OUT

Keeping the kids amused
Budget £300-£400 for a family of four
Getting around Tube, walking, boat.
Allow plenty of time in your schedule for
last-minute wee stops, getting lost and
other child-rearing distractions.

Morning

The trick with many of London's greatest
attractions is getting out early – which
can be a problem if you've multiple kids
to corral, but it always pays off in reduced
crowds. Get out at Tower Hill on the
District and Circle lines and head down the
steps to the **Tower of London** (*see p234*).
There's lots to see and do here, with the
experience enhanced by the presence of
affable red-coated beefeaters (who are
resident in the Tower: you can sometimes
see their laundry hanging out to dry).
Hustle to the Crown Jewels first thing,
though. Queues build up rapidly to glide on
the travelator past Her Majesty's baubles.

Afternoon

Grab a snack before heading east on the
District Line to Mile End and then the
Central Line to Stratford for the **Queen
Elizabeth Olympic Park** (*see p276*).
Enjoy a picnic in the park, or head to the
Timber Lodge Café for lunch; it's right next
to the Tumbling Bay Playground. Older
kids might prefer the Last Drop café at
the foot of the **ArcelorMittal Orbit** (*see
p277*). After a couple of hours exploring
the park, catch the Jubilee Line to North
Greenwich, where you can pick up a

ArcelorMittal Orbit

Thames Clipper (*see p407*) back into
central London, with views of **Maritime
Greenwich** (*see p282*) and **Canary
Wharf** (*see p274*) en route. (Children
under 16 get a 50 per cent discount on
fares, and under-fives are free.) Pass under
Tower Bridge (*see p237*) and alongside
the **Shard** (*see p94*), before leaving the
boat at Bankside Pier (if you want a stroll
along the South Bank) or at Festival Pier (if
little legs are tired).

Evening

There's plenty to see along the **South
Bank**, and it's particularly magical in the
evening when the fairy lights come on. If
your luck's in, there'll be free child-focused
entertainment in the foyer of the **Royal
Festival Hall** (*see p82*); if there isn't, the
combination of crowds and entertainers
will keep the nippers happy. There are
reliable chain restaurants here too for
an early supper. Finish at the **London
Eye** (*see p84*) to enjoy the constantly
changing vistas as the sun goes down.
(Book your timeslot in advance for the
cheapest tickets.) Return to your hotel
from Waterloo station.

Thames Clipper crusies past the Tower of London

When to Visit

London by season

London doesn't really have an off-season, with interesting things going on all through the year (see *pp308-318* Events). The weather is never predictable, but nor is it particularly harsh – in winter you might even bless our polluted air, which keeps the temperature a degree or two higher than the surrounding countryside.

Spring

Our favourite time of year. This is a surprisingly green city, with blossoming cherry trees and crocuses, primroses and daffodils in the Royal Parks that ring central London. Spring weather can be mixed, but Easter holidays aside, there tend to be fewer crowds than in the summer. The Old Smoke can feel lively, pretty and far more cheerful than our fellow Brits would ever believe.

Summer

At the slightest sniff of fine weather, Londoners are boozing at pavement tables like some fantasy of the South of France. The Tube becomes a sweaty hellhole, but suck it up: this is the season of al fresco cinema, music festivals in the parks and sipping Camparis with the trendsters.

Autumn

Autumn has a good share of clear, crisp days, which often seem to fall kindly for Diwali and Bonfire Night fireworks. The kids are back at school after the summer holidays, but it is rarely unpleasantly cold, so autumn is a great time of year for busy sightseeing.

Winter

There's plenty of fun to be had in the run-up to the big C, with roaring fires in trad pubs, the giant Christmas tree arriving in Trafalgar Square from Norway and the West End illuminations going up. Just don't count on seeing any snow. Christmas Day is pretty much the only time London closes down: there's no public transport and few attractions, shops or restaurants bother to open.

Buckingham Palace

Soho Square

Bonfire Night

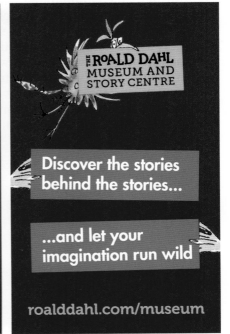

London Today

Is this global city prepared for what Brexit might bring?

What a difference a couple of years can make. In 2016, London's optimism seemed unbounded. The city's cosmopolitan outlook was perfectly in tune with our globalised era. Although widely scorned as pointless and ugly, the new skyscrapers popping up everywhere were at least a testament to the gazillions of pounds of foreign investment flowing in. Though slowed by government austerity, recovery from the late-noughties recession was underway. Most promisingly, our new mayor had defeated a divisive election campaign, promising the city genuinely affordable homes and action on air pollution and crime.

March for a second referendum on Brexit, October 2018

Fast-forward to early 2019, and the picture looks a little different. The UK's referendum on EU membership set Remain-voting London at odds with the country's Leave majority. Although the final destination is still uncertain, Brexit could have serious effects on the capital's economy. Meanwhile, Mayor Sadiq Khan is beleaguered by rising knife crime, the failure of two big infrastructure projects and slow progress on his flagship policies. And London's big, tough problems – air pollution, gentrification, social divisions and a desperate lack of public money – haven't gone away. For now, on paper, the city remains largely as it was before the shock of the Brexit vote. But most Londoners can't remember a time when the Big Smoke's future and its place in the world seemed less certain.

The Mayor of London is responsible for an annual budget of £17 billion.

The troubles of Sadiq

Back in May 2016, Labour politician Sadiq Khan become the third directly elected Mayor of London, with more personal votes than any other politician in British history. Khan was raised on a south London council estate, the son of a bus driver and his wife who had emigrated to London from Pakistan in 1968: a biography that became one of Khan's most effective (and most regularly deployed) weapons in his mayoral race against Conservative candidate Zac Goldsmith, the son of a billionaire financier.

Despite dog-whistle attacks by Goldsmith's campaign, Khan's sensible centre-left platform – more homes for low-income Londoners, stronger action on the environment, making transport more affordable, action to make London a better place for women and minorities as well as pedestrians and cyclists – seemed to offer a refreshing change from the bluster and vanity projects of his Conservative predecessor, Boris Johnson. (Khan swiftly emphasised that difference by moving to scrap an unfinished Boris folly, the proposed Garden Bridge over the Thames in central London.)

Then came 2017, an *annus horribilis* for London. As well as the horrific Grenfell Tower fire, which claimed 72 victims in one of the poorest parts of London, the capital suffered no fewer than five terrorist attacks, killing nine people and injuring more than a hundred. Four of the assaults were associated with radical Islamism; the fifth was a revenge attack by a white extremist on a north London mosque. Khan's comments from 2016 that terror threats were 'part and parcel' of living in a major city came back to haunt him.

Londoners can't remember a time when the Big Smoke's future and its place in the world seemed less certain

Crime on the rise

Next came a huge rise in knife crime, which – although also affecting large swathes of the UK – has become particularly associated with London, and specifically with young black Londoners. In February 2018, the city briefly outstripped New York's murder rate for the first time on record, and levels of knife crime hit record heights by October. For the vast majority, the chances of being caught up in an incident are still low, but with police overstretched and government spending on youth centres down by two thirds, the headlines are enough: Londoners are more genuinely scared of violent crime than they have been for years.

Not helping matters is US President Donald Trump, who has made melodramatic public remarks about blood on London hospital floors. Trump's supporters at home and in the UK have taken to calling the city 'Londonistan' and slamming its mayor, motivated at least in part by his Muslim faith. Khan has consistently spoken out against Trump too: a fairly smart move in a city that Trump avoided during his 2018 visit to the UK due to fears of massive protests. Londoners crowdfunded a giant, inflatable orange 'Baby Trump' to fly during the visit; a counter-protest with an inflatable effigy of Sadiq Khan followed a few months later, marking a pretty spectacular new low for the city's political discourse.

Londoners crowdfunded a giant, inflatable orange 'Baby Trump' to fly during the Presidential visit in 2018.

Severe delays

Inflatables aside, two years of mostly negative headlines have seen a serious downturn in Khan's once-soaring popularity. The planned pedestrianisation of Oxford Street by the end of 2018, one of the mayor's most eye-catching manifesto pledges, was unilaterally cancelled by Westminster Council after a small number of locals objected. Even more disastrously, the long-awaited Crossrail project – a new railway crossing London and slashing journey times from east to west – was postponed in late summer 2018 and is now unlikely to arrive before 2020. Nor have things been helped by a perception that the mayor has failed to do enough to tackle some of the big issues facing the city.

City Hall points to statistics showing that the percentage of affordable housing on new developments is heading up, air quality is improving and the number of music and nightlife venues (which plummeted under Khan's predecessor) has stabilised – but progress is achingly slow, and drastic changes are still a long way off. The next mayoral election in 2020 will see Khan pitted against the Conservative candidate, Shaun Bailey. Bailey has already been widely mocked as a lightweight, but he's no billionaire's son – his own working-class London background and the inevitable anti-Khan mudslinging from the *Evening Standard* newspaper (now edited, controversially, by former Conservative chancellor of the exchequer George Osborne) might make the path rocky for the incumbent. But if Khan does fail to get a new mandate, it will be his own failures, not his opponent's qualities, that are to blame.

Home truths

Housing continues to be the most serious problem. The London property boom of the

London's house prices are unaffordable for those on low or average incomes.

Most young Londoners and key workers still don't have a hope of ever buying a place in the city

early 2010s has cooled slightly – house prices and rents are rising far more slowly than they have for years, partly due to the uncertainty of Brexit – but most young Londoners and key workers still don't have a hope of ever buying a place in the city. Fed up of waiting for the political wind to change to allow them to build large-scale housing themselves, several local authorities have jumped into bed with major property developers, prompting local protests and even (in the case of Haringey borough) a council coup. Many working-class areas feel threatened by new development, and there's no shortage of examples for them to point to, of former council housing blocks mysteriously becoming swanky flats for overseas investors and buy-to-let landlords. The tone from City Hall may have changed since the days of Boris Johnson but, despite Khan's inclusive rhetoric, the gap between London's haves and have nots doesn't feel as though it's narrowed since 2016.

Cultural and leisure venues are under threat too, with government tax rises and increasing rents in gentrifying areas becoming a dangerous combination for pubs, bars, restaurants and arts venues. Councils across town have shown ambivalence towards live music and nightlife: superclub Fabric was temporarily closed in 2017, and, in 2018, Hackney, one of London's hardest-partying boroughs, introduced licensing restrictions on new venues. Khan followed the model of Amsterdam in appointing a Night Czar to encourage London to become a '24-hour city', and the Night Tube service on Fridays and Saturdays has opened up areas of London that would previously have been too remote to draw a crowd, such as Tottenham. But venue owners still complain of finding it nearly impossible to turn a profit, and a reported rise in underground raves suggests some promoters are simply ignoring the bureaucratic hurdles.

Khan has followed the model of Amsterdam in appointing a 'Night Czar' to encourage London to become a 24-hour city

Gasping for air

London is one of the worst cities in Europe when it comes to air pollution, and 'black bogeys' (a rite of passage for new Londoners) aren't the worst of it. Across the city, more than 9,000 premature deaths a year are associated with long-term exposure to polluting particles. Under Mayor Khan, the trend towards more cycle lanes has been extended and exhaust-belching buses have been moved off major high streets. The Ultra Low Emission Zone introduced in 2019 charges the most polluting vehicles to enter central London. But with outer boroughs, especially, still heavily dependent on cars, and more private-hire vehicles on the roads than ever before (Uber's licence to operate was suspended in 2017, then reinstated), the current aim of making London entirely carbon-free by 2050 seems unlikely to be achieved.

Transport for London has introduced Cycle Superhighways in an attempt to alleviate pollution.

Can't live if living is without EU?

As London struggles to get on top of crime, air pollution and a housing crisis that's starting to feel like it may never end, decisions are being tortuously made at a national and international level that will affect the city's future in ways that nobody seems to be able to predict. Over the last four decades, the UK capital transformed itself from a quaint little place on the edge of Europe to the continent's *de facto* cultural, commercial and financial capital. EU rules on freedom of movement, government relaxation of immigration restrictions and accelerating globalisation meant that a generation of young Europeans, raised speaking English as a second language, had the legal right to visit, settle and work here. And, in their millions, they did. London had always been an international city, but EU citizens made it even more outward-looking and multicultural. The city's financial, hospitality and construction

Decisions are being tortuously made at a national and international level that will affect the city's future in ways that nobody seems to be able to predict

sectors were swelled with European workers, and by the time of the census of 2011, one in ten Londoners held non-British EU citizenship.

Since the Brexit referendum in 2016, in which 52 per cent of the UK population voted to leave the EU, the mood in London has been particularly bleak. The capital had defied the national result: 60 per cent of Londoners voted to stay in the EU, with six boroughs topping 75 per cent and the Streatham constituency in south London registering the highest Remain vote in the entire country. But it seemed the majority of the country was determined to sever the capital's European ties for good. Reports of xenophobic attacks in the wake of the vote were an extra kick in the teeth for our supposedly tolerant city.

Since then, debate within the UK and negotiations in Brussels have been fierce, with Prime Minister Theresa May trying to thrash out a withdrawal agreement that will somehow deliver Brexit without jeopardising jobs, trade and security.

Ultra-Brexiteers favour a 'no-deal' exit, ignoring expert warnings of an instant economic meltdown. Meanwhile, diehard Remainers from a variety of political parties (including London mayor Sadiq Khan, with his slogan 'London is Open') have demanded a second referendum with the option to keep the UK in the EU. In October 2018, an estimated 700,000 people marched through London to back such a 'people's vote', the second-biggest protest the city had ever seen. But May (who supported Remain in 2016) has continued to work towards delivering Brexit, her options severely limited by the raging internal politics of her Conservative party.

The UK's withdrawal agreement was signed off by EU leaders in November 2018, but as this guide went to press, the political wranglings looked set to continue right up to the last minute. As the pundits offer competing visions of how events could unfold, and the nation slumps

In October 2018, an estimated 700,000 people marched through London to call for a second referendum on Brexit.

further into anger, division and frustration with the whole process, the clock continues to tick down towards 29 March 2019, when the UK is set to leave the EU... with or without a deal.

The impact on London over the next decade could be enormous, with a surprise downward trend in population growth in 2017 perhaps acting as the first rumbling of a pretty serious decline. While the sense of history-in-the-making does give city life a certain frisson, these are anxious times for the cosmopolitan, outward-looking capital. But if London could survive Boudicca, the Black Death and the Blitz, it can surely weather Brexit.

London survived Boudicca, the Black Death and the Blitz; it can surely weather Brexit

A ray of hope

London's fabled resilience is one reason to be cheerful. But the main cause for optimism is the fact that the city remains extraordinarily, world-beatingly vibrant. It houses pretty much all of the UK's (and many of the planet's) greatest cultural institutions. It's an essential stop for the biggest musical artists – that is, the ones that don't already live here. Its art exhibitions are bigger, better and more Instagrammable than ever before. Its streets are an incredible mixture of history and innovation, with new squares and buildings opening up all the time in previously industrial areas like King's Cross. The diversity and quality of its food scene, with 73 Michelin stars ranking it above any city but Tokyo, Paris and Osaka, is unprecedented. It's greener and cleaner than New York; friendlier than Paris; more convenient than Los Angeles; more laidback than Tokyo. Like every city, London has its problems – and any Londoner (especially black cab drivers) will be more than happy to vent about them. But grumble as we might, you'll never get us to admit that this is anything but the greatest city in the world.

In the know
Illuminated River

The Thames is the setting for the huge light installation 'Illuminated River', designed by artist Leo Villareal and architects Lifschutz Davidson Sandilands. The project will light up 15 bridges in the capital, starting with London Bridge, Southwark Bridge, Cannon Street Railway Bridge and Millennium Bridge in 2019.

BAG YOURSELF
A BARGAIN

Whether it's food, drink, theatre or
events, we've got exclusive offers
and the best tickets in town.

Eating

Welcome the world on to your plate

'No longer can it be said that London is only a great city between meals,' wrote the *New York Times* in late 2018. 'What was once a sallow and predictable dining experience is now salubrious and full of surprises, befitting a metropolis of such diversity and ingenuity.' It's been a hell of a long time since 'sallow' and 'predictable' were adjectives accurately applied to London eating – but the *Times* got one thing right: London's restaurant scene is an absolute banger. It's hard to think of a city, save perhaps Tokyo or LA, that surpasses it for sheer thrill factor, as well as cosmopolitan breadth. From gutsy British cuisine to Korean-infused haute-junk, cutting-edge African and modern European fare (plus everything else in-between), you'll find a superlative form of almost every food within zones 1 and 2. It's time to loosen that belt and empty your wallet. Happy eating.

Modern British

For at least a decade we banged on about it – then, in 2009, Michelin caught on and gave **St John** (*see p216*) a star. This modest whitewashed restaurant effectively reinvented British food. The idea was simple: take out-of-favour but flavour-packed cuts of meat and bits of animal (bone marrow, pig's trotters, hearts) and offer them in simple preparations that let the unique qualities of the ingredients shine – this was to become known as 'nose-to-tail' eating. From that moment on, every new restaurant in London seemed to claim its 'modern British' culinary heritage, and indeed chefs from St John cropped up across London: the **Anchor & Hope** (*see p87*) and **Rochelle Canteen** (*see p266*) are notable. In truth, St John had struck upon a couple of key themes: localism (sourcing superb ingredients from as close to home as possible, rather than flying them in from across the globe) and the newly

The Barbary

casual gourmet diner, who was willing to pay for fine food but didn't relish the flim-flam of Mayfair haute cuisine.

Of course, this stripped-back, blackboard menu approach doesn't disguise the fact that this is serious cooking, often for top dollar. And things have become even more elaborate at meticulous, tasting-menu-led trendsetters like Isaac Hale's **Clove Club** (*see p264*) and James Lowe's **Lyle's** (*see p266*) in Shoreditch. That said, there's still plenty of room in town for what visitors might consider 'British' without the 'modern' appendage: you might fancy fish and chips at **Poppies** (*see p260*) or **Hook** (*see p243*), for instance, or to indulge in the post-colonial excess of a leisurely afternoon tea (*see p45*). There's also a handful of historic places serving what was, for a century, the staple diet of the London working man: eels, pie and mash. **M Manze** (*see p97*) is our pick because it's relatively central, has classic utilitarian tiled premises and continues to serve eels. A word of advice, though: unless you've sturdy Cockney genes, always avoid jellied in favour of stewed.

The world in one city

The reinvention of British cooking has long since slid off the cutting edge to be superseded by wave after wave of global food. Eastern Mediterranean cuisine has been riding high for the last few years, pioneered by **Ottolenghi** (*see p250*), and exemplified by the likes of **The Barbary** (*see p185*) and **Palomar** (*see p176*). **Moro** (and its little sibling, **Morito**; *see p219* for both) brought a fusion of Spanish and North African cooking to grateful diners in the late nineties. A few years later came Peruvian, with **Ceviche Soho** (*see p164*) still a top place to dine. Noodles had their moment: fast, casual, delicious bowls of goodness can be enjoyed at **Kanada-ya** (*see p186*) or **Shoryu Ramen** (*see p156*). Nordic cuisine and influences were everywhere for a while and remain very

❤ **Best of British**

Lyle's *p266*
Beautiful, seasonal small plates in a former tea factory.

M Manze *p97*
Proletarian cuisine, the way the Victorians knew it: pie or eels, mash, parsley sauce. Proper.

Regency Café *p112*
Fry-up in a post-war art deco caff – save it for when your hangover really deserves one.

St John *p216*
The mod Brit pioneer: 'nose-to-tail' ingredients, in simple and excellent combinations.

❤ **Best walk-in restaurants**

10 Greek Street *p164*
Modern British with Mediterranean touches – book at lunch if you will, or prepare to queue for dinner.

The Barbary *p185*
Entertainingly excellent Middle Eastern grub.

Franco Manca *p290*
A Neapolitan pizza pioneer in Brixton Market.

Hoppers *p164*
Sri Lankan street food.

Padella *p92*
Excellent Italian at Borough Market.

Som Saa *p260*
Thai the way it should be.

present: fine exponents include the very different **Snaps & Rye** (*see p300*).

This is hardly a new phenomenon. You might choose to trace it back to curry's popularity in London following mass immigration from Bangladesh in the 1970s – with chicken tikka masala hailed as Britain's national dish by the 2000s. But before that there was Chinese (now ably represented in Chinatown by the likes of **Baiwei**, *see p176*, and **Shuang Shuang**, *p177*, and the Taiwanese **Bao**, *see p172*); Italian (check out **Bocca di Lupo**, *see p169*), and French. We could even cite the coffeehouses that flooded London from the Ottoman Empire during the 17th century, much to Charles II's consternation.

What's notable is how food arrives in London from abroad as cheap national cuisine, becomes dramatically popular, consolidates, and is then reinvented as a luxury. The plurality of pricey Italians in Chelsea and Mayfair is one example; the excellent **Gymkhana** (*see p159*) might be another. But one does not replace the other. There are finally terrific, affordable curry options in the centre of town – **Tandoor Chop House** (*see p187*) and its forebear **Dishoom** (*see p185*) – as well as a growing number of decent options near (if not yet on) Brick Lane, which has for a long time failed to live up to its international fame: the long-standing **Tayyabs** (*see p263*) and **Needoo Grill** (*see p263*) have been joined by the excellent **Gunpowder** (*see p259*).

Veg is king

Perhaps the most notable shift in London eating habits in the last couple of years has been the rise in the popularity and quality of vegetarian and vegan food. Prompted by a collective reaction to the ecological and ethical impact of animal farming, by the relative expense of meat and by healthy eating advice (plus, a big slice of modish 'clean eating'

♥ Best veggie and vegan eats

Ethos *p207*
Fitzrovia's serene, green, pay-by-weight café serves tip-top veggie salad bowls and global 'hot pods'.

Farmacy *p298*
Notting Hill's premier plant-based spot specialises in 'clean indulgence'.

Lyle's *p266*
The elegant seasonal vegetarian menu more than holds its own against the meaty mains.

Oldroyd *p250*
Visit on a Monday for a menu of delectable, inventive vegan and veggie fare.

Temple of Seitan *p46*
Seitan, the vegan's secret superfood, is fashioned into uncannily delicious fried 'chicken' burgers and wings.

Oldroyd

Lyle's

♥ Afternoon tea

Allegedly introduced in 1840 by the seventh Duchess of Bedford, afternoon tea was designed to combat what the Duchess described as 'that sinking feeling' around 5pm. This most decadent of meals was eagerly adopted by the capital's grand hotels, who remain the foremost exponents of the classic afternoon tea – think crustless cucumber sandwiches, bone china teapots and fat little scones – but now other venues offer quirkier riffs on convention: how about lager-braised bacon jam, cannabis-infused chocolates or Manolo Blahnik gingersnap stilettos?

For traditionalists, the ultimate tea can be found in the art deco foyer and reading room at **Claridge's** (*see p399*; 2.45-5.30pm daily, from £65 pp). Musicians serenade you; the scent of roses surrounds you, as you elegantly stuff yourself on sandwiches and just-baked scones. Crane your neck discreetly to check out your dining companions: our money's on at least one A-lister being present. **Fortnum & Mason** (*see p119*; from 11.30am daily, from £52.50 pp) offers an equally lavish spread in the pastel-painted Jubilee Salon. Cosseting staff go beyond the call of duty and the super-buttery scones are exceptional, but the star of this show is the Battenberg cake. There's a dedicated children's tea available too. Other trad treats include the English Tea Room at **Brown's Hotel** (Albemarle Street, W1S 4BP, noon-6pm daily, from £55 pp) and the Palm Court at the **Langham** (*see p145*; from noon daily, from £55 pp).

For renegades, the options feel limitless. Highlights include a 'Tipsy Tea' at **Mr Fogg's Residence** in Mayfair (*see p159*; 2-6.45pm Sat, 3-5pm Sun, from £40 pp), where you can get sozzled on bottomless gin tea while surrounded by interesting taxidermy. The plant-based afternoon tea at Westbourne Grove's **Farmacy** (*see p298*; 3.30-5pm Fri-Sun, £42 pp) promises 'clean indulgence': no dairy bits, refined sugars or artificial additives here, but instead you'll get cannabis choccies, savoury fancies and tea-infused cocktails. And anyone wanting, desperately, to take a selfie in a loo at teatime should head to dandy-esque Mayfair pleasure dome **Sketch** (9 Conduit Street, W1S 2XG, from 11.30am daily, from £58 pp) for a classic tea through the looking glass: the scones are nice, sure, but don't miss the egg-shaped toilets, where birdsong is piped into each pod.

Finally, if you're on a short trip to the capital and want to cram in as many London traditions as possible, hop aboard **B Bakery's Afternoon Tea Bus** (b-bakery. com, from £45 pp), which departs from Victoria or Northumberland Avenue several times a day for a tour of central London. Sightseeing? Check. Vintage Routemaster bus? Check. Delicious afternoon tea? Check.

▶ *For more great tea-time options, see timeout. com/london/restaurants/ afternoon-tea-in-london.*

Mr Fogg's Residence

mumbo-jumbo), the humble vegetable is now king of the restaurant kitchen. The trend for veggie and plant-based food isn't new, but the places doing it have recently got good enough to attract the attention of serious foodies. Not only are there interesting exclusively veggie and vegan eateries around – the four branches of **Mildred's** (www.mildreds.co.uk), for example, or **Temple of Seitan** (templeofseitan.co.uk) in Camden and Hackney for vegan junk food, and **Itadaki Zen** (139 King's Cross Road, 7278 3573, www.itadakizen-uk.com) for vegan bento – but there are other notable restaurants explicitly eschewing meat on a part-time basis: **Oldroyd** (*see p250*) does meat-free Mondays and **Lyle's** (*see p266*) has vegan and veggie tasting menus. What's more, places like **Coal Rooms** in Peckham (*see p288*), **Ikoyi** in Piccadilly (*see p118*) and **Bao** (*see p172*) offer vegan plates that are among the best dishes on their menus.

It's good to share

Another trend that Londoners have made their own is… well, what to call it? 'Small plates' seems a pedestrian description for the parade of exquisite dishes served in reduced portions at many of our favourite London eateries and, anyway, Spanish tapas and Chinese dim sum had nailed the concept long before anyone thought it needed an English name. Any round-up of London's best restaurants should include a good handful of superb tapas restaurants: most notably **Barrafina**, **Ember Yard** (*see p169*) and **Morito** (*see p219*). Then there's the enduring popularity of the *cicchetti* (Venetian bar snacks) served at Russell Norman's Polpo mini-chain (**Polpo Soho**) or the Mexican tacos served in a party atmosphere at **El Pastór**. For dim sum, try **Royal China** or the luxury offerings at **Yauatcha** (*see p170*). The small plates concept proper is behind venues such as the **Shed**, while Jason Atherton's **Social Eating House** (*see p174*)

♥ Best for small plates and sharing

Barrafina *p185*
Best tapas in London but be prepared to queue.

El Pastór *p92*
Tacos that are worth the wait… and the hype.

Polpo Soho *p172*
Venetian street food was the making of this terrific mini-chain.

Royal China *p134*
Some of the best dim sum in London.

Shed *p303*
Anything the Spaniards can do… Fine modern British tapas.

♥ Best for brunch

Caravan King's Cross *p205*
Relaxed and boozy brunches on a fine modern square.

Duck & Waffle *p237*
At the top of a skyscraper in the heart of the city.

Good Egg *p272*
Jewish-inspired weekend plates at a Stoke Newington staple.

Wolseley *p118*
Grand setting, fine food – omelette Arnold Bennett, say.

El Pastór

HAKATA TONKOTSU RAMEN BAR

Specialising in authentic Hakata tonkotsu ramen from the Southern Island of Kyushu, Japan

London | Manchester | Oxford
Book now: www.shoryuramen.com

sells jars of pâté and nibbles to get diners dipping in and off to a suitably convivial start.

No bookings and other 'dirty' notions

Somewhere between the green-lobby farmers' markets and the rise of the 'dirty' burger (the one your doctor warned you about), street food found its foothold in London and began a city-wide takeover. There are now gatherings of stalls all over place (*see right* Street food). Again there has been a welcome gentrification in the genre: the brilliant, wickedly unhealthy burgers at **Bleecker** (*see p112*) now have a permanent address, while **Bar Boulud** (*see p135*) does a very upmarket take on the subject. The aged cheeseburger tacos at **Temper** (*see p170*) are a different tack on the same basic culinary navigation.

Taking a related – but rather different – approach to risk-free catering is the enduring trend for no-booking 'walk-in' restaurants. The attraction for the restaurateur is obvious: no empty tables and the chance to generate a buzz. The attraction for the punter may be less obvious (long waits and long queues are standard), but whatever our misgivings, many of these places are really worth the effort – *see p43* Best walk-in restaurants – and, as a visitor free from the exigencies of a working life, you can always opt to visit at unconventional times and thereby avoid the worst of the crowds.

Top 20

❤ Street food

Now that London is a Russian oligarch's playground, eating out is wildly unaffordable – right? Wrong: some of the most inventive, delicious food in the city is to be found for under a fiver and eaten with a wooden fork. Whether you're after an atmospheric stroll through East London's cobbled streets, doughnut in hand, or a gourmet hot dog on the go in Canary Wharf, London's food markets are at your service. Just don't be afraid to get your hands (and face) dirty.

The Big Daddies of London street food are **Kerb** (www.kerbfood.com) and **Street Feast** (www.streetfeast.com). Kerb was founded in 2012 by Petra Barran, who once ran a mobile chocolate business from an ice-cream van. She saw an opportunity to cluster together the best of the capital's food vendors and bring an element of cooperative organisation to this previously ad hoc industry. Kerb now has six locations hosting a rotating line-up of vendors: at Granary Square, West India Quay, Paddington, the Gherkin, St Katherine Docks and, from summer 2019, Seven Dials in Covent Garden.

Street Feast was founded in the same year by Jonathan Downey. Its six markets feature a similar mix of food and drink vendors but locates them in derelict and disused spaces, creating an urban festival vibe. Its Shoreditch hub, **Dinerama** (19 Great Eastern Street, EC2A 3EJ, 5pm-midnight Wed-Sat) is set in a 1,000-capacity former bullion truck yard – great if you enjoy booming house music with your vegan taco.

Savage Salads

With the support of these collectives, stall-owners are able to trial a foodie idea and make some money, without immediately taking on the heavy burden of renting a London restaurant space. Many have since gone on to greater things. Fried chicken supremos **Mother Clucker** (*see right*) were able to open a permanent shop on Exmouth Market thanks to the success of their market stall; **Som Saa** (*see p260*) financed the transition from street vendor to restaurant through an insanely popular crowdfunding appeal; and **Kricket** (*see p172*), another much-admired restaurant, started out in a shipping container in Brixton.

For those in search of a more traditional London street food experience, **Borough Market** (*see p93*) is still the grandaddy of them all, but the cognoscenti increasingly head a little further east to the less touristy **Maltby Street** and **Spa Terminus** (*see p98*) and even further south to **Brockley Market** (Lewisham College Carpark, SE4 1UT, from 10am Sat). Another top spot is **Broadway Market** in Hackney (*see p271*), which has been peddling fruit and vegetables since the 1890s. Today the trad traders are supplemented by stalls selling lobster-infused mac & cheese and roasted duck burgers. Equally charming are Soho's old-world **Berwick Street Market** (*see p170*) and historic covered **Greenwich Market**. But if you fancy a weirder, shinier, more space-age sort of street food adventure, head for Street Feast's **Giant Robot** (Crossrail Place, E14 5AR) in Canary Wharf, a hulking silver 'rooftopia' bursting with everything from crispy squid to experimental ice-cream.

❤ (Some of the) best street food

BBQ Dreams
(bbqdreamz.co.uk) Filipino backyard barbecue. Available at Kerb (*see left*).

Club Mexicana
(clubmexicana.com) Mexican-inspired vegan street food. Available Thur-Sat at Dinerama (*see left*).

Luxury Flats
(www.luxuryflats.co) Gourmet flatbreads. Available at Netil Market (*see p273*).

Mother Clucker
(motherclucker.co.uk) Fried chicken. Available at Exmouth Market (59-61 Rosebery Avenue, EC1R 4SD); the Truman Brewery (*see p258*); Flat Iron Square (Union Street, SE1 1TD), and Street Feast Hawker House (Canada Street, SE16 7PJ).

Savage Salads
(www.savagesalads.co.uk) Nutritious and delicious salads. Available at Berwick Street Market (*see p170*); Flat Iron Square (Union Street, SE1 1TD), and Strutton Ground (Westminster, SW1P 2JT).

Sub Cult
(sub-cult.co.uk) Gourmet deli-style sub rolls. Available at Boxpark, Shoreditch (*see p267*) and Brockley Market (*see left*).

Club Mexicana

Gastropubs and beautiful brasseries

Another kind of eaterie whose dominance of the London scene has waned, without it showing the remotest signs of disappearing, is the gastropub: restaurant-quality food, eaten in the relaxed atmosphere of a boozer that serves good beer and, generally, above-average wine. A few years ago every pub that wasn't already a gastro was in the process of turning into one – now a lot of London pubs have realised that being a superb place for a drink is a perfectly solid ambition. Still, for a substantial – and often terrific, usually hearty – meal that doesn't demand you pull on a suit or cocktail dress, the gastropub is great: the **Harwood Arms** (*see p139*) and the **Drapers Arms** (www.thedrapersarms.com) are established favourites, but foodie scholars could do worse than visit the **Eagle** (*see p218*), widely celebrated as the originator of the genre back in the 1990s.

Taking on a similar role of providing noon till night dining – albeit with a more Continental flavour, generally higher price bracket and considerably greater interest in providing brunch and breakfast opportunities – are what we'll call the brasseries. The kings of London in this field are Chris Corbin and Jeremy King, who seem incapable of opening a dud: the **Wolseley** (*see p118*), **Fischer's** (*see p149*) and **Delaunay** (*see p191*) are all great, combining a kind of Viennese glamour with very approachable menus. There are plenty of worthy competitors, though, among them **Quo Vadis** (*see p168*), which does some heavy lifting restoring the spirits of Soho's dissolute media workers, and **Bistrotheque** (*see p269*), putting an idiosyncratic east London spin on the idea of all-day comfort food.

Prices you'll like – and waiting that you won't

Dining in London can be expensive, and it certainly will be if you insist on dinner at

❤ Best cheap eats

Bao *p172*
Fiery Taiwanese street food.

Brasserie Zédel *p172*
This *grand café*'s prix-fixe is the city's best bargain.

Chick'n'Sours *p185*
Cracking Korea-inflected chicken sandwiches.

Herman ze German *p167*
Sausages. Yup, pretty much just that – top-quality imported German sausages.

Hoppers *p164*
Authentically wonderful Sri Lankan dishes.

Roti Chai *p146*
Indian street food, served canteen style.

Borough Market

❤ Best for a blow-out

Bosi at Bibendum *p131*
Claude Bodi's modern French, Michelin-themed powerhouse.

Hutong *p97*
Chinese with a view – from the Shard's 33rd floor.

Roka *p209*
Beautifully presented raw and robata-grilled Asian deliciousness.

Social Eating House *p174*
The finest establishment from one of London's finest chefs, Jason Atherton.

Roka

posh City or Mayfair restaurants where the expense account rules. Remember: as a tourist, you're more flexible than the locals. Many of the swankiest venues offer exceptionally good value prix-fixe lunches, especially so if you're happy not to drink wine with your meal. Still too expensive? Most of the global food options we've discussed – not to mention the street food – are both tasty and inexpensive. If you're happy to experiment, you'll be able to eat extremely well without breaking the bank. There's bad news, though: that combination of good value and good quality often makes places busy. If you want to eat at a popular destination restaurant, then you'll need to book in advance, or, if it's a no-booking venue, then be prepared to queue. Again, make use of your flexibility: Londoners are time-constrained, but you can eat whenever you want to.

Where to eat

The **South Bank** (*see p78*), close to foodie-magnets Borough Market and Maltby Street, offers plenty of quality chain options strung along the riverside, but **Soho** (*see p162*), just north of the Thames and less than half an hour's walk from the Southbank Centre,

If you're happy to experiment, you'll be able to eat extremely well without breaking the bank

In the know
Essentials

Most restaurants accept credit cards (although American Express is least popular), but some of the cheaper places still only accept cash; if you're anywhere informal, like a street food stall, you should expect to use money rather than plastic. Service charges are frequently included in café and restaurant bills, but not always. Check: if such a charge hasn't been added, paying a tip of 10%-15% is usual. If you can, tip in cash: it's most likely to go directly to your server that way.

is probably the best place in London for eats, both cheap and chic: Bun House does a brisk takeaway trade not far from Jeremy Lee's upmarket and timeless Quo Vadis and trend-setting 10 Greek Street, for example. East of Soho, **Covent Garden** (*see p178*) remains a busy tourist trap, but some very decent eating options have emerged. Expense-account eats are concentrated in **Mayfair** (*see p157*), where celebrity executive chefs thrive in the dining rooms of posh hotels. Further west, **Marylebone** (*see p147*) is another foodie enclave, replete with top-notch delis and cafés, as well as terrific restaurants including Fischer's and the Chiltern Firehouse. **South Kensington and Chelsea** (*see p122*) does expensive, special-occasion destinations, but runs to more affordable fare too at venues like Gallery Mess. **The City** (*see p210*) remains relatively poor for evening and weekend eats, but **Clerkenwell** (*see p216*), just beyond the old City walls, is a culinary hotspot: from the Modern Pantry to the Eagle, from St John to Moro, most London restaurant trends have kicked off here. However, the biggest change to London's dining geography over the last few years has been the growth of exciting options in the neighbourhoods, partly due to new restaurants struggling to meet steep rents in central London: try **Peckham** (*see p286*), **Brixton** (*see p289*), or any of the huge number of places in **East London** (*see p254*).

The biggest change to London's dining geography over the last few years has been the growth of exciting options in the neighbourhoods

In the know
Late lunch

As you'll need to book a long way ahead for dinner at many of London's coolest restaurants, it is worth checking out lunchtimes, especially late lunches.

Salut! p250

Drinking

Trad ales or craft beers? Classic cocktails or crazy new confections? Pull up a bar stool – we've got it all here

It's the combination of rich traditions and a long history of bohemian revelry with a real taste for innovation that makes drinking in London such a pleasure these days. Any sense of rivalry with New York over which city is the world capital of booze is mostly a media confection: the truth is that London learnt the art of the bar from the Big Apple – and learnt that lesson surprisingly well – but we continue to own the pub. And recent years have proved the resilience of London's drinking scene: pubs are no longer shutting at the alarming rate that they did during the 2008/9 recession, while rising rents in central London have only encouraged a neighbourhood cocktail movement to thrive. You'll find a drinking culture with a conscience, too – with bars focused on sustainability and pubs supporting local brands and producers, especially with the continuing vogue for craft beer and small-batch gin. Above all, there's entertainment by the pint from spirited landlords, cocktail visionaries and the clued-up barflies who stand on the other side of the counter. When you're down the local, this city doesn't feel so sprawling after all.

Bar Américain *p174*

Pub it and be damned

'The local' – the public house, with its colourful characters and cosy interior – remains the symbolic heart of boozing culture in the capital. Sure, the carcasses of street-corner pubs are littered around the city, often converted into luxury flats or chicken shops, but London's enduring love of the local is proved by a smattering of charming boozers saved by patrons who've campaigned for their protection from property developers. A drink in 'saved' pubs like the **Ivy House** (*see p288*) and the **Chesham Arms** (15 Mehetabel Road, Hackney E9 6DU, 8986 6717, www.cheshamarms.com) comes with a genuine sense of community.

Some pubs have stood the test of time without such a fight. Indeed, a handful of historic inns all claim to be the oldest pub in the capital. **Ye Olde Cheshire Cheese** (*see p221*), **Ye Olde Mitre** (*see p216*) and the **Prospect of Whitby** (*see p274*) are just a few of the pubs that have held licences since the 1600s. These creaking London legends are the best places to

❤ Best beer

Cask *p111*
No looker, but great ales.

Cock Tavern *p272*
Hackney's finest.

Lyric *p170*
Central location, 20 taps.

Waterloo Tap *p86*
A great selection and handy for the South Bank.

Prospect of Whitby

soak up a spot of history, warmed by the fire, ducking under low ceiling beams to fetch a pint of lukewarm ale before settling in for a Sunday roast with all the trimmings.

Glasses full of creativity

London's front-running bars demonstrate the same level of craft, skill and reverence shown by the capital's best kitchens, some of them even using techniques derived from so-called 'molecular gastronomy'. The cocktail scene never takes itself too seriously, though, offering a good time at most hours of the day and night. (Certainly, cocktail o'clock is no longer limited by traditional working hours and former licensing restrictions to 5.30pm.) You'll find quirkiness in presentation – witness drinks themed around childhood stories at **Blind Pig** (*see p174*) and those that appear in a puff of smoke at **Purl** (*see p151*) – or in the very setting: you can drink in an underground public toilet at **Ladies & Gentlemen** (*see p243*). There are plenty of places to get the classics done to perfection, but increasingly, people are seeking out new levels of boozy wizardry. One of the leading lights is cocktail maestro Ryan Chetiyawardana, who is fast becoming a household name (albeit under his pseudonym, Mr Lyan) thanks to drinks that incorporate madcap ideas, techniques and ingredients but never compromise on flavour. Check out his concoctions at **Lyaness** on the South Bank. Other innovative bars include **69 Colebrooke Row**, which has a lab upstairs, and stripped-back, sophisticated **Swift**. Wherever you end up, cocktails in the capital are more than ever about quality over quantity – even when they come with a good dose of fun.

Trending tipples

Whatever else you do, make sure you tap into London's craft beer 'revolution', another American import that we've taken to heart and

❤ **Best cocktails**

69 Colebrooke Row *p251*
More mixmeister magic.

Connaught Bar *p159*
Pure Mayfair class.

Lyaness *p86*
The latest incarnation of Mr Lyan's constantly evolving cocktail bars.

Purl *p151*
Classic speakeasy.

Satan's Whiskers *p270*
East London trendies and fabulous booze.

Swift *p168*
Glamorous Soho bar.

> ## London's front-running bars demonstrate the same level of craft, skill and reverence shown by the capital's best kitchens

Swift

made our own. Most pubs and bars (and even restaurants) these days will serve something interesting, from the keg or in a bottle, usually hoppy and often brewed in London. It's a scene that's particularly active on the periphery, with grungy brewery taprooms and hip neighbourhood bottle shops where you can try and buy springing up on the outskirts of London, but there are plenty of poshed-up pubs in the centre of town that have dedicated themselves to the humble hop too.

While grapes from around the world are well represented in a few wonderfully unstuffy new wine bars (try **Sager + Wilde**, *see p270*, or **Terroirs**, *see p187*), it's fair to say you won't find quite the same fervour for vino. More booze fanaticism is instead reserved for gin. 'Mother's ruin' first wreaked havoc on the capital in the 1700s, when home production made the spirit the crystal meth of the day; the government's attempts to crack down on gin distilling in the capital led to riots. London's current gin craze is far more refined: the Chiswick-based distiller **Sipsmith** (*see p304* Boozy Tours) helped push through new laws for small-batch production in the UK, and local gin-making has since spread across the country. You can sample it at source on a distillery tour or trail, or opt for one of the numerous bars claiming to stock the most varieties of gin in London.

Strait-laced supping

Millennials have waved goodbye to by-numbers binge drinking. Mocktails are now common on London bar menus, so locals no longer need to deploy the designated-driver excuse (which never really stood up anyway in the face of London transport). Indeed, non-alcoholic bar **Redemption** (www.redemptionbar.co.uk) is so popular that it's opened three venues (Notting Hill, Shoreditch and Covent Garden) dedicated to booze-free good times. You might also choose to hang out with fashion-forward

♥ Best pubs

Bradley's Spanish Bar *p209*
A cosy and unassuming little boozer, just off Oxford Street.

Coach & Horses *p168*
French House *p168*
A venerable pair of Soho classics.

Cross Keys *p187*
What's this? A genuinely good pub in touristy Covent Garden, you say?

Jerusalem Tavern *p219*
Former coffeehouse turned quintessence of London pub.

Ye Olde Mitre *p216*
A gem of an old pub down a blink-and-you'll-miss-it alley.

Monmouth Coffee Company serves coffee for connoisseurs.

Redemption proves that no alcohol doesn't have to mean no fun.

types at one of London's juice bars: **Ham's Yard Press Juice Bar** (6 Denman Street, Soho, W1D 7HD, 7287 2462, press-london.com) has plenty of cold-pressed delights.

Of course, you needn't go completely vice-free. Coffee is as big as ever, thanks to the proliferation of masterful bean techniques – and, no doubt, to the fast pace of London life. You'll find on-site roasters, a plethora of brew technology and lab-style equipment, and beans sourced from far-flung places. Some coffee shops are well established on the caffeine scene – check out **Monmouth** (27 Monmouth Street, Covent Garden, WC2H 9EU, 7232 3010, monmouthcoffee.co.uk) – but don't ignore the new generation of stylish roastery-cum-cafés including **Allpress Espresso Bar** (*see p265*), **Ozone Coffee** (11 Leonard Street, Hackney, EC2A 4AQ, 7490 1039, ozonecoffee. co.uk) and **Workshop Coffee** (workshopcoffee. com), which has five coffee bars dotted around central London.

The where and when of London drinking

Soho retains its reputation as the bohemian centre of the capital, for all that the razzle-dazzle naughtiness has now mostly been replaced by tech entrepreneurs and middle-aged media types. It still hosts character-filled pubs, but these have been joined by increasing numbers of chic cocktail bars. **Shoreditch** – its days as the epitome of cool receding fast as its denizens grow up – is still a lively part of town, packed with drinkers, but in-the-know boozers seem to have drifted north into **Hackney** or south to **Peckham** and **Brixton**, where creative drinks scenes are flourishing; here, you'll find cocktails at the £8-£10 mark as opposed to the £12-£14 prices of central London. If hell-raising hipsters aren't your bag, stick to **Mayfair**, **Covent Garden** or **West London**, where drinks are served with a side of sophistication, but heftier price tags exclude the hoi polloi.

♥ **Best outdoor venues**

Boundary London *p400*
The rooftop bar at Conran's finest hotel is an east London must.

Earl of Essex *p252*
A purveyor of fine beer with a fine beer garden.

Frank's *p288*
Campari. Multistorey carpark. Peckham. Don't miss it.

Scottish Stores *p206*
Rare pub roof terrace in central London.

Sushisamba *p237*
Swish cocktails at the restaurant's Tree Bar on the 38th floor.

Sipsmith Distillery was in the vanguard of London's gin craze.

Mondays are mostly a sober affair as Londoners recover from the weekend, but during the rest of the week there's enthusiastic after-work drinking; certainly, Thursday nights are every bit as big as Fridays for the post-work crowds. Pubs host relaxed, all-day drinking sessions as soon as the weekend hits, while an ever-increasing number of restaurants have adopted the trend for bottomless brunches (for the price of your food, the booze comes unlimited). It's the new Sunday lunch for London's weekend socialites.

In summer, locals go a bit drink crazy. They'll flock to rooftop bars – many making the pilgrimage to Peckham to visit **Frank's Cafe** (*see p288*), now a long-term seasonal highlight – or to the riverside pubs of east London's Docklands or to the almost bucolic pubs that line the Thames in Hammersmith and Putney.

The liberalisation of the licensing laws means that any pub or bar can apply to open late, but noise-nuisance restrictions mean most still close their doors around midnight, with only a handful of places staying open past 1am. In all cases, you'll have to be over 18 to be served alcohol (or even admitted to many venues at night), while many bars embrace a Challenge 21 policy – if you're fresh-faced, expect to have to show ID.

> **Pubs host relaxed, all-day drinking sessions and many restaurants have adopted the trend for bottomless brunches**

Frank's Cafe

Shopping

Fashion, flowers, food and famous labels

With two of the world's most prestigious design colleges (Central Saint Martins and the London School of Fashion) at its centre, London's fashion scene has an energy that radiates throughout the city. As so often in the capital, it's all in the mix – for every catwalk look on New Bond Street, there is an inspiring street style to be seen in Shepherd's Bush Market; for every neatly attired Dalston hipster, there's a devil-may-care transvestite in a home-made frock. From glossy department stores peddling everything from Prada to panettone, to flower markets, to cheap-and-chic high-street chains, there are very few things in this city that money can't buy. And, although you can shop the world's finest if you have the cash, there are vintage stores, market stalls and budget brands on offer if you don't.

It's the fashion

We'd argue London is currently the fashion capital of the world. So it should be no surprise that some of the world's finest fashion retailers are here, from small independents – like Soho's **Machine-A**, a tireless champion of the most exciting emerging designers – all the way up to the big department stores. Part of the secret is that the big guys who might be in danger of slowing down have learnt to collaborate with the little guys who are still quick on their feet.

Selfridges (*see p146*) is a fine example. Opened in 1909, it is one of a handful of central London department stores to have thrived ever since the Edwardian shopping boom – and the innovative spirit of founder Harry Gordon Selfridge has remained intact. From hosting pantos in the basement, to curating a collection from Primark on the street-fashion floor, you can always expect the unexpected (as well as the best of the world's designer labels).

A city of shoppers, London is a kind of petri dish – and we're not talking about germs. Big brands use the capital as a testing ground, so Londoners are exposed to all the latest initiatives and launches. After years of perfecting everything from the cut of the silk shirts to the scribbly font on the carrier bags,

❤ Best for fashion

Browns Fashion *p160*
One of the most influential fashion boutiques, credited with discovering Alexander McQueen, John Galliano and Christopher Kane.

Dover Street Market *p119*
Exclusive fashion, affordable streetwear and an excellent café.

Machine-A *p171*
A platform for London's most exciting emerging designers.

Shop at Bluebird *p188*
The dreamy fashion concept store has decamped from Chelsea to Covent Garden.

Machine-A

In the know
Opening hours

Shops are generally open 10am-6pm Monday to Saturday, with few closing on bank holidays (Christmas is the sole exception to that rule). Most don't open until around noon on Sundays, which gives you plenty of time to refuel for a day of pavement pounding with a good brunch (see *p46* Best brunches). In general the shops in central London close later on Thursday nights, with the Oxford Street stores staying open until 10pm.

it was here that the H&M family launched the first branch of **& Other Stories** (*see p156*) in 2013 and the Swedish behemoth followed it up in 2017 with its first lifestyle concept store, **Arket** (www.arket.com).

It's not all about the high street, either: Japanese designer Rei Kawakubo of Comme des Garçons stuck with London when she moved her ground-breaking concept store **Dover Street Market** from the street that gave it its name. In the event, she took it just up the road to St James's.

Dover Street Market

Department stores and chain reactions

The sheer number of top-class designers creates fierce competition, so even the retail stalwarts have to remain fresh to survive. **Selfridges** is always the pioneer, opening London's first gender-neutral department in 2015; installing a negroni fountain on the roof in 2017; staffing the tech department with robots and unveiling a sculpture park in store in 2018. Meanwhile **Liberty** (*see p155*), which still trades William Morris pattern scarves from grand half-timbered premises like it's 1893, is also a hotbed of exciting new labels and beauty brands. In 2018, it opened a new hair art salon, which weaves Liberty printed scarves into chic new braids. A fitting metaphor.

Elsewhere a high-street giant like **Topshop** (*see p146*) might rest on its laurels, complacent in its confidence that customers would always come through the doors. Not in London: the mammoth flagship store keeps things lively with a revolving roster of concessions, an in-store tattooist and a branch of Bleach hairdressers.

Only in London

While the city's particular strength is fashion, London has more to offer than posh frocks and directional sweatshirts. There's a wealth of niche shops, specialising in traditional umbrellas (**James Smith & Sons**, *see p188*),

In the know
Remember this

Not all souvenir shops are full of junk. Single-handedly rebuilding their tarnished reputation, **We Built this City** (*see p175*) is full of witty, cool and creative London-themed mementos. It's the kind of shop that can make a tea towel a pretty decent gift.

We Built this City

cheese (**Neal's Yard Dairy**, *see p188*) and gourmet teas (**Postcard Teas**, *see p161*) – even, in the mustachioed heartlands of east London, cacti (**Prick**, 492 Kingsland Road, E8 4AE, www.prickldn.com) and hand-carved wooden spoons (**Barn the Spoon**, 260 Hackney Road, E2 7SJ, barnthespoon.com).

Market up

East London is also home to two of the city's best markets: **Columbia Road** (*see p270*) and **Broadway Market** (*see p271*). The source of their success is very different: Columbia Road kept true to its flower-selling traditions, while Broadway Market underwent stunning reinvention in the 2000s. If you're really just after a stroll (and the jam-packed crowds are part of the fun), Columbia Road's the one: stop to smell the roses before investigating the dinky independent shops round the corner. Broadway Market is the nexus of dress-down catwalk and street eats, but it's still possible to pick up an intriguing little something from the accessory and apparel stalls, not to mention those selling something altogether more mouth-watering. For gifts to take back home, though, we say nip

Broadway Market

Columbia Road Market

Where To Spend It

London's shopping districts – the cheat sheet

Marylebone *p151*

Marylebone is a really lovely part of the city for a shopaholic wander. It has brilliant shops for contemporary design, but is also home to **Daunt Books**, with its stained-glass windows and titles arranged by country. Then there's Chiltern Street, blessed with both pretty Victorian Gothic architecture and great independent shops, particularly for men: vintage Americana from **John Simons** (no.46, www.johnsimons.co.uk) and a branch of trad British brand **Sunspel** (nos.13-15, www.sunspel.com).

Soho *p166, p170*

The fear is that Soho will one day soon lose all its individuality to a developer-led invasion of faceless national brands. For the moment, it remains one of the most exciting places to shop in the city, with a slew of brilliant boutiques carrying independent labels: start with **OTHER/Shop**, now on Berwick Street, and Brewer Street's **Machine-A**, before taking on one-off international flagships, like contemporary Swedish sneaker brand **Axel Arigato**. And while nearby Carnaby Street may not be crawling with mods anymore, it has a healthy mix of affordable fashion stores from international brands such as **Monki** and **Vans**.

Covent Garden *p187*

Less stressful than busy Oxford Street, Covent Garden is full of chains (don't turn your nose up: there's a particularly good H&M with a separate beauty hall) but happily has a wealth of independent stores too. It plays host to **Nigel Cabourn Army Gym** – his only stand-alone retail concept outside Japan – and the **Vintage Showroom**, where menswear designers go to find inspiration. There's the prettiest, daintiest jewellery from **Laura Lee** (42 Monmouth Street, www.lauraleejewellery.com) and, next door, quirky plastic accessories at **Tatty Devine** (www.tattydevine.com).

Islington *p252*

Islington is well served by stylish little shops, often with an interiors bias. Head down Camden Passage for teensy boutiques – **Annie's** (no.12, www.anniesvintageclothing.co.uk) and wool shop **Loop** (no.15, www.loopknitting.com) are favourites, dinky cafés and the bargain-filled antique stalls for which it's famous. Upper Street is dominated by chain stores, but there's also covetable menswear at **Sefton** (no.196, www.seftonfashion.com) and stand-out indie homewares from **twentytwentyone** and **Aria**. And, if you head down Essex Road, you'll find **Molly Meg** at no.111 (www.mollymeg.com), one of the sweetest kids' shops in London, and, just off the main road at 26 Cross Street, a careful edit of brilliant brands and fine coffee at **Paper Mache Tiger** (www.papermachetiger.com).

Shoreditch *p267*

This neighbourhood now attracts a mash-up of serious shoppers and people doing the Jack the Ripper walking tour. Nonetheless, it has managed to keep its individuality, with **Redchurch Street** (*see p265*) a chic shopping destination in its own right, where independents such as Miista mix with cool global brands APC and the like. Shoreditch is also home to **Boxpark**, which hosts a changing roster of brands in its shipping containers, and the **House of Hackney**, a maximalist print boutique with in-house florist. **Rough Trade East** (*see p262*) on Brick Lane is probably the capital's best record shop.

round the corner to Netil Market, a great little space dedicated to local designer-makers and the perfect spot to pick up locally made gifts.

The two other key markets are at opposite ends of town. At the far end of the tourist-magnet South Bank, **Borough Market** (*see p93*) rejuvenated its noble history of food wholesaling with street eats and gourmet snacking – a reinvention that worked so well that the cognoscenti now sniffily head a little further east of London Bridge to **Maltby Street** (*see p98*). Then, in west London, Notting Hill's **Portobello Road** (*see p300*) has stall after stall of vintage goodies – with admittedly few bargains, but great atmosphere. Up-and-coming designers come out in force on Fridays.

You're booked

The bookshop didn't die, it turns out. Like everywhere else, their survival in London comes down to creatively selected stock, helpful and informed sellers, fine events and, wherever possible, a café. At different ends of the spectrum, the **London Review Bookshop** (*see p201*) and **Foyles** (*see p166*) tick all these boxes. The former is a tiny place with stock that's all killer and no filler; the latter is a multistorey book palace, pragmatically redeveloped a few years ago. To these can be added historic beauties, like **Daunt Books** (*see p151*) in Marylebone, specialists like comics emporium **Gosh!** (*see p171*), and the combination of both that is **Cecil Court** (*see p177*).

While we're being all old-fashioned... vinyl, eh? Bricks-and-mortar record-selling also survives, even thrives, when it knows its niche. In Soho, record shops keep on spinning near **Berwick Street** (*see p170*), while **Honest Jon's** (*see p300*) in Notting Hill and Brick Lane's **Rough Trade East** (*see p262*) are institutions – if, by institution, you mean something that's still full of life after decades doing what it does. Much like London itself.

In the know
Museum shops

In London, shopping opportunities crop up all the time. You might find yourself being all cultural at the **Barbican** (see p227), only to realise you're within grabbing distance of a carefully curated design, art and architecture gift shop. The same is true of **Tate Modern** (see p89), full of artist-designed exclusives; the new **Design Museum** (see p302), a trove of ingenious gadgets and sleek homeware; and the **V&A** (see p128), chock-a-block with bold jewellery and unusual gifts.

Honest Jon's

LONDON

LOOP

Gorgeous knitting, crochet & embroidery supplies

Explore

■■■	**Getting Started**	**72**
■■■	**South Bank & Bankside**	**78**
■■■	**Westminster & St James's**	**100**
■■■	**South Kensington & Chelsea**	**122**
■■■	**Oxford Street, Marylebone & Mayfair**	**140**
■■■	**Soho & Leicester Square**	**162**
■■■	**Covent Garden & the Strand**	**178**
■■■	**Bloomsbury & King's Cross**	**192**
■■■	**The City**	**210**
■■■	**North London**	**238**
■■■	**East London**	**254**
■■■	**South London**	**278**
■■■	**West London**	**294**

Tower Bridge

Getting Started

Plan, pre-book and orientate yourself before you start exploring

The key to London's geography is that it is two cities, not one. The City is the area originally walled by the Romans, which, through its mercantile wealth and the weakness of English kings, secured considerable independence from Westminster. Westminster is where the monarchs and, latterly, Parliamentarians reside. Around these poles, the patchwork of districts grew up that are now central London.

For this guide, we first take a roughly clockwise journey through central London, starting with the district that has become over the last two decades its premier tourist area. A pleasant Thameside stroll takes throngs of visitors along the **South Bank** (*see p78*) past such key attractions as Tate Modern, Shakespeare's Globe and the Shard. Across the river lies **Westminster** (*see p100*), where you'll find Westminster Abbey, the Houses of Parliament and, overlooking delightful St James's Park, Buckingham Palace; to its north, Trafalgar Square is the official centre of London. **South Kensington & Chelsea** (*see p122*) is the land of plenty for cash-flash non-doms, but also boasts the immense cultural riches of the Natural History Museum, Science Museum and, our favourite, the V&A. We then explore

💚 **Best viewpoints**

Alexandra Palace *p343*
Come for the vista and stay for a gig or festival.

London Eye *p84*
This Millennium big wheel is still a Thameside hit.

Monument *p235*
Anything we can do... Wren already did. This 17th-century memorial to the Great Fire is a fine historic viewpoint.

Primrose Hill *p244*
The picture-postcard view of the London skyline is especially memorable at dusk.

Sky Garden *p236*
Glorious at sunset – and admission is free with a pre-booked ticket.

View from the Shard *p94*
Recognisable from across London and offering views of every bit of the city.

The Shard *p94*

Whitehall

the West End – that part of London west of the City – from the shops of **Oxford Street & Marylebone** (*see p140*) via the restaurants and bars of formerly naughty **Soho** (*see p162*) – just north of Leicester Square – to the boutiques of **Covent Garden** (*see p178*), also home to the fine London Transport Museum. To the north, academic **Bloomsbury** (*see p192*) leads up to the revitalised **King's Cross** area (*see p202*), with the British Museum and British Library the major points of interest. Finally, we come to London's busy financial centre, the **City** (*see p210*), where you'll find St Paul's Cathedral, the Tower of London and the Museum of London, an essential stop to gain an understanding how London came to be.

Around these central areas is a doughnut of other sights you won't want to miss: Camden Market in **North London** (*see p244*); trendier-than-thou **East London** (*see p254*), where you'll find Spitalfields, Brick Lane and Shoreditch, with Dalston further north; **South London** (*see p278*), which combines the historic appeal of Greenwich and Kew Gardens with freshly funky Peckham; and **West London** (*see p294*), where Notting Hill is neighbour to the fabulous Design Museum.

> **In the know**
> **Appy travels**
>
> Central London is easy to get around: if you're in doubt, get the nearest Tube from where you are to where you want to be. But, as more and more exciting things crop up in more peripheral neighbourhoods, you'll have to master 'multimodal' transport – in other words, travel like a Londoner using a mixture of the Tube, trains, buses and walking. The best advice? Download the free transport app **Citymapper** to your smartphone before arriving. Provide an address, point of interest or postcode and it lays out all your transport options, with connections, fares and time estimates for each. Want to find out what to do while you're out and about? Also download the digital edition of the free **Time Out** to your phone or tablet to get our editors' selection of the best culture, food and fun each week.

Getting around

London's a big city, but might not feel it. In the centre, many attractions are surprisingly close to each other: the **Transport for London walking distance map** (content.tfl.gov.uk/walking-tube-map. pdf) reveals, to cite only the best known example, that Covent Garden station is only four minutes' walk from Leicester Square station. It looks much further on the schematic Underground map. When you do need public transport, it offers good coverage of the city through a combination of underground trains (the Tube), surface trains (rail and Overground services), buses, cabs and taxis, even Thames boats and an official bike hire scheme; for details, *see pp404-409.*

Information and advice

There are tourist information centres in two of the focal sightseeing areas of London: the **City of London Information Centre** (7332 3456, www.cityoflondon.gov.uk) is next to St Paul's Cathedral (see *p224*) at the top of the slope down to the Millennium Bridge and across the Thames to Tate Modern, while the **Greenwich Tourist Information Centre** (0870 608 2000, www.visitgreenwich.org. uk) is in one of the halls of the historic Old Royal Naval College *(see p283).* An easy walk from Covent Garden, there's a further

information point outside Holborn tube: the **Holborn Information Kiosk** (closed weekends). **Travel Information Centres** at King's Cross, Euston, Liverpool Street and Victoria rail stations, and Piccadilly Circus tube *(see p152)* sell tickets for transport – and for some attractions.

Prices and discounts

There's good news for price-conscious visitors to London: admission to the permanent collections of almost all the key museums is absolutely free (they only charge for blockbuster temporary exhibitions). That means paid-for discount cards such as the **London Pass** (www. londonpass.com) only make sense if you're planning to do several of the eligible attractions: among them St Paul's *(see p224)*, Westminster Abbey *(see p108)*, the London Transport Museum *(see p183)*, London Zoo

18 Stafford Terrace
Step back in time to 1899
Open Wednesdays and weekends

 Leighton House Museum
www.leightonhouse.co.uk

Routemasters

London's original hop-on, hop-off double decker bus

Trundling the streets since the 1950s, the hugely popular Routemaster bus, London's original hop-on, hop-off double-decker, was retired in 2005 – to howls of protest. Former mayor Boris Johnson vowed to resurrect the service – and did so with a fleet of handsomely designed red double-deckers, officially known as the New Routemaster (but routinely dubbed the 'Boris Bus'). The new fleet briefly offered the hop-on, hop-off service that was central to their design, but this proved pointlessly expensive and was quietly dropped, leaving the rear-access doors largely redundant. Found to be uncomfortably hot on the top deck in summer, the buses also used a hybrid engine technology that has been overtaken by cleaner, cheaper alternatives, so new mayor Sadiq Khan cancelled future orders in September 2016. Still, 195 more New Routemasters arrived in summer 2017, so they'll be running through London for a good while yet. But for a real nostalgia kick, you can still ride refurbished 1960-64 Routemasters for the same price as any other bus. A heritage service runs on route 15 (between Trafalgar Square and Tower Hill); head to stop F, on the Strand to the east of the square. Buses run every 15 minutes from around 9.30am; you must have a ticket or valid card before boarding (see p405).

(see p245), Kew Gardens (see p292) or any of the Historic Royal Palaces (including the Tower of London, see p234). All our listings give pricing information. For travel, by far the cheapest option is to use an **Oyster card** or **contactless credit/debit card** (see p405). And if you're partial to posh nosh, do check out the prix fixe lunches offered by most of London's swankier restaurants – especially in Mayfair. They aren't always cheap, but can be astonishingly good value for the quality.

Tours

On foot

For free, self-guided walking tours, head to **www.walklondon.org.uk** or the Greater London section of the Royal Geographical Society's **www.discoveringbritain.org**. Good choices for paid group tours include **And Did Those Feet** (www.chr.org.uk) and **Original London Walks** (www.walks.com). More idiosyncratic outings include London seen through its old maps (www.londontrails.wordpress.com), public conveniences (lootours.com), art scene (www.foxandsquirrel.com), fashion trends (www.urbangentry.com) and the radical history of the East End (www.eastendwalks.com). **Unseen Tours** (07514 266774, www.sockmobevents.org.uk) are noteworthy: they are led by homeless guides, who bring their own perspective to well-known landmarks and the quirkier nooks of the city.

By bicycle

The **London Bicycle Tour Company** (7928 6838, www.londonbicycle.com) runs a range of tours from the South Bank, while **Boris Bikes** (see p409) can be an affordable option for self-starters.

By boat

Explore the River Thames by speedboat with **Thames RIB Experience** (3613 2307, www.thamesribexperience.com; £26.50-£55, £23.50-£39 reductions), by canoe with **London Kayak Tours** (0845 453 2002, www.londonkayaktours.co.uk, from £39) or take a more conventional hop-on, hop-off tour with **City Cruises** (7740 0400, www.citycruises.com; from £10, £8 reductions). There are narrowboat tours from Camden with **Jason's Trip Canal Boats** (www.jasons.co.uk; £10 single, £9 reductions; £15 return, £14 reductions; Apr-Nov).

By bus

Big Bus Company (7808 6753, bigbustours.com; from £34, £17 reductions, free under-5s) and **Original London Sightseeing Tour** (8877 1722, www.theoriginaltour.com; £32, £15-£29 reductions, free under-5s) both offer multiple hop-on, hop-off stops near the key central London sights, with the price of the ticket including a river cruise.

By car

Offering fun takes on London's motor-car culture are **Black Taxi Tours of London** (7935 9363, www.blacktaxitours.co.uk, £150 per cab) and **Small Car Big City** (7839 6737, smallcarbigcity.com, from £119 per car) in a groovy Mini Cooper.

By air

Money no object? Take an eye-popping aerial tour with **Adventure Balloons** (01252 844222, adventureballoons.co.uk; from £249; late Apr-late July) or the **London Helicopter** (7887 2626, www.thelondonhelicopter.com; from £200).

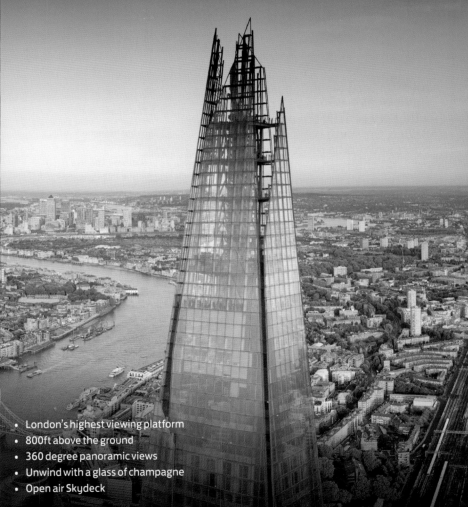

SEE FURTHER THAN THE EYE CAN SEE

- London's highest viewing platform
- 800ft above the ground
- 360 degree panoramic views
- Unwind with a glass of champagne
- Open air Skydeck

BOOK YOUR TICKETS NOW

theviewfromtheshard.com

Open daily from 10am till late ⊖ London Bridge

THE VIEW
FROM THE SHARD

South Bank & Bankside

An estimated 14 million people come this way each year, and it's easy to see why. Between the London Eye and Tower Bridge, the south bank of the Thames offers a two-mile procession of diverting arts and entertainment venues and events.

The area's modern-day life began in 1951 with the Festival of Britain, staged to boost morale in the wake of World War II. The Royal Festival Hall stands testament to the inclusive spirit of the project; it was later expanded into the Southbank Centre, alongside the BFI Southbank cinemas and the concrete ziggurat of the National Theatre.

The riverside really took off in the new millennium, with the arrival of the London Eye, the Millennium Bridge and Tate Modern, and the expansion of Borough Market, but it has continued to thrive in the years since, with the Shard and the Tate Modern's Blavatnik Building adding to the parade of show-stopping structures.

❤ **Don't miss**

1 The Shard *p94*
The bird's-eye view not every bird has the energy to flap up to.

2 National Theatre *p360*
Cultural powerhouse by the Thames.

3 Shakespeare's Globe *p88 & p363*
Top-notch productions in an authentic theatre.

4 Tate Modern *p89*
Power station turned burgeoning artistic powerhouse.

5 Imperial War Museum *p86*
Conflict histories in refreshed displays.

6 Borough Market *p93*
The oldest market in town is a foodie favourite.

El Pastór *p92*

SOUTH BANK & BANKSIDE

Restaurants

1. Anchor & Hope *p87*
2. Baltic *p87*
3. Casse-Croûte *p96*
4. Elliot's *p92*
5. Hutong *p97*
6. M Manze *p97*
7. Oxo Tower *p86*
8. Padella *p92*
9. El Pastór *p92*
10. Pizarro restaurant *p98*
11. Restaurant Story *p98*
12. Sea Containers & Lyaness *p86*
13. Swan at Shakespeare's Globe *p90*

Pubs & bars

1. Doodle Bar *p98*
2. Elephant & Castle *p88*
3. Gông *p98*
4. Royal Oak *p93*
5. Skylon *p86*
6. Waterloo Tap *p86*

Shops & services

1. Bermondsey Square Antiques Market *p98*
2. Borough Market *p93*
3. Maltby Street & Spa Terminus *p98*

SOUTH BANK

▶*Embankment or Westminster tube, or Waterloo tube/rail.*

Thanks to the sharp turn the Thames makes around Waterloo, **Lambeth Bridge** lands you east of the river, not south, opposite the Tudor gatehouse of **Lambeth Palace**. Since the 12th century, it's been the official residence of the Archbishop of Canterbury. The palace is not normally open to the public, except on holidays. The church next door, St Mary at Lambeth, is now the **Garden Museum**, while worshippers of the cult of Damien Hirst do well to check out his ambitious new **Newport Street Gallery**. The benches along the river here are great for viewing the Houses of Parliament opposite, before things get crowded after **Westminster Bridge**, where London's major riverside tourist zone begins.

Next to the bridge is **County Hall**, once the seat of London government, now home to the **Sea Life London Aquarium** and the **London Dungeon**. In front of these attractions, in full view of the lovely **Jubilee Gardens**, the wheel of the **London Eye** rotates serenely.

When the **Southbank Centre** (*see p357*) was built in the 1950s and 1960s, the big concrete boxes that together contain the Royal Festival Hall (RFH), the Queen Elizabeth Hall (QEH), the Purcell Room and the Hayward Gallery were hailed as a daring statement of modern architecture. Along with the National Theatre, they comprise one of the largest and most popular arts districts in the world.

The centrepiece is Sir Leslie Martin's handsome **Royal Festival Hall** (1951), given a £91-million overhaul in 2007, which enhanced the acoustics and refurbished the seating of the main auditorium. The

upper floors include an improved Poetry Library and event rooms, in which readings are delivered against the backdrop of the Eye and, on the far side of the river, Big Ben. Behind the hall, **Southbank Centre Square** hosts a food market every weekend, and there are cafés and chain restaurants all around.

Next door to the Royal Festival Hall, and just across the building housing the QEH and the Purcell Room, the **Hayward Gallery** is a landmark of brutalist architecture – all three venues underwent a multi-million pound 'Let the Light In' refurbishment programme and reopened in 2018.

Tucked under Waterloo Bridge is **BFI Southbank** (*see p323*); the UK's premier arthouse cinema, it's run by the British Film Institute. At the front is a second-hand book market – fun, but not brilliant for real finds. Due to its relative height and location just where the Thames bends from north–south to east–west, **Waterloo Bridge** provides some of the finest views of London, especially at dusk. It was designed by Sir Giles Gilbert Scott, the man behind Tate Modern, in 1942. East of the bridge is Denys Lasdun's terraced **National Theatre** (*see p360*), another brutalist concrete structure, recently much improved.

Shaded by trees dotted with blue LEDs, the river path leads past a rare sandy patch of riverbed, busy with sand sculptors in warm weather, to **Gabriel's Wharf**, a collection of eateries and small independent shops that range from stylish to kitsch.

Next door, the deco tower of **Oxo Tower Wharf** was designed to circumvent advertising regulations for the stock-cube company that used to own the building. Saved by local action group Coin Street Community Builders, it now provides affordable housing, interesting designer

---

❤ Time to eat, drink & shop

A taste of old London town
M Manze *p97*

Beer! Beer! Beer!
Waterloo Tap *p86*

Booze with a view
Gŏng *p98*

France in Bermondsey
Casse-Croûte *p96*

Michelin-starred innovations
Restaurant Story *p98*

Party-time tacos
El Pastór *p92*

Quick pasta fix
Padella *p92*

The go-to for gourmets
Borough Market *p93*,
Maltby Street *p98*

Hay's Galleria

shops and galleries, and restaurants (including a rooftop restaurant and bistro with more wonderful views). Next door, **Sea Containers London** (*see p399*) has brought a bit of buzz to this part of the South Bank.

Sights & museums

Florence Nightingale Museum
St Thomas' Hospital, 2 Lambeth Palace Road, SE1 7EW (7188 4400, www.florence-nightingale.co.uk). Westminster tube or Waterloo tube/rail. **Open** *10am-5pm daily.* **Admission** *£7.50; £4.80 reductions; £15 family; free under-5s.* **Map** *p80 N10.*

The nursing skills and campaigning zeal that made Nightingale a Victorian legend are honoured here. Reopened for the centenary of her death in 2010, the museum is a chronological tour through a remarkable life via three key themes: family life, the Crimean War, health reformer. Among the period mementoes – clothing, furniture, books, letters and portraits – are Nightingale's lantern and stuffed pet owl, Athena.

Garden Museum
5 Lambeth Palace Road, SE1 7LB (7401 8865, www.gardenmuseum.org.uk). Lambeth North tube or Waterloo tube/rail. **Open** *10.30am-5pm Tue-Fri, Sun; 10.30am-4pm Sat; check website for occasional closures.* **Admission** *Museum £10; £5-£8.50 reductions; free under-6s. Tower £3, free under-18s.* **Map** *p80 M11.*

Saved from demolition in the 1970s, the deconsecrated church of St Mary's is a fitting site for the world's first horticulture museum: it was the last resting place of intrepid plant hunter and gardener to Charles I, John Tradescant (c1570-1638). Reopened in May 2017 after a £7.5 million redevelopment, the museum's interior features seven galleries containing gardening memorabilia from 1600 to the modern day, including Britain's oldest watering can and Harold Gilman's intriguing *Portrait of a Black Gardener*. The courtyard extension contains a garden of rare plants, designed by Dan Pearson, and a café. You can climb the 14th-century tower and explore the Ark Gallery – based on the Tradescants' 17th-century cabinet of curiosities – as well as visiting temporary exhibitions. It's a quiet place for reflection too.

The extension was built without foundations due to the 20,000 bodies buried on the site – some dating back to the Norman Conquest. During the works a vault containing no fewer than five lost archbishops was found. The stone

Southbank Centre

London Eye

sarcophagus containing the remains of William Bligh, the captain of the mutinous HMS *Bounty*, is also here.

Hayward Gallery
Southbank Centre, 337-338 Belvedere Road, SE1 8XX (7960 5211, www.southbankcentre. co.uk). Embankment tube or Waterloo tube/ rail. **Open** *11am-7pm Mon, Wed, Fri-Sun; 11am-9pm Thur.* **Map** *p80 N9.*

The 1960s brutalist Hayward Gallery reopened in 2018 after a two-year multi-million pound refurbishment project. Now, 66 glass pyramid rooflights let controlled natural lighting into the upper galleries for the first time, transforming the visitor experience. The improved environment makes the gallery's versatile programme of thought-provoking contemporary art all the more appealing. It has no permanent collection, but has always hosted (often sell-out) exhibitions, among them Anthony Gormley's fog-filled chamber for 'Blind Light,' and Carsten Holler's roller-coaster slides. In 2018, the gallery's 'Shape Shifters' exhibition showcased mind-bending works by Anish Kapoor, Yayoi Kusama and Larry Bell.

London Dungeon
Riverside Building County Hall, Westminster Bridge Road, SE1 7PB (www.thedungeons. com/london). Westminster tube or Waterloo tube/rail. **Open** *10am-5pm Mon-Fri, Sun; 10am-6pm Sat. Times vary during school hols.* **Admission** *£30; £24 reductions; free under-3s. Book online for 30% reductions.* **Map** *p80 N9.*

Visitors to this jokey celebration of torture, death and disease journey back in time to London's plague-ridden streets (rotting corpses, rats, vile boils, projectile vomiting) and meet some of the city's least savoury characters, from Guy Fawkes to Sweeney Todd. A cast of blood-splattered actors are joined by 'virtual' guests, such as Brian Blessed as Henry VIII, as well as 18 different shows and 'surprises' – which could see you on the run from Jack the Ripper or getting lost in London's Victorian sewers. There are two thrill rides too: a turbulent boat trip down the Thames for execution, and a dark drop ride that plunges three storeys in the pitch black.

London Eye
Jubilee Gardens, SE1 7PB (www.londoneye. com). Westminster tube or Waterloo tube/ rail. **Open** *varies.* **Admission** *£27; £22 reductions; free under-3s. Ticket office in County Hall, next to London Eye. Book online for reduced prices.* **Map** *p80 N9.*

The Eye is up there with Tower Bridge and 'Big Ben' among the capital's most postcard-friendly tourist assets. Assuming you choose a clear day, a 30-minute circuit on the Eye affords predictably great views of the city, with touchscreens in each of the 32 pods providing a guide to what you can see. Take a few snaps from the comfort of your pod and, there, your sightseeing's just about done – and the fact that the vista changes makes it a doughty competitor to the Shard (*see p94*). The Eye was the vision of husband-and-wife architect team Julia

Barfield and David Marks, who entered a 1992 competition to design a structure for the millennium. Their giant wheel idea came second, but the winning entry is conspicuous by its absence. The Eye was planned as a temporary structure but its removal now seems unthinkable.

Newport Street Gallery

Newport Street, SE11 6AJ (3141 9320, www. newportstreetgallery.com/about). Vauxhall tube/rail or Lambeth North tube. **Open** *10am-6pm Tue-Sun.* **Admission** *free.* **Map** *p80 N11.*

Damien Hirst, the Young British Artist par excellence, isn't a man to do things by halves – unless, that is, taking half a street of listed warehouses and converting them into a huge gallery. Across two levels, six exhibition spaces and some 37,000sq ft of floor, his private collection of 3,000 works is displayed in temporary exhibitions: with holdings that include Picasso, Francis Bacon and Jeff Koons alongside YBA chums like Sarah Lucas and Gavin Turk, he's got plenty of art to choose from, but there's also taxidermy, indigenous art from the Pacific Northwest and anatomical models. The space was brilliantly reworked by the architects Caruso St John, who won the 2017 Stirling Prize for their work. The in-house restaurant, **Pharmacy 2**, designed by Hirst, serves a casual modern-British menu overseen by chef Mark Hix.

Sea Life London Aquarium

County Hall, Westminster Bridge Road, SE1 7PB (www2.visitsealife.com/london). Westminster tube or Waterloo tube/rail. **Open** *10am-6pm Mon-Fri; 9.30am-7pm Sat, Sun. School holidays varies.* **Admission** *£26; £21 reductions; free under-3s. Book online for reductions.* **Map** *p80 N10.*

This is one of Europe's largest aquariums, and a huge hit with kids – perhaps too huge: it does get awfully crowded in the school holidays and at weekends. The inhabitants are grouped by geographical origin, beginning with the Atlantic, where blacktail bream swim alongside the Thames Embankment. The 'Rainforests of the World' exhibit has introduced poison arrow frogs, crocodiles and piranhas. The Ray Lagoon is still popular, though touching the friendly flatfish is no longer allowed (it's bad for their health). Starfish, crabs and anemones can be handled in special open rock pools instead, and the clown fish still draw crowds. There's a mesmerising Seahorse Temple, a tank full of turtles and enchanting Gentoo penguins. The centrepieces, though, are the massive Pacific and Indian Ocean tanks, with menacing sharks quietly circling fallen Easter Island statues.

Hayward Gallery

Shrek's Adventure!

Riverside Building, County Hall, Westminster Bridge Road, SE1 7PB (www.shreksadventure. com/london). Westminster tube or Waterloo tube/rail. **Open** *10am-4pm Mon-Fri; 10am-6pm Sat; 10am-5pm Sun.* **Admission** *£27.50; £22 reductions. Book online for 30% reductions.* **Map** *p80 N10.*

Opened in 2015, Shrek's Adventure! takes you on an immersive journey ('4D', in the jargon) through the worlds of the golden-hearted green ogre and other DreamWorks characters. It happens onboard a red double-decker bus, with Donkey as your driver to the Kingdom of Far, Far Away. Here you and your six- to 12-year-olds find yourselves part of the story, solving clues, joining in the occasional singsong and generally doing silly things on a quest for that 'happy ever after' ending. With excellent set design and plenty of surprises, it's an engaging and amusing 75-minute trip into Shrek's off-kilter fairytale world.

Restaurants

Clustered around the **Royal Festival Hall**, you'll find plenty of chain restaurants (including Ping Pong, Giraffe, Pizza Express, Wahaca and Wagamama). There are also crêpe and pizza restaurants at **Gabriel's Wharf**, along the bank to the east, and good drinking and dining options in the **National Theatre** (*see p360*) and **BFI Southbank** (*see p323*). For quality dining with a view, try the **Oxo Tower Restaurant** (Bargehouse Street, SE1 9PH, 7803 3888, www.oxotower.co.uk, £££ ❼) or **Sea Containers Restaurant** (20 Upper Ground, SE1 9PD, 3747 1063, www. seacontainersrestaurant.com, £££ ⓬).

Pubs & bars

For cocktails, **Lyaness** has taken over from the all-conquering Dandelyan on the ground-floor of Sea Containers London (*see p399*). In the Royal Festival Hall, the bar at **Skylon** (7654 7800, www.skylon-restaurant.co.uk ❺) has one of the best river views in town.

❤ Waterloo Tap ££

Corner of Sutton Walk & Concert Hall Approach, SE1 8RL (3455 7436, www. waterlootap.com). Waterloo tube/rail. **Open** *noon-11pm Mon-Tue; noon-11.30pm Wed, Thur; noon-midnight Fri; 11am-midnight Sat; 11am-10pm Sun.* **Map** *p80 N9* ❻

Tucked away in a railway arch a short dash from Waterloo station, the Tap has bucked the trend towards the new breed of high-alcohol brews and stuck to its roots as a more traditional alehouse. You'll find no filament bulbs or scruffily chalked-up beer lists here. The 20-strong keg collection is very

British-focused, with the north especially well represented (no surprise, given the original Tap is in Sheffield). If they're on, try something from Manchester's Cloudwater Brew Co, whose one-off, seasonal brews are never around for long.

WATERLOO & LAMBETH

▶ *Waterloo tube/rail or Lambeth North tube.*

Surprisingly, perhaps, there's plenty of interest around the stone-meets-glass rail terminus of London Waterloo. The most obvious attraction is the massive **BFI IMAX** (*see p322*), located in the middle of a roundabout at the southern end of Waterloo Bridge. The £20-million cinema makes use of a desolate space that, in the 1990s, was notorious for its 'Cardboard City' of homeless residents.

South, on the corner of Waterloo Road and the Cut, is the restored Victorian façade of the **Old Vic** theatre (*see p362*), which has settled comfortably into life after artistic director Kevin Spacey. Further down the Cut is the **Young Vic** (*see p368*), a hotbed of theatrical talent with a stylish balcony bar. Both bring a touch of West End glamour across the river.

Further south, into Lambeth, is the impressive – and steadily revamped – **Imperial War Museum**. The imposing premises were built in 1814 as a lunatic asylum (the Bethlehem Royal Hospital, aka Bedlam). After the inmates were moved out in 1930, the central block became the war museum, only to be damaged by air raids. Today, it provides a compelling and frequently hard-hitting history of armed conflict since World War I.

Sights & museums

❤ Imperial War Museum

Lambeth Road, SE1 6HZ (7416 5000, www. iwm.org.uk). Lambeth North tube or Elephant & Castle tube/rail. **Open** *10am-6pm daily.* **Admission** *free. Special exhibitions vary.* **Map** *p80 O11.*

One of London's great museums – but probably the least famous of them – IWM London focuses on the military action of British and Commonwealth troops during the 20th century. One of the highlights, built to commemorate the centenary, is a state-of-the-art First World War gallery that takes a more considered, contemporary look at the conflict, examining the Home Front as much as the Western Front. Alongside huge set pieces like a walk-through trench is a heart-stopping collection of small, personal items and medical objects, including a magnet used to pull shrapnel from wounds. The Central Hall is an attention-grabbing repository of major artefacts: guns, tanks and aircraft hang from the ceiling (not least a Harrier GR9 that saw action in Afghanistan). Terraced galleries allow this section of the museum also to show a Snatch Land Rover from Iraq and an Argentine operating table from the Falklands.

The museum's tone darkens as you ascend. On the third floor, the Holocaust Exhibition (not recommended for under-14s) traces the history of European anti-Semitism and its nadir in the concentration camps. Upstairs, Crimes Against Humanity (unsuitable for under-16s) is a minimalist space in which a film exploring contemporary genocide and ethnic violence rolls relentlessly. At the top, a new gallery explores contemporary conflicts.

Restaurants

Anchor & Hope ££
36 The Cut, SE1 8LP (7928 9898, www.anchorandhopepub.co.uk). Southwark tube or Waterloo tube/rail. **Open** *5-11pm Mon; 11am-11pm Tue-Sat; noon-5pm Sun. Food served 6-10.30pm Mon; noon-2.30pm, 6-10.30pm Tue-Sat; 12.30-3.15pm Sun.* **Map** *p80 O9* ① *Gastropub*

Open for more than a decade, the Anchor & Hope is still a leading exponent of using offal and unusual cuts of meat in simple but artful combinations, served in a relaxed setting. Bookings aren't taken, so most evenings you'll join the waiting list for a table (45 minutes midweek is typical) and have to hover at the crammed bar. But the food is terrific: beautifully textured venison kofte, say, served on perkily dressed gem lettuce leaves; or rabbit served savagely red, with salty jus, fat chips and béarnaise sauce.

Baltic ££
74 Blackfriars Road, SE1 8HA (7928 1111, www.balticrestaurant.co.uk). Southwark tube. **Open** *5.30-11.15pm Mon; noon-3pm, 5.30-11.15pm Tue-Sat; noon-4.30pm, 5.30-10.30pm Sun.* **Map** *p80 O9* ② *Eastern European*

A modern take on Polish/central European classics is served in surroundings of understated glamour, with pared-down monochrome decor punctuated by a supersized chandelier dripping shards of golden amber. You'll struggle to find such enjoyable buckwheat blinis topped with smoked salmon or tender herring elsewhere. Home-style pleasures abound, such as rabbit braised in a fragrant broth flavoured with sweet prune and smoky bacon, served with little knobbly spätzle dumplings. Start with a classy clear vodka such as Zytnia (rye), then move on to one of Baltic's own tasty ginger or spicy orange varieties.

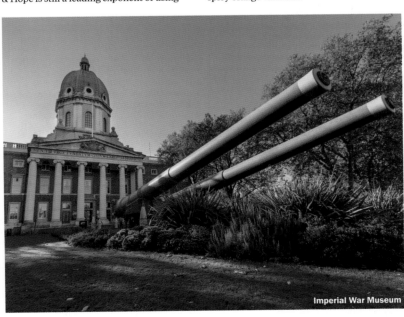

Imperial War Museum

Pubs & bars

Elephant & Castle

119 Newington Causeway, SE1 6BN (7403 8124, elephantandcastlepub.com). Elephant & Castle tube/rail. **Open** *noon-midnight Mon-Wed, Sun; noon-1am Thur; noon-2am Fri, Sat.* **Map** *p80 P11* ②

Pub histories don't come much better than that of the Elephant & Castle. Back in the 18th century, the entire area was named after it. In 1991, DJ Matt 'Jam' Lamont's Sunday morning raves made it the birthplace of UK Garage. Then, in 2015, it lost its licence. Nearly suffering the ignominious fate of being turned into an estate agent, it was saved by the council, which gave it protected status as an asset of community value. It's now a trendy joint, with craft beer on tap.

BANKSIDE

▶ *Borough or Southwark tube, or Blackfriars or London Bridge tube/rail.*

In Shakespeare's day, the area known as Bankside was the centre of bawdy Southwark, neatly located just beyond the jurisdiction of the City fathers. As well as playhouses such as the Globe and the Rose, there were the famous 'stewes' (brothels) presided over by the bishops of Winchester, who made a tidy income from the fines they levied on the area's 'Winchester Geese' (or, in common parlance, prostitutes). There's less drinking, carousing and mischief-making here these days, but the area's cultural heritage remains alive thanks to the reconstructed **Shakespeare's Globe** and, pretty much next door to it, the recently dramatically extended **Tate Modern**, a former power station that's now a gallery.

Spanning the river in front of the Tate, the **Millennium Bridge** for pedestrians opened in 2000, when it became the first new Thames crossing in London since Tower Bridge (1894). Its early days were fraught with troubles: after just two days, the bridge was closed because of a pronounced wobble caused by the resonance of thousands of people crossing together, and didn't reopen until 2002. Its difficulties long behind it, the bridge is an elegant structure – a 'ribbon of steel' in the words of its conceptualists, architect Lord Foster and sculptor Anthony Caro. Cross it and you're at the foot of the stairs leading up to St Paul's Cathedral (*see p224*); to the west, the massively refurbished **Blackfriars** rail station not only has an entrance on the south bank of the river, but runs train platforms right across the river on the podiums of an earlier, incomplete version of **Blackfriars Bridge**.

Shakespeare's Globe

Sights & museums

Bankside Gallery

48 Hopton Street, SE1 9JH (7928 7521, www. banksidegallery.com). Blackfriars tube/rail or Southwark tube. **Open** *(during exhibitions) 11am-6pm daily.* **Admission** *free; donations appreciated.* **Map** *p80 P8.*

In the shadow of Tate Modern, this tiny gallery is the home of the Royal Watercolour Society and the Royal Society of Painter-Printmakers. The gallery runs a changing programme of exhibitions, with many of the displayed works for sale.

♥ Shakespeare's Globe

21 New Globe Walk, SE1 9DT (7902 1400, www.shakespearesglobe.com). Blackfriars tube/rail or Southwark tube. **Exhibition** *9am-5pm daily.* **Tours** *9.30am-5pm daily (except during performances).* **Admission** *£17; £10-15.50 reductions; £46 family; free under-5s.* **Map** *p80 P8.*

The original Globe Theatre, where many of William Shakespeare's plays were first staged and which he co-owned, burned to the ground in 1613 during a performance of *Henry VIII.* Nearly 400 years later, it was rebuilt not far from its original site, using construction methods and materials based on as much historical detail as could be found.

A visit here isn't just a history lesson. The Globe is also a fully operating open-air theatre (*see p363*) and the productions are among the best in London. Each season (from 23 April – conventionally regarded as the Bard's birthday – into early October) includes several Shakespeare classics, performed by a company of established and upcoming actors, but works of other writers are also programmed.

The Globe also now offers performances in the Sam Wanamaker Playhouse – a candlelit indoor theatre alongside the Globe, which presents plays in a traditional and intimate Jacobean setting.

Even if you're not attending a play, you can do the Globe Exhibition and Tour: the tours run all year, even out of season (allow 90 minutes for the visit).

♥ Tate Modern

Bankside, SE1 9TG (7887 8888, www.tate.org. uk). Blackfriars tube/rail or Southwark tube. **Open** *10am-6pm Mon-Thur, Sun; 10am-10pm Fri, Sat.* **Admission** *free. Temporary exhibitions vary.* **Map** *p80 P8.*

Thanks to its industrial architecture, this powerhouse of modern art is awe-inspiring even before you enter. Built after World War II as Bankside Power Station, it was designed by Sir Giles Gilbert Scott, architect of Battersea Power Station. The power station shut in 1981; nearly 20 years later, it opened as an art museum, and has enjoyed spectacular popularity ever since. The gallery attracts five million visitors a year – twice as many as the original building was intended for, hence the ten-storey extension that rose from the power station's former fuel tanks to completion in 2016. Known first as the Switch House – then renamed the Blavatnik Building after major donor Len Blavatnik – this vast, partly folded tower has increased exhibition space by 60 per cent and features a top-floor viewing level, restaurant, and three new floors of galleries. It has allowed for a 'progressive rehang' of Tate Modern's permanent collection across both the Blavatnik Building and current Tate Modern building, with more room for lesser-known international art. The cavernous Turbine Hall, used to jaw-dropping

Tate Modern

Southwark Cathedral

effect for the massive Hyundai Commission installation each year, has become what the Tate is calling 'the street' that connects both buildings, with walkways at different points.

Beyond, the permanent collection draws from the Tate's many post-1900 international works, featuring heavy-hitters such as Matisse, Rothko and Beuys – but the grouping by theme rather than chronology can make it hard to pilot your way through, by contrast to the gallery's much-improved elder sibling, Tate Britain (see p113). Many visit for the very busy blockbuster shows – or the views from the extension platform, notwithstanding the overworked lifts – without spending much time on the permanent collection.

Restaurants

There are some handy chain restaurants (Pizza Express, The Real Greek, Tas Pide) on the river near the Globe Theatre, plus more (Tsuru, Leon) behind Tate Modern on Canvey Street. **Tate Modern Café: Level 2** is good for those with children.

Swan at Shakespeare's Globe £££
21 New Globe Walk, SE1 9DT (7928 9444, www.swanlondon.co.uk). London Bridge tube/rail. Open noon-3pm, 5pm-10.15pm Mon-Sat; 11.30am-5.30pm Sun. Map p80 P8 ⓭
Modern British

Attached to the Globe theatre, the Swan is a decent (if pricey) option for canny pre- and post-performance diners. And it's worth a trip just for the view. By night, the river aspect of an illuminated St Paul's is a stunner. It's a lovely room too: smart, chic and airy, a foil to the rammed bar downstairs. The modern British cooking is picture-perfect if a little one-dimensional.

BOROUGH

▶ *Borough or Southwark tube, or London Bridge tube/rail.*

On the east side of Southwark Bridge, you'll find the **Anchor Bankside** pub (34 Park Street, SE1 9EF, 7407 1577, www.greeneking-pubs.co.uk). Built in 1775 on the site of an even older inn, the Anchor has, at various points, been a brothel, a chapel and a ship's chandler. The outside terrace, across the pathway, offers fine river views – a fact lost on no one each summer, when it's invariably crammed with people.

All that's left of the Palace of Winchester, home of successive bishops, is the ruined rose window of the Great Hall on Clink Street. It stands next to the site of the bishops' former Clink prison, where thieves, prostitutes and debtors all served their sentences; it's now the **Clink Prison Museum** (1 Clink Street, SE1 9DG, 7403 0900, www.clink.co.uk). At the other end of Clink Street, St Mary Overie's dock contains a terrific full-scale replica of Sir Francis Drake's ship, the **Golden Hinde**.

The main landmark here is the Anglican **Southwark Cathedral**, formerly St Saviour's and before that the monastic church of St Mary Overie. Shakespeare's brother Edmund was buried in the graveyard; there's a monument to the playwright inside. Just south of the cathedral is **Borough Market**, a busy covered food market dating from the 13th century, although with its new glass-fronted premises you'd hardly think so. There's still plenty of Victorian ironwork to enjoy. This is London's 'foodiest' public food market; stalls are limited on Mondays and Tuesdays, but it is crammed with buyers and sellers for the rest of the week. It's surrounded by good places to eat and drink. Not far away, the **George** (75-77 Borough High Street, SE1 1NH, 7407 2056, www.greeneking-pubs.co.uk) is London's last surviving galleried coaching inn. Owned by the National Trust, it hosted Charles Dickens, among many others.

Fans of gore should head to the interesting and thoroughly grisly **Old Operating Theatre, Museum & Herb Garret**, with its body parts and surgical implements.

Sights & museums

Golden Hinde

Pickfords Wharf, Clink Street, SE1 9DG (7403 0123, www.goldenhinde.com). London Bridge tube/rail. **Open** *10am-5pm daily.* **Admission** *£5; £15 family; free under-3s.* **Map** *p80 Q9.*

This meticulous replica of Sir Francis Drake's 16th-century flagship is thoroughly seaworthy: the ship has even reprised the privateer's circumnavigatory voyage. You can visit by means of a self-guided tour, but if you've got kids it's much more fun to join in on a 'living history' experience (some overnight): participants dress in period clothes, eat Tudor fare and learn the skills of the Elizabethan seafarer; book well in advance. At weekends, the ship swarms

with children dressed up as pirates for birthday dos.

Old Operating Theatre, Museum & Herb Garret

9A St Thomas' Street, SE1 9RY (7188 2679, oldoperatingtheatre.com). London Bridge tube/rail. **Open** *2-5pm, 10.30am-5pm Mon, Tue-Sun.* **Admission** *£6.50; £3.50-£5 reductions; £15 family.* **Map** *p80 R9.*

The tower that houses this reminder of the surgical practices of the past used to be part of the chapel of St Thomas' Hospital. Before moving there, operations took place in the wards. Visitors enter via a vertiginous spiral staircase to inspect a pre-anaesthetic operating theatre dating from 1822, with tiered viewing seats for students. The operating tools look more like torture implements.

Southwark Cathedral

London Bridge, SE1 9DA (7367 6700, www. cathedral.southwark.anglican.org). London Bridge tube/rail. **Open** *8am-6pm Mon-Fri; 8.30am-6pm Sat, Sun (closing times vary on religious holidays). Services 8am, 8.15am, 12.30pm, 12.45pm, 5.30pm Mon-Fri; 9am, 9.15am, 4pm Sat; 8.30am, 9am, 11am, 3pm, 6pm Sun.* **Admission** *free; suggested donation £4.* **Map** *p80 Q9.*

Golden Hinde

El Pastór

The oldest bits of this building date back more than 800 years. The retro-choir was the setting for several Protestant martyr trials during the reign of Mary Tudor. Inside, there are memorials to Shakespeare, John Harvard (benefactor of the American university) and Sam Wanamaker (the motivation and driving force behind the reconstruction of the Globe); Chaucer features in the stained glass. There are displays throughout the cathedral explaining its history. The courtyard is one of the area's prettiest places for a rest; there's also a café.

Restaurants

Borough Market, full of stalls selling all kinds of wonderful food, is a superb foraging place for street-food enthusiasts, as well as the home of one of London's finest restaurants, **El Pastór** (*see right*).

Elliot's ££

12 Stoney Street, SE1 9AD (7403 7436, www. elliotscafe.com). London Bridge tube/ rail. **Open** *noon-3pm, 6-10pm Mon-Fri; noon-4pm, 6-10pm Sat.* **Map** *p80 Q9* 4
Brasserie

Light and airy, with stripped brick walls and a contemporary feel, Elliot's is a busy spot. The choices are to sit out front while watching the world going by, to perch at the bar or to take a seat in the bright back area. The seasonal menu is short but innovative, and the ingredients are carefully sourced. Smaller plates, such as pickled mackerel with apple and rye cracker, are listed alongside larger dishes such as lox cheek, polenta horse radish and pickled walnut. Drinks include a selection of natural wines (orange wines are listed alongside the expected white, red and rosé).

♥ Padella ££

6 Southwark Street, SE1 1TQ (www.padella. co). London Bridge tube/rail. **Open** *noon-3.45pm, 5-10pm Mon-Sat; noon-3.45pm, 5-9pm Sun.* **Map** *p80 Q9* 8 *Italian*

This sleek pasta bar, from the duo behind Islington's **Trullo** (*see p251*), is ideal for a classy express lunch. There's a changing mix of classics and lesser-spotted varieties, such as *tagliarini* (skinny tagliatelle) or *pici* (a kind of hand-rolled no-egg noodle from Siena), which is smothered in a simple yet moreish *cacio e pepe* sauce of parmesan, butter and cracked black pepper. The eight-hour beef shin ragu served over pappardelle is a perennial favourite, while the smoked eel and cream tagliatelle – with just a hint of Sicilian lemon – is sublime. Dishes are small enough (and, at around £5-£9, cheap enough) to let you to order three between two.

♥ El Pastór ££

7A Stoney Street, SE1 9AA (www.tacoselpastor. co.uk). London Bridge tube/rail. **Open** *noon-3pm, 5-11pm Mon-Fri; noon-4pm, 6-11pm Sat; noon-4pm Sun.* **Map** *p80 Q9* 9 *Mexican*

El Pastór is a taco joint in a railway arch next to foodie magnet Borough Market (*see p93*) and it doesn't accept bookings. The wait can, at peak times, be up to two hours. But once you've got a table you might try a tuna tostada, a bowl of fresh guac and a prawn taco on a nicely firm corn tortilla. Or the signature 24-hour marinated 'al pastór' pork – just the thought of which makes us smile. With the pork, make sure you get 'gringa' quesadilla: a dirty and delicious quarter slice of a large tortilla, served 'open-faced', with a messy tumble of meat, melted cheese, coriander and salsa. Every bite brings sweet, salt, fire, squidge and crunch. El Pastór knows how to throw a fiesta, with excellent, Latin-vibey music cranked up loud; staff who are smiley and obliging; and the lighting set to 'looking good, baby'.

Pubs & bars

Royal Oak

44 Tabard Street, SE1 4JU (7357 7173, www.royaloaklondon.co.uk). Borough tube. **Open** *11am-11pm Mon-Fri; noon-11pm Sat; noon-7.45pm Sun. Food served noon-2.45pm, 5-9.30pm Mon-Fri; noon-4pm, 5-9.30pm Sat; noon-9pm Sun.* **Map** *p80 Q10* 4

Perfectly treading the line between old-man boozer and cutesy retro watering hole, this Victorian corner pub's a lovely blend of the scruffy and the pretty. Selling mainly ales from Harvey's brewery in Sussex (which runs the pub), drinkers are largely men in their thirties and older. But the most important thing about this characterful boozer: it's curiously unbothered by the crowds you'll find in other Borough pubs, making it perfect for a quiet few pints.

Shops & services

♥ Borough Market

8 Southwark Street, SE1 1TL (7407 1002, www.boroughmarket.org.uk). London Bridge tube/rail. **Open** *10am-5pm Mon-Thur; 10am-6pm Fri; 8am-5pm Sat.* **Map** *p80 Q9* 2 *Market*

The food hound's favourite market is also London's oldest, dating back to the 13th century. It's the busiest, too, occupying a sprawling site near London Bridge. In its long history, Borough Market has survived fire, riot, terrorism and redevelopment – a busy rail line has been thrice installed and extended above the market itself. Now all it has to contend with are the hordes of tourists and Londoners who flock here to grab a gourmet goodie: from fresh loaves and rare-breed meats, via fish, game, fruit and veg, to cakes and all manner of preserves, oils and teas; head out hungry to take advantage of the numerous free samples. Market Hall, facing on to Borough High Street, acts as a kind of greenhouse for growing plants (including hops), as well as hosting workshops, tastings and foodie demonstrations. You can also nip in with your snack if the weather's poor.

In the know
Timing is everything

Although Borough Market is open on Monday and Tuesday, those days are mainly for tradespeople, and there are fewer stalls open to the general public. Given that weekends are almost always mobbed, Wednesday and Thursday are normally the best days on which to visit.

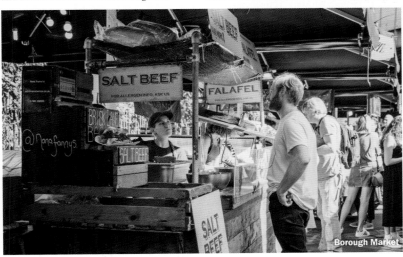

Borough Market

LONDON BRIDGE TO TOWER BRIDGE

▶ *Bermondsey tube or London Bridge tube/rail.*

Nothing can compete with the colossal, 1,016-foot **Shard** development at London Bridge station – it towers over the immediate area, and the London skyline, from pretty much everywhere – but there are more modest discoveries to be made further to the east.

Next to the Thames is **Hay's Galleria**. Once an enclosed dock, it's now dominated by a peculiar kinetic sculpture called *The Navigators*. Exiting on the riverside, you can walk east past the great grey hulk of **HMS Belfast** to Tower Bridge. Beyond the battleship you'll pass the pristine environs of the **More London** complex – sold off to Kuwaiti investors in a £1.7-billion property deal – part of which is **City Hall**, home of London's current government. A pleasant outdoor area called the 'Scoop' is used for outdoor events, with the **Bridge Theatre** (*see p366*) just to the east.

South of here, many of the historic houses on Bermondsey Street now host hip design studios or funky shops. This is also where you'll find the **Fashion & Textile Museum**, as well as Jay Jopling's largest **White Cube** art gallery (nos.144-152, 7930 5373, www. whitecube.com, 10am-6pm Tue-Sat, noon-6pm Sun). At the street's furthest end, the redevelopment of Bermondsey Square created an arthouse cinema and the Bermondsey Square Hotel, alongside a charming cemetery park, but old-timers linger on: the classic eel and pie shop **M Manze** and a Friday **antiques market** – great for browsing, but get there early. If the Borough Market crowds are getting too much for you on a Saturday, head east from Bermondsey Street to the winning cluster of food stalls that form **Maltby Street Market**. For those looking to buy and eat the food, rather than just Insta-snap it, this area is a better bet than Borough, although it's no longer the preserve of gourmets in the know. South again is **Spa Terminus**, a collective of food and drink producers who have set up shop in the railway arches of the Dockley Road Industrial Estate. Bermondsey's craft beer producers are also concentrated in this area (*see p99*).

Back on the riverfront, a board announces when Tower Bridge is next due to be raised. The bridge is one of the lowest to span the Thames, hence its twin lifting sections (or bascules). The original steam-driven machinery can be seen at the **Tower Bridge Exhibition** (*see p237*). Further east, the former warehouses of **Butler's Wharf** are now mainly given over to dining: they are pleasant enough for watching the river if you're not particularly watching the pennies.

💙 The Shard

32 London Bridge Street, SE1 9SG (0844 499 7111, www.theviewfromtheshard.com). London Bridge tube/rail. **Open** *10am-10pm daily.* **Admission** *£30.95; £24.95 reductions; free under-4s. Book online for reductions.* **Map** *p80 R9.*

You can't miss the Shard – which is, after all, the point of the structure. Looking oddly similar to Saruman's tower in *The Lord of the Rings*, it shoots into the sky 'like a shard of glass' – to use the words of its architect, Renzo Piano, who doodled the idea for this vast edifice for its developer, Irving Sellar, on the back of a menu. In 2011, the Shard became the tallest building in the EU, but wasn't to reach its full height until 2012, when it topped out at 1,016ft (310m). As is the fate of skyscrapers, the Shard's claims to be the tallest are relative: it's beaten in Moscow, the Arab Emirates and across South-east Asia.

But height isn't everything: it's the shape of this slim, slightly irregular pyramid that makes it noteworthy, an instantly recognisable centrepiece of views from pretty much everywhere in London – except, ironically, from the Victorian alleys at its foot, where the monstrous building plays peek-a-boo with visitors as they scurry around looking for a good snapshot.

Once you're inside, high-speed lifts whisk passengers up 72 floors to enjoy stunning 360°, 40-mile views, but the real joy of a visit is looking down: even seasoned London-watchers find peering down on the likes of the Tower of London from this extreme height oddly revelatory, like Google Earth in real time.

If you've got a few quid in your pocket, a stay at the Shangri-La (*see p400*) gives you plenty of time to take it all in without the hoi polloi – and with the opportunity to swim in a rather narrow infinity pool on the 52nd floor. But you don't have to be resident to enjoy cocktails at Gŏng (also on the 52nd floor; *see p98*) or local Bermondsey beer and live music at Bar 31 on the ground floor (31 St Thomas Street, SE1 9QU, bar31.com). Of the Shard's four restaurants (Aqua Shard, Level 31; Oblix, Level 32; Hutong, Level 33; Ting, Level 35) – Hutong is our favourite (*see p97*).

▶ *If you're planning to take your time up there, note there are no toilets on the viewing platforms.*

Sights & museums

Fashion & Textile Museum

83 Bermondsey Street, SE1 3XF (7407 8664, www.ftmlondon.org). London Bridge tube/rail. **Open** *11am-6pm Tue, Wed, Fri, Sat; 11am-8pm Thur; 11am-5pm Sun.* **Admission** *£9.90; £7-£8.80 reductions; free under-12s.* **Map** *p80 R10.*

As flamboyant as its founder, fashion designer Zandra Rhodes, this pink and orange museum holds 3,000 of Rhodes's garments and her archive of paper designs, sketchbooks, silk screens and show videos. The varied and always interesting temporary exhibits explore the work of trend-setters or themes such as the development of underwear. A quirky shop sells wares by new designers.

HMS Belfast

The Queen's Walk, SE1 2JH (7940 6300, www.iwm.org.uk). London Bridge tube/rail. **Open** *Mar-Oct 10am-6pm daily. Nov-Feb 10am-5pm daily.* **Admission** *£17; £8.50-£13.60 reductions; free under-5s.* **Map** *p80 S9.*

This 11,500-ton 'Edinburgh' class large light cruiser is the last surviving big-gun World War II warship in Europe. It's also a floating branch of the Imperial War Museum, and is a popular if unlikely playground for children, who tear around its complex of gun turrets, bridge, decks and engine room. The *Belfast* was built in 1936, ran convoys to Russia, supported the Normandy Landings and helped UN forces in Korea before being decommissioned in 1963.

In the know
Kapow!

Wondering where those big forward guns on **HMS Belfast** are pointing? Exploiting an effective range of a bit less than 12 miles, they'd put a shell through the plate-glass windows of a service station on the M1 motorway.

Restaurants

♥ Casse-Croûte £££

109 Bermondsey Street, SE1 3XB (7407 2140, cassecroute.co.uk). London Bridge tube/rail. **Open** *noon-10pm Mon-Sat; noon-4pm Sun.* **Map** *p80 R10* ❸ *French*

Romantically lit, with checked tablecloths and a tiny bar lined with digestifs, Casse-Croûte is a shot of warm, villagey France in Bermondsey. On the site of a former sandwich shop, Hervé Durochat's intimate bistro has space for just over 20 covers and feels genuinely familial. Best of all, the sensibly priced blackboard menu of boldly chosen French classics really delivers. From delicate shavings of calf's head in a tangy sauce *ravigote* to creamy mackerel fillets pepped up with a scoop of mustard ice-cream, dishes are fresh, simple and smartly executed. **Other location** Pique Nique, Tanner Street Park, SE1 3LD (7403 9549, pique-nique.co.uk).

Hutong £££££
The Shard, Level 33, 31 St Thomas Street, SE1 9RY (3011 1257, hutong.co.uk). London Bridge tube/rail. **Open** *noon-2.30pm, 6-10.30pm Mon-Fri; 11.30am-3.30pm, 6-10.30pm Sat, Sun.* **Map** *p80 R9* ⑤ *Chinese*

Like the original Hutong in Hong Kong, the Shard version is a glitzy place with amazing views, ersatz Old Beijing decor, and a Sichuan/northern Chinese menu. The traditionally fiery cuisine, big on chilli and sichuan pepper, has been toned down a little for the *gweilo* (Western) palate, but there's plenty to set the tastebuds alight. Delicate starters of chilled sliced scallops served with pomelo segments or octopus salad with hot and sour sauce are followed by mouthwatering mains such as prawn wantons with *ma-la* ('numbing, spicy hot' sauce), a 'red lantern' of softshell crabs or Mongolian-style barbecue rack of lamb. It's not cheap but then this is the Shard, not Chinatown.

♥ M Manze £
87 Tower Bridge Road, SE1 4TW (7407 2985, www.manze.co.uk). Bus 1, 42, 188. **Open** *11am-2pm Mon; 10.30am-2pm Tue-Thur; 10am-2.30pm Fri; 10am-2.45pm Sat.* **Map** *p80 R11* ⑥ *Pie & mash*

One of the few remaining purveyors of the dirt-cheap traditional foodstuff of London's working classes. It's the oldest pie shop in town, established in 1902, with tiles, marble-topped tables and wooden benches – and is almost as beautiful as L Manze's on Walthamstow High Street, now Grade II-listed. Orders are simple: minced beef pies or, for braver souls, stewed eels with mashed potato and liquor (a thin parsley sauce).

HMS Belfast and Tower Bridge

Pizarro Restaurant ££

*194 Bermondsey Street, SE1 3TQ (7378 9455, www.pizarrorestaurant.com). Borough tube or London Bridge tube/rail. **Open** noon-11pm Mon-Sat; noon-10pm Sun. **Map** p80 R11* ⑩ *Spanish*

José Pizarro's restaurant continues in the style set in his tapas-only bar, **José**, up the street. Menus are more extensive here; the mostly traditional dishes are prepared with care and skill, using fine ingredients, and usually include an expertly slow-braised beef stew. The space artfully combines old-Spanish touches – tiles, warm wood, exposed brick – with a stripped-down 'New Bermondsey' look. **Other locations** José Tapas Bar, 104 Bermondsey Street, SE1 3UB (7403 4902); José Pizarro Broadgate, 36 Broadgate Circle, EC2M 2QS (7256 5333).

❤ Restaurant Story ££££

*199 Tooley Street, SE1 2JX (7183 2117, restaurantstory.co.uk). London Bridge tube/ rail. **Open** 6.30-9pm Mon; noon-5pm, 6.30-9pm Tue-Sat. **Map** p80 S10* ⑪ *British*

Story, from starry young chef Tom Sellers, continues this area's rise to foodie heaven, having secured a Michelin star within months of opening. It's set in a sparse room – all the better to emphasise the view of the Shard through floor-to-ceiling windows, and, of course, the food: an enjoyable procession of modernist dishes layered with culinary puns (bread and dripping, for instance, features a lit candle made from dripping) and tastebud challenges (mackerel versus green strawberries).

Pubs & bars

This is one of the best bits of London in which to explore the extraordinary proliferation of craft breweries (*see opposite* Bermondsey Beer Mile).

Doodle Bar

*60 Druid Street, SE1 2EZ (7403 3222, www. thedoodlebar.com). Bermondsey tube. **Open** 5-11pm Wed; noon-11pm Thur; noon-midnight Fri, Sat; noon-6pm Sun. **Map** p80 S10* ①

One of London's more original pop-up bars, Doodle now resides in an atmospheric Bermondsey railway arch. The concrete floor is high gloss, there's table football by the bar, and a street food van parks outside on weekends. But the real action is at the back: a narrow arch of a room with ping pong tables, where drinkers are encouraged to draw all over the walls. A well-curated wine list is accompanied by a handful of cocktails and the bar's own-brewed pale ale.

❤ Gŏng

*Level 52, The Shard, 31 St Thomas Street, SE1 9QU (7234 8208, www.gong-shangri-la.com). London Bridge tube/rail. **Open** noon-1am Mon-Sat; noon-midnight Sun. **Map** p80 R9* ③

Take the express lift up the Shard to the 52nd floor to find London's highest bar. At this altitude, it's actually not so easy to pick out landmarks, but the views of the City are simply spectacular, especially if you book a two-hour slot across sunset. Be warned: you'll pay a premium for drinking in such an elevated location. Look No Hands, for example, made with CopperDog whisky, Triple Sec and Fernet-Branca is a punchy aperitif, but you won't get any change from a £20 note.

There's usually a minimum £30 spend per person, but on Sunday, Monday or Tuesday (except bank holidays) you can enjoy the view for up to 90 minutes for just the price of a bottle of beer or a glass of wine.

Shops & services

Bermondsey Square Antiques Market

*Corner of Bermondsey Street & Long Lane, SE1 3UN (bermondseysquare.net). Borough tube or London Bridge tube/rail. **Open** 6am-2pm Fri. **No cards**. **Map** p80 R11* ① *Antiques*

Following the redevelopment of Bermondsey Square, the antiques market – which started in 1855 in north London – continues in an expanded space that now accommodates 200 stalls. Traditionally good for china and silverware, as well as furniture and glassware, there are now also food, fashion and crafts stalls. It's famous for being the spot where, back in the day, thieves could sell their goods with impunity: it's half car boot sale, half chic Parisian fleamarket. Get there early – lunchtime arrivals will be disappointed to find grouchy antiques sellers (well, they did start work at 4am) packing up.

❤ Maltby Street & Spa Terminus

*Maltby Street, SE1 3PA & Dockley Road, SE16 3SF (www.maltby.st, www.spa-terminus. co.uk). Bermondsey or Southwark tube. **Open** 10am-5pm Sat; 11am-4pm Sun. **Map** p80 S10* ③ *Food & drink*

Borough Market's trade has been challenged by former stallholders who have set up camp under the railway arches around Maltby Street and further south. Head here for delicious raclette from Kappacasein (Arch 1), chocolate heaven from Bad Brownie (badbrownie. co.uk) and craft beer from Kernel Brewery (*see p99* Bermondsey Beer Mile). Most producers are open on Saturday mornings, some on Sundays too – the website has a useful map showing locations and opening hours.

Bermondsey Beer Mile

Tap into London's craft ale scene

London has always been awash with beer – literally in 1814, when an exploding brewery on Tottenham Court Road created the London Beer Flood – but the current ubiquity of craft ale is remarkable. For a taster, explore Bermondsey's 'Beer Mile': more than a dozen bottleshops and breweries occupying railway arches south of London Bridge. All open their tap rooms – the small bar attached to the brewery – every Saturday, allowing curious drinkers to savour some of London's tastiest brews in an intoxicating crawl. Start with a stomach-lining breakfast at Maltby Street Market (*see left*) before following the route on www.bermondsey-beer-mile.co.uk. Be sure to bring cash and to charge your phone, as the walk isn't straightforward... especially after a few pints.

The grandaddy of the scene is **Kernel** (Arch 11, Dockley Industrial Estate, SE16 3SF), which set up in the first wave of the London beer renaissance in 2007, but is now only open as a bottle shop. It was followed by **Partizan** (8 Almond Street, SE16 3LR), which used some of Kernel's old equipment, then **Brew By Numbers** (79 Enid Street, SE16 3RA), **Fourpure** (22 Bermondsey Trading Estate, Rotherhithe New Road, SE16 3LL) and **Anspach & Hobday** (118 Druid Street, SE1 2HH) – Anspach & Hobday also opens on Friday and Sunday, which are generally less busy than Saturday.

Collectively, they offer tasty evidence of the way London has embraced craft beer. When Kernel began, there were less than half a dozen breweries in London; now they are in almost every neighbourhood. As drinking habits have been transformed, pubs that once served gassy lagers and tasteless bitters now compete to serve the widest range of new beers. As one Hackney landlord commented, 'You might not get more customers if you serve good beers, but you will definitely lose them if you don't.'

For once London was behind the curve. The microbrewery trend started in the United States in the 1980s, and parts of Scotland have had thriving scenes for years. But when it hit London, it hit big. That moment came with the 2008 recession, which lowered costs for new businesses. Craft ale was part of a wider foodie trend that celebrated local produce and embraced more complex tastes.

But London was also able to tap into a strong, lost tradition of brewing: IPAs, porters and several other varieties were created in London centuries ago, allowing canny current brewers to provide an experience that felt new and exciting, but was also deep in taste and rich in history.

Where better to enjoy that heady brew than under a railway arch in south-east London?

Westminster & St James's

The whole of the United Kingdom is ruled from this small portion of London. The monarchy has been in residence in Westminster since the 11th century, when Edward the Confessor moved west out of the walled City, and as the role of British kings and queens became increasingly ceremonial, Parliament was already here to take on the real business of government. It's a key destination for visitors as well, with the most significant area designated a UNESCO World Heritage Site back in 1987.

As well as being home to some of London's most impressive buildings – Westminster Abbey and the Houses of Parliament among them – it's also packed with culture: Tate Britain, the National Gallery and the National Portrait Gallery are all here. And for such an important part of London, it's surprisingly spacious. St James's Park is one of London's finest green spaces, Trafalgar Square is a tourist hotspot – and thanks to pedestrianisation along its northern edge, not an unpleasant one – while the Mall offers a regally broad approach route to Buckingham Palace.

❤ Don't miss

1 Houses of Parliament *p107*
Don't just gawp at the exterior, join a tour and discover the history of this fascinating place.

2 Tate Britain *p113*
The original Tate gallery, handsomely revamped.

3 St James's Park *p117*
Central London's prettiest park, replete with pelicans.

4 Westminster Abbey *p108*
Magnificent, sacred and packed to its reredos with history.

5 National Gallery *p105*
One masterpiece after another.

6 Fortnum & Mason *p119*
Historic department store with trad foodie treats.

Westminster Abbey

WESTMINSTER & ST JAMES'S

Restaurants

1 Bleecker p112
2 Ikoyi p118
3 Kerridge's Bar & Grill p106
4 National Dining Rooms p106
5 Regency Café p112
6 St James's Café p118
7 Saka no Hana p118
8 Wolseley p118

Pubs & bars

1 Boisdale of Belgravia p112
2 Cask p111
3 Dukes Bar p119
4 Red Lion p110
5 Stephen's Tavern p110
6 Westminster Arms p110

Shops & services

1 Dover Street Market p119
2 Dr Harris p119
3 Floris p119
4 Fortnum & Mason p119
5 James J Fox p119
6 Lock & Co Hatters p120
7 Waterstones Piccadilly p120

WESTMINSTER & ST JAMES'S

TRAFALGAR SQUARE

▶ *Leicester Square tube or Charing Cross tube/rail.*

Laid out in the 1820s by John Nash, Trafalgar Square is the heart of modern London. Tourists come in their thousands to pose for photographs in front of **Nelson's Column**. It was erected in 1840 to honour Vice Admiral Horatio Nelson, who died at the point of victory at the Battle of Trafalgar in 1805. The statue atop the 150-foot (46-metre) Corinthian column is foreshortened to appear in perfect proportion from the ground. The granite fountains were added in 1845; Sir Edwin Landseer's bronze lions joined them in 1867 – the metal has in places been worn very thin by tourists clambering over them. Stay off!

Once surrounded on all sides by busy roads, the square was improved markedly in 2003 by the pedestrianisation of the North Terrace, right in front of the **National Gallery**. A ban on feeding pigeons was another positive step. The square feels more like public space now, and is a focus for performance and celebration.

Around the perimeter are three plinths bearing statues of George IV and two Victorian military heroes, Henry Havelock and Sir Charles James Napier. The long-empty fourth plinth, which never received its planned martial statue, has been used since 1998 to display temporary, contemporary art. Michael Rakowitz's *The Invisible Enemy Should Not Exist*, based on an ancient Assyrian statue destroyed by Daesh in Iraq, will be replaced in 2020 by Heather Phillipson's *THE END*.

Other points of interest around the square include an equestrian statue of Charles I dating from the 1630s. A dogged bunch of royalists gathers here every 31 January to mark Charles I's execution. Behind the statue, a plaque marks the original site of Edward I's **Eleanor Cross**, the official centre of London. (A Victorian replica of the cross is outside Charing Cross Station, *see p189*.) At the square's north-east corner is **St Martin-in-the-Fields**.

❤ Time to eat & drink

A beauty for brunch
Wolseley *p118*

Art deco café
Regency Café *p112*

Best burgers
Bleecker *p112*

London's finest martini?
Dukes Bar *p119*

West African surprise
Ikoyi *p118*

Whisky a gogo
Boisdale of Belgravia *p112*

❤ Time to shop

Classic department store
Fortnum & Mason *p119*

New premises, same style
Dover Street Market *p119*

Sensational old-school scents
Floris *p119*

Trad titfers
Lock & Co Hatters *p120*

St Martin-in-the-Fields

🖤 National Gallery

Trafalgar Square, WC2N 5DN (7747 2885, www.nationalgallery.org.uk). Charing Cross tube/rail. **Open** *10am-6pm Mon-Thur, Sat, Sun; 10am-9pm Fri.* **Tours** *11am Mon-Fri.* **Admission** *free. Special exhibitions vary.* **Map** *p102 L8.*

Founded in 1824 to display 36 paintings, the National Gallery is now one of the world's great repositories for art. There are masterpieces from virtually every European school of art, from austere 13th-century religious paintings to the sensual delights of Titian, Caravaggio and Van Gogh. Dr Gabriele Finaldi, who became the gallery's director in 2015, has overseen major exhibitions such as 'Beyond Caravaggio' and 'Goya: The Portraits', which attracted record numbers of visitors.

The gallery itself is huge. Furthest to the left of the main entrance, the modern Sainsbury Wing extension contains the gallery's earliest works: Italian paintings by masters such as Giotto and Piero della Francesca, as well as the *Wilton Diptych*, one of the finest medieval pictures in the collection, showing Richard II with the Virgin and Child.

In the West Wing (left of the main entrance) are Italian Renaissance masterpieces by Correggio, Titian and Raphael. Straight ahead on entry, in the North Wing, are 17th-century Dutch, Flemish, Italian and Spanish Old Masters, including works such as Rembrandt's *A Woman Bathing in a Stream* and Caravaggio's *Supper at Emmaus*. Velázquez's *Rokeby Venus* is one of the artist's most famous paintings. Also in this wing are works by the great landscape artists Claude and Poussin. Turner insisted that his *Dido Building Carthage* and *Sun Rising Through Vapour* should hang alongside two Claudes here that particularly inspired him.

In the East Wing are some of the gallery's most popular paintings: you'll find works by the French Impressionists and Post-Impressionists, including Monet's *Water-Lilies*, one of Van Gogh's *Sunflowers* and Seurat's *Bathers at Asnières*. Don't miss Renoir's astonishingly lovely *The Skiff* (*La Yole*).

Downstairs, the opening of Gallery B – the first new gallery space in 26 years – transformed the ground floor in 2017 by connecting the once isolated Gallery A and main Ground Floor Galleries. 'Rubens and Rembrandt', a special display of paintings from the National Gallery's extensive collection of Dutch and Flemish art, kicked off the programme of free temporary exhibitions here.

Top of Nelson's Column, Trafalgar Square

WESTMINSTER & ST JAMES'S

You shouldn't plan to see everything in one visit, but free guided tours and audio guides help you make the best of your time.

National Portrait Gallery

St Martin's Place, WC2H 0HE (7306 0055, www.npg.org.uk). Leicester Square tube or Charing Cross tube/rail. **Open** *10am-6pm Mon-Thur, Sat, Sun; 10am-9pm Fri.* **Admission** *free. Special exhibitions vary.* **Map** *p102 L8.*

Portraits don't have to be stuffy. The NPG has everything from oil paintings of stiff-backed royals to photographs of soccer stars and gloriously unflattering political caricatures. On the ground floor, director Nicholas Cullinan (who joined in 2015) programmes interesting temporary exhibitions, not least a revealing pairing of cult surrealist Claude Cahun with (no longer quite so) Young British Artist Gillian Wearing, alongside permanent galleries of contemporary portraiture in different media. Portraits of musicians, scientists, artists, philanthropists and celebrities are then arranged in chronological order from the top of the gallery to the bottom. On the second floor are the earliest works, portraits of Tudor and Stuart royals and notables, including Holbein's 'cartoon' of Henry VIII and the 'Ditchley Portrait' of his daughter, Elizabeth I, her pearly slippers placed firmly on a colourful map of England. On the same floor, the 18th-century collection features Georgian writers and artists, with one room devoted to the influential Kit-Cat Club of bewigged Whig (leftish) intellectuals, the playwright Congreve and the poet Dryden among them. More famous names include Wren and Swift. The second floor also shows Regency greats, military men such as Wellington and Nelson, plus Byron, Wordsworth and other Romantics. The first floor is devoted to the Victorians (Dickens, Brunel, Darwin) and to 20th-century luminaries, such as TS Eliot and Ian McKellen.

St Martin-in-the-Fields

*Trafalgar Square, WC2N 4JH (7766 1100, www.smitf.org). Leicester Square tube or Charing Cross tube/rail. **Open** 8.30am-6pm Mon-Fri; 9am-6pm Sat, Sun. Brass Rubbing Centre 10am-6pm Mon-Wed; 10am-7.45pm Thur-Sat; 11am-5pm Sun. **Admission** free. Brass rubbing £4.50. **Map** p102 M8.*

There's been a church 'in the fields' between Westminster and the City since the 13th century, but the current one was built in 1726 by James Gibbs, using a fusion of neoclassical and Baroque styles. The parish church for Buckingham Palace (note the royal box to the left of the gallery), St Martin's bright interior was restored a few years back, with Victorian furbelows removed and the addition of a brilliant altar window that shows the Cross, stylised as if rippling on water. Downstairs in the crypt are a fine café and the London Brass Rubbing Centre.

The lunchtime and evening concerts in the church (which rarely wander far from the embrace of Mozart and Bach) are often delightful, especially when candlelit.

Restaurants

Aside from all shine and no soul chains and tourist traps, there are few dining options. The **National Dining Rooms** (7747 2525, www.peytonandbyrne.co.uk, **££** ④) in the Sainsbury Wing of the National Gallery are one peaceful but middling choice. Otherwise, head a few steps east to **Barrafina** (*see p185*), the **Tandoor Chophouse** (*see p187*) and **Terroirs** (*see p187*) or southeast to **Kerridge's Bar & Grill** in the Corinthia Hotel (10 Northumberland Avenue, 7321 3244, www. kerridgesbarandgrill.co.uk, **£££** ❸).

WHITEHALL TO PARLIAMENT SQUARE

▶ *Westminster tube or Charing Cross tube/rail.*

The offices of the British government are lined along Whitehall, itself named after Henry VIII's magnificent palace, which burned to the ground in 1698. Walking south from Trafalgar Square, you pass the old Admiralty Offices and War Office, the Ministry of Defence, the Foreign Office and the Treasury, as well as the **Banqueting House**, one of the few buildings to survive the blaze. Also here is **Horse Guards**, headquarters of the Household Cavalry, the elite army unit that protects the Queen (*see p116* Household Cavalry Museum).

Either side of **Downing Street** – home to the prime minister (no.10) and chancellor (no.11), but closed to the public after IRA attacks in the 1980s – are significant war memorials. The millions who died in the service of the nation in World Wars I and II are commemorated by Sir Edwin Lutyens' dignified **Cenotaph**, focal point of Remembrance Day (*see p317*), while a separate memorial to the women of World War II, by sculptor John Mills, recalls the seven million women who contributed to the war effort. Just past the Cenotaph and hidden beneath government offices at the St James's Park end of King Charles Street, the claustrophobic **Churchill War Rooms** are where Britain's wartime prime minister planned the struggle.

The broad sweep of Whitehall is an apt introduction to the cluster of iconic buildings around **Parliament Square**, most notably the **Houses of Parliament** (*see p107*) and **Westminster Abbey** (*see p108*). Despite all the statues (Disraeli, Churchill, Lincoln, Mandela, Gandhi, and, since 2018, Millicent Fawcett), Parliament Square can

---

In the know
Reacting to terror

In 2017 a car and knife attack on Westminster Bridge and within the grounds of the Houses of Parliament left more than 50 people injured, six of them fatally. This event, and other terrorist attacks at London Bridge and Borough Market, prompted the construction of concrete and steel barriers along Westminster Bridge, an increase in the number of armed officers on patrol and more stringent security measures – including airport-style bag searches – for visitors to the Parliament buildings. Be prepared for queues at busy times.

💙 Houses of Parliament

Parliament Square, SW1A 0AA (Commons information 7219 4272; Lords information 7219 3107; tickets 7219 4114, www.parliament. uk/visiting). Westminster tube. **Tours** *every Sat plus weekdays when not in session.* **Public galleries** *Mon-Fri when in session (check the website for further details).* **Audio tour** *£20.50 (£18.50 in advance); £8.50-£18 (£7.50-£16 in advance) reductions; free under-5s.* **Guided tour** *£28 (£25.50 in advance); £12-£23 (£11-£21 in advance) reductions; free under-5s.* **Map** *p102 M10.*

The British Parliament has an extremely long history, with the first parliamentary session held in St Stephen's Chapel in 1275. The Palace of Westminster, however, only became the permanent seat of Parliament in 1532, when Henry VIII moved to a new des-res in Whitehall. The current Palace is a wonderful mish-mash of styles, dominated by Gothic buttresses, towers and arches. It looks much older than it is: the Parliament buildings were designed in 1860 by Charles Barry (ably assisted by Augustus Pugin) to replace the original building, which had been destroyed by fire in 1834. Now, the compound contains 1,000 rooms, 11 courtyards, eight bars and six restaurants, plus a small cafeteria for visitors. Of the original palace, only the Jewel Tower (*see p110*) and, within the Parliament buildings, Westminster Hall, remain.

Visitors are welcome (subject to stringent security checks at the Cromwell Green entrance, the only public access point into Parliament) either to tour the palace buildings, or to observe the political debates in the House of Lords and House of Commons. The experience of listening in on the Houses of Parliament in session is often soporific, but Prime Minister's Question Time at noon on Wednesday is often sparky: the PM has alternately to rebuff a barrage of hostile questions from the opposition (and occasionally their own rebellious backbenchers) and massage value out of soft questions from loyal backbenchers eager to present the government in a good light.

For more insight into the history, architecture and arcane practices of parliament, book a 60-minute audio tour or (better) the revealing 90-minute guided tour, which takes in both Houses, Westminster Hall, the Queen's Robing Room and the Royal Gallery. (The Elizabeth Tower housing Big Ben is, however, inaccessible until 2021 due to restoration work.)

▶ *It's best (and cheapest) to book parliamentary tours online in advance, but they can also be bought on the day from the ticket office at the front of Portcullis House on Victoria Embankment (10am-4pm Mon-Fri, 8.45am-4.45pm Sat).*

In the know
What's happened to Big Ben?

Visitors to Westminster may be disappointed to see that the Elizabeth Tower is shrouded in scaffolding, ruining that long-imagined Instagram shot of the iconic tower. Essential refurbishment works began in early 2017 and are expected to last until 2021, during which time Big Ben remains silent except for important national events.

WESTMINSTER & ST JAMES'S

seem little more than a glorified traffic island – especially when you're trying to cross the roads to have a closer look. But its symbolic value has been brought back into focus as a site for political protest: most recently over Brexit. This is the beating heart of Westminster, inscribed as a UNESCO World Heritage Site in 1987. Any part of it alone would feature on most visitors' itineraries, but the combination – especially on a sunny day, when the yellow stone of Parliament is at its best – is an extraordinary historic and cultural nexus.

Whether viewed from the square or from the river, the outrageous neo-Gothic parliament building dazzles. It is still formally known as the Palace of Westminster, though the only remaining parts of the medieval palace are Westminster Hall (which can be visited on one of the brilliant tours) and the undervisited **Jewel Tower**.

At the north end of the palace is the 315-foot (96-metre) clocktower housing the huge 'Big Ben' bell that gives the clocktower its popular name; more than seven feet tall, the bell (itself formally known as the 'Great Bell') weighs over 13 tons. The tower was renamed the **Elizabeth Tower** in 2012 – in honour of the Queen's Diamond Jubilee. On the opposite side of Bridge Street, **Portcullis House** opened in 2001 to house MPs' offices, with Westminster tube station directly below it. A spear-brandishing statue of Boadicea (the fierce British chieftain Boudica, misnamed by Classics-obsessed Victorians) aims her chariot at the heart of Parliament from the end of Westminster Bridge nearby.

Before you hot-foot it to the Gothic splendour of Westminster Abbey, note the other buildings on Parliament Square: the neo-Gothic Middlesex Guildhall, housing the **Supreme Court**, on the west side, and **St Margaret's Church** dwarfed by the Abbey to the south.

Sights & museums

Banqueting House

Whitehall, SW1A 2ER (3166 6000, www.hrp. org.uk/banqueting-house). Westminster tube. Open 10am-5pm daily; phone to check. Admission £6.10; £5.10 reductions; free under-16s. Map p102 M9.

This handsome Italianate mansion, which was designed by Inigo Jones and constructed in 1620, was the first true Renaissance building in London. The sole surviving part of the Tudor and Stuart kings' Whitehall Palace, the Banqueting House features a lavish painted ceiling by Rubens, glorifying James I, 'the wisest fool in Christendom'. Regrettably,

♥ Westminster Abbey

*20 Dean's Yard, SW1P 3PA (information 7222 5152, tours 7654 4834, www. westminster-abbey.org). St James's Park or Westminster tube. **Open** May-Aug 9.30am-3.30pm Mon, Tue, Thur-Sat; 9.30am-3.30pm, 4.30-6pm Wed. Sept-Apr 9.30am-3.30pm Mon, Thur, Fri; 2-3.30pm Tue; 9.30am-3.30pm, 4.30-6pm Wed; 9.30am-1.30pm Sat. Check the website for opening times of the Abbey Museum, Chapter House and College Gardens. **Admission** (incl audio guide) £20; £9-£17 reductions; £45 family; free under-5s. Tours £5. **Map** p102 L10.*

The cultural, historic and religious significance of Westminster Abbey is impossible to overstate, but also hard to remember as you're shepherded around, forced to elbow fellow tourists out of the way to read a plaque or see a tomb. The best plan is to get here as early in the day as you can – although it also quietens down towards closing time.

Edward the Confessor commissioned a church dedicated to St Peter on the site of a seventh-century version, but it was only consecrated on 28 December 1065, eight days before he died. (Today, all that remains from Edward's time are the round arches and supporting columns of the undercroft and the Pyx Chamber in the cloisters.) William the Conqueror subsequently had himself crowned here on Christmas Day 1066 and, with just two exceptions, every English coronation since has taken place in the Abbey. The Coronation Chair, dating from 1300, is on display in St George's Chapel.

Construction of the current Gothic Abbey started in the middle of the 13th century under King Henry III and continued for several hundred years. In fact, the Abbey's distinctive west towers weren't added until the 18th century, to a design by Nicholas Hawksmoor.

Many royal, military and cultural notables are interred in the Abbey. The shrine of Edward the Confessor and other medieval royals can be found by the High Altar, but the most haunting memorial is the Grave of the Unknown Warrior, in the nave. Elaborate resting places in side chapels are taken up by the tombs of Elizabeth I and Mary Queen of Scots. In Innocents Corner lie the remains of two lads believed to be Edward V and his brother Richard (their bodies were found at the Tower of London), as well as two of James I's children. Poets' Corner is the final resting place of Chaucer, who was the first writer to be buried here. Few of the other writers who have stones here are buried in the Abbey, but the remains of Dryden, Johnson, Browning and Tennyson are all present. Henry James, TS Eliot and Dylan Thomas have dedications – on the floor, fittingly for Thomas.

Hidden for over 700 years, the Triforium (the gallery set into the walls above the nave) reopened in June 2018 as the **Queen's Diamond Jubilee Galleries**. The galleries tell the long and complex history of this glorious place through a series of symbolic royal documents and historical oddities, such as Prince William and Kate Middleton's marriage licence, 21 funeral effigies (including Henry VII's) and a chunk of England's oldest surviving altarpiece.

Elsewhere, other highlights include Henry VII's **Lady Chapel**, which has an exquisite pendant fan-vaulted ceiling (a dull name for architecture of such intricacy) and an array of saints in niches along the walls, among them a bearded lady – St Wilgefortis.

Even when the abbey is at its most crowded, the 900-year-old **College Garden** – one of the oldest cultivated spaces in Britain, with some lovely mulberry trees – remains tranquil. Ask one of the staff to direct you there; they are very knowledgeable, so collaring the right person brings the abbey to life in a way the audioguide never can.

For snacks, there's a refectory-style restaurant – the **Cellarium Café & Terrace** (7222 0516, www.benugo.com/restaurants/cellarium-cafe-terrace) – next to the little souvenir shop.

In the know
Stained glass

The latest addition to the Abbey's collection of stained glass is the **Queen's Window** in the north transept. Designed by David Hockney and dedicated in 2018, it's a characteristically colourful depiction of the Yorkshire Wolds, which the artist designed on an iPad.

James's successor, Charles I, did not rule so wisely. After losing the English Civil War to Cromwell's Roundheads, he was executed in front of Banqueting House in 1649 – the subject of a set of displays here.

Churchill War Rooms

Clive Steps, King Charles Street, SW1A 2AQ (7930 6961, www.iwm.org.uk). St James's Park or Westminster tube. Open 9.30am-6pm daily. Admission £21; £10.50-£16.80 reductions; free under-5s. Map p102 L10.

Out of harm's way beneath Whitehall, this cramped and spartan bunker was where Winston Churchill planned the Allied victory in World War II, and the rooms powerfully bring to life the reality of a nation at war. The cabinet rooms were sealed on 16 August 1945, keeping the complex in a state of suspended animation: every pin stuck into the vast charts was placed there in the final days of the conflict. The humble quarters occupied by Churchill and his deputies give a tangible sense of wartime hardship, an effect reinforced by the wailing sirens and wartime speeches on the audio guide (free with admission).

Jewel Tower

Abingdon Street, SW1P 3JY (7222 2219, www. english-heritage.org.uk). Westminster tube. Open Apr-Oct 10am-6pm Thur-Sat. Nov-Mar 10am-4pm Sat, Sun. Admission £5.40, £3.20-£4.90 reductions; free under-5s. Map p102 M10.

This easy-to-overlook little stone tower opposite Parliament was built in 1365 to house Edward III's treasure, complete with a moat that ran into the Thames. It is, with Westminster Hall, all that remains of the medieval Palace of Westminster. Over three storeys, joined by a spiral staircase, the tale is told: the Crown Jewels were evicted in 1512 (they are now displayed in the **Tower of London**, *see p234*) and the tower became an archive for parliamentary records, then, in the 19th-century, a testing site for standardised measurements. A fascinating and neglected piece of Westminster history.

St Margaret's Church

Parliament Square, SW1P 3PA (7654 4840, www.westminster-abbey.org/st-margarets-church). St James's Park or Westminster tube. Open 9.30am-3.30pm Mon-Fri; 9.30am-1.30pm Sat; 2-4.30pm Sun (times vary due to services). Services times vary; check website for details. Admission free. Map p102 M10.

Tucked in next to the grandeur of Westminster Abbey, this little church was founded in the 12th century; since 1614, it's

served as the official church of the House of Commons. The interior features some of the most impressive pre-Reformation stained glass in London. The east window (1509) commemorates the marriage of Henry VIII and Catherine of Aragon; others celebrate Britain's first printer, William Caxton (buried here in 1491), explorer Sir Walter Raleigh (executed in Old Palace Yard in 1618) and writer John Milton (1608-74), who married his second wife here in 1656.

Supreme Court

Parliament Square, SW1P 3BD (7960 1900, www.supremecourt.uk). St James's Park or Westminster tube. Open 11am-4pm Mon; 10.30am-4pm Tue-Fri. Tours 11am, 2pm, 3pm Fri. Admission free. Tours £7; £5 reductions; free under 16s. Map p102 L10.

In 2005, Parliament made a momentous decision – not that anyone noticed. The right to adjudicate final appeals was taken from the House of Lords and given to a new, independent Supreme Court, which was duly opened by the Queen in 2009, directly opposite Parliament. Part of the notion was to open up higher processes of law to the public – in plain English, you can visit any time you like (through airport-style security gates) to see lawyers debate 'points of law of general public importance' in front of the country's most senior judges. Recent cases have included whether an MP can be tried in a magistrate's court for alleged criminal misconduct within Parliament, and how binding a prenuptial agreement should be. You can also look around the lovely Grade II*-listed, neo-Gothic premises, built for Middlesex County Council in 1913. There's even a café and souvenirs on sale.

▶ *The Supreme Court doesn't sit on Friday; visitors are still welcome but it isn't as interesting as when the court is in session.*

Pubs & bars

While the **Red Lion** (48 Parliament Street, SW1A 2NH, 7930 5826, redlionwestminster. co.uk ④) is, by tradition, the politicians' favourite pub and the **Westminster Arms** (9-10 Storey's Gate, SW1P 3AT, 7222 8520, www.westminsterarms.co.uk ⑥) has its own 'division bell' to summon drinkers back into the House to vote, most MPs nowadays prefer to drink in the privacy of Parliament's own taxpayer-subsidised bars.

Opposite Big Ben, **Stephen's Tavern** (10 Bridge Street, SW1A 2JR, 7925 2286, ststephenstavern.co.uk ⑤), done out with dark woods, etched mirrors and Arts and Crafts-style wallpaper, is neither too touristy nor too busy.

MILLBANK

▶ *Pimlico or Westminster tube.*

Running south from Parliament along the river, Millbank leads eventually to **Tate Britain** (see *p113*). If you're walking that way (which is a good idea), look out on the left for **Victoria Tower Gardens**. Often overlooked, the gardens are a wonderful spot that is sometimes occupied by nothing more than its commemorative furniture: a distinguished statue of suffragette Emmeline Pankhurst, a fine cast of Rodin's *The Burghers of Calais* and a magnificent neo-Gothic folly/water fountain that celebrates the abolition of slavery. Less eye-catching is a small green plaque on the river wall dedicated to Peirson Frank, 'the man who saved London from drowning'. His covert rapid-response unit was responsible for mending the Thames wall during the Blitz: hit more than 120 times, it was never breached. The gardens have also been designated the site of a new £50 million National Holocaust Memorial – but given Brexit and government cuts, don't expect its arrival any time soon.

On the other side of the road, Dean Stanley Street leads to Smith Square, home to the architecturally striking **St John's Smith Square** (see *p357*), built as a church in grand Baroque style and now a venue for classical music. Lord North Street, the Georgian terrace running north from here, has long been a favourite address of politicians; note the directions on the wall for wartime bomb shelters.

Across the river from Millbank is **Vauxhall Cross**, the oddly conspicuous HQ of the Secret Intelligence Service (SIS), commonly referred to by its old name, MI6. In case any enemies of the state were unaware of its location, the cream-and-green block appeared as itself in the 1999 James Bond film *The World is Not Enough* – reprising the role (and suffering impressively serious bomb damage) in 2012's *Skyfall*.

Pubs & bars

Cask
6 Charlwood Street, Pimlico, SW1V 2EE (7630 7225, www.caskpubandkitchen.com). Pimlico tube. **Open** *noon-11pm Mon-Sat; noon-10.30pm Sun. Food served noon-3pm, 5-10pm Mon-Fri; 12.30-9.30pm Sat, Sun.* **Map** *p102 K12* ❷

It's not much to look at – an awkward shape at the bottom of a newbuild block – but Cask has been blazing the trail for better beer for years. Its fridges and cellar are filled with an absurdly generous range of the finest brews

from London, Britain and beyond, with something to satisfy the most ardent hophead or convert the most timid quaffer of fizzy yellow lager. Staff really know their stuff too – ask for a recommendation and you won't be disappointed.

VICTORIA

▶ *Pimlico tube or Victoria tube/rail.*

Victoria is chaotic. The rail station is a major hub for trains to southern seaside resorts and ferry terminals, while the nearby coach station is served by buses from all over Europe, and theatres dotted around the area add up to a kind of western outpost of the West End's Theatreland. But there's no real focus here, just one stand-out attraction: **Westminster Cathedral**. Not to be confused with Westminster Abbey (*see p108*), it is the headquarters of the Roman Catholic Church in England. South and east of Victoria Station are the Georgian terraces of Pimlico and Belgravia. Antiques stores and restaurants line Pimlico Road, and Tachbrook Street has some intriguing independent shops.

North of Victoria Street, towards Parliament Square, is **Christchurch Gardens**, burial site of Thomas ('Colonel') Blood, who stole the Crown Jewels in 1671. He was apprehended making his getaway but, amazingly, managed to talk his way into a full pardon. Also in the area is the former site of New Scotland Yard, sold to private investors for £370 million, with the Met moved to a new police headquarters on Victoria Embankment by the Ministry of Defence in 2016 – taking the name and famous revolving sign with them. The fabulous art deco former headquarters of London Underground at 55 Broadway is also now in private hands. Public outrage about Jacob Epstein's graphic nudes on the façade almost led to the resignation of the managing director in 1929; there was no such outrage at this more recent management decision.

Sights & museums

Westminster Cathedral
42 Francis Street, SW1P 1QW (7798 9055, www.westminstercathedral.org.uk). Victoria tube/rail. **Open** *6.30am-7pm Mon-Fri; 7.30am-7.30pm Sat; 7.30am-8pm Sun.* **Admission** *free; donations appreciated.* **Map** *p102 K11.*

With its domes, arches and soaring tower, the most important Catholic church in England looks surprisingly Byzantine. There's a reason: architect John Francis Bentley, who built it between 1895 and 1903, was heavily influenced by Hagia Sophia in Istanbul. Compared to the candy-cane exterior, the interior is surprisingly restrained (in fact, it's unfinished), but there are still some impressive marble columns and mosaics. Eric Gill's sculptures of the Stations of the Cross (1914-18) were dismissed as 'Babylonian' when they were first installed, but worshippers have come to love them. An upper gallery holds the 'Treasures of the Cathedral' exhibition, where you can see an impressive Arts and Crafts coronet, a Tudor chalice, holy relics and Bentley's amazing architectural model of his cathedral, complete with tiny hawks.

Restaurants

💜 Bleecker £

205 Victoria Street, SW1E 5NE (www. bleeckerburger.co.uk). Victoria tube/rail. **Open** *11am-11pm daily.* **Map** *p102 J11* ❶
Burgers

The first bricks-and-mortar shop from this popular street-food burger outfit is pure filth… in the best possible way. Made with rare-breed, dry-aged beef, the burgers don't compromise on quality but there's nothing pretentious about them – they're just bun, cheese and killer pucks of meat. Serious carnivores will adore the award-winning 'Bleecker black': two pink patties sandwiching a slice of black pudding. But given the inevitable, crippling post-scoff food coma, be sure to come hungry and eat fast.

💜 Regency Café £

17-19 Regency Street, SW1P 4BY (7821 6596, regencycafe.co.uk). St James's Park tube or Victoria tube/rail. **Open** *7am-2.30pm, 4-7.15pm Mon-Fri; 7am-noon Sat.* **Map** *p102 L11* ❺ *Café*

Behind this black-tiled art deco exterior, this classic caff has been here since 1946. Customers sit on brown plastic chairs at Formica-topped tables, watched over by muscular boxers and Spurs stars of yore, whose photos hang on the tiled walls.

In the know
View halloo

While we hesitate to recommend a sacred space merely for the secular pleasures it affords – ah, who are we kidding? Shin up the extraordinary 201-foot (61-metre) campanile (bell tower) at **Westminster Cathedral** for views that, while neither the highest or the most encompassing in London, offer a really impressive vista. Entry is £6 (£3 reductions).

Lasagne, omelettes, salads, every conceivable cooked breakfast and mugs of tannin-rich tea are meat and drink to the Regency. Still hungry? The improbably gigantic cinnamon-flavoured bread and butter pud will see you right for the rest of the week.

Pubs & bars

💜 Boisdale of Belgravia

15 Eccleston Street, SW1W 9LX (7730 6922, www.boisdale.co.uk). Victoria tube/rail. **Open** *noon-1am Mon-Fri; 6pm-1am Sat.* **Admission** *free before 9-10pm (times vary), then £12.* **Map** *p102 J11* ❶

There's nowhere quite like this posh, Scottish-themed enterprise, and that includes its sister branches in the City, Mayfair and Canary Wharf. If you're here to drink, there's a terrific choice of single malts. That said, the outstanding wine list is surprisingly affordable, with house selections starting at just over £20. Additional appeal comes from live jazz (six nights a week) and a heated cigar terrace. **Other locations** Swedeland Court, 202 Bishopsgate, the City, EC2M 4NR (7283 1763); Cabot Place, Canary Wharf, E14 4QT (7715 5818); 12 North Row, Mayfair, W1K 7DF (3873 8888).

ST JAMES'S

▶ *Green Park or Piccadilly Circus tube.*

One of London's most refined residential areas, St James's was laid out in the 1660s for royal and aristocratic families, some of whom still live here. It's a rewarding district, a sedate bustle of intriguing mews and grand squares. Bordered by Piccadilly, Haymarket, the Mall and Green Park, the district is centred on St James's Square.

Just south of the square, **Pall Mall** is lined with members-only gentlemen's clubs (in the old-fashioned sense of the word). Polished nameplates reveal such prestigious establishments as the **Reform Club** (nos.104-105), site of Phileas Fogg's famous bet in *Around the World in Eighty Days*, and the **Institute of Directors** (no.116). Around the corner on St James's Street, the **Carlton Club** (no.69) is the official club of the Conservative Party, founded in 1832; until the club's rules were finally changed in 2008, Lady Thatcher was the only woman to have been granted full membership. The world's oldest fine-art auctioneers, **Christie's** (7839 9060, www.christies.com), is on King Street.

At the south end of St James's Street, **St James's Palace** was built for Henry VIII in the 1530s. Extensively remodelled over

🖤 Tate Britain

Millbank, SW1P 4RG (7887 8888, www.tate. org.uk). Pimlico tube. **Open** *10am-6pm daily. Tours 11am, noon, 2pm, 3pm daily.* **Admission** *free. Special exhibitions vary.* **Map** *p102 G5.*

Especially since the opening of its dramatic Blavatnik extension in 2016, **Tate Modern** (*see p89*) has been getting all the attention. But (whisper it) we prefer the original Tate Gallery – or Tate Britain, as it's now known. This isn't nostalgia. Tate Britain was handsomely refurbished a few years ago, has a better organised collection than its illustrious counterpart and is much less busy, which makes viewing art more enjoyable. Tate Modern is undeniably amazing. But as you queue for the overburdened lifts to whizz up to its viewing platform, you may find yourself wondering if it's become more of a tourist attraction than a place to love art.

While the international scope and themed presentation of Tate Modern are laudable, the effect for visitors can be disorientating – some argue that this arrangement covered gaps in the collection that might be cruelly exposed were it to be displayed chronologically. No such anxieties at Tate Britain, where the main floor is a logical journey through the history of British Art from Holbein in the 1540s, while key artists are given more substantial treatment:

Blake and Henry Moore have their own rooms, while JMW Turner occupies his own extensive Clore Gallery.

Founded by sugar magnate Sir Henry Tate, Tate Britain opened in a stately riverside building in 1897 – built on the site of the pentagonal Millbank Prison, which held criminals destined for transportation to Botany Bay – with a display of 245 British paintings. Now, the collection is rather more extensive. Constable, Millais, Whistler, Hogarth and Bacon are all represented; the blockbuster exhibitions – not least a stunning Hockney retrospective in 2017 – are increasingly excellent.

Tate Britain has also been surreptitiously stealing a bit of the limelight back from its starrier sibling with a long-term redevelopment plan called the Millbank Project. In an initial £45 million tranche of improvements, architects Caruso St John improved the fabric of the oldest part of the building, conserving original features, upgrading the galleries, opening new spaces to the public and adding a new café. Sturdier floors meant that more sculpture could be displayed, and the amount of natural light was increased. The Millbank entrance is lovely these days, with its stained glass and striking spiral staircase; downstairs in the restaurant, a new Alan Johnston ceiling mural complements the restored 1926-27 Rex Whistler wall mural *Pursuit of Rare Meats.*

Buckingham Palace

Pall Mall became too crowded. On the south side of the park, Wellington Barracks contains the **Guards Museum**; to the east, Horse Guards contains the **Household Cavalry Museum**.

Carlton House Terrace, on the north flank of the Mall, was the last project completed by John Nash before his death in 1835. Part of the terrace now houses the **ICA**. Just behind is the Duke of York column, commemorating Prince Frederick, Duke of York, who led the British Army against the French. He's the nursery rhyme's 'Grand old Duke of York', who marched his 10,000 men neither up nor down Cassel hill in Flanders.

Sights & museums

Buckingham Palace & Royal Mews
The Mall, SW1A 1AA (Palace 0303 123 7300, Royal Mews 0303 123 7302, Queen's Gallery 0303 123 7301, www.royalcollection.org.uk). Green Park tube or Victoria tube/rail. **Open** *admission times & prices vary.* **Map** *p102 J10.*

Although the nearby St James's Palace remains the official seat of the British court, every monarch since Victoria has used Buckingham Palace as their primary home. Originally known as Buckingham House, the present home of the British royals was constructed as a private house for the Duke of Buckingham in 1703, but George III liked it so much he purchased it for his German bride Charlotte in 1761. George IV decided to occupy the mansion himself after taking the throne in 1820 and John Nash was hired to convert it into a palace befitting a king. Construction was beset with problems, and Nash – whose expensive plans had always been disliked by Parliament – was dismissed in 1830. When Victoria came to the throne in 1837, the building was barely habitable. The job of finishing the palace fell to the reliable but unimaginative Edward Blore ('Blore the Bore'). The neoclassical frontage now in place was the work of Aston Webb in 1913.

the centuries, the red-brick palace is still the official address of the Royal Court, even though every monarch since 1837 has lived at Buckingham Palace. Here, Mary Tudor surrendered Calais, Elizabeth I led the campaign against the Spanish Armada, and Charles I was confined before his 1649 execution. The palace is home to the Princess Royal (the title given to the monarch's eldest daughter, currently Princess Anne); it's closed to the public, but you can attend Sunday services at its historic **Chapel Royal** (Oct-Mar 8.30am, 11.15am Sun).

Adjacent to St James's Palace is **Clarence House**, former residence of the Queen Mother; a few streets north, delightful **Spencer House** is the ancestral home of the family of the late Princess Diana. Across Marlborough Road lies the pocket-sized **Queen's Chapel**, designed by Inigo Jones in the 1620s for Charles I's Catholic queen Henrietta Maria, at a time when Catholic places of worship were officially banned. The Queen's Chapel can only be visited for Sunday services (Easter-July; 8.30am, 11.15am).

To the south is the wonderful **St James's Park** (*see p117*), surely London's loveliest park. Along the park's northern boundary, **the Mall** connects Buckingham Palace with Trafalgar Square. It looks like a classic processional route, but the Mall was actually laid out as a pitch for Charles II to play 'pallemaille' (an early version of croquet imported from France) after the pitch at

WE'LL TELL YOU WHERE TO GO

Wherever you're exploring, we've got
the insider insight on the world's best

As the home of the Queen, the palace is usually closed to visitors, but you can view the interior for a brief period each year while the Windsors are away on their holidays; you'll be able to see the State Rooms, still used to entertain dignitaries and guests of state, and part of the garden. There's even a café – paper cups, sadly, but coloured a pretty blue-green and clearly marked with the palace crest for souvenir-hunters. At any time of year, you can visit the Queen's Gallery to see her personal collection of treasures, including paintings by Rubens and Rembrandt, Sèvres porcelain and the Diamond Diadem crown. Further along Buckingham Palace Road, the Royal Mews is a grand garage for the royal fleet of Rolls-Royces and home to the splendid royal carriages and the horses, individually named by the Queen, that pull them.

Clarence House

St James's Palace, the Mall, SW1 1BA (7766 7303, www.royalcollection.org.uk). Green Park tube. **Open** *Aug 10am-4.30pm Mon-Fri; 10am-5.30pm Sat, Sun. Closed Sept-July.* **Tours** *£10.30; £6.20 reductions; free under-5s.* **Map** *p102 K9.*

Currently the official residence of Prince Charles and the Duchess of Cornwall, this austere royal mansion was built between 1825 and 1827 for Prince William Henry, Duke of Clarence, who stayed on in the house after his coronation as King William IV. Designed by John Nash, the house has been much altered. Five receiving rooms and the late Queen Mother's British art collection are open to the public in August.

Guards Museum

Wellington Barracks, Birdcage Walk, SW1E 6HQ (7414 3428, www.theguardsmuseum. com). St James's Park tube. **Open** *10am-4pm daily.* **Admission** *£8; £2-£5 reductions; free under-16s.* **Map** *p102 K10.*

Just down the road from Horse Guards, this small museum tells the 350-year story of the Foot Guards, using flamboyant uniforms, period paintings, medals and intriguing memorabilia, such as the stuffed body of Jacob the Goose, the Guards' Victorian

In the know
On your guard

The Guards assemble on the parade ground at Wellington Barracks before marching on to the palace for Changing the Guard. The Cavalry assemble for their version of the ceremony on the parade ground outside the Household Cavalry Museum. See p311 Changing the Guard.

mascot, who was regrettably run over by a van in barracks. Appropriately, the shop is well stocked with toy soldiers of the British regiments.

Household Cavalry Museum

Horse Guards, Whitehall, SW1A 2AX (7930 3070, www.householdcavalrymuseum. co.uk). Westminster tube or Charing Cross tube/rail. **Open** *Apr-Oct 10am-6pm daily. Nov-Mar 10am-5pm daily.* **Admission** *£8; £6 reductions; £20 family; free under-5s.* **Map** *p102 L9.*

Household Cavalry is a fairly workaday name for the military peacocks who make up the Queen's official guard. They tell their stories through video diaries at this small but entertaining museum, which also offers the chance to see medals, uniforms and shiny cuirasses (breastplates) up close. You also get a peek – and sniff – of the magnificent horses that parade just outside every day: the stables are separated from the main museum by no more than a screen of glass.

ICA (Institute of Contemporary Arts)

The Mall, SW1Y 5AH (7930 0493 information, 7930 3647 tickets, www.ica.org.uk). Piccadilly Circus tube or Charing Cross tube/rail. **Open** *11am-11pm Tue-Sun. Galleries (during exhibitions) 11am-6pm Tue, Wed, Fri-Sun; 11am-9pm Thur.* **Admission** *free Tue; £1 Wed-Sun.* **Map** *p102 L9.*

Founded in 1947 by a collective of poets, artists and critics, the ICA moved to its current location on the Mall in 1968. Here it offers exhibitions, arthouse cinema, performance art, philosophical debates, art-themed club nights and anything else that might challenge convention – but 'convention' is so much harder to challenge now that everyone's doing it. Perhaps new director Stefan Kalmár – whose CV includes stints at New York's Artists Space and Munich's Bonner Kunstverein – will make it a must-visit for the culturati once more.

St James's Piccadilly

197 Piccadilly, W1J 9LL (7734 4511, www. sjp.org.uk). Piccadilly Circus tube. **Open** *8am-6.30pm daily. Evening events times vary.* **Admission** *free.* **Map** *p102 K8.*

Consecrated in 1684, St James's is the only church Sir Christopher Wren built on an entirely new site. A calming building with few architectural airs or graces, it was almost destroyed in World War II, but painstakingly reconstructed. Grinling Gibbons, the woodcarver, created the delicate limewood garlanding around the sanctuary which thankfully survived the bombing and is one of the few real frills. Beneath a new tiled roof, the church stages regular classical concerts,

💗 St James's Park

St James's Park tube. **Open** *5am-midnight daily.* **Map** *p102 L9.*

There's only one London park where you might spot a pelican swallow a pigeon. St James's Park, a 90-acre wedge of green between Westminster, Trafalgar Square and Buckingham Palace, is the oldest of eight royal parks – those parks that are Crown rather than municipal property. It is also one of London's finest, with narrow lanes meandering round a lake and gorgeous sculpted flower beds, a lakeside café, copious wildfowl and one of the most romantic views in the city. This comes from a bridge across the graceful central lake, which was created from a more formal canal by John Nash in the 1820s. Look east and, above the trees in the near distance, hover the spires, pinnacles and domes of Whitehall – with no square modern towers in sight, it looks like something from Prague or Disneyland; look west and, if the leaves are off the trees, you'll see **Buckingham Palace** (*see p114*).

The city is blessed with numerous parks, many formed from Crown or common land, some from land donated by wealthy philanthropists. **Regent's Park** (*see p244*), slightly north of the centre, is St James's closest rival, less genteel but every bit as much loved; further afield, Greenwich, Richmond, Brixton's Brockwell and east London's Victoria Park are all a rewarding wander. St James's is the finest of London's three central parks, more relaxed than **Hyde Park** (*see p132*), whose wide green spaces are ideal for sport, and more interesting than dull old **Green Park** (*see p120*). These three parks almost interlink, making a stroll east from Kensington Gardens to St James's a delight. St James's itself is the place for a wistful wander, or parking your posterior on a deckchair for a weekend summer concert at the bandstand. It's a peaceful place – except when it's used for ceremonial events like **Trooping the Colour** (*see p311*).

It's quite a transformation for a park, formed from a marshy field attached to a leper hospital, that later became a haunt of prostitutes. Henry VIII was the first to use the land for leisure, creating a bowling alley and ground for hunting. James I had more formal gardens laid out and imported a menagerie that included two crocodiles. In the 17th century, Charles II had it redesigned again, by the French landscape gardener from Versailles, adding a pair of pelicans that had been a gift from the Russian ambassador – pelicans have been resident ever since. In fact, wildlife has been a constant theme. Early occupants included deer, leopards and an elk, but by the 18th century the park was being used to graze cows – fresh milk could be bought here until 1905. Now, wildfowl are the draw, with 17 different species splashing about in the central lake. Those bag-jawed pelicans are fed between 2.30pm and 3pm daily.

WESTMINSTER & ST JAMES'S

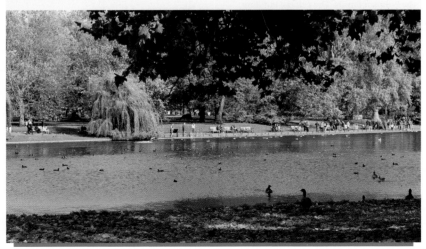

provides a home for the William Blake Society (Blake was baptised here) and hosts markets in the churchyard: food on Monday, antiques on Tuesday, and arts and crafts from Wednesday to Saturday. There's a handy café in the basement with plenty of tables – and the church's hospitality extends to the homeless, who come to sleep in the pews. Blake would certainly approve.

Spencer House
27 St James's Place, SW1A 1NR (7514 1958, www.spencerhouse.co.uk). Green Park tube. **Open** *Sept-Jul 10am-4.30pm Sun. Last tour 4.45pm.* **Admission** *£15; £12 reductions. Under-10s must be accompanied by an adult.* **Map** *p102 K9.*

One of the last surviving private residences in St James's, this handsome mansion was designed for John Spencer by John Vardy, but was completed in 1766 by Hellenophile architect James Stuart, hence the mock Greek flourishes. Lady Georgiana, the 18th-century socialite and beauty – played by Keira Knightley in *The Duchess* (2008) – lived here, but the Spencers left generations before their most famous scion, Diana, married into the Windsor family. The palatial building has painstakingly restored interiors, and a wonderful garden, which is sometimes open to the general public.

Restaurants

In St James's Park, **St James's Café** (7839 1149, www.benugo.com ⑥) is a good place to pick up some breakfast or lunchtime ciabatta. It's fairly low key but the setting (overlooking the duck lake, with trees all around and the London Eye in the distance) is really wonderful.

♥ Ikoyi £££-£££
1 St James's Market, Piccadilly, SW1Y 4AH (3583 4660, ikoyilondon.com). Piccadilly Circus tube. **Open** *noon-3pm (last orders 2.45pm), 5.30pm-midnight (last orders 10.15pm) Mon-Sat.* **Map** *p102 L8* ② *West African*

London may have a trough-load of upscale north African eateries, but there are not so many from the rest of the continent. Hooray, then, for Ikoyi, a hip little joint in an otherwise staid area of town. The room is a warm terracotta, decorated with hanging clay lamps and plants, creating a lovely vibe that nods to Africa without being kitsch. The same could be said for the menu, which zips across West Africa, showcasing a host of fusiony flavours that'll be truly new to most foodie Londoners: fried buttermilk plantain with smoked scotch bonnet; rib of lamb with *asun* relish; chicken with *benne* (a sesame-like seed) and okra; papaya marinated in *zobo* (a Nigerian drink made from roselle flowers) served with soft meringue. Heat, it's worth pointing out, is a thing here. Sweltering, face-sweating pepper heat. It's not a place for the faint-hearted.

Sake no Hana ££££
23 St James's Street, SW1A 1HA (7925 8988, sakenohana.com/london). Green Park tube. **Open** *noon-3pm, 6-11pm Mon-Thur; noon-3pm, 5.30-11.30pm Fri; noon-3.15pm, 5.30-11.30pm Sat.* **Map** *p102 K9* ⑦ *Japanese*

As you'd expect from the Hakkasan restaurant group, Sake no Hana is beautifully designed. That and the fine range of contemporary Japanese dishes and slick service make it a popular place for business lunches and well-heeled families. For a filling meal, the 'Taste of Sake no Hana' (£29) consists of miso soup, a choice of *sukiyaki*, tempura or grilled dish, a handful of sushi and a dessert. There's also plenty for wine and saké buffs to get stuck into. Don't forget to glance upwards while you're dining: the sculptural wood slatting above your head definitely deserves a look.

♥ Wolseley £££
160 Piccadilly, W1J 9EB (7499 6996, www. thewolseley.com). Green Park tube. **Open** *7am-11pm (last orders) Mon-Fri; 8am-11pm (last orders) Sat, Sun.* **Map** *p102 K8* ⑧ *Brasserie*

A self-proclaimed 'café-restaurant in the grand European tradition', the Wolseley combines London heritage and Viennese grandeur. The kitchen is much celebrated for its breakfasts, and the scope of the main menu is admirable. From oysters, steak tartare or soufflé suisse, via wiener schnitzel or grilled halibut with wilted spinach and béarnaise, to Portuguese custard tart or apple strudel, there's something for everyone. On Sunday afternoons, three-tiered afternoon tea stands are in abundance. The Wolseley's owners, Chris Corbin and Jeremy King, run a number of London's favourite venues, including the **Delaunay** (*see p191*) and **Bar**

Américain (*see p174*), and have opened their first hotel, the **Beaumont** (*see p399*).

Pubs & bars

❤ Dukes Bar
*Dukes Hotel, 35 St James's Place, SW1A 1NY (7491 4840, www.dukeshotel.com/dukes-bar). Green Park tube. **Open** 2-11pm Mon-Sat; 4-10.30pm Sun. **Map** p102 K9* ❸

If you want to go out for a single cocktail, strong and expensive and very well made, go to Dukes. It's in a luxury hotel, but you're sure to get the warmest of welcomes – as long as you're not wearing trainers. There are three small rooms, all decorated in discreetly opulent style; you feel cocooned. The bar is famous for the theatre of its Martini-making – at the table, from a trolley, using vermouth made exclusively for them at the Sacred distillery in Highgate – but other drinks are just as good.

Shops & services

Heading west on Piccadilly, the shops become increasingly upmarket. **Jermyn Street**, dating back to 1664 when Charles II authorised Henry Jermyn to develop the area, has become a byword for bespoke gentlemen's clothing, with resident tailors including Turnbull & Asser, Hawes & Curtis and T M Lewin.

❤ Dover Street Market
*18-22 Haymarket, SW1Y 4DG (7518 0680, www.doverstreetmarket.com). Green Park tube. **Open** 11am-7pm Mon-Sat; noon-6pm Sun. **Map** p102 L8* ❶ *Fashion*

No longer on Dover Street (which gave this globally renowned store its name), DSM took over the old Burberry HQ in 2016. Combining the energy of London's indoor markets with rarefied labels, Rei Kawakubo's ground-breaking multistorey store is a mecca for the fashion obsessed. Housing some of London's brightest stars – Grace Wales Bonner's wonderfully elegant menswear and Molly Goddard's dream dresses woven out of tulle – it's a real champion of the capital's pioneering fashion designers. All 14 of the Comme des Garçons collections are here, alongside exclusive lines from such designers as Lanvin and Azzedine Alaïa.

DR Harris
*29 St James's Street, SW1A 1HB (7930 3915, www.drharris.co.uk). Green Park or Piccadilly Circus tube. **Open** 8.30am-6pm Mon-Fri; 9.30am-5pm Sat. **Map** p102 K9* ❷ *Health & beauty*

In a city overtaken by characterless chain pharmacies, the venerable DR Harris has remained unfazed – it's hung on tight to its identity since 1790 and demurely holds a royal warrant. A visit is much like stepping through a door into times past. Polished wooden cabinets are filled with bottles and jars with old-fashioned shaving brushes and manicure kits. Traditional it may be, but DR Harris appeals to modern sensibilities – none of the products are tested on animals, the use of palm oil is limited and nearly all packaging is recyclable. **Other location** 52 Piccadilly, W1J 0DX (7930 3915).

❤ Floris
*89 Jermyn Street, SW1Y 6JH (7747 3612, www.florislondon.com). Green Park tube. **Open** 9.30am-6.30pm Mon-Sat; 11.30am-5.30pm Sun. **Map** p102 K8* ❸ *Health & beauty*

Enterprising young Spaniard Juan Floris set up his fragrance shop in 1730 and it has been run by the same family ever since. One imagines not too much has changed. Everything is behind glass cabinets and oak-panelled counters in the manner of an old-fashioned apothecary, and smartly dressed men and women guide you through the selection process; much more civilised than a department store.

❤ Fortnum & Mason
*181 Piccadilly, W1A 1ER (7734 8040, www.fortnumandmason.co.uk). Green Park or Piccadilly Circus tube. **Open** 10am-9pm Mon-Sat; noon-6pm Sun (11.30am for browsing). **Map** p102 K8* ❹ *Department store*

In business for over 300 years, Fortnum & Mason is as historic as it is inspiring. A sweeping spiral staircase soars through the four-storey building, while light floods down from a central glass dome. The iconic eau de nil blue and gold colour scheme with flashes of rose pink abounds on both the store design and the packaging of the fabulous ground-floor treats, such as chocolates, biscuits, teas and preserves. A food hall in the basement has a good range of fresh produce; Fortnum's Bees honey comes from beehives on top of the building. There are various eateries, including an ice-cream parlour. The famous hampers start from £60 – though they rise to a whopping £6,000 for the most luxurious.

James J Fox
*19 St James's Street, SW1A 1ES (7930 3787, www.jjfox.co.uk). Green Park tube. **Open** 10am-8pm Mon-Fri; 10am-5.30pm Sat. **Map** p102 K9* ❺ *Cigars*

There are other cigar shops in London, but Fox is the grandest and most storied. Oscar

Wilde died owing it money and the iconic image of Winston Churchill, with a cigar clenched between his teeth, is down to the fact he used to buy his Montecristos here. It's worth a visit just to see the clientele: a curious mixture of ageing Euro playboys, old Etonians and Mayfair gents. There's also a small museum.

❤ Lock & Co Hatters

6 St James's Street, SW1A 1EF (7930 8874, www.lockhatters.co.uk). Green Park tube. **Open** *9am-5.30pm Mon-Fri; 9.30am-5pm Sat.* **Map** *p102 K9* **6** *Milliners*

Lock & Co is perhaps the most famous hat shop in the world. It is certainly one of the oldest, dating from 1759, and has been frequented by such names as Charlie Chaplin and Admiral Lord Nelson. But, history aside, it is simply very good. It has one of the most comprehensive selections of classic hats to be found anywhere in London: bowlers, top hats, homburgs, berets, panamas – all exquisitely made.

Waterstones Piccadilly

203-206 Piccadilly, W1J 9HD (7851 2400, www.waterstones.co.uk). Piccadilly Circus tube. **Open** *9am-10pm Mon-Sat; noon-6.30pm Sun.* **Map** *p102 K8* **7** *Books*

The flagship store of the chain is located in a handsome art deco former department store, where six floors are now stuffed with some 200,000 books, as well as two Café Ws (one on the lower ground-floor, one on the mezzanine) and, on the top floor, the 5th View Bar & Restaurant. The programme of readings, reading groups and workshops is lively and varied. London's only rival to **Foyles** (*see p166*).

GREEN PARK & HYDE PARK CORNER

▶ *Green Park or Hyde Park Corner tube.*

Just east of Green Park tube station, smartly uniformed doormen mark the entrance to the **Ritz** (150 Piccadilly, W1J 9BR, 7493 8181, www.theritzlondon.com). To the southwest is the flat green expanse of **Green Park**; it's rather dull, except in spring, when the daffodils jolly things up.

Work your way along Piccadilly, following the northern edge of Green Park past the queue outside the **Hard Rock Café** (where the Vault's displays of memorabilia are free to visit and open every day; www.hardrock. com) to the Duke of Wellington's old home, **Apsley House**, opposite Wellington Arch. This is hectic **Hyde Park Corner**; Buckingham Palace (*see p114*) is just a short

walk south-east, while Hyde Park and the upper-crust enclave of Belgravia are to the west. There is a collection of memorials that are worth lingering over. The newest is the Bomber Command Memorial. Unveiled in 2012, it recognises the sacrifice of the 55,573 men of Bomber Command, killed between 1939 and 1945 as they pulverised Nazi-held Europe into submission. But we find Charles Sargeant Jagger's thoughtful tribute to the 49,076 men of the Royal Regiment of Artillery, slain between 1914 and 1919, to be more deeply moving. It's both vast – a huge Portland stone slab with giant gunners on three sides – and strangely muted, with a dead soldier lying peacefully in giant hobnail boots on the monument's north side.

Sights & museums

Apsley House

149 Piccadilly, W1J 7NT (7499 5676, www. english-heritage.org.uk). Hyde Park Corner tube. **Open** *Nov-Mar 10am-4pm Sat, Sun.*

Apr-Oct 11am-5pm Wed-Sun. **Tours** *by arrangement.* **Admission** *£10; £6-£9 reductions; £26 family; free under-5s. Joint ticket with Wellington Arch £12.70; £7.60-£11.40 reductions; £33 family.* **Map** *p102 H9.*

Called No.1 London because it was the first London building encountered on the road to the city from the village of Kensington, Apsley House was built by Robert Adam in the 1770s. The Duke of Wellington kept it as his London home for 35 years. Although his descendants still live here, several rooms are open to the public, providing a superb feel for the man and his era. Admire the extravagant porcelain dinnerware and plates or ask for a demonstration of the crafty mirrors in the scarlet and gilt picture gallery, where a fine Velázquez and a Correggio hang near Goya's portrait of the Iron Duke after he defeated the French in 1812. This was a last-minute edit: X-rays have revealed that Wellington's head was painted over that of Joseph Bonaparte, Napoleon's brother. In winter, the twilight tours at Apsley House are very atmospheric.

Wellington Arch

Hyde Park Corner, W1J 7JZ (7930 2726, www.english-heritage.org.uk). Hyde Park Corner tube. **Open** *Apr-Oct 10am-5pm daily. Nov-Mar 10am-4pm daily.* **Admission** *£5.40; £3.20-£4.90 reductions; £14 family; free under-5s. Joint ticket with Apsley House £12.70; £7.60-£11.40 reductions; £33 family.* **Map** *p102 H9.*

Built in the late 1820s to mark Britain's triumph over Napoleonic France, Decimus Burton's Wellington Arch was initially topped by an out-of-proportion equestrian statue of Wellington. However, Captain Adrian Jones's 38-ton bronze *Peace Descending on the Quadriga of War* has finished it with a flourish since 1912. The arch has three floors, with an English Heritage bookshop and various displays, covering the history of the arch and the Blue Plaques scheme, and the Quadriga Gallery providing space for excellent temporary exhibitions. There are great views from the balcony in winter (leafy trees obscure the sightlines in spring and summer).

Wellington Arch

South Kensington & Chelsea

There can be few cities in the world with a square mile so crammed with cultural highlights as you'll find in South Kensington: three of the world's greatest museums, a grand concert hall, university campuses and an expansive park. Neighbouring Knightsbridge, on the other hand, has no cultural pretensions: a certain type of Londoner comes here to spend, spend, spend – or hang around with the non-doms and hyperwealthy incomers who are spend, spend, spending in the designer shops and world-famous department stores. Chelsea, running between them and the river, has long since left its raffish youth behind – but there are pleasures to be found amid its red-brick gentility.

❤ Don't miss

1 Victoria & Albert Museum *p128*
A palace for global applied arts.

2 Chelsea Physic Garden *p137*
A place of botanical delight.

3 Science Museum *p127*
From maths to medicine: how the world works.

4 Natural History Museum *p126*
Life on earth from prehistory to now.

5 Harrods *p135*
Legendary department store.

Queensway

Diana, Princess
of Wales Memorial
Playground

Peter Pan
Statue

The Long Water

West Carriage Drive (The Ring)

Hyde
Park

Serpentine
Sackler
Gallery

Kensington
Gardens

Round
Pond

Serpentine Road

The Serpentine

Kensington
Palace

The Broad Walk

Palace Avenue

Serpentine
Gallery

Rotten Row

KENSINGTON

Kensington Road

Albert
Memorial

South Carriage Drive

Royal
College
of Art

Kensington Gore

Kensington Road

Jay Mews

Royal
Albert
Hall

De Vere Gdns

Palace Gate

Victoria Rd

Hyde Park Gate

Ennismore Gdns

Rutland Gate

Trevor Pl

Montpelier St

Trevor Sq

Douro St

Kensington
Gate

Prince Consort Rd

Princes Gdns

Harrods

St Albans Gr

Victoria Gr

Queen's Gate Mews

Royal
College
of Music

KNIGHTSBRIDGE

Hans Rd

Brompton Pl

Cottesmore
Gardens

Queen's Gate Terrace

Imperial
College
London

Goethe
Institute

Beauchamp Pl

Eldon Rd

Peterslain

Queen's Gate

Gore St

Imperial College Road

Brompton
Square

Cheval Pl

Ovington St

Brompton Road

Lennox St

Cornwall Gardens

La

Gate Pl

Science
Museum

Victoria &
Albert
Museum

Cornwall Gardens

Granville Pl

Queen's Gate Gdns

Natural
History
Museum

Brompton
Oratory

Egerton Terr

Walton Street

Hasker St

First St

Halsey St

Emperor's
Gate

Cromwell
Hospital

McLeod's
Mews

SOUTH
KENSINGTON

Thurloe Sq

BROMPTON

Denver St

Rawlings St

Cromwell Road

Cromwell Pl

Egerton Gdns

Mossop St

Draycott Avenue

Sloane Avenue

Courtfield Gdns

Collingham Rd

Ashburn
Gdns

Ashburn Pl

Gloucester
Rd

Gloucester Road

Stanhope Gdns

Harrington Rd

Pelham
Mews

Bute St

South Terrace

South
Kensington

South Terrace

Pelham St

Pelham Cres

Lucan Pl

Michelin
House

Whitehead's Gr

Courtfield Gdns

Harrington Gardens

Wetherby Gardens

Bina Gdns

Rosary Gdns

Clareville Gdns

Clareville St

Onslow Sq

Summer Pl

Onslow Sq

Pond Pl

Ixworth Pl

Elystan St

Elystan Pl

Bramham Gdns

Bolton Gdns

Drayton Gardens

Cresswell Place

Roland Gdns

Old Brompton Road

Cranley Gdns

Cranley Pl

Onslow Gdns

Selwood Terr

Neville St

Foulis Terr

Burn Wk

Royal
Marsden
Hospital

Cale Street

Danube St

Astell St

Jubilee Pl

Markham St

Elystan Pl

King's Rd

EARL'S
COURT

The Little Boltons

The Boltons

Cranley Mews

Evelyn
Gdns

Cranley Gdns

South Parade

Royal
Brompton
Hospital

Sydney Street

Britten St

Dovehouse St

King's Rd

Smith St

Redcliffe Gardens

Harcourt Ter

Tregunter Road

Priory Walk

Gilston Road

Fulham Road

Elm Park Gdns

Elm Park Rd

The Vale

Carlyle Sq

Manresa Rd

CHELSEA

Old Church Street

Chelsea
Old Town
Hall

Radnor Walk

Sheffield St

Redesdale St

Flood Street

Redburn St

Finborough Road

Coleherne Rd

Cathcart Road

Seymour Wk

Fawcett St

Redcliffe
Place

Redcliffe Place

Chelsea &
Westminster
Hospital

Limerston Street

Park Walk

Callow St

Beaufort St

Elm Park La

Beaufort St

Chelsea Park Gdns

Paultons
Square

King's Road

Bramerton St

Chelsea
Antiques
Market

Carlyle's
House

Oakley St

Upper Cheyne Row

Old Church St

Oakley
Gdns

Margaretta Terr

Chelsea Manor Street

Cheyne Walk

Brompton
Cemetery

Edith Gr

Gertrude St

Beaufort St

Crosby
Hall

Cheyne Walk

Chelsea

124

SOUTH KENSINGTON & CHELSEA

Restaurants

1. Bar Boulud *p135*
2. Claude Bosi at Bibendum *p131*
3. Colbert *p138*
4. Daquise *p131*
5. Gallery Mess *p138*
6. Harwood Arms *p139*
7. Medlar *p139*
8. Mona Lisa *p139*
9. Rabbit *p139*
10. Royal China *p134*

Pubs & bars

1. The Hour Glass *p131*
2. K Bar *p131*

Shops & services

1. Boutique 1 *p139*
2. Conran Shop *p131*
3. Harrods *p135*
4. Harvey Nichols *p135*
5. John Sandoe *p139*

© Copyright Time Out Group 2019

SOUTH KENSINGTON

▶ *Gloucester Road or South Kensington tube.*

As far as cultural and academic institutions are concerned, this is the land of plenty. It was Prince Albert who oversaw the inception of its world-class museums, colleges and concert hall, using the profits of the 1851 Great Exhibition; the area was nicknamed 'Albertopolis' in his honour. Here you'll find the **Natural History Museum**, the **Science Museum** and the **Victoria & Albert Museum** (*see p128*), **Imperial College**, the **Royal College of Art** and the **Royal College of Music** (Prince Consort Road, 7591 4300, www.rcm.ac.uk; call for details of the musical instrument museum). The last forms a unity with the **Royal Albert Hall** (*see p356*), open since 1871 and variously used for boxing, motor shows, marathons, table-tennis tournaments, fascist rallies and rock concerts. Directly opposite is the endearingly pompous **Albert Memorial**.

Sights & museums

Albert Memorial

Kensington Gardens (0300 061 2000, www. royalparks.org.uk). South Kensington tube. Tours Mar-Dec 2pm, 3pm 1st Sun of mth. Admission £9; £8 reductions. Map p124 E9.

'I would rather not be made the prominent feature of such a monument,' was Prince Albert's reported response when the subject of his commemoration arose. Hard, then, to imagine what he would have made of this extraordinary thing, unveiled 15 years after his death. Created by Sir George Gilbert Scott,

it centres on a giant, gilded Albert holding a catalogue of the 1851 Great Exhibition, guarded on four corners by the continents of Africa, America, Asia and Europe. The pillars are crowned with bronze statues of the sciences, and the frieze at the base depicts major artists, architects and musicians. It's one of London's most dramatic monuments.

♥ Natural History Museum

Cromwell Road, SW7 5BD (7942 5000, www. nhm.ac.uk). South Kensington tube. Open 10am-5.50pm daily. Admission free. Special exhibitions vary. Tours free. Map p124 E11.

Both a research institution and a fabulous museum, the NHM opened in Alfred Waterhouse's purpose-built, Romanesque palazzo on the Cromwell Road in 1881. Now joined by the splendid Darwin Centre extension, the original building still looks quite magnificent. The pale blue and terracotta façade just about prepares you for the natural wonders within.

The vast entrance hall, previously home to the iconic Diplodocus skeleton, now displays another huge beast: a blue whale. The 82ft-(25m) long, 4.5-tonne skeleton is suspended dramatically from the ceiling, taking centre-stage as part of an exhibition that tells the tale of evolution and of human impact on the natural world.

From the entrance hall, a left turn leads into the west wing, or Blue Zone, where queues form to see animatronic dinosaurs – especially the endlessly popular T rex. Here too, is the Mammals Hall, where you can stare out all manner of stuffed animals from a polar bear to a pygmy shrew. A display on biology features an illuminated, human-sized model of a foetus in the womb along

♥ Time to eat & drink

Brit with a twist
Rabbit *p139*

French and fancy
Claude Bosi at Bibendum *p131*

Meaty feasts
Bar Boulud *p135*

Perfect for people-watching
Colbert *p138*

♥ Time to shop

Great gifts
Natural History Museum, Science Museum and V&A shops, *p131*

Old-school bookselling
John Sandoe *p139*

Shopping as theatre
Harrods *p135*

Top-notch fashion
Boutique 1 *p139*

In the know
Clues to the queues

Especially in school holidays, there are often long queues at the main entrance of the Natural History Museum on Cromwell Road. Try the side entrance on Exhibition Road, instead: it is usually less busy and provides an impressive introduction to the collections as you ascend the escalator up into the Earth Galleries. Tickets to the dinosaur room can be booked online for free and allow you to enter at a specific time slot rather than queue.

with graphic diagrams of how it might have got there.

A right turn from the central hall leads past the Creepy Crawlies exhibition to the Green Zone. Stars include a cross-section through a giant sequoia tree and an amazing array of stuffed birds, plus the chance to compare the egg of a hummingbird smaller than the nail on your little finger with that of an elephant bird (now extinct), almost football-sized.

Beyond is the Red Zone, where a Stegosaurus skeleton takes pride of place. Earth's Treasury is a mine of information on a variety of precious metals, gems and crystals; From the Beginning is a brave attempt to give the expanse of geological time a human perspective; Volcanoes and Earthquakes explores the immense energy and power of the natural world through dramatic film footage, interactive games and an earthquake simulator.

Many of the museum's 22 million insect and plant specimens are housed in the Darwin Centre, where they take up nearly 17 miles of shelving. With its eight-storey Cocoon, this is also home to the museum's research scientists, who can be watched

at work. But a great deal of this amazing institution is hidden from public view, given over to labs and specialised storage.

Outside, the delightful Wildlife Garden (Apr-Oct only) showcases a range of British lowland habitats, including a 'Bee Tree', a hollow tree trunk that opens to reveal a busy hive.

♥ Science Museum

Exhibition Road, SW7 2DD (7942 4000, www.sciencemuseum.org.uk). South Kensington tube. **Open** *10am-6pm daily.* **Admission** *free. £10; £8-£9 reductions; £2 off per ticket for families. Special exhibitions vary.* **Map** *p124 E10.*

The Science Museum is a celebration of the wonders of technology in the service of our daily lives. On the ground floor, the shop – selling brilliant toys, not least because you can pretend they're educational – is part of the Energy Hall, which introduces the museum's collections with impressive 18th-century steam engines. In Exploring Space, rocket science and the lunar landings are illustrated by dramatically lit mock-ups and full-size models, before the museum gears up for its core collection in Making the

Natural History Museum

❤ Victoria & Albert Museum

Cromwell Road, SW7 2RL (7942 2000, www.vam.ac.uk). South Kensington tube. **Open** *10am-5.45pm Mon-Thur, Sat, Sun; 10am-10pm Fri. Tours 10.30am, 12.30pm, 1.30pm, 3.30pm daily.* **Admission** *free. Special exhibitions vary.* **Map** *p124 F11.*

It comes to something when a museum can lay claim to having been opened as Queen Victoria's last public engagement. In 1899, the current premises of the V&A enjoyed that privilege. It has gone on to become one of the world's – let alone London's – most magnificent museums. It is a superb showcase for applied arts from around the globe, appreciably calmer than its tearaway cousins the **Science Museum** (*see p127*) and **Natural History Museum** (*see p126*) on the other side of Exhibition Road. All three South Ken museums would be must-visits in another city, but it is the sheer beauty of the V&A that keeps it closest to our heart.

The details? There are some 150 grand galleries over seven floors. They contain countless pieces of furniture, ceramics, sculpture, paintings, posters, jewellery, metalwork, glass, textiles and dress, spanning several centuries. You could run through the highlights for the rest of this guide, but key artefacts include the seven Raphael Cartoons, painted in 1515 as tapestry designs for the Sistine Chapel; the finest collection of Italian Renaissance sculpture outside Italy; the Ardabil carpet, the world's oldest and arguably most splendid floor covering, in the Jameel Gallery of Islamic Art; and

the Luck of Edenhall, a 13th-century glass beaker from Syria. The fashion galleries run from 18th-century court dress right up to contemporary chiffon numbers, while the architecture gallery has videos, models, plans and descriptions of various styles.

Over more than a decade, the V&A's ongoing FuturePlan transformation has been a revelation – more than 85 per cent of its public spaces have been restored and redesigned. The completely refurbished Medieval & Renaissance Galleries are stunning, but there are many other eye-catching new or redisplayed exhibits: they were preceded by the restored mosaic floors and beautiful stained glass of the 14th- to 17th-century sculpture rooms, just off the central John Madejski Garden, and followed by the Furniture Galleries – another immediate hit. The ambitious Europe 1600-1815 Galleries – centred around a stunning four-metre-long table fountain, painstakingly reconstructed from 18th-century fragments – collect European clothes, furnishings and other artefacts.

In the know
Monumental

Of all the wonders in the V&A, it was the magnificent Cast Courts we first fell in love with. Here you can ogle an 18ft-high plaster-cast of *David* and other monumental sculptures – faultless, full-scale facsimiles of Renaissance cathedral doorways and the like – in a painstakingly restored double-height gallery that dates to 1873. At least one of the copies here – of the late 15th-century Lubeck relief depicting Christ washing the feet of the Apostles – has outlasted its original.

Or there's the Toshiba Gallery of Japanese Art, exhibiting 550 works running from the sixth century AD to the first Sony Walkman and an origami outfit by Issey Miyake. On a smaller scale, the Ceramics Galleries have been renovated and supplemented with an eye-catching bridge; and the Theatre & Performance Galleries took over where Covent Garden's defunct Theatre Museum left off. Newer additions include the museum's 'Rapid Response Collection', which features examples of contemporary design and architecture reflecting important news events, while the major temporary exhibitions – Alexander McQueen, David Bowie – are frequently blockbuster sell-outs.

Summer 2017 saw the opening of a new entrance, directly into the heart of the museum from Exhibition Road, through the porcelain-tiled Sackler Courtyard to the purpose-built Sainsbury Gallery. It's a fitting introduction to a fabulous museum.

▶ *The V&A also runs the Museum of Childhood in Bethnal Green (see p269).*

Science Museum

Modern World. Introduced by Puffing Billy, the world's oldest steam locomotive (built in 1815), the gallery also contains Stephenson's Rocket. Also here are the Apollo 10 command module, classic cars and an absorbing collection of everyday technological marvels from 1750 up to the present.

In the main body of the museum, the second floor has a couple of newer additions. There's the Media Space, for excellent temporary exhibitions drawn from the museum's impressive photographic archive, and Information Age, the UK's first permanent gallery dedicated to the history of communications technology. It follows developments from the 19th-century establishment of an international telegraph network through broadcasting all the way up to the worldwide web. The stunning Winton Gallery, designed by Zaha Hadid Architects using equations of airflow used in the aviation industry, reveals how mathematics has shaped the modern world.

The centrepiece is a 1929 Handley Page aircraft designed as part of a competition to build safe planes. Other displays explore how maths is driven by real-world problems, from foetal monitoring and artificial intelligence to World War II code-breaking and astronomy. Here too is the Clockmakers' Museum, recently moved from the Guildhall and containing a John Harrison chronometer – he was the man who solved the problem of longitude.

The third floor is dedicated to flight, among other things, including the hands-on Launchpad Gallery, which has levers, pulleys, explosions and all manner of experiments for children (and their associated grown-ups). It is also home to Wonderlab: The Statoil Gallery (entry costs from £8), whose exhibits are dedicated to communicating the properties and principles of the physical world by encouraging visitors to play with them. Fun mirrors help to explain geometry, plasma globes are effectively bottled lightning, and the chemistry bar is home to live experiments that let you get messy and spectacular with crystals, dry ice, bubble volcanoes and non-Newtonian fluids.

Beyond Making the Modern World, bathed in an eerie blue light, are the three floors of the Wellcome Wing, where the museum makes sure it stays on the cutting edge of science. On the ground floor, Antenna is a web-savvy look at breaking science stories, displaying video interviews and Q&As with real research scientists alongside the weird new objects they've been working on. Upstairs is the enjoyable and troubling Who Am I? gallery. A dozen silver pods surround brightly lit cases of objects with engaging interactive displays – from a cartoon of

In the know
Kids' stuff

The Science Museum is great for kids – but everyone knows that, so be sure to arrive early if you don't like crowds and queues. Specifically child-friendly attractions include interactive experimental play in the Garden (basement; for three- to seven-year-olds), the Pattern Pod (ground floor; three- to eight-year-olds) and Engineer your Future (Level 3; 11- to 16-year-olds), but the mathematics gallery (Level 2; over-11s), Wonderlab (Level 3; all ages) and Fly Zone flight simulators (Level 3; all ages) are usually a hit. There's a charge for Wonderlab and the simulators.

ethical dilemmas that introduces you to your dorsolateral prefrontal cortex to a chance to find out what gender your brain is. Compelling objects include a jellyfish that's 'technically immortal', the statistically average British man (he's called Jose), a pound of human fat, displayed alongside a gastric band, and half of Charles Babbage's brain (good luck seeing the other half: it's in the Hunterian Museum, which is now closed until 2021).

Restaurants

❤ Claude Bosi at Bibendum ££££
Michelin House, 81 Fulham Road, SW3 6RD (7581 5817, www.bibendum.co.uk). South Kensington tube. Open 6.30-9.45pm Tue-Wed; noon-2.15pm, 6.30-9.45pm Thur, Fri; noon-2.15pm, 6.30-10pm Sat; noon-2.15pm, 6.30-9pm Sun. Map p124 F11 ❷ *French*

First opened more than 30 years ago, Bibendum is a bona fide London institution. For a start, the building (the massive old Michelin House) is a spectacular art deco pile and one of the city's most striking bits of architecture. Wander through the cavernous former garage forecourt (now Bibendum's **Oyster Bar**, 7589 1480) and up to London's nattiest dining room. With grey leather banquettes, fine art and those awesome Michelin Man-stained glass windows, it's an absolute picture. Gawp all you want, but you come here to eat. Bibendum is home to French fine dining powerhouse Claude Bosi. The food is overwhelmingly excellent and meticulous: from the delicate choux pastry amuse-bouches through mains of turbot *à la grenobloise* or tripe and cuttlefish gratin to exquisite desserts such as black fig millefeuille. Blow the budget and be blown away.

Daquise ££
20 Thurloe Street, SW7 2LT (7589 6117, daquise.co.uk). South Kensington tube. Open noon-11pm daily. Map p124 F11 ❹ *Polish*

This much-loved grande dame of London Polish restaurants (established 1947) offers a home-from-home ambience with a stylish twist. In the shabby-chic, light and airy interior, enlivened with fresh flowers, robust, flavourful, no-nonsense traditional dishes are served with great charm. Classic cold starters of meltingly tender herring with cream, apple, onion and flax oil, or beetroot with subtly warming horseradish, are ladled directly from capacious earthenware bowls, while mains are assembled directly at the table from well-worn saucepans, borne by the chefs who lovingly prepared the dishes.

Pubs & bars

Hour Glass
279-283 Brompton Road, SW3 2DY (7581 2497, hourglasspub.co.uk). South Kensington tube. Open noon-11pm Mon-Sat; noon-9pm Sun. Map p124 F11 ❶

In the posh-shop-big-museum nexus around South Kensington, this nice old pub has been scrubbed up by a couple of lads who own the nearby Brompton Food Market. There are two floors with plenty of standing, leaning and sitting room to enjoy an ale and a pork pie or two.

K Bar
The Kensington, 109-113 Queen's Gate, SW7 5LP (7589 6300, townhousekensington. com/k-bar). South Kensington tube. Bar 4pm-midnight Mon-Fri; noon-midnight Sat, Sun. Food served 6.30-10.30pm Mon-Fri; 7-11am, noon-10.30pm Sat, Sun. Map p124 E11 ❷

Not just any old hotel bar, K Bar buzzes from early evening, with guests preparing for a night out, right through to the nightcap crowd. It's a relatively small area with large, comfy sofas lining the oak-panelled walls and a marble-topped bar adding an air of opulence. Table service is efficient and the competitively priced cocktails are expertly mixed; there's even menu of dessert drinks: bring a sweet tooth if you're trying the Crème Brûlée Martini.

Shops & services
The **V&A** has a superb gift shop, stuffed with stylish exhibition-related buys; the **Science Museum** has a lively range of geek-free science presents for kids, and the **Natural History Museum** has cute cuddly dinosaurs.

Conran Shop
Michelin House, 81 Fulham Road, SW3 6RP (7589 7401, www.conranshop.co.uk). South Kensington tube. Open 10am-6pm Mon, Tue, Fri, Sun; 10am-7pm Wed, Thur; 10am-6.30pm Sat. Map p124 F11 ❷ *Homewares*

Sir Terence Conran's flagship store in the Fulham Road's beautiful 1909 Michelin Building showcases furniture and design for every room in the house as well as the garden. In addition to design classics, such as the Eames DAR chair, there are plenty of portable accessories, gadgets, books, stationery items and toiletries that make great gifts or souvenirs. **Other location** 55 Marylebone High Street, W1U 5HS (7723 2223).

HYDE PARK & KENSINGTON GARDENS

▶ *Hyde Park Corner, Knightsbridge, Lancaster Gate or Queensway tube.*

At one and a half miles long and about a mile wide, **Hyde Park** (0300 061 2114, www.royalparks.org.uk) is one of the largest of London's Royal Parks. The land was appropriated in 1536 from the monks of Westminster Abbey by Henry VIII for hunting deer. Although opened to the public in the early 1600s, the parks were favoured only by the upper echelons of society. At the end of the 17th century, William III, averse to the dank air of Whitehall Palace, relocated to **Kensington Palace**. A corner of Hyde Park was sectioned off to make grounds for the palace and closed to the public, until King George II opened it on Sundays to those wearing formal dress. Nowadays, **Kensington Gardens** is delineated from Hyde Park only by the line of the Serpentine and the Long Water. Beside the Long Water is a bronze statue of **Peter Pan**, erected in 1912: it was in Kensington Gardens beside the Round Pond eight years earlier that playwright JM Barrie met Jack Llewelyn Davies, the boy who was the inspiration for Peter. The **Diana, Princess of Wales Memorial Playground** is a kids' favourite, as is Kathryn Gustafson's ring-shaped **Princess Diana Memorial Fountain**. Near the fountain, Simon Gudgeon's giant bird *Isis* was in 2009 the first sculpture added to the park for half a century. There are changing exhibitions of contemporary art at the **Serpentine Gallery**, which also has a Zaha Hadid-designed counterpart, the **Serpentine Sackler** just across the bridge.

The **Serpentine** itself is London's oldest boating lake, home to ducks, coots, swans, tufty-headed grebes and, every summer, gently perspiring blokes rowing their children or lovers about. The lake is at the south end of Hyde Park, which isn't a beautiful park, but is of historic interest. The legalisation of public assembly in the park led to the establishment of **Speakers' Corner** in 1872 (close to Marble Arch tube), where political and religious ranters – sane and otherwise – still have the floor every Sunday afternoon. Marx, Lenin, Orwell and the Pankhursts all spoke here. It has made the park a traditional destination for protest marches: notably the million opponents of the Iraq War in 2003. There is also a moving memorial in the south-east corner of the park to the 52 people killed by Islamist suicide bombers on 7 July 2005. Their commemoration, set between the Lovers' Walk and busy Park Lane, consists of 52

In the know
Alternative play

The Diana Memorial Playground often has queues to get in. If you get bored of waiting, head to the south of the park and the **Hyde Park Playground**. It has a slide, nest swing and 'jungle area' for nature quests.

Kensington Palace

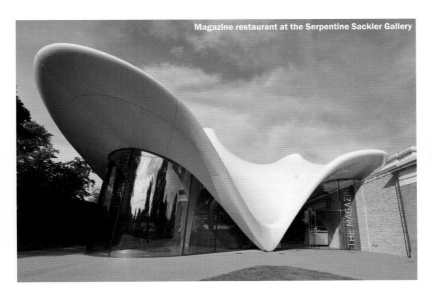

ten-foot-tall, square steel columns marked with the date, time and location of each person's death.

The park perimeter is popular with skaters, as well as with bike- and horse-riders. If you're exploring on foot and the vast expanses defeat you, look out for the **Liberty Drives** (May-Oct). Driven by volunteers, these electric buggies, each with space for a wheelchair, pick up groups of sightseers and ferry them around; there's no fare, but offer a donation if you can.

Sights & museums

Diana, Princess of Wales Memorial Playground

Near Black Lion Gate, Broad Walk, Kensington Gardens, W8 (0300 061 2000, www.royalparks.org.uk). Bayswater or Queensway tube. **Open** *Summer 10am-7.45pm daily. Winter 10am-dusk daily.* **Admission** *free; adults admitted only if accompanied by under-12s.* **Map** *p124 D8.*

Bring buckets and spades, if you can, to this superb playground: the focal attraction is a huge pirate ship, moored in a sea of sand. Other highlights include a tepee camp and a treehouse encampment with walkways, ladders, slides and 'tree phones'. Many of the playground's attractions appeal to the senses (scented shrubs, whispering willows and bamboo are planted throughout), and much equipment has been designed for use by children with special needs.

Kensington Palace

Kensington Gardens, W8 4PX (information 0844 482 7777, reservations 0844 482 7799 or 3166 6000, www.hrp.org.uk). High Street Kensington or Queensway tube. **Open** *Mar-Oct 10am-6pm daily. Nov-Feb 10am-4pm daily.* **Admission** *£19.50; £9.70-£15.50 reductions; free under-5s. Book online for reductions.* **Map** *p124 D9.*

Sir Christopher Wren extended this Jacobean mansion to palatial proportions on the instructions of William III, initiating the palace's long love affair with royalty – which culminated with the floral memorials for one particular resident, Princess Diana, that were placed at the palace's gate after her fatal accident in 1997. Wren's work was also adapted, under George I, with the addition of intricate trompe l'oeil ceilings and staircases. Visitors can now follow a whimsical trail that focuses on four 'stories' of former residents – Diana, of course; William and Mary, and Mary's sister Queen Anne; Georges I and II; Queen Victoria – unearthing the facts through handily placed 'newspapers'. Artefacts include paintings by the likes of Tintoretto, contemporary art and fashion installations, and even Victoria's (tiny) wedding dress.

Serpentine & Serpentine Sackler galleries

Kensington Gardens, near Albert Memorial, W2 3XA (7402 6075, www.serpentinegalleries. org). Lancaster Gate or South Kensington tube. **Open** *10am-6pm daily.* **Admission** *free; donations appreciated.* **Map** *p124 E9 & F8.*

The Serpentine Gallery – much-loved for its sometimes challenging exhibitions of contemporary art – originally had just the one secluded location in a small 1930s tea-house building south-west of the Long Water and Serpentine, into which were squeezed exhibition spaces and a bijou bookshop. Here, the rolling two-monthly programme of exhibitions features a mix of up-to-the-minute artists and edgy career retrospectives, but – perhaps symbolic of the gallery's limitations of space – every spring it also commissions a renowned architect, who's never before built in the UK, to build a temporary pavilion outside. The pavilion then hosts a packed programme of cultural events (June to September).

A permanent solution to the issue of space was found in 2013, when the gallery opened a second location, the Serpentine Sackler, just across the bridge from the original. Devoted to emerging art in all forms, the Sackler is a Grade II-listed, Palladian former gunpowder store, with a clean-lined restaurant over which the late architect Zaha Hadid cast a billowing white cape of a roof.

Restaurants

Royal China ££
13 Queensway, W2 4QJ (7221 2535, www.theroyalchina.co.uk). Bayswater or Queensway tube. **Open** *noon-11pm Mon-Thur; noon-11.30pm Fri, Sat; 11am-10pm Sun.* **Map** *p124 D8* ⑩ *Chinese*

Not far beyond the north side of the park, this stalwart of London's dim sum scene is always a pleasure to visit. Its perennial popularity ensures a lively atmosphere, and the authentic, perfectly prepared little dishes are head and shoulders above most of Chinatown's lazy offerings. The main menu features wonderfully light beef balls enlivened with strong accents of ginger and water chestnuts, while the delicious wun tun soup has light dumplings floating in a rich broth with an undertone of five-spice. Opt for dim sum and you can choose from the likes of crab and spinach steamed dumplings or prawn and chive packages in batter.

KNIGHTSBRIDGE

▶ *Knightsbridge tube.*

Knightsbridge in the 11th century was a village celebrated for its taverns, highwaymen and the legend that two knights once fought to the death on the bridge spanning the Westbourne River (later dammed to form Hyde Park's Serpentine lake). In modern Knightsbridge, urban princesses would be too busy unsheathing the credit card to notice such a farrago. Voguish **Harvey Nichols** holds court at the top of Sloane Street, which leads down to **Sloane Square**. Expensive brands – Gucci, Prada, Chanel – dominate. East of Sloane Street is **Belgravia**, characterised by a cluster of embassies around **Belgrave Square**. Hidden behind the stucco-clad parades fronting the square are numerous mews, worth exploring for the pubs they conceal, notably the **Nag's Head** (53 Kinnerton Street, SW1X 8ED, 7235 1135).

For many tourists, Knightsbridge means one thing: **Harrods**. From its olive-green awning to its green-coated doormen, it's an instantly recognisable retail legend. Further along is the imposing **Brompton Oratory**.

Sights & museums

Brompton Oratory
Thurloe Place, Brompton Road, SW7 2RP (7808 0900, www.bromptonoratory.co.uk). South Kensington tube. **Open** *6.30am-8pm daily.* **Admission** *free; donations appreciated.* **Map** *p124 F11.*

The second-biggest Catholic church in the country (after Westminster Cathedral; see *p111*) is formally the Church of the Immaculate Heart of Mary, but almost universally known as the Brompton Oratory. Completed in 1884, it feels older, partly because of the Baroque Italianate style but also because much of the decoration pre-dates the structure: Mazzuoli's 17th-century apostle statues, for example, are from Siena Cathedral. During the Cold War, KGB agents used the Brompton Oratory as a dead-letter box. The church is popular with young, traditionally minded Catholics: the 11am Solemn Mass sung in Latin on Sundays is enchanting, as are Vespers, at 3.30pm; the website has details.

Restaurants

There's a branch of the popular – and self-explanatory – mini-chain **Burger & Lobster** in **Harvey Nichols** (*see opposite*).

Shops & services

♥ Harrods

87-135 Brompton Road, SW1X 7XL (7730 1234, www.harrods.com). Knightsbridge tube. **Open** *10am-9pm Mon-Sat; noon-6pm Sun (browsing from 11.30am).* **Map** *p124 G10* ❸
Department store

It might be unashamedly ostentatious, stuffed with tourists and in possession of the world's most vulgar statue (Dodi and Diana in bronze by the Egyptian escalators), but Harrods – London's most famous department store – is still spectacular. Serious shoppers browse the elegantly tiled and fragrant food halls on the ground floor or the wealth of exclusives in the beauty halls. But indulge the excesses too: Harrods has an art gallery, a stunning new interiors department and a kitchenware floor that hosts live cooking lessons from household names. Got kids? Head straight to Toy Kingdom on the third floor, with its enchanted forest, intergalactic science lab and bespoke sweets-maker. Elsewhere, Harrods excels at shoes – with a gargantuan footwear department stocking labels such as Ferragamo, Charlotte Olympia and Giuseppe Zanotti – and the Fashion Lab, on the fourth floor, is dedicated to young designer labels such as Zadig & Voltaire, Wildfox and the Kooples.

Harvey Nichols

109-125 Knightsbridge, SW1X 7RJ (7235 5000, www.harveynichols.com /store/ knightsbridge). Knightsbridge tube. **Open** *10am-8pm Mon-Sat; noon-6pm Sun (browsing from 11.30am).* **Map** *p124 G10* ❹
Department store

Once the watchword for luxury Knightsbridge shopping, Harvey Nicks lost ground to **Liberty** (*see p155*), **Selfridges** (*see p146*) and even Harrods, which were engaging better with their customers and seemed to get the idea of hosting dynamic shopping events. But it's beginning to fight back. Makeup junkies should head to the ground floor beauty space to pick up established brands like Charlotte Tilbury and Shu Uemura, or try something new with Beauty Bites – a lovely series of mini cosmetics, featuring up-and-coming brands. On the third floor, Sneaker Concept showcases high-fashion sports shoes. The clothing rails are full of top labels such as Alexander Wang, Balenciaga and Givenchy, and there's an excellent array of accessories and beauty buys from luxurious brands such as Tom Ford and COR (whose soap contains real silver). Finish off proceedings with lunch on the fifth floor, where the buzzy food department is located along with a branch of **Burger & Lobster** (0207 201 8676, noon-10.30pm Mon-Sat, noon-10pm Sun).

Harrods

♥ Bar Boulud £££

Mandarin Oriental Hyde Park, 66 Knightsbridge, SW1X 7LA (7201 3899, www. barboulud.com). Knightsbridge tube. **Open** *noon-10.30pm Mon-Wed, Sun; noon-11pm Thur-Sat.* **Map** *p124 G10* ❶ *French*

Overseen by renowned chef Daniel Boulud, the restaurant has an eye-catching view of the open-plan kitchen, where chefs work in meditative calm. Charcuterie from Gilles Verot is a big draw, as are the elegant French brasserie options and finger-licking American staples. We've had burgers here and loved every bite – try a beef patty topped with pulled pork and green chilli mayonnaise – but other culinary gems might include a robust French onion soup, resplendent with caramelised onions and topped with molten gruyère.

CHELSEA

▶ *Sloane Square tube then various buses.*

Chelsea is where London's wealthy classes play in cultural and geographical isolation. Originally a fishing hamlet, the area was a 'village of palaces' by the 16th century, home to the likes of Henry VIII's ill-fated advisor Sir Thomas More. Artists and poets (Whistler, Carlyle, Wilde) followed from the 1880s, before the fashionistas arrived with the opening of Mary Quant's Bazaar in 1955. Soon after, Chelsea had acquired a raffish reputation and was at the forefront of successive youth-culture revolutions. Synonymous with the Swinging Sixties and immortalised by punk, the dissipated phase of the **King's Road** is now a matter for historians as the street teems with pricey fashion houses and air-conditioned poodle parlours. Yet on a sunny day, it does make a vivid stroll. For one thing, you don't have to take yourself as seriously as the locals. And for another, the area is figuratively rich in historical associations, and literally so with the expensive red-brick houses that slumber down leafy mews and charming, cobbled side streets.

At the top (east end) of the King's Road is **Sloane Square**. It's named after Sir Hans Sloane, whose collections formed the basis of the British Museum (*see p198*). The shaded benches in the middle of the square provide a lovely counterpoint to the looming façades of Tiffany & Co and the enormous Peter Jones department store, in a 1930s building with excellent views from its top-floor café. A certain edginess is lent to proceedings by the **Royal Court Theatre** (*see p362*), which shocked the nation with its 1956 première of John Osborne's *Look Back in Anger*.

To escape the bustle and fumes, head to **Duke of York Square**, a pedestrianised enclave of boutiques and restaurants presided over by a statue of Sir Hans. In the summer, the cooling fountains attract hordes of children, their parents sitting to watch from the outdoor café tables or taking advantage of the Saturday food market. The square is also home to the mercilessly modern art of the **Saatchi Gallery**, housed in former military barracks.

The once-adventurous shops on the King's Road are now a mix of trendier-than-thou fashion houses and high-street chains. Wander **Cale Street** for some pleasing boutiques, or head for the **Chelsea Farmers' Market** on adjoining Sydney Street to find a clutter of artfully distressed rustic sheds housing restaurants and shops selling everything from cigars to garden products. Sydney Street leads to **St Luke's Church**, where Charles Dickens married Catherine Hogarth in 1836.

Towards the western end of the King's Road is **Bluebird**, a dramatic art deco former motor garage housing a café and restaurant (although the Shop at Bluebird, one of Chelsea's most notable boutiques, has moved to Covent Garden; *see p188*.) A little further up the road, the **World's End** store (no.430) occupies what was once Vivienne Westwood's notorious leather- and fetishwear boutique Sex; a green-haired Johnny Rotten auditioned for the Sex Pistols here in 1975 by singing along to an Alice Cooper record on the shop's jukebox.

Running parallel to the King's Road, Chelsea's riverside has long been noted for its nurseries and gardens, lending a village air that befits a place of retirement for the former British soldiers living in the **Royal Hospital Chelsea**. In summer, the Chelsea Pensioners, as they're known, regularly don red coats and tricorn hats when venturing beyond the gates. The Royal Hospital's lovely gardens host the **Chelsea Flower Show** (*see p313*) each spring. Almost next door is the **National Army Museum**.

West from the river end of Royal Hospital Road is **Cheyne Walk**. Its river-view benches remain good spots for a sit-down, but the tranquillity of the **Chelsea Physic Garden** – established on land bought by Sir Hans Sloane – is the real treat.

Further west on Cheyne Walk, the park benches of **Chelsea Embankment Gardens** face Albert Bridge, where signs still order troops to 'Break step when marching over this bridge'. In the small gardens, you'll find a statue of the great historian Thomas Carlyle – the 'sage of Chelsea', whose home is preserved (**Carlyle's House**). Nearby, a gold-faced statue of Sir Thomas More looks out over the river from the garden of **Chelsea Old Church**, where he once sang in the choir and may well be (partially) buried. Legend has it that the Thomas More Chapel, on the south side, contains More's headless body somewhere under the walls (his head, having been spiked on London Bridge, was 'rescued' and buried in a family vault in St Dunstan's church, Canterbury). Follow Old Church Street north and you'll find the **Chelsea Arts Club** (no.143), founded in 1871 by Whistler and now host to occasional public events, including classical recitals.

North of the western extremity of Cheyne Walk are **Brompton Cemetery** (suffragette Emmeline Pankhurst is buried here; *see p303*) and the home ground of London's first Champions League winners: Chelsea FC. Tickets for league games are hard to come by, but **Stamford Bridge** (Fulham Road, SW6 1HS, 0371 811 1955, www.chelseafc. com) does have the excellent **Chelsea Centenary Museum**.

Sights & museums

Carlyle's House

24 Cheyne Row, SW3 5HL (7352 7087, www. nationaltrust.org.uk/carlyles-house). Sloane Square tube or bus 11, 19, 22, 49, 170, 211, 319. **Open** *Mar-Oct 11am-5pm Wed-Sun. Closed Nov-Feb.* **Admission** *£7; £3.50 children; £17.50 family. No cards.* **Map** *p124 F13.*

Thomas Carlyle and his wife Jane moved to this four-storey, Queen Anne house in 1834. The house was inaugurated as a museum in 1896, 15 years after Carlyle's death, offering an intriguing snapshot of Victorian life. The writer's quest for quiet (details of his valiant attempts to soundproof the attic) strikes a chord today: he was plagued by the sound of revelry from Cremorne Pleasure Gardens.

Chelsea Centenary Museum

Stamford Bridge, Fulham Road, SW6 1HS (0371 811 1955, events.chelseafc.com/room-item/museum). Fulham Broadway tube. **Open** *9.30am-5pm daily.* **Admission** *£12; £10-£11 reductions; free under-5s.*

Opened in 1877 as an athletics track (it was thought track and field had a more promising financial future than mere Association Football), Stamford Bridge was soon a football ground in search of a team. It became the home of the Blues in 1905; for its 100th anniversary the club celebrated with the opening of this fine museum. It provides a terrific social history of the game, helped along by the narrative of Chelsea's journey from music-hall joke to oil-money-funded Premier League titans. There are interactives, trophies – Chelsea are the only London club to have won the prestigious Champions League (in 2012) and the only British club to have won all the major European trophies (adding the Europa League, 2013; Cup Winners' Cup, 1971, 1998; and Super Cup, 1998) – and some ace memorabilia, including a photo of Raquel Welch in Chelsea strip making a valiant attempt to side-foot the ball.

♥ Chelsea Physic Garden

66 Royal Hospital Road, SW3 4HS (7352 5646, www.chelseaphysicgarden.co.uk). Sloane Square tube or bus 11, 19, 22. **Open** *Apr-June, Sept, Oct 11am-5pm Mon; 11am-6pm Tue-Fri, Sun. July, Aug 11am-5pm Mon; 11am-6pm Tue, Thur, Fri, Sun; 11am-10pm Wed. Nov-Mar 11am-3pm Mon-Fri.* **Tours** *times vary; phone to check.* **Admission** *£9.50; £6.25 reductions; free under-5s.* **Tours** *free.* **Map** *p124 G13.*

Passing through these modest red-brick walls is like stepping into a secret garden: a place by the Thames but with its own microclimate, where rare plants from Britain and across the globe have been collected – and now

thrive. Set up by apothecaries in 1673, Chelsea Physic Garden contains the world's oldest rock garden, created in 1773 from black Icelandic basalt imported by Joseph Banks (the most-famous plant hunter of all) and decorated with masonry from the Tower of London. Today, the garden is also home to Britain's first garden of ethnobotany (the study of the botany of different ethnic groups and indigenous peoples), and a Garden of Medicinal Plants, tracing the chronology of plant remedies over almost an acre, from ancient Greek herbs to plants that are likely to be used in future medicine. The half-acre World Woodland Garden, which celebrates useful and medicinal plants from the

Chelsea Physic Garden

Americas, Europe and East Asia, is home to more than 150 species of plant. Visitors can weave through it on a serpentine path or learn more about the collection from garden volunteers in one of the woodland clearings. There's also a shop where visitors can buy unusual plants, and a café serving very good homemade cakes.

National Army Museum

Royal Hospital Road, SW3 4HT (7730 0717, www.nam.ac.uk). Sloane Square tube or bus 170. **Open** *10am-5.30pm daily; until 8pm 1st Wed of the mth.* **Admission** *free.* **Map** *p124 G13.*

The National Army Museum reopened in 2017 after a three-year, £24m redesign – and a major rethink. A huge atrium has been carved out of the middle of the building, and the whole place is much lighter and less gloomy, but the structural redevelopment isn't the biggest change. The museum now reflects evolving perceptions of the history of the British Army. As one graph on display reveals, there are fewer people serving in the regular army today than at any time in the last 200 years, yet its public profile has never been higher. To reflect this, the museum has five new galleries representing different aspects of the armed forces, with a much keener focus on social history and diversity. Some old-fashioned models of battles (notably Waterloo) and uniforms remain, of course, along with favourite exhibits such as Major Michael 'Bronco' Lane's frost-bitten fingertips and the skeleton of Napoleon's horse Marengo. In Play Base, under-eights can take on an assault course, climb aboard a command liaison vehicle or develop their fieldcraft skills.

Royal Hospital Chelsea

Royal Hospital Road, SW3 4HT (7881 5200, www.chelsea-pensioners.co.uk). Sloane Square tube or bus 11, 19, 22, 137, 170. **Open** *10am-4pm Mon-Fri.* **Admission** *free.* **Map** *p124 H13.*

Around 350 Chelsea Pensioners (retired soldiers) live at the Royal Hospital, founded in 1682 by Charles II for those 'broken by age or war' and designed by Sir Christopher Wren (with adjustments by Robert Adam and Sir John Soane). Retired soldiers are still eligible to apply for a final posting here if they're over 65 and in receipt of an Army or War Disability Pension for Army Service. The pensioners have their own club room, bowling green and gardens, and get tickets to Chelsea FC home games. The museum (same times) has more about their lives. The annual Chelsea Flower Show (*see p313*) is held in the grounds.

Saatchi Gallery

Duke of York's HQ, King's Road, SW3 4RY (7811 3070, www.saatchigallery.com). Sloane Square tube. **Open** *10am-6pm daily.* **Admission** *free.* **Map** *p124 G12.*

Charles Saatchi's gallery offers 50,000sq ft (4,645sq m) of space for temporary exhibitions. Given his fame as a promoter in the 1990s of what became known as the Young British Artists – Damien Hirst, Tracey Emin, Gavin Turk, Sarah Lucas et al – it will surprise many that the focus of exhibitions here has been internationalist in outlook, with China, Africa and India all featuring. Still, Richard Wilson's superb oil-sump installation *20:50* has survived from the Saatchi Gallery's previous incarnations and remains here as the only permanently displayed artwork.

Restaurants

♥ Colbert £££

50-52 Sloane Square, SW1W 8AX (7730 2804, www.colbertchelsea.com). Sloane Square tube. **Open** *8am-11pm Mon-Sat; 8am-10pm Sun.* **Map** *p124 H12* ❸ *Brasserie*

Paying homage to Continental grand cafés with marble, linen napkins and mirrors aplenty, Colbert feels more casual and local than its siblings – the Wolseley (see *p118*), the Delaunay (see *p191*) and Brasserie Zédel (see *p172*) – and the posters in the booth-lined bar area advertising performances by Olivier and Vivien Leigh at the Royal Court Theatre next door (see *p362*) lend a sense of history. It also trumps the others with pavement tables from which to admire the beautiful people. More importantly, it serves the best lunch in the area: perhaps a deliciously decadent smoked haddock florentine with spinach, poached egg and a buttery cream sauce; or a croque madame – brioche filled with comté cheese, jambon blanc and béchamel sauce, topped with a fried egg.

Gallery Mess ££

Saatchi Gallery, Duke of York's HQ, King's Road, SW3 4RY (7730 8135, www.saatchigallery.com/gallerymess). Sloane Square tube. **Open** *10am-11.30pm Mon-Sat; 10am-7pm Sun.* **Map** *p124 G12* ❺ *Brasserie*

As befits its Chelsea location, this welcoming brasserie at the Saatchi art gallery is smarter than most, with white linen tablecloths, exposed brickwork and impressive bar all somewhat in thrall to the vaulted ceiling and expansive curtain of floor-to-ceiling arched windows. There's also a large outdoor terrace. Service is disarmingly friendly and mains offer comforting flavours and proportions. So you'll find haddock and chips, steak, charcuterie and smoked fish platters, caesar salad and afternoon tea.

Harwood Arms £££

Corner of Walham Grove & Farm Lane, SW6 1QP (7386 1847, harwoodarms.com). Fulham Broadway tube. **Open** *6.15-9.15pm Mon; noon-2.15pm, 6.15-9.15pm Tue-Fri; noon-2.45pm, 6.15-9.15pm Sat, Sun.* **Map** *p124 C13* **6** *British*

It might look like an upmarket pub, but the Harwood Arms is a serious restaurant with wine list to match. It showcases prime British produce through skilled, imaginative modern cooking. The mounted deer's head is a reminder that game and wild food are a speciality, with mains such as grilled haunch of Berkshire roe deer accompanied by beetroot, slivers of roast onion and pickled mushrooms. Expect fine dining, rather than pub portions, and you'll be more than happy. Be sure to book ahead.

Medlar £££

438 King's Road, SW10 0LJ (7349 1900, www. medlarrestaurant.co.uk). Fulham Broadway tube or bus 11, 22. **Open** *noon-3pm, 6.30-10.30pm Mon-Fri; noon-3pm, 6-10.30pm Sat; noon-3pm, 6-9.30pm Sun.* **Map** *p124 E13* **7** *Modern European*

The decor here is understated: a soothing grey-green colour scheme and unobtrusive artwork. The real artistry arrives on the plates, dishes of astounding excellence. Assemblies are complex and have lengthy names: crisp calf's brain with smoked duck breast, aïoli, pink fir potatoes and *tardivo* (raddichio), for example. But every ingredient justifies its place in entirely natural-seeming juxtapositions of flavour, texture and colour. And the execution is nearly flawless. Save room for wonderful (and relatively simple) puddings, such as cardamom custard with saffron oranges, pomegranate and langues de chat.

Mona Lisa £

417 King's Road, SW10 0LR (7376 5447, https://mona-lisa.business.site). Fulham Broadway tube or bus 11, 22. **Open** *7am-11pm Mon-Sat; 8.30am-5.30pm Sun.* **Map** *p124 E13* **8** *Italian/café*

Not much to look at, either inside or out, the Mona Lisa is hidden away at the 'wrong' end of the King's Road, just beyond World's End. But the bonhomie is infectious, and if you order the right thing, such as the meltingly tender calf's liver *alla salvia* (with butter and sage), served with old-school potatoes and veg, you won't give a fig about the decor. The menu ranges across breakfasts, sandwiches, burgers, omelettes, jacket potatoes and pastas to three-course blow-outs (at lunch, the latter is a real bargain).

♥ Rabbit £££

172 King's Road, SW3 4UP (3750 0172, www. rabbit-restaurant.com). Sloane Square tube. **Open** *6-11pm (last orders 10.30pm) Mon; noon-midnight (last orders 10.30pm) Tue-Sat; noon-5pm (last orders 4pm) Sun.* **Map** *p124 F12* **9** *British*

More than a restaurant, Rabbit feels a bit like a theme bar that does food, right down to a 'stable door' entrance, outside which smokers linger. But to see it as a party venue does the cooking a disservice: the Gladwins dish up inventive mouthfuls of joy that warm you up for heavy, slow-cooked mains (perhaps pigs' cheeks with malt, stout, garlic and pennywort) and lighter, faster-cooked dishes (such as tempura duck liver). However, the 'British with a twist' ethos is best summed up by the desserts: try a Viennetta parfait made of Magnum ice-cream lollies, or an intriguing cep and white-chocolate bourbon. Rabbit's older sibling, The Shed (*see p303*) in Notting Hill is the Gladwin brothers' original 'wild' food eaterie.

Shops & services

♥ Boutique 1

127/128 Sloane Street, SW1X 9AS (7118 0111, www.boutique1.com). Sloane Square tube. **Open** *10am-7pm Mon-Sat; noon-6pm Sun.* **Map** *p124 G11* **1** *Fashion/accessories*

Selling the kind of clothes you'd consider going temporarily homeless for, since they cost a month's rent, Boutique 1 is the first European outpost of a swish Middle Eastern retailer. The stylish range of accessories, jewellery, shoes and beachwear are set out across two spacious floors, like a miniature department store. Even if you're not buying, come for swanky April's Café, the in-store eaterie. With its low-hanging lighting, pale wooden furniture, scattered House of Hackney cushions and, through the windows, an urban garden, it's like being in the kitchen of your Scandi dreams.

♥ John Sandoe

10-12 Blacklands Terrace, SW3 2SR (7589 9473, www.johnsandoe.com). Sloane Square tube. **Open** *9.30am-6.30pm Mon-Sat; 11am-5pm Sun.* **Map** *p124 G12* **5** *Books & music*

Tucked away on a side street, this 50-year-old independent has always looked just as a bookshop should, with stock literally packed to the rafters. The enthusiasm and knowledge of the staff can be taken as, forgive us, read – several have worked here for decades, their passion for books undimmed.

Oxford Street, Marylebone & Mayfair

Oxford Street is working hard to stay top of London's shopping destinations, with a revamped roundabout at Marble Arch, wider pavements, the innovative pedestrian crossings at Oxford Circus, and an all-new 'eastern gateway' development near the shiny new Tottenham Court Road superstation in anticipation of Crossrail's eventual arrival.

North of London's busiest commercial artery are the luxury cafés and boutiques of Marylebone, bounded by Regent's Park at the furthest edge, with the Arab shisha cafés and juice bars of the Edgware Road to divide it from scruffy Paddington. South of Oxford Street, Mayfair oozes wealth, while to the south-east, neon-lit Piccadilly Circus is a bit of town every Londoner does their best to avoid.

❤ **Don't miss**

1 Liberty *p155*
A sweet combination of tradition and fashion.

2 Royal Academy of Arts *p158*
Impressive home to blockbuster shows.

3 Selfridges *p146*
London's leading department store.

4 The Connaught Bar *p159*
A place for civilised cocktailing.

5 Wallace Collection *p148*
A grand townhouse museum, full of art, armour and exquisite *objets*.

Liberty

OXFORD STREET, MARYLEBONE & MAYFAIR

Restaurants
1. Bentley's Oyster Bar & Grill p154
2. Busada Eathai p145
3. Chiltern Firehouse p149
4. Fischer's p149
5. Gymkhana p159
6. Kitty Fisher's p159
7. Providores & Tapa Room p150
8. Rasa W1 p159
9. Roti Chai p146
10. Shorya Ramen p156
11. Twist p150
12. Zoilo p150

Pubs & bars
1. The Connaught Bar p159
2. Mr Fogg's Residence p159
3. Purl p151

Shops & services
1. & Other Stories p156
2. Alexander McQueen p160
3. Alfie's Antiques Market p151
4. Berry Bros & Rudd p160
5. Browns p160
6. Burberry p156
7. Burlington Arcade p160
8. Cadenhead's Whisky Shop & Tasting Room p151
9. Collaborative Store p151
10. Daunt Books p151
11. Drake's p160
12. Gallery of Everything p151
13. Grays Antique Market & Grays in the Mews p161
14. Hamleys p156
15. J Crew p156
16. John, Bell & Croyden p151
17. KJ's Laundry p152
18. Liberty p155
19. Paul Smith p161
20. Postcard Teas p161
21. Prism p152
22. Rigby & Peller p161
23. Selfridges p146
24. Smythson p161
25. Stella McCartney p161
26. Topshop/Topman p146
27. Victoria Beckham p161

OXFORD STREET

▶ *Bond Street, Marble Arch, Oxford Circus or Tottenham Court Road tube.*

Official estimates put the annual footfall at somewhere near 200 million people per year, but few Londoners love **Oxford Street**. A shopping district since the 19th century, it's unmanageably busy on weekends and in the run-up to Christmas. Even outside these times, it's rarely pretty, lined as it is with over-familiar chain stores and choked with bus traffic. The New West End Company (www.newwestend.com) has been charged with changing all that: Oxford Circus, Marble Arch and Regent Street are beginning to feel the benefits, with Tottenham Court Road next on the list.

The street gets smarter as you walk from east to west. The eastern end around Tottenham Court Road station is emerging from major development for Crossrail, which should begin services in autumn 2019. Its lack of destination shops had already been solved by the opening of teen-magnet fashion flagship **Primark** (nos.14-28, 7580 5510, www.primark.com). The string of classy department stores – including **John Lewis** (nos.278-306, 7629 7711, www. johnlewis.com) and **Selfridges** – begins west of Oxford Circus, always chaotic with shoppers. Next stop along, Bond Street station has reopened after its Crossrail redevelopment.

Apart from the art deco splendour of Selfridges, architectural interest along Oxford Street is largely limited to Oxford Circus's four identical convex corners, constructed between 1913 and 1928. The crowds and traffic make it hard to enjoy the architecture, although the situation has improved since the council widened the pavements, removed street clutter and

Oxford Street

❤ **Time to eat & drink**

Cocktails with class
The Connaught Bar *p159*, Mr Fogg's Residence *p159*

Global small plates
Providores & Tapa Room *p150*, Zoilo *p150*

Indian street food
Roti Chai *p146*

Modern European blow-out
Kitty Fisher's *p159*

Viennese-style brasserie
Fischer's *p149*

❤ **Time to shop**

Best department stores
Selfridges *p146*, Liberty *p155*

Beautiful books
Daunt Books *p151*

Curated fashion
Browns *p160*

Mall shopping the old-fashioned way
Burlington Arcade *p160*

Outsider art on celeb street
Gallery of Everything *p151*

Trendy threads for the teenage hordes
Topshop/Topman *p146*

Under-the-radar labels
Collaborative Store *p151*

created diagonal pedestrian crossings. Mayor Khan's more ambitious plans to pedestrianise the whole of Oxford Street came to nothing.

At the western end of Oxford Street, stands **Marble Arch**, with its Carrara marble cladding and sculptures celebrating Nelson and Wellington. It was designed by John Nash in 1827 as the entrance to a rebuilt Buckingham Palace, but the arch was moved here in 1851, after – it is said – a fuming Queen Victoria found it to be too narrow for her coach. Now given a £2 million revamp, it's been joined by renovated water fountains and gardens that contain an ongoing series of large-scale public sculpture commissions.

Oxford Street gained notoriety as the route by which condemned men were conveyed from Newgate Prison to the old Tyburn gallows, stopping only for a last pint at the **Angel** (61-62 St Giles High Street, 7240 2876), at the eastern end of the street, in the shadow of Centre Point. At the western end, for over six centuries, crowds would gather to watch executions at Tyburn. Held in 1783, the final execution to be carried out here is marked by the most euphemistic circular plaque in London: around a humble cross, it says just 'The site of the Tyburn Tree'. This was the gallows that was London's main place of execution from 1388, silent witness to the death of highwayman Jack Sheppard (who drew crowds of 200,000) and the hanging of Cromwell's exhumed corpse.

North of Oxford Circus

▶ *Great Portland Street, Oxford Circus or Regent's Park tube.*

North of Oxford Circus runs **Langham Place**, notable for the Bath stone façade of John Nash's **All Souls Church** (Langham Place, 2 All Souls Place, 7580 3522, www.allsouls.org). Its bold combination of a Gothic spire and classical rotunda wasn't popular: in 1824, a year after it opened, the church was condemned in Parliament as 'deplorable and horrible'; a statue of Nash now stands outside, looking forlornly away.

Tucked to one side of the church you'll find the BBC's **Broadcasting House**, an oddly asymmetrical art deco building, much extended by recent redevelopment. Over the road is the **Langham Hotel** (1C Portland Place, W1B 1JA, 7636 1000, www.langham hotels.com), which opened in 1865 as Britain's first grand hotel and has been home at various points to Mark Twain, Napoleon III and Oscar Wilde.

North, Langham Place turns into **Portland Place**, designed by Robert and James Adam as the glory of 18th-century London. Its Georgian terraced houses are now mostly occupied by embassies and swanky offices.

At no.66 is the **Royal Institute of British Architects** (RIBA). Parallel to Portland Place are **Harley Street**, famous for its high-cost dentists and doctors, and **Wimpole Street**, erstwhile home to the poet Elizabeth Barrett Browning (no.50), Sir Paul McCartney (no.57) and Sir Arthur Conan Doyle (2 Upper Wimpole Street).

Sights & museums

BBC Broadcasting House

Portland Place, Upper Regent Street, W1A 1AA (0370 901 1227, www.bbc.co.uk). Oxford Circus tube. **Map** p142 J6.

Completed in 1932, this was Britain's first purpose-built broadcast centre; in 2013, it acquired a neighbour, New Broadcasting House. Tours are not currently offered to members of the public due to security concerns, but you can eat and drink in the café, which has views into the glass-sided newsroom. The Radio Theatre in the original BBC building is especially gorgeous; there you can join the audience for radio and TV shows, with ticketing information at www. bbc.co.uk/showsandtours/shows.

Restaurants

Busaba Eathai £

8-13 Bird Street, W1U 1BU (7518 8080, www.busaba.com/locations/busaba-st-christophers-place). Bond Street tube. **Open** *11.30am-11pm Mon-Thur; 11.30am-11.30pm Fri, Sat; 11.30am-10pm Sun.* **Map** *p142 H7* ❷ *Thai*

Busaba is a 16-strong chain – but it's not your average Thai joint. The dark, handsome interior combines dark wood, incense and dimly lit lanterns. With spacious shared tables, no reservations and brisk service, it remains a great spot for a casual meal with friends. Among the Thai classics, you'll find a few dishes that aren't often seen in London, such as *sen chan pad thai* (a pimped *pad thai* with crab originating from the Chanthaburi province of eastern Thailand).

♥ Roti Chai ££

3 Portman Mews South, W1H 6AY (7408 0101, www.rotichai.com). Marble Arch tube. **Dining room** *noon-2.30pm, 5-10.30pm Mon-Fri; 5-10.30pm Sat; 5-9pm Sun.* **Street kitchen** *noon-10.30pm Mon-Sat; 12.30-9pm Sun.* **Map** *p142 H7* ⑨ *Pan-Indian*

The ground-floor 'street kitchen', with its utilitarian furniture and canteen vibe, is ideal for a swift midday feed – and the alert young staff keep things pacy. The menu is modelled on those of urban India's snack shacks, so you'll find food such as bhel pooris, chilli paneer and pani puri. Larger dishes include 'railway lamb curry' (tender meat and potato in a rich gravy spiced with star anise and cinnamon bark). In the basement, the 'dining room' is a darker, sexier (and pricier) space.

Shops & services

♥ Selfridges

400 Oxford Street, W1A 1AB (0800 123400, www.selfridges.com). Bond Street or Marble Arch tube. **Open** *9.30am-10pm Mon, Tue; 9am-10pm Wed-Sat; noon-6pm Sun (browsing from 11.30am).* **Map** *p142 H7* ㉓ *Department store*

With its plethora of concession boutiques, store-wide themed events and collections from all the hottest brands, Selfridges is as dynamic as a department store can be. Although the store layout changes regularly, the useful floor plans make navigating the place easy-peasy. While the basement is chock-full of hip home accessories and stylish kitchen equipment, it's Selfridges' fashion floors that really get hearts racing. With a winning combination of new talent, hip and edgy labels, high-street brands and luxury high-end designers, the store stays ahead of the pack. Highlights include the huge denim section, the extensive Shoe Galleries and, on the fifth floor, the 37,000sq ft (3,437m sq) Body Studio, a temple of top-notch activewear that aims to kit out people of all shapes and sizes. Level 4 hosts the predictably excellent Toy Shop. There are always new excitements in the food hall, ranging from great deli and bakery produce to classy packaged goods, while regularly changing pop-ups and special events keep customers on their toes.

♥ Topshop/Topman

36-38 Great Castle Street, W1W 8LG (7927 7644, www.topshop.com). Oxford Circus tube. **Open** *9.30am-10pm Mon-Sat; 11.30am-6pm Sun.* **Map** *p142 K7* ㉖ *Fashion*

Topshop has been the queen of the British high street for the past decade, and walking into the busy Oxford Street flagship of this massive chain, it's easy to see why. Spanning five huge floors, the place lays claim to being the world's largest fashion shop, and is always buzzing with fashion-forward teens and twentysomethings keen to get their hands on the next big trends. The store covers a huge range of styles and sizes, and includes free personal shoppers, boutique label concessions, capsule collections, a Cheeky nail salon, Hershesons Blow Dry Bar, Bleach London and Blink Brow Bar, as well as a café and sweet shop.

Topman is as on-the-ball and innovative as its big sister, stocking niche menswear labels such as Garbstore, and housing a trainer boutique, a suit section, and a new personal shopping suite, featuring consultation rooms, Xbox 360s and an exhibition space. Both shops are even more of a hive of activity than normal during London Fashion Week, when they host a series of special events.

Marble Arch p145

MARYLEBONE & BAKER STREET

▶ *Baker Street, Bond Street, Marble Arch, Oxford Circus or Regent's Park tube.*

North of Oxford Street, the moneyed district known to its boosters as 'Marylebone Village' became a magnet for fashionable Londoners following the opening of André Balazs's **Chiltern Firehouse** hotel in 2013. However, most visitors to the area head directly for the unfashionable but deathlessly popular waxworks of **Madame Tussauds**, or make their way to the northern end of Baker Street to pay their respects to the world's favourite freelance detective at the **Sherlock Holmes Museum**. The Beatles painted 94 Baker Street with a psychedelic mural before opening it in December 1967 as the Apple Boutique, a clothing store run on such whimsical hippie principles that it had to close within six months due to financial losses. Fab Four pilgrims head to the **London Beatles Store** (no.231, 7935 4464, www.beatlesstorelondon.co.uk), where the ground-floor shop offers a predictable array of Beatles-branded accessories alongside some genuinely collectible items.

The area's beating heart for locals was always **Marylebone High Street**, which still teems with interesting shops – not least a hot drink and Gaultier collaboration at **Kusmi Tea** (no.15), Sicilian perfumier **Ortigia** (no.23) and the unapologetically British and thoroughly lovely **Daunt Books**. **St Marylebone Church** stands in its fourth incarnation at the northern end of the street. The church's garden hosts designer clothing and artisan food stalls at the **Cabbages & Frocks** market on Saturdays (www.cabbagesandfrocks.co.uk). The name of the neighbourhood is a contraction of the church's earlier name, St Mary by the Bourne; the 'bourne' in question, Tyburn stream, still filters into the Thames near Pimlico, but its entire length is now covered. Just north of here, across busy Marylebone Road is the **Royal Academy of Music**, with its small and oft-overlooked museum (7873 7373, www.ram.ac.uk), and the York Gate entrance to fabulous **Regent's Park** (*see p244*).

Lovely boutiques can be found on winding **Marylebone Lane**, among them **KJ's Laundry**, and the **Golden Eagle** (no.59, 7935 3228) hosts regular singalongs around its piano. There's fine food here too, with smart, often upmarket eateries snuggling alongside delicatessens such as **La Fromagerie** (2-6 Moxon Street, W1U 4EW, 7935 0341, www.lafromagerie.co.uk) and century-old lunchroom **Paul Rothe & Son** (35 Marylebone Lane, 7935 6783).

Marylebone Farmers' Market takes place in the Cramer Street car park every Sunday.

But if you're on trend and have money in your pocket, Marylebone's all about **Chiltern Street** these days. Eat at the Chiltern Firehouse if you can get a table, but on your way down the street, also note **Cadenhead's**, **Prism**, the **Gallery of Everything**, that little sitar shop and – since you don't really have a reservation – the cool little **Monocle Café** (no.18, 7135 2040, cafe.monocle.com), the coffee shop of Tyler Brûlé's magazine.

Further south, the soaring neo-Gothic interior of the 19th-century **St James's Roman Catholic Church** (Spanish Place, 22 George Street, 7935 0943, www.sjrcc.org.uk) is lit dramatically by stained-glass windows; Vivien Leigh (née Hartley) married barrister Herbert Leigh Hunt here in 1932. Other cultural diversions include the **Wallace Collection** and the **Wigmore Hall** (*see p358*).

Part of the Romans' Watling Street from Dover to Wales, **Edgware Road** rules a definite north–south line marking the western edge of the West End. It's now the heart of the city's Middle East end: if you want to pick up your copy of *Al Hayat*, cash a cheque at the Bank of Kuwait or catch Egyptian football, head here.

That the name Paddington has been immortalised by a certain small, ursine Peruvian émigré (check out the 2014 and 2017 films) is appropriate, given that the area has long been home to refugees and immigrants. It was a country village until an arm of the Grand Union Canal arrived in 1801, linking London to the Midlands, followed in the 1830s by the railway. **Paddington Station**, with its fine triple roof of iron and glass, was built in 1851 to the specifications of the great engineer Isambard Kingdom Brunel. (If you've a smartphone, there's interactive information available at Brunel's statue in the station.) Paddington's proximity to central London eventually drew in developers. To the east of the station, gleaming **Paddington Central** now provides a million square feet of office space, canalside apartments and restaurants. In St Mary's Hospital, the old-fashioned **Alexander Fleming Laboratory Museum** gives a sense of what the district used to be like.

Sights & museums

Alexander Fleming Laboratory Museum

St Mary's Hospital, Praed Street, W2 1NY (3312 6528, www.medicalmuseums.org). Paddington tube/rail. **Open** *10am-1pm Mon-Thur. By appt 2-5pm Mon-Thur; 10am-5pm*

Fri. Admission £4; £2 reductions; free under-5s. No cards. Map pull-out E6.

Buzz in at the entrance on your left as you enter the hospital and head up the stairs to find this tiny, dusty, instrument-cluttered lab. Enthusiastic guides conjure up Professor Alexander Fleming who, in 1928, noticed that mould contamination had destroyed some *Staphylococcus* bacteria on a set-aside culture plate: he had discovered penicillin. The keen entrepreneurs across the street immediately began to advertise their pub's healthful properties, claiming the miracle fungus had blown into the lab from them. The video room has a documentary on Fleming's life and discovery.

Madame Tussauds

Marylebone Road, NW1 5LR (www. madametussauds.com/london). Baker Street tube. Open ticketed time slots only; book online. Admission £35; £30 reductions; free under-3s. Cheaper tickets available online in advance. Map p142 H5.

Streams of humanity jostle excitedly here for the chance to take pictures of one another planting a smacker on a waxen visage of fame and fortune. Madame Tussaud brought her show to London in 1802, 32 years after it was founded in Paris, and it's been expanding ever since on these very premises since 1884. There are now some 300 figures in the collection: current movie A-listers who require no more than a first name (Angelina, Brad), as well as their illustrious forebears for whom the surname seems more fitting (Chaplin); a bevy of Royals (not least Wills and Kate, and Harry and Meghan), and sundry sports stars including Bobby Moore and Mo Farah. Rihanna and One Direction can be found hanging out among the Music Megastars, while Dickens, Einstein and Madame Tussaud herself kick back in the Culture section. Proving they remain right on top of trends and current affairs, there's a section dedicated to YouTube stars Zoe and Alfie, as well as a Donald Trump alongside political luminaries such as Nelson Mandela, Martin Luther King and Barack Obama. What must they be thinking.

Tussauds also hosts Marvel Super Heroes 4D, where interactives and waxworks of Iron Man, Spider-Man and an 18ft Hulk provide further photo ops, but the highlight is the nine-minute film in '4D' (as well as 3D projections, there are 'real' effects such as a shaking floor and smoke in the auditorium). There's a truly impressive Star Wars area, with expertly finished sets spread over two floors, so visitors can explore Yoda's swamp and the lava fields of Mustafar, where Anakin turns to the dark side. Waxworks show Luke Skywalker fighting Darth Vader,

Obi-Wan Kenobi and (teenage boys and their dads take note) a captive Princess Leia in Jabba's Throne Room. For an extra £8, you can visit the Sherlock Holmes Experience and choose from one of the theatrical experiences, such as the King Kong-themed Skull Island Experience, complete with 18ft-tall animatronic gorilla head, or Alien: Escape Experience, featuring Michael Fassbender's first wax figure.

Sherlock Holmes Museum

221B Baker Street, NW1 6XE (7224 3688, www.sherlock-holmes.co.uk). Baker Street tube. Open 9.30am-6pm daily. Admission £15; £10 reductions. Map p142 G5.

Founded in 1989 at what used to be no.239, the museum fought long and hard for the right to claim the address 221B Baker Street as its own. When you visit, you are likely to be greeted by an august person wearing a bowler hat and whiskers; this, you will deduce, is Dr Watson. And every lovingly recreated detail – murder weapons, Victoriana, waxwork tableaux of key scenes from Conan Doyle's stories – conspires to persuade visitors to suspend their disbelief and feel themselves travelling back in time to a preserved fragment of historical reality. Perhaps most interesting is a folder of letters upstairs in Mrs Hudson's room: they were all actually sent to Holmes by fans from all over the world, asking for help or offering their assistance as wannabe sleuths.

❤ Wallace Collection

Hertford House, Manchester Square, W1U 3BN (7563 9500, www.wallacecollection.org). Bond Street tube. Open 10am-5pm daily. Admission free. Map p142 H6.

Built in 1776 and tucked away on a quiet square, this handsome house contains an exceptional collection of 18th-century French furniture, paintings and *objets d'art*, as well as an amazing array of medieval armour and weaponry taking up much of the ground floor. It all belonged to Sir Richard Wallace, who, as the illegitimate offspring of the fourth Marquess of Hertford, inherited in 1870 the treasures his father had amassed in the last 30 years of his life. Room after grand room contains Louis XIV and XV furnishings and

In the know
Roald Dahl Museum & Story Centre

Rather than paying a premium for Madame Tussauds, families might prefer to catch a train from Marylebone station to Great Missenden to visit the home and museum of the great children's author. For full details, see www.roalddahl.com/museum.

Sèvres porcelain; the galleries are hung with paintings by Titian, Gainsborough and Reynolds, as well as Fragonard's *The Swing*.

Thoroughly refurbished, the Wallace is looking wonderful these days, especially upstairs, where the West Galleries display 19th-century and Venetian paintings (including a room of Canalettos) and the East Galleries are dedicated to Dutch paintings, among them a wonderful Rembrandt self-portrait hung directly opposite his less characterful painting of Titus, his son. At the back, the Great Gallery – following painstaking improvements to lighting and decor – is now the loveliest gallery room in London, with Franz Hals's *Laughing Cavalier*, Poussin's *A Dance to the Music of Time*, Velázquez's *The Lady with a Fan* and Rubens' *The Rainbow Landscape* shown to their very best advantage.

Restaurants

Chiltern Firehouse £££££
*1 Chiltern Street, W1U 7PA (7073 7676, www. chilternfirehouse.com). Baker Street tube. **Open** 7-10.30am, noon-3pm, 5.30-10.30pm Mon-Fri; 8-10am, 11am-3pm, 6-10.30pm Sat, Sun. **Map** p142 H6* ❸ *Modern European*

This lovely 1889 Grade II-listed Victorian Gothic fire brigade building was rebuilt from the inside out to create one of London's most hyped hotels, but the discreetly gated garden is also the entrance to one of London's finest restaurants. The kitchen can do fiddly and pretty, exemplified by appetisers such as the tiny, slider-like 'doughnuts' filled with crab meat, but pretty is only part of the story. The

In the know
Holmes from home

Studious fans of the Victorian sleuth may find more of interest among the books and photos of the Sherlock Holmes Collection, which is now held at **Westminster Reference Library** (7641 1206, by appointment only), just south of Leicester Square.

restaurant's success is built on its reputation as a celeb-magnet but when that fades, the flavour combinations and exemplary modern cooking techniques, as 'curated' by Portuguese superchef Nuno Mendes, will remain. The best seats are at the kitchen counter, from which you can watch the chefs work their magic.

❤ Fischer's £££
*50 Marylebone High Street, W1U 5HN (7466 5501, www.fischers.co.uk). Baker Street or Regent's Park tube. **Open** 7.30am-10.30pm Mon; 7.30am-11pm Tue-Sat; 8am-10.30pm Sun. **Map** p142 H5* ❹ *Austrian*

Chris Corbin and Jeremy King have made a habit of producing destination restaurants that don't feel stand-offish. This revival of the Mittel-European grand café is no exception. It's another celebrity hotspot – they love both Fischer's ageless elegance and its two-track booking system (fast-track for slebs; sidings for the hoi polloi) – but the prices here, in a setting where the monthly bill for wood polish might cause a Habsburg lip to tremble, are not as inflated as you'd expect. The main menu would be familiar to someone touring

Sherlock Holmes Museum

Wallace Collection p148

the Austro-Hungarian Empire in their charabanc, but there is fabulous sachertorte and strudel for those who can't manage a full meal.

♥ Providores & Tapa Room £££

109 Marylebone High Street, W1U 4RX (7935 6175, www.theprovidores.co.uk). Baker Street or Bond Street tube. **Providores** *noon-3pm, 6-10.30pm Mon-Fri; 10am-3pm, 6-10.30pm Sat; 10am-3pm Sun.* **Tapa Room** *8-11.30am, noon-10.30pm Mon-Fri; 9am-3pm, 4-10.30pm Sat; 9am-3pm, 4-10pm Sun.* **Map** *p142 H6* ❼ *Fusion*

Fusion cuisine is common in London these days, but Peter Gordon was one of the pioneers – and his flagship restaurant continues to shine. On the ground floor is the Tapa Room, a casual, buzzy space heaving with well-dressed locals knocking back top-quality coffee, New Zealand wines and an all-day menu of small plates. Upstairs is the more formal but still intimate Providores restaurant, where everything is ratcheted up a notch. The menu of small plates – roughly a sonnet in length and style – might include scallops with a bright salad and *beurre noisette* hollandaise or coconut laksa with a fish dumpling and quail's eggs.

Twist £££

42 Crawford Street, W1H 1JW (7723 3377, www.twistkitchen.co.uk). Edgware Road or Marylebone tube. **Open** *noon-3pm, 6-10.30pm Mon-Sat.* **Map** *p142 G6* ⓫ *Mediterranean*

It's not often you see an Italian chef embrace small plates, but that's precisely the twist Neapolitan Eduardo Tuccillo has put on the food at this charming little restaurant. Rather than stick to southern Italian dishes, he's mixed it up with Spanish and other Mediterranean influences. Top-flight ingredients are in evidence throughout, with perfectly made pasta slathered with a creamy mushroom sauce heady with truffle, or juicy prawns cooked *a la plancha* with chilli and garlic and served on a purée of Jerusalem artichoke. Dishes are on-trend without being pretentious, with an honest commitment throughout to quality cooking.

♥ Zoilo ££

9 Duke Street, W1U 3EG (7486 9699, www. zoilo.co.uk). Bond Street tube. **Open** *5.30-10pm Mon; noon-2.30pm, 5.30-10.30pm Tue-Sat.* **Map** *p142 H7* ⓬ *Argentinian*

If the idea of deconstructed, small-plates Argentinian cooking seems a contradiction in terms, pull up a counter seat and prepare to be amazed. With few actual tables, most of the seating is around the ground-floor bar or the downstairs kitchen – it shouts 'watch us work, look how good we are!'. Diners can witness the creation of dazzling offerings like octopus cooked *sous vide*, fried *queso de chancho* ('head cheese'), or miniature steak, each rustled up with flair and a feel for authenticity. Desserts run from a traditional, ultra-sweet 'tres leches' milk cake to a tart passionfruit sorbet, and most of the all-Argentinian wine list is available by the glass or small carafe. Plates might be small, but when flavours are as compelling as these, you want as many different dishes as you can get.

Pubs & bars

Purl
50-54 Blandford Street, W1U 7HX (7935 0835, www.purl-london.com). Bond Street tube. **Open** *5-11.30pm Mon-Thur; 5pm-midnight Fri, Sat.* **Map** *p142 H6* ❸

Purl, one of London's first speakeasy-style bars, remains popular, which means that booking is advisable – though walk-ins will be seated if there's space. The layout of the bar, over a number of smallish spaces in a vaulted basement, gives the opportunity for genuine seclusion, if that's what you're looking for. And if you're interested in cutting-edge cocktail making, you're also in luck. Novel methods and unusual ingredients are used in many of the drinks, but the classics are always sound. And the music is chosen by someone who has very good taste in jazz.

Shops & services

Alfie's Antique Market
13-25 Church Street, NW8 8DT (7723 6066, www.alfiesantiques.com). Edgware Road tube or Marylebone tube/rail. **Open** *10am-6pm Tue-Sat.* **No cards.** **Map** *p142 F5* ❸ *Antiques*

Over almost four decades now, Alfie's three floors and basement have hosted at least a hundred dealers in vintage furniture and fashion, art, books, maps and the like behind the rather bold art deco façade. Alfie's has been an encouragement – and, in some cases, a stepping stone – for other dealers to set up businesses near here. But before you take on what is now the cluster of shops, many focused on 20th-century collectibles, at the east end of Church Street, repair to Alfie's pleasant rooftop café to revive flagging spirits.

Cadenhead's Whisky Shop & Tasting Room
26 Chiltern Street, W1U 7QF (7935 6999, www.whiskytastingroom.com). Baker Street tube. **Open** *10.30am-6.30pm Mon-Thur; 11am-6.30pm Fri; 10.30am-6pm Sat.* **Map** *p142 H6* ❽ *Food & drink*

Cadenhead's is a survivor of a rare breed – the independent whisky bottler – and its shop is one of a kind, at least in London. Cadenhead's selects barrels from distilleries all over Scotland and bottles them without filtration or any other intervention.

♥ Collaborative Store
58 Blandford Street, W1U 7JB (7935 8123, www.thecollaborativestore.co.uk). Baker Street tube. **Open** *11am-7pm Mon-Sat; noon-6pm Sun.* **Map** *p142 H6* ❾ *Fashion*

Following a couple of great pop-ups, this concept store found a permanent place to call home. Only stocking independent designers and makers, it features plenty of under-the-radar brands. In the same space, you can pick up delicate, geometric jewellery from Clerkenwell's Miya Bonner, colourful furniture from Jennifer Newman and brilliant shoes from Ganor Dominic – all of them London-based. Every month the store also hosts workshops and pop-up events.

♥ Daunt Books
83-84 Marylebone High Street, W1U 4QW (7224 2295, www.dauntbooks.co.uk). Baker Street tube. **Open** *9am-7.30pm Mon-Sat; 11am-6pm Sun.* **Map** *p142 H6* ❿ *Books & music*

This beautiful Edwardian shop's elegant three-level back room – complete with oak balconies, viridian-green walls and stained-glass window – houses a much-praised travel section featuring guidebooks, maps, language reference, travelogues and related fiction. Travel aside, Daunt is also a first-rate stop for literary fiction, biography, gardening and more, with a good range of author readings to boot. There are branches throughout the city, but this is by far the most handsome.

♥ Gallery of Everything
4 Chiltern Street, W1U 7PS (7486 8908, shop.musevery.com). Baker Street tube. **Open** *11am-6.30pm Tue-Sat; 2-6pm Sun.* **Map** *p142 H6* ⓬ *Art & merchandise*

It all started in a former dairy in Camden – or perhaps with Duchamp's urinal. The former was, in 2009, the site of the hugely popular Museum of Everything exhibition of outsider or non-academic or naïve or private or... well, of art you don't usually see in galleries. Further exhibitions followed, here and in other cities, all delivered with a winning pop sensibility and a shrewd eye for artistry and interest. This gallery-shop continues the good work – even if you're not in the hunt for original art, the excellent merchandise makes winningly idiosyncratic souvenirs.

John, Bell and Croyden
50-54 Wigmore Street, W1U 2AU (7935 5555, johnbellcroyden.co.uk). Bond Street tube. **Open** *8.30am-7pm Mon-Fri; 9.30am-8pm Sat; noon-6pm Sun.* **Map** *p142 J6* ⓰ *Pharmacy*

Daunt Books p151

After two centuries of dishing out cures for Londoners' maladies, this venerable pharmacy has undergone a multimillion-pound revamp. Intriguing bits of antique paraphernalia are dotted among of-the-moment wellness fads – JB&C houses a royal prescription book, so you can gawp at Queen Victoria's beauty secrets (cold cream and Coraline toothpaste, FYI). The store is also home to a globetrotting selection of fancy brands, from French cult favourites (Embryolisse, La Roche Posay) to under-the-radar Antipodean suncare.

KJ's Laundry

*74 Marylebone Lane, W1U 2PW (7486 7855, www.kjslaundry.com). Bond Street tube. **Open** 10am-7pm Mon-Sat; 11am-5pm Sun. **Map** p142 J6 ⑰ Fashion*

Since opening in 2006, proprietors Kate Allden and Jane Ellis have curated a delightful mix of both established and lesser-known designers from around the globe, with an emphasis on timeless elegance rather than cutting-edge style. Luxury knits, skinny jeans, floaty tops, cowboy boots and charm jewellery are all hardy perennials here.

Prism

*54 Chiltern Street, W1U 7QX (7635 5407, prismlondon.com). Baker Street tube. **Open** 9.30am-6pm Mon-Wed, Fri; 10.30am-7pm Thur; 11am-7pm Sat; noon-5pm Sun. **Map** p142 H6 ㉑ Fashion*

Designer Anna Laub's clothing label was founded entirely according to her own wish list. After failing to find a bikini that fitted her body shape, she created a swimwear collection for the non-standard-sized woman,

with 12 variations of the same bikini – including skimpy bottoms, '50s-style pants and jumbo retro granny pants, which can be matched with triangle tops, bandeaux, bras and moulded cups. Everything in store is designed with the same particular eye, from the rubber-soled espadrilles to a beach bag that doubles as carry-on-luggage.

PICCADILLY CIRCUS & REGENT STREET

▶ *Oxford Circus or Piccadilly Circus tube.*

Busy **Piccadilly Circus** is an uneasy mix of the tawdry and the grand, a mix that has little to do with the vision of its architect. John Nash's 1820s design for the intersection of Regent Street and Piccadilly, two of the West End's most elegant streets, was a harmonious circle of curved frontages. But 60 years later, Shaftesbury Avenue muscled in and ruined it all. Still, a revamp of the traffic junction by the same design consultants who successfully remodelled Oxford Circus (here they ripped out a mile of railings to ease pedestrian access) has made it a bit more pleasant.

Alfred Gilbert's memorial fountain in honour of child-labour abolitionist Earl Shaftesbury was erected in 1893. It's properly known as the **Shaftesbury Memorial**, with the statue on top intended to show the Angel of Christian Charity, but critics and public alike recognised the likeness of **Eros** and their judgement has stuck.

The illuminated advertising panels around the intersection (www.piccadillylights.co.uk) appeared late in

Gunther von Hagens' Original

BODY WORLDS
THE MUSEUM EXPERIENCE

A UNIQUE JOURNEY UNDER YOUR SKIN

⊖ **PICCADILLY CIRCUS | BODYWORLDS.CO.UK**

the 19th century and have been there ever since; a Coca-Cola ad has been here since 1955, making it the world's longest-running advertisement. Previously the lights have only been turned off during World War II, for Winston Churchill's funeral in 1965 and Princess Diana's funeral in 1997, but in January 2017, Piccadilly went dark for a major upgrade: Europe's largest single digital screen was unveiled nine months later.

Opposite the memorial, the **London Pavilion** has seen several ventures come and go, in a prime but tired location. Ripley's Believe It or Not Odditorium occupied the site until 2017, to be replaced by Gunther von Hagens' globally successful **Body Worlds** exhibition of real human cadavers.

Connecting Piccadilly Circus to Oxford Circus to the north and Pall Mall to the south, **Regent Street** was designed by Nash in the early 1800s with the aims of improving access to Regent's Park and bumping up property values in Haymarket and Pall Mall. Much of Nash's architecture was destroyed in the early 20th century, but the street's broad curve retains some of the grandeur Nash intended for it.

Sights & museums

Body Worlds

London Pavilion, 1 Piccadilly Circus, W1J 0DA (0330 223 3233, bodyworlds.co.uk). Piccadilly Circus tube. **Open** *9.30am-7pm Sun-Thur (last entry 5.30pm); 9.30am-9pm Fri, Sat (last entry 7.30pm).* **Admission** *prices vary; book online.* **Map** *p142 L8.*

Gunther von Hagens' famous collection of human bodies preserved via his own 'plastination' technique has found a permanent home at Piccadilly Circus. It's unsettling to move from the throngs of people outside into an exhibition that lays humanity bare in such a stark way. Visitors report finding the skinless cadavers sincerely life-affirming, sometimes even spurring them on to give up the booze and start exercising.

Restaurants

Bentley's Oyster Bar & Grill £££

11-15 Swallow Street, W1B 4DG (7734 4756, www.bentleys.org). Piccadilly Circus tube. **Oyster Bar** *11.30am-11pm Mon-Sat; 11.30am-10pm Sun.* **Restaurant** *noon-3pm, 5.30-11pm Mon-Fri; 5.30-11pm Sat.* **Map** *p142 K8* ❶ *Fish & seafood*

Richard Corrigan first overhauled this grande dame of the capital's restaurant scene (established 1916) in 2005. The interior remains as polished as ever, with art deco

♥ Liberty

Regent Street, W1B 5AH (7734 1234, www.liberty.co.uk). Oxford Circus tube. **Open** *10am-8pm Mon-Sat; noon-6pm Sun (browsing from 11.30am).* **Map** *p142 K7* ⑱ *Department store*

Founded in 1875, Liberty's present site was built in 1925 – its distinctive half-timbered frontage constructed from the remains of a couple of decommissioned warships, HMS *Hindustan* and HMS *Impregnable*. Which goes a good way to summarising the place: it's a superbly loveable mix of tradition and fashion. The store's interconnecting jumble of rooms, with the odd fireplace and cushioned window seat, have an intimate feel – as if you've strayed into a private room in a stately home. It's no accident: founder Arthur Lasenby Liberty wanted customers to feel as if they were exploring someone's home, keeping the shopping galleries small, albeit linked to three rather grand atriums.

Although Liberty trades well on its history, it has spent the last half decade squeezing innovation into its wood-panelled rooms. At the main entrance to the store is Wild at Heart's exuberant floral concession, and just off from here you'll find yourself in a room devoted to the store's own label. Fashion brands focus on high-end British designers, such as Vivienne Westwood and Christopher Kane. But despite being up with the latest fashions, Liberty still respects its dressmaking heritage with a range of cottons in the third-floor haberdashery department.

Back in 2011 it expanded its men's floor, adding a huge tailoring and accessories chamber packed full of posh undies. The Paper Room soon followed on the ground floor, with micro-floral Liberty print stationery and gifts, and then the Dining Room opened – quirky cookware and gadgetry in a space modelled on the kitchen in *Downton Abbey*.

French publishing powerhouse Assouline opened its Literary Lounge on the ground floor, where you can flick through fashion, art and photography coffee-table books (which are, oddly, the size of coffee tables). The Beauty Hall then doubled in size – stocking cult brands such as Aesop, Le Labo and Byredo, and skincare from the much-celebrated Egyptian Magic, at counters manned by an eerily beautiful staff – and three new treatment rooms were added.

For all its pomp and fizz, Liberty doesn't take itself too seriously – there's a genuine sense of whimsy in its approach to retail. Collaborations with brands such as Puma and Nike produce floral sneakers (that instantly sell out) and, via its Art Fabrics project, Liberty has worked with babydoll-dress fancier Grayson Perry and even Hello Kitty to create exclusive fabrics. The store still has a little sewing school, with crafty classes for aspiring seamstresses. Visitors can also have their moustache expertly trimmed and waxed at Murdock barbers or their barnacles plucked off by expert chiropodists in the Margaret Dabbs Sole Spa.

windows, the original marble oyster bar and wood panelling. Week nights in the more formal first-floor Grill restaurant have a restrained business-dinner vibe, but the downstairs oyster bar is pleasingly laid-back. Theatrics at the gleaming marble counter (part staff speedily shucking, part competitive knocking 'em back) provide entertaining distraction as you decide between menu classics and imaginative daily specials.

Shoryu Ramen £

9 Regent Street, SW1Y 4LR (no phone, www. shoryuramen.com). Piccadilly Circus tube. **Open** *11.15am-midnight Mon-Sat; 11.15am-10.30pm Sun.* **Map** *p142 L8* ⓾ *Japanese*

Shoryu pips its West End *tonkotsu* rivals when it comes to the texture and stock of its broth. As well as Hakata-style ramen (noodles in a rich, boiled-down, pork-bone broth), the other notable feature is speed. Both help to ease the hassle of no-bookings dining. Dracula *tonkotsu* – with caramelised garlic oil, balsamic vinegar and garlic chips – packs a flavoursome punch. Extra toppings such as bamboo shoots and boiled egg are to be expected, but *kaedama* (plain refill noodles) are a godsend for anyone sharing soup stock between small children. There's a varied choice of sides, sakés and sweets. **Other locations** throughout the city.

Shops & services

& Other Stories

256-258 Regent Street, W1B 3AF (3402 9190, www.stories.com). Oxford Circus tube. **Open** *10am-9pm Mon-Sat; noon-6pm Sun.* **Map** *p142 K7* ❶ *Fashion*

While the name of H&M's sister label, & Other Stories, may not exactly roll off the tongue, the clothes and location are bang on the money. This capacious store is spread over two floors and handily located for fashion-savvy shoppers between Topshop and Liberty. What started as a beauty concept in 2010, quickly evolved into a fully fledged fashion brand offering accessories, lipsticks, lingerie and soft, clean, tailored fashion that won't break the bank. **Other locations** throughout the city.

Burberry

121 Regent Street, W1B 4TB (7806 8904, www. burberry.com). Piccadilly Circus tube. **Open** *10am-9pm Mon-Sat; 11.30am-6pm Sun.* **Map** *p142 K8* ❻ *Fashion*

The flagship store of the Burberry brand melds together the building's near-200 years of history with the attributes of hyper-modern retailing. Interactive mirrors react to microchipped products and respond with

bespoke informative content. Welcoming assistants are armed with iPads, a 38sq ft TV live-streams shows, and acoustic performances are held on a hydraulic stage. But the gracious surroundings and an emphasis on natural light create a welcoming atmosphere. There's a beauty room here, as well as fashion and accessories.

Hamleys

188-196 Regent Street, W1B 5BT (0371 704 1977, www.hamleys.com). Oxford Circus tube. **Open** *10am-9pm Mon-Fri; 9.30am-9pm Sat; noon-6pm Sun.* **Map** *p142 K7* ⓮ *Children*

Visiting Hamleys is certainly an experience – whether a good one or not will depend on your tolerance for noisy, over-excited children, especially during school holidays and the run-up to Christmas, when the store runs special kids' events. As you doubtless know, Hamleys is a ginormous toy shop, perhaps the most ginormous toy shop, with attractive displays of all this season's must-have toys across five crazed floors, and perky demonstrators ramping up the temptation levels.

J Crew

165 Regent Street, W1B 4AD (7292 1580, www.jcrew.com). Oxford Circus tube. **Open** *10am-8pm Mon-Sat; noon-6pm Sun.* **Map** *p142 K8* ⓯ *Fashion*

Established in 1983 as a catalogue label, J Crew has become one of America's most successful fashion brands. Happily the US export has brought with it American-style customer service: the staff are ultra-attentive and beam when they serve you. Go here for luxurious wardrobe basics for men, women and kids from cashmere knits to neat blazers.

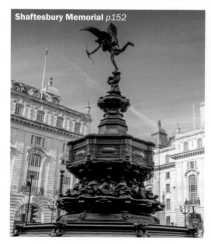
Shaftesbury Memorial *p152*

MAYFAIR

▶ *Bond Street or Green Park tube.*

The gaiety suggested by the name of Mayfair, derived from a long-gone spring celebration, isn't matched by its atmosphere today. Even on Mayfair's busy shopping streets, you may feel out of place without the reassuring heft of a platinum card in your pocket. Nonetheless, there are many pleasures to enjoy if you fancy a stroll, not least the rapidly changing roster of blue-chip commercial art galleries.

The Grosvenor and Berkeley families bought the rolling green fields that would become Mayfair in the middle of the 17th century. In the 1700s, they developed the pastures into a posh new neighbourhood, focused on a series of landmark squares. The most famous of these, **Grosvenor Square** (1725-31), is dominated by the supremely inelegant former US Embassy building. The Embassy moved to new premises in Vauxhall in 2017, and the Grosvenor Square site is set to become a hotel, redesigned by architect Sir David Chipperfield. Out front, pride of place is taken by a statue of President Dwight Eisenhower, who stayed in nearby **Claridge's** (*see p399*) when in London; Roosevelt presides over the square itself, and its rather eloquent 9/11 memorial: 'Grief is the price we pay for love'. About the Ronald Reagan statue – complete with some of his oratorical greatest hits – the less said the better.

Brook Street has impressive musical credentials: GF Handel lived and died at no.25, and Jimi Hendrix roomed briefly next door at no.23, adjacent buildings that have been combined into **Handel & Hendrix in London**. For most visitors, however, this part of town is all about shopping. Connecting Brook Street with Oxford Street to the north, **South Molton Street** is home to the fabulous boutique-emporium **Browns** and the excellent **Grays Antique Market**, while **New Bond Street** is an A-Z of top-end, mainstream fashion houses.

East of New Bond Street, **Hanover Square** is another of the area's big squares, now a busy traffic chicane. Just to the south is **St George's Church**, built in the 1720s and

once everyone's favourite place in which to be seen and to get married. Handel, who married nobody, attended services here. South of St George's, salubrious **Conduit Street** is where fashion shocker Vivienne Westwood (no.44) faces staid **Rigby & Peller**, corsetière to the Queen.

Running south off Conduit Street is the most famous Mayfair shopping street of all, **Savile Row**. Gieves & Hawkes (no.1) is a must-visit for anyone interested in the history of British menswear; at no.15, the estimable Henry Poole & Co has cut suits for clients including Napoleon III, Charles Dickens and 'Buffalo' Bill Cody. No.3 was the home of the Beatles' Apple Records and scene of their rooftop farewell concert.

Two streets west, **Cork Street** was long the heart of the West End art scene – but Fitzrovia's Eastcastle Street these days mounts a pretty serious challenge. Still, **Flowers Central** (21 Cork Street, 7439 7766, www.flowersgallery.com) is one of Mayfair's notable small galleries, facing off against heavy competition from major US art dealers: notably, the 10,000 square foot (929 square metre) **David Zwirner** gallery (24 Grafton Street, 3538 3165, www.davidzwirner.com). **Pace** (6 Burlington Gardens, 3206 7600, www.pacegallery.com), also stages arresting shows.

Also on Burlington Gardens is an entrance to the **Royal Academy of Arts**, which hosts several lavish, crowd-pleasing shows each year. The Academy's main building is former Burlington House (1665) on Piccadilly. Next door is the entrance to the renovated **Burlington Arcade**, the oldest and most famous of the area's Regency shopping arcades, where 'beadles' – top-hatted security staff with fancy-pants braiding on their jackets – ensure there's no singing, whistling or hurrying: such uncouth behaviour is prohibited by archaic by-laws. A couple of streets over is Albemarle Street, where you'll find the **Royal Institution**.

Just west of Albemarle Street, **44 Berkeley Square** is one of the original houses in this grand square. Built in the 1740s, it was described by architectural historian Nikolaus Pevsner as 'the finest terrace house of London'. Curzon Street, which runs off the south-west corner of Berkeley Square, was home to MI5, Britain's secret service, from 1945 until the '90s. It's also the northern boundary of **Shepherd Market**, named after a food market set up here by architect Edward Shepherd in the early 18th century and now a curious little enclave. From 1686, this was where the raucous May Fair was held, until it was shut down in the late 18th century due to 'drunkenness, fornication, gaming

---

In the know
Piccadilly

Piccadilly's name is derived from the 'picadil', a type of suit collar that was in vogue during the 18th century. The first of the area's main buildings was built by tailor Robert Baker and nicknamed 'Piccadilly Hall' to indicate the source of his wealth.

Royal Academy of Arts

restored, with his bedroom detailed down to the discarded fag butts. But here the life of the former occupant really comes through: in addition to the period bedroom, there's a timeline room with a few artefacts and plenty of audio and film, and a brilliant, revealing annex where Jimi's record collection is itemised and explored. Yes, vinyl nerds, he did vibe on his illustrious former neighbour, buying both the *Messiah* and *Water Music* from HMV.

♥ Royal Academy of Arts

*Burlington House, W1J 0BD (7300 8000, www.royalacademy.org.uk). Green Park or Piccadilly Circus tube. **Open** 10am-6pm Mon-Thur, Sat, Sun; 10am-10pm Fri (last admission 30mins before closing time). **Admission** free. Exhibitions vary. **Map** p142 K8.*

Britain's first art school was founded in 1768 and moved to the extravagantly Palladian Burlington House a century later, but it's now best known not for education but for exhibitions. Ticketed blockbusters are generally held in the Sackler Wing or the main galleries; shows in the John Madejski Fine Rooms are drawn from the RA's holdings, which range from Constable to Hockney, and are free. The biggest event here is the annual Summer Exhibition, which for more than two centuries has drawn from works entered by the public. The RA's restaurant, the Keeper's House, has a little courtyard 'garden'.

The RA also occupies a 19th-century building on a parallel street: 6 Burlington Gardens. Coveniently located directly behind the main location, it exhibits unabashedly contemporary art, from Tracey Emin and David Hockney to lightworks by Mariko Mori. There's a Peyton & Byrne café here, and the Studio Shop.

As part of its 250th anniversary celebrations in 2018, the Royal Academy unveiled its New RA, a £56 million redevelopment by architect David Chipperfield. Linking together Burlington House and Burlington Gardens for the first time, the new expanded campus includes gallery spaces, cafés, a lecture theatre and learning centre.

and lewdness'. You'll still manage the drunkenness easily enough at a couple of good pubs, but the flavour of the place is now captured by the presence of a tobacconist and a couple of leather-bag makers.

▶ *For details of the venues on the south side of Piccadilly, including Fortnum & Mason, the Wolseley and the Ritz, see p118 and p120.*

Sights & museums

Handel & Hendrix in London

*25 Brook Street, W1K 4HB (7495 1685, handelhendrix.org). Bond Street tube. **Open** 11am-6pm Mon-Sat (last entry 5pm). **Admission** £10; £5 reductions; free under-5s. **Map** p142 J7.*

Separated by just a brick wall are the former homes of two of history's most innovative and influential musicians – George Frideric Handel (1685-1759) and Jimi Hendrix (1942-1970). George Frideric Handel moved to Britain from his native Germany aged 25 and settled in this house 12 years later, remaining here until his death in 1759. The house – where he composed his *Messiah, Music for the Royal Fireworks* and several operas – has been faithfully restored, with original and recreated furnishings, paintings and some of the composer's scores. The programme of events includes Thursday recitals on the museum's several period instruments, which – along with engaging staff – enliven what is otherwise a bit of a worthy experience. The Hendrix section of the museum couldn't be more different. The upstairs flat at no.23 where, in 1968, Jimi lived with one of his girlfriends has also been painstakingly

---

**In the know
Phone's home**

The red phonebox in the arch leading into the Royal Academy (*see above*) is the last wooden 1924 prototype of the classic Giles Gilbert Scott design, its roof modelled on the Soane mausoleum at Old St Pancras church (*see p204*).

Royal Institution & Faraday Museum

21 Albemarle Street, W1S 4BS (7409 2992, www.rigb.org). Green Park tube. **Open** *9am-5pm Mon-Fri. Closes for events; phone ahead.* **Admission** *free.* **Map** *p142 K8.*

The Royal Institution was founded in 1799 for 'diffusing the knowledge... and application of science to the common purposes of life'; from behind its neoclassical façade, it's been at the forefront of London's scientific achievements ever since. In 2008, Sir Terry Farrell completed a £22 million rebuild, hoping to improve accessibility and lure people in with more open frontage, a licensed café and spruced-up events. Instead, the RI found itself in a recession and saddled with major debt – after reports in early 2013 that the premises would have to be sold, illustrious benefactors stepped in to help. So the RI continues to deliver its terrific rolling programme of talks and demonstrations. The Michael Faraday Laboratory, a replica of the great scientist's former workspace, is in the basement, alongside a working laboratory in which Royal Institution scientists can be observed researching their current projects. Some 1,000 of the RI's 7,000-odd scientific objects are on display, including the world's first electric transformer, a prototype Davy lamp and, from 1858, a print of the first transatlantic telegraph signal.

Restaurants

Gymkhana £££

42 Albemarle Street, W1S 4JH (3011 5900, www. gymkhanalondon.com). Green Park tube. **Open** *noon-2.30pm, 5.30-10.15pm Mon-Sat. Bar open until 1am.* **Map** *p142 K8* ❺ *Indian*

Justly lauded, Gymkhana looks and feels like an Indian colonial club, with its retro ceiling fans, marble-topped tables and yesteryear photos of polo and cricket team triumphs. It serves a splendid spread of modern Indian dishes based on regional masalas and marinades: a starter of South Indian fried chicken wings, steeped in chilli batter, perhaps, followed by Goan pork vindaloo – slow-cooked chunks of suckling pig cheek, with a vinegary red chilli and garlic masala, spiced with sweet cinnamon and coriander.

♥ Kitty Fisher's ££££

10 Shepherd Market, W1J 7QF (3302 1661, www.kittyfishers.com). Green Park tube. **Open** *noon-2.30pm, 6-9.30pm Mon-Sat.* **Map** *p142 J9* ❻ *Modern European*

Named after an 18th-century courtesan, known for her wit and extravagance, Kitty Fisher's will leave you with a big smile on your face – if you don't mind paying for the privilege. The signature dish is beef cut from a ten- to

12-year-old Galician milking cow, chargrilled and served with cheese-stuffed salad potatoes and blackened onion (£80, serves two). To cut your bill in half, stick to small plates (£6-£12.50) such as melted taleggio with London honey, wholegrain mustard and loads of shaved truffle, or whipped cod's roe on dainty soldiers. The basement dining room is intimate and hugely atmospheric, but tables do get booked up well in advance.

Rasa W1 £

6 Dering Street, W1S 1AD (7629 1346, rasarestaurants.com). Oxford Circus or Bond Street tube. **Open** *noon-3pm, 6-11pm Mon-Sat; 1-3pm, 6-9pm Sun.* **Map** *p142 J7* ❽ *Indian*

The bright pink walls of this branch of the Rasa minichain are as bold as the flavours in their south Indian dishes – but a lot less tasteful. This Keralan joint offers the same wholesome and moreish basics as its Stoke Newington forebear – lentil daals and chewy coiled paratha – alongside more unusual dishes like *moru kachiathu*, a turmeric-infused, sweet-sour runny yoghurt dish made with mango and green banana. The eat-in or takeaway lunchboxes are sensational value for Mayfair at £5-£6.

Pubs & bars

♥ The Connaught Bar

The Connaught, Carlos Place, W1K 2AL (7499 7070, www.the-connaught.co.uk). Bond Street or Green Park tube. **Open** *11am-1am Mon-Sat; 11am-midnight Sun.* **Map** *p142 J8* ❶

Inside one of the more discreet of London's mega-expensive hotels, the Connaught Bar is all about old-school style and glamour. Designed by David Collins, its mirrors, low lighting, silver leaf and tasteful palette will put you in mind of a deco steamship. Even if you can only stretch to a single drink, it's worth it, especially if you order a martini – a trolley is wheeled up beside you and the drink mixed on top.

If the Connaught Bar is too lively for you, try the hotel's other drinking spot: the splendidly upholstered **Coburg** feels more like a country club.

♥ Mr Fogg's Residence

15 Bruton Lane, W1J 6JD (7036 0608, mr-foggs.com/residence). Green Park tube. **Open** *4.01pm-2.01am Mon-Fri; 1.31pm-2.01am Sat; 3.01pm-12.01am Sun.* **Map** *p142 J8* ❷

For sheer spectacle, Mr Fogg's is hard to beat. The place is stuffed with the detritus left by the titular Victorian explorer: every wall is covered with hunting rifles, stuffed animals, weathered flags and maps – all imaginary souvenirs of course, but that doesn't make the profusion of clutter any less fun. With an interior like this, it would be easy for cocktails to take second place, but seriously knowledgeable bar staff make sure the drinks are punchy and altogether sensational.

Shops & services

This is a focal area for British designer showcases, with **Stella McCartney** and **Alexander McQueen** our top picks.

The Royal Arcades are a throwback to shopping of the past – the **Burlington Arcade** is both the largest and grandest, but the **Piccadilly Arcade**, opposite it, and the **Royal Arcade**, at 28 Old Bond Street, are also worth a visit.

Alexander McQueen

4-5 Old Bond Street, W1S 4PD (7355 0088, www.alexandermcqueen.com). Green Park tube. **Open** *10.30am-6pm Mon-Wed, Fri, Sat; 10am-7pm Thur; noon-6pm Sun.* **Map** *p142 K8* ❷ *Fashion*

The late Alexander McQueen's collections are more wearable than ever. The UK's only store – where you can see the best of his designer womenswear – is a very posh contemporary space, full of baroque wood panels, marble and gilt mirrors. But – as with all things McQueen – in among the splendour something sinister must lurk. Look at the feet of chairs and tables and you'll see claws and hoofs. Gargoyles and skulls grimace and twist furtively from the flora and fauna of the moulded plaster panels. A real shopping experience.

Once you've checked out the flagship store, pay a visit to **Menswear** (9 Savile Row, W1S 3PF, 7494 8840), which has similarly macabre touches – as well as a bespoke tailoring workshop in the basement – and the diffusion line, **McQ** (14 Dover Street, W1S 4LW, 7318 2220, www.mcq.com).

Berry Bros & Rudd

3 St James's Street, SW1A 1EG (0800 280 2440/7022 8973, www.bbr.com). Green Park tube. **Open** *10am-9pm Mon-Fri; 10am-5pm Sat.* **Map** *p142 K9* ❹ *Food & drink*

Britain's oldest wine merchant has been trading in the same premises since 1698, and its heritage is reflected in its panelled sales and tasting rooms. Burgundy- and claret-lovers will drool at the hundreds of wines, but there are also decent selections from elsewhere in Europe and the New World. **Other location** 63 Pall Mall, SW1Y 5HZ.

♥ Browns

23-27 South Molton Street, W1K 5RD (7514 0016, www.brownsfashion.com). Bond Street tube. **Open** *10am-7pm Mon-Wed, Sat; 10am-8pm Thur, Fri; noon-6pm Sun.* **Map** *p142 J7* ❺ *Fashion*

The buying team at Browns are magicians, with an uncanny ability to pull in the most interesting, talking-point pieces of a designer's collection. Having been owned by Joan Burnstein and her family for the past four decades, Browns was acquired by fashion website Farfetch in 2015, with the aim of bringing technological innovation to its offerings. Among the 100-odd designers jostling for attention across five interconnecting shops are fashion heavyweights Chloé, Dries Van Noten and Balenciaga. You'll also find designs from rising stars, and shop exclusives are common. No.24 now houses Browns Focus, a younger and more casual look; while Labels for Less is loaded with last season's leftovers.

♥ Burlington Arcade

51 Piccadilly, W1J 0QJ (7493 1764, www. burlingtonarcade.com). Green Park tube. **Open** *9am-7.30pm Mon-Sat; 11am-6pm Sun.* **Map** *p142 K8* ❼ *Mall*

In 1819, Lord Cavendish commissioned Britain's very first shopping arcade. Nearly two centuries later, the Burlington is still one of London's most prestigious shopping 'streets', patrolled by 'beadles' decked out in top hats and tailcoats. Highlights include collections of classic watches at David Duggan, established British fragrance house Penhaligon's, and Sermoneta, selling Italian leather gloves in a range of bright colours. High-end food shops come in the form of Luponde Tea and Ladurée; head to the latter for exquisite Parisian macaroons. Burlington also houses a proper shoe-shine boy working with waxes and creams. This may not offer the best shopping in London, but it's certainly one of the best shopping experiences.

Drake's

3 Clifford Street, W1S 2LF (7734 2367, www.drakes.com). Green Park tube. **Open** *10am-6pm Mon-Sat; noon-5pm Sun.* **Map** *p142 K8* ⓫ *Menswear*

The subtle interplay between exuberance and understatement is what makes Drake's unique. Its parquet floors and soft white walls provide a neutral backdrop to showcase the Drake's look: classic British style, as it might be imagined by Italians. The place to release your inner gent.

Grays Antique Market & Grays in the Mews

58 Davies Street, W1K 5LP & 1-7 Davies Mews, W1K 5LP (7629 7034, www.graysantiques. com). Bond Street tube. **Open** *10am-6pm Mon-Fri; 11am-5pm Sat.* **Map** *p142 J7* ⑱ *Antiques*

Sibling of Alfie's (*see p151*), Grays gathers more than 200 dealers in a smart covered market building. They sell everything from antique furniture and rare books to vintage fashion and jewellery.

Paul Smith

9 Albemarle Street, W1S 4BL (7493 4565, www.paulsmith.co.uk). Green Park tube. **Open** *10am-6pm Mon-Wed; 10am-7pm Thur-Sat; noon-6pm Sun.* **Map** *p142 K8* ⑲ *Fashion*

The Paul Smith flagship is as big, glossy and imposing as an oligarch's art gallery, with the whimsical flourishes that made Smith Britain's most popular designer replaced by something on a much grander scale. There's that huge wrought-iron façade, which jars brilliantly with the Georgian elegance of the surrounding buildings, and white pillars within that spring from the parquet floor to showcase nostalgic record players and vintage radios. The full men's and women's collections are here, displayed on more wrought-iron and on chunks of reclaimed wood. Samples and previous season's stock are sold at discounts of up to 50% at the **Paul Smith Sale Shop** (23 Avery Row, W1K 4AX, 7493 1287).

Postcard Teas

9 Dering Street, W1S 1AG (7629 3654, www. postcardteas.com). Bond Street or Oxford Circus tube. **Open** *10.30am-6.30pm Mon-Fri; 11am-6.30pm Sat. Tastings £20; £15 reductions.* **Map** *p142 J7* ⑳ *Food & drink*

The range in this exquisite little shop is not huge, but it is selected with great care, and all teas are sourced from small cooperatives. There's a central table for those who want to try a pot; or book in for one of the tasting sessions held on Saturdays between 10am and 11am. Stunning tea-ware and accessories are also sold.

Rigby & Peller

22A Conduit Street, W1S 2XT (7491 2200, www.rigbyandpeller.co.uk). Oxford Circus tube. **Open** *9.30am-6pm Mon-Wed, Fri, Sat; 9.30am-7pm Thur; 11am-5pm Sun.* **Map** *p142 J7* ㉒ *Fashion*

Rigby & Peller make Elizabeth II's smalls – if it's good enough for Her Majesty, it's good enough for us. Established in 1939, the brand's royal warrant was granted in 1960. Book an appointment for the bespoke bra-making service or to be expertly fitted for ready-to-wear lingerie and swimwear. Premium brands such as Aubade, Lejaby, Huit and Simone Perele are also stocked, along with sports, bridal, mastectomy and maternity bras.

Smythson

131-132 New Bond Street, W1S 2DE (3535 8009, www.smythson.com). Bond Street tube. **Open** *10am-8pm Mon-Sat; noon-6pm Sun.* **Map** *p142 J7* ㉔ *Stationery*

London's poshest stationers is a veritable paradise for paper-lovers. Established in 1887, Smythson made its name from selling extraordinarily desirable pigskin diaries, notebooks and personalised stationery – it has designed invitations and notelets for everyone from Stella McCartney to the Queen herself.

Stella McCartney

23 Old Bond Street, W1S 4PZ (7518 3100, www. stellamccartney.com). Piccadilly Circus or Green Park tube. **Open** *10am-6.30pm Mon-Sat; noon-6pm Sun.* **Map** *p142 K8* ㉕ *Fashion*

It's hard not to adore Stella's flagship, all super-sleek in shiny black with the brand emblazoned on it in fuchsia. Her current collection presides over a main space decked out in lots of white marble with pops of pink: if you can't afford £1,000 for a chic tailored blazer or this year's 'It' bag, look to signature shades or some delicate jewellery. There's children's wear in a well-lit atrium towards the back, just before you get to the footwear shrine in a cosy back chamber. And there's a simply gigantic fitting room, where you have all the space you need to play dress up.

Victoria Beckham

36 Dover Street, W1S 4NH (7042 0700, www. victoriabeckham.com). Bond Street tube. **Open** *11am-7pm Mon-Sat; noon-5pm Sun.* **Map** *p142 J8* ㉗ *Fashion*

This stunning space, with a dramatic atrium that runs the height of the building, is divided into three floors: the basement is for pop-ups and personal shopping; the ground floor houses a wall of luxury accessories and an edit of the slightly cheaper Victoria by Victoria Beckham label, while the first floor features the catwalk collection – familiar to fashion-watchers from its popularity with Hollywood's finest. Customers get first dibs on designs from the runway immediately after London's Fashion Week, and there are always in-store exclusives too: colourways on handbags or VVB T-shirts that you won't find anywhere else. Occasionally, the designer herself surprises customers with an appearance on the shop floor.

Soho & Leicester Square

For more than two centuries, poseurs, spivs, tarts, toffs, drunks and divas have gathered in Soho. But the district's time as the focus of all that's benevolently naughty – and a proportion of the truly wicked too – has gone. Prostitution has largely been cleared out; many of the area's music, film and advertising businesses have moved on, and even the once-thriving gay scene faces frequent venue closures. Instead, the sizeable residential community that remains is faced with an almost inconceivable number of bars, restaurants and shops. There are more chains among them than there used to be, but independents still dominate.

Just to the south of Soho, beyond London's bustling Chinatown, Leicester Square – known for cinemas and, for many years, drunk out-of-towners – is inching towards a classier reputation.

❤ Don't miss

1 Carnaby Street *p174*
Bringing West Soho back into fashion.

2 Bars and restaurants *p164*
Eat and drink your way around the streets.

3 Algerian Coffee Stores *p168*
An aromatic piece of Soho history.

4 Foyles *p166*
The most impressive of London's large bookshops.

5 Berwick Street Market *p170*
Fruit 'n' veg 'n' street food.

Kingly Street

SOHO SQUARE & AROUND

▶ *Tottenham Court Road tube.*

Forming the area's northern gateway, Soho Square was laid out in 1681. It was initially called King's Square; a weather-beaten statue of Charles II stands in it. One of the square's benches is dedicated to singer Kirsty MacColl, in honour of her song named after the square.

Two classic Soho streets run south from the square. **Greek Street**, its name a nod to a church that once stood here, is lined with restaurants and bars, among them **Bar Hercules** (no.7, 7437 1179), formerly known as the Pillars of Hercules, where the literati once enjoyed long, liquid lunches. Just by the Pillars, an arch leads to Manette Street and Charing Cross Road, where you'll find the bookshop **Foyles**. Back on Greek Street, no.49 was once Les Cousins, a folk venue (note the mosaic featuring a musical note); Casanova lived briefly at no.46.

Parallel to Greek Street is **Frith Street**, once home to Mozart (1764-65, no.20) and painter John Constable (1810-11, no.49). Humanist essayist William Hazlitt died in 1830 at no.6, now a discreet hotel named in his memory (no.6, 7434 1771, www.hazlittshotel.com). Further down the street are **Ronnie Scott's** (*see p350*), Britain's best-known jazz club, and, across from Ronnie's, the similarly mythologised 24-hour coffee haunt **Bar Italia** (no.22, 7437 4520).

Restaurants

♥ 10 Greek Street ££
10 Greek Street, W1D 4DH (7734 4677, www.10greekstreet.com). Tottenham Court Road tube. **Open** *noon-2.30pm, 5.30-10.15pm Mon, Tue; noon-2.30pm, 5.30-10.45pm Wed-Sat; noon-8.45pm Sun. Lunch bookings taken; dinner walk-in only.* **Map** *p165 L7* ❶ *Modern European*

This small, unshowy restaurant has made a name for itself with a short but perfectly formed menu and an easygoing conviviality. Dishes are seasonal and the kitchen produces lots of interesting but ungimmicky combinations – such as a special of halibut fillet with yellow beans, chilli and garlic, on a vivid romesco sauce. It's good value too. Tables are closely packed, and in the evening it can get noisy; bookings are taken for lunch but not dinner.

♥ Ceviche ££
17 Frith Street, W1D 4RG (7292 2040, www.cevicheuk.com). Leicester Square tube. **Open** *noon-3pm, 5-11.30pm Mon-Fri; noon-11.30pm Sat; noon-10pm Sun.* **Map** *p165 L7* ❼ *Peruvian*

Ceviche showcases citrus-cured fish. It is available in half a dozen different forms, though the menu also includes everything from terrific chargrilled meat and fish skewers (*anticuchos*) to a simple but perfectly executed corn cake. Factor in the seating options (trendy at the steel counter-bar, more comfortable in the rear dining area), the charismatic, attentive staff and the party atmosphere, and it's no wonder this place has been such a huge hit.

♥ Hoppers £
49 Frith Street, W1D 4SG (www.hopperslondon.com). Tottenham Court Road or Leicester Square tube. **Open** *noon-2.30pm, 5.30-10.30pm Mon-Thur; noon-10.30pm Fri, Sat. No reservations.* **Map** *p165 L7* ⓫ *Sri Lankan*

For those not familiar with Sri Lankan cuisine, a hopper is a bowl-shaped savoury crêpe, usually eaten at breakfast, and this small stylish joint has them down to a T. Decor is an effortless mix of old and new; exposed brick meets wood panelling; pretty patterned tiles meet carved-wood devil masks. The menu, likewise, gives traditional Sri Lankan street food a fashionable lift: slender breaded and deep-fried mutton rolls come with a ginger, garlic and chilli 'ketchup'; a dinky dish of roast bone marrow is treated to a fiery 'dry' sauce, and the guinea fowl curry is unapologetically spicy.

♥ Time to eat & drink

Drink in the history
French House *p168*

Exceptional foodie innovations
Social Eating House *p174*

Good pub, great location
The Lyric *p170*

Hot buns on a budget
Bao *p172*, Bun House *p167*

Perfect Peruvian
Ceviche *p164*

Sri Lankan street food
Hoppers *p164*

Superb small plates
10 Greek Street *p164*

Top cocktails
Bar Américain *p174*, Bar Termini *p168*, Swift *p168*

♥ Time to shop

Bibliophile's delight
Cecil Court *p177*, Foyles *p166*

London fashion forward
Machine-A *p171*, YMC *p175*

Manicure as masterpiece
WAH Nails *p171*

Record shop with soul
Sounds of the Universe *p171*

wooden counter. The range of coffees is broad, with house blends sold alongside single-origin beans; some serious teas and brewing hardware are also available. If you're just passing, pick up an espresso or latte to go.

WARDOUR STREET & AROUND

▶ *Leicester Square or Tottenham Court Road tube.*

Parallel to Dean Street, Wardour Street provides offices for film and TV production companies, but is also known for its rock history. No.100 was, for nearly three decades, the Marquee, where Led Zeppelin played their first London gig and Hendrix appeared four times. The latter's favourite Soho haunt was the nearby **Ship** pub (no.116), still with a sprinkling of music-themed knick-knacks. There's more music history at Trident Studios on nearby St Anne's Court: Lou Reed recorded *Transformer* here, and David Bowie cut both *Hunky Dory* and *The Rise and Fall of Ziggy Stardust* on the site.

When he was still known as David Jones, Bowie played a gig at the Jack of Clubs on **Brewer Street**. But this corner of Soho is most famous not for music but for its position at the heart of Soho's almost vanished but still notorious sex trade. The Raymond Revuebar opened on the neon alleyway of Walker's Court in 1958, swiftly becoming London's most famous strip club. It closed in 2004, became a series of short-lived gay clubs, then reopened as celebrity-infested, exclusive alt-cabaret club the **Box** (11-12 Walker's Court, W1F 0SD, 7434 4374, www.theboxsoho.com), the London branch of a New York original.

North of here, **Berwick Street** clings on to its mix of old-school London raffishness and new-Soho style. The former comes courtesy of the fruit and veg market, and the egalitarian, old-fashioned and unceasingly popular **Blue Posts** pub (no.22, 7437 5008), where builders, post-production editors, restaurateurs and market traders gabble and glug as one beneath a portrait of Berwick Street-born star of stage and radio Jessie Matthews (1907-81). The fruit and veg have been here since 1778, but there's less fresh produce nowadays: instead stalls sell takeaway food – anything from a virtuous but vivid salad of couscous with charred vegetables to a juicy, dripping cheeseburger. Alongside the street eats, the likes of coffee bar **Flat White** (no.17, 7734 0370, flatwhitesoho.co.uk) and **Ember Yard** herald the area's likely future of upscale eating and drinking.

Restaurants

Bocca di Lupo ££

12 Archer Street, W1D 7BB (7734 2223, www. boccadilupo.com). Piccadilly Circus tube. **Open** *noon-3pm, 5.15-11pm Mon-Sat; noon-3.30pm, 5-9.30pm Sun.* **Map** *p165 L8* ❺ *Italian*

The buzz is as important as the food at this popular restaurant. The menu is a slightly confusing mix of small and large plates to share: buttery brown shrimp on soft, silky white polenta, say, or a deep-fried mix of calamari, soft-shell crab and lemon. The radish, celeriac, pomegranate and pecorino salad with truffle dressing is a much-imitated Bocca di Lupo signature.

> **In the know**
> **Ice, ice baby**
>
> The team behind Bocca di Lupo also runs **Gelupo**, the *gelateria* at 7 Archer Street (7287 5555, www.gelupo.com). The blood-orange *granita* – dark, intense and made with only fruit and cane sugar – is one of our favourite desserts.

Copita ££

27 D'Arblay Street, W1F 8EP (7287 7797, www. copita.co.uk). Oxford Circus tube. **Open** *noon-11pm Mon-Sat. Food served noon-4.30pm, 5.30-10.30pm Mon-Fri; noon-10.30pm Sat.* **Map** *p165 K7* ❽ *Tapas*

For an authentic taste of modern Spain, you can't go far wrong with Copita. Avoiding the standards of *patatas bravas* and *ensalada rusa*, the menu ventures admirably off the well-trodden tapas path with dishes such as sherry-braised pig cheeks, *empanadillas de carne*, or sweet and smoky aubergine stew with tahini and mint. Each tapa should be accompanied by a little glass (*copita*) of Spanish wine or sherry from the well-informed list. Equally triumphant desserts include delicate rosemary ice-cream or lightly scented rosewater ice-cream with stewed strawberries. Like its sister restaurant, Barrica (*see p209*), the properly tapa-sized dishes mean you can get stuck into the menu without needing a crane to lift you out afterwards.

Ember Yard ££

60 Berwick Street, W1F 8SU (7439 8057, emberyard.co.uk). Oxford Circus or Tottenham Court Road tube. **Open** *noon-11pm Mon-Fri; noon-midnight Sat; noon-10pm Sun.* **Map** *p165 K7* ❾ *Tapas*

The third in a chain of new-style tapas bars, Ember Yard follows the winning template of its forebears – combining Italian and Spanish influences – but it places an even greater emphasis on the grill. The result is reminiscent of the fabulous charcoal-grill restaurants of the Basque country, especially if you're sitting near the glowing coals. Every flavour combination here is a winner, with the bar snacks among the best in Soho.

Temper ££

25 Broadwick Street, W1F 0DF (3879 3834, temperrestaurant.com). Oxford Circus tube. **Open** *4-10.30pm Mon; noon-10.30pm Tue, Wed; noon-11pm Thur-Sat; noon-9pm Sun.* **Map** *p165 K7* ⑱ *Barbecue*

This Soho joint, from Scottish chef Neil Rankin, sources top-notch slabs of meat (think incredibly juicy pork or full-flavoured smoked goat) that are grilled or smoked over charcoal before being served up in small affordable portions. Flatbreads (basically a *roti* made with rendered animal fat and puffed up on the grill) come with exotic sprinkles and salsas (all homemade). Standout dishes include the aged cheeseburger, beef fat tacos and smoked goat flatbread. Desserts, including the molten cookie dough pudding, are equally appealing.

Yauatcha ££££

15-17 Broadwick Street, W1F 0DL (7494 8888, www.yauatcha.com). Leicester Square, Piccadilly Circus or Tottenham Court Road tube. **Open** *noon-10.30pm Mon-Sat (last reservation); noon-10pm Sun (last reservation).* **Map** *p165 K7* ⑲ *Chinese*

Such acutely stylish venues rarely last, but after more than a decade Yauatcha can add longevity to its enviable list of attributes. The sensual basement of this Michelin-starred self-styled tea house has a nightclub vibe, with a long bar, spot-lit back tables and illuminated fish tank. Day-and-night dim sum offers exquisite combinations such as scallop and edamame crystal dumplings, while main courses hold interest with offerings of sea bass with shiitake and wolf berry. Exotic teas and East-West fusion desserts (yuzu brûlée tart) are further highlights, though grazing on exquisite snacks is undoubtedly the primary draw.

Pubs & bars

♥ The Lyric

37 Great Windmill Street, W1D 7LT (7434 0604, www.lyricsoho.co.uk). Piccadilly Circus tube. **Open** *11am-11.30pm Mon-Thur; 11am-midnight Fri, Sat; noon-10.30pm Sun. Food served noon-10pm daily.* **Map** *p165 L8* ⑦

Small, slightly shambolic and with a jovial share-a-table vibe, the Lyric is a longstanding favourite, not least because of its location near a fantastically crowded part of London where disappointing, pricey tourist traps are the norm. The Victorian pub's 18 taps pour out reliable pints, including Camden Hells and Brooklyn Lager, as well as more unusual guests – perhaps the hyper-citrussy High Wire Grapefruit brew from Magic Rock.

Shops & services

Berwick Street is really the heart of Soho, with its breezy street market (8am-6pm Mon-Sat), one of London's oldest. Dating back to 1778, it's seeing a bit of a revival with popular street-food stalls. The indie record shops that used to cluster here took a pasting in the noughties, but **Reckless Records** (no.30, 7437 4271, reckless.co.uk) and **Sister Ray** (no.75, 7734 3297) are now

Temper

beneficiaries of the vinyl revival – along with nearby **Sounds of the Universe**.

Axel Arigato
19-23 Broadwick Street, W1F 0DF (7494 1728, axelarigato.com). Piccadilly Circus tube. **Open** *11am-7pm Mon-Wed; 11am-8pm Thur-Sat; noon-6pm Sun.* **Map** *p165 K7* ❸ *Shoes*

After successfully building a fan base online, Swedish footwear brand Alex Arigato opened its flagship store in 2016. The handcrafted designer trainers are meticulously displayed on marbled pedestals and stone podiums, while the white colour scheme, concrete and mirrored surfaces of the shop's interior reflect its minimalist aesthetic. There are accessories and clothing too, as well as a selection of Japanese literature and objects that inspired the collection.

Gosh!
1 Berwick Street, W1F 0DR (7437 0187, www. goshlondon.com). Oxford Circus tube. **Open** *10.30am-7pm daily.* **Map** *p165 L7* ❻ *Books & music*

There's nowhere better to bolster your comics collection. There's a huge selection of manga, but graphic novels take centre stage, from early classics such as *Krazy Kat* to Alan Moore's erotic Peter Pan adaptation *Lost Girls*. Classic children's books, of the *This is London* vein, are another strong point. First port of call? The central table, where you'll find new releases – sometimes even before official publication.

♥ Machine-A
13 Brewer Street, W1F 0RH (7734 4334, www. machine-a.com). Oxford Circus tube. **Open** *11am-7pm Mon-Wed; 11am-8pm Thur-Sat; noon-6pm Sun.* **Map** *p165 L7* ❿ *Fashion*

Hats off (make it an Alex Mattsson baseball cap) to Machine-A for championing London's most exciting emerging designers at this Soho concept store. It's the natural habitat for the young, bold and brave, a small space full of pieces that practically sizzle with energy. Outside, the neon signage is a cheeky nod to its massage-parlour neighbours on Brewer Street.

OTHER/shop
3 Berwick Street, W1F 0DR (7734 6846, www. other-shop.com). Oxford Circus tube. **Open** *10.30am-6.30pm Mon-Sat; noon-5pm Sun.* **Map** *p165 L7* ⓬ *Fashion*

Founders of B Store, Matthew Murphy and Kirk Beattie, have more than a decade's experience of running an indie boutique. With a subtle industrial look, highlighter-yellow tiles and use of mixed materials to cover the walls – from exposed brick to reams of fabric – OTHER/shop specialises in wearable clothes for men and women with a creative twist. This applies to both its own range and guest labels including Peter Jensen and Christophe Lemaire.

♥ Sounds of the Universe
7 Broadwick Street, W1F 0DA (7734 3430, soundsoftheuniverse.com). Tottenham Court Road tube. **Open** *10am-7.30pm Mon-Sat; 11.30am-5.30pm Sun.* **Map** *p165 L7* ⓭ *Music*

SOTU's remit is broad. This is especially true on the ground floor (new vinyl and CDs), where grime and dubstep 12-inches jostle for space alongside new wave cosmic disco, electro-indie re-rubs and Nigerian compilations. The second-hand vinyl basement is big on soul, jazz, Brazilian and alt-rock.

Supreme
2-3 Peter Street, W1F 0AA (7437 0493, www. supremenewyork.com). Piccadilly or Leicester Square tube. **Open** *11am-7pm Mon-Sat; noon-6pm Sun.* **Map** *p165 L7* ⓮ *Fashion*

The London outpost of New York's legendary skate shop brings together the cult brand's skatewear, including apparel, accessories and decks. Ongoing collaborations with musicians, artists and designers ensures Supreme maintains the edgy style it originally made its name with back in 1994.

Universal Works
26 Berwick Street, W1F 8RG (3581 1501, www. universalworks.co.uk). Tottenham Court Road tube. **Open** *11am-7pm Mon-Sat; noon-5pm Sun.* **Map** *p165 K7* ⓯ *Menswear*

One of a number of newish men's brands that draw on Brit heritage in terms of design and craftsmanship, Universal Works has a street-orientated outlook on style. There's an aversion to flashiness, which lends individual pieces and the store that displays them a quiet, understated feel.

♥ WAH Nails
4 Peter Street, W1F 9AD (7439 8586, wah-london.com). Leicester Square tube. **Open** *11am-8pm Mon-Wed, Fri; 11am-9pm Thur; 11am-5pm Sat.* **Map** *p165 L7* ⓰ *Nail salon*

Any self-respecting nail-art fanatic will have heard of WAH, whose fanzine kicked off the nail art craze in London a few years ago. Its two-floor flagship salon offers the usual manicures, but also has room for a 'play and discover' area with immersive virtual-reality experiences, nail-printing and a product-testing zone. The futuristic space, complete with industrial concrete walls and cool cocktail bar, feels more like a club than a salon.

WEST SOHO

▶ *Piccadilly Circus or Oxford Circus tube.*

The area west of Berwick Street was rebranded 'West Soho' in a bid to give it some kind of upmarket identity – a foolish notion – but Brewer Street does have star restaurant **Hix**, with its hip **Mark's Bar** downstairs. On Great Windmill Street is the **Windmill Theatre** (nos.17-19), which gained fame in the 1930s and '40s for its 'revuedeville' shows with erotic 'tableaux' – naked women who remained stationary in order to stay within the law. The place is now a lap-dancing joint. North of Brewer Street is **Golden Square**. Developed in the 1670s, it became the political and ambassadorial district of the late 17th and early 18th centuries, and remains home to some of the area's grandest buildings (many now bases for media firms) and a purveyor of cinnamon buns: the **Nordic Bakery** (no.14A, 7734 7837, www.nordicbakery.com).

Just short of Golden Square is **Carnaby Street**, which became a fashion mecca shortly after John Stephen opened His Clothes here in 1956; Stephen, who went on to own more than a dozen fashion shops on the street, is now commemorated with a plaque at the corner with Beak Street. After thriving during the Swinging Sixties, Carnaby Street became a rather seamy commercialised backwater. However, along with nearby **Newburgh Street** and **Kingly Court**, it's revived, with the tourist traps and chain stores joined by a wealth of independent stores.

A little further north, just short of Oxford Street, is the **Photographers' Gallery**.

Sights & museums

Photographers' Gallery

16-18 Ramillies Street, W1F 7LW (7087 9300, www.thephotographersgallery.org. uk). Oxford Circus tube. **Open** *10am-6pm Mon-Wed, Fri, Sat; 10am-8pm Thur during exhibitions; 11am-6pm Sun.* **Admission** *£4; £2.50 reductions; free before noon. Temporary exhibitions vary.* **Map** *p165 K7.*

Given a handsome refit by Irish architects O'Donnell+ Tuomey, this old, brick corner building reopened in 2012 as the new home for London's only gallery dedicated solely to the photographic arts. The upper floors have two airy exhibition spaces, while a bookshop, print sales room and café (10am-6pm daily) are tucked into the ground floor and basement. The exhibitions are varied, and enhanced by quirky details such as the camera obscura in the third-floor Eranda Studio and a projection wall in the café.

Restaurants

Set in a grand art deco basement just off Piccadilly Circus, **Brasserie Zédel** is a huge, all-day French eaterie run by the team behind the **Wolseley** (*see p118*); good on its own terms, it's also home to the excellent **Bar Américain** (*see p174*).

🧡 Bao £

53 Lexington Street, W1F 9AS (baolondon. com). Oxford Circus or Piccadilly Circus tube. **Open** *noon-3pm, 5.30-10pm Mon-Wed; noon-3pm, 5.30-10.30pm Thur; noon-10.30pm Sat; noon-5pm Sun. No reservations.* **Map** *p165 K7* ❸ *Taiwanese*

This slick Taiwanese operation has successfully made the journey from market pop-up to permanent Soho establishment. The tantalising menu is fresh and innovative, based on Taiwanese street food dishes, with *xiao chi* (small eats) and of course *bao* (fluffy white steamed buns) stuffed with braised pork, soy-milk-marinated chicken, or even Horlicks ice-cream. Complementing the moreish food is the drinks list. Sakés, artisanal ciders, well-matched beers and hot oolong teas vie for attention alongside creations such as foam tea – a chilled light oolong artistically topped with foamed cream. Arrive hungry, leave happy.

Kricket ££

12 Denman Street, W1D 7HH (7734 5612, www.kricket.co.uk). Piccadilly Circus tube. **Open** *noon-2.30pm, 5.15-10.30pm Mon-Sat.* **Map** *p165 K8* ⓬ *Indian*

A spin-off of a tiny but brilliant Brixton original, Kricket is stylish and sophisticated: exposed brick and sleek monogrammed bar stools are dominated by an L-shaped counter, where you can dine looking over into a gleaming open kitchen. Just as good-looking is the menu. Indian-inspired small plates include delights such as tender kid goat *raan* dotted with pomegranate seeds; or perfectly creamy butter garlic crab with poppadoms perched on top for dipping. Comforting desserts, including delicately aromatic cardamom *kheer* rice pudding, should be accompanied by a glass or two of delicious spiced *masala chai* – with or without a shot of rum.

Polpo Soho ££

41 Beak Street, W1F 9SB (7734 4479, www. polpo.co.uk). Piccadilly Circus tube. **Open** *11.30am-11pm Mon-Sat; 11.30am-10pm Sun.* **Map** *p165 K7* ⓮ *Italian*

This Italian restaurant pioneered both London's small plates trend and its no-bookings culture. With peeling paint and battered wooden panelling, the decor may

IT'S SHOWTIME

Book the best of the West End, from big-hitting musicals to brand new shows and all of our critics' top picks.

 TIMEOUT.COM/
LONDON/THEATRE

not look like much, but you won't find better Venetian food anywhere in W1. Brown paper menus and chunky tumblers for wine glasses underline the sense of squatter chic, as does sharing small plates of unfussy food. These stretch from humble plates of olives to tasty crab *arancini*, sirloin steak and calf's liver, or spinach and egg *pizzette*.

♥ Social Eating House ££££
58 Poland Street, W1F 7NR (7993 3251, www. socialeatinghouse.com). Oxford Circus tube. **Open** *noon-2.30pm, 6-10.30pm Mon-Sat.* **Map** *p165 K7* **16** *British*

One of nine Jason Atherton restaurants in the capital, Social Eating House has head chef Paul Hood at the helm. Dishes display a trademark playfulness. Try smoked duck 'ham', egg and chips, perhaps: the 'ham' is cured and smoked from duck breast on the premises, served with a breadcrumbed duck egg that's molten in the middle, but with an aroma of truffle oil. Or savour the umami in a roast cod main course that uses powdered Japanese *kombu* seaweed in a glaze, served with a creamy sauce of roasted cockles and just-in-season St George's mushrooms.

Presentation is a strong point of Hood's work, just as it is for his mentor, and the desserts show similar inventiveness, imagination and attention to detail. The ground-floor dining room has a mirrored ceiling to create the sensation of space in a low room, while the smart cocktail bar upstairs, called the Blind Pig (*see below*), has a separate entrance and is a destination in its own right.

Pubs & bars
♥ Bar Américain
Brasserie Zédel, 20 Sherwood Street, W1F 7ED (7734 4888, www.brasseriezedel.com). Piccadilly Circus tube. **Open** *1pm-midnight Mon-Wed; 1pm-1am Thur-Sat; 1-11pm Sun.* **Map** *p165 K8* **1**

We love the simplicity of the cocktail list here: around 20 drinks, most of them tried and tested classics. Expertly rendered martinis, manhattans and daiquiris sit alongside inventive house specialities like the Danse Banane, which includes ginger liquer, pickled banana, pineapple and lemon. Fancy a quiet drink in the West End without having to pay through the nose? You can't do much better than the Américain's beautiful art deco interior.

Blind Pig
Social Eating House, 58 Poland Street, W1F 7NR (7993 3251, www.socialeatinghouse.com). Oxford Circus tube. **Open** *noon-midnight Mon-Sat; last entry 10.30pm.* **Map** *p165 K7* **3**

If you fancy getting straight to the booze, Social Eating House's excellent cocktail bar isn't immediately obvious at street level: look under the vintage 'Optician' sign and you'll find a door knocker marked with a blindfolded hog. Once inside, you can get stuck into mighty fine cocktails with mighty silly names: who could resist a Slap 'n' Pickle (gin, brandy and pickle brine), Kindergarten Cup (incorporating 'Skittles-washed Ketel One'), or a Robin Hood, Quince of Thieves (brandy, quince liqueur, mead)?

Mark's Bar
Hix, 66-70 Brewer Street, W1F 9UP (7292 3518, www.marksbar.co.uk). Piccadilly Circus tube. **Open** *3-10.30pm Mon; 3-11.30pm Tue-Thur; 3pm-12.30am Fri; noon-12.30am Sat; noon-5.30pm Sun.* **Map** *p165 K8* **8**

The always busy basement cocktail bar at Mark Hix's restaurant is a first-rate establishment. Cocktails are king – especially the historical drinks, which manage to be both interesting and good, but the gin and scotch lists also repay steady investigation. The bar 'snax' are terrific, and the place looks great, with its big, smoked mirrors.

Milk & Honey
61 Poland Street, W1F 7NU (7065 6800, www.mlkhny.com). Oxford Circus tube. **Open** *3-10.30pm Mon; 3-11.30pm Tue-Thur; 3pm-12.30am Fri; noon-12.30am Sat; noon-5.30pm Sun.* **Map** *p165 K7* **9**

This London outpost of the top-drawer Manhattan bar is a members' bar, but non-members can book the ground floor or basement bar up to 11pm. Reservation made, look for a tiny sign next to a buzzer on Poland Street, and proper cocktails made in a civilised but unstuffy atmosphere will be your reward. House rules state that the bar doesn't like noise, it doesn't like rowdy, it doesn't like poseurs or pickups; but then who does?

Shops & services

As famous as the King's Road back when the Sixties swung, **Carnaby Street** was, until the noughties, more likely to sell you a postcard of the Queen snogging a punk rocker than a fishtail parka. But Carnaby is cool again, with **Kingly Court** home to several hip boutiques.

Albam
23 Beak Street, W1F 9RS (3157 7000, www. albamclothing.com). Oxford Circus tube. **Open** *11am-7pm Mon-Sat; noon-5pm Sun.* **Map** *p165 K7* **1** *Menswear*

With contemporary, pared-down British menswear having a bit of a renaissance, it's easy to forget who did it first and best. These days, big ticket items such as Shetland wool jumpers, floral printed cagoules and quilts abound, but Albam can still pull off a tapered chino, crisp shirt and a brilliant basic tee.

Kingly Court
Carnaby Street, opposite Broadwick Street, W1B 5PJ (7333 8118, www.carnaby.co.uk). Oxford Circus tube. Open 10am-7pm Mon-Sat; noon-6pm Sun. Restaurants 8am-midnight daily. Map p165 K7 ⑧ *Mall*

If you want to shop modern Carnaby Street, Kingly Court is the place to start – in fact, it's also the place that started the area's revival as a cool shopping destination. It's a three-tiered complex that contains a funky mix of established chains, independents, vintage and vintage-style boutiques. There's an increasing emphasis on food outlets, including cafés in the central courtyard.

MAC Carnaby
30 Great Marlborough Street, W1F 7JA (0370 192 5555, www.maccosmetics.co.uk). Oxford Circus tube. Open 10am-8pm Mon, Tue, Sat; 10am-9pm Wed-Fri; 11.30am-7pm Sun. Map p165 K7 ⑨ *Cosmetics*

This impressive outpost of beauty heavyweight MAC features the brand's ever-popular collaborations and tongue-in-cheek limited edition lines – Haute Dogs, for instance, whose lipsticks were inspired by pedigree pooches. There are also nine kaleidoscopic make-up stations, for quick drop-in demos or longer, bookable lessons. Upstairs is dedicated to Mac's Pro line, beloved of make-up artists and drag queens alike. With an exhaustive selection of products, it's shopping nirvana for slap-happy amateurs and studious pros.

Monki
37 Carnaby Street, W1V 1PD (8018 7400, www. monki.com/gb). Oxford Circus tube. Open 10am-8pm Mon-Sat; noon-6pm Sun. Map p165 K7 ⑪ *Fashion*

Hailing from Sweden, Monki's aesthetic is a bold urban one featuring cute animal prints, oddly shaped sweater dresses and eccentric accessories – current hits include the animal-print backpacks, chunky leather ankle boots and cute woolly mittens emblazoned with big logos for less than a fiver.

We Built This City
56B Carnaby Street, W1F 9QF (3642 9650, www.webuilt-thiscity.com). Oxford Circus tube. Open 10am-7pm Mon-Wed; 10am-8pm Thur-Sat; 11am-6.30pm Sun. Map p165 K7 ⑰ *Fashion*

Tired of all the tourist tat? If you're after funky souvenirs, We Built This City is the place for you. It sells a selection of pieces by London artists inspired by the city among them from premises given a supercool graphic look, inside and out, by east London artist Camille Walala.

♥ YMC
11 Poland Street, W1F 8QA (7494 1619, www. youmustcreate.com). Oxford Circus tube. Open 11am-7pm Mon-Sat; noon-6pm Sun. Map p165 K7 ⑱ *Fashion*

Impeccably designed staples are the forte of this London label. It's the place to head to for simple vest tops and T-shirts, stylish macs, tasteful knits and chino-style trousers, for both men and women.

CHINATOWN & LEICESTER SQUARE

▶ *Leicester Square tube.*

Shaftesbury Avenue is the very heart of Theatreland. The Victorians built seven grand theatres here, six of which still stand. The most impressive is the gorgeous **Palace Theatre** on Cambridge Circus, which opened in 1891 as the Royal English Opera House; when grand opera flopped, the theatre reopened as a music hall two years later. Appropriately, it's most famous for the musicals it has staged: *The Sound of Music* (1961) and *Jesus Christ Superstar* (1972) had their London premières here, and *Les Misérables* racked up 7,602 performances between 1985 and 2004. (The *Les Mis* juggernaut continues to rumble a few blocks west on Shaftesbury Avenue: there, the **Queen's Theatre** proudly proclaims it the world's longest-running musical; for our selection of the best of the West End, *see p365*.)

Marks & Co, the shop that was made famous by Helene Hanff's book *84 Charing Cross Road*, used to stand just opposite the Palace Theatre, on a road that was once a byword for bookselling. Barely any second-hand bookshops remain on Charing Cross Road, though some appealing new shops are opening in their stead; bibliophiles should keep on south towards Leicester Square, where **Cecil Court** continues to fight the good fight for readers. West of Charing Cross Road and south of Shaftesbury Avenue, officially just outside Soho, is London's **Chinatown**.

The Chinese are relative latecomers to this part of town. The city's original Chinatown was set around Limehouse in east London, but hysteria about Chinese opium dens and criminality led to 'slum clearances' in 1934 (interestingly, the surrounding slums were deemed to be in less urgent need of clearance). It wasn't until the 1950s that the Chinese put down roots here, attracted by the cheap rents along Gerrard and Lisle streets.

The ersatz oriental gates, stone lions and pagoda-topped phone boxes around Gerrard Street suggest a Chinese theme park, but this remains a close-knit residential and working enclave, a genuine focal point for London's Chinese community. The area is crammed with restaurants, Asian grocery stores, great bakeries and a host of small shops selling iced-grass jelly, speciality teas and cheap air tickets to Beijing, but even here rising rents are pricing out some long-established family businesses.

South of Chinatown, **Leicester Square** was one of London's most exclusive addresses in the 17th century; in the 18th, it became home to the royal court of Prince George (later George II). Satirical painter William Hogarth had a studio here (1733-64), as did 18th-century artist Sir Joshua Reynolds – busts of both once resided in the small gardens at the heart of the square, along with a now vanished statue of Charlie Chaplin. They've been swept away in the fine refurbishment of the square, which has left just a statue of a wistful Shakespeare presiding over modish white 'ribbon' seating and the cut-price theatre-tickets booth, **tkts** (*see p360*).

For many years, locals left the square to the unimaginative tourists and drunk suburban kids that were its only denizens. But the arrival in 2011 of a couple of high-class hotels (for the **W**, *see p401*) and the reopening in 2012 of the Frank Matcham-designed, castle-like, red-brick **Hippodrome** (on the corner of Cranbourn Street and Charing Cross Road) as a high-rolling casino gave the area a bit of pull. Not all memories of the square's cheerfully tacky phase have gone, however: the Swiss glockenspiel has returned, with its 27 bells and mechanical mountain farmers chiming out the time on behalf of Switzerland Tourism.

Film premières are still regularly held in the monolithic **Odeon Leicester Square** (*see p323*), which once boasted the UK's largest screen and probably still has the UK's highest ticket prices. It underwent a major refurbishment in 2018, ready for it to host the **London Film Festival** in October 2019 (*see p326*). Get a price-conscious cinema fix just north of the square on Leicester Place, at the excellent **Prince Charles** rep cinema (*see p323*).

Chinatown

Restaurants

Baiwei ££

8 Little Newport Street, WC2H 7JJ (7494 3605). Leicester Square tube. **Open** *noon-11pm daily.* **Map** *p165 L8* ❷ *Chinese*

'One dish, one style; a hundred dishes, a hundred tastes.' Baiwei (which means 'a hundred flavours' in Chinese) exemplifies this Sichuanese culinary adage. Despite the Mao-era decor, it's a cosy place where authentic home-style cuisine is served with uncommonly friendly service. South-western dishes are typically robust, with an abundance of dried chillies, pepper and fragrant garlic and Baiwei's variations on Sichuan standards offer a pleasing contrast of flavours. Try the *gong bao* tofu (silky pieces of pan-fried egg tofu coated in lustrous sweet and sour sauce, then lavished with crunchy peanuts and dried chillies) or long beans mixed with lightly marinated fried minced pork.

Palomar ££

34 Rupert Street, W1D 6DN (7439 8777, thepalomar.co.uk). Leicester Square or Piccadilly Circus tube. **Open** *noon-2.30pm, 5.30-11pm Mon-Sat; 12.30-3.30pm, 6-9pm Sun.* **Map** *p165 L8* ⓫ *Israeli*

Pulse-quickening dance music, free-flowing drink and vibrantly flavoured dishes are common in Israel's fashionable eateries, but were a rarity among London's once po-faced Jewish restaurants. That was until Palomar, run by Israeli-born nightclub entrepreneurs, became an unlikely West End hit and sparked a trend for modern Jewish cuisine. The menu takes influences from Spain, North Africa and the Levant, so you might start with Yemeni-style bread, *kubaneh* – a yeast bread served with rich tahini and tomato dips – and continue with Moroccan-style chermoula-stuffed sardines. Jew or Gentile doesn't matter: bring an appetite for fun as well as for food.

Shuang Shuang ££

64 Shaftesbury Avenue, W1D 6LU (7734 5416, www.shuangshuang.co.uk). Piccadilly Circus or Leicester Square tube. **Open** *noon-11pm Mon-Thur, Sun; noon-11.30pm Fri, Sat.* **Map** *p165 L8* **17** *Chinese*

Specialising in hotpot (an Asian version of a meat fondue, using broth to do the 'cooking'), Shuang Shuang requires concentration. Once you've picked from the mind-boggling array of raw ingredients whizzing round on the *kaiten* (sushi-bar conveyor belt), there's a choice of five broths and eight dipping sauces to decide on – or you can make your own. Each customer then cooks in their own personal bubbling cauldron, which should be turned up high then – once it's bubbling – low again. You'll be equipped with a timer and the friendly staff are on hand to advise. If that all sounds a bit complicated, fill up on snacks such as golden fritters of scallop and prawn with chilli and fresh herbs, or strips of deep-fried pig ear with heaps of cumin, salt and chilli.

Xu ££

30 Rupert Street, W1D 6DL (3319 8147, xulondon.com). Piccadilly Circus tube. **Restaurant** *noon-3pm, 5-11pm Mon-Sat; noon-3pm, 5-10pm Sun.* **Teahouse** *noon-5pm daily.* **Map** *p165 L8* **20** *Taiwanese*

Vintage is the vibe at Xu (pronounced 'Shu'. Not 'Joo'. Not 'Sue'.) The first 'smart' restaurant from the crew behind cult hit Bao (*see p172*), it's a love letter to 1930s Taipei. The narrow, potentially awkward two-floor space has been reformatted as a bundle of mini dining spots, each with its own air of intimacy. The upstairs room even has a teeny bar at its centre. As for the food, it's magnificent, layered with the full spectrum of sweet, sour and spice. First up, a pancake filled not with duck but tender short rib, enriched with bone marrow and served in the hollowed-out canoe of a calf shin with a potato 'crumb' on top. Then, a stunning

cold tomato and smoked eel soup-of-sorts, oscillating between sweet and salty, smoky and tangy. And chilli egg drop crab: a creamy curry, full of crabby flavour and punchy chilli, with the odd blob of wibbly egg and delicious briny accents, when the salmon roe pops on your tongue.

Pubs & bars

Experimental Cocktail Club

13A Gerrard Street, W1D 5PS (www.chinatownecc.com). Leicester Square tube. **Open** *6pm-3am Mon-Sat; 6pm-midnight Sun.* **Admission** *£5 after 11pm.* **Map** *p165 L8* **5**

ECC is all elegant opulence, arranged over three floors of an old townhouse. Booking isn't essential (half of the capacity is kept for walk-ins) but is recommended (email only, between noon and 5pm). The cocktails are among London's best: sophisticated, complex and strong – try the Havana (cigar-infused bourbon, marsala wine, Bruichladdich Octomore single malt 'wash').

Shops & services

♥ Cecil Court

Between Charing Cross Road & St Martin's Lane, WC2N (www.cecilcourt.co.uk). Leicester Square tube. **Map** *p165 L8* **4** *Books & music*

Quaint Cecil Court is known for its antiquarian book, map and print dealers, housed in premises that haven't changed in a hundred years. Notable residents include children's specialist Marchpane (no.16, 7836 8661); 40-year veteran David Drummond of Pleasures of Past Times (no.11, 7836 1142), with his playbills and Victoriana; and the mystical, spiritual and occult specialist Watkins Books (nos.19-21, 7836 2182).

Japan Centre

35B Panton Street, SW1Y 4EA (3405 1246, www.japancentre.com). Piccadilly Circus tube. **Open** *10am-9.30pm Mon-Sat; 11am-8pm Sun.* **Map** *p165 L8* **7**

This well-regarded centre offers all things Japanese, from specialist food ingredients to kitchenware and homewares. In the basement food hall, specialist rooms for tea, saké and miso are set around open kitchens and a central dining area. For an even more immersive Japanese experience, head west to the Japan Centre's food hall in Shepherd's Bush. Located in the Westfield London shopping centre, **Ichiba** (Lwr Ground Floor, www.ichibalondon.com) is the biggest of its kind in Europe and has everything from hot food counters and groceries to large sections of homewares and gifts.

Covent Garden & the Strand

Covent Garden has always been an index of the extremes of London life: on one hand, it used to be the capital's wholesale fruit and veg market; on the other, it has been home since the 1700s to the Royal Opera House, purveyor of that most refined of all the arts.

The masses now descend daily on the restored 19th-century market and its cobbled 'piazza' to peruse the increasingly high-end shops and gawp at the street entertainment, with even the most crowd-averse Londoner finding some aspects appealing: grudgingly the buskers; eagerly the London Transport Museum.

Down towards the Thames on the grubbily historic Strand, the vast courtyard of Somerset House is another attraction.

♥ **Don't miss**

1 London Transport Museum *p183*
Fun for all the family, especially train and bus geeks.

2 Royal Opera House *p184*
New public spaces and in-depth tours have democratised this bastion of high culture.

3 Shopping *p187*
High-end brands, quirky independents, trad shops and market stalls.

4 Courtyard at Somerset House *p190*
Fountains in summer, an ice-rink in winter.

5 Beaufort Bar *p191*
Drink in the classic opulence at London's most famous hotel.

The Shop at Bluebird *p188*

COVENT GARDEN

►*Covent Garden or Leicester Square tube.*

Covent Garden was once the property of the medieval Abbey ('convent') of Westminster. After Henry VIII dissolved the monasteries, it passed to John Russell, first Earl of Bedford, in 1552; his family still owns land hereabouts. During the 16th and 17th centuries, they developed the area: the fourth Earl employed Inigo Jones to create the Italianate open square that remains the area's centrepiece.

A market was first documented here in 1640 and grew into London's pre-eminent fruit and vegetable wholesaler, employing over 1,000 porters; its success led to the opening of coffeehouses, theatres, gambling dens and brothels. A flower market was added (which has been, since 1980, the location of the London Transport Museum).

In the second half of the 20th century, it became obvious that the congested streets of central London were unsuitable for such market traffic and the decision was taken to move the traders out. In 1974, with the market gone, the threat of property development loomed for the empty stalls and offices. It was only through demonstrations that the area was saved. It's now a pleasant place for a stroll, especially if you catch it early before the crowds descend.

Covent Garden Piazza

The area centred on Covent Garden Piazza now offers a combination of gentrified shops, restaurants and cafés, supplemented by street artists and busking musicians in the lower courtyard and under the portico of **St Paul's Covent Garden**. Tourists favour the 180-year-old covered market, which combines upmarket chain stores with a collection of small, sometimes quirky but often rather twee independent shops. Its handsome architecture is best viewed from the terrace of the Restaurant on Level 5 in the **Royal Opera House**.

In the last decade or so, a slew of ho-hum shops on the Piazza, King Street, James Street, Long Acre and beyond have been replaced by high-street heavyweights and luxury brands. Fred Perry, Kurt Geiger, Ralph Lauren's Rugby brand and Burberry Brit are all here, as is a flagship **Apple Store** and the beautiful **Shop at Bluebird**. Classy restaurateurs have also been lured in: **Terroirs** and **Delaunay** are near, while celeb-magnet the Ivy has a sister restaurant, **Ivy Market Grill**, right on the piazza.

Change is less evident elsewhere. The **Apple Market**, in the North Hall, still has arts and crafts from Tuesday to Sunday, and antiques on Monday. Across the road, the tackier **Jubilee Market** deals mostly in novelty T-shirts and other tat. And the always excellent **London Transport Museum** remains the stand-out attraction.

♥ Time to eat & drink

A proper pub
Cross Keys *p187*

Cocktails with class
Beaufort Bar *p191*

Fish is the dish
J Sheekey *p186*

Korean fried chicken
Chick'n'Sours *p185*

Middle East fun
The Barbary *p185*

Punjabi grills
Tandoor Chop House *p187*

Use your noodle
Kanada-Ya *p186*

Wine and sharing plates
Barrafina *p185*, Terroirs *p187*

♥ Time to shop

Beautiful brollies
James Smith & Sons *p188*

Chompable cheese
Neal's Yard Dairy *p188*

Covetable fashion
The Shop at Bluebird *p188*

Marvellous menswear
Nigel Cabourn Army Gym *p188*, Vintage Showroom *p188*

Naughty but nice
Coco de Mer *p188*

COVENT GARDEN & THE STRAND

Restaurants

1. The Barbary *p185*
2. Barrafina *p185*
3. Battersea Pie *p185*
4. Chick'n'Sours *p185*
5. Delaunay *p191*
6. Dishoom *p185*
7. Fernandez & Wells *p191*
8. Frenchie *p186*
9. Great Queen Street *p186*
10. Hawksmoor Seven Dials *p186*
11. Ivy Market Grill *p186*
12. Kanada-Ya *p186*
13. J Sheekey *p186*
14. Tandoor Chop House *p187*
15. Terroirs *p187*
16. Wahaca *p185*

Pubs & bars

1. Beaufort Bar *p191*
2. Cross Keys *p187*

Shops & services

1. Apple Store *p187*
2. Arthur Beale *p187*
3. Benjamin Pollock's Toy Shop *p187*
4. Blackout II *p187*
5. Coco de Mer *p188*
6. James Smith & Sons *p188*
7. Neal's Yard Dairy *p188*
8. Nigel Cabourn Army Gym *p188*
9. Shop at Bluebird *p188*
10. Vintage Showroom *p188*

Neal's Yard

Elsewhere in Covent Garden

Outside Covent Garden Piazza, the area offers a mixed bag of entertainment, eateries and shops. Nearest the markets, most of the more unusual shops have been superseded by a homogeneous mass of cafés, while big fashion chains – and the **St Martin's Courtyard mall** (www.stmartinscourtyard. co.uk) – have all but domesticated Long Acre. There are more interesting stores north of here on Neal Street and Monmouth Street; Earlham Street is also home to the **Donmar Warehouse** (*see p366*), a former banana-ripening depot that's now an intimate and groundbreaking theatre. On tiny Shorts Gardens next door is the **Neal's Yard Dairy**, purveyor of exceptional UK cheeses; down a passageway one door along

is Neal's Yard itself, a pleasant courtyard with communal seating.

South of Long Acre and east of the Piazza, historical depravity was called to account at the former **Bow Street Magistrates Court**. Once home to the Bow Street Runners, the precursors of the Metropolitan Police, this was also where the Krays were famously tried and Oscar Wilde entered his plea when arrested for 'indecent acts' in 1895. It was snapped up by Qatari investors in 2016 and is set to become a £125-million luxury hotel.

To the south, Wellington and Catherine streets mix restaurants and theatres, including the grand **Theatre Royal** (0844 412 4660, www.reallyusefultheatres.co.uk). Other diversions in and around Covent Garden include the museum at **Freemasons' Hall** (7395 9257, www.freemasonry.london. museum, call for details of tours), the eye-catchingly bombastic white stone building where Long Acre becomes Great Queen Street; and the **Coliseum** (*see p358*), home of the English National Opera.

Sights & museums

London Film Museum
*45 Wellington Street, WC2E 7BN (7836 4913, www.londonfilmmuseum.com). Covent Garden tube. **Open** 10am-6pm daily. Last entry 1hr before closing time. **Admission** £14.50; £9.50 reductions; £38 family; free under-5s. Tickets are available online in advance. **Map** p181 M7.*

💙 London Transport Museum

Covent Garden Piazza, WC2E 7BB (7379 6344, www.ltmuseum.co.uk). Covent Garden tube. **Open** *10am-6pm daily.* **Admission** *£17.50; £15 reductions; free under-18s.* **Map** *p181 M7.*

Londoners and their transport, eh? There's no need to keep banging on about it, you might think. We beg to differ. Most Londoners spend more time commuting than they do having lunch, and their city's prodigious growth in Victorian times into the biggest, most flabbergastingly exciting and frankly unpleasant city the world had ever known was largely down to transport infrastructure, which supported an unprecedented population explosion.

It is this story that the London Transport Museum tells so well, tracing the city's transport history from the horse age to the present day. The museum also raises some interesting and important questions about the future of public transport in the city, even offering a fanciful imagining of London's travel network in the years ahead.

Engaging and inspiring, the Transport Museum's focus is on social history and design, which are illustrated by a superb array of preserved buses, trams and trains, backed up by some impressively solid temporary exhibitions. The collections are in broadly chronological order, beginning with the Victorian gallery, where a replica of Shillibeer's first horse-drawn bus service from 1829 takes pride of place. Along the way there is a Northern Line simulator to drive, and train carriages and buses to jump on and climb up.

A new permanent gallery, London by Design, explores how, under the leadership of Frank Pick in the early 20th century, London Transport developed one of the most coherent brand identities in the world: that roundel, which now means Tube station with no need for words, is down to him. The gallery also explores some of the network's enduring industrial design and arresting poster art from the likes of Abram Games, Graham Sutherland and Ivon Hitchens.

All in all, it's a great place for families, with younger children especially enjoying the small but terrific play zone, All Aboard, where they can repair a mini Tube train, make passenger announcements and operate the Emirates Air Line cable car – get there early if you don't want your gorgeous child overrun by everyone else's herberts.
▶ *For the Acton depot, see opposite.*

Royal Opera House

'Bond In Motion', an exhibition of swanky vehicles from the James Bond films, has become a permanent feature at the London Film Museum's Covent Garden showroom. On display are cars, boats, motorbikes, sleds and jets including the Rolls-Royce Phantom III from *Goldfinger* (1964), the Aston Martin DB5 from *GoldenEye* (1995) and 'Wet Nellie' the underwater Lotus Esprit S1 from *The Spy Who Loved Me* (1977). The display also features action sequence boards, vehicle concept art, props and miniature models including the one third scale model of AgustaWestland's AW101 helicopter, used during the filming of *Skyfall* (2012).

♥ Royal Opera House

*Bow Street, WC2E 9DD (7304 4000, www. roh.org.uk). Covent Garden tube. **Open** from 10am daily. Guided tours Mon-Sat; see the website for details. **Admission** Tours £15; £12 reductions. **Map** p181 M7.*

The ROH was founded in 1732 by John Rich on the profits of his production of John Gay's *Beggar's Opera*; the current Grade 1-listed building, constructed roughly 150 years ago but extensively remodelled since, is the third on the site. After the most recent three-year 'Open Up' refurbishment, the Royal Opera House reopened in September 2018, with a new café, bar and restaurant, plus an extensive programme of daytime events that have succeeded in making the building much more accessible to the general public. Check out the glass-roofed Paul Hamlyn Hall, the Crush Bar (so named because in Victorian times the only thing served during intermission was orange and lemon crush)

and the Restaurant on Level 5, which has great views over the covered market. For a more in-depth look at the massive eight-floor building, including the main auditorium, the costume workshops and sometimes even a rehearsal, join an organised themed tour (details and bookings via the website). For music and ballet at the **Royal Opera House**, *see p359 and p369.*

St Paul's Covent Garden

*Bedford Street, WC2E 9ED (7836 5221, www. actorschurch.org). Covent Garden tube. **Open** 8.30am-5pm Mon-Fri; 9am-1pm Sun (5pm when there is Evensong). Times vary Sat; phone for details. **Services** 1.10pm Tue, Wed; 11am Sun. Choral Evensong 4pm 2nd Sun of mth. **Admission** free; donations appreciated. **Map** p181 M8.*

Known as the Actors' Church for its long association with Covent Garden's theatres, this pleasingly spare building was designed by Inigo Jones in 1631. A lovely limewood wreath by the 17th-century master carver Grinling Gibbons hangs inside the front door

---

In the know
Cinema-bilia

The **London Film Museum** (see *p182*) is stuffed with eye-catching props and memorabilia, but serious film buffs might prefer the **Cinema Museum** (see *p322*), whose collection spans a longer time period – all the way back to the 1890s – and includes projects, signage and other rarities.

as a reminder that he and his wife are interred in the crypt. But most visitors come to see the memorial plaques: many thespians are commemorated here, among them Vivien Leigh, Charlie Chaplin and Hattie Jacques of *Carry On* fame.

Restaurants

There's a branch of the reliably fun Mexican food chain **Wahaca** on Chandos Place (no.66, WC2N 4HG, 7240 1883, www.wahaca. co.uk, £, ⑯).

❤ The Barbary ££
16 Neal's Yard, WC2H 9DP (thebarbary. co.uk). Covent Garden tube. **Open** *noon-3pm, 5-10pm Mon-Fri; noon-10pm Sat; noon-9.30pm Sun. No reservations.* **Map** *p181 M7* ❶ *North African*

The Barbary takes everything that's good about its sister restaurant Palomar (*see p176*) and reinvents it. Seating is on 24 stools arranged at a horseshoe-shaped counter bar. Down one wall, there's a standing counter, where they'll feed you snacks like deep-fried pastry 'cigars' filled with cod, lemon and Moroccan spices while you wait for a seat. And the food – inspired by the eponymous Barbary coast, which stretches from Morocco to Egypt – is heady with smoke and North African spices. The signature *naan e beber*, made to an ancient recipe, emerges from the fiercely hot tandoor deliciously fluffy and blistered. Main courses such as slow-braised octopus with oranges cooked over a coal-fired robata are impossibly tender; while *knafeh* (filo pastry filled with goat's cheese and pan-fried until it's crispy on the outside, chewy on the inside, and sprinkled with roasted pistachio nuts) is dessert heaven.

❤ Barrafina ££
10 Adelaide Street, WC2N 4HZ (7440 1456, www.barrafina.co.uk). Charing Cross or Leicester Square tube. **Open** *noon-3pm, 5-11pm Mon-Sat; 1-3.30pm, 5.30-10pm Sun. No reservations.* **Map** *p181 M8* ❷ *Tapas*

Like its predecessor in Soho, Barrafina Covent Garden takes no reservations, so arrive early – or late – if you don't want to queue at this perennially popular tapas restaurant. The menu is studded with tempting Mallorcan and Catalan dishes, but watch out if you're properly hungry: the bill adds up fast. Despite the fancy prices, remember that Barrafina is a modern Spanish tapas bar rather than a restaurant per se – that means that the list of sherries, cavas and other wines by the glass are as much a part of the appeal as the food, and perfect for experimenting with as you nibble. For the latest triumph from the same owners, *see p92*.

Battersea Pie £
Lower ground floor, 28 The Market, WC2E 8RA (7240 9566, www.batterseapiestation. co.uk). Covent Garden tube. **Open** *11am-7.30pm Mon-Fri; 10am-8pm Sat; 11am-7pm Sun.* **Map** *p181 M8* ❸ *British*

Serving proper British food at bargain prices, this pie-and-mash house is something of an anomaly in Covent Garden Market. Housed in one of the refurbished subterranean arches, it retains the traditional exterior and flagstone floor, but the fixtures and fittings are stylish and modern: bright white tiles, polished marble tables and a shiny counter. Besides traditional fillings such as steak and mushroom with stout are less expected versions, such as butternut squash and goat's cheese. Even for a counter-service place, this is a terrific little caff.

❤ Chick'n'Sours £
1A Earlham Street, WC2H 9LL (3198 4814, chicknsours.co.uk). **Open** *noon-2.30pm, 5-10pm Mon-Wed; noon-10.30pm Thur-Sat; noon-8pm Sun.* **Map** *p181 L7* ❹ *Korean*

Combining KFC (that's Korean Fried Chicken, food fans) with cocktails has proved to be a winning formula. Set in a basement, the vibe is somewhere between house party and Prohibition speakeasy. There's a bar in the middle, a playlist of feel-good tunes and the food comes served on granny's best china plates. The speciality K-Pop burger is impossibly juicy and over four inches tall; it's double-fried for crunchiness and served with *gochujang* (an umami-tastic red chilli paste) mayo, fiery sriracha, kimchi, chilli vinegar and Asian slaw. Follow it up with sweet-sticky disco wings and a peanut and pickled watermelon salad. Or go for an Asian mash-up of Shin Cup fries (with sriracha sour cream and spring onions) and Seoul Destroyer burger (with Korean schmaltz, nacho cheese and kimchi). **Other locations** 390 Kingsland Road, Haggerston E8 4AA (3620 8728); 62 Upper Street, Islington, N1 0NY (7704 9013).

Dishoom ££
12 Upper St Martin's Lane, WC2H 9FB (7420 9320, www.dishoom.com). Covent Garden or Leicester Square tube. **Open** *8am-11pm Mon-Thur; 8am-midnight Fri; 9am-midnight Sat; 9am-11pm Sun.* **Map** *p181 M7* ❻ *Pan-Indian*

A swish, self-styled 'Bombay café', Dishoom is filled with retro features: whirring ceiling fans, low-level lighting and vintage Bollywood posters. The place is crowded all day, from breakfast (for bacon naan rolls with chilli jam) to dinner (for the usual curries and tandoori grills). Quality can vary: *vada pau* (potato croquettes with sharp chutney in a fluffy Portuguese-style bun) and *bhel* (crunchy puffed rice with tangy tamarind chutney) are tasty; kebabs and curries are fairly standard renditions. There are other branches in Kensington, Shoreditch, King's Cross and Soho; see the website for details.

Frenchie £££

16 Henrietta Street, WC2E 8QH (7836 4422, www.frenchiecoventgarden.com). Covent Garden or Leicester Square tube. **Open** *noon-2.30pm, 5.30-10.30pm daily.* **Map** *p181 M8* ❽ *French*

You'll have to be patient to secure a booking at Gregory Marchand's tiny Parisian-style bistro but, like its original French counterpart, it's worth the wait. Tucked away down a cobbled alley, Frenchie is all about impeccably composed modern European small plates – the menu might only list three ingredients but each dish is deceptively sophisticated. Playful starters include maple-sweetened bacon scones, still warm from the oven, or rich eggs mimosa with strands of black truffle. The signature pulled pig slider is a must-try, thanks to its house-smoked meat and lightly pickled, crunchy red cabbage. Be sure to pace yourself for a dazzling pud: the moist lemon polenta cake, served with silky ice-cream and morsels of honeycomb (for sweet) and dehydrated kalamata olives (for salt).

Great Queen Street ££

32 Great Queen Street, WC2B 5AA (7242 0622, www.greatqueenstreetrestaurant.co.uk). Covent Garden or Holborn tube. **Restaurant** *noon-2.30pm, 5.30-10.30pm Mon-Sat; noon-3.30pm Sun.* **Bar** *5pm-midnight Tue-Sat.* **Map** *p181 M7* ❾ *British*

The excellent location ensures Great Queen Street's popularity. The outdoor tables are almost never vacant, but walk-ins may find space at the bar, where the full menu is served. The menu changes daily, is produce-led and is predominantly British. There's minimal fussing with ingredients: a plump piece of bone-in smoked mackerel might be served with a dollop each of cooked gooseberries and horseradish; slow-cooked pork could arrive in a stew with a generous quantity of cockles.

Hawksmoor Seven Dials £££

11 Langley Street, WC2H 9JG (7420 9390, thehawksmoor.com). Covent Garden tube. **Open** *noon-3pm, 5-10.30pm Mon-Thur; noon-3pm, 5-11pm Fri; noon-11pm Sat; noon-9.30pm Sun.* **Map** *p181 M7* ❿ *Steakhouse*

The short main menu centres on steak (rib-eye, T-bone, porterhouse, fillet, sirloin and more), at serious prices, plus the likes of grilled chicken, lobster with garlic butter,

monkfish grilled over charcoal, and a meat-free choice for the odd misplaced vegetarian. A good kick-off is one of Hawksmoor's renowned cocktails. There are other branches in Borough, Spitalfields, Knightsbridge and the City; see the website for details.

Ivy Market Grill £££

1A Henrietta Street, WC2E 8PS (3301 0200, www.theivymarketgrill.com). Covent Garden tube. **Open** *8am-12.30am Mon-Sat; 8am-11.30pm Sun.* **Map** *p181 M8* ⓫ *Modern European*

If you're after a culinary superstar, go elsewhere, but this is no mere cash-in on the celeb-courted **Ivy** (1-5 West Street, WC2H 9NQ, 7836 4751, www.the-ivy.co.uk) – and it's bang on the Piazza. The interior's lovely, in a classy, bourgeois brasserie, my-family-own-Dorset kind of way, and the menu's a good read too, with a pleasingly retro Continental feel to dishes that use mainly British ingredients. You aren't going to spot any A-listers round here, but we like the place: it's good-looking, with good service, opens late and serves breakfast, tea and all-day snacks.

♥ Kanada-Ya £

64 St Giles High Street, WC2H 8LE (7240 0232, www.kanada-ya.com). Tottenham Court Road tube. **Open** *noon-3pm, 5-10.30pm Mon-Sat; noon-8.30pm Sun. No reservations.* **Map** *p181 L7* ⓬ *Japanese*

Small, brightly lit and minimal, this is not the place for a leisurely meal: there are always lengthy mealtime queues outside its doors. But there's a reason for Kanada-Ya's already-large fan base: exceptional ramen. If you don't eat pork, forget it; but those pork bones are simmered for 18 hours to create the smooth, rich, seriously savoury *tonkotsu* broth – one of the best in London. If you don't have much time, the wait at Ippudo, just opposite, is always more bearable than that at Kanada-Ya. **Other locations** 25 Upper Street, Islington, N1 0PN (7288 2787); 3 Panton Street, Soho, SW1Y 4DL (7930 3511).

♥ J Sheekey £££

28-32 St Martin's Court, WC2N 4AL (7240 2565, www.j-sheekey.co.uk). Leicester Square tube. **Open** *noon-3pm, 5pm-midnight Mon-Sat; noon-3.30pm, 5.30-10.30pm Sun.* **Map** *p181 L8* ⓭ *Fish & seafood*

After well over a century of service, Sheekey's status as a West End institution is assured. With its monochrome photos of stars of stage and screen, wooden panelling and cream crackle walls, and array of silver dishes atop thick white tablecloths, it oozes old-fashioned glamour. The menu runs from super-fresh oysters and shellfish via old-fashioned snacks (herring roe on toast) to upmarket classics (dover sole, lobster thermidor). The fish pie – a rich, comforting treat – is acclaimed, but we feel the shrimp and scallop burger merits similar status.

Adjoining Sheekey restaurant, **J Sheekey Atlantic Bar** (nos.33-35, www.jsheekeyatlanticbar.co.uk) serves a similar menu – with an expanded range of oysters – to customers sitting at the counter.

♥ Tandoor Chop House ££
8 Adelaide Street, WC2N 4HZ (3096 0359, tandoorchophouse.com). Charing Cross tube. **Open** *noon-11pm Mon-Thur; noon-11.30pm Fri, Sat; 1-10pm Sun.* **Map** *p181 M8* ⓮ *Indian*

TCH is slightly less hectic and slightly more refined than **Dishoom** (*see p185*). With cheerfully attentive service and a bustling Bombay vibe, it's a twist on what you'd get in an old-fashioned Brit 'chop house', only using Indo-Punjabi spices and swapping the grill for the tandoor. Plates are small and meant for sharing. Start with the pistachio-studded seekh kebab strewn with pomegranate seeds and coriander, or the 'beef dripping' keema naan. For mains, be sure to try the thickly marinated, fatty-edged lamb chops, all soot and spice, or the juice spice-rubbed rib-eye. But don't stop there: the malted kulfi ice cream is silky smooth and intense, served with chunks of caramelised banana and salted peanuts.

♥ Terroirs £££
5 William IV Street, WC2N 4DW (7036 0660, www.terroirswinebar.com). Charing Cross tube/rail. **Open** *noon-11pm Mon-Sat.* **Map** *p181 M8* ⓯

Terroirs – a wine bar with excellent food – is really two places under one roof. The always-crowded ground floor has a casual feel and a menu to match, focused on small plates for sharing. You can sample some of the same dishes in the atmospheric and surprisingly roomy basement, which feels more like a restaurant: the menu here, with its focus on rustic French dishes, seems designed to guide diners towards a more traditional starter-main-dessert approach. The wine list is an encyclopaedia of organic and biodynamic bottles.

Pubs & bars
♥ Cross Keys
31 Endell Street, WC2H 9BA (7836 5185, www.crosskeyscoventgarden.com). Covent Garden tube. **Open** *11am-11pm Mon-Sat; noon-10.30pm Sun.* **Map** *p181 M7* ❷

Central London pubs with a local vibe are the rarest of things, but the Cross Keys is precisely that. With its canopy of copper implements, garish carpet and walls covered in vintage beeraphernalia, it feels like it hasn't changed for 30 years. Despite the local competition, it makes zero effort to appeal to tourists, which is ironic, since sipping a pint in the failing sunlight amid wafts from the nearby chippie is one of the most perfectly London experiences you'll get in the West End.

Shops & services
Apple Store
1-7 The Piazza, WC2E 8HB (7447 1400, www.apple.com/uk/retail). Covent Garden tube. **Open** *10am-8pm Mon-Sat; noon-6pm Sun.* **Map** *p181 M7* ❶ *Electronics & photography*

A temple to geekery, this has separate rooms – set out over three storeys – devoted to each product line. The exposed brickwork, big old oak tables and stone floors make it an inviting place. In the Start Up Room staff will help to set up your new iPad, iPhone, iPod or Mac, or transfer files from your old computer to your new one – all for free.

Arthur Beale
194 Shaftesbury Avenue, WC2H 8JP (7836 9034, www.arthurbeale.co.uk). Tottenham Court Road tube. **Open** *10am-7pm Mon-Wed, Fri, Sat; 10am-8pm Thur; 11am-5pm Sun.* **Map** *p181 M7* ❷ *Boat equipment*

There are some odd shops in London, but few beat the surprise factor of finding a yacht chandler in Shaftesbury Avenue. It may look old-fashioned but, for sailors, Arthur Beale's stock is as useful now as it ever was. On the ground floor you'll find everything from reels of rope, ship's bells, barometers and navigation lights to boating hardware such as cleats, fairleads and lacing hooks. Upstairs, there are books, boots and lifejackets for the real or wannabe sailor.

Benjamin Pollock's Toy Shop
44 The Market, WC2E 8RF (7379 7866, www.pollocks-coventgarden.co.uk). Covent Garden tube. **Open** *10.30am-6pm Mon-Wed; 10.30am-6.30pm Thur-Sat; 11am-6pm Sun.* **Map** *p181 M7* ❸ *Children*

Best known for its Victorian-style cardboard toy theatres, Pollock's is also great for traditional toys such as knitted animals, china tea sets, masks, glove puppets, cards, spinning tops and fortune-telling fish.

Blackout II
52 Endell Street, WC2H 9AJ (7240 5006, www.blackout2.com). Covent Garden tube. **Open** *11am-7pm Mon-Fri; 11.30am-6.30pm Sat.* **Map** *p181 M7* ❹ *Vintage clothing*

There are dozens of good vintage stores in London, but this remains a firm favourite. Blackout II has been providing bright and beautiful frocks, handbags, shoes and all the trimmings for more than two-and-a-half decades. Here, you will find a wonderful array of dress-up clothes, from 1930s cocktail frocks to full-skirted '50s dresses and some slinky numbers that might have graced the sets of *Dynasty*. It's a magpie's dream of costume jewellery, and also does clothing hire.

♥ Coco de Mer

23 Monmouth Street, WC2H 9DD (7836 8882, www.coco-de-mer.com). Covent Garden tube. **Open** *11am-7pm Mon-Sat; noon-6pm Sun.* **Map** *p181 M7* ❺ *Accessories*

London's most glamorous erotic emporium sells a variety of tasteful books, toys and lingerie, from glass dildos that double as objets d'art to a Marie Antoinette costume of crotchless culottes and corset. Trying on items can be fun as well: the peepshow-style velvet changing rooms allow your lover to peer through and watch you undress from a 'confession box' next door.

♥ James Smith & Sons

Hazelwood House, 53 New Oxford Street, WC1A 1BL (7836 4731, www.james-smith. co.uk). Holborn or Tottenham Court Road tube. **Open** *10am-5.45pm Mon, Tue, Thur, Fri; 10.30am-5.45pm Wed; 10am-5.15pm Sat.* **Map** *p181 M7* ❻ *Accessories*

Nearly 190 years after it was established, this charming shop, with Victorian fittings still intact, is holding its own in the niche market of umbrellas and walking sticks. The stock here isn't the throwaway type of brolly that breaks at the first sign of a breeze. The lovingly crafted brollies – perhaps a classic City umbrella with a malacca cane handle at £175 – are built to last. A repair service is also offered.

♥ Neal's Yard Dairy

17 Shorts Gardens, WC2H 9AT (7500 7520, www.nealsyarddairy.co.uk). Covent Garden tube. **Open** *10am-7pm Mon-Sat.* **Map** *p181 M7* ❼ *Food & drink*

Neal's Yard buys from small farms and creameries and matures the cheeses in its own cellars until they're ready to sell in peak condition. Names such as Stinking Bishop and Lincolnshire Poacher are as evocative as the aromas in the shop. It's best to walk in and ask what's good today: you'll be given tasters by the well-trained staff. **Other location** Borough Market, 6 Park Street, SE1 9AB.

♥ Nigel Cabourn Army Gym

28 Henrietta Street, WC2E 8NA (7240 1005, www.cabourn.com). Covent Garden tube. **Open** *11am-6.30pm Mon-Wed, Fri, Sat; 11am-7pm Thur; noon-5pm Sun.* **Map** *p181 M8* ❽ *Menswear*

This is the only Cabourn shop outside Japan, selling the hallowed designer's vintage-inspired collections, dreamed to life by consulting his vast personal archive of over 4,000 pieces. As the name might suggest, you're guaranteed to be able to get hold of some camo here, but there's also a solid amount of smart tailoring and shirting, all drawing on the best of British design.

♥ The Shop at Bluebird

Carriage Hall, Floral Street, WC2E 9DP (7351 3873, theshopatbluebird.com). Covent Garden tube. **Open** *10am-7pm Mon-Sat; noon-6pm Sun.* **Map** *p181 M7* ❾ *Fashion & homewares*

This chic lifestyle boutique relocated from the King's Road to Covent Garden. Inside you'll find a broad selection of designer clothing, shoes, accessories, books, music (both CDs and vinyl) and the odd piece of furniture. There's also a slew of hard-to-find niche skincare brands, including New York's Bigelow, Ole Henriksen, DCL and Kaeline. Fashion is wide-ranging; London-based designers Emma Cook and Peter Jensen are to be found here, as are US faves Alexander Wang and Marc by Marc Jacobs, and Japanese heavyweights Junya Watanabe and Comme des Garçons. Look out for lesser-known labels as well, such as the rock-inspired Rika and Isabel Marant, and vintage-inspired eyewear from hip label Prism.

♥ Vintage Showroom

14 Earlham Street, WC2H 9LN (7836 3964, www.thevintageshowroom.com). Covent Garden tube. **Open** *11am-7pm Mon-Sat; noon-6pm Sun.* **Map** *p181 L7* ❿ *Vintage menswear*

In the old FW Collins & Sons ironmongery, Roy Luckett and Doug Gunn show a tiny selection of their famous west London menswear archive, which they routinely loan out to big-name designers, denim brands and vintage obsessives. With stock sourced from around the world (Roy and Doug have some hair-raising stories of dealings with collectors and hoarders in obscure locations), it follows that the pair occasionally find it hard to part with an item, and they've been known to try to dissuade shoppers from buying the rarer pieces on display. But the shop has London's best men's vintage collection, with an emphasis on Americana (denim, sweats, a few choice tees) and classic military and British pieces.

THE STRAND, EMBANKMENT & ALDWYCH

▶ *Embankment or Temple tube, or Charing Cross tube/rail.*

Until as recently as the 1860s, the Strand ran beside the Thames; indeed, it was originally the river's bridlepath. In the 14th century, it was lined with grand residences with gardens that ran down to the water. It wasn't until the 1870s that the Thames was pushed back with the creation of the Embankment and its adjacent gardens. By the time George Newnes's famed *Strand* magazine was introducing its readership to Sherlock Holmes (1891), the street boasted the Cecil Hotel (long since demolished), **Simpson's-in-the-Strand** (still going), King's College and **Somerset House**. Prime Minister Benjamin Disraeli described it as 'perhaps the finest street in Europe'. While nobody would make such a claim today, there's still plenty to interest visitors.

In 1292, the body of Eleanor of Castile, consort to King Edward I, completed its funerary procession from Lincoln to the small hamlet of Charing, at the western end of what is now the Strand. The occasion was marked by the erection of the last of 12 elaborate crosses. A replica of the **Eleanor Cross** (originally set just south of nearby Trafalgar Square; *see p104*) was placed in 1865 on the forecourt of Charing Cross Station; it remains there today, looking like the spire of a sunken cathedral. Across the road, behind **St Martin-in-the-Fields** (*see p104*), is Maggi Hambling's weird memorial to a more recent queen, *A Conversation with Oscar Wilde*.

The Embankment itself can be reached down Villiers Street. Pass through the tube station to the point at which boat tours with on-board entertainment depart. Just to the east stands **Cleopatra's Needle**, an obelisk presented to the British nation by the viceroy of Egypt, Mohammed Ali, in 1820 but not set in place by the river for a further 59 years. The obelisk was originally erected around 1500 BC by the pharaoh Tuthmosis III at a site near modern-day Cairo, before being moved to Alexandria, Cleopatra's capital, in 10 BC. By this time, however, the great queen was 20 years dead.

Back on the Strand, the majestic **Savoy** (7836 4343, www.fairmont.com/savoy-london) is the hotel from which Monet painted the Thames, where Vivien Leigh met Laurence Olivier, where Londoners learned to love the martini. It was first opened in 1889, financed by profits from Richard D'Oyly Carte's productions of Gilbert and Sullivan's light operas at the neighbouring **Savoy Theatre**. The theatre,

Savoy

which pre-dates the hotel by eight years, was the first to use electric lights. Two grand hotels guard Aldwych, at the eastern end of the Strand: **One Aldwych** (7300 1000, www.onealdwych.com) and, directly opposite, **ME London** (7395 3400, www.melia.com). This grand crescent dates only from 1905, but the name 'ald wic' (old settlement or market) has its origins in the tenth century. To the south is **Somerset House**. Almost in front of it is **St Mary-le-Strand** (7836 3126, www.stmarylestrand.org, 11am-4pm Mon-Fri, 10am-3pm Sun), James Gibbs's first public building, completed in 1717. On Strand Lane, reached via Surrey Street, is the so-called 'Roman' bath where Dickens took the waters – you have to peer through a dusty window.

On a traffic island just east of Aldwych is **St Clement Danes** (7242 8282, www.raf.mod.uk/stclementdanes). It's believed that a church was first built here by the Danish in the ninth century and dedicated to one

---

In the know
Cashing in

As a rule, we're not the kind of travel guide that recommends cashpoints – but the lobby of the Law Courts branch of Lloyds bank (222 Strand, WC2R 1BB), just east of **St Clement Danes** (*see above*), is a thing of beauty – all richly coloured Doulton tiles and Victorian domestic-industrial loveliness. It opened as a restaurant in 1883, failed, failed again, and reopened as a Lloyds in 1895.

of the many patron saints of mariners, but the current building is mainly Wren's handiwork. It's the principal church of the RAF. Just beyond the church are the **Royal Courts of Justice** and the original site of **Temple Bar** (*see p222 and p223*).

Sights & museums

Benjamin Franklin House

36 Craven Street, WC2N 5NF (7839 2008, www.benjaminfranklinhouse.org). Charing Cross tube/rail. **Open** *box office 10.30am-5pm Mon, Wed-Sun. Entry by tour only. Historical tours at noon, 1pm, 2pm, 3.15pm, 4.15pm Wed-Sun. Architectural tours at noon, 1pm, 2pm, 3.15pm, 4.15pm Mon.* **Admission** *£6-£8; £3-£6 reductions; free under-16s.* **Map** *p181 M8.*

This is the house where Franklin – scientist, diplomat, philosopher, inventor and Founding Father of the US – lived between 1757 and 1775. It isn't a museum in the conventional sense: there are few artefacts on display. Rather, the house is explored through 45-minute 'historical experiences' (booking advised). These are led by an actress playing Franklin's landlady's daughter, Polly Hewson, using sound and visual projections on the plain walls of the house to conjure up the world in which Franklin lived. On Mondays, as an alternative to the Historical Experience tours, there are 20-minute Architectural tours.

Courtauld Gallery

Somerset House, Strand, WC2R 0RN (7848 2777, www.courtauld.ac.uk/gallery). Temple tube. **Open** *Closed until at least 2020.* **Map** *p181 N8.*

Located for the last two decades in the north wing of **Somerset House** (*see right*), the Courtauld has one of Britain's greatest collections of paintings, including several works of world importance. Although there are some outstanding early works (Cranach's *Adam & Eve*, for one), the collection's strongest suit is in Impressionism and Post-Impressionism. Popular masterpieces here include Manet's *A Bar at the Folies-Bergère*, but there are also superb works by Monet and

Cézanne, important Gauguins, and some Van Goghs and Seurats. On the top floor, there's a selection of gorgeous Fauvist pieces and a lovely room of Kandinskys. Note that the gallery is closed for refurbishment until autumn 2020.

♥ Somerset House & the Embankment Galleries

Strand, WC2R 1LA (7845 4600, www. somersethouse.org.uk). Temple tube. **Open** *10am-6pm Mon, Tue, Sat, Sun (last entry to galleries 5pm); 11am-8pm Wed-Fri (last entry to galleries 7pm). Tours Tue, Thur, Sat.* **Admission** *Courtyard & terrace free. Embankment Galleries prices vary. Tours free; check website for details.* **Map** *p181 N8.*

The original Somerset House was a Tudor palace commissioned by the Duke of Somerset. In 1775, it was demolished to make way for the first purpose-built office block in the world. Architect Sir William Chambers spent the last 20 years of his life working on this neoclassical edifice overlooking the Thames, built to accommodate learned societies such as the Royal Academy and government departments. The taxmen are still here, but the rest of the building is open to the public. Attractions include the **Courtauld** (*see left*), the handsome fountain court and several eating options: from a terrace café and **Fernandez & Wells** to Skye Gyngell's **Spring**, a pricey Italian restaurant. Several rooms around the courtyard are used

Fountains at Somerset House

to host lively art exhibitions. Downstairs on the Thames side of the building, the **Embankment Galleries** house exhibitions on a grander scale. But perhaps the most appealing part of the complex is the huge courtyard, where choreographed fountains lure children in the summer, while parents watch idly from cafe tables. In winter, an ice rink takes over the space (bookings 0333 320 2836, £11, £8.50 reductions), ringed by festive shopping and food stalls.

Restaurants

Delaunay £££

*55 Aldwych, WC2B 4BB (7499 8558, www. thedelaunay.com). Covent Garden or Temple tube. **Open** 7am-11pm Mon-Fri; 8am-11pm Sat; 9am-10pm Sun. **Map** p181 N7* ⑤ *Brasserie*

European grand cafés are the inspiration here, resulting in a striking interior of green leather banquette seating, dark wood, antique mirrors and a black-and-white marble floor. The menu runs from breakfast to dinner, taking in afternoon tea (try the Austrian-biased cakes, all made in-house). There's a dish of the day, soups, sandwiches, salads and egg dishes, plus savouries and crustacea. If the restaurant at Delaunay is full, try the no-bookings Counter café next door for cakes.

Fernandez & Wells £

*East Wing, Somerset House, Strand, WC2R 1LA (7420 9408, www.fernandezandwells. com). Temple tube. **Open** 8am-10pm Mon, Tue; 8am-11pm Wed-Fri; 10am-10pm Sat; 10am-6pm Sun. **Map** p181 N8* ⑦ *Café*

Four rooms in the east wing of Somerset House (*see opposite*) are set up for all-day grazing. Meat is central: the 'ham room' has carved slices of *lomito ibérico, jamón de lampiño*, or wild fennel Tuscan salami, while *morcilla* and the like arrive from an open grill. Breakfasts are simple but good. There's a scattering of Fernandez & Wells throughout the city.

Pubs & bars

❤ Beaufort Bar

*The Savoy, Strand, WC2R 0EZ (7836 4343, www.fairmont.com/savoy-london). Charing Cross tube/rail or Embankment tube. **Open** 5pm-1am Mon-Sat. **Map** p181 M8* ①

Set in London's most famous hotel, the ultra-suave Beaufort Bar is quite possibly the most attractive space to sip a drink in the city. Just off the busy lobby, it's a hideaway of supreme style and opulence, with jet-black walls, theatrical lighting and enough discreet touches of gold to remind you you're somewhere special. The drinks live up to the ambience, pushing the boundaries of mixology and incorporating fizz to great effect.

Ice rink at Somerset House

Bloomsbury & King's Cross

London's neighbourhoods north of Oxford Street are bookish and bohemian. Bloomsbury is best known as the home of the British Museum, but also has a handful of delightful small museums. To the west, Fitzrovia is a favourite source of stories for London nostalgists, but the days of post-war spivs and drunken poets have given way to an era of new-media offices. At least they keep the pubs lively and the quality of the restaurants high. To the north of Bloomsbury, the legendarily seedy King's Cross has gone the way of formerly raffish Fitzrovia, with the arrival of the British Library, the rebirth of St Pancras Station as an international rail hub and the emergence of the shiny new King's Cross Central district.

❤ Don't miss

1 British Museum *p198*
A treasure trove.

2 Wellcome Collection *p200*
Science made scintillating.

3 Coal Drops Yard *p203*
Eat, drink and shop in artfully refurbed industrial surroundings.

4 Novelty Automation *p197*
Coin-op giggles.

5 London Review Bookshop *p201*
Find yourself some inspiration.

BLOOMSBURY & KING'S CROSS

Restaurants

1. Barrafina p205
2. Berners Tavern p207
3. Caravan King's Cross p205
4. Casa Pastor p205
5. Dishoom p205
6. Ethos p207
7. German Gymnasium p205
8. Homeslice p207
9. Honey & Co p207
10. Icco p207
11. Kerb p205
12. Koba p208
13. Lady Ottoline p201
14. Lantana p208
15. Lima London p208
16. Portland p208
17. Roka p209

Pubs & bars

1. All Star Lanes p201
2. Barrica p209
3. Booking Office p206
4. Bradley's Spanish Bar p209
5. Lamb p201
6. Museum Tavern p201
7. Scottish Stores p206
8. Spiritland p206

Shops & services

1. Blade Rubber Stamps p201
2. Heal's p209
3. Lewis Leathers p209
4. London Review Bookshop p201
5. Pentreath & Hall p202
6. Persephone Books p202
7. Skoob p202

© Copyright Time Out Group 2019

BLOOMSBURY

▶ *Euston Square, Holborn, Russell Square or Tottenham Court Road tube.*

Bloomsbury's florid name is, prosaically, taken from 'Blemondisberi' – the manor ('bury') of William Blemond, who acquired the area in the 13th century. It remained rural until the 1660s, when the fourth Earl of Southampton built **Bloomsbury Square** around his house. The Southamptons intermarried with the Russells, the Dukes of Bedford; together, they developed the area as one of London's first planned suburbs.

Over the next two centuries, the group built a series of grand squares. **Bedford Square** (1775-80) is London's only complete Georgian square (regrettably, its central garden is usually closed to the public); huge **Russell Square** has been restored as a public park with a popular café. To the east, the cantilevered postwar **Brunswick Centre** is full of shops, flats, restaurants and a cinema. The nearby streets, particularly Marchmont Street, are some of the more characterful in the West End.

Bloomsbury's charm is the sum of its parts, best experienced on a meander through its bookshops (many on Great Russell Street), pubs and squares. The blue plaques are a *Who's Who* of literary modernists – TS Eliot, Virginia Woolf, WB Yeats – with a few interlopers from more distant history: Edgar Allan Poe (83 Southampton Row), Anthony Trollope (6 Store Street) and, of course, Dickens (48 Doughty Street; now the **Charles Dickens Museum**).

On Bloomsbury's western border, Malet, Gordon and Gower streets are dominated by the **University of London**. The most notable building is Gower Street's University College, founded in 1826. Inside is the 'autoicon' of utilitarian philosopher and founder of the university, Jeremy Bentham: his preserved cadaver, fully clothed, sits in a glass-fronted cabinet. The university's main library is housed in towering Senate House on Malet Street, one of the city's most imposing examples of monumental art deco. It was the model for Orwell's Ministry of Truth in *1984* – but don't be scared to step inside: the lower floors and little café are open to the public.

South of the university sprawls the must-see **British Museum** (*see p198*). Running off Great Russell Street, where you'll find the museum's main entrance, are three attractive parallel streets (Coptic, Museum and Bury) and, nearby, the **Cartoon Museum**; also close by, Bloomsbury Way is home to Hawksmoor's restored **St George's Bloomsbury**. Across from here, Sicilian Avenue is an Italianate, pedestrian precinct of colonnaded shops – which has a smattering of places to eat and drink.

North-east of the British Museum, Lamb's Conduit Street is a convivial thoroughfare lined with interesting shops. At the north end of the street is **Coram's Fields**, a delightful children's park on the grounds of the former Thomas Coram's Foundling Hospital. Coram's legacy is commemorated in the **Foundling Museum**.

Sights & museums

Charles Dickens Museum

48 Doughty Street, WC1N 2LX (7405 2127, www.dickensmuseum.com). Chancery Lane or Russell Square tube. **Open** *10am-5pm Tue-Sat. Tours by arrangement.* **Admission** *£9.50; £4.50-£7.50 reductions; free under-6s.* **Map** *p194 N5.*

London is scattered with plaques marking addresses where Dickens lived, but this is the only one to have been preserved as a museum. He lived here from 1837 to 1840, writing *Nicholas Nickleby* and *Oliver Twist* while in residence. Ring the doorbell to gain access to four floors of Dickensiana, collected over the years from various former residences. Some rooms are arranged as they might have been when he lived here

---

❤ **Time to eat & drink**

Best for brunch
Caravan King's Cross *p205*

Culinary magic
Portland *p208*

For an Asian feast
Roka *p209*

If music be the food of love
Spiritland *p206*

Tasty and affordable lunches
Honey & Co *p207*

Upmarket boozer – with a roof terrace
Scottish Stores *p206*

When atmosphere is everything
Bradley's Spanish Bar *p209*

❤ **Time to shop**

Bloomsbury's best bookstore
London Review Bookshop *p201*

Classic biker leathers
Lewis Leathers *p209*

Unusual souvenirs
Blade Rubber Stamps *p201*

(especially atmospheric during the occasional candlelit openings); others deal with different aspects of his life, from struggling hack to famous performer. But the study has the key artefact: the chair and desk at which Dickens wrote *Great Expectations*, bought for the nation by the National Heritage Memorial Fund in 2015. Refurbishment has created a pleasant downstairs café and courtyard garden.

Coram's Fields

93 Guilford Street, WC1N 1DN (7837 6138, www.coramsfields.org). Russell Square tube. **Open** *9am-dusk daily.* **Admission** *free; adults admitted only if accompanied by under-16s.* **Map** *p194 M5.*

This historic site dates to 1747, when Thomas Coram established the Foundling Hospital (now a museum; *see below*), but it only opened as a park in 1936. It is now probably the best playground in London – with the Diana, Princess of Wales Memorial Playground (*see p133*) its only real rival. It has sandpits, a small petting zoo, ride-on toys and several well-designed areas for different age groups, with the most challenging including a zip wire and some superb spiral slides.

Foundling Museum

40 Brunswick Square, WC1N 1AZ (7841 3600, www.foundlingmuseum.org.uk). Russell Square tube. **Open** *10am-5pm Tue-Sat; 11am-5pm Sun.* **Admission** *£10; £7.50 reductions; free under-16s.* **Map** *p194 M5.*

This museum recalls the social history of the Foundling Hospital, set up in 1739 by shipwright and sailor Thomas Coram. Returning to England from America in 1720, Coram was appalled by the number of abandoned children he saw. Securing royal patronage, he persuaded Hogarth and Handel to become governors; it was Hogarth who made the building Britain's first public art gallery; works by artists as notable as Gainsborough and Reynolds are on display. The most heart-rending display is a tiny case of mementoes that were all mothers could leave the children they abandoned here.

Grant Museum of Zoology

University College London, Rockefeller Building, 21 University Street, WC1E 6DE (3108 2052, www.ucl.ac.uk/culture/grant-museum). Goodge Street tube. **Open** *1-5pm Mon-Sat.* **Admission** *free.* **Map** *p194 L5.*

Now rehoused in a former Edwardian library belonging to University College, the Grant Museum retains the air of an avid Victorian collector's house, but visitors are engaged in dialogue about the distant evolutionary past via the most modern means available, including iPads and smartphones. The

museum's 67,000 specimens include the remains of many rare and extinct creatures, including skeletons of the dodo and the zebra-like quagga (which lived in South Africa and was hunted out of existence in the 1880s), as well as pure oddities, not least the jar of moles. Don't miss the Micrarium – a kind of booth walled with little illuminated microscope slides.

Museum of Comedy

The Undercroft, St George's Church, Bloomsbury Way, WC1A 2SR (7534 1744, www. museumofcomedy.com). Holborn tube. **Open** *1-10pm Mon-Fri; noon-10pm Sat; 4-10pm Sun.* **Admission** *free; show prices vary.* **Map** *p194 M6.*

The crypt below St George's Church in Bloomsbury is the unlikely location of the country's first museum dedicated to comedic artefacts. It's the brainchild of Martin Witts, owner of the Leicester Square Theatre. Over decades working alongside the heroes of British comedy, Witts has collected thousands of curiosities, including Tommy Cooper's magic props (all made by Cooper himself) and the Two Ronnies' glasses. These are on permanent display – along with temporary photographic exhibitions. Taking a charmingly old-school approach to interactivity, the museum has a portable TV on which you can watch, yes, videos of old comedy shows, as well as a record player for the collection of LPs. Attached to the museum, the Cooper Room is a 100-seat stand-up/theatre venue. And you can sup a lager (the comic's drink of choice) at the Comedians' Arms bar – itself an artefact, since the counter was recycled from Wilton's Music Hall (*see p367*).

♥ Novelty Automation

1A Princeton Street, WC1R 4AX (novelty-automation.com). Chancery Lane or Holborn tube. **Open** *Term time 11am-6pm Mon-Wed, Fri, Sat; noon-8pm Thur. School holidays daily; hours vary.* **Admission** *free; tokens £1 each.* **Map** *p194 N6.*

Want a divorce? Fancy a cheap holiday? Need to launder money or lose weight? All these things and many others can be achieved for the modest outlay of a pound (sometimes two) at the nutty slot machines of Novelty Automation in a small shabby space behind a Bloomsbury shopfront. Once displayed in the Cabaret Mechanical Theatre on the lower level of Covent Garden's Apple Market, these lovingly crafted moving sculptures are almost all the work of cartoonist Tim Hunkin. Highlights include Test Your Nerve – a slot machine that invites you to place your hand beneath the jowls of a huge, red-eyed, growling dog; and Microbreak, which

❤ British Museum

*Great Russell Street, WC1B 3DG (7323 8299, www.britishmuseum.org). Russell Square or Tottenham Court Road tube. **Galleries** 10am-5.30pm Mon-Thur, Sat, Sun; 10am-8.30pm Fri. **Great Court** 9am-6pm Mon-Thur, Sat, Sun; 9am-8.30pm Fri. Multimedia guides available 10am-4.30pm Thur, Sat, Sun; 10am-7.30pm Fri. **Admission** free; donations appreciated. Temporary exhibitions vary. Multimedia guides £7; £6 reductions. Eye Opener tours free. Highlights tours (Fri-Sun, 90mins) £12. **Map** p194 L6.*

Officially the country's most popular tourist attraction, with more than six million visitors a year, the British Museum opened in 1759. The first national museum to open to the public anywhere in the world was free to visit (and, since 2001, is so again) so that 'studious and curious persons' could pass through its doors and look upon strange objects collected from all over the globe.

It opened in Montagu House, which then occupied this site, but the current building is a neoclassical marvel built in 1847 by Robert Smirke, one of the pioneers of the Greek Revival style. In 2000, Lord Foster added a glass roof to the Great Court, now claimed to be 'the largest covered public square in Europe' and a popular public space ever since. This £100-million landmark surrounds the domed Reading Room, where Marx, Lenin, Dickens, Darwin, Hardy and Yeats once worked. (This was used by the British Library until its move to purpose-built quarters in King's Cross, *see p203*.) In 2014, the museum added a new building to its western corner, containing the Sainsbury Exhibitions Gallery, dedicated to the museum's fabulous, sell-out blockbuster shows, including Rodin & the Art of Ancient Greece in 2019. Previous exhibitions included a rare visit from China's Terracotta Army and an eye-opening tour of Ice Age art.

In the know
In translation

The Rosetta Stone (Room 1) is almost always invisible behind a crowd – head to the King's Library in the opposite wing and you can scrutinise a perfect replica at your leisure.

In the museum proper, star exhibits include ancient Egyptian artefacts – the Rosetta Stone on the ground floor, mummies upstairs – and Greek antiquities, including the marble friezes from the Parthenon known as the Elgin Marbles. Room 41 displays Anglo-Saxon artefacts, including the famous Sutton Hoo treasure. Also upstairs, the Celts gallery has Lindow Man, killed in 300 BC and so well preserved in peat you can see his beard, while the ground-floor Wellcome Gallery of Ethnography holds an Easter Island statue and regalia collected during Captain Cook's travels. The King's Library provides a calming home to a permanent exhibition entitled 'Enlightenment: Discovering the World in the 18th Century', a 5,000-piece collection devoted to the extraordinary formative period of the museum. The remit covers archaeology, science and the natural world; the objects displayed range from Indonesian puppets to a beautiful orrery (a mechanical solar system model).

You won't be able to see everything in one day, so, unless you plan on making several visits, use the worthwhile multimedia guide (which includes interactive maps as well as audio commentaries) to help you pick out the show-stoppers or to guide you around a particular area of the museum. There is also a host of trails, tours and talks to ensure you make the most of the overwhelming collection; check the website for details.

Lely's Venus

❤ Best overlooked artefacts

Assyrian lion hunt reliefs *Room 10a*
Created for the palace at Nineveh (in modern-day Iraq) in the mid seventh century BC.

Egyptian prosthetic toe *Room 63*
Made from wood and dating from the sixth century BC.

Helmet and crushed skull *Room 56*
From the ancient Mesopotamian city of Ur, c2,500 BC.

Marble horse *Room 21*
A fourth-century BC statue from the Mausoleum at Halikarnassos.

Three human figurines *Room 59*
From Bab edh-Dhra, near the Dead Sea, c3,000 BC.

Assyrian lion hunt reliefs

Living with Buildings, Wellcome Collection

simulates 'all the benefits of a holiday with none of the downsides' – you even get a hot blast of sun, courtesy of the lamp on top of the telly in front of you. Great fun.

Petrie Museum of Egyptian Archaeology

*University College London, Malet Place, WC1E 6BT (7679 2884, www.ucl.ac.uk/ culture/petrie-museum). Warren Street tube. **Open** 1-5pm Tue-Sat. **Admission** free; donations appreciated. **Map** p194 L5.*

The Petrie Museum of Egyptian Archaeology – set up in 1892 by eccentric traveller and diarist Amelia Edwards – is named after Flinders Petrie, tireless excavator of ancient Egypt. Where the British Museum's Egyptology collection is strong on the big stuff, the Petrie is an extraordinary selection of minutiae (amulets, pottery fragments, tools, weapons, weights and measures, stone vessels, jewellery), which provide an insight into how people lived and died in the Nile Valley. Highlights include colourful tiles, carvings and frescoes from heretic pharaoh Akhenaten's capital Tell el Amarna. The museum also has the world's largest collection of mummy portraits from the Roman period (first to second centuries AD). Computers offer 3D views of select objects from the 80,000-strong collection.

St George's Bloomsbury

*Bloomsbury Way, WC1A 2SA (7242 1979, www.stgeorgesbloomsbury.org.uk). Holborn or Tottenham Court Road tube. **Open** hours vary. Services 9am Tue, Thur; 9am, 1.10pm Wed, Fri; 10.30am Sun. **Admission** free. **Map** p194 M6.*

Consecrated in 1730, St George's is a grand and disturbing Nicholas Hawksmoor church, with an offset, stepped spire that was inspired by Pliny the Elder's account of the Mausoleum at Halicarnassus. Highlights include the mahogany reredos and sculptures of lions and unicorns clawing at the base of the steeple. The opening hours are erratic, but on Sundays, the church always remains open for visitors after the regular service. Do head down to the Undercroft for a compelling (and free) little exhibition on the building of the church above (as well as the Museum of Comedy, *see p197*), and check online for details of concerts.

♥ Wellcome Collection

*183 Euston Road, NW1 2BE (7611 2222, www. wellcomecollection.org). Euston Square tube or Euston tube/Overground. **Galleries** 10am-6pm Tue, Wed, Fri, Sat; 10am-10pm Thur; 11am-6pm Sun. **Library** 10am-6pm Mon-Wed, Fri; 10am-8pm Thur; 10am-4pm Sat. **Admission** free. **Map** p194 L5.*

Wellcome Collection is a free museum and library for the 'incurably curious'. Celebrating its tenth birthday in 2017, this gathering of international and medical oddities (Napoleon's toothbrush, Victorian amulets, Polynesian medical aids) is complemented by brilliant temporary exhibitions that explore art, health and what it means to be human. ('Bedlam' explored mental health and asylums; 'Teeth' focused on our pearly whites, from folk remedies to barber-surgeons). Over its first decade, the museum has grown to attract far more visitors than the original premises could cope with, so the ground-floor exhibition gallery, shop and café-restaurant, and well-displayed historic collection (Medicine Man) and science-themed contemporary art gallery (Medicine Now) upstairs have been enhanced by a typically ingenious adaptation. Connected to the lower floors with a showpiece spiral staircase, space has been found upstairs for a new restaurant, an extra gallery and the handsome Reading Room. The latter has a slightly studious air and a mezzanine stuffed with medical and scientific books, but it's a public space too, manned by explainers and librarians who can introduce you to historic artwork (some of it in boxes that must be opened with protective white gloves) and extraordinary artefacts (a dentist's workstation, a Smoky Sue Smokes for Two pregnancy doll). Fascinating interactives include the 'Virtual Autopsy' table – effectively a giant tablet where you can swipe cuts through 3D cadavers – and a replica of Freud's couch. Now with two temporary exhibition spaces and a compelling year-round programme of live events, Wellcome Collection is livelier than ever.

Restaurants

Lady Ottoline £££
11A Northington Street, WC1N 2JF (7831 0008, www.theladyottoline.net). Chancery Lane or Russell Square tube. **Open** *noon-11pm Mon-Sat; noon-5pm Sun. Food served noon-3pm, 6-9.45pm Mon-Sat; noon-4pm Sun.* **Map** *p194 N5* ⑬ *Gastropub*

This upmarket gastropub has a commitment to drink as well as food, with space for drinkers and a selection that runs from cocktails and real ales to a thoughtful wine list. Food is served in the ground-floor bar at the Lady Ottoline, but for a more sedate meal, it's best to dine in the pleasant first-floor room. The menu is a bit more adventurous than most – witness creamy rabbit pie with pomegranate salad.

Pubs & bars

Check out the fine cask beers at the historic **Museum Tavern** (49 Great Russell Street, 7242 8987, ⑥), opposite the British Museum. It actually pre-dated the museum as the Dog & Duck, but changed its name to cash in on the new institution in the 1760s.

All Star Lanes
Victoria House, Bloomsbury Place, WC1B 4DA (7025 2676, www.allstarlanes.co.uk). Holborn tube. **Open** *11am-11.30pm Mon-Wed; 11am-midnight Thur; 11am-2am Fri, Sat; 11am-10.30pm Sun.* **Map** *p194 M6* ①

Of Bloomsbury's two subterranean bowling dens, this is the one with aspirations. Walk past the lanes and smart, diner-style seating, and you'll find yourself in a comfortable, subdued side bar with chilled glasses, classy red furnishings, an unusual mix of bottled lagers and some impressive cocktails. There's an American menu and, at weekends, DJs. **Bloomsbury Bowling Lanes** (basement of Tavistock Hotel, Bedford Way, WC1H 9EU, 7183 1979, bloomsburybowling.com) offers a pints-and-worn-carpets take on the same game – as well as gigs and private karaoke booths.

Lamb
94 Lamb's Conduit Street, WC1N 3LZ (7405 0713, www.thelamblondon.com). Holborn or Russell Square tube. **Open** *11am-11pm Mon-Wed; 11am-midnight Thur-Sat; noon-10.30pm Sun. Food served noon-9.30pm daily.* **Map** *p194 N5* ⑤

The standard range of Young's beers is dispensed from a central horseshoe bar in this 300-year-old pub, around which are ringed original etched-glass snob screens, used to prevent Victorian gentlemen from being seen when liaising with 'women of dubious distinction'. A sunken back area gives access to a convenient square of summer patio.

Shops & services

♥ Blade Rubber Stamps
12 Bury Place, WC1A 2JL (7831 4123, www.bladerubberstamps.co.uk). Holborn or Tottenham Court Road tube. **Open** *10.30am-6pm Mon-Fri; noon-6pm Sat; 11.30am-4.30pm Sun.* **Map** *p194 M6* ① *Stationery*

Blade Rubber Stamps is a shrine to wooden-handled rubber stamps. Neatly stacked shelves display arty stamps depicting chandeliers, cityscapes, images of Henry VIII, London buses, *Alice in Wonderland* characters, cutesy puppies and telephone boxes. Handy potential purchases include homework stamps ('check spelling', 'keep trying') and adorable love-letter writing kits. Unmounted sheets of rubber stamps, ink pads in every shade, glitters, glues, stencils, stickers, sticks of sealing wax, and a range of magazines and books complete the stock.

♥ London Review Bookshop
14 Bury Place, WC1A 2JL (7269 9030, www.londonreviewbookshop.co.uk). Holborn or Tottenham Court Road tube. **Open** *10am-6.30pm Mon-Sat; noon-6pm Sun.* **Map** *p194 M6* ④ *Books*

From the inviting and stimulating presentation to the quality of the books selected, this is an inspiring bookshop. Politics, current affairs and history are well represented on the ground floor; downstairs, audio books lead on to exciting poetry and philosophy sections, everything you'd expect from a shop owned by the purveyor of long-form critical writing that is the *London Review of Books*. Browse through your purchases in the adjoining London Review Cakeshop.

Pentreath & Hall

17 Rugby Street, WC1N 3QT (7430 2526, www.pentreath-hall.com). Holborn tube. **Open** *11am-6pm Mon-Sat.* **Map** *p194 N5* ❺ *Homewares*

This petite store looks like the drawing room of a smart country house scaled to the size of a Shoreditch studio flat, scattered with beautifully made decorative artefacts and accessories such as watercolours above the mantelpiece, vintage maps and fine chinaware mugs. Alongside design and architecture books (Ben Pentreath is an architect), there's a notable range of découpage plates and trays from Bridie Hall (the designer is a joint owner of the shop) with designs from archival natural history and geographical sources.

Persephone Books

59 Lamb's Conduit Street, WC1N 3NB (7242 9292, www.persephonebooks.co.uk). Russell Square tube. **Open** *10am-6pm Mon-Fri; noon-5pm Sat.* **Map** *p194 N5* ❻ *Books*

Persephone Books independently publishes the works of 20th-century women writers (and a few men) in beautifully rendered publications. Pick from a range that includes Diana Athill's *Midsummer Night in the Warehouse*, a classic memoir about a failed love affair, or Virginia Woolf's *A Writer's Diary*. The shop itself spills over into the Persephone office at the back (or is it the other way around?), giving the store a slightly ramshackle, writer's room feel, with herbal tea and upscale literary chit-chat always seeming to be on the table.

Skoob

Unit 66, The Brunswick Centre, WC1N 1AE (7278 8760, www.skoob.com). Russell Square tube. **Open** *10.30am-8pm Mon-Sat; 10.30am-6pm Sun.* **Map** *p194 M5* ❼ *Books*

A back-to-basics basement beloved of students from the nearby University of London, Skoob showcases some 50,000 second-hand titles covering virtually every subject, from philosophy and biography to politics and the occult. Prices are reasonable, with discounts for students, but the organisational dial is set to browse rather than strict alphabetical efficiency.

KING'S CROSS & ST PANCRAS

▶ *King's Cross St Pancras tube/rail.*

North-east of Bloomsbury, King's Cross is becoming a major European transport hub, thanks to a £500-million makeover of the area. The renovated and restored **St Pancras International** was the key arrival, but neighbouring **King's Cross** station has since benefited with a handsomely restored 1851 façade overlooking a public square, nicely balancing the splendidly restored **Great Northern Hotel** (*see p400*), plus an expanded station concourse with snazzy cascading roof, much-improved restaurants and cafés, and – yes – a sawn-in-half luggage trolley that symbolises Harry Potter's **Platform 9¾**. If joining the queue for a photo-op doesn't satisfy your cravings, there are plenty of souvenirs in the **Harry Potter Shop** (3196 7375, www.harrypotterplatform934.com).

It's the area to the north that holds our attention, however. The King's Cross development has its own postcode, N1C, and is impressive in stats alone: 67 acres, 20 new streets, 1,900 new homes, three new bridges, ten new parks and squares, and 400 trees planted. The concept behind the numbers is interesting too. The developers have tried to create from scratch a 'mixed-use' development – one with the virtues of multiplicity and resilience normally found in communities that have grown up over time. To this end, they have paid careful attention to honouring the area's industrial heritage, to attracting a mix of residents, and to hosting the kind of events that might draw in visitors. So, heading north-east from the station, King's Boulevard leads directly over the Regent's Canal to **Granary Square**. Filled with choreographed fountains (1,080 water spouts, operating 8am-8pm daily, and lit in many colours at night), the square's terracing down to the canal is populated most sunny days. No wonder: there's a ready supply of students from UAL Central Saint Martins college of art, which in 2011 moved into the building behind – a sensitively and impressively converted, Grade II-listed 1850s granary. Fronting on to the square are restaurants and a café, with the **House of Illustration** tucked around the corner. From Wednesday to Friday, the square hosts **Kerb**, a regularly changing roster of street-food vendors. Adjacent to Granary Square is **Coal Drops Yard**, a complex of brick viaducts and warehouses built in the 1850s to handle the vast quantities of coal delivered to the capital. In the 1990s, the rundown site became the focus for London's rave scene. Following redevelopment by Heatherwick Studio, Coal Drops Yard reopened as a shopping and lifestyle district in October 2018, with enticing bars, restaurants and shops. There are more public spaces north and east of Coal Drops Yard, including **Gasholder Park**, created within the frame of one of the gasholders that once dominated the King's Cross skyline.

The development has given the area a sense of context and cohesion, meaning that the pioneering **Kings Place** arts complex (*see p355*) and old timers like the **London Canal Museum** and **St Pancras Old Church** no longer feel like isolated attractions.

Sights & museums

British Library
96 Euston Road, NW1 2DB (01937 546060, www.bl.uk). Euston or King's Cross St Pancras tube/rail. **Open** *9.30am-8pm Mon-Thur; 9.30am-6pm Fri; 9.30am-5pm Sat; 11am-5pm Sun.* **Admission** *free; donations appreciated.* **Map** *p194 L4.*

'One of the ugliest buildings in the world,' opined a parliamentary committee on the opening of the new British Library in 1997. But don't judge a book by its cover: the interior is a model of cool, spacious functionality, the collection is unmatched (150 million items and counting), and the reading rooms (open only to cardholders) are so popular that regular users complain that they can't find a seat. The focal point of the building is the King's Library, a six-storey glass-walled tower housing George III's collection, but the library's main treasures are on permanent display in the John Ritblat Gallery: the Lindisfarne Gospels, a Diamond Sutra from AD 868, original Beatles lyrics. There is also a great programme of temporary exhibitions and associated events: the Folio Society Gallery, a floor up from the entrance,

Coal Drops Yard

is free and hosts focused little shows based around key artefacts, while the engaging blockbuster shows to the left are ticketed but cover meaty themes such as sci-fi, Gothic literature, the 800th anniversary of Magna Carta and the English language itself.

Camley Street Natural Park
12 Camley Street, N1C 4PW (7833 2311, www. wildlondon.org.uk /reserves/camley-street-natural-park). King's Cross St Pancras tube/rail. Open 10am-5pm daily (closes at 4pm in winter). Admission free. Map p194 M3.

A small but thriving green space on the site of a former coal yard, Camley Street is London Wildlife Trust's flagship reserve. It hosts pond-dipping and nature-watching sessions for children, and its new visitor centre has a café and educational space.

Francis Crick Institute
1 Midland Road, NW1 1AT (3796 0000, www. crick.ac.uk). King's Cross St Pancras tube/rail. Open 10am-8pm Wed; 10am-4pm Thur-Sat. Admission free. Map p194 L3.

Come out of the eastern exit from St Pancras and, just north of the British Library (*see* p203), you'll see a 46ft (14m) sculpture of different triangles in weathered steel: this is *Paradigm*, by Conrad Shawcross. It marks the entrance to the Crick, an altar to biomedical research, where a crack team of around 1,500 scientists are dedicated to gaining a better understanding of disease. Completed in 2016, the building opened an exhibition space in 2017 where members of the public can learn about the cutting-edge work going on next door and the future of human health. A busy events programme includes 'Meet the Scientist' evenings.

House of Illustration
2 Granary Square, N1C 4BH (3696 2020, www.houseofillustration.org.uk). King's Cross St Pancras tube/rail. Open 10am-6pm Tue-Sun. Admission £7.50; £4-£5 reductions; family £18; free under-5s. Map p194 M3.

The world's first gallery dedicated to the art of illustration has demonstrations, talks, debates and hands-on workshops covering all aspects of illustration, from children's books and scabrous cartoons to advertising and animation, as well as a regular programme of temporary exhibitions, usually dedicated to a single illustrator: Quentin Blake, for instance, or EH Shepard, who drew the captivating pictures for *Winnie-the-Pooh*.

London Canal Museum
12-13 New Wharf Road, off Wharfdale Road, N1 9RT (7713 0836, www.canalmuseum.org. uk). King's Cross St Pancras tube/rail. Open
10am-4.30pm Tue-Sun (until 7.30pm 1st Thur of mth). Admission £5; £2.50-£4 reductions; family £12.50; free under-4s. Map p194 N3.

Housed on two floors of a former 19th-century ice warehouse, the London Canal Museum has a barge cabin to sit in and models of boats, but the displays on the history of the ice trade (photos and videos about ice-importer Carlo Gatti) are perhaps the most interesting. The canalside walk (download a free MP3 audio tour from the museum website) from Camden Town to the museum is lovely, and in summer don't miss the tours – organised by the museum – that explore dank Islington Tunnel, an otherwise inaccessible Victorian canal feature.

St Pancras International
Euston Road, N1C 4QP (7843 7688, www. stpancras.com). King's Cross St Pancras tube/rail. Open 24hrs daily. Admission free. Map p194 M4.

The redeveloped St Pancras station has become a destination in more ways than the obvious, now containing large sculptures, the self-proclaimed 'longest champagne bar in Europe', high-end boutiques – even a gastropub and farmers' market. But the new additions are mere window-dressing for the stunning original structures: famously, George Gilbert Scott's grandiloquent red-brick exterior (much of which is now the **St Pancras Renaissance hotel**), but even more impressively William Barlow's Victorian glass-and-iron roof to the train shed, a single span that is airy and light, as though he wished to create some kind of cathedral to 19th-century industry and transport.

St Pancras Old Church & St Pancras Gardens
Pancras Road, NW1 1UL (7424 0724, www.posp.co.uk/st-pancras-old-church). Mornington Crescent tube or King's Cross St Pancras tube/rail. Church & gardens 9am-dusk. Services times vary; check website for details. Admission free. Map p194 L3.

St Pancras Old Church has been ruined and rebuilt many times. The current structure is handsome, but it's the churchyard that delights. Among those buried here are writer William Godwin and his wife, Mary Wollstonecraft; over their grave, their daughter Mary Godwin (author of *Frankenstein*) declared her love for poet and future husband Percy Bysshe Shelley. Also here is the last resting place of Sir John Soane, one of only two Grade I-listed tombs (the other is that of Karl Marx, in Highgate Cemetery; *see* p249). Designed for his wife, the tomb's dome influenced Gilbert Scott's design for the classic red British phone box.

St Pancras Old Church & St Pancras Gardens

Restaurants

The new area behind King's Cross station is shaping up to be something of a gastronomic destination, with a host of restaurants along King's Boulevard, around Granary Square and in Coal Drops Yard. Check out Bombay-style **Dishoom** (5 Stable Street, www.dishoom.com, **5**; see p185); tapas star **Barrafina** (Coal Drops Yard, www.barrafina.co.uk, **1**; see p185), and Mexico-via-Bermondsey darling **Casa Pastor** (Coal Drops Yard, www.tacoselpastor.co.uk, **4**; see p92). The station forecourt and Granary Square also host street food vendors for lunches on the go.

♥ Caravan King's Cross ££
*Granary Building, 1 Granary Square, N1C 4AA (7101 7661, www.caravankingscross. co.uk). King's Cross St Pancras tube/rail. **Open** 8am-10.30pm Mon-Fri; 10am-10.30pm Sat; 10am-4pm Sun. **Map** p194 M3* **3** *Global*

This is an altogether bigger, more urbane operation than the original Caravan on Exmouth Market. The ethos is the same, however: welcoming staff and a menu of what they call 'well-travelled food'. Most are small plates – deep-fried duck egg with baba

ganoush, chorizo oil and crispy shallots, say, or grits, collard greens and brown shrimp butter – plus a few large plates and (at King's Cross only) a handful of first-class pizzas. Recent favourites include a naughty-but-nice crispy fried chicken with jerk mayo and pawpaw salsa. The setting, overlooking the fountains of Granary Square, is another plus, and there's a good range of drinks, including cocktails.

German Gymnasium ££-£££
*1 King's Boulevard, N1C 4BU (7287 8000, www.germangymnasium.com). King's Cross St Pancras tube/rail. **Open** 8am-11pm Mon-Fri; 10am-11pm Sat; 10am-10pm Sun. **Map** p194 M3* **7** *European*

England's first purpose-built gymnasium was constructed in 1865 for the German Gymnastics Society and hosted the indoor events at the Olympic Games in 1866. Today, the vast Victorian surroundings provide an inspired setting for three floors of stylish eating and drinking. There's an expansive Grand Café on the ground floor for poshed-up Germanic lunches (think beef broth with liver dumplings or schnitzel with lingonberry sauce); a sophisticated modern European restaurant on the first floor and glamorous cocktails in the Meister Bar. Going to the gym has never been more fun.

Kerb £
*Granary Square, NC1 (www.kerbfood.com/ kings-cross). King's Cross St Pancras tube/ rail. **Open** noon-2pm Wed-Fri. **Map** p194 M3* **11** *Street food*

Street food collective Kerb pitches up in various sites across London – and has led a peripatetic existence around King's Cross over the last several years. Now back on Granary Square, where it all began, traders

In the know
Ticking the Cross

For information about the area's ongoing development and some neat merchandise, visit the **King's Cross Visitor Centre** (Western Transit Shed, 11 Stable Street, N1C 4AB, 3479 1795, www.kingscross. co.uk/visitor-centre, 10am-5pm Mon-Fri; 10am-4pm Sat).

dish up some seriously tasty food to hundreds of hungry passers-by. The stalls rotate, so there's always something new to try, whether Sri Lankan *kothu roti* or barbecue ribs, houmous salads or black pudding rolls. The website has details of who's selling what on any particular day.

Pubs & bars
Booking Office
St Pancras Renaissance Hotel, Euston Road, NW1 2AR (7841 3540, www.stpancraslondon. com). King's Cross St Pancras tube/rail. **Open** *6.30am-midnight Mon-Wed; 6.30am-1am Thur-Sat; 7am-midnight Sun.* **Map** *p194 M4* ❸

Sit indoors at this smart cocktail bar and you'll gaze at Sir George Gilbert Scott's lofty interior, a stirring example of the Victorian architect's interpretation of Gothic revival. Outside, under spacious canopies, you'll have a nearly ceiling-level view of St Pancras International station. The cocktail list gives prominent place to traditional punches, served in mugs, but the list is a long one. Martinis are well made, and the Victorian Gimlet (vodka, lime juice and seasonal fresh fruit juice) is a wonderful and refreshing potion. Warning: the free bar snacks – coated peanuts – are dangerously addictive.

♥ Scottish Stores
2-4 Caledonian Road, N1 9DT (3384 6497, www.thescottishstores.co.uk). King's Cross St Pancras tube/rail. **Open** *noon-11pm Mon-Wed; noon-midnight Thur-Sat; noon-10.45pm Sun.* **Map** *p194 M4* ❼

Transformed from a seedy strip club into a handsome wood-panelled pub, the Scottish Stores is a reflection of the area's transformation from grotty to gleaming over the last decade or so. Run by a good old-fashioned gentleman, it specialises in interesting beers, such as the Basqueland Brewing Project IPA, as well as some more traditional draught options, all of which can be enjoyed out on the roof terrace – quite a find in this area.

♥ Spiritland
9-10 Stable Street, N1C 4AB (3319 0050, spiritland.com). King's Cross St Pancras tube/rail. **Open** *8am-midnight Mon, Tue; 8am-1am Wed-Fri; 10am-1am Sat; 10am-10pm Sun.* **Map** *p194 M2* ❽

A true labour of love, Spiritland (named after a surprisingly funky Elkie Brooks song) puts its audiophile sound system, robust decks and rotary DJ mixer centre stage. At its core, it's a bar and eatery on Granary Square. But the quality of record selectors that pass

through the space are on another level, and make it a truly rewarding destination for music lovers.

Shops & services
Coal Drops Yard (www.coaldropsyard. com) is the focus for retail therapy in this area, with posh shops like Cos, Rains, Aesop and sportswear specialist The Sports Edit all in residence.

FITZROVIA

▶ *Goodge Street or Tottenham Court Road tube.*

Squeezed in between Tottenham Court Road, Oxford Street, Great Portland Street and Euston Road, Fitzrovia isn't as famous as Bloomsbury, but its history is just as rich. The origins of the name are hazy: some believe it comes from **Fitzroy Square**, named after Henry Fitzroy (son of Charles II); others insist it's due to the famous **Fitzroy Tavern** (16 Charlotte Street, 7580 3714), focal venue for London bohemia of the 1930s and '40s and a favourite with the likes of Dylan Thomas and George Orwell. Fitzrovia also had its share of artists: James McNeill Whistler lived at 8 Fitzroy Square, later taken over by British Impressionist Walter Sickert, while Roger Fry's Omega Workshops, blurring the distinction between fine and decorative arts, had its studio at no.33. Fitzrovia's raffish image is largely a thing of the past, but a clutch of galleries – notably the likes of **Pilar Corrias** (54 Eastcastle Street, W1W 8EF, 7323 7000, www. pilarcorrias.com) – gives the district some artistic clout, even if local rents mean it will never again be home to the dissolute.

The district's icon is the **BT Tower**, completed in 1964 as the Post Office Tower. Its revolving restaurant and observation deck featured in any film that wanted to prove how much London was swinging (*Bedazzled* is just one example). The restaurant is now reserved for corporate functions, but Charlotte Street and neighbouring byways have plenty of good options for food and drink.

Sights & museums
All Saints
7 Margaret Street, W1W 8JG (7636 1788, www.allsaintsmargaretstreet.org.uk). Oxford Circus tube. **Open** *7am-7pm mon-Fri; 11am-7pm Sat. Services 7.30am, 8am, 1.10pm, 6pm, 6.30pm Mon-Fri; noon, 6pm, 6.30pm Sat; 8am, 11am, 5.15pm, 6pm Sun.* **Admission** *free.* **Map** *p194 K6.*

Providing respite from the tumult of Oxford Street, this 1850s church was designed by William Butterfield, one of the great exponents of the Victorian Gothic revival. The church looks as if it has been lowered on to its tiny site, so tight is the fit; its lofty spire is the second-highest in London. Behind the polychromatic brick façade, the lavish interior is one of the capital's finest, with luxurious marble, flamboyant tile work and glittering stones built into its pillars.

Cartoon Museum

63 Wells Street, W1T 3PT (www. cartoonmuseum.org). Oxford Circus/ Tottenham Court Road tube. **Open** *10.30am-5.30pm Tue-Sun; late opening Thur.* **Admission** *£7; free under 18s.* **Map** *p194 K6.*

The best of British cartoon art is displayed here. The displays start in the early 18th century, when high-society types back from the Grand Tour introduced the Italian practice of caricatura to polite company. From Hogarth, it moves through Britain's cartooning 'golden age' (1770-1830) to examples of wartime cartoons, ending up with modern satirists such as Gerald Scarfe and the wonderfully loopy Ralph Steadman. There's also original 1921 Rupert Bear artwork by Mary Tourtel, Frank Hampson's Dan Dare, Leo Baxendale's Bash Street Kids and a painted Asterix cover by that well-known Briton, Albert Uderzo. The museum hosts numerous events and workshops throughout the year; check the website for details.

Pollock's Toy Museum

1 Scala Street, W1T 2HL (7636 3452, www. pollockstoys.com). Goodge Street tube. **Open** *10am-5pm Mon-Sat.* **Admission** *£7; £4-£6 reductions; free under-3s.* **Map** *p194 K6.*

Named after Victorian toy theatre printer Benjamin Pollock, this place is in turns beguiling and creepy, a nostalgia-fest of old board games, tin trains, porcelain dolls and gollies. It is fascinating for adults but less so for children: describing a pile of painted woodblocks in a cardboard box as a 'Build a skyscraper' kit may make them feel lucky to be going home to *Minecraft*. Having said that, the Pollock's Toy Museum shop is good for wind-up toys and other funny little gifts for children.

Restaurants

Need a pizza fix? Go for a wood-fired slice of delight at **Homeslice** (52 Wells Street, W1T 3PR, 3151 9273, www.homeslicepizza.co.uk, £ ⑧) or join the feeding frenzy at budget-fave **Icco** (46 Goodge Street, W1T 4LU, 7580 9688, www.icco.co.uk, £ ⑩).

Berners Tavern £££

10 Berners Street, W1T 3NP (7908 7979, www.bernerstavern.com). Oxford Circus or Tottenham Court Road tube. **Open** *7-10.30am, noon-midnight Mon-Fri; 7-10.30am, noon-4pm, 5pm-midnight Sat, Sun.* **Map** *p194 K6* ❷ *Modern European*

The huge lobby bar of the London Edition hotel (*see p400*) looks fabulous, but the vast dining room, with its ornate plasterwork, framed pictures and lively bar area, looks even better. Food is playful and appealing: tender pork belly with capers, golden raisins and apple coleslaw, and cod with fennel and cider sauce, are sublime. Any caveats? Sometimes dizzy service; frequent upselling of extras; and lighting so low it's hard to read the menu. But Berners Tavern is glamtastic. Wear your best threads, and book ahead for a preliminary cocktail in the candle-lit **Punch Room** bar (7781 0000, www.editionhotels. com/london) – at the back of the hotel.

Ethos £

48 Eastcastle Street, W1W 8DX (3581 1538, ethosfoods.com). Oxford Circus or Tottenham Court Road tube. **Open** *8-11am, noon-10pm Mon-Fri; 11.30am-10pm Sat; 11am-5pm Sun.* **Map** *p194 K7* ❻ *Vegetarian*

Ethos is a vegetarian, self-serve buffet, where you pay for your food by its weight. It opens early in the day with a short breakfast menu (avocado on toast, fruit salad, granola, porridge), then rolls on through to lunch and dinner with dishes with a pretty broad global range. Although it's most popular as a midday spot, the drinks list (three beers and a dozen wines) and the rarity of affordable vegetarian eateries in the West End mean it's also a good dinner destination.

♥ Honey & Co £

25A Warren Street, W1T 5LZ (7388 6175, honeyandco.co.uk). Warren Street tube. **Open** *8am-10.30pm Mon-Fri; 9.30am-10.30pm Sat.* **Map** *p194 K5* ❾ *Middle Eastern*

A bijou delight, with small tables and chairs packed closely together. The kitchen is run by an accomplished Israeli husband-and-wife team. This pedigree shines in a daily-changing menu that draws influences from across the Middle East. The meze selection includes fabulously spongy, oily bread, sumac-spiked tahini, smoky taramasalata, crisp courgette croquettes with *labneh*, pan-fried feta and a bright salad with lemon and radishes. A main might be a whole baby chicken with lemon and a chilli and walnut *muhamara* paste. It's imaginative home-style cooking, and service is charming.

Berners Tavern p207

Koba ££

11 Rathbone Street, W1T 1NA (7580 8825, www.kobalondon.com). Goodge Street or Tottenham Court Road tube. **Open** *noon-2.45pm, 5.30-10.45pm Mon-Sat; noon-2.45pm, 5.30-10pm Sun.* **Map** *p194 K6* ⑫
Korean

Koba is one of the strongest players on the West End Korean scene. Barbecue meats such as beef *kalbi* or *bulgogi* are well marinated, and grilled at the table by efficient staff. Barbecued squid is fresh as a daisy, with just the right amount of tongue-tingling heat in the vibrant red sauce. Stews make a sound choice too, with umami-rich stocks and accompanying bowls of pearly rice. Service is polished but not too formal, and the dark, modern, east Asian meets industrial, interior is slick. Drinks include Korean beers, *soju* and a short wine list.

Lantana £

13 Charlotte Place, W1T 1SN (7637 3347, www.lantanacafe.co.uk). Goodge Street tube. **Open** *8am-6pm Mon-Fri (kitchen closes 3.30pm); 9am-5pm Sat, Sun (kitchen closes 4pm).* **Map** *p194 K6* ⑭ *Café*

Lantana is a lively spot. Its look – wooden tables, mismatched chairs, small pieces of art on white walls – is now commonplace, but the staff pride themselves on their coffee-making and baking skills, and rightly so. The flat whites are super-smooth and go well with a moist raspberry friand or an Aussie 'cherry ripe' cake slice. The breakfast

and brunch menu includes the likes of maple French toast with streaky bacon, grilled banana and candied pecans. Savoury dishes can be ordered with a glass of wine. The kiosk next door sells some dishes as takeaways.

Lima London ££

31 Rathbone Place, W1T 1JH (3002 2640, www.limalondongroup.com/fitzrovia). Tottenham Court Road tube. **Open** *noon-2.30pm, 5.30-10.30pm Mon-Sat; noon-2.30pm, 5.30-9.30pm Sun.* **Map** *p194 L6* ⑮ *Peruvian*

Part of the 'Peruvian wave' of restaurants that hit the capital back in 2012, Lima London pitched itself squarely at the high end. The modish rear dining room mixes the hum of low-level beats with polite chatter. Well-drilled staff bring out a medley of carefully crafted small plates, the likes of sea bream ceviche flecked with hot *aji limo* chilli and pieces of roasted corn, and thick wedges of suckling pig – part dense meat, part salty, crispy crackling – matched by a rough corn mash spiked with two kinds of peppers.

♥ Portland £££

113 Great Portland Street, W1W 6QQ (7436 3261, portlandrestaurant.co.uk). Oxford Circus tube. **Open** *6-10pm Mon, Tue; noon-2.30pm, 6-10pm Wed-Sat.* **Map** *p194 J6* ⑯ *Contemporary European*

It is rare to go to a restaurant and be astonished, but chef Merlin Labron-Johnson cooks like a wizard. Favourite dishes include pig's head croquettes, aged mimolet cheese and granola, or pickled shiitake mushrooms. Desserts – such as 'chocolate bar, peanut butter praline, peanut ice-cream' – are skilfully executed and the wine list is short but imaginative. It's a small, bare-wood, no-frills kind of place, but it's very attractive and the flavours are sensational.

♥ Roka ££££

*37 Charlotte Street, W1T 1RR (7580 6464, www.rokarestaurant.com). Goodge Street or Tottenham Court Road tube. **Open** noon-3.30pm, 5.30-11.30pm Mon-Fri; 12.30-4pm, 5.30-11.30pm Sat; 12.30-4pm, 5.30-10.30pm Sun. **Map** p194 K6* 🟠 *Japanese*

Roka gets top marks for glitz and glamour. Much of the action takes place at the central robata grill, where a repertoire of contemporary *izakaya*-inspired food is created in full view. The 13-course tasting menu is popular with first-time diners, taking them on a spin of the best Roka has to offer: elegant dishes such as hand-made *kimchi*, sashimi and sticky skewers of *tebasaki* (chicken wings) are finished off with a trio of desserts, featuring delights such as Pocky-style chocolate and sesame biscuit sticks. It isn't cheap, but each dish is impeccable.

Pubs & bars

Barrica

*62 Goodge Street, W1T 4NE (7436 9448, www.barrica.co.uk). Goodge Street or Tottenham Court Road tube. **Open** noon-3pm, 5.30-10.30pm Mon-Fri; noon-10.30pm Sat. **Map** p194 K6* 🟠

With its canary-yellow walls, rich wood and marble, Barrica is a little taste of laidback Spain in the busy West End. The speciality? Sherry: a selection of over 20, from the intensely sweet to the bone-dry and salty. There are also around 100 wines, selected by the bar's oenophile owner. It's not just about the impressive alcohol offerings, though: be sure to try a few dishes off the brilliant tapas menu too.

♥ Bradley's Spanish Bar

*42-44 Hanway Street, W1T 1UT (7636 0359, www.bradleysspanishbar.com). Tottenham Court Road tube. **Open** noon-11.30pm Mon-Thur; noon-midnight Fri, Sat; 1-10.30pm Sun. **Map** p194 L7* 🟠

There's something of the Barcelona dive bar about this place, with San Miguel or Cruzcampo on draught, but Bradley's isn't really very Spanish. In fact, it's not even a bar. Bradley's is definitely a pub, and with its jumble sale decor and tattered furniture,

it sure puts the 'shabby' in 'shabby chic'. But don't be put off: Londoners love Bradley's for its low-key and unpretentious vibe and shoppers and foreign exchange students fill the cramped two-floor space. After all, there's a good jukebox (playing vinyl, retro fans) and a good atmosphere – what more could anyone want?

Shops & services

The electronics shops that once congregated at the south end of Tottenham Court Road have pretty much vanished, but the rebirth of little-loved Tottenham Court Road tube as a Crossrail station is driving a minor revival north of the previously scruffy end of Oxford Street.

Heal's

*196 Tottenham Court Road, W1T 7LQ (7636 1666, www.heals.com). Goodge Street tube. **Open** 10am-7pm Mon-Wed, Fri, Sat; 10am-8pm Thur; noon-6pm Sun. **Map** p194 L6* 🟠 *Homewares*

Heal's may be the grand old dame of interiors stores, on this site since 1840, but its commitment to sourcing new designers is impressive. Established names such as Orla Kiely, Clarissa Hulse and LSA are also well represented among the mirrors, rugs, bed linen, clocks, cushions, art and photography. The ground floor has a cornucopia of kitchenware and gift items, plus a terrific lighting department with such delights as Tom Dixon's Beat pendant shades. Most of the furniture is upstairs, and for midcentury modern fans, there's a great selection of vintage Danish makes. Don't miss the Ambrose Café upstairs - it's quiet, comfortable and the perfect place to pause before you splurge on that £3,000 sofa.

♥ Lewis Leathers

*Mottram House, 3-5 Whitfield Street, W1T 2SA (7636 4314, www.lewisleathers.com). Tottenham Court Road tube. **Open** 11am-6pm Mon-Sat. **Map** p194 L6* 🟠 *Fashion*

It's the heritage leather biker brand that boasts Cara Delevigne and Kate Moss as customers. Established in 1892, the history of Lewis Leathers is plastered on the wall in nostalgic posters from TT racer days of the 1920s through to the '70s. Here, you can pick and choose from a wide range of leather goods, whether it's a classic racer jacket, trousers, a studded belt or some seriously sleek heeled boots. The shop also stocks a variety of denim, T-shirts, sneakers, goggles and even books, including its current issue of Nick Clements' *Men's File Archive*. Of course, quality leather like this costs (jackets retail at upwards of £600).

The City

The City's current fame as the financial heart of London does no justice to its 2,000-year history. Here – on top of a much more ancient ritual landscape – the Romans founded the city they called Londinium, building a bridge to the west of today's London Bridge. They left a forum-basilica, an amphitheatre, public baths and the defensive wall that still defines what we now call the Square Mile (an area, in fact, of 1.21 square miles).

Although the City has just over 9,000 residents, 330,000 people arrive each weekday to work as bankers, lawyers and traders, taking over 85 million square feet (nearly eight million square metres) of office space. Tourists come, too, to see St Paul's Cathedral, the Tower of London and the Museum of London. There is much else besides: no area of London offers quite so much in so small a space. Roman ruins? Medieval churches? Iconic 21st-century towers? You've come to the right place.

We begin this chapter with a couple of rather more lived-in adjuncts on the western border of the City proper. Holborn is a half-way house in terms of both geography and atmosphere between the City and Bloomsbury, while Clerkenwell has some of London's best places to eat and drink.

♥ **Don't miss**

1 St Paul's Cathedral *p224*
Sir Christopher Wren's masterpiece.

2 Tower of London *p234*
Crown Jewels, Beefeaters, armour: a historic attraction par excellence.

3 Sir John Soane's Museum *p215*
Architect and antiquarian's former home, packed with art, furniture and ornaments.

4 Sky Garden *p236*
London's best view? Head up 20 Fenchurch Street.

5 Museum of London *p227*
Life in the city from prehistory to the present.

6 Postal Museum & Mail Rail *p217*
Take an atmospheric journey on the capital's underground postal service.

7 Barbican Centre *p227*
Art, film, plays and concerts amid 1970s brutalist architecture.

St Paul's Cathedral *p224*

THE CITY

Restaurants

① Bad Egg *p229*
② Café Sou *p224*
③ Chiswell Street Dining Rooms *p229*
④ City Càphê *p232*
⑤ The Coach *p217*
⑥ Duck & Waffle *p237*
⑦ Eagle *p218*
⑧ Exmouth Market *p218*
⑨ Jugged Hare *p229*
⑩ Look Mum No Hands *p218*
⑪ Modern Pantry *p218*
⑫ Moro *p219*
⑬ St John *p219*
⑭ Sweetings *p226*

Pubs & bars

① Blackfriar *p222*
② Black Rock *p229*
③ Café Kick *p219*
④ City Social Bar *p237*
⑤ Draft House *p237*
⑥ Jerusalem Tavern *p219*
⑦ Ye Olde Mitre *p216*
⑧ Oriole *p229*
⑨ Princess Louise *p216*
⑩ ZTH Cocktail Lounge *p219*

Shops & services

① One New Change *p226*
② Royal Exchange *p232*

HOLBORN

▶ *Holborn tube.*

A sharp left turn out of Holborn tube on to Kingsway and then another left leads to the unexpectedly lovely **Lincoln's Inn Fields**. Surely London's largest square (indeed, it's more of a park), it's blessed with gnarled oaks casting dappled shade over a tired bandstand. On the south side of the square, the neoclassical façade of the Royal College of Surgeons hides the **Hunterian Museum** (35-43 Lincoln's Inn Fields, WC2A 3PE (7869 6560, www.rcseng.ac.uk/museums), a fascinating collection of grisly artefacts including half of Charles Babbage's brain and Churchill's dentures, sadly closed for redevelopment until 2021. Facing it from the north is the equally curious **Sir John Soane's Museum**.

East of the square lies **Lincoln's Inn** (7405 1393, www.lincolnsinn.org.uk), one of the city's four Inns of Court. Its grounds are open to the public, with an odd mix of Gothic, Tudor and Palladian buildings. On nearby Portsmouth Street lies the **Old Curiosity Shop** (nos.13-14, WC2A 2ES, 7405 9891, www.the-old-curiosity-shop.com), its timbers apparently known to Dickens, but now selling decidedly modern shoes. Gray's Inn Road runs north from Holborn alongside the sculpted gardens at **Gray's Inn** (7458 7800, www.graysinn.org.uk). Known as the Walks, they date to 1606 and are open noon-2.30pm weekdays.

Opened in 1876 on Chancery Lane as a series of strongrooms in which the upper classes could secure their valuables, the **London Silver Vaults** (7242 3844, www.thesilvervaults.com) are now a hive of dealers buying, selling and repairing silverware. There are also glittering displays on **Hatton Garden**, the city's jewellery and diamond centre – which suffered a dramatic heist in 2015. It's no distance to walk but a million miles in nature from the Cockney fruit stalls and sock merchants of the market on **Leather Lane** (10am-2pm Mon-Fri).

Further on is **Ely Place**, its postcode absent from the street sign as a result of it not falling under the jurisdiction of the City of London; instead, it is a private road with its own beadles to police it. The church garden of ancient **St Etheldreda** produced strawberries so delicious that they made the pages of Shakespeare's *Richard III*; a celebratory Strawberrie Fayre is still held on the street each June. The 16th-century **Ye Olde Mitre** is one of the city's most atmospheric pubs, hidden down a barely marked alley.

Sights & museums

St Etheldreda

14 Ely Place, EC1N 6RY (7405 1061, www. stetheldreda.com). Chancery Lane tube. **Open** *8am-5pm Mon-Sat; 8am-12.30pm Sun.* **Admission** *free; donations appreciated.* **Map** *p212 O6.*

Dedicated to the saintly seventh-century Queen of Northumbria, this is Britain's oldest Catholic church and London's only surviving example of 13th-century Gothic architecture; it was saved from the Great Fire by a change in the wind. The crypt is darkly atmospheric, untouched by traffic noise, and the stained glass (actually from the 1960s) is stunning. It's a peaceful place.

♥ Time to eat & drink

Best boozers
Jerusalem Tavern *p219*, Princess Louise *p216*

Fabulous fusion
Modern Pantry *p218*

Food that's Moorish
Moro *p219*

Highly inventive cocktails
ZTH Cocktail Lounge *p219*

Modern British
St John *p219*

Sky-high breakfasts
Duck & Waffle *p237*

Whisky from an oak
Black Rock *p229*

In the know
Getting started

Newcomers to the City are advised to head straight to **St Paul's** (see *p224*), not just for the beauty of the architecture, but because the spiky-roofed **City of London Information Centre** (7332 3456, www.cityoflondon.gov.uk) is there, on the river side of the cathedral. Open daily (9.30am-5.30pm Mon-Sat; 10am-4pm Sun), it has information on sights, events, walks and talks, as well as offering tours with specialist guides, and has free Wi-Fi.

💜 Sir John Soane's Museum

13 Lincoln's Inn Fields, WC2A 3BP (7405 2107, www.soane.org). Holborn tube. **Open** *10am-5pm Wed-Sun.* **Admission** *free; donations appreciated. Tours £12.50-£15.* **Map** *p212 N6.*

When he wasn't designing notable buildings (among them the original Bank of England), Sir John Soane (1753-1837) obsessively collected art, furniture and architectural ornamentation. In the 19th century, he turned his house into a museum to which, he said, 'amateurs and students' should have access. The result is this perfectly amazing place.

The modest rooms were modified by Soane with ingenious devices to channel and direct daylight, and to expand space, including walls that fold out to display paintings by Canaletto, Turner and Hogarth. The Tivoli Recess – the city's first gallery of contemporary sculpture, with a stained-glass window and plaster sunbursts – has been restored, and further stained glass illuminates a bust of Shakespeare. The Breakfast Room has a beautiful domed ceiling, inset with convex mirrors, while the Monument Court contains a sarcophagus of alabaster, so fine that it's almost translucent, that was carved for the pharaoh Seti I (1291-78 BC) and discovered in the Valley of the Kings. There are also numerous examples of Soane's eccentricity, not least the cell for his imaginary monk 'Padre Giovanni'.

In 2016, the museum completed a £7-million project to restore previously unseen parts of the building and to create a new shop, exhibition gallery and flexible space for displays and events. The second-floor Model Room holds Britain's largest collection of historical architectural models.

Formerly a treasured secret of the cognoscenti, the museum now welcomes 93,000 people a year: arrive early and expect to queue – but you won't regret it. For details of open evenings, tours and other special events, see the website.

In the know
When to visit the City

To understand the City properly, visit on a weekday when the great economic machine is running at full tilt and the commuter is king. Despite efforts by the City authorities to improve the district's prospects as a weekend leisure destination, many of the streets still fall eerily quiet on Saturday and Sunday. If you do visit at the weekend, try the Cheapside shops; take in the view from one of the growing number of skyscrapers; drop in on the always wonderful **Museum of London** (*see p227*); or just do as a discerning minority of locals do – potter about the place's odd nooks and crannies, from unexpected parks to disregarded churches.

Sir John Soane's Museum

Restaurants

Leather Lane has daytime street food and good coffee bars: **Department of Coffee & Social Affairs** (nos.14-16, EC1N 7SU, www.departmentofcoffee.com) and **Prufrock Coffee** (nos.23-25, EC1N 7TE, 7242 0467, www.prufrockcoffee.com), while **Catalyst** is on parallel Gray's Inn Road (no.48, WC1X 8LT, www.catalyst.cafe).

Pubs & bars

Ye Olde Mitre

1 Ely Court, Ely Place, EC1N 6SJ (7405 4751, www.yeoldemitreholborn.co.uk). Farringdon tube/rail. **Open** *11am-11pm Mon-Fri. Food served 11.30am-9.30pm Mon-Fri.* **Map** *p212 O6* ⑦

Largely due to its location – down a barely marked alley between Hatton Garden's jewellers and Ely Place – this little traditional pub, the foundation of which dates to 1546, is a favourite of 'secret London' lists. There's always a good range of ales on offer at the tiny central bar, but people come for the atmosphere: lots of cosy dark wood and some overlooked curiosities, such as the tree in the front bar. It's a cherry tree that Good Queen Bess is said to have danced around, but now supports a corner of the bar.

❤ Princess Louise

208 High Holborn, WC1V 7EP (7405 8816, princesslouisepub.co.uk). Holborn tube. **Open** *11am-11pm Mon-Fri; noon-11pm Sat; noon-6.45pm Sun. Food served noon-2.30pm, 6-8.30pm Mon-Thur; noon-2.30pm Fri.* **Map** *p212 M6* ⑨

With its magnificent Victorian interior restored to its former glory by the Sam Smith's Brewery, the old Louise oozes charm. The ground-floor saloon is spectacularly ornate with etched glass, mirrors, buffed wood panelling and a warren of Victorian frosted-glass booths, each with direct access to the bar. An open fire completes the atmosphere. While the pub is busiest at weekends, a preponderance of stools and bright lighting give the Princess a post-work rather than pre-night-out vibe.

CLERKENWELL & FARRINGDON

▶ *Farringdon tube/rail.*

Few places encapsulate London's capacity for reinvention quite like Clerkenwell, an erstwhile religious centre that takes its name from the parish clerks who once performed Biblical mystery plays on its streets. The most lasting holy legacy is that of the 11th-century knights of the Order of St John; the remains of their priory can still be seen at St John's Gate, a crenellated gatehouse that dates from 1504 and is home to the **Museum of the Order of St John**. For a little peace and quiet, stroll by the Charterhouse in Charterhouse Square. This Carthusian monastery, founded in 1370, is now Anglican almshouses which retain the original 14th-century chapel and a 17th-century library. In 2017 it opened to the public for the first time, as **Revealing the Charterhouse**.

By the 17th century, Clerkenwell was a fashionable locale, but the Industrial Revolution soon buried it under warehouses and factories. Printing houses were established, and the district gained a reputation as a safe haven for radicals, from 15th-century Lollards to 19th-century Chartists. In 1903, Lenin is believed to have met Stalin for a drink in what is now the **Crown Tavern** (43 Clerkenwell Green, EC1R 0EG, 7253 4973, www.thecrowntavernec1. co.uk), one year after moving the publication of the newspaper *Iskra* to no.37A (now the **Marx Memorial Library**; 7253 1485, www.marx-memorial-library.org).

Industrial dereliction and decay were the theme until property development in the 1980s and '90s turned Clerkenwell into a desirable area to live in and visit. The process was aided by a slew of artfully distressed gastropubs (following the lead of the **Eagle**), and the food stalls, fashion boutiques, restaurants and bars along the colourful strip of **Exmouth Market**. The area became one of London's dining powerhouses, with **St John** the acknowledged pioneer of modern British cuisine – reviving the taste for unfavoured cuts of meat and offal under the catchy motto of 'nose-to-tail eating'.

Sights & museums

Islington Museum

245 St John Street, beneath Finsbury Library, EC1V 4NB (7527 2837, www.islington.gov.uk). Angel tube. **Open** *10am-5pm Mon, Tue, Thur-Sat.* **Admission** *free.* **Map** *p212 P4.*

The museum covers local history and the political and ethical credentials of the borough, exemplified by local residents such as reformist preacher John Wesley, playwright Joe Orton and eminent feminist Mary Wollstonecraft.

Museum of the Order of St John

*St John's Gate, St John's Lane, EC1M 4DA (7324 4005, www.museumstjohn.org. uk). Farringdon tube/rail. **Open** Oct-June 10am-5pm Mon-Sat. July-Sept 10am-5pm daily. Tours 11am, 2.30pm Tue, Fri, Sat. **Admission** free. Suggested donation £5; £4 reductions. Tours free. **Map** p212 P5.*

Now best known for its ambulance service, the Order of St John's roots lie in Christian medical practices from the Crusades of the 11th to 13th centuries. Artefacts related to the Order of Hospitaller Knights, from Jerusalem, Malta and the Ottoman Empire, are displayed (among them Caravaggio's *The Cardsharps*); there's a separate collection relating to the ambulance service. A major refurbishment has reorganised the galleries in the Tudor gatehouse and, across St John's Square, opened to the public the Priory Church (10.30am-12.30pm, 2-4pm, by prior arrangement), its secluded garden and the pleasingly gloomy 12th-century crypt.

♥ Postal Museum & Mail Rail

*Phoenix Place, WC1X 0DA (www. postalmuseum.org). Russell Square tube or Farringdon tube/rail. **Open** 10am-5pm daily. **Admission** £17.05; £10.45-£15.40 reductions (incl donation). Family play area (45min session) £5; £1.50 with Mail Rail ticket. **Map** p212 N5.*

One hundred years ago, the Post Office built a secret railway under central London. Stretching six-and-a-half miles from Paddington to Whitechapel and linking post offices across the city, the driverless electric line carried up to four million letters a day. But in 2003, after 75 years of service, this wonder of engineering was shut down. The postmen left and the tunnels fell silent. Since autumn 2018, the Mail Rail has been back in service – but this time two battery-powered trains take passengers rather than letters through the tunnels as part of the revamped Postal Museum. The museum charts 500 years of the pioneering British postal service. It's got original Penny Black stamps, pneumatic tubes, a superb kids' play area called Sorted! and a nifty five-wheeled post bike that wouldn't look out of place on the streets of Shoreditch. But the main event is across the street at the old Mail Rail engineering depot, where you can hop on board for a 15-minute journey that's deeper than the tube. You'll learn what it took to make London's post arrive on time, hear about the men who spent their lives down here, and see the roof of the interwar tunnel passing inches above your head.

Revealing the Charterhouse

*Charterhouse Square, EC1M 6AN (3818 8873, www.thecharterhouse.org). Barbican tube. **Open** 11am-5.20pm Tue-Sun. Standard tour 11.30am, noon, 2pm Tue-Sat; 2pm, 3.15pm Sun. Brother's tour 2.15pm Tue-Thur, Sat, Sun. **Admission** free. Tours £10-£15. **Map** p212 P6.*

This tiny museum documents the history of the Charterhouse from the Black Death to the present day – or, more accurately, from the present day to the Black Death, since the chronology runs backwards, from details of the lives of some of the Brothers who still live in these almshouses, past some neat artefacts – not least a sacred statue recut into the shape of a brick that was built into a wall after the 16th-century Dissolution of the Monasteries – to the touchingly displayed skeleton of a victim of that most deadly mid 13th-century plague. Be sure to drop into the chapel (past a plaque dedicated the author William Thackeray), where an old wooden door – half burnt down – records how close the Charterhouse came to destruction in the Blitz. The tours last an hour (two hours if you opt for one led by a Brother) and are well worth the money: not only do you hear the whole history of the place, but you get access to private areas of the Charterhouse – such as the Great Hall and the solitary monks' cells, complete with hatch by the main door where food came in and, er, rubbish came out.

Restaurants

The Coach ££-£££

*26-28 Ray Street, EC1R 3DJ (3954 1595, thecoachclerkenwell.co.uk). Farringdon tube/ rail. **Open** 7.30am-11pm Mon-Fri; 11am-11pm Sat; noon-10pm Sun. **Map** p212 O5* ⑤
Gastropub

This former Victorian pub still has a bar area, albeit one decked out like the lounge of a gentlemen's club, but the focus here is on eating, rather than boozing. The elegant dining room is the perfect backdrop for a menu created by the mighty Henry Harris, formerly of upmarket Knightsbridge bistro Racine. It's a line-up of rustic Gallic food plus a few trad Brit faves, including rare carnivore treats such as buttery calves' brains, served with vinegary capers and flecks of fresh parsley. A leg of rabbit is accompanied by brittle rashers of smoked bacon and a wee jug of creamy, mustard-spiked sauce. This is timeless food, for a chilled-out crowd, in a lovely spot.

Eagle ££

159 Farringdon Road, EC1R 3AL (7837 1353, www.theeaglefarringdon.co.uk). Farringdon tube/rail. **Open** *noon-11pm Mon-Sat; noon-5pm Sun. Food served noon-3pm, 6.30-10.30pm Mon-Fri; 12.30-3.30pm, 6.30-10.30pm Sat; 12.30-4pm Sun.* **Map** *p212 O5* ❼ *Gastropub*

Widely credited with launching the revolutionary notion of serving restaurant-quality food in a boozer when it opened in its current form in 1991, the Eagle has long since passed into both legend and middle age. But this high-ceilinged corner room remains a cut above the gastropub competition. Globetrotting mains are chalked twice daily above the bar/open kitchen. You can just drink but few do, aware they're missing the big-flavoured likes of moreish tomato and bread soup; a classic steak sandwich; and succulent leg of lamb with jansson's temptation (a potato gratin-style Swedish dish).

Exmouth Market £

Exmouth Market, EC1 (www.exmouth-market.com). Farringdon tube/rail. **Open** *noon-3pm Mon-Fri.* **Map** *p212 O5* ❽ *Street food*

On weekdays the stalls here serve takeaway food in sufficient variety to compete with the street's permanent eateries. Regular attendees include Spinach & Agushi, with their Ghanaian stews, Pasean pastas, Mac &

Cheese, Meat Head BBQ, Spanish dishes from La Cochinita, and Freebird burritos.

Look Mum No Hands £

49 Old Street, EC1V 9HX (7253 1025, www.lookmumnohands.com). Barbican tube or Old Street tube/rail. **Open** *7.30am-10pm Mon-Fri; 8.30am-6pm Sat; 9am-6pm Sun.* **Map** *p212 Q5* ❿ *Café*

Look Mum is a cycle-friendly café-bar with cycle parking in a courtyard, a small workshop and plenty of space to hang out, snack, use the Wi-Fi and – in the evenings – drink bottled beer or well-priced wine. Live afternoon screenings of cycle races take place in the big main room. The food is simple: expect cured meat platters, baked tarts, pastries and cakes.

♥ Modern Pantry £££

47-48 St John's Square, EC1V 4JJ (7553 9210, www.themodernpantry.co.uk). Farringdon tube/rail. **Open** *8-11am, noon-9pm Mon; 8-11am, noon-10pm Tue-Fri; 9am-4pm, 6-10pm Sat; 9am-4pm, 5-9pm Sun.* **Map** *p212 P5* ⓫ *International*

Chef Anna Hansen creates enticing fusion dishes that make the most of unusual ingredients sourced from around the globe. Antipodean and Asian flavours (yuzu, tamarind) pop up frequently, alongside plenty of seasonal British fare (wild garlic, purple sprouting broccoli); the combinations can seem bewildering on the page, but

Postal Museum & Mail Rail *p217*

rarely falter in execution, and the signature dish of sugar-cured prawn omelette with chilli, coriander and spring onion is always a winner. The stylish ground-floor café is quite feminine in feel, with soothing white and grey paintwork, white furniture and burnished copper light fittings; there's a more formal restaurant upstairs.

♥ Moro ££
34-36 Exmouth Market, EC1R 4QE (7833 8336, www.moro.co.uk). Farringdon tube/rail or bus 19, 38, 341. **Open** *noon-2.30pm, 5.15-10.45pm Mon-Sat; noon-3.30pm, 5-9.45pm Sun. Tapas available all day Mon-Sat from the bar.* **Map** *p212 O5* ⑫ *North African/ Spanish*

Back in 1997, in a former supermarket on Exmouth Market, Sam(antha) and Sam Clark set the benchmark for a distinctly British style of Mediterranean cooking that puts a North African twist on Iberian food. Their restaurant (accompanied by a range of beautifully produced cookbooks) is still in London's culinary front rank some 20 years later. Moro provides a spectacular showcase for modern Spanish and Portuguese wines, and vibrantly fresh food that throws out surprising and pleasurable flavours at every turn.

Next door to Moro is its offshoot **Morito** (no.32, EC1R 4QE, 7278 7007, www.morito. co.uk), a fine no-bookings tapas bar.

♥ St John £££
26 St John Street, EC1M 4AY (7251 0848, stjohnrestaurant.com). Barbican tube or Farringdon tube/rail. **Restaurant** *noon-3pm, 6-11pm Mon-Fri; 6-11pm Sat; 12.30-4pm Sun.* **Bar** *11am-11pm Mon-Fri; 6-11pm Sat; noon-5pm Sun.* **Map** *p212 P6* ⑬ *British*

Fergus Henderson and Trevor Gulliver's restaurant has been praised to the skies for reacquainting the British with the full possibilities of native produce, and especially anything gutsy and offal-ish. Perhaps as influential, however, has been its almost defiantly casual style. The mezzanine dining room in the former Smithfield smokehouse has bare white walls, battered floorboards and tables lined up canteen-style. St John's cooking is famously full-on, but also sophisticated, concocting flavours that are delicate as well as rich, as in black cuttlefish and onions, with a deep-flavoured ink-based sauce with a hint of mint. The airy bar here is a great place for a drink and a no-fuss snack.

Pubs & bars

Clerkenwell has a compelling claim to being the birthplace of the now ubiquitous gastropub: the **Eagle** (*see p218*), which kicked things off, is a perfectly decent place for a drink, while Brit cuisine pioneer **St John** (*see left*) is a good option for a relaxed glass of wine.

Café Kick
43 Exmouth Market, EC1R 4QL (7837 8077, www.cafekick.co.uk). Angel tube or Farringdon tube/rail. **Open** *11am-11pm Mon-Wed; 11am-midnight Thur-Sat; 11am-10.30pm Sun. Food served noon-3pm Mon-Fri; noon-10pm Sat, Sun.* **Map** *p212 O5* ③

Clerkenwell's most likeable bar is this table football gem. The soccer paraphernalia is authentic, retro-cool and mainly Latin (you'll find a Zenit St Petersburg scarf amid the St Etienne and Lusitanian gear); bar staff, beers and bites give the impression you could be in Lisbon. A modest open kitchen ('we don't microwave or deep-fry') dishes out tapas, sandwiches and charcuterie platters. The **Bar Kick** on Shoreditch High Street (at no.127) is a bit more of a barn, but also good fun.

♥ Jerusalem Tavern
55 Britton Street, EC1M 5UQ (7490 4281, www.stpetersbrewery.co.uk/london-pub). Farringdon tube/rail. **Open** *noon-11pm Mon-Fri.* **Map** *p212 P6* ⑥

Despite the carefully scuffed wooden floors, peeling paint and tables that look as if they've had centuries-worth of pints spilled on them, the Jerusalem Tavern has actually only been a pub since 1990 – it was originally a coffeehouse. Still, the place feels embedded in the history of the area, notwithstanding nods to modernity from the poshed-up bar snacks, taxidermy cabinets and beer from the excellent St Peter's Brewery in Suffolk that includes premium-strength IPAs and whisky-accented ale. Crowds frequently spill out onto the side streets.

♥ ZTH Cocktail Lounge
Zetter Townhouse Clerkenwell, 49-50 St John's Square, EC1V 4JJ (7324 4545, www. thezettertownhouse.com). Farringdon tube/ rail. **Open** *7am-midnight Mon-Wed, Sun; 7am-1am Thur-Sat.* **Map** *p212 P5* ⑩

The decor at Townhouse embodies a 'more is more' philosophy: every square inch of surface area is occupied by something lovely. The result: one of the most beautiful bars in London. The cocktail list is high quality, devised by the team behind the brilliant 69 Colebrooke Row (*see p251*), among others. The original drinks here are fairly simple and restrained, as well as being typically wonderful. Among the house cocktails, check out the Köln Martini. Service is friendly and helpful.

TEMPLE, FLEET STREET & AROUND

▶ *Temple tube or Blackfriars tube/rail.*

At the eastern end of the arterial Strand is **Temple Bar**, the boundary between the City of London and neighbouring Westminster; during the Middle Ages, the monarch was allowed to pass through the Temple Bar into the City only with the approval of the Lord Mayor of London. In the 17th century, the site was marked with a great gateway by Sir Christopher Wren, which is now in Paternoster Square beside St Paul's (*see p223*). A newer, narrower, but still impressive wyvern-topped monument marks the original spot. The area has long been linked to the law, and here stands the splendid neo-Gothic **Royal Courts of Justice**. On the other side of the road, stretching almost to the Thames, are the several courtyards that make up **Middle Temple** (7427 4800, www.middletemple.org.uk) and **Inner Temple** (7797 8250, www.innertemple.org.uk), two of the Inns of Court that provided training and lodging for London's medieval lawyers. Anybody may visit the grounds, but access to the grand, collegiate buildings is for lawyers and barristers only.

Middle Temple was the HQ of the Knights Templar, a religious order of warrior monks founded in the 12th century to protect pilgrims to the Holy Land. The Templars built the original **Temple Church** in 1185, but fell foul of Philip IV of France, who pressured the pope into suppressing their order.

Almost due south of Temple Bar, alongside Middle Temple, is the immensely popular and generally fabulous **Two Temple Place**.

In the know
No piss take

One of many bits of Victorian arcana that Lee Jackson's fine sanitary history, *Dirty Old London*, revealed to us was the 'urine deflector'. Before public conveniences, to stop men relieving themselves in dark corners, sloping shelves were built into walls that would deposit any urine on the would-be urinator's shoes. We were delighted to discover one remains in the wall of the Bank of England (*see p389*) no less, near the corner of Lothbury and Bartholomew Lane. But Jackson himself found the finest array: a row on Clifford's Inn Passage, off Chancery Lane.

Fleet Street

Without Fleet Street, the daily newspaper might never have been invented. Named after the vanished River Fleet, Fleet Street was a major artery for the delivery of goods into the City, including the first printing press, which was installed behind **St Bride's Church** in 1500 by William Caxton's assistant, Wynkyn de Worde, who also set up a bookstall in the churchyard of St Paul's. London's first daily newspaper, the *Daily Courant*, rolled off the presses in 1702; in 1712, Fleet Street saw the first of innumerable libel cases when the *Courant* leaked the details of a private parliamentary debate.

By the end of World War II, half a dozen offices were churning out scoops and scandals between Strand and Farringdon Road. Most of the newspapers moved away after Rupert Murdoch won his war with the print unions in the 1980s; the last of the news agencies, Reuters, finally followed suit in 2005. Until recently, the only periodical published anywhere near Fleet Street was a comic, the much-loved *Beano*, but in 2009 left-wing weekly the *New Statesman* moved into offices around the corner on Carmelite Street. Relics from the media days remain: the Portland-stone **Reuters building** (no.85), the Egyptian-influenced **Daily Telegraph building** (no.135) and the sleek, black **Daily Express building** (no.120), designed by Owen Williams in the 1930s and arguably the finest art deco building in London. Tucked away on an alley behind St Bride's Church is the **St Bride Foundation** (7353 3331, www.sbf.org.uk), dedicated to printing and typography. There's an interesting programme of events and courses, a library and temporary exhibitions that show off the foundation's collections, which include rare works by Eric Gill and maquettes for Kinnear and Calvert's distinctive road signs.

At the top of Fleet Street itself is the church of **St Dunstan-in-the-West** (7405 1929, www.stdunstaninthewest.org), where the poet John Donne was rector in the 17th century. The church was rebuilt in the 1830s, but the eye-catching clock dates from 1671. The clock's chimes are beaten by clockwork giants who are said to represent Gog and Magog, tutelary spirits of the City. Next door, no.186 is the house where Sweeney Todd, the 'demon barber of Fleet Street', reputedly murdered his customers before selling their bodies to a local pie shop. The legend, sadly, is a porky pie: Todd was invented by the editors of a Victorian penny dreadful in 1846 and propelled to fame rather later by a stage play.

Fleet Street was always known for its pubs; half the newspaper editorials in London were composed over liquid lunches, but there were also more literary imbibers. If you walk down Fleet Street, you'll see **Ye Olde Cheshire Cheese** (no.145, 7353 6170), a favourite of Dickens and Yeats. In its heyday, it hosted the bibulous literary salons of Dr Samuel Johnson, who lived nearby at 17 Gough Square (**Dr Johnson's House**). It also had a famous drinking parrot, the death of which prompted hundreds of newspaper obituaries. At no.66, the **Tipperary** (7583 6470) is the oldest Irish pub outside Ireland: it sold the first pint of Guinness on the British mainland in the 1700s. Just south of Fleet Street, near Blackfriars station, is the **Black Friar**, a lovely, art nouveau meets Arts and Crafts pub. **Blackfriars Bridge** – designed by Thomas Cubitt and dating from 1869 – is a handsome beast, with its red-and-white painted ironwork, and now runs alongside London's first cross-river railway platforms. Now commuters can peer along the Thames without bothering to leave Blackfriars station. Less famous than the view from Waterloo Bridge, this is still one of the finest in London.

Sights & museums

Dr Johnson's House

*17 Gough Square, off Fleet Street, EC4A 3DE (7353 3745, www.drjohnsonshouse.org). Chancery Lane tube or Blackfriars tube/ rail. **Open** May-Sept 11am-5.30pm Mon-Sat. Oct-Apr 11am-5pm Mon-Sat. Tours by arrangement; groups of 10 or more only. **Admission** £7; £3.50-£6 reductions; £15 family; free under-5s. Tours £5. No cards. **Map** p212 O7.*

Famed as the author of one of the first – as well as the most significant and unquestionably the wittiest – dictionaries of the English language, Dr Samuel Johnson (1709-84) also wrote poems, essays, literary criticism, a novel and an early travelogue, an acerbic account of a tour of the Western Isles with his biographer James Boswell. You can tour the stately Georgian townhouse where he came up with his inspired definitions – 'to make dictionaries is dull work' was his definition of the word 'dull' while 'oats' is a 'grain, which in England is generally given to horses, but in Scotland supports the people'.

THE CITY

St Bride's Church *p222*

Royal Courts of Justice

Strand, WC2A 2LL (7947 6000, www. theroyalcourtsofjustice.com). Temple tube. **Open** *9.30am-4.30pm Mon-Fri.* **Admission** *free. Tours £13; £10 reductions; under 15s free.* **Map** *p212 N7.*

Two of the highest civil courts in the land sit in these imposing buildings: the High Court and the Appeals Court. Visitors are welcome to observe the process of law in any of the 88 courtrooms, but very little happens in August and September.

St Bride's Church

Fleet Street, EC4Y 8AU (7427 0133, www. stbrides.com). Temple tube. **Open** *8am-6pm Mon-Fri; 10am-3.30pm Sat; 10am-6.30pm Sun. Tours 2.15pm Tue.* **Admission** *free. Tours £6.* **Map** *p212 O7.*

Hidden down an alley south of Fleet Street, St Bride's is known as the journalists' church: in the north aisle, a shrine is dedicated to hacks killed in action. Down in the crypt, a surprisingly interesting little museum displays fragments of the churches that have existed on this site since the sixth century, as well as some portions of Roman tessellated floor, which you can view using a pair of angled mirrors.

An 18th-century Fleet Street pâtissier, William Rich, was famous for tiered wedding cakes, which he modelled on the lovely Wren-designed spire of St Bride's – the template for such cakes ever since, as the tour guides never tire of explaining. Intriguingly, the church's marital connections might run much deeper than that. It's likely that the holy well that gave the original church its location had been a site of pagan worship – including the blessing of relationships.

Temple Church

Off Fleet Street, EC4Y 7BB (7353 3470, www. templechurch.com). Chancery Lane or Temple tube. **Open** *varies.* **Admission** *£5; £3 reductions; free under 16s.* **Map** *p212 O7.*

Inspired by Jerusalem's Church of the Holy Sepulchre, the Temple Church was the chapel of the Knights Templar. The rounded apse contains the worn gravestones of several Crusader knights, but the church

---

In the know
Just our cup of tea

At Temple Bar, the sweet Strand branch of **Twinings** (no.216, 7353 3511, www. twinings.co.uk) is London's oldest tea shop (dating to 1717), with some interesting memorabilia in the rear.

---

was refurbished by Wren and the Victorians, and was damaged in the Blitz. Not that this puts off the wild speculations of fans of Dan Brown's *The Da Vinci Code*. There are organ recitals most Wednesdays at 1.15pm.

Two Temple Place

2 Temple Place, WC2R 3BD (7836 3715, www. twotempleplace.org). Temple tube. **Open** *Exhibitions late Jan-mid Apr 10am-4.30pm Mon, Thur-Sat; 10am-9pm Wed; 11am-4.30pm Sun. Private tours only mid Apr-late Jan.* **Admission** *free. Tours free but must be booked in advance.* **Map** *p212 N8.*

The pale Portland stone exterior and oriel windows here are handsome – but the interior is extraordinary. You get a hint about what's to come before you open the door: look right and there's a cherub holding an old-fashioned telephone to his ear. Built as an estate office in 1895 to the close specifications of William Waldorf Astor, Two Temple Place now opens to the public for three months a year with immensely popular exhibitions of 'publicly-owned art from around the UK', arranged by an up-and-coming curator. Ring the bell and you're warmly welcomed by volunteers into a house with decor that combines sublime, extravagant craftsmanship with a thorough lack of interest in coherence: above porphyry tiles, the Three Musketeers adorn the banisters of a staircase; intricately carved literary characters crowd the first floor, mixing Shakespeare with Fenimore Cooper; the medieval-style Great Hall, with lovely stained glass, crams together 54 random busts – Voltaire, Marlborough and Anne Boleyn enjoying the company of Mary Queen of Scots.

Pubs & bars

Blackfriar

174 Queen Victoria Street, EC4V 4EG (7236 5474, www.nicholsonspubs.co.uk). Blackfriars tube/rail. **Open** *10am-11pm Mon-Fri; 9am-11pm Sat; noon-10.30pm Sun.* **Map** *p212 P7* ⓘ

Built in 1875 on the site of a medieval Dominican friary, the Blackfriar had its interior completely remodelled in the Arts and Crafts style. It is now part of the Nicholson's stable – the group runs most of the trad pubs in the City, serving moderate food but decent real ales – so you'll come here for the intricate friezes and carved slogans ('Industry is Ale', 'Haste is Slow') of the main saloon bar. You're basically sinking an ale in the middle of a stunning work of art. Admittedly, there's a far more prosaic bar adjoining it, but this remains one of London's most interesting pub interiors.

ST PAUL'S & AROUND

▶ *St Paul's tube.*

The towering dome of **St Paul's Cathedral** is, excluding the 'Big Ben' clocktower, probably the definitive symbol of traditional London and an architectural two fingers to the Nazi bombers that pounded the city in 1940 and 1941. North of the cathedral is the redeveloped **Paternoster Square**, a modern plaza incorporating a sundial that rarely tells the time. The name harks back to the days when priests from St Paul's walked the streets chanting the Lord's Prayer (*Pater noster*, Latin for 'Our Father').

Also of interest is Wren's statue-covered **Temple Bar**. It once stood at the intersection of Fleet Street and Strand, marking the City's western boundary. The archway was dismantled as part of a Victorian road-widening programme in 1878 and became a garden ornament for a country estate in Hertfordshire, before being installed in its current location, as the gateway between St Paul's and Paternoster Square, in 2004. The gold-topped pillar in the centre of the square looks as if it commemorates something important, but it's just an air vent for the Underground.

South of St Paul's, steps cascade down to the **Millennium Bridge**, which spans the river to Tate Modern (*see p89*) and now offers the main gateway to the City for tourists. The grand **St Lawrence Jewry Memorial Fountain** is another peripatetic monument: kept in storage since the 1970s after it was removed from the church (*see p231*), it was placed here in 2011. The

structure dates to 1866. The stairs take you close to the 17th-century **College of Arms** (130 Queen Victoria Street, EC4V 4BT, 7248 2762, www.college-of-arms.gov.uk), official seat of British heraldry. Originally created to introduce competing knights at medieval jousting tournaments, coats of arms soon became an integral part of family identity for the landed gentry of Britain. Scriveners still work here to create beautiful heraldic certificates, but only the Earl Marshal's Court is open to the general public.

East of the cathedral is the huge **One New Change** shopping mall and office development. Designed by French architect Jean Nouvel, its most interesting aspects are a gash that gives views straight through the building to St Paul's and, for a fine roof-level panorama, the sixth-floor public terrace and bar-restaurant. Meekly hidden among the alleys behind it, you'll find narrow Bow Lane. At one end sits **St Mary-le-Bow** (7248 5139, www.stmarylebow.co.uk; closed Sat, Sun), built by Wren between 1671 and 1680. The church bells' peals once defined anyone born within earshot as a true Cockney. At the other end of Bow Lane is **St Mary Aldermary** (7248 9902, www.moot. uk.net; closed Sat). With a pin-straight spire designed by Wren's office, this was the only Gothic church by him to survive World War II. Inside, there's a fabulous moulded plaster ceiling and original wooden sword rest (London parishioners carried arms until the late 19th century).

There are more Wren creations south of St Paul's. On Garlick Hill, named for the medieval garlic market, is **St James Garlickhythe** (7236 1719,

Old Bailey *p224*

www.stjamesgarlickhythe.org.uk, closed
Fri-Sun). The official church of London's
vintners and joiners, it was built by Wren in
1682. Hidden in the tower are the naturally
mummified remains of a young man,
nicknamed Jimmy Garlick, discovered
in the vaults in 1855. The church was hit
by bombs in both World Wars, and partly
ruined by a falling crane in 1991, but the
interior has been convincingly restored.
On Queen Victoria Street, **St Nicholas Cole
Abbey** was the first church rebuilt after the
Great Fire.

Built on the site of the infamous Newgate
Prison to the north-west of the cathedral is
the **Old Bailey**. A remnant of the prison's
east wall can be seen in Amen Corner.

Sights & museums

Old Bailey (Central Criminal Court)
*Corner of Newgate Street & Old Bailey,
EC4M 7EH (7192 2739, www.cityoflondon.
gov.uk). St Paul's tube.* **Open** *Public gallery
9.55am-12.40pm, 1.55-3.40pm Mon-Fri.
Reduced court sitting Aug.* **Admission** *free.
No under-14s; 14-16s only if accompanied by
adults.* **Map** *p212 P7.*

A gilded statue of blind (meaning impartial)
justice stands atop London's most famous
criminal court. The current building was
completed in 1907; the site itself has hosted
some of the most famous trials in British
history, including that of Oscar Wilde.
Anyone is welcome to attend a trial, but bags,
cameras, dictaphones, mobile phones and
food are banned (and no storage facilities are
provided).

In the know
Get me out of here!

A blocked-up door in **St Sepulchre Without**,
opposite the Old Bailey, is the visible
remains of a priest tunnel into the court;
the Newgate Execution Bell is also kept in
the church.

Restaurants

Gordon Ramsay's brasserie **Bread Street
Kitchen** (10 Bread Street, EC4M 9AJ, 3030
4050, www.gordonramsayrestaurants.com)
is the best of several eating options in One
New Change (*see p226*).

Café Sou £
*The Ned, 27 Poultry, EC2R 8AJ (3828
2002, www.thened.com). Bank tube/DLR.*
Restaurant *6am-10pm Mon-Fri.* **Wine bar**
5-10pm Mon-Fri. **Map** *p212 Q7* ❷ *French*

♥ St Paul's Cathedral

*St Paul's Churchyard, EC4M 8AD (7246 8348,
www.stpauls.co.uk). St Paul's tube.* **Open**
*8.30am-4.30pm Mon-Sat. Galleries, crypt &
ambulatory 9.30am-4.15pm Mon-Sat. Tours
of cathedral & crypt 10am, 11am, 1pm, 2pm
Mon-Sat. Special events may cause closure;
check before visiting.* **Admission** *Cathedral,
crypt & gallery (incl tour) £18; £8-£16
reductions; £44 family; free under-6s. Book
online for reductions.* **Map** *p212 P7.*

St Paul's Cathedral hasn't been lucky
through most of its history, but it has been
at the centre of some of London's most
momentous events. The first cathedral
to St Paul was built on this site in 604,
but fell to Viking marauders. Its Norman
replacement, a magnificent Gothic structure
with a 490ft (149m) spire (taller than any
London building until the 1960s), burned
in the Great Fire – its spire having already
collapsed many years before. The current
church was commissioned in 1673 from Sir

THE CITY

Christopher Wren, as the centrepiece of London's resurgence from the ashes, and though modern buildings now encroach on the cathedral from all sides, the passing of three centuries has done nothing to diminish the appeal of the master architect's finest work. After a £40-million restoration removed most of the Victorian grime from the outside walls, the extravagant main façade looks as brilliant today as it must have when the last stone was placed in 1708.

The vast open spaces of the interior contain memorials to national heroes such as Wellington and Lawrence of Arabia. The statue of John Donne, metaphysical poet and former Dean of St Paul's, is often overlooked, but it's the only monument to have been saved from old St Paul's. There are also more modern works, including a Henry Moore sculpture and Bill Viola's video installation *Martyrs (Earth, Air, Fire, Water)*.

The Whispering Gallery, inside the dome, is reached by 259 steps from the main hall; the acoustics here are so good that a whisper can be bounced clearly to the other side of the dome. Steps continue up to first the Stone Gallery (119 tighter, steeper steps), with its high external balustrades, then outside to the Golden Gallery (152 steps), with its giddying views.

Before leaving St Paul's, head down to the maze-like crypt (through a door whose frame is decorated with skull and crossbones), which contains a shop and café, and memorials to such dignitaries as Alexander Fleming, William Blake and Admiral Lord Nelson, whose grand tomb (purloined from Wolsey by Henry VIII but never used by him) is right beneath the centre of the dome. To one side is the small, plain tombstone of Christopher Wren himself, inscribed by his son with the epitaph, 'Reader, if you seek a monument, look around you'; at their request, Millais and Turner were buried near him.

In the know
Triforium tours

As well as tours of the main cathedral and self-guided audio tours (which are free), you can join special tours of the Triforium, visiting the library and Wren's 'Great Model' – the ruinously expensive prop he used to sell his design to the church commissioners – at 11.30am and 2pm on Monday and Tuesday and at 2pm on Friday (pre-book on 7246 8357, £8 on top of general ticket price). On the tour you'll see the exquisite Dean's Staircase – one of the loveliest features in the whole church. Each step rests elegantly on the previous one, with such perfect balance that no central support is required, giving the curves an airiness that is quite enchanting.

Located at the far end of the Ned's gargantuan banking hall, Café Sou is the hotel's least formal foodie offering: the Soho House Group's attempt at a grand railway café in the Parisian mould. *Très jolie* it is too. The simple menu includes baguettes, quiches, omelettes, *rillettes* and a few salads, plus some decent wines for lunchtime lushes. For swiftly sensational nosh in the City, Café Sou is hard to beat.

▶ *The Ned has seven other eateries, plus two bars. Most of these occupy the former bank's main hall. Imagine a giant food court with different restaurant zones under one ridiculously high roof, each serving a different menu: sort of Harrods Food Hall meets the Wolseley. For details of the hotel itself, see p399.*

Sweetings ££££
39 Queen Victoria Street, EC4N 4SA (7248 3062, www.sweetingsrestaurant.co.uk). Mansion House tube. **Open** *11.30am-3pm Mon-Fri.* **Map** *p212 Q7* **14** *Fish & seafood*

Things don't change much at this enduring City classic, and that's the way everyone likes it. The walls remain covered with photos of old sports teams, and many of the staff have been here for years. Lobster and crab bisques preface a choice of fish and seafood dishes that read and taste like upmarket versions of a pub-side stall – smoked fish, whitebait, trout and so forth. Top-quality fish are then served fried, grilled or poached to order. The handful of more elaborate dishes includes an excellent fish pie.

Shops & services
One New Change
New Change Road, EC4M 9AF (7002 8900, www.onenewchange.com). Mansion House or St Paul's tube or Bank tube/DLR. **Open** *10am-6pm Mon-Wed, Sat; 10am-8pm Thur, Fri; noon-6pm Sun; check website for opening hours of individual shops.* **Map** *p212 Q7* **1** *Mall*

This sprawling Jean Nouvel-designed development is opposite the east end of St Paul's Cathedral, and features a warren of high-street retailers, office buildings and restaurants (Jamie Oliver's Barbecoa, Wahaca, Ramsay's Bread Street Kitchen). Nicknamed the 'stealth building' due to its dark, low-slung design, the place is unsurprisingly popular with City workers on lunchbreaks or post-work spending sprees among predictable chain stores. Take the glass elevator up to the top floor, though, and you'll be rewarded with an unexpected view – St Paul's, yes, but on a level with its roof rather than above or below it. Enjoy it for free, or accompanied by a pricey drink or tapas.

NORTH OF ST PAUL'S

▶ *Barbican or St Paul's tube.*

North of St Paul's Cathedral on Foster Lane is **St Vedast-alias-Foster** (7606 3998, www.vedast.org.uk), another finely proportioned Wren church, restored after World War II using spare trim from other churches in the area. Further west on Little Britain (named after the Duke of Brittany) is **St Bartholomew-the-Great**, founded along with **St Bartholomew's Hospital** in the 12th century. Popularly known as Bart's, the hospital treated air-raid casualties throughout World War II; shrapnel damage from German bombs is still visible on the exterior walls. Scottish nationalists now come here to lay flowers at the monument to William Wallace, executed in front of the church on the orders of Edward I in 1305.

Just beyond Bart's is the fine ironwork of **Smithfield Market**. The market had been under almost constant threat of redevelopment, usually with promises to maintain historic façades, but now seems to have landed itself a rather wonderful future tenant: the Museum of London (*see p227*), funding permitting, will move here in 2022. Smithfield's provides a colourful, not to say visceral, link to an age when the quality of British beef was a symbol of national virility and good humour. Meat has been traded here for a millennium; the current market, designed by Horace Jones, opened in 1868, though it's since been altered (in part thanks to World War II bombs). At weekends, one former cold storage warehouse opposite the market opens as the indefatigable superclub **Fabric** (*see p339*).

Museum of London & the Barbican

From Bart's, the road known as **London Wall** runs east to Bishopsgate, following the approximate route of the old Roman wall. Tower blocks have sprung up here like daisies, but the odd lump of weathered stonework can still be seen poking up between the office blocks, marking the path of the old City wall. You can patrol the remaining stretches of the wall, with panels (some barely legible) pointing out highlights all the way to the Tower of London. Also of interest is peaceful **Postman's Park**, next to one of the exit staircases from the current **Museum of London**, which is due to relocate to the Smithfield Market.

The area north of London Wall was reduced to rubble by German bombs in World War II. In 1958, the City of London and London County Council clubbed together to buy the land for the construction of 'a

In the know
Urban jungle

The Barbican has the second-largest conservatory in London, stuffed with 2,000 tropical plants and trees, plus some fish and turtles in its ponds. It's a great place to hide away from the concrete outside. **The Conservatory** is open on most Sundays and Bank Holidays, noon-5pm. Admission is free, unless you book onto a guided tour (£12.50) or indulge in an afternoon tea among the greenery (noon and 2.30pm, £35 per person).

genuine residential neighbourhood, with schools, shops, open spaces and amenities'. What Londoners got was the **Barbican**, a vast concrete estate of 2,000 flats that feels a bit like a university campus after the students have gone home. Casual visitors may get the eerie feeling they have been miniaturised and transported into a giant architect's model, but design enthusiasts will recognise the Barbican – with its landmark saw-toothed towers – as a prime example of 1970s brutalism, softened a little by time and rectangular ponds of friendly resident ducks. Learn to love the place by taking one of the regular, 90-minute architectural tours of the complex (www. barbican.org.uk/education, £12.50, £10 reductions) – which will also help you to navigate its famously confusing layout.

The main attraction here is the **Barbican Centre** (www.barbican.org), a world-class arts complex, with library, cinema (see p323), theatre (see p362) and concert hall (see p354), plus the **Barbican Art Gallery**. Marooned amid the towers is the only pre-war building in the vicinity: the restored 16th-century church of **St Giles Cripplegate** (7638 1997, www.stgilesnewsite.co.uk), where Oliver Cromwell was married and John Milton buried.

North-east of the Barbican on City Road are **John Wesley's House** and **Bunhill Fields**, the nonconformist cemetery where William Blake, the preacher John Bunyan and novelist Daniel Defoe are buried.

Sights & museums
Barbican Art Gallery

Barbican Centre, Silk Street, EC2Y 8DS (7638 8891, www.barbican.org.uk/artgallery). Barbican tube or Moorgate tube/rail. **Open** *11am-8pm Mon-Wed, Sat, Sun; 11am-9pm Thur, Fri. Last entry 1hr before closing.* **Admission** *varies.* **Map** *p212 Q6.*

The art gallery on the third floor at the Barbican Centre isn't quite as 'out there' as it

would like you to think, but the exhibitions on architecture, fashion, design and pop culture are usually diverting at the very least – and accompanied by interesting programmes of events. On the ground floor, the Curve is a second – long, thin and, yes, curved – gallery that commissions large-scale installations. They're free, and can be superb.

John Wesley's House & the Museum of Methodism

Wesley's Chapel, 49 City Road, EC1Y 1AU (7253 2262, www.wesleysheritage.org. uk). Moorgate or Old Street tube/rail. **Open** *10am-4pm Mon-Wed, Fri, Sat; 10am-12.45pm, 1.30-4pm Thur; after the service until 1.45pm Sun. Tours available.* **Admission** *free; donations appreciated.* **Map** *p212 R5.*

John Wesley (1703-91), the founder of Methodism, was a man of legendary self-discipline. You can see the minister's nightcap, preaching gown and personal experimental electric-shock machine on a tour of his austere home on City Road. The adjacent chapel has a small museum on the history of Methodism and fine memorials of dour, sideburn-sporting preachers. Downstairs (to the right) are some of the finest public toilets in London, built in 1899 with original fittings by Sir Thomas Crapper.

♥ Museum of London

150 London Wall, EC2Y 5HN (7001 9844, www.museumoflondon.org.uk). Barbican or St Paul's tube. **Open** *10am-6pm daily.* **Admission** *free; suggested donation £5.* **Map** *p212 Q6.*

One of the original settlements established by the Romans after their first invasion in AD43, Londinium – as it was known then – has survived war, plague and fire to become the bustling metropolis it is today. This journey, from ancient marshland to one of the greatest cities on earth, is documented through a mind-boggling array of exhibits alongside innovative interactive displays.

On the entrance floor, the social history of London is told in chronological displays that begin with 'London Before London', where

In the know
Street-wise museum

The **Museum of London** (see above) and sister-museum the **Museum of London Docklands** (see p274) have issued a number of excellent free apps, including Streetmuseum and Streetmuseum Londinium. They offer archive images and/or information about historic sites, geolocated to where you're standing.

THE CITY

227

artefacts include flint axes from 300,000 BC, found near Piccadilly, and the bones of an aurochs, an extinct type of wild cattle. 'Roman London' includes an impressive reconstructed dining room complete with mosaic floor. Windows overlook a sizeable fragment of the City wall, whose Roman foundations have clearly been built on many times over the centuries. Sound effects and audio-visual displays illustrate the medieval, Elizabethan and Jacobean city, with particular focus on the plague and the Great Fire, which marked 400-year anniversaries in 2016.

Downstairs, the lower-ground-floor gallery tells the story of the city from 1666 to the present day. This newer space features everything from an unexploded World War II bomb, suspended in a room where the understated and very moving testimony of ordinary Blitz survivors is screened, to clothes by the late Alexander McQueen and the impressive golden Lord Mayor's Coach (it dates from 1757). There are displays and brilliant interactives on poverty (an actual debtor's cell has been reconstructed, complete with graffiti), finance, shopping and 20th-century fashion, including a recreated Georgian pleasure garden, with mannequins that sport Philip Treacy masks and hats. Some displays are grand flourishes – the suspended installation that chatters London-related web trivia in the Sackler Hall, a printing press gushing changing news-sheets, a grand gallery space for Thomas Heatherwick's delicate flower 'Cauldron' from the 2012 Olympics – while others ingeniously solve problems: games to engage the kids, glass cases in the floors to maximise display space.

The museum's biggest obstacle had always been its location: the entrance is two floors above street level, and hidden behind a dark and rather featureless brick wall. With visitor numbers higher than ever, the museum is set to move half a mile from its current location to take up residence in the abandoned Victorian market at Smithfield – the architects' design (by Stanton Williams and Asif Khan) has already been selected for a putative grand opening in 2022.

Museum of St Bartholomew's Hospital

*North Wing, St Bartholomew's Hospital, West Smithfield, EC1A 7BE (bartshealth. nhs.uk/bartsmuseum). Barbican tube or Farringdon tube/rail. **Open** 10am-4pm Tue-Fri. **Admission** free; donations appreciated. Tours £7; £6 reductions; children free. **Map** p212 P6.*

Be glad you're living in the 21st century. Many of the displays in this small museum inside St Bart's Hospital relate to the days before anaesthetics, when surgery and carpentry

were kindred occupations. Every Friday at 2pm, visitors can take a guided tour of the museum that takes in the Hogarth paintings in the Great Hall, the little church of St Bartholomew-the-Less, neighbouring St Bartholomew-the-Great and Smithfield.

Postman's Park

*Entrances from St Martin's Le-Grand, Aldersgate Street or King Edward Street. St Paul's tube. **Open** 8am-7pm (or dusk) daily. **Map** p212 P7.*

A soothing little park in itself, Postman's Park is best known for the Watts Memorial to Heroic Sacrifice: a wall of ceramic plaques, established in 1900, each of which commemorates a heroic but doomed act of bravery. Most date to Victorian times – pantomime artiste Sarah Smith, for example, who received 'terrible injuries when attempting in her inflammable dress to extinguish the flames which had engulfed her companion (1863)' – but the first new plaque for 70 years was added in 2009. It was dedicated to 30-year-old Leigh Pitt, who died while saving a child from drowning.

St Bartholomew-the-Great

*West Smithfield, EC1A 9DS (7600 0440, www.greatstbarts.com). Barbican tube or Farringdon tube/rail. **Open** 8.30am-5pm Mon-Fri (until 4pm Nov-Feb); 10.30am-4pm Sat; 8.30am-8pm Sun. **Admission** £5; £4.50 reductions; £12 family; free under-7s. **Map** p212 P6.*

This atmospheric medieval church was built over the remains of the 12th-century priory hospital of St Bartholomew, founded by Prior Rahere, a former courtier of Henry I. The church was chopped about during Henry VIII's reign and the interior is now firmly Elizabethan, although it also contains donated works of modern art. You may recognise the main hall from *Shakespeare in Love* or *Four Weddings and a Funeral*. If you need refreshment, the church has a bar-café in the 15th-century cloister, serving coffee, monastery beers and home-made weekday lunches.

Restaurants

The Barbican Centre has a handful of eating and drinking options but better venues can be found elsewhere. The **Jugged Hare** (49 Chiswell Street, EC1Y 4SA, 7514 0134, www.thejuggedhare.com ❾) has a well-regarded game-focused menu, while the **Chiswell Street Dining Rooms** (56 Chiswell Street, EC1Y 4SA, 7614 0177, www.chiswellstreetdining.com ❸) is an upscale alternative nearby. But, for a slap-up lunch on the go there are some cheap-and-cheerful offerings at the energetic food market (11am-5pm Mon-Fri) on Whitecross Street.

Bad Egg £

*Unit 1B, City Point, 1 Ropemaker Street, EC2Y 9AW (3006 6222, www.badegg.london). Moorgate tube/rail. **Open** 8am-10pm Mon-Fri; 10am-7.30pm Sat; 10am-5pm Sun.* **Map** *p212 R6* ❶ *Diner*

In the brutalist shadow of the Barbican, Bad Egg's an idiosyncratic little brunch spot run by London 'barbecue king' Neil Rankin. A mash-up of Tex-Mex diner-style grub (nachos, tacos, buffalo rib tips, sandwiches et al) and more modish plates (kimchi on toast, 'macanchini' balls), the menu is a relentless parade of fiery, funky hits. Famished/hungover types should hit the bottomless brunch: endless booze or softies plus three plates per person. Eggs abound. As do head-sweltering chipotle-infused bits and synthetic cheese. This is unrepentantly filthy stuff, but being bad never tasted so good.

Pubs & bars

For cocktails, book ahead to visit **Oriole** (East Poultry Avenue, Central Markets, EC1A 9LH, 3457 8099, www.oriolebar.com ❽), showy little sister of Nightjar (barnightjar. com) and elder sibling to Swift (*see p168*).

❤ Black Rock

*9 Christopher Street, EC2A 2BS (7247 4580, http://blackrock.bar). Liverpool Street tube/Overground/rail. **Open** 5pm-midnight Mon-Wed; 5am-1am Thur; 5pm-2am Fri, Sat.* **Map** *p212 R6* ❷

Tucked away in the maze-like streets behind Liverpool Street station, this dimly lit subterranean whisky lounge is the place for connoisseurs to blow a hole in their bank accounts. One side of the room is lined with cabinets filled with over 250 bottles, while down the middle a table made from half of an English oak tree has two booze-filled channels hewn in the wood. Choose from the Cherry River – bourbon and morello with spices – or the Table Whisky, an ever-evolving house blend.

BANK & AROUND

▶ *Mansion House tube or Bank tube/DLR.*

Above Bank station, seven streets come together to mark the symbolic heart of the Square Mile, ringed by some of the most important buildings in the City. Constructed from Portland stone, the Bank of England, the Royal Exchange and Mansion House form a stirring monument to the power of money: most decisions about the British economy are still made within this small precinct. Few places in London have quite the same sense of pomp and circumstance.

Easily the most dramatic building is the **Bank of England**, founded in 1694 to fund William III's war against the French. It's a fortress, with no accessible windows and just one public entrance (leading to the **Bank of England Museum**). The outer walls were designed in 1788 by Sir John Soane, whose own museum can be seen in Holborn (**Sir John Soane's Museum**, *see p215*). Millions have been stolen from its depots elsewhere in London, but the bank itself has never been robbed. Today, it's responsible for printing the nation's banknotes and setting the base interest rate. On the south side of the junction is the Lord Mayor of London's official residence, **Mansion House** (7626 2500, www.cityoflondon.gov.uk), an imposing neoclassical building constructed by George Dance in 1753; there are tours at 2pm on Tuesday. It's the only private residence in the country to have its own court and prison cells for unruly guests. Just behind Mansion House is the superbly elegant church of **St Stephen Walbrook** (7626 9000, www.ststephenwalbrook.net, 10am-4pm Mon, Tue, Thur, 11am-3pm Wed, 10am-3.30pm Fri), built by Wren in 1672. Its gleaming domed, coffered ceiling was borrowed from Wren's original design for St Paul's; other features include an incongruous modernist altar, sculpted by Sir Henry Moore and cruelly dubbed 'the camembert'. The Samaritans was founded here in the 1950s.

To the east of Mansion House is the **Royal Exchange**, flanked by statues of James Henry Greathead, who invented the machine that cut the tunnels for the London Underground, and Paul Reuter, who founded the Reuters news agency here in 1851. In 1972, the exchange shifted to offices on Threadneedle Street, thence to Paternoster Square in 2004, where it remains.

The period grandeur is undermined by the monstrosity on the west side of the junction, **No.1 Poultry**. The name fits: it's a turkey. A short walk down Queen Victoria Street is the **London Mithraeum Bloomberg Space**, site of the Roman

Temple of Mithras. The remains of the temple were discovered in the shell of a bombsite in 1954 and had contemporary Londoners transfixed, dominating news reports and attracting 30,000 visitors. Then the whole thing was dismantled to make way for post-war construction and moved 100 metres away to the roof of a car park, with decidedly non-Roman crazy paving on the floor. In 2009, tech and media giant Bloomberg bought up the original location for its multi-million-pound HQ and announced plans to 'rebuild' the Temple of Mithras.

Further south, a left on to Cannon Street leads to the traditional site of the **London Stone**, a dull chunk of oolitic limestone with an interesting history – and fascinating mythology. Perhaps a Roman milestone, it was mentioned by both Shakespeare and William Blake. The removal of the stone is said to presage the fall of London – and it *has* been removed for redevelopment of its former home at no.111 and is currently on display in the Museum of London. Roughly opposite the address is the late Wren church of **St Michael Paternoster Royal** (7248 5200, 9am-5pm Mon-Fri), the final resting place of Richard 'Dick' Whittington. Later transformed into a rags-to-riches pantomime hero, the real Dick Whittington was a wealthy merchant elected Lord Mayor of London four times between 1397 and 1420. The role of Dick Whittington's cat is less clear – many now believe that 'cat' was actually slang for a ship – but an excavation to find Whittington's tomb in 1949 did uncover a mummified medieval moggy. The happy pair are shown in the stained-glass windows.

Returning to Bank, stroll north along Prince's Street, beside the Bank of England's blind wall. Look right along Lothbury to find **St Margaret Lothbury** (7606 8330,

www.stml.org.uk, 7am-6pm Mon-Fri). The grand screen dividing the choir from the nave was designed by Wren himself; other works here by his favourite woodcarver, Grinling Gibbons, were recovered from various churches damaged in World War II. Lothbury also features a beautiful neo-Venetian building, now apartments, built by 19th-century architect Augustus Pugin, who worked with Charles Barry on the Houses of Parliament.

South-east of Bank on Lombard Street is Hawksmoor's striking, twin-spired church of **St Mary Woolnoth** (7626 9701, 9.30am-4.30pm Mon-Fri), squeezed in between what were 17th-century banking houses. Only their gilded signboards now remain, a hanging heritage artfully maintained by the City's planners.

Further east on Lombard Street is Wren's **St Edmund the King** (7621 1391, www.lcsd.org.uk, open by arrangement), which now houses a centre for modern spirituality. Other significant churches in the area include Wren's handsome red-brick **St Mary Abchurch**, off Abchurch Lane, and **St Clement**, on Clement's Lane, immortalised in the nursery rhyme 'Oranges and Lemons'. Over on Cornhill are two more Wren churches: **St Peter-upon-Cornhill**, mentioned by Dickens in *Our Mutual Friend*, and **St Michael Cornhill**, which contains a bizarre statue of a pelican feeding its young with pieces of its own body – a medieval symbol for the Eucharist, it was sculpted by someone who had plainly never seen a pelican.

North-west of the Bank of England is the **Guildhall**, the City of London headquarters. 'Guildhall' can either describe the original banqueting hall or the cluster of buildings around it. These include the **Guildhall Art Gallery**, **Guildhall Library** and the **City of London Police Museum** (7332 1868,

www.cityoflondon.police.uk, closed Sun),
a free and thoroughly diverting account
of seeking Jack the Ripper and fighting
cybercrime and terrorism. Also here is the
church of **St Lawrence Jewry** (7600 9478,
www.stlawrencejewry.org.uk, 8am-1pm
Mon-Thur). St Lawrence is another restored
Wren church, with an impressive gilt ceiling.
Within, you can hear the renowned Klais
organ at lunchtime organ recitals (usually
from 1pm Tue).

Glance north along Wood Street to see the
isolated tower of **St Alban**, built by Wren
in 1685 but ruined in World War II and now
an eccentric private home. At the end of the
street is **St Anne & St Agnes**, laid out in the
form of a Greek cross, and now home to a
music charity.

Sights & museums

Bank of England Museum

*Entrance on Bartholomew Lane, EC2R 8AH
(3461 4878, www.bankofengland.co.uk/
museum). Bank tube/DLR. **Open** 10am-5pm
Mon-Fri. **Admission** free. **Map** p212 R7.*

Housed inside the former Stock Offices of the
Bank of England (there's a full-size recreation
of Sir John Soane's Bank Stock Office from
1693), this surprisingly lively museum
explores the history of the national bank. As
well as ancient coins and original artwork for
British banknotes, the museum offers a rare
chance to lift nearly 30lbs (14kg) of gold bar
(you reach into a secure box, closely monitored
by CCTV) and displays Kenneth Grahame's
resignation letter – the *Wind in the Willows*
author worked here for three decades.

Guildhall

*Gresham Street, EC2V 7HH (7332 1313, www.
guildhall.cityoflondon.gov.uk). St Paul's tube
or Bank tube/DLR. **Open** 10am-4.30pm daily.
Great Hall closes for functions; phone ahead.
Admission free. **Map** p212 Q7.*

The City of London and its progenitors have
been holding grand ceremonial dinners in
this hall for eight centuries. Memorials to
national heroes line the walls, shields of
the 100 livery companies grace the ceiling,
and every Lord Mayor since 1189 gets a
namecheck on the windows. Many famous
trials have taken place here, including the
treason trial of 16-year-old Lady Jane Grey,
'the nine days' queen', in 1553. Above the
internal entrance to the Guildhall are statues
of Gog and Magog, mythical giants who are
said to protect the City. (They originate in
the medieval legend of an exiled Trojan who
wrestled a giant Briton, Gogmagog, whose
name over time was split into a pair of giants.)
The current statues replaced 18th-century
forebears that were destroyed in the Blitz.

Guildhall Art Gallery

*Guildhall Yard, off Gresham Street, EC2V
5AE (7332 3700, www.cityoflondon.org.
uk). St Paul's tube or Bank tube/DLR.
Open 10am-5pm Mon-Sat; noon-4pm Sun.
Admission free. Temporary exhibitions vary.
Map p212 Q7.*

The City of London's gallery has always been
a favourite of ours. Upstairs is the entertaining
and informative thematic Victorian Collection,
where you'll find lushly romantic and suberbly
camp Pre-Raphaelite works by Frederic
Leighton, Dante Gabriel Rossetti and John
Everett Millais; you wouldn't mess with
Clytemnestra, as painted by John Collier in
1832. A few steps down from the entrance, a
mezzanine gallery holds sun-filled abstracts by
Matthew Smith; continuing to the Undercroft
you'll find various London-themed pieces,
some of historical and sociological more than
artistic merit, but fascinating nonetheless.
There are also neat heritage displays of Roman
artefacts and medieval charters that explain
the background to Dick Whittington, Gog and
Magog and various other topics. Still towering
over the temporary exhibition spaces on
this floor is John Singleton Copley's *Defeat
of the Floating Batteries at Gibraltar*, all two
storeys of it.

London Mithraeum Bloomberg Space

*12 Walbrook, EC4N 8AA (www.
londonmithraeum.com). Bank tube or
Cannon Street rail. **Open** 10am-6pm Tue-Sat;
noon-5pm Sun; 10am-8pm on 1st Thur of mth.
Admission free; online booking advised.
Map p212 Q7.*

The glossy waffle-shaped Bloomberg London
HQ contains a full reconstruction of the
Roman Temple of Mithras, whose remains
were discovered on this site in the 1950s. On
the first floor, impressive artefacts discovered
during the archaeological dig in 2012 are
displayed behind glass. Among the worn
leather shoes and broken pots, you'll find
a wooden tablet from AD 57, with marks on

THE CITY

its surface: one of the oldest handwritten documents found in the UK. The main event is below ground level: an atmospheric re-imagining of the temple, built with the help of mud casts and archive material. Almost 1,800 years ago, the temple hosted the men-only cult of Mithras, which worshipped a deity known for slaying a primordial bull. Audio and light installations contribute to the evocative atmosphere.

Restaurants

City Càphê £

17 Ironmonger Lane, EC2V 8EY (www. citycaphe.com). Bank tube/DLR. **Open** 11.30am-4.30pm Mon-Fri. **Map** p212 Q7 ❹
Vietnamese

Long before you see this charming Vietnamese café, you'll smell enticing aromas wafting down the street. At lunchtime, you can expect to see a queue at the door; staff are calmly efficient, so don't baulk at the length – it disappears in next to no time. The menu is easy to follow and most options are available with beef, pork, chicken or tofu. Seating in the bright, modern interior is limited, so City Càphê is not the place for a long lunch, but it's perfect for a quick bite or a tasty takeaway.

Shops & services

Royal Exchange

Bank, EC3V 3LR (7283 8935, www. theroyalexchange.co.uk). Bank tube/DLR. **Shops** 10am-6pm Mon-Fri. **Restaurants** 8am-11pm Mon-Fri. Check individual outlets for details. **Map** p212 R7 ❷ *Mall*

This Parthenon-like building is the former home of the London Stock Exchange, founded by ace financier Sir Thomas Gresham back in 1565 to facilitate the newly invented trade in stocks and shares with Antwerp. Destroyed by the Great Fire, and again in 1838, the current premises date to 1844, when they were opened by Queen Victoria, but trading stopped in 1939. The Exchange reopened in 2001 as a rather upmarket mall, with a grand champagne bar and expensive fashion and gift shops – if your desire for a fancy fountain pen or flash watch subsides, it's still worth a look to see City dwellers in repose.

> **In the know**
> **Hop to it**
>
> The gilded grasshopper hanging over 68 Lombard Street is the heraldic emblem of Sir Thomas Gresham, founder of the Royal Exchange (see above).

MONUMENT & THE TOWER OF LONDON

▶ *Aldgate, Monument or Tower Hill tube, Liverpool Street tube/Overground/rail, or Tower Gateway DLR.*

From Bank, King William Street runs south-east towards London Bridge, passing the small square containing the **Monument**. South on Lower Thames Street is the moody-looking church of **St Magnus the Martyr**; nearby are several relics from the days when this area was a busy port, including the old Customs House and **Billingsgate Market**, London's main fish market until 1982 (when it moved to east London).

North of the Monument along Gracechurch Street is the atmospheric **Leadenhall Market**, constructed in 1881 by Horace Jones (who also built the market at Smithfield; *see p226*). The vaulted roof was restored to its original Victorian finery in 1991, and City workers come here in droves to lunch at the pubs, cafés and restaurants, including the historic **Lamb Tavern**. Fantasy fans may recognise the market as Diagon Alley in *Harry Potter & the Philosopher's Stone*.

Behind the market is Lord Rogers' high-tech **Lloyd's of London** building, constructed in 1986, with all its ducts, vents, stairwells and lift shafts on the outside, like an oil rig dumped in the heart of the City. Rogers was also responsible for the **Cheesegrater** (122 Leadenhall) directly opposite. By the mid-2020s, this distinctive building will be overshadowed by the **Diamond**, a planned 864-foot (263-metre) tower at 100 Leadenhall Street. The original Lloyd's Register of Shipping, decorated with evocative bas-reliefs of sea monsters and nautical scenes, is on Fenchurch Street, where the next in the sequence of City skyscrapers emerged: Rafael Viñoly's 20 Fenchurch Street, nicknamed the **Walkie Talkie** due to its distinctive top-heavy shape, and now providing wonderful views from the **Sky Garden**. South of Fenchurch Street, on Eastcheap (derived from the Old English *ceap*, meaning 'barter'), is Wren's **St Margaret Pattens**, with an original 17th-century interior.

Several more of the City's tallest buildings are nearby. To the north, the ugly and rather dated **Tower 42** (25 Old Broad Street) was the tallest building in Britain until the construction of One Canada Square in Docklands in 1990. And topping out at 755 feet (230 metres, including a radio mast), **Heron Tower** (110 Bishopsgate, www.herontower.com) became the City's tallest building at the end of 2009. It has since been overtaken by **22 Bishopsgate**, which will reach 912 feet (278 metre) when completed; this in turn will be usurped by a planned skyscraper at 1 Undershaft, which is due to hit 951 feet (290 metres). Also on Bishopsgate, behind Tower 42, is **Gibson Hall**, the ostentatious former offices of the National Provincial Bank of England.

A block south, St Mary Axe is an insignificant street named after a vanished church that is said to have contained an axe used by Attila the Hun to behead English virgins. It is now known for Lord Foster's **Gherkin** (30 St Mary Axe), one of London's finest modern buildings, which now has a restaurant and bar on its top floors (searcysatthegherkin.co.uk). In autumn 2018, Foster + Partners submitted plans for a new 1,000-foot (305-metre) skyscraper called the Tulip (more like a gherkin on a stick) to be built next door. On curved stone benches either side of 30 St Mary Axe are inscribed the 20 lines of Scottish poet Ian Hamilton Finlay's 'Arcadian Dream Garden', a curious counterpart to Lord Foster's building. Nearby are two medieval churches that survived the Great Fire: **St Helen's Bishopsgate** and **St Andrew Undershaft**. The latter, right at the foot of the Cheesegrater, contains a Hobbit-sized statue of John Stow, who wrote London's first guidebook, the *Survey of London*, in 1598. The quill his effigy holds is replaced by the Lord Mayor every three years.

The north end of St Mary Axe intersects with two interesting streets. The more northerly, **Houndsditch**, is where Londoners threw dead dogs and other rubbish in medieval times – the ditch ran outside the London Wall, dividing the City from the East End. The southerly one is Bevis Marks, home to the superbly preserved **Bevis Marks Synagogue** (7621 1188, www.sephardi.org.uk/bevis-marks, closed Sat, £5, £2.50-£4 reductions), founded in 1701 by Sephardic Jews fleeing the Spanish Inquisition. Services are still held in Portuguese as well as Hebrew.

South along Bevis Marks are **St Botolph's-without-Aldgate** and the tiny stone church of **St Katharine Cree** (7488 4318, www. sanctuaryinthecity.net, 9.30am-4pm Mon-Fri) on Leadenhall Street, one of only eight churches to survive the Great Fire. Inside is a memorial to Sir Nicholas Throckmorton, Queen Elizabeth I's ambassador to France, who was imprisoned for treason on numerous occasions, despite – or perhaps because of – his friendship with the temperamental queen.

Further south, towards the Tower of London, streets and alleys have evocative names: Crutched Friars, Savage Gardens, Pepys Street and the like. The famous diarist lived in nearby Seething Lane and

Heron Tower

observed the Great Fire of London from **All Hallows by the Tower**. Pepys is buried in the church of **St Olave** (7488 4318, www. sanctuaryinthecity.net, 10am-5pm Mon-Fri) on Hart Street, nicknamed 'St Ghastly Grim' by Dickens due to the skulls above the entrance.

Marking the eastern edge of the City, the **Tower of London** was the palace of the medieval kings and queens of England. Home to the Crown Jewels and the Royal Armoury, it's one of Britain's best-loved tourist attractions and, accordingly, is mobbed by visitors seven days a week. Overlooking the Tower from the north,

---

In the know
London's tallest buildings

The Shard 1016ft (310m; *see p94*)
1 Undershaft 951ft (290m; planned)
22 Bishopsgate 912ft (278m; *see opposite*)
The Diamond 863ft (263m; planned)
One Canada Square 771ft (235m; *see p274*)
Spire London 771ft (235m; under construction at Canary Wharf)
Landmark Pinnacle 764ft (233m; under construction at Canary Wharf)
Heron Tower 755ft (231m; *see opposite*)
Cheesegrater 738ft (225m; *see opposite*)

💙 Tower of London

Tower Hill, EC3N 4AB (3166 6000, www. hrp.org.uk /tower-of-london). Tower Hill tube or Tower Gateway DLR. **Open** *Mar-Oct 10am-5.30pm Mon, Sun; 9am-5.30pm Tue-Sat. Nov-Feb 10am-4.30pm Mon, Sun; 9am-4.30pm Tue-Sat.* **Admission** *£26.80; £12.70-£20.90 reductions; £48.40-£68.10 family; free under-5s. Book online for reductions.* **Map** *p212 S9.*

If you haven't been to the Tower of London before, you should go now. Despite the exhausting crowds and long climbs up barely accessible, narrow stairways, this is one of Britain's finest historical attractions. Who wouldn't be fascinated by a close-up look at the crown of Queen Victoria or the armour (and prodigious codpiece) of King Henry VIII? Or, indeed, a castle that's barely an arrow-shot away from the financial heart of Britain? The buildings of the Tower span 900 years of – mostly violent – history, and the bastions and battlements house a series of interactive displays on the lives of British monarchs, and the often excruciatingly painful deaths of traitors. The oldest part is the central **White Tower**, built by William the Conqueror in 1078 as a symbol of Norman hegemony; it is surrounded by a complex of later medieval buildings set within two defensive walls

and a moat. There's easily enough to do here to fill a whole day, which makes the steep entry price pretty good value, and it's worth joining one of the highly recommended and entertaining free tours led by the Yeoman Warders (or Beefeaters).

Make the **Crown Jewels** your first stop. Beyond satisfyingly solid vault doors, you get to glide along a set of travelators (each branded with the Queen's official 'EIIR' badge) past such treasures of state as the Monarch's Sceptre, mounted with the Cullinan I diamond, and the Imperial State Crown, which is worn by the Queen each year for the opening of Parliament.

The other big draw is the **Royal Armoury** in the central White Tower, with its swords, armour, poleaxes, morning stars (spiky maces) and other gruesome tools for separating human beings from their body parts. The reassembled Line of Kings, a collection of arms and armour (some belonging to monarchs), life-sized wooden horses and the carved heads of kings, is eccentric pro-monarchy propaganda that dates from the Restoration. Kids are entertained by swordsmanship games, coin-minting activities and even a child-sized longbow. The garderobes (medieval toilets) also seem to appeal.

Royal Armoury

Back outside, **Tower Green** – where executions of prisoners of noble birth were carried out (the last execution, of World War II German spy Joseph Jakobs, was in 1941) – is marked by a stiff glass pillow, sculpted by poet/artist Brian Catling. Overlooking the green, **Beauchamp Tower**, dating from 1280, has an upper floor full of intriguing graffiti by the prisoners who were held here. The Tower only ceased functioning as a prison in 1952 and over the years counted Anne Boleyn, Rudolf Hess and the Krays among its inmates.

On the south side, the 13th-century **Bloody Tower** is another must-see that gets overwhelmed by numbers later in the day. The ground floor is a reconstruction of Sir Walter Raleigh's study; the upper floor details the fate of the Princes in the Tower.

In the Thameside wall of the Tower is the unexpectedly beautiful **Medieval Palace**, with its reconstructed bedroom and throne room, as well as spectacularly complex stained glass in the private chapel. On a hot day, the whole palace is deliciously cool – welcome respite when you've been struggling round with the throng on a hot summer's day.

In the know
Gem of an idea

It's best to visit the Crown Jewels as early in the day as you possibly can: if you wait until you've pottered around a few other things, the queues are usually immense.

White Tower

beside the tube station, **Trinity Square Gardens** contain a humbling memorial to the tens of thousands of merchant seamen killed in the two World Wars, as well as a set of four plaques commemorating more than 125 Catholics who were executed at the Tower Hill scaffold between 1381 and 1747. Across the road is the small square in which London's druids celebrate each spring equinox with an elaborate ceremony. Just beyond is one of the City's finest Edwardian buildings: the former **Port of London HQ** at 10 Trinity Square, with a huge neoclassical façade and gigantic statues symbolising Commerce, Navigation, Export, Produce and Father Thames. It's now a luxury hotel, run by Four Seasons. Next door is **Trinity House**, the home of the General Lighthouse Authority, founded by Henry VIII for the upkeep of shipping beacons along the river.

At the south-east corner of the Tower is **Tower Bridge**, built in 1894 and still London's most distinctive bridge. Used as a navigation aid by German bombers, it escaped the firestorm of the Blitz. East across Bridge Approach is **St Katharine Docks**, the first London docks to be formally closed. The restaurants around the marina, slightly hidden behind modern office blocks, offer more dignified dining than those around the Tower.

Sights & museums

All Hallows by the Tower

Byward Street, EC3R 5BJ (7481 2928, www. ahbtt.org.uk). Tower Hill tube or Tower Gateway DLR. **Open** *8am-5pm Mon-Fri; 10am-5pm Sat, Sun. Tours Apr-Oct 2-4pm most weekdays; donation requested.* **Admission** *free; donations appreciated.* **Map** *p212 S8.*

Often described as London's oldest church, All Hallows is built on the foundations of a seventh-century Saxon church. Much of what survives today was reconstructed after World War II, but several Saxon details can be seen in the main hall, where the Knights Templar were tried by Edward II in 1314. The undercroft contains a museum with Roman and Saxon relics and a Crusader altar. William Penn, the founder of Pennsylvania, was baptised here in 1644.

Monument

Monument Street, EC3R 8AH (7626 2717, www.themonument.info). Monument tube. **Open** *Apr-Sept 9.30am-6pm daily. Oct-Mar 9.30am-5.30pm daily.* **Admission** *£4.50; £2.30-£3 reductions; free under-5s.* **Map** *p212 R8.*

One of 17th-century London's most important landmarks, the Monument is a magnificent

Portland stone column, topped by a landmark golden orb with more than 30,000 fiery leaves of gold – it looks decidedly like the head of a thistle. The Monument was designed by Sir Christopher Wren and his (often overlooked) associate Robert Hooke as a memorial to the Great Fire. The world's tallest free-standing stone column, it measures 202ft (62m) from the ground to the tip of its golden flames, exactly the distance east to Farriner's bakery in Pudding Lane, where the fire is supposed to have begun on 2 September 1666. The viewing platform is surrounded by a lightweight mesh cage, but the views are great – you have to walk 311 steps up the internal spiral staircase to enjoy them, though. At least, everyone who makes it to the top gets a certificate.

St Botolph's-without-Aldgate

*Aldgate High Street, EC3N 1AB (7283 1670, www.stbotolphs.org.uk). Aldgate tube. **Open** 9am-3pm Mon-Fri. Eucharist 1.05pm Tue, Thur; 10.30am Sun. **Admission** free; donations appreciated. **Map** p212 S7.*

The oldest of three churches of St Botolph in the City, this handsome monument was built at the gates of Roman London as a homage to and to ask the intercession of the patron saint of travellers. The building was reconstructed by George Dance in 1744 and a beautiful ornamental ceiling was added in the 19th century by John Francis Bentley, who also created Westminster Cathedral.

St Ethelburga Centre for Reconciliation & Peace

*78 Bishopsgate, EC2N 4AG (7496 1610, www.stethelburgas.org). Bank tube/DLR or Liverpool Street tube/Overground/rail. **Open** 11am-3pm 1st & 3rd Mon of the mth, or by prior arrangement. **Admission** free; donations appreciated. **Map** p212 S7.*

Built around 1390, the tiny church of St Ethelburga was reduced to rubble by an IRA bomb in 1993 and rebuilt as a centre for peace and reconciliation. Behind the chapel is a Bedouin tent where events are held to promote dialogue between the faiths (phone or check the website for details), an increasingly heated issue in modern Britain.

St Helen's Bishopsgate

*Great St Helen's, off Bishopsgate, EC3A 6AT (7283 2231, www.st-helens.org.uk). Bank tube/ DLR or Liverpool Street tube/Overground/rail. **Open** 9.30am-12.30pm Mon-Fri; afternoons by appointment. **Admission** free. **Map** p212 S7.*

Founded in 1210, St Helen's Bishopsgate is actually two churches knocked into one, which explains its unusual shape. The church survived the Great Fire and the Blitz, only to be partly wrecked by IRA bombs in 1992 and 1993. The hugely impressive 16th- and

17th-century memorials inside include the grave of Thomas Gresham, founder of the Royal Exchange (*see p232*).

St Magnus the Martyr

*Lower Thames Street, EC3R 6DN (7626 4481, www.stmagnusmartyr.org.uk). Monument tube. **Open** 10am-4pm Tue-Fri. Mass 12.30pm Tue-Fri; 11am Sun. **Admission** free; donations appreciated. **Map** p212 R8.*

Downhill from the Monument, this looming Wren church marked the entrance to the original London Bridge. There's a scale model of the old bridge inside the church, and the porch has a timber from the original version. There's also a statue of axe-wielding St Magnus, the 12th-century Earl of Orkney. The church is mentioned at one of the climaxes of TS Eliot's *The Waste Land*: 'Where the walls/Of Magnus Martyr hold/Inexplicable splendour of Ionian white and gold.'

In the know
Poetry corners

St Mary Woolnoth (see p230) and **St Magnus Martyr** (see above), both feature in TS Eliot's *The Waste Land*: keeping 'the hours/With a dead sound on the final stroke of nine'.

♥ Sky Garden

*20 Fenchurch Street (entrance via Philpot Lane), EC3M 8AF (7337 2344, skygarden. london). Monument tube. **Open** 10am-6pm Mon-Fri; 11am-9pm Sat, Sun. Advance booking required. **Admission** free. Photo ID required. **Map** p212 R8.*

The distinctive but not widely admired skyscraper, 20 Fenchurch Street, aka the Walkie-Talkie, has a major calling card. The airport-style security in the unprepossessing lobby gives no hint of the splendid experience in store upstairs. You're funnelled into a lift that zips 35 floors up the building; when you walk out you'll be knocked sideways by the soaring space on the top floors. Flanked by flights of steps rising through lush, leafy plants to a series of terraces, this vast open-air piazza commands outstanding views of the capital. There are irritations: the health-and-safety glass screens deny you the sense of intimacy with the city outside the Sky Garden – a feeling emphasised by the guards refusing to let you stick your phone up over the parapet. But this is a space that changes with the light, with the rewards becoming richer as darkness falls. If you're lucky enough to get a decent sunset, it's truly spectacular, with the detailed panorama transformed into an impressionistic night scene before your eyes.

► Visitors must book a 90-minute timeslot on the Sky Garden website at least three days in advance. If no slots are available, try booking a table at the Sky Pod Bar or at one of the two restaurants (the Darwin Brasserie is cheaper than the Fenchurch Restaurant): all three also give access to the viewing floors.

Tower Bridge Exhibition

Tower Bridge Road, SE1 2UP (7403 3761, www.towerbridge.org.uk). Tower Hill tube or Tower Gateway DLR. **Open** *Apr-Sept 10am-5.30pm daily. Oct-Mar 9.30am-5pm daily.* **Admission** *£9.80; £4.20-£6.80 reductions; £14.10-£22.50 family; free under-5s.* **Map** *p212 S9.*

Opened in 1894, this is the 'London Bridge' that wasn't sold to America. Originally powered by steam, the drawbridge is now opened by electric rams when big ships need to venture upstream (check when the bridge is next due to be raised on the bridge's website or follow the Twitter feed). An entertaining exhibition on its history is displayed in the old steamrooms and the west walkway, which provides a crow's-nest view along the Thames. Since 2014, when glass panels were placed in the walkways, you've also been able to look directly down past your own feet at the river below – assuming you're not prone to vertigo.

Restaurants

♥ Duck & Waffle £££

Floor 40, Heron Tower, 110 Bishopsgate, EC2N 4AY (3640 7310, duckandwaffle. com). Liverpool Street tube/Overground/ rail. **Open** *24hrs daily. Food served 6-11am, 11.30am-4pm, 5-11pm, 11.30pm-5am Mon-Fri; 6am-4pm, 5-11pm, 11.30pm-5am Sat, Sun.* **Map** *p212 S7* ❻ *Modern European*

There's a dedicated entrance in Heron Tower from which a glass lift whizzes you up to the Duck & Waffle on the 40th floor. The views are stunning – if you're facing the right way and, preferably, sitting at a window table (many of which are for couples). Food is an on-trend mix of pricey small plates, raw offerings (oysters, ceviche) and a few main courses (including the namesake duck confit and waffle), as well as sensational barbecue-spiced crispy pigs' ears. Service wavers between keen and offhand, and the acoustics are terrible. But Duck & Waffle is open 24/7 – even though the menu is limited between midnight and 5am, all-night dining is pretty much unheard of in London.

► *One floor below Duck & Waffle, Sushisamba (3640 7330, www.sushisamba. com) has two small bars and an outdoor*

roof terrace with arguably better views; if you can tear your attention away from the panorama, then sushi and saké are the best things on the fusion menu.

Pubs & bars

City Social Bar

Tower 42, 25 Old Broad Street, EC2N 1HQ (7877 7703, citysociallondon.com). Liverpool Street tube/Overground/rail. **Open** *noon-late Mon-Fri; 4pm-late Sat.* **Map** *p212 R7* ❹

Chef-about-town Jason Atherton (*see p174*) took over what had been a pretty run-of-the-mill City restaurant on the 24th floor of what used to be the NatWest Tower – and made it pretty terrific. It is mighty expensive, however, so we recommend the attached bar, which anyone can just show up to – having negotiated two lots of security, an escalator and at least one lift. Still, the bar food and drink is of a far higher standard than you might expect. The cocktails are great, with just enough invention to make them worth the lofty prices: The Soybean Car, for example, comprises Remy Martin 1738, citrus, vanilla, light soy, and orange and dark chocolate powder. Bar snacks give you a sense of Atherton's culinary prowess.

Draft House

14-15 Seething Lane, EC3N 4AX (7042 7468, www.drafthouse.co.uk). Tower Hill tube or Tower Gateway DLR. **Open** *noon-11pm Mon-Wed, Fri, Sat; noon-midnight Thur; noon-8pm Sun.* **Map** *p212 S8* ❺

Pretty much the archetypal 'beer bars', members of the Draft House chain focus on serving a brilliant range of superb beers, simple but relaxed surroundings, and eats that don't deviate far from the sausage/burger/hot dog booze-fodder axis. In addition to its handy location, this branch has a big screen for sporting events – which it shows with great verve and much audience advice to the players.

In the know
Savouring the view

In the last few years, the proliferation of high-rise buildings in the Square Mile has increased the number of restaurants and bars with knock-out views. Not all have the food to match the vistas, but good bets include the Duck & Waffle (*see left*), City Social (*see above*) and the Sky Pod Bar (*see left*). For an alternative view of the City, head south across the river to the Oxo Tower Restaurant (*see p86*) or Hutong at the Shard (*see p97*).

THE CITY

North London

North London's list of famous former residents gives a good idea of the scope of the area – from Amy Winehouse and Liam Gallagher to Karl Marx, John Keats and Charles Dickens, a huge variety of people have been drawn to its mix of pretty, sleepy retreats and buzzing, creative party zones. First stop is normally Camden Town, with its markets, indie pubs and general alternative vibe, but there's further joy to be found in the leafy squares of Islington. Further to the north, Hampstead and Highgate offer genteel village life and a glorious public space: Hampstead Heath.

❤ **Don't miss**

1 ZSL London Zoo *p245*
If you don't love this zoo, then you haven't seen the penguins yet.

2 Kenwood House/Iveagh Bequest *p248*
See a Rembrandt, have a café lunch and head out onto the Heath.

3 Camden Market *p244*
Heaven for teens, hell for grown-ups, an experience for everyone.

4 Regent's Park *p244*
Royal hunting ground turned people's playground.

Camden High Street

CAMDEN & AROUND

▶ *Camden Town tube, Chalk Farm tube or Camden Road Overground.*

Despite the pressures of gentrification, Camden refuses to leave behind entirely its grungy history as the cradle of British rock music. Against a backdrop of social deprivation, venues such as the **Electric Ballroom** (184 Camden High Street, electricballroom. co.uk – but seemingly always under threat of redevelopment) and **Dingwalls** (Middle Yard, Camden Lock, 01920 823098, www.dingwalls. com) provided a platform for musical rebels. By the 1990s, the Creation label was based in nearby Primrose Hill (*see p244*), unleashing My Bloody Valentine and the Jesus & Mary Chain on the world, before making it big with Oasis. The Gallagher brothers were often seen trading insults with Blur at the **Good Mixer** (30 Inverness Street, 3076 0002, www. thegoodmixer.com). The music still plays at the **Roundhouse** (*see p345*) in the north, at Koko (*see p344*) to the south, and at any number of pubs and clubs between.

Before the Victorian expansion of London, this was no more than a watering stop on the highway to Hampstead, with two notorious taverns – the Mother Black Cap and Mother Red Cap – frequented by highwaymen and brigands. (The latter is now the World's End.) After the gaps between the pubs were filled in with terraced houses, the borough became a magnet for Irish and Greek railway workers, many of them working in the engine turning-house that is now the Roundhouse. The area's squalor had a powerful negative influence on the young Charles Dickens, who lived briefly on Bayham Street – you can see a blue plaque that commemorates his residence there.

From the 1960s, things started to pick up, helped by an influx of students, lured by low rents and the growing arts scene that nurtured punk, then indie, then Britpop – and now any number of short-lived indie-electro and alt-folk hybrids, whose young protagonists will all tell you with great fervour about the Camden they knew before it went upmarket.

Parts of Camden still have a rough quality, but the hardcore rebellion of the rock 'n' roll years has been replaced by a more laid-back carnival vibe, as young shoppers join the international parade of counterculture costumes. Tourists travel here in their thousands for the sprawling mayhem of **Camden Market**, which stretches north from the tube along boutique-lined Camden High Street and Chalk Farm Road.

Cutting through the market is **Regent's Canal** (*see p242*), which opened in 1820

to provide a link between east and west London for horse-drawn narrowboats loaded with coal.

Camden's single avowed 'sight' is west of Camden Town – the excellent **Jewish Museum** – but it remains a good bit of town for rough-and-ready gigs. As well as Koko and the Roundhouse, there are plenty of pub stages where this year's hopefuls try to get spotted: try **Camden Assembly**, **Underworld** and the **Dublin Castle** (94 Parkway, 7485 1773), where Madness and, later, Blur were launched. The **Jazz Café** and the **Blues Kitchen** offer a different vibe. For details of these and other live music venues, *see pp336-351*.

North-east of Camden, scruffy **Kentish Town** used to be where you came for gigs at the **Forum** (*see p344*), but it has quietly become a great place for eating and drinking too – and it's just a tube stop or bus ride from the craziness of the market.

Sights & museums

Jewish Museum

*Raymond Burton House, 129-131 Albert Street, NW1 7NB (7283 7384, www.jewishmuseum. org.uk). Camden Town tube. **Open** 10am-5pm Mon-Thur, Sat, Sun; 10am-2pm Fri. **Admission** £7.50; £3.50-£6.50 reductions; free under-5s. **Map** p241 J2.*

This museum is a brilliant exploration of Jewish life in Britain since 1066, combining fun interactives – you can wield the iron in a tailor's sweatshop, sniff chicken soup, pose for a wedding photo or take part in some Yiddish theatre – with serious history. There's a powerful Holocaust section, using the testimony of a single survivor, Leon Greenman, to bring tight focus to the unimaginable horror of it all. Opposite, a beautiful room of religious artefacts, including a 17th-century synagogue ark and silver Torah ornaments, does an elegant job of introducing Jewish ritual. Access is free to the downstairs café, located beside an ancient ritual bath, and to the shop.

Zabludowicz Collection

*176 Prince of Wales Road, NW5 3PT (7428 8940, www.zabludowiczcollection.com). Chalk Farm tube or Kentish Town West Overground. **Open** noon-6pm Thur-Sun. **Admission** free. **Map** p241 H1.*

This former Methodist chapel – a remarkable neoclassical building that makes a superb setting for art exhibitions – holds three shows a year, enabling artists to create experimental new work and curators to build exhibitions around the Collection's global emerging art in all media.

▶ *Some of the areas discussed in this chapter are shown on the pull-out map at the back of this guide.*

CAMDEN & AROUND

Restaurants

1 Arancini Brothers Factory *p242*
2 The Cheese Bar *p242*
3 Engineer *p246*
4 Hook Camden Town *p243*
5 Lansdowne *p246*
6 Lemonia *p246*

Shops & services

1 Camden Lock Market *p244*
2 Stables Market *p244*

❤ **Time to eat & drink**

Affordable haute cuisine
Salut! *p250*

All-day eats
Ottolenghi *p250*

**Beer in a fine
Georgian pub**
Earl of Essex *p252*

Creative cocktails
69 Colebrooke Row *p251*

Excellent Italian
Trullo *p251*

❤ **Time to shop**

**Arts, crafts and
everything between**
Cass Art *p252*

Heaven for teens
Camden Market *p244*

Hot home accessories
Aria *p252*

Regent's Canal

Ditch the car and follow this waterway through north London

The Victorian Regent's Canal was built to link the Grand Union Canal in the west of London with the River Thames at Limehouse. No longer of much industrial value, it is now used by an increasing number of narrowboats, walkers and cyclists who appreciate this car-free route through the capital. From Camden Lock (see p244), you can catch a jolly tour boat run by the **London Waterbus Company** (7482 2550, 2550, www.londonwaterbus. co.uk) or **Walker's Quay** (7485 6210, www.walkersquay.com).

These pass through London Zoo, Regent's Park and the short Maida Hill tunnel en route to Little Venice, just north of Paddington. Home to a community of boat-dwelling Londoners, **Little Venice** (pull-out map D5) is a picturesque enclave where the Regent's Canal meets the Grand Union Canal to form Brownings Pool, named after the poet Robert Browning who lived nearby.

Alternatively, it's an enjoyable half-hour walk east then south from Camden Lock on the Regent's Canal to Granary Square, Camley Street Natural Park and the **London Canal Museum** (see p204). Keep going east from here – you'll need to allow a couple of hours – and you'll eventually reach the Thames at Limehouse marina.

Restaurants

For tasty street food to take away, head to Camden Market's **West Yard** (Camden Lock Place, NW1 8AF, 11am-6pm daily, extended hours in summer), where more than 30 vendors offer street food from around the world. In Kentish Town, the Soho House group serves up a double-whammy at 79 Highgate Road: on the ground floor is **Pizza East** (www.pizzaeast.com/kentish-town, £-££), which offers rustic pizza and other wood-fired goodies, while **Chicken Shop** (www. chickenshop.com, £) in the diner basement dishes up marinated rotisserie chicken.

Arancini Brothers Factory £

115A Kentish Town Road, NW1 8PB (3583 2242, www.arancinibrothers.com). Kentish Town tube/rail. **Open** *8am-9.30pm Mon-Fri; 9.30am-9.30pm Sat, Sun.* **Map** *p241 K1* ❶

Italian

Deep-fried risotto balls are the stars here, but breakfast, sandwiches and great coffee all play their part at this Kentish Town favourite. The wheat-free and vegetarian risotto are slowly cooked with herbs, onions and garlic and then bound together with a vegetable stock and a variety of flavours, like mozzarella, cheddar, parsley and lemon. They are then rolled into balls and fried in rice flour until crispy. But that's not all, there are also lamb wraps and burgers, salad boxes and stew pots up for grabs.

The Cheese Bar ££

Unit 93/94 Camden Stables, North Yard, Chalk Farm Road, NW1 8AH (7428 6441, www.thecheesebar.com). Chalk Farm tube. **Open** *noon-9pm Mon-Thur; noon-9.30pm Fri; 11am-9.30pm Sat; 11am-7pm Sun.* **Map** *p241 J1* ❷ *Cheese*

In 2017, the people behind bright yellow street food legend the Cheese Truck opened this permanent eaterie underneath a burlesque club in Camden Stables Market. The intimate space is dominated by a sleek, rectangular marble counter where friendly and relaxed bartenders talk you through the cheese-centric menu. Try indecently creamy truffled baron bigod, followed by the indulgently oily 'young buck' stilton raclette – a hot mess of fried potatoes, sharp blue cheese and smoky strips of meat. Best of all are those grilled-cheese sandwiches that made the Cheese Truck Insta-famous. Piping-hot and perfectly greasy, they're a hangover cure to beat any bloody mary on earth.

Hook Camden Town £
63-65 Parkway, NW1 7PP (7482 0475, www. hookrestaurants.com). Camden Town tube. **Open** *noon-3pm, 5.30-9pm Mon; noon-3pm, 5.30-10pm Tue-Thur; noon-3.30pm, 7.30-10.30pm Fri; noon-10.30pm Sat; noon-9pm Sun.* **Map** *p241 J2* ❹ *Fish & chips*

Hook will make you feel as if you're at the seaside. The simple, maritime-themed furnishings are reminiscent of a beach hut. The walls are painted blue like sea and sky. And, as on any seaside visit, you'll be eating fish and chips. The menu changes daily: Hook gets some fish from Cornish day boats. Other fish are farmed, and Hook isn't afraid to use lesser-known species such as ling. Fish is served tempura as well as breaded, and there are some lovely home-made sauces alongside the usual tartare.

Pubs & bars

The **Lock Tavern** (*see p341*) is a good Camden DJ bar, while the **Blues Kitchen**, the **Dublin Castle** and the **Camden Assembly** supply live music (*see pp346-349*). **Camden Town Brewery** is actually based in Kentish Town and has a brewery tap (55-59 Wilkin Street Mews, NW5 3NN, 7485 1671, www.camdentownbrewery.com).

Ladies & Gentlemen
2 Highgate Road, NW5 1NR (7813 7562, www. ladiesandgents.co). Kentish Town tube/ rail. **Open** *5pm-midnight Mon-Thur, Sun; 5pm-late Fri, Sat.*

Housed in a former underground toilet in Kentish Town, Ladies & Gentlemen makes the most of its unusual space: two moodily underlit rooms (one seriously tiny) at a V-shaped angle to each other, with a small bar at in between. There are a few seats at the bar, but mostly it's table service – delivered with a smile and loads of enthusiasm. The cocktails may not be the best in the city, but the unusual surroundings, retro music and welcoming vibe have made this former public convenience a neighbourhood favourite.

Pineapple
51 Leverton Street, Kentish Town, NW5 2NX (7284 4631, www.facebook.com/ ThePineapplePub). **Open** *noon-11pm Mon-Thur; noon-midnight Fri, Sat; noon-10.30pm Sun.*

So great is Kentish Town's love of the Pineapple that when the pub was threatened with redevelopment into flats in 2002, locals started a campaign to save it – and got the place listed by English Heritage in just eight days. This backstreet boozer dates back to the mid 19th century, and you can feel the history in the weathered wood of the joyously unmodernised main bar. There's also a conservatory at the back, and outdoor tables when the weather's good. The Pineapple

Camden Town Brewery

hosts a variety of special events, including semi-annual beer festivals, but it's at its best on an ordinary weekend, when the locals crowd in for a pint and a gab-fest. And there's cheap Thai food if you want to settle in for the long haul.

Shops & services

Camden's sprawling collection of markets colonise a prime chunk of Camden Town. Together, they attract around 250,000 visitors a week, making them one of the capital's most popular visitor attractions. This means they're pretty hectic, especially at peak times, so it's best to plan ahead. The markets have undergone major gentrification in recent years, so they're no longer the smörgåsbord of street culture that they once were. You might still see the odd goth or punk rooting out fetish clothing, skull rings and vinyl, but they are massively outnumbered by teenage tourists and street-food junkies.

♥ Camden Market
3763 9900, www.camdenmarket.com. Camden Town or Chalk Farm tube. **Open** *10am-6pm daily.* **Map** *p241 J1.*

There are two main areas to Camden Market proper. **Camden Lock Market** (Camden Lock Place, off Chalk Farm Road, NW1 8AF ❶) next to the Regent's Canal lock, is an arts and crafts haven packed with covered retail units and pop-ups specialising in scarves, shoes, hand-stitched leather goods, Fairtrade jewellery and loads more. It's also the place to go when you're hungry, thanks to the 30-plus global street-food stalls at West Yard (the cobbled bit next to the canal and behind Lock 17).

Further along Chalk Farm Road, the **Stables Market** (opposite Hartland Road, NW1 8AH ❷) is in the midst of a multimillion-pound redevelopment. The grade II listed Horse Hospital (where horses injured from pulling barges along the canal were treated) and a warren of stables known as the Triangle are now home to an eclectic mix of cool urban clothing outlets, handmade crafts and one-off vintage items. North Yard has become a mecca for foodies with its artisan bakery, cafés and the boutique fine produce store, the Camden Grocer.

▶ *On the south side of the Regent's Canal, a short walk from Camden Town tube station, Buck Street Market is a separate entity to Camden Market itself. After extensive renovations, it is set to re-open in summer 2020 with a mix of new and former retailers housed in 50 shipping containers, with a focus on upcycling and sustainability.*

REGENT'S PARK & AROUND

▶ *Regent's Park, Great Portland Street, Baker Street, St John's Wood or Camden Town tube.*

Regent's Park (www.royalparks.org.uk, 5am-dusk daily) is one of London's most delightful open spaces. Originally a hunting ground for Henry VIII, it remained a royals-only retreat long after it was formally designed by John Nash in 1811; only in 1845 did it open to the public. Attractions run from the animal noises and odours of **ZSL London Zoo** to the fragrant blooms of roses in **Queen Mary's Garden** and the enchanting **Open Air Theatre** (*see p362*); rowing-boat hire, lovely waterfowl lakes, ice-cream stands and the **Espresso Bar** (7935 5729, open 8am-4pm daily) complete the picture. West of Regent's Park, beyond the golden dome of the **London Central Mosque** (www.iccuk. org), is the wealthy district of St John's Wood (*see below*); exit to the south and you're in Marylebone (*see p147*).

To the north of Regent's Park, it's worth walking up steep little **Primrose Hill** for postcard-worthy views of the city's skyline. Visit at sunset to enjoy the vista at its best. To the east, celebrities frequent fashionable gastropubs and quaint cafés along Regent's Park Road and Gloucester Avenue.

St John's Wood

The woodland that gives St John's Wood its name was part of the great Middlesex Forest, before the land was claimed by the Knights of St John of Jerusalem. Areas of forest were cleared for private villas in the mid 19th century, but the district has retained its green and pleasant glow – proximity to the western edge of Regent's Park helps. Some uncharacteristically sensitive redevelopment during the 1950s has left the area smart and eminently desirable to those with the money. The expensive tastes of the locals are reflected in the posh boutiques along the High Street. The main tourist attraction is **Lord's** cricket ground, but a steady stream of music fans pay tribute to

ZSL London Zoo

the Beatles on the zebra crossing in front of **Abbey Road Studios** (3 Abbey Road, NW8 9AY, 7266 7000, www.abbeyroad. com). The studio, founded in 1931 by Sir Edward Elgar, is still used to record albums and film scores, including soundtracks to the *Lord of the Rings* trilogy, *Star Wars* prequels and *Harry Potter* films. Up the Finchley Road from St John's Wood is **Swiss Cottage**, worth a visit for the modernist library designed by Sir Basil Spence in the early '60s.

Sights & museums

Lord's Tour & MCC Museum

St John's Wood Road, NW8 8QN (7616 8500, www.lords.org). St John's Wood tube. Entry to museum as part of a tour; times vary. **Tickets** *£24; £15-£18 reductions; £50 family; free under-5s.* **Map** *pull-out F4.*

Lord's is more than just a cricket ground. As the headquarters of the Marylebone Cricket Club (MCC), it is the official guardian of the sport's rules – and, consequently, a portion of the nation's heart – and celebrated its bicentenary (on the current site) in 2014. Opened in 1953, the museum's highlight is the unfeasibly tiny urn containing the Ashes: this coveted trophy, battled over since 1882-83, never leaves Lord's, so it will still be here no matter what happens when we take on Australia again down under in 2017/18. There's also memorabilia celebrating legends

of the game (Jack Hobbs, Don Bradman, Shane Warne and, above all, WG Grace) and plenty of pleasing oddities, not least a stuffed sparrow mounted on the cricket ball that killed it on 3 July 1936.

♥ ZSL London Zoo

Regent's Park, NW1 4RY (7722 3333, www. zsl.org/london-zoo). Baker Street or Camden Town tube then bus 274, C2. **Open** *daily, times vary; check website for details.* **Admission** *£29.75; £22-£26.80 reductions; free under-3s. Book online for reductions.* **Map** *p241 H3.*

London Zoo has been open in one form or another since 1826. Spread over 36 acres and containing more than 600 species, it cares for many of the endangered variety – part of the entry price (pretty steep at nearly £30 in peak season) goes towards the ZSL's projects around the world. Regular events include 'Animals in Action' and keeper talks. Exhibits are entertaining: look out, for example, for the re-creation of a kitchen overrun with large cockroaches. In the fabulous 'In with the Lemurs' exhibit, you get to walk through jungle habitat with the long-tailed primates leaping over your head. Other major attractions are 'Tiger Territory', where Sumatran tigers can be watched through floor-to-ceiling windows, and 'Gorilla Kingdom'. The relaunched 'Rainforest Life' biodome and the 'Meet the Monkeys' attractions allow you to walk through enclosures that recreate the natural

Hampstead Heath

habitat of, respectively, tree anteaters and sloths, and black-capped Bolivian squirrel monkeys. Personal encounters of the avian kind can be had in the Victorian Blackburn Pavilion – as well as at Penguin Beach, where the black-and-white favourites are plainly visible as they swim underwater; responses to the snakes and crocodiles in the Reptile House tend to involve a good proportion of shudders. Bring a picnic and you could easily spend the day here.

Restaurants

The restaurants fill up fast in Primrose Hill. Try upmarket Greek bistro **Lemonia** (89 Regent's Park Road, NW1 8UY, 7586 7454, www.lemonia.co.uk ⑥). For a gastropub feed, head to Gloucester Avenue: both the **Engineer** (no. 65, NW1 8JH, 7483 1890, www.theengineerprimrosehill.co.uk ③) and **Lansdowne** (no. 90, NW1 8HX, 7483 0409, www.thelansdownepub.co.uk ⑤) are here.

Singapore Garden £££
83 Fairfax Road, NW6 4DY (7624 8233, www. singaporegarden.co.uk). Swiss Cottage tube. **Open** *noon-3pm, 6-11pm Mon-Thur; noon-3pm, 6-11.30pm Fri, Sat; noon-5pm, 6-11pm Sun. Singaporean & Malay*

In a capital city that represents the cuisine of nearly every nation in the world, from Iceland to India, Nepal to New Zealand, it's surprisingly difficult to find Singaporean and Malay food. But at this Swiss Cottage stalwart you can feast not only on Malaysian dishes, but on specialities from the Singapore Straits – an island melting-pot whose majority Chinese population and shared history (and border) with Malaysia makes for some very interesting happenings on your plate. Skip the everyday Cantonese stuff in favour of Straits classics: mouthwatering sambals, curries and noodles. It's hawker-style food, but served in a stylish, restaurant setting.

Tamada £££
122 Boundary Road, NW8 0RH (7372 2882, www.tamada.co.uk). Kilburn Park or St John's Wood tube, or Kilburn High Road Overground. **Open** *6-11pm Tue-Fri; 1-3.30pm, 6-11pm Sat; 1-3.30pm, 6-9pm Sun. Georgian*

Those unfamiliar with Georgian cuisine will find themselves pleasantly surprised at this understated neighbourhood restaurant. A crossroads between East and West, delicately spiced plates such as *kuchmachi* (tender cubes of pork heart, liver and lung in a rich, mildly spicy gravy spiked with tangy pomegranate seeds) or *lobio* (a red bean vegetarian stew the consistency of porridge, boosted by coriander, served with pickled green tomatoes and gherkins) offer a highly satisfying meal.

HAMPSTEAD

▶ *Hampstead tube, or Gospel Oak or Hampstead Heath Overground.*

It may have been absorbed into London during the city's great Victorian expansion, but hilltop Hampstead still feels like a Home Counties village. It has long been a favoured roost for literary and artistic types: Keats and Constable lived here in the 19th century, and sculptors Barbara Hepworth and Henry Moore took up residence in the 1930s. However, the area is now popular with City workers, who are among the only people able to afford what is some of London's priciest property.

The undisputed highlight of the district is **Hampstead Heath**, the vast and in places wonderfully overgrown tract of countryside between Hampstead village and Highgate that is said to have inspired CS Lewis's Narnia. The heath covers 791 acres of woodland, playing fields, swimming ponds and meadows of tall grass that attract picnickers and couples in search of privacy.

NORTH LONDON

The south end of the heath is where you'll find dinky Hampstead village, all genteel shops and cafés, restaurants and lovely pubs such as the **Holly Bush**. While you're there, tour the gorgeous sunken gardens and antique collection at **Fenton House** or gaze at the stars from the **Hampstead Scientific Society Observatory** (Lower Terrace, www.hampsteadscience.ac.uk/astro), open on clear Friday and Saturday evenings and Sunday lunchtimes from mid September to mid April. A stroll along nearby Judges Walk reveals a line of horse chestnuts and limes virtually unchanged since they appeared in a Constable painting in 1820. Constable was buried nearby at **St John-at-Hampstead Church** (7794 5808, www.hampsteadparishchurch.org.uk), as was the comedian Peter Cook. At the top of Hampstead, North End Way divides the main heath from the wooded West Heath, one of London's oldest gay cruising areas (but perfectly family-friendly by day).

You can swim here too, in bucolic majesty. **Hampstead Heath Swimming Ponds** (www.cityoflondon.gov.uk/hampstead; £2, £1 reductions) are the only places in the UK to offer life-guarded open-water public swimming all year round. Competent swimmers aged eight and above are allowed in, but remember there's no shallow end – you just jump straight in.

East of Hampstead tube, a maze of postcard-pretty residential streets shelters **Burgh House** (New End Square, 7431 0144, www.burghhouse.org.uk), a Queen Anne house with a small local history museum and gallery. Also in the area are **2 Willow Road**, architect Ernö Goldfinger's self-designed 1930s residence, and **40 Well Walk**, Constable's home for the last ten years of his life. Downhill towards Hampstead Heath Overground station is **Keats House**.

Further west, and marginally closer to Finchley Road tube, is the **Freud Museum**, while the contemporary art exhibitions of **Camden Arts Centre** are almost opposite Finchley Road & Frognal Overground station.

Sights & museums

2 Willow Road

*2 Willow Road, NW3 1TH (7435 6166, www.nationaltrust.org.uk/2-willow-road). Hampstead tube or Hampstead Heath Overground. **Tours** Mar-Oct 11am, noon, 1pm, 2pm Wed-Sun. **Admission** £7; £3.50 reductions; £17.50 family; free under-5s. Joint ticket with Fenton House £13; £6.50 reductions.*

A surprising addition to the National Trust's collection of historic houses, this small modernist building was designed by Hungarian-born architect Ernö Goldfinger. The house was made to be flexible, with ingenious movable partitions and folding doors. Home to the architect and his wife until their deaths, it contains a fine, idiosyncratic collection of art by the likes of Max Ernst and Henry Moore. Goldfinger also designed Notting Hill's Trellick Tower. Ian Fleming despised the architect and named a James Bond villain after Goldfinger.

Camden Arts Centre

*Arkwright Road, NW3 6DG (7472 5500, www.camdenartscentre.org). Finchley Road tube or Finchley Road & Frognal Overground. **Open** 10am-6pm Tue, Thur-Sun; 10am-9pm Wed. **Admission** free.*

Under director Martin Clark, this 50-year-old gallery eclipses larger, younger venues. The annual artist-curated shows – sculpture, automata, film works – have been among the most memorable in recent history. The Centre also hosts a comprehensive programme of talks, events and workshops, and boasts a good bookshop and a great café, which opens on to a surprisingly tranquil garden.

Fenton House

*3 Hampstead Grove, NW3 6RT (7435 3471, www.nationaltrust.org.uk). Hampstead tube. **Open** Mar-Oct 11am-5pm Wed-Sun. Closed Nov-Feb. **Admission** House & gardens £8; £4 reductions; £20 family; free under-5s. Gardens £2. Joint ticket with 2 Willow Road £13, £6.50 reductions.*

Set in a gorgeous garden, with a 300-year-old apple orchard, this manor house is notable for its 17th- and 18th-century harpsichords, virginals and spinets, which are still played at lunchtime and evening concerts (usually Wed; phone for details). Also on display are European and Chinese porcelain, Chippendale furniture and some artful and intricate 17th-century needlework.

Freud Museum

*20 Maresfield Gardens, NW3 5SX (7435 2002, www.freud.org.uk). Finchley Road tube. **Open** noon-5pm Wed-Sun. **Admission** £8; £4-£6 reductions; free under-12s.*

Driven from Vienna by the Nazis, Sigmund Freud lived in this quiet house in north

---

In the know
A dream in green

Just off North End Way is the secluded and overgrown **Hill Garden & Pergola** (7332 3977, dawn-dusk daily), which was built by Lord Leverhulme using soil from the excavation of the Northern Line's tunnels.

Kenwood House

London with his wife Martha and daughter Anna until his death in 1939. Now a museum with temporary exhibitions, the house displays Freud's antiques, art and therapy tools, including his famous couch. Unusually, the building has two blue plaques, one for Sigmund and another for Anna, a pioneer in child psychiatry.

Keats House

10 Keats Grove, NW3 2RR (7332 3868, www.cityoflondon.gov.uk/things-to-do/keats-house). Hampstead tube, Hampstead Heath Overground or bus 24, 46, 168. **Open** *11am-5pm Wed-Sun.* **Admission** *£6.50; £3.25-5.50 reductions; free under-18s.*

Keats House was the Romantic poet's last British home before tuberculosis forced him to Italy and death at the age of only 25. A leaflet guides you through each room, starting from the rear, as well as providing context for Keats's life and that of his less famous friend and patron, Charles Brown. Painstaking renovation has ensured the decorative scheme is entirely accurate, down to pale pink walls in Keats's humble bedroom. The garden, in which he wrote 'Ode to a Nightingale', is particularly pleasant.

♥ Kenwood House/Iveagh Bequest
Hampstead Lane, NW3 7JR (8348 1286, www.english-heritage.org.uk). Hampstead tube, or Golders Green tube then bus 210. **Open** *10am-5pm daily.* **Admission** *free.*

Set in lovely grounds at the top of Hampstead Heath, Kenwood House is every inch the country manor house. Built in 1616, the mansion was remodelled in the 18th century for William Murray, who made the pivotal

court ruling in 1772 that made it illegal to own slaves in England. The house was purchased by brewing magnate Edward Guinness, who was kind enough to donate his art collection to the nation in 1927. After extensive, splendid renovations, it reopened in 2014. The interiors have been returned to a state that enhances such highlights of the collection as Vermeer's *The Guitar Player*, Gainsborough's *Countess Howe*, and one of Rembrandt's finest self-portraits (dating to c1663). There's a terrific kids' room with games and activities too.

Pubs & bars

The well-regarded **Bull & Last** gastropub (168 Highgate Road, NW5 1QS, 7267 3641, www.thebullandlast.co.uk) will reopen after refurbishment in autumn 2019. We're hoping it doesn't change too much.

Holly Bush
22 Hollymount, NW3 6SG (7435 2892, www.hollybushhampstead.co.uk). Hampstead tube or Hampstead Heath Overground. **Open** *noon-11pm Mon-Sat; noon-10.30pm Sun. Food served noon-3.30pm, 6-10pm Mon-Thur; noon-4.30pm, 6-10pm Fri, Sat; noon-8pm Sun.*

As the trend for gutting old pubs claims yet more Hampstead boozers, this place's cachet increases. Located on a quiet hilltop backstreet, this Grade II-listed building was originally built as a house in the 1790s and used as the Assembly Rooms in the 1800s, before becoming a pub in 1928. A higgledy-piggledy air remains, with three low-ceilinged bar areas and one bar counter at which decent pints are poured. Sound food and a good choice of wines by the glass are further draws.

HIGHGATE

▶ *Archway or Highgate tube.*

Taking its name from the tollgate that once stood on the High Street, Highgate is inexorably linked with London's medieval mayor, Richard 'Dick' Whittington. As the story goes, the disheartened Whittington, having failed to make his fortune, fled the City as far as Highgate Hill, but turned back when he heard the Bow bells peal out 'Turn again, Whittington, thrice Mayor of London'. Today, the area is best known for the atmospheric grounds of **Highgate Cemetery**. Adjoining the cemetery is pretty **Waterlow Park**, created by low-cost housing pioneer Sir Sydney Waterlow in 1889, with ponds, a mini-aviary, tennis courts, and a cute garden café in 16th-century **Lauderdale House** (8348 8716, www.lauderdalehouse.co.uk), former home of Charles II's mistress, Nell Gwynn. North of Highgate tube, shady **Highgate Woods** are preserved as a conservation area, with a nature trail, an adventure playground and a café that hosts live jazz during the summer. It is a surviving remnant of the vast Middlesex Forest that once spread in every direction.

Sights & museums

Highgate Cemetery
Swains Lane, N6 6PJ (8340 1834, www. highgate-cemetery.org). Archway tube. **Open** *East Cemetery Mar-Oct 10am-5pm daily. Nov-Feb 10am-4pm daily. Tours 2pm Sat. West Cemetery by tour only, check website for times.* **Admission** *£4; free under-18s. Tours East Cemetery £8, £4 reductions. West Cemetery £12; £6 reductions.*

The final resting place of some very famous Londoners, Highgate Cemetery is a wonderfully overgrown maze of ivy-cloaked Victorian tombs and time-shattered urns. Visitors can wander at their own pace through the East Cemetery, with its memorials to Karl Marx, George Eliot and Douglas Adams, but the most atmospheric part of the cemetery is the foliage-shrouded West Cemetery, laid out in 1839. Only accessible on an organised

In the know
George Michael

The late Wham! singer lived at The Grove, Highgate. Since his death on Christmas Day 2016, his home has become a place of pilgrimage for fans from all over the world. A vast array of tributes to the star were finally cleared from the square in 2018.

tour (book ahead, dress respectfully and arrive 30 minutes early), the shady paths wind past gloomy catacombs, grand Victorian pharaonic tombs, and the graves of notables such as poet Christina Rossetti, scientist Michael Faraday and poisoned Russian dissident Alexander Litvinenko.

▶ *Highgate Cemetery closes during burials, so call ahead before you visit – even if you're only planning a mooch round the East Cemetery.*

Pubs & bars

The Bull
13 North Hill, N6 4AB (8341 0510, www. thebullhighgate.co.uk). Highgate tube. **Open** *noon-11pm Mon-Thur, Sun; noon-midnight Fri; 10am-midnight Sat. Food served until 10pm Mon-Sat; until 9pm Sun.*

First impressions would suggest the Bull is just another suburban gastropub, but note the enamelled beer memorabilia on the walls and garlands of hop flowers: this pub holds beer in extremely high esteem. You might catch a glimpse of the Willy Wonka tubing and brass vats of the brewing equipment, and the beer taps reveal almost nothing recognisable from the average high-street chain pub. Five of the pumps dispense the fine products of the London Brewing Company, made on the premises, and keg fonts advertise the likes of Sierra Nevada Torpedo and Veltins Pils.

ISLINGTON

▶ *Angel tube or Highbury & Islington tube/ Overground.*

Islington started life as a country village beside one of Henry VIII's expansive hunting reserves. It soon became an important livestock market, supplying the Smithfield meat yards, before being enveloped into Greater London. The 19th century brought industrial development along the Regent's Canal and later industrial decay, but locals kept up their spirits at the area's music halls, launchpads for such working-class heroes as Marie Lloyd, George Formby and Norman Wisdom. From the 1960s, there was an influx of arts and media types, who gentrified the Georgian squares and Victorian terraces, and opened cafés, restaurants and boutiques around Upper Street and Essex Road.

Close to Angel station on Upper Street, the **Camden Passage** antique market bustles with browsing activity on Wednesdays and Saturdays. The music halls have long gone, but locals still take advantage of the celluloid offerings at the **Screen on the Green** (*see p324* Everyman & Screen Cinemas) and the stage productions at the **Almeida** theatre (*see p366*).

North of Angel, Regency-era Canonbury Square was once home to George Orwell (no. 27) and Evelyn Waugh (no. 17A). One of the handsome townhouses now contains the **Estorick Collection of Modern Italian Art**. Nearby, on Compton Terrace, the Grade I-listed Gothic masterpiece **Union Chapel** (*see p350*) is still a working church, but also a help centre for London's homeless and a superb music venue. Just beyond the end of Upper Street is **Highbury Fields**, where 200,000 Londoners fled in 1666 to escape the Great Fire. The surrounding district is best known as the home of Arsenal Football Club, who abandoned the charming Highbury Stadium in 2006 for the gleaming 60,000-seat behemoth that is the **Emirates Stadium** (Hornsey Road, N7 7AJ). Fans can either take a fine self-guided audio tour of the stadium or check out the memorabilia at the **Arsenal Museum** (7619 5000, www. arsenal.com). Dedicated football fans will enjoy walking a couple of blocks east to Avenell Road, where Archibald Leitch's palatial East Stand has been preserved as offices; on parallel Highbury Hill, a single painted house marks the entrance to the vanished West Stand.

Sights & museums

Estorick Collection of Modern Italian Art

39A Canonbury Square, N1 2AN (7704 9522, www.estorickcollection.com). Highbury & Islington tube/Overground or bus 271. **Open** *11am-6pm Wed-Sat; noon-5pm Sun.* **Admission** *£6.50; £4.50 reductions; free under-16s, students.*

Originally owned by American political scientist and writer Eric Estorick, this is a wonderful repository of early 20th-century Italian art – substantially renovated for its reopening in 2017. It is one of the world's foremost collections of futurism, Italy's brash and confrontational contribution to international modernism. The galleries are full of movement, machines and colour, while the temporary exhibits meet the futurist commitment to fascism full on. There is also a shop and café.

Restaurants

Other good choices include ever-popular gastropub, the **Draper's Arms** (44 Barnsbury Street, N1 1ER, 7619 0348, www.thedrapersarms.com) and **Rök Islington** (149 Upper Street, N1 1RA,

7686 8024, www.roklondon.com), a branch of the Scandi-Brit smokehouse.

Oldroyd ££

344 Upper Street, N1 0PD (8617 9010, www. oldroydlondon.com). Angel tube. **Open** *noon-11pm Mon-Thur; noon-11.30pm Fri, Sat; noon-9.30pm Sun.* **Map** *pull-out P3. Modern European*

The first solo restaurant from Tom Oldroyd (former chef-director at Polpo, *see p172*) is a small place with big ambition. If you've eaten at Polpo, you won't be surprised by the high-impact flavourings and combinations, but here the menu draws on France and Spain as well as Italy. The tiny kitchen offers a set lunch of stunning small plates (£16 for two courses or £19 for three) and a similarly exquisite dinner a la carte: dishes might include goat's curd, violet artichokes, girolles and pea shoots, or monkfish tail, chicken liver sauce, grilled apricot, runner beans and almond. There's hardly enough room to swing a cat, but it's a tasty menu by a renowned chef at very reasonably prices.

▶ *Tom Oldroyd also runs the Duke of Richmond pub and dining room in Hackney (316 Queensbridge Road, E8 3NH, 7923 3990, www.thedukeofrichmond.com).*

♥ Ottolenghi ££

287 Upper Street, N1 2TZ (7288 1454, www. ottolenghi.co.uk). Angel tube or Highbury & Islington tube/Overground. **Open** *8am-10.30pm Mon-Sat; 9am-7pm Sun. Café*

Hit cookbooks have made this flagship branch of the burgeoning Ottolenghi empire a point of pilgrimage for foodies the world over. French toast made from brioche and served with crème fraîche and a thin berry and muscat compote makes a heady start to the day. Or there's welsh rarebit, scrambled eggs with smoked salmon or a lively chorizo-spiked take on baked beans served with sourdough, fried egg and black pudding. In the evening (when bookings are taken), the cool white interior works a double shift as a smart and comparatively pricey restaurant serving elegant fusion dishes for sharing.

♥ Salut! ££

412 Essex Road, N1 3PJ (3441 8808, salut-london.co.uk). Essex Road rail. **Open** *6-11pm Tue-Thur; noon-3pm, 6-11pm Fri-Sun. Modern European*

Salut offers a relaxed take on modern European haute cuisine. The menu is understated but everything on it demonstrates exquisite attention to detail: on one recent visit, king crab and watercress came with unexpected crab roe foam and micro herb pesto; the 'selection of onions'

69 Colebrooke Row

with a juicy pork belly was three colourful piles of alliums that were in turn pickled, caramelised and charred to perfection; poached pear was perfectly complemented by fermented berries, rich fruit jelly, hazelnut crumble and white chocolate foam. These beautiful plates of food taste as good as they look – without breaking the bank.

Smokehouse ££
63-69 Canonbury Road, N1 2DG (7354 1144, www.smokehouseislington.co.uk). Highbury & Islington tube/Overground. **Open** *noon-11pm Mon-Fri; noon-midnight Sat; noon-10.30pm Sun. Barbecue*

It may be a barbecue restaurant, but the menu extends to French bistro dishes, carefully sourced British produce and even Korean flavours. The mutton chops come from the grill, not the barman's cheeks, and they come fatty and full-flavoured. Mullet is smoked, cut into translucent slivers and served with white pickled clams, radishes and sea purslane. Pit-roasted corn on the cob, slathered with buttery smoked béarnaise sauce, shows that a barbecue isn't all about meat.

♥ Trullo ££
300-302 St Paul's Road, N1 2LH (7226 2733, www.trullorestaurant.com). Highbury & Islington tube/Overground. **Open** *12.30-2.45pm, 6-10.15pm Mon-Sat; 12.30-2.45pm, 6-9.15pm Sun. Italian*

While evenings are still busy-to-frantic in this two-floored contemporary trattoria, lunchtime finds Trullo calm and the cooking relaxed and assured. Grills and roasts from the carte might include Black Hampshire pork chop and cod with cannellini beans and mussels, while pappardelle with beef shin ragù has been a staple since Trullo's early days and remains a silky, substantial delight.

Pubs & bars

The **Old Queen's Head** (*see p341*) is a boisterous and lively pub.

♥ 69 Colebrooke Row
69 Colebrooke Row, N1 8AA (07540 528 593, www.69colebrookerow.com). Angel tube. **Open** *5pm-midnight Mon-Wed, Sun; 5pm-1am Thur; 5pm-2am Fri, Sat.*

It's not easy to get a seat in Tony Conigliaro's flagship bar without booking. Punters come for the outstanding cocktails – some of which may push the boundaries of what can be put in a glass, but they always maintain the drinkability of the classics. Take the Terroir, for instance, which lists as its ingredients 'distilled clay, flint and lichen', and tastes wonderfully like a chilled, earthy, minerally vodka. It's made in the upstairs laboratory, which also produces bespoke cocktail ingredients such as Guinness reduction, paprika bitters, rhubarb cordial and pine-infused gin. There's a subtle jazz-age vibe in the small, low-lit room and – on certain nights – a pianist belts out swinging standards.

Craft Beer Company

55 White Lion Street, N1 9PP (7278 0318, www.thecraftbeerco.com/islington). Angel tube. **Open** *4-11pm Mon-Thur; noon-1am Fri, Sat; noon-10.30pm Sun. Food served 4-10pm Mon-Thur; noon-3pm, 4-10pm Fri; noon-10pm Sat; noon-9pm Sun.* **Map** *pull-out O3*

Each of London's Craft Beer Co pubs has dozens of taps, but this Islington outpost is the only one that could also be labelled cosy. A comfortable pub with an excellent beer list is a dangerous proposition. You could certainly spend many happy hours (and rather a lot of money – the list is long but not cheap) finding a new favourite pint with the help of the knowledgeable, friendly bar staff. Outdoor tables and a covered yard offer the beer buffs who flock here the option of a little daylight, too.

♥ Earl of Essex

25 Danbury Street, N1 8LE (7424 5828, www.earlofessex.net). Angel tube. **Open** *noon-11.30pm Mon-Thur; noon-midnight Fri, Sat; noon-11pm Sun.*

The first thing you notice on entering this backstreet Georgian pub is the beautiful island back-bar with a 1960s 'Watney Red Barrel' sign; the second is the vast list of beers on offer. There are 13 on keg, three on cask, plus a couple of quality ciders. The range covers Britain (including a pouring from the on-site Earl's Brewery), Europe and the USA. Staff are happy to offer tastings and know their stuff. On the menu, dishes are all listed with beer recommendations. Whether you really need a suggested beer match for a fishfinger sandwich is a matter of opinion, but it's a nice touch.

Shops & services

Islington isn't the shopping area it once was – many of the boutiques have been replaced by chains – but Upper Street still rewards a stroll and Camden Passage is full of little cafés and boutiques, not least crafters' favourite wool shop **Loop** at no.15 (www.loopknittingshop.com).

♥ Aria

Barnsbury Hall, Barnsbury Street, N1 1PN (7704 6222, www.ariashop.co.uk). Angel tube or Highbury & Islington tube/Overground. **Open** *10am-6.30pm Mon-Sat; 11am-5pm Sun. Homewares*

Housed in an impressive Victorian-era former concert hall, Aria is one of London's best design destinations. As well as mid-range contemporary designed kitchenware, clocks and lighting by Alessi, Marimekko and Kartell, there are quirkier international treasures, including vintage Indian trestle market tables and Finnish folklore cushions from Klaus Haapaniemi.

♥ Cass Art

66-67 Colebrooke Row, N1 8AB (7354 2999, www.cassart.co.uk). Angel tube. **Open** *9.30am-8pm Mon-Fri; 10am-8pm Sat; noon-6pm Sun. Art supplies*

This cavernous store, hidden down a back street by Tony Conigliaro's cocktail bar *(see p251)*, houses a dazzling array of art materials. Everything is here, from sable brushes and oil paints to Winsor & Newton inks and artists' mannequins. You'll find all you need for crafting too, with full accessories for screen printing, calligraphy and découpage. It's absolutely brilliant for kids, with stickers, origami and paper-doll sets from hip French brand Djeco, art toys like Etch-a-Sketch and more felt-tip pens and glitter pots than you can shake a glue stick at.

twentytwentyone

274-275 Upper Street, N1 2UA (7288 1996, www.twentytwentyone.com). Angel tube or Highbury & Islington tube/Overground. **Open** *10am-6pm Mon-Sat; 11am-5pm Sun. Homewares*

There's a definite Scandi-slant to furniture store twentytwentyone. Set over two spacious floors, its sleek lines, muted colours and clean outlines display minimalistic furniture, accessories and ceramics at their most appealing. We love the functionality of the Lonneberga Wood stacking beds, which will transform a study into a guest room, and the off-kilter angles of Martino Gamper's colourful Arnold Circus stool. The El Baúl golf-ball-like storage box is perfect for hiding kids' toys somewhere chic. You can also find the world's most stylish smoke alarm here – a tactile pastel ingot that simply sticks to the ceiling.

COME HERE, YOU

Get to know the London attractions with pulling power, and book them for less with Time Out.

 TIMEOUT.COM/
LONDON/ATTRACTIONS

THE BEST OF THE CITY

East London

Browse Instagram today, and it's hard to believe how recently east London was notorious for slums and cursed with the city's smelliest and most unpleasant industries. Jack the Ripper stalked through Whitechapel; the presence of the docks – the sanitised remains of which can be enjoyably explored at Wapping and Limehouse – later attracted some of the most brutal bombing during the Blitz. How things change. East London now comprises much of what is most vibrant about the capital: Spitalfields and Brick Lane, Shoreditch and Hoxton, Dalston and Hackney are all must-visits, while the Olympic Park and Docklands also have plenty of interest.

♥ **Don't miss**

1 Redchurch Street *p265*
London's best shopping street. Period.

2 Broadway Market *p273*
Shop and people-watch by the canal in Hackney.

3 Columbia Road Market *p270*
Sunday flower power and a street packed with independent shops.

4 ArcelorMittal Orbit *p277*
Slide down a sculpture.

Emirates Air Line *p277*

EAST END

Restaurants

1. Bistrotheque *p269*
2. Brat *p264*
3. Brick Lane Beigel Bake *p259*
4. Clove Club *p264*
5. Cub *p264*
6. E Pellicci *p269*
7. Gunpowder *p259*
8. The Kitchens *p259*
9. Lyle's *p266*
10. Marksman *p270*
11. Monty's Deli *p266*
12. Needoo Grill *p263*
13. Oklava *p266*
14. Poppies *p260*
15. Rochelle Canteen *p266*
16. Smokestak *p260*
17. Smoking Goat *p266*
18. Som Saa *p260*
19. Tayyabs *p263*

Pubs & bars

1. Bounce Old Street *p267*
2. Draughts Café *p272*
3. Happiness Forgets *p267*
4. Mayor of Scaredy Cat Town *p270*
5. Old Blue Last *p267*
6. Sager + Wilde Paradise Row *p270*
7. Satan's Whiskers *p270*
8. Wenlock Arms *p267*

Shops & services

1. Atika *p260*
2. Boxpark *p267*
3. Broadway Market *p273*
4. Colombia Road Market *p270*
5. Goodhood Store *p267*
6. House of Hackney *p268*
7. Hoxton Street Monster Supplies *p268*
8. Libreria *p261*
9. Mercantile London *p261*
10. Old Spitalfields Market *p261*
11. Rough Trade East *p262*
12. Tatty Devine *p262*

SPITALFIELDS & BRICK LANE

▶ *Aldgate East tube, Liverpool Street tube/ rail or Shoreditch High Street Overground.*

Approach this area from Liverpool Street Station, up Brushfield Street, and you'll know you're on the right track when the magnificent spiky spire of **Christ Church Spitalfields** comes into view. The area's other signature sight, **Old Spitalfields Market**, has upmarket stalls and restaurants, gathered underneath a vaulted Victorian roof, now alongside a rather sterile redeveloped square and office blocks.

Outside, along Brushfield Street, the shops look as if they're from Dickens' day, but most are recent inventions. Settle any anxieties about gentrification by heading a few streets south: on Sundays, the salt-of-the-earth **Petticoat Lane Market** hawks knickers and cheap electronics around Middlesex Street.

A block north of Spitalfields Market is **Dennis Severs' House**, while across from the market, on the east side of Commercial Street and in the shadow of Christ Church, the **Ten Bells** (84 Commercial Street, 7247 7532, www.tenbells.com) is where one of Jack the Ripper's victims drank her last gin. On the next corner, Sandra Esqulant's **Golden Heart** pub (no.110, 7247 2158) has hosted every Young British Artist of note, ever since the day Gilbert & George decided to pop in on their new local.

The streets between here and Brick Lane to the east are dourly impressive, lined with tall, shuttered Huguenot houses; 19 Princelet Street opens to the public a few times a year as the **Museum of Immigration and Diversity** (7247 5352, www.19princeletstreet.org.uk). This unrestored 18th-century house was home first to French silk merchants and later to Polish Jews who built a synagogue in the garden; its spare exhibition now serves as a symbol of the many changes this area has witnessed.

Join the crowds flowing east from Spitalfields Market along Hanbury Street at the weekend, and the direction you turn at the end determines which **Brick Lane** you see. Turn right and you'll know you're in 'Banglatown', the name adopted by the ward back in 2002: until you hit the bland modern offices beside the kitsch Banglatown arch, it's almost all Bangladeshi cafés, curry houses, grocery stores, money-transfer services and sari shops – plus the **Pride of Spitalfields** (3 Heneage Street, 8089 5014), an old-style East End boozer serving ale to all-comers. Between Fournier Street and Princelet Street, **Jamme Masjid Mosque** is a key symbol of Brick Lane's hybridity. It began as a Huguenot chapel, became a synagogue and was converted, in 1976, into a mosque – in other words, immigrant communities have been layering their experiences on this street at least since 1572, when the St Bartholomew's Day Massacre forced many French Huguenots into exile.

If you turned left when you hit Brick Lane, you'll find yourself in a land of boho gentrification. On Sunday, there's a lively street market, complemented by the trendier UpMarket and Backyard Market (for arts and crafts), which are both held in the **Old Truman Brewery** (nos.91-95). Here, pedestrianised Dray Walk, full of hip

💙 **Time to eat & drink**

Breakfast of champions
E Pellicci *p269*, Good Egg *p272*

Brilliant boozers
Grapes *p275*, Wenlock Arms *p267*

Cocktails to savour
Cub *p264*, Happiness Forgets *p267*, Satan's Whiskers *p270*

Fiery Thai
Som Saa *p260*

Gastro sensation
Marksman *p270*

Winning wine bars
P Franco *p272*, Sager + Wilde Paradise Row *p270*

💙 **Time to shop**

Amazing Perspex jewellery
Tatty Devine *p262*

East London in microcosm
Broadway Market *p273*

Flowers galore
Columbia Road Market *p270*

Hip, home-grown interiors
House of Hackney *p268*

London's best boutiques
Redchurch Street *p265*

Old-school, tech-lite bookshop
Libreria *p261*

Vinyl treats
Rough Trade East *p262*

Christ Church Spitalfields

independent businesses, is crowded every day. As you head north on Brick Lane, you'll find bars, cafés and vintage fashion shops.

Sights & museums

Christ Church Spitalfields

Commercial Street, E1 6LY (7377 2440, www. christchurchspitalfields.org). Liverpool Street tube/rail or Shoreditch High Street Overground. **Open** *10am-4pm Mon-Fri; 1-4pm Sun.* **Admission** *free.* **Map** *p256 T6.*

Built in 1729 by architect Nicholas Hawksmoor, this splendid church has in recent years been restored to its original state (tasteless alterations had been made to the building following a lightning strike in the 19th century). Most tourists get no further than cowering before the wonderfully overbearing spire, but the revived interior is impressive too, its pristine whiteness in marked contrast to its architect's dark reputation. The formidable 1735 Richard Bridge organ is almost as old as the church. Regular concerts are held here, notably during the annual Spitalfields Music Festival (*see p318*).

Dennis Severs' House

18 Folgate Street, E1 6BX (7247 4013, www.dennissevershouse.co.uk). Liverpool Street tube/rail or Shoreditch High Street Overground. **Open** *noon-2pm, 5-9pm Mon; 5-9pm Wed, Fri; noon-4pm Sun.* **Admission** *daytime visits £10; £5 reductions; evening visits £15-£50.* **Map** *p256 S6.*

The ten rooms of this original Huguenot house have been decked out to recreate vivid snapshots of daily life in Spitalfields between 1724 and 1914. A tour through the compelling 'still-life drama', as American creator Dennis Severs dubbed it, takes you through the cellar, kitchen, dining room, smoking room and upstairs to the bedrooms. With hearth and candles burning, smells lingering and objects scattered apparently haphazardly, it feels as though the inhabitants have deserted the building only moments before you arrived.

Spitalfields City Farm

Buxton Street, E1 5AR (7247 8762, www. spitalfieldscityfarm.org). Shoreditch High Street Overground. **Open** *Oct-Mar 10am-4pm Tue-Sun. Apr-Sept 10am-4.30pm Tue-Sun.* **Admission** *free.* **Map** *p256 U5.*

A taste of the countryside in the scruffy city, this is a welcoming and brilliantly maintained green spot. Friendly residents up for a pat include Bayleaf the donkey and a loveable pair of hairy hogs. The farm shop sells homegrown produce – the range of veg is remarkable for the location – but for tourists

the café is a more likely destination. There's always something going on, from laid-back weekend festivals to the kids' Wild Club.

Restaurants

Despite Brick Lane's global reputation for quality curries, most of the food on offer there is disappointing. There are some good restaurants nearby, however: try **Needoo Grill** or **Tayyabs** (*for both, see p263*) on the Whitechapel Road, or **Gunpowder**. Alternatively, opt for Bengali sweets from the **Madhubon Sweet Centre** at 42 Brick Lane.

Brick Lane Beigel Bake £

159 Brick Lane, E1 6SB (7729 0616). Shoreditch High Street Overground. **Open** *24hrs daily.* **Map** *p256 T5* ❸ *Jewish*

This little East End institution rolls out perfect bagels (egg, cream cheese, salt beef, at seriously low prices), good bread and moreish cakes. Even at 3am, fresh-baked goods are pulled from the ovens at the back; no wonder the queue for bagels trails out the door when the local bars and clubs close. Note: this is essentially a takeaway operation – don't expect to be able to linger.

Gunpowder ££

11 Whites Row, E1 7NF (7426 0542, www. gunpowderlondon.com). Aldgate East tube or Liverpool Street tube/rail. **Open** *noon-3pm, 5.30-10.30pm Mon-Sat.* **Map** *p256 T6* ❼ *Indian*

Despite its 'Curry Mile' reputation, it's still surprisingly hard to find a good Indian restaurant in the Brick Lane area. This tiny family-run restaurant – with a kitchen headed by Nirmal Save, once a chef at Mayfair's storied Tamarind – aims to bring quality small-plate eating to Indian food, ditching stomach-bursting breads and creamy sauces for delights such as *rasam ke bomb*, chilli cheese toast and Chettinad pulled duck served with homemade *oothappam*. The place oozes passion without a hint of pretension; at weekends it positively buzzes.

The Kitchens £-££

Old Spitalfields Market, 16 Horner Square, E1 6EW (oldspitalfieldsmarket.com). Liverpool Street tube/rail or Shoreditch High Street Overground. **Open** *11am-8pm Mon-Fri; 11am-6pm Sat; 11am-5pm Sun.* **Map** *p256 S6* ❽

As part of the Old Spitalfields Market refurbishment, ten kitchen units serve up first-rate nosh from some of London's highly rated eateries, all curated by superstar chef Nuno Mendes of Chiltern Firehouse. Look out for cult dumplings from the Dumpling Shack, nose-to-tail, open-fire cooking at Flank and possibly the best sandwich in the city from Monty's Deli (*see p266*).

Poppies £

6-8 Hanbury Street, E1 6QR (7247 0892, www.poppiesfishandchips.co.uk). Liverpool Street tube/rail or Shoreditch High Street Overground. **Open** *11am-11pm Mon-Thur; 11am-11.30pm Fri, Sat; 11am-10.30pm Sun.* **Map** *p256 T6* ⓮ *Fish & chips*

Poppies' pick and mix assortment of shiny British kitsch – including a jukebox, mini red telephone box and a monochrome photo of heart-throb Cliff Richard – makes it look like a simulation of a fish and chip shop. But the food on the plate is excellent, and offered grilled as well as fried. Extending beyond the staples of cod and haddock, the menu encompasses mackerel, seafood platters and jellied eels. The bill, however, gives the game away – Poppies is a cut above the average chippie.

Smokestak £

35 Sclater Street, E1 6LB (3873 1733, smokestak.co.uk). Liverpool Street tube/rail or Shoreditch High Street Overground. **Open** *noon-3pm, 5.30-11pm Mon-Fri; noon-11pm Sat; noon-9.30pm Sun.* **Map** *p256 T5* ⓰ *Street food*

Having built a cult following for its smokehouse meats, Smokestak did the decent thing, opening up a restaurant proper: this semi-industrial space with a hum of throbbing beats. There's a man-tastic, meat-lovin' vibe, the place full of bearded blokes in their 30s supping craft beers and cocktails. Beef brisket is the signature dish, coming as a single hunk of flesh in a bun. Smoked overnight, for 12-14 hours, over English oak, it's moist, smoky, sweet and salty – and priced at a fiver. That's scandalously good value for London. The sticky toffee pud is insanely good, but may push you over the edge. Come here hungry – we mean *caveman* hungry – and be sure to order plenty of the citrussy fennel and celery slaw as palate-cleansing yin to all that meaty yang.

❤ Som Saa £££

43A Commercial Street, E1 6BD (7324 7790, www.somsaa.com). Shoreditch High Street Overground. **Open** *6-10pm Mon; noon-2.30pm, 6-10.30pm Tue-Fri; noon-3pm, 6-10.30pm Sat.* **Map** *p256 T6* ⓲ *Thai*

Som Saa isn't somewhere you come for a cheeky green curry and a plate of pad thai – this is authentic, red-hot food from Thailand's north-eastern provinces. Take the deep-fried seabass with Isaan (north-eastern) herbs, for instance. The delicate flesh comes

Libreria

loose easily, leaving a cartoon fish skeleton and crunchy roasted-rice-battered skin, herbs (mint, coriander, Thai basil), mandolin-thin shallots and a puddle of sweet-sour-salt-fire sauce. The effect is thrilling: like setting off ooh-aahh fireworks of taste and texture.

Pubs & bars

Mayor of Scaredy Cat Town

12-16 Artillery Lane, E1 7LS (7078 9639, www. themayorofscaredycattown.com). Liverpool Street tube/rail or Shoreditch High Street Overground. **Open** *5pm-midnight Mon-Thur; 3pm-midnight Fri; noon-midnight Sat; noon-10.30pm Sun.* **Map** *p256 S6* ❹

Part of the trend for 'secret' speakeasies, this one is a basement bar beneath the Breakfast Club. The entrance is the one that looks like a big Smeg fridge door. Go inside and you'll find a quirky, dimly lit cocktail bar clad in exposed brick and wood: it's all a bit like a cabin from *Twin Peaks*. The drinks menu makes an amusing mockery of more self-conscious 'underground' venues. The cocktails– classics and house specials – are well crafted on the whole.

Shops & services

Atika

55-59 Hanbury Street, E1 5JP (7377 0730, atikalondon.co.uk). Shoreditch High Street Overground. **Open** *11am-7pm Mon-Sat; noon-6pm Sun.* **Map** *p256 T6* ❶ *Fashion*

The vintage emporium formerly known as Blitz has been jazzed up and born again. You'll still find the capital's hugest and most impressive pre-loved wares here, but they now sit alongside an edit of new lifestyle and fashion pieces from the likes of Barry the Cactus and Illustrated People. There are also manis from Wah and frequent in-store events... that's before you've even got to the vintage clothes and furniture, which is clean, well-presented and dazzling in its variety and quantity.

♥ Libreria
65 Hanbury Street. E1 5JP (libreria.io). Shoreditch High Street Overground. **Open** *10am-6pm Tue, Wed; 10am-8pm Thur-Sat; 11am-6pm Sun.* **Map** *p256 T6* **❽** *Books*

This tech-free bookshop is so into printed words on physical pages that using your mobile phone is banned. 'Techpreneur' – and former special advisor to David Cameron – Rohan Silva founded the analogue bookshop as a reaction against digital distractions. The shelves were designed by Slade School artists, their contents arranged to maximise the possibility of chance book discoveries, and there is a whisky bar for events and a risograph printing press downstairs.

Mercantile London
17 Lamb Street, E1 6EA (7377 8926, www. themercantilelondon.com). Shoreditch High Street Overground. **Open** *10.30am-7pm Mon-Sat; 11am-6pm Sun.* **Map** *p256 T6* **❾** *Fashion*

This boutique, full of independent labels (not to mention an in-store dog called Robert), is enough to restore your faith in the future of London retail. Founder Debra McCann has a good eye for striking fashion that ordinary women will covet, so labels err on the side of tasteful rather than daft – think high-waisted jeans, batwing silk blouses and cool ankle boots at sensible prices (£70-£100 for a silk top, £150 for well-made leather boots).

Old Spitalfields Market
Brushfield Street, E1 6AA (www. oldspitalfieldsmarket.com). Liverpool Street tube/rail or Shoreditch High Street Overground. **Open** *10am-5pm Mon-Fri, Sun; 11am-5pm Sat.* **Map** *p256 S6* **❿** *Market*

Old Spitalfields Market is one of east London's busiest shopping hubs. Built in the late 1800s, the market hall was restored and refurbished in the early 2000s and further revamped by Foster + Partners in 2017. Edging the giant covered space are numerous permanent boutiques from big brands such as Mac, Hackett, Dr Martens and Chanel, but it's the heart of the market that's the most exciting. Here you'll find two concourses packed with traders selling arts, crafts, clothing and knick-knacks seven days a week. There's an antiques market every Thursday for vintage maps, books, furniture,

Old Spitalfields Market

fashion and collectibles, and a vinyl market twice a month. These days no London market is complete without a serious food offering: at Spitalfields it comes courtesy of The Kitchens (*see p259*).

❤ Rough Trade East

*Dray Walk, Old Truman Brewery, 91 Brick Lane, E1 6QL (7392 7788, www.roughtrade. com). Shoreditch High Street Overground. **Open** 9am-9pm Mon-Thur; 9am-8pm Fri; 10am-8pm Sat; 11am-7pm Sun. **Map** p256 T6* ⑪ *Music*

The indie music label Rough Trade – perhaps most famous for signing the Smiths in the early 1980s – set up this 5,000sq ft (465sq m) record store, café and gig space in the noughties when the death of music shops in the face of internet price-cutting was widely accepted as inevitable. Perversely, Rough Trade instead offered a physical space where music-lovers could browse a dizzying range of vinyl and CDs, spanning punk, indie, dub, soul, electronica and more, providing them with 16 listening posts and a stage for live sets. Now its triumph seems like it was always certain.

❤ Tatty Devine

*236 Brick Lane, E2 7EB (7739 9191, www. tattydevine.com). Shoreditch High Street Overground. **Open** 10am-6pm Mon-Fri; 11am-6pm Sat; 11am-5pm Sun. **Map** p256 T5* ⑫ *Jewellery*

Shoreditch pioneers Tatty Devine (AKA art-school pals Harriet Vine and Rosie Wolfenden) began making and selling their distinctive perspex jewellery from this bijou boutique in 2001. Since then, they've opened a store in Covent Garden and a concession in Selfridges (*see p146*), collaborated with everyone from Ashish to Rob Ryan, and seen their designs sold in over 200 shops worldwide. As well as now-classic perspex pieces such as the anchor and dinosaur necklaces and volume-control brooch, you'll find rings, cufflinks and earrings in enamel, wood and silver.

WHITECHAPEL

▶*Aldgate East tube or Whitechapel tube/ Overground.*

Not one of London's prettier thoroughfares, busy but anonymous Whitechapel Road sets the tone for this area. One bright spot is **Whitechapel Gallery**, west from the foot of Brick Lane, while a little to the east, the **Whitechapel Bell Foundry** (nos.32 & 34) made its last bell on 22 March 2017, having been in business in these premises since 1738, during which time it produced Philadelphia's Liberty Bell and 'Big Ben' (*see p107*). At Whitechapel's foremost place of worship, it isn't bells but a muezzin that summons the faithful each Friday: the **East London Mosque**, founded elsewhere

Whitechapel Gallery

in 1910 and now the focal point for the largest Muslim community in Britain, can accommodate 10,000 worshippers. Behind is Fieldgate Street and the dark mass of **Tower House**, a former doss house whose 700 rooms have, inevitably, been redeveloped into flats. Joseph Stalin and George Orwell (researching his book *Down and Out in Paris and London*) kipped here for pennies.

East again is the frontage of the Royal London Hospital – the hospital itself is now in the vast blue tower block looming over it from behind – and in the alleys to the south, a small crypt on Newark Street holds the **Royal London Hospital Archives & Museum** (7377 7608, bartshealth. nhs.uk, 10am-4pm Tue-Fri, archives by appointment only). Inside are reproduction letters from Jack the Ripper (including the notorious missive 'From Hell', delivered with an enclosed portion of human kidney) and information on Joseph Merrick, the 'Elephant Man', rescued by Royal London surgeon Sir Frederick Treves. Behind the hospital is the high-tech **Centre of the Cell** (4 Newark Street, 7882 2562, www. centreofthecell.org), which gives visitors a lively, interactive insight into cell biology in a purpose-built pod, suspended over labs investigating cancer and tuberculosis.

Sights & museums

Whitechapel Gallery

*77-82 Whitechapel High Street, E1 7QX (7522 7888, www.whitechapelgallery.org). Aldgate East tube. **Open** 11am-6pm Tue, Wed, Fri, Sat; 11am-9pm Thur; 11am-6pm Sun. **Admission** free. Temporary exhibitions vary. **Map** p256 T7.*

This East End stalwart, a perennial favourite of avant-garde aficionados and art students, continues to build on a stellar reputation as a contemporary art pioneer that began with exhibitions of Picasso – *Guernica* was shown here in 1939 – Jackson Pollock, Mark Rothko and Frida Kahlo. The Grade II-listed building underwent a 21st-century refurb that saw it expand into the similarly historic former library next door – rather brilliantly, the architects left the two buildings stylistically distinct rather than trying to smooth out their differences. As well as nearly tripling its exhibition space, the Whitechapel gave itself a research centre and archives, plus a café/bar. With no permanent collection, there's a rolling programme of temporary shows, but an increasing number of artists have contributed permanently to the fabric of the building: a few years back, Rachel Whiteread added gold vine leaves to the gallery's frontage.

Restaurants

Needoo Grill £

*85-87 New Road, E1 1HH (7247 0648, www. needoogrill.co.uk). Whitechapel tube/ Overground. **Open** noon-11.30pm daily. **Map** p256 U7 ⑫ Pakistani*

This squashed space doesn't suffer from the same problem of endless queues as its rival Tayyabs, though you will usually have a wait. Bright red walls, leather benches and blaring flatscreen TVs are the order of the day, yet with curries this good, the decor just fades into the background. What you get are succulent karahi dishes and specials that include *nihari* (lamb on the bone) and a very passable biriani. Service is swift and friendly.

Tayyabs £

*83-89 Fieldgate Street, E1 1JU (7247 6400, www.tayyabs.co.uk). Aldgate East tube or Whitechapel tube/Overground. **Open** noon-11.30pm daily. **Map** p256 U6 ⑲ Pakistani*

Tayyabs is a full-on, hectic, loud, in-and-out sort of place, and if you come here without booking, expect to wait for up to an hour for a table. But we recommend this Punjabi stalwart because of the cheapness and boldness of the food. Fiery grilled lamb chops are a must. The rest of the menu is all about rich dhals and *masala channa*; unctuous, slow-cooked lamb curries; and good versions of North Indian staples – spice-rubbed tikka, hot, buttery breads and juicy kebabs. The corkage-free bring-your-own-bottle policy doesn't do its popularity any harm.

SHOREDITCH & HOXTON

▶ *Old Street tube/rail, or Hoxton or Shoreditch High Street Overground.*

The story is familiar: in the 1980s, impecunious artists moved into the derelict warehouses in the triangle formed by Old Street, Shoreditch High Street and Great Eastern Street, and quickly turned it into the place to be. At which point, rising rents drove the artists out. They've been replaced by the tech-hip denizens of 'Silicon Roundabout' – a tongue-in-cheek name for the area around Old Street roundabout that became a focus for digital start-ups, the beginning of **East London Tech City** (www.technation.io).

Nightlife permeates the area (linking conveniently to Brick Lane), with centres on Curtain Road, the lower end of Kingsland Road and around Hoxton Square. But the nature of the scene has changed dramatically: growing up in some people's eyes, losing its edge for others. Hotels, smart shops and cocktail bars are more prevalent than bug-eyed rave holes. There's culture of yet another type to come – or, more accurately, return – since the remains of two Shakespearean theatres have been found in the area. The **Theatre** on New Inn Broadway was rediscovered by archaeologists in 2008. Built by James Burbage in 1576, this was the first early modern playhouse and staged plays by Shakespeare, Marlowe and Kidd, before being closed down in 1598. Elements of the dismantled structure were used to build the Globe on Bankside (*see p88*). A short distance south of the Theatre on Hewett Street was the **Curtain Theatre**, which opened in 1577 and continued staging plays until 1624. Unlike its contemporaries, the Curtain was rectangular and featured a very wide stage suitable for sword-fighting. From late 2019 in-situ remains of the Theatre will go on display on New Inn Broadway, while the ongoing redevelopment of the Curtain site will eventually include a permanent Shakespeare exhibition.

At present, apart from seemingly countless galleries – Wharf Road neighbours **Parasol Unit** (no.14, N1 7RW, 7490 7373, www.parasol-unit.org) and **Victoria Miro** (no.16, N1 7RW, 7336 8109, www.victoria-miro.com) and not-for-profit pioneer **Raven Row** (56 Artillery Lane, E1 7LS, 7377 4300, www.ravenrow.org) are notable – the area's sole bona fide tourist attraction is the exquisite **Geffrye Museum**, a short walk north up Kingsland Road. The surrounding area is dense with good, cheap Vietnamese restaurants: **Sông Quê** (134 Kingsland Road, E2 8DY, 7613 3222) is our favourite.

To the east, it's a short walk towards Bethnal Green and **Columbia Road flower market**.

Sights & museums

Geffrye Museum

136 Kingsland Road, E2 8EA (7739 9893, www.geffrye-museum.org.uk). Hoxton Overground. **Open** *closed until 2020. Almshouse tours 1st Sat, 1st & 3rd Tue, Wed of mth.* **Admission** *donations appreciated. Almshouse tours £5; free under-16s.* **Map** *p256 S4.*

Housed in a set of 18th-century almshouses, the Geffrye Museum has for more than a century offered a vivid physical history of the English interior. Displaying original furniture, paintings, textiles and decorative arts, the museum recreates a sequence of typical middle-class living rooms from 1600 to the present. It's an oddly interesting way to take in domestic history, with any number of intriguing details to catch your eye – from a bell jar of stuffed birds to a particular decorative flourish on a chair. There's an airy restaurant overlooking the lovely gardens, which include a walled plot for herbs and a chronological series in different historical styles. The museum is closed for major redevelopment until 2020, but will continue to host events in the garden and run tours of the almshouses; see the website for details.

Restaurants

Brat £££

First floor, 4 Redchurch Street, E1 6JL (www.bratrestaurant.com). Shoreditch High Street Overground. **Open** *noon-3pm, 6-10pm Mon; noon-3pm, 6-11pm Tue-Sat; noon-5pm Sun.* **Map** *p256 S5* ②

A set of pokey steps go up to a room above a former pub, where you'll find glorious original features – wood panelling, arched windows, parquet floors – and chefs bustling around a large island kitchen. This is a handsome, buzzy chophouse serving a no-frills menu of meat and fish from a wood-fired oven, propped up by modern Brit small plates. Highlights include a subtle soused red mullet and an expertly cooked shorthorn beef chop.

Clove Club ££££

Shoreditch Town Hall, 380 Old Street, EC1V 9LT (7729 6496, www.thecloveclub.com). Old Street tube/rail or Shoreditch High Street Overground. **Open** *6-10.30pm Mon; noon-1.45pm, 6.30-10.30pm Tue-Sat.* **Map** *p256 S5* ④ *Modern European*

It can sometimes be hard to know if a restaurant is trying to make food that you will savour and enjoy, or simply creating dishes for Instagram. Taking no chances, Clove Club does both. Its tasting menu is economically worded in describing a succession of small plates, seasonal and championing British produce, yet oddly esoteric. The best dishes tend to be the ones that aren't trying too hard to impress: the pine fried chicken, perhaps, or a dish of Ruby Red beef, ramson and potato. Shorter four- and six-course menus are available for lunch.

♥ Cub ££

153 Hoxton Street, N1 6PJ (3693 3202, lyancub.com). Hoxton Overground. **Open** *5-11.45pm Tue; 5pm-midnight Wed, Thur, Sun; 5pm-1am Fri, Sat.* **Map** *p256 S4* ⑤ *Plant-based*

Never one to rest on his laurels, meister mixologist Ryan Chetiyawardana ('Mr Lyan') closed his pioneering cocktail bar White Lyan in 2017 and opened Super Lyan and Cub in its place. Super Lyan moved to Amsterdam a year later, but Cub continues to serve a no-choice menu of inventive small plates teamed with equally creative cocktails, all made from sustainable ingredients. It's not technically

💜 Redchurch Street

Map p256 S5.

For the cognoscenti, this is London's best shopping street. As late as the 2000s it was an almost entirely anonymous – even rather grim – cut-through from the north end of Brick Lane to Shoreditch High Street, but this part of London was changing unimaginably fast.

First had come the artists and bug-eyed clubbers, who loved the low rents and space provided by post-industrial semi-dereliction, as well as the freedom they found here from the restrictions that suburban neighbours impose on late-night living. The oft-parodied, tiresomely self-conscious hipster was to follow – and a much-missed restaurant, Les Trois Garçons, which took over a corner pub on Redchurch Street, filled the gap between these generations, providing fine dining in a thoroughly idiosyncratic style, amid flamboyant decor that combined rococo chandeliers and taxidermy.

As Shoreditch went mainstream, Les Trois Garçons morphed into an interiors shop – then departed for Marylebone. But smart, individualistic fashion and homewares shops had by now found their feet on Redchurch Street – in the lee of London's financial powerhouse, the City – a sweet spot between disposable incomes and urban cool. It helped when Terence Conran opened his superb

Boundary London hotel (*see p400*) here; **Soho House** soon followed round the corner on Ebor Street (*see p402*). Some saw the death of Shoreditch and high-tailed it north into Dalston, where the party continues; but many welcomed an impressive growth in civilised, imaginative, independent-minded shopping – driven by art and fashion.

While the artists are long gone from Shoreditch and the clubbers now outnumbered by hen parties, Redchurch Street calmly goes about its business. Aussie botanical beauty shop **Aesop** (no.44) and classic menswear brand **Sunspel** (no.7) anchor one end of the street. Further up are high-quality, eminently wearable clothes at **Modern Society** (no.33), the darkly lit headquarters of fashion store **Hostem** (nos.41-43), and vintage-style up-dos and manicures at **Painted Lady** (no.65). **Labour & Wait** (no.85) sells aesthetically pleasing mops, bread bins and other simply designed essentials, and there are Finnish folk-arty interiors at **Klaus Haapaniemi & Co** (no.81) and cutting-edge design at concept store **Monologue London** (no.93).

There's the sweet boutique cinema **Electric Shoreditch**, beneath multistorey beauty and grooming emporium **Barber & Parlour** (nos.64-66), and plenty of refuelling options: **Brat** (no.4; *see p264*), the **Owl & Pussycat** gastropub (no.34) and New Zealand-born **Allpress Espresso Bar** (no.58).

EAST LONDON

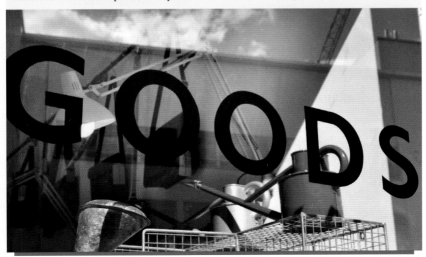

a vegetarian restaurant, but the food is light and plant-dominated, with animal products only making fleeting guest appearances. The Midweek Supper Menu on Wednesdays and Thursdays features three food courses and three drinks for £45 per person. Super-friendly, savvy staff ensure the vibe is more like a house party than a restaurant.

Lyle's £££

Tea Building, 56 Shoreditch High Street, E1 6JJ (3011 5911, lyleslondon.com). Shoreditch High Street Overground. **Open** *8am-11pm Mon-Fri; noon-11pm Sat. Food served noon-2.30pm, 6-10pm Mon-Sat.* **Map** *p256 S5* **9** *British*

Dinner at Lyle's is a long, leisurely affair. You can book and stay as long as you like, as there's no turning tables. The pricing is fair: the no-choice menu costs £59, which gets you four small courses (plus bread, petits fours and filtered tap water), served in a drawn-out procession. The chef is James Lowe, one of the most talented cooks in town; the sweet staff know their food, and the semi-industrial setting (polished concrete floors, exposed girders, whitewashed brick walls) makes for a thoroughly relaxing setting. Set aside two and a half hours or so – then settle in and enjoy your meal.

Monty's Deli £

227-229 Hoxton Street, N1 5LG (7729 5737, www.montys-deli.com). Hoxton Overground. **Open** *11am-10pm Wed-Sun.* **Map** *p256 S3* **11** *Delicatessen*

To say that Monty's has a cult following would be a bit of an understatement. Once a stall at achingly hip Maltby Street Market, it crowdfunded to open a permanent restaurant in 2017. The compact, retro menu echoes a New York kosher-style deli, offering packed sarnies, chicken soup, bagels, chopped liver, latkes, pastries, salads and sauerkraut. But if this is your first time, order one thing: the salt beef. Monty's makes its own, from scratch, and it shows. Try some in the signature reuben sandwich: toasted rye, melted swiss cheese, a lick of mustard, 'Russian dressing' (a piquant mayo-ketchup), a pile of finely shredded kraut, and, finally, lashings of salt beef. It sounds like a lot, but it's perfection.

Oklava ££

74 Luke Street, EC2A 4PY (7729 3032, www.oklava.co.uk). Old Street tube/rail. **Open** *noon-3pm, 5.30-10pm Tue-Sat.* **Map** *p256 S5* **13** *Turkish*

The streets east of Old Street are paved with cheap kebab shops, but Oklava isn't that kind of Turkish. The look is contemporary chic, with an open kitchen and sleek designer furnishings. As for the cooking, Selin Kiazim

has gone back to her Turkish-Cypriot roots in a modish, creative way, showing off skills learnt at Providores (*see p150*). Plates are small, made for sharing, and bursting with flavour: mostly bold and southern-Med-meets-Middle-Eastern, but with dashes and splashes from other parts of the planet. On our last visit service was exceptional, the ambience vibrant, and prices very reasonable.

Rochelle Canteen ££

Rochelle School, 16 Playground Gardens, Arnold Circus, E2 7FA (7729 5677, www.arnoldandhenderson.com). Shoreditch High Street Overground. **Open** *9-11am, noon-3pm Mon-Wed, Sun; 9-11am, noon-3pm, 6-9pm Thur-Sat.* **Map** *p256 T5* **15** *British*

Eating at Melanie Arnold and Margot Henderson's spot remains a distinctive treat: entry is via a buzzer on a tiny door in the wall around an old Victorian school, now a hub of creative studios. Inside, a handful of outdoor tables and a former bike shed converted into an airy, modern space act as the canteen for those creatives – and lucky outsiders in the know. The short but enticing menu might include pea soup with bantam egg and mint; grilled quails and green sauce; rabbit rillettes; and a pork chop with mustard and chard. Newcomers to the Shoreditch dining scene can come and go, but Rochelle Canteen stands firm, and stands out.

Smoking Goat £

64 Shoreditch High Street, E1 6JJ (www.smokinggoatbar.com). Shoreditch High Street Overground. **Open** *noon-3pm, 5.30-11pm Mon-Wed; noon-3.30pm, 5.30pm-1am Thur, Fri; 10am-4pm, 5pm-1am Sat; 10am-4pm, 5-10pm Sun.* **Map** *p256 S5* **17** *Thai*

Got £3.80 in your pocket? Great. Because that's all you'll need for Smoking Goat's lardo-fried rice, aka the best fried rice in London: it's the colour of autumn, the taste of long-haul holidays and the ultimate hangover cure. The restaurant feels like the pub it once was, but with an open-counter kitchen in place of the bar and tightly packed tables that ensure a friendly, noisy buzz. The food is in your face, featuring an abundance of volcanically hot chillies and heaps of fresh herbs. Try fragrant seafood tom yum; 'drunken noodles' – a twist on Cantonese beef ho fun; fish-sauce chicken wings, or, if you're reckless enough, the indecently fiery laab-style pork.

Pubs & bars

Late-night hangout **Charlie Wright's International Bar** (*see p348*) and the multitasking **Book Club** (*see p340*) are at least as much about drinking as the events they host.

Bounce Old Street

*241 Old Street, EC1V 9EY (3657 6525, www.
bouncepingpong.com). Old Street tube/rail.
Open 4-11pm Mon, Tue; 4pm-midnight Wed;
4pm-1am Thur; 1pm-1am Fri; noon-1am Sat;
1-10.30pm Sun. **Map** p256 R5* ①

Whether you're a ping-pong pro or whiff-
whaff wally, there's fun to be had here, the
second of two vast bars dedicated to table
tennis. Like its Holborn predecessor, Bounce
Old Street buzzes with fun as balls land
everywhere but the table and glow under the
UV lights. There's an open-plan restaurant
serving traditional Italian pizzas along a
25ft counter, and suave cocktails at the
bar. Neither of which are likely to improve
your game.

♥ Happiness Forgets

*8-9 Hoxton Square, N1 6NU (7613 0325, www.
happinessforgets.com). Old Street tube/rail
or Shoreditch High Street Overground. **Open**
5-11pm daily. **Map** p256 S4* ③

From the moment you walk in, the staff
will know how to make you happy. The
short list of original cocktails is unfailingly
good: lots of nice twists on classic ideas
but never departing from the essential
cocktail principles of balance, harmony and
drinkability. Star turns: Mr McRae, Perfect
Storm and Tokyo Collins. But the classics
are brilliantly handled too, the food is
fabulous and so is the service. This is a very
special place but not very large: booking is a
good idea.

Old Blue Last

*38 Great Eastern Street, EC2A 3ES (www.
theoldbluelast.com). Old Street tube/rail or
Shoreditch High Street Overground. **Open**
noon-midnight Mon-Wed, Sun; noon-1am
Thur; noon-2am Fri, Sat. **Map** p256 S5* ⑤

Despite being at the heart of the Shoreditch
party scene, the Old Blue Last defies
preconceptions. Absent are the clichéd
bare lightbulbs and brick walls, and,
while London- and US-made craft beers
are available, low-brow big-brand brews
like Heineken and Grolsch get prime
representation. Furniture is minimal,
something you'll be thankful for from 7pm
onwards, when nearby digital drones flock
in to decompress over pints. Its enduring
popularity – and reputation for first-class live
music – keep the Old Blue Last noteworthy
among the East End newcomers.

♥ Wenlock Arms

*26 Wenlock Road, N1 7TA (7608 3406, www.
wenlockarms.com). Old Street tube/rail.
Open 3-11pm Mon; noon-11pm Tue, Wed,
Sun; noon-midnight Thur; noon-1am Fri, Sat.
Map p256 Q4* ⑧

Hoxton Street Monster Supplies *p268*

On an unremarkable backstreet, this old pub
was the tap for a nearby brewery, and poured
its first pint in 1836; it closed with its parent
brewery in the 1960s, then reopened in 1994,
whereupon it won awards for the quality of
its real ale and plaudits for the toastiness
of its real fire. Having fought off threats of
redevelopment and spruced itself up with a
new paint job, new furniture and even more
beer fonts, the Wenlock is the quintessence of
all that is good about pubs – minimal decor,
minimal food and a great range of ace beer.

Shops & services

Once a shabby cut-through, **Redchurch
Street** (*see p265*) has gone on to become
a strong contender for London's
best shopping street.

Boxpark

*2-10 Bethnal Green Road, E1 6GY (7033 2899,
www.boxpark.co.uk). Shoreditch High Street
Overground. **Open** 11am-7pm Mon-Wed, Fri,
Sat; 11am-8pm Thur; noon-6pm Sun. **Map**
p256 S5* ② *Mall*

Refitted shipping containers plonked
underneath the elevated Shoreditch High
Street Overground station make up this
contemporary 'shopping mall'. Installed in
2011, the units of Boxpark are full of high-
street labels (Lllamasqua and Tigi Hair),
but also contain an impressive array of
independents, usually some street food and
an endless stream of pop-ups. The food stalls
are open daily from 8am to 11pm (10am to
10pm on Sunday).

Goodhood Store

*151 Curtain Road, EC2A 3QE (7729 3600,
www.goodhood.co.uk). Old Street tube/
rail. **Open** 10.30am-6.30pm Mon-Fri;
10.30am-7pm Sat; noon-6pm Sun. **Map** p256
S5* ⑤ *Fashion*

A first stop for East End trendies, Goodhood is owned by streetwear obsessives Kyle and Jo. Japanese independent labels are well represented, while other covetable brands include Pendleton, Norse Projects and Wood Wood.

❤ House of Hackney
131 Shoreditch High Street, E1 6JE (7739 3901, www.houseofhackney.com). Old Street tube/ rail or Shoreditch High Street Overground. **Open** *10am-7pm Mon-Sat; 11am-5pm Sun.* **Map** *p256 S5* ❻ *Homewares*

House of Hackney has the makings of a new Liberty (*see p155*): buy your future design classics now, we say. This is one of the most gorgeous retail establishments in London – bedecked in the deliberately over-the-top juxtapositions of print-on-print-on-print that have made the brand's name, and with the entrance full of flowers. Upstairs, you'll find rolls of gorgeous paper, fabric, trays, mugs, fashion and collaborative designs with brands such as Puma; downstairs are generously proportioned sofas and plump armchairs in more-is-more combinations of print and texture.

Hoxton Street Monster Supplies
159 Hoxton Street, N1 6PJ (7729 4159, www. monstersupplies.org). Hoxton Overground. **Open** *1-5pm Thur, Fri; 11am-5pm Sat.* **Map** *p256 S4* ❼ *Children*

Purveyor of quality goods for monsters of every kind, this curious little shop stocks jars of Thickest Human Snot and pots of Salt Made From Tears of Anger – oddly reminiscent of lemon curd and of smoked sea salt. Follow the creepy music past a pinboard plastered with notices for missing brains and gravestone engravers, and you'll find a wall of cabinets piled high with Milk Tooth chocolate bars, Witches' Brew tea and Tinned Fear (a can of stories courtesy of Zadie Smith, Joe Dunthorne and Meg Rosoff). Proceeds support the Ministry of Stories' creative writing and mentoring centre for local children. Mind the invisible cat on your way out.

BETHNAL GREEN

▶ *Bethnal Green tube/Overground, Cambridge Heath Overground or Mile End tube.*

Once a gracious suburb of spacious townhouses, by the mid 19th century Bethnal Green was one of the city's poorest neighbourhoods. As in neighbouring Hoxton, an upturn in fortunes over the last couple of decades was in part occasioned by Bethnal Green's adoption as home by a new generation of artists, with the **Maureen Paley** gallery (21 Herald Street, E2 6JT, 7729 4112, www.maureenpaley.com) having set up here in 1984, but the new Bethnal Green was typified by the arrival of the ambitious **Town Hall Hotel** (Patriot Square, E2 9NF, 7871 0460, www.townhallhotel.com, £££) in

House of Hackney

2016. For a taste of the old Bethnal Green, take a seat at **E Pellicci**, the exemplary traditional London caff.

The **V&A Museum of Childhood** is close to Bethnal Green tube station, but the area's other main attraction is a bit of a walk away (almost in Shoreditch). Nonetheless, a visit to the weekly **Columbia Road flower market** is a lovely way to fritter away a Sunday morning. A microcosmic retail community has grown up around the market: check out **Angela Flanders** (no.96, 7739 7555) for perfume and cult London jeweller **Jacey Withers** (no.110a, www.jaceywithers.com). To refuel, pop into **Jones Dairy** (23 Ezra Street, 7739 5372, www.jonesdairy.co.uk) for organic and local produce, or sink a locally brewed pint at the **Nelson's Head** (32 Horatio Street, E2 7SB, 7613 4434, www.nelsonshead.uk).

Sights & museums

Ragged School Museum
46-50 Copperfield Road, E3 4RR (8980 6405, www.raggedschoolmuseum.org.uk). Mile End tube. **Open** *10am-5pm Wed, Thur; 2-5pm 1st Sun of mth. Tours by appt.* **Admission** *free; donations appreciated.* **Map** *p256 W6.*

Ragged schools were an early experiment in public education: they provided tuition, food and clothes for destitute children. This one was the largest in London, and Dr Barnardo himself taught here. It's now a sweet local museum that contains complete mock-ups of a ragged classroom and Edwardian kitchen, with displays on vanished local history.

V&A Museum of Childhood
Cambridge Heath Road, E2 9PA (8983 5200, www.vam.ac.uk/moc). Bethnal Green tube/Overground or Cambridge Heath Overground. **Open** *10am-5.45pm daily.* **Admission** *free; donations appreciated.* **Map** *p256 V4.*

Home to one of the world's finest collections of children's toys, dolls' houses, games and costumes, the Museum of Childhood is part of the Victoria & Albert Museum (*see p128*). It has been amassing childhood-related objects since 1872 and continues to do so, with *Incredibles* figures complementing bonkers 1970s puppets, Barbie dolls and Victorian praxinoscopes. The museum has lots of hands-on stuff for kids dotted about the many cases of historic artefacts, including dressing-up boxes and soft play areas, though the cases themselves might be of more interest to nostalgic adults than their spawn. Regular small exhibitions are held upstairs, while the café in the central space helps to revive flagging spirits.

Viktor Wynd Museum of Curiosities
11 Mare Street, E8 4RP (7998 3617, www.thelasttuesdaysociety.org). Bethnal Green tube/Overground. **Open** *3-11pm Tue; noon-11pm Wed-Sat; noon-10.30pm Sun.* **Admission** *£6.* **Map** *p256 V3.*

This oddity is both on the art circuit and determinedly off any beaten track. Peek through the windows and you'll see a world in which velvet-cloaked Victorians might reside. Entering the shop, which is also the spiritual home of the esoterically minded Last Tuesday Society, reveals a wunderkammer of shells, skulls, taxidermy specimens and assorted weirdness and tat, from a two-headed lamb to McDonald's Happy Meal toys and condoms used by the Rolling Stones. Art gets a designated space in the first-floor gallery, where the shows tend towards the eerily surreal. There's a cocktail bar and café if you need bracing up again; admission includes the price of a cup of tea.

Restaurants

Bistrotheque ££
23-27 Wadeson Street, E2 9DR (8983 7900, www.bistrotheque.com). Bethnal Green tube/Overground. **Open** *6-10.30pm Mon-Thur; 6-11pm Fri; 11am-4pm, 6-11pm Sat; 11am-4pm, 6-10.30pm Sun. Bar 5.30pm-midnight Mon-Fri; 11am-midnight Sat; 11am-10.30pm Sun.* **Map** *p256 V3* ❶
French

Head to the first floor of this East End trendsetter for the light, white restaurant and big oval bar (where walk-ins can eat and good cocktails are mixed). Although the hipster count is high, the service is friendly, and there's a level of professionalism that's missing from many local restaurants. The kitchen is capable of highs – we've had a stellar duck confit with puy lentils and mushrooms – but a steady B-plus is more usual; the generous prix fixe costs £25 for three good-sized courses. The menu (and short wine list) is more French-leaning than truly Gallic and the popular weekend brunch adds the likes of US-style pancakes with bacon and maple syrup. Less welcome at brunch are the 90-minute dining slots.

❤ E Pellicci £
332 Bethnal Green Road, E2 0AG (7739 4873, epellicci.com). Bethnal Green tube/Overground or bus 8. **Open** *7am-4pm Mon-Sat.* **No cards.** **Map** *p256 U5* ❻ *Café*

You go to Pellicci's as much for the atmosphere as for the food, although the food is more than edible. Opened in 1900, and still in the hands of the same family, this Bethnal Green landmark has chrome and Vitrolite

Columbia Road Market

outside, wood panelling with deco marquetry, Formica tabletops and stained glass within – it earned the café a Grade II-listing in 2005. Fry-ups are first rate, and the fish and chips, daily grills and Italian specials aren't half bad.

♥ Marksman ££
*254 Hackney Road, E2 7SJ (7739 7393, www.marksmanpublichouse.com). Hoxton Overground. **Open** 11am-midnight Mon-Thur; 11am-1am Fri, Sat; 10am-11pm Sun. Food served 6-10pm Mon-Thur; noon-3pm, 6-10pm Fri; noon-4pm, 6-10pm Sat; 10am-4pm, 6-9pm Sun. **Map** p256 T4* ⑩
Modern British

Michelin Pub of the Year 2017, the Marksman is one of Hackney Road's growing crop of refurbed bars and restaurants. Owned and run by head chefs Tom Harris and Jon Rotheram, it combines convivial pub surroundings with a first-rate modern British menu that strays far and wide from the standard gastropub script. Come for the unbeatable Sunday roast (£33 for three courses); at other times, try the signature beef and barley bun with horseradish cream or the curried duck with sourdough roti and tomato chutney. For dessert, the brown butter and honey tart is a masterpiece of culinary engineering.

Pubs & bars

♥ Sager + Wilde Paradise Row
*250 Paradise Row, E2 9LE (7613 0478, www.sagerandwilde.com). Bethnal Green tube/Overground. **Open** 5-10pm Mon; noon-3pm, 5-10.30pm Tue-Fri; 11am-3pm, 5-11pm Sat; 11am-3pm, 5-10pm Sun. **Map** p256 V4* ⑥

This bar-restaurant lies in a railway arch, low lit in the evenings, with a cathedral-like vaulted ceiling the colour of Carrara marble and a spacious courtyard which faces the traffic-free street. The wine list is intimidatingly vast, but, thankfully, the staff know it well and adroitly help you navigate it. Abundant beverages aside, the food is excellent, having enlisted the talents of Chris Leach (formerly of Kitty Fisher) to produce British dishes with European flourishes.

♥ Satan's Whiskers
*343 Cambridge Heath Road, E2 9RA (7739 8362). Bethnal Green tube/Overground or Cambridge Heath Overground. **Open** 5pm-midnight daily. **Map** p256 V4* ⑦

Satan's Whiskers might sound like a Captain Haddock curse, but it refers to a classic cocktail containing gin, orange and vermouth topped with Grand Marnier and orange bitters. It's a staple on the otherwise daily changing menu here, along with seductive alternatives – this tiny bar was set up by three bartenders, and they really know their stuff. Leather booths, an illuminated ice box and taxidermy for decor all add to the atmosphere.

Shops & services

♥ Columbia Road Market
*Columbia Road, E2 7RG (www.columbiaroad. info). Hoxton Overground or Bethnal Green tube/Overground. **Open** 8am-3.30pm Sun. **Map** p256 T4* ④ *Market*

On Sunday mornings, this unassuming East End street is transformed into a delightful swathe of fabulous plant life and the air is fragrant with blooms and the shouts of old-school Cockney stallholders (most offering deals for 'a fiver'). It's worth shopping around; don't be afraid to barter, and prepare for it to get very busy. The market is popular with both locals and tourists; during the midday rush it is rammed with people elbowing their way to that perfect pot plant. If you can't bear crowds or just want to guarantee the pick of the crop, arrive when the market opens. Or wait till after 2pm to pick up bargains. When you've bought your blooms, head behind the stalls and down side streets to find cute cafés, independent restaurants, delis, shops, antique dealers, vintage stalls and small galleries, many of which follow the market's opening hours.

DALSTON & HACKNEY

▶ *Dalston Junction, Dalston Kingsland, Hackney Central or London Fields Overground.*

Occupying the area around the junction of Balls Pond Road and Kingsland Road, scruffy **Dalston** is a typical East London mash-up that combines African-flavoured Ridley Road market, with delicious Turkish *ocakbaşı* (grill restaurants) along Stoke Newington Road, and throngs of hipsters OMGing over sharing plates and the latest 'dirty' food pop-up. In truth, even as the brand managers descend, Dalston remains a cool and lively part of London. All tribes play together happily enough at the appealingly urban **Dalston Jazz Bar** (4 Bradbury Street, 7254 9728, www.dalstonjazzclubrestaurant.co.uk), the brilliant **Vortex Jazz Club** (*see p350*) and **Café Oto** (*see p349*). Also nearby is an appealing 'micropark', the delightfully urban **Dalston Eastern Curve Garden** (13 Dalston Lane, E8 3DF, dalstongarden.org).

Neighbouring **Stoke Newington** is the richer cousin of Dalston and poorer cousin of Islington. At weekends, pretty **Clissold Park** (www.clissoldpark.com) is overrun with picnickers and mums pushing prams. Most visitors head here for bijou **Church Street**. This curvy road is lined with second-hand bookshops, cute boutiques and kids' stores, and superior cafés and restaurants – Keralan vegetarian restaurant **Rasa** (no.55, 7249 0344, www.rasarestaurants.com) was the pioneer in what is now a bit of a foodie hotbed. Another local highlight is **Abney Park Cemetery** (www.abney-park.org), a wonderfully wild, overgrown Victorian boneyard and nature reserve.

North of Bethnal Green and east of Stoke Newington, **Hackney Central** has few blockbuster sights, but has been one of London's fastest gentrifying areas. Its administrative centre is Town Hall Square on Mare Street, where you'll find a century-old music hall, the **Hackney Empire** (291 Mare Street, E8 1EJ, 8985 2424, www.hackneyempire.co.uk); an art deco town hall; and the fine little **Hackney Museum** (1 Reading Lane, E8 1GQ, 8356 3500, www.hackney.gov.uk/cm-museum.htm) in the 21st-century library. Opposite, an ambitious failed music venue has become a terrific cinema (**Hackney Picturehouse**; *see p325*). Within walking distance to the east is the historic **Sutton House**.

In the southern part of Hackney, the area of **London Fields** demonstrates the area's changing demographics. Once a failing fruit and veg market, **Broadway Market** is now brimming with young urbanites and trendy families. From here, you can walk east – dodging cyclists and joggers – along the Regent's Canal to **Victoria Park**. Opened in 1845 to give the impoverished working classes access to green space, this sprawling, 290-acre oasis was designed by Sir James Pennethorne, a pupil of John Nash; its elegant landscaping (with rose garden and waterfowl lake) is indeed reminiscent of Nash's Regent's Park (*see p244*). There's also a terrific vegetarian café. At the eastern end of the park, across a nasty dual carriageway, is the mish-mash of artist-colonised post-industrial buildings that makes up **Hackney Wick**.

Sights & museums

Sutton House & Breaker's Yard
2-4 Homerton High Street, E9 6JQ (8986 2264, www.nationaltrust.org.uk/sutton-house). Hackney Central Overground. **Open** *times vary; check website for details. Closed Jan.* **Admission** *6.30; £3.50 reductions; £17.50 family; free under-5s.*

The oldest house in east London, red-brick Sutton House is owned by the National Trust and was built in 1535 for Henry VIII's first secretary of state, Sir Ralph Sadleir. It has been sensitively restored, retaining the authentic original decor: you'll be able to see a Tudor kitchen, Jacobean and Georgian interiors, an Edwardian chapel, medieval foundations in the cellar and 1980s graffiti up under the roof. Sutton House also has one London's oldest loos (a 16th-century garderobe, boarded up in the 1700s) and, in the Breaker's Yard, a crisply contemporary community garden whose highlight is the Grange – chopped-up caravans rebuilt into a parody stately home.

Restaurants

♥ Good Egg £
93 Church Street, Stoke Newington, N16 0AS (3869 8629, www.thegoodegg.co). Stoke Newington rail. **Open** *9am-5pm Mon; 9am-11pm Tue-Fri; 10am-11pm Sat, Sun.* Middle Eastern

From the slatted bench that runs round one wall, it's interesting to sit and contemplate what an efficient job the owners have done with a small space – it's compact but not packed, stylish but not slavishly so, with an open kitchen, bar, high stools and central service stations all fitted in. The 'plates' here are Middle Eastern-influenced, but convincing: perhaps an Iraqi pitta with fried aubergine, chopped egg and mango pickle inside airy bread, or keenly priced spicy and crunchy *za'atar* fried chicken. There are also bigger dishes like Persian smoked brisket or whole roast cauliflower with tahini and pomegranate. The Good Egg is open all day (except Monday evenings), with tempting breakfasts ensuring this little space is full morning to night.

Jidori ££
89 Kingsland High Street, E8 2PB (7686 5634, www.jidori.co.uk). Dalston Kingsland Overground. **Open** *6-11pm Mon, Tue; noon-3pm, 6-11pm Wed, Thur; noon-3pm, 6pm-midnight Fri; noon-4pm, 6pm-midnight Sat; noon-4pm Sun.* Japanese

The *izakaya* – a kind of Japanese pub, but with better food and worse beer – serves almost anything chicken-related, grilled on a stick: juicy hearts, intestines, skin. Essentially there to mop up the saké, they just happen to be really great bar snacks. At Brett Redman's yakitori restaurant each skewer is great and they're all very different: perhaps the wing with shiso and lemon – crisp, pleasantly sweet and a little sharp – or the moreish *tsukune* skewers, packed full of chives and served with a raw egg to dip the meat into. There's a nice selection of craft beer – local and Japanese – plus a well-curated cocktail menu.

♥ P Franco ££
107 Lower Clapton Road, E5 0NP (8533 4660, www.pfranco.co.uk). Hackney Central or Hackney Downs Overground. **Open** *4-9pm Tue, Wed; 4-10pm Thur; 4-11pm Fri; 2-11pm Sat; 2-10pm Sun. Food served 6-9pm Thur; 6-10pm Fri, Sat; 2-9pm Sun.* Wine bar

London's hardly bereft of wine bars with food, but P Franco – a diddy, no-reservations spot in Clapton – is not just another cheeseboard-and-plonk kinda place. Rather, it's a place that learned gourmands and restaurant pros

say reverent things about in hushed voices. To accompany the modish natural wines, a rotating selection of chefs – each resident for six months at a time – knocks out a consistently interesting selection of small plates, all cooked on two induction hobs. These might segue from decent charcuterie to pitch-perfect pasta to peripatetic and globally-inflected riffs on Modern European dishes… The flavours may change but the quality remains unfailingly excellent.

Pubs & bars

Cock Tavern
315 Mare Street, E8 1EJ (no phone, www.thecocktavern.co.uk). Hackney Central Overground. **Open** *noon-11pm Mon-Thur; noon-1am Fri, Sat; noon-10.30pm Sun.*

The Cock is the sort of place you walk into and think: this is a bloody good pub. It's dark, uncomplicated and resonant with merry conversation. Put simply, it's a room for grown-ups to stand in and drink beer. It's timelessly classic – aside from the Victorian beards on the bar staff, it could be any era since 1920. It's usually rammed, which is mainly down to the fabulous beer and cider: the pub cellar is home to the Howling Hops microbrewery, whose output is mostly drunk on the premises, while plenty of guest beers pop up on the 22 taps. A bartop cabinet displays scotch eggs and pork pies, and there's a jar of pickled eggs.

Draughts Café
337 Acton Mews, E8 4EA (07930 936237, www.draughtslondon.com). Haggerston Overground. **Open** *noon-11pm Mon; 10am-11pm Tue-Thur, Sun; 10am-midnight Sat.* **Map** *p256 S2* ②

If the phrase 'Let's play Seven Wonders' appeals more than making a DJ request, Draughts is for you. This bar-café has a library of more than 500 board games, from Articulate and Cranium to newer (and more complex) classics Carcassonne and Pandemic. Admission is £5 per person, which buys you

In the know
Books on board

A 1920s Dutch barge has been lovingly transformed into **Word on the Water**, a floating bookshop that can be found somewhere along the Regent's Canal, often near Broadway Market (see right). As well as keenly priced books, it has a wood-burning stove, a friendly dog and occasional live jazz performances. Visit www.facebook.com/wordonthewater for the current location.

unlimited play and, crucially, the help of a 'game guru', who'll offer guidance on rules and which game would suit your party. Food, craft beer, ale, cider and wine are available.

Shops & services

♥ Broadway Market

Broadway Market, E8 4QL (www. broadwaymarket.co.uk). London Fields Overground or bus 394. **Open** *9am-5pm Sat.* **Map** *p256 U3* ❸ *Market*

The coolest and most ridiculous of east London's young trendies can be found at this endearing market, where fruit-and-veg sellers trade alongside vintage clothes 'specialists'. It's as busy as a beehive, but the slew of cafés, pubs, restaurants and boutiques along the street – plus the market itself, plus the nearby **Netil Market** for further street food, plus Saturday's **School Yard Market**, plus the overspill of drunks and slumming may-do-wells on London Fields when there's even a whiff of sunshine – is a fine education in new London.

Hackney Walk

Morning Lane, E9 6LH (7287 9601, www. hackneywalk.com). Hackney Central or Homerton Overground. **Open** *10am-6pm Mon-Sat; 11am-5pm Sun. Fashion*

Is there a more unlikely part of town for a fashion nexus? From Hackney Central station, you stroll past junkyards, a supermarket, tower blocks and takeaways. But thanks to a £2-million fund to regenerate the area, Hackney's Morning Lane has become the home of London's first luxury retail outlet. The developer (Manhattan Loft Corporation, which was behind the rebirth of St Pancras International) capitalised on footfall to the nearby **Burberry** factory outlet (29-31 Chatham Place, E9 6LP) by renting neighbouring property to **Aquascutum** (7-8 Ram Place, E9 6LT) and, in a converted pub, **Pringle** (90 Morning Lane). The jewel in the crown of an already glitzy development is the **Matches Fashion** outlet, which offers archive designs from Stella McCartney to Emilia Wickstead at big reductions. Come on a Thursday if you can – that's when the

new stock arrives. For refreshments, there are cocktails and snazzy wallpaper at **Every Cloud** (11 Morning Lane, E9 6NU, 3441 9850, everycloudbar.com), and coffee from **Black Box** (blackboxcoffee.co.uk) is served outside Folli Follie/Nicole Fahri 10am-2pm Sat.

Kristina Records

44 Stoke Newington Road, N16 7XJ (7254 2130, www.kristinarecords.com). Dalston Kingsland Overground. **Open** *noon-8pm Mon, Wed-Fri; 11am-8pm Sat, Sun. Music*

Kristina is a living, breathing experience for living, breathing music fans, with a clean and uncluttered layout that makes shopping for vinyl the kind of pleasure that websites can never replicate. For the dedicated dance-music fan, the racks of new house and techno are a goldmine, while expertly chosen soul and jazz oldies are also represented.

LN-CC

18-24 Shacklewell Lane, E8 2EZ (3174 0744, www.ln-cc.com). Dalston Kingsland Overground. **Open** *by appointment 10am-6pm Mon-Sat. Fashion, books & music*

'Late Night Chameleon Club' is as mysterious as its name suggests. Accessed via a basement-level door in an unlikely Shacklewell warehouse building, the store is a Tim Burton-like wonderland rendered in natural wood with a secret dancefloor, tree house, listening library and London's most unique edit of super-rare fashion. Ostensibly a showroom for internet boutique LN-CC. com, the space is a gallery for upscale design, selling super-posh brands such as Rick Owens, Givenchy, Lanvin and any number of hard-to-pronounce rarities. With vinyl, art books and eyewear, and stock in different themed zones, LN-CC is a shop like no other.

Mare Street Market

115 Mare Street, E8 4RT (www. marestreetmarket.com). **Open** *8am-11pm Mon; 8am-midnight Tue-Thur; 8am-1am Fri; 9am-1am Sat; 9am-11pm Sun. Shopping hall*

It might be a bit of a stretch to call this spot a market as it's housed inside what was once a Job Centre. Rather, the refurbished building, which is just a stone's throw from Broadway Market, operates more as a shopping hall. In this 10,000sq ft (3,048sq m) space you'll find a deli selling charcuterie and cheese, an off-licence selling local beers and organic wines, a florist and a record stall. If you're after hot food, there's the Open Kitchen restaurant and the Dining Room, which also operates as a furniture shop. What's more, the whole place is cashless, and there's no plastic packaging to be found anywhere.

In the know
Trad eats

If your tastes extend to the old East End, dig into some stewed eels at **F Cooke** (9 Broadway Market, 7254 6458), a pie and mash place that's been in operation since the early 1900s.

EAST LONDON

DOCKLANDS

London's docks were fundamental to the prosperity of the British Empire. Between 1802 and 1921, ten separate docks were built between Tower Bridge in the west and Woolwich in the east, employing tens of thousands of people. Yet by the 1960s, the shipping industry was changing irrevocably. The new 'container' system of cargo demanded larger, deep-draught ships, as a result of which the work moved out to Tilbury, whence lorries drove the containers into the city. By 1980, the London docks had closed.

The London Docklands Development Corporation (LDDC), founded in 1981, spent £790 million of public money on redevelopment, only for a country-wide property slump in the early 1990s to leave the shiny new high-rise offices and luxury flats unoccupied. Nowadays, though, focal **Canary Wharf** is a booming rival to the City, supporting an estimated 90,000 workers. It is at the heart of the **Isle of Dogs** peninsula, the origin of whose name – first recorded in 1588 – remains uncertain; one theory claims Henry VIII kept his hunting dogs here. In the 19th century, a huge system of docks and locks transformed what had been just drained marshland, with the West India Docks cutting right across the peninsula, so the Isle of Dogs finally lived up to the island part of its name.

Almost all the interest for visitors is to be found in the vicinity of Cesar Pelli's **One Canada Square**, which was the country's tallest habitable building from 1991 to 2012, when it was topped by the Shard (see p94). Once dramatic, the building now almost disappears amid similarly sized office-block clones. Shopping options are limited to the mall beneath the towers (www.mycanarywharf.com), but you'll find a crisp garden behind Canary Wharf tube station and a selection of upmarket chain restaurants. Across a floating bridge over the basin to the north, the brilliant **Museum of London Docklands** is flanked by a pub and a couple of bar-restaurants.

From Canary Wharf, it's well worth heading south on the DLR to Island Gardens station at the tip of the Isle of Dogs. From narrow **Island Gardens** park, there's a famous view of Greenwich (see p280) – and the entrance to the Victorian pedestrian tunnel. Nearby to the north, at **Mudchute Park & Farm** (Pier Street, 7515 5901, www.mudchute.org), a complete farmyard of animals ruminate in front of the skyscrapers. But, to gain a sense of the docklands in times past, alight from the DLT at Shadwell, from where you can walk south to **Wapping**. In 1598, London chronicler John Stowe described Wapping High Street as 'a filthy strait passage, with alleys of small tenements or cottages, inhabited by sailors' victuallers'. This can still be imagined as you walk along it now, flanked by tall Victorian warehouses. The historic **Town of Ramsgate** pub (no.62, 7481 8000), dating from 1545, helps. Here, 'hanging judge' George Jeffreys was captured in 1688, trying to escape to Europe in disguise as a woman. Privateer Captain William Kidd was executed in 1701 at Execution Dock, near Wapping New Stairs; the bodies of pirates were hanged from a gibbet until seven tides had washed over them. Further east, the touristy but appealing **Prospect of Whitby** (57 Wapping Wall, 7481 1095) dates from 1520 and counted Pepys and Dickens among its regulars. It has a riverside terrace and balcony outside, and a handsome pewter bar counter and flagstone floor within.

Sights & museums

Museum of London Docklands
*No.1 Warehouse, West India Quay, Hertsmere Road, E14 4AL (7001 9844, www. museumoflondon.org.uk/museum-london-docklands). Canary Wharf tube/DLR or West India Quay DLR. **Open** 10am-6pm daily. **Admission** free. Temporary exhibitions vary.*

Housed in a 19th-century warehouse (itself a Grade I-listed building), this museum explores the complex history of London's docklands and the river over two millennia. Displays spreading over three storeys take you from the arrival of the Romans all the

Museum of London Docklands

way to the docks' 1980s closure and the area's subsequent redevelopment. The Docklands at War section is very moving, while a haunting new permanent exhibition sheds light on the dark side of London's rise as a centre for finance and commerce, exploring its involvement in the slave trade. You can also walk through full-scale mock-ups of a quayside and a dingy riverfront alley. Temporary exhibitions are set up on the ground floor, where you'll also find a café and a docks-themed play area. Just like its elder sibling, the Museum of London (*see p227*), the MoLD has a great programme of special events.

Restaurants

Docklands is short of destination restaurants – but long on upmarket chains, especially around Canary Wharf.

Giant Robot £-££

Crossrail Place, Canary Wharf, E14 5AR (7719 1325, www.streetfeast.com). Canary Wharf tube/DLR. Open 11am-late Mon-Sat. Street food

A big shiny box on a low-rise Canary Wharf rooftop, Giant Robot is from the Street Feast team, also responsible for hip outdoor food hangouts Dinerama and Model Market. It looks sort of like a boat. Or something with a massive quiff. Inside, it's like a cross between an airport departure lounge and a nightclub. Concrete floors, retro furnishings, groovy

tunes. Plus four street food vendors, two bars and a coffee shack. Outside, there's access to the wharf's glorious 'rooftopia'. You've got it: a landscaped rainforest on a roof. It's all under a translucent, wood-framed dome, meaning shelter from the rain, but they've taken lots of panels out, so there's breeze and birds, too. This is the best eating option in Docklands by a mile.

Pubs & bars

♥ Grapes

76 Narrow Street, Limehouse, E14 8BP (7987 4396, thegrapes.co.uk). Limehouse or Westferry DLR. Open noon-11pm Mon-Sat; noon-10.30pm Sun. Food served noon-9.30pm daily.

If you're trying to evoke the feel of the Thames docks before their Disneyfication into Docklands, these narrow, ivy-covered and etched-glass 1720 riverside premises in Limehouse are a good place to start: the downstairs is all wood panels and nautical jetsam; upstairs is plainer, but it's easier to find seats for Sunday lunch. Expect good ales and a half-dozen wines of each colour by glass and bottle.

▶ *Not far from the Grapes at the mouth of Limehouse Basin, the Narrow (44 Narrow Street, E14 8DQ, 7592 7950, www. gordonramsayrestaurants.com/the-narrow) has a good Thameside terrace as well as a wraparound conservatory.*

EAST LONDON

275

OLYMPIC PARK & LEA VALLEY

▶ *Stratford tube/DLR/Overground.*

The Olympic Park, scene of the 2012 Games, is a square mile of the Lower Lea Valley in east London. That sporting summer, which exceeded most predictions and won over many critics, is long gone but the contentious business of 'legacy' remains: arguments over what benefits have been brought to Londoners by the £8.77 billion that was spent on the Games may continue for generations. The physical legacy, at least, is clear: the **Queen Elizabeth Olympic Park** (www.queenelizabetholympicpark. co.uk), as it was renamed, comprises immaculate parklands to the north, laced by a network of paths and waterways. By the Timber Lodge café, the Tumbling Bay Playground is especially good for kids, and this is where you'll find the Lee Valley VeloPark. The 7,500-seat Copper Box Arena has provided a flexible indoor venue for sport (notably boxing) and concerts. In the southern part of the park are the handsome Zaha Hadid-designed Aquatics Centre (www.londonaquaticscentre.org), which is open to the public, further children's play areas, walking trails and a couple of dozen public artworks, not least the landmark **ArcelorMittal Orbit**. The **Olympic Stadium** is the home ground of West Ham Football Club, which took up residence for the 2016-17 season, but it continues to host other major sporting events, including the IAAF World Championships and the World Para Athletics Championships in 2017. There are now ambitious plans to create a cultural hub here, named the East Bank, involving the V&A, University College London, the BBC, Sadler's Wells and even the Smithsonian – an eastern rival for South Ken's 'Albertopolis'. The main entrance to the park is from Stratford town centre, just to the east, which has the **Discover Children's Story Centre** (383-387 High Street, E15 4QZ, 8536 5555, www.discover. org.uk), the UK's first creative-learning centre, which offers all sorts of imaginative exploration and interactive exhibitions.

For a good vantage point on the park, head to the **Common Greenway Café** (9am-5pm daily) in the brightly painted, recycled shipping containers of the **View Tube** (The Greenway Marshgate Lane, E15 2PJ, theviewtube.co.uk) or, if you've a chunk of time on your hands, stroll south along the River Lea to **Three Mills Island**, which has an impressive new playground.

ArcelorMittal Orbit

If you make it all the way down the Lea to the Thames, you'll find **Trinity Buoy Wharf**, while the impressively vast **Royal Docks** lie further to the east – it's best to get the DLR to Royal Victoria or Royal Albert stations for them. As well as the ExCeL conference centre, you'll find the black and pointy **Crystal** exhibition space and the **Emirates Air Line** cable car, which takes travellers high over the river to the **O2** (*see p344*) on the far bank. Down by the river, the **Thames Barrier Park** opened in 2001 as London's first new park in half a century. It has a lush sunken garden of waggly hedges and offers perhaps the best land views of the Thames Barrier (*see p285*). If you don't fancy walking, enter the park from Pontoon Dock DLR.

In the know
Palace of putrification

Victorian sewer engineer Sir Joseph Bazalgette's extraordinary, Byzantine-style **Abbey Mills Pumping Station** can be seen near Three Mills Island (*see opposite*). Admire it from the nearby Greenway footpath; there's no public access.

Unless you're checking in at **London City Airport** (*see p413*), keep on the DLR as far as King George V to get a free ferry (every 15mins daily; *see p285*) that chugs pedestrians and cars across the river, or stay in your carriage as the DLR passes under the river all the way to its final stop at Woolwich Arsenal.

Sights & museums

♥ ArcelorMittal Orbit

3 Thornton Street, Queen Elizabeth Olympic Park, Stratford, E20 2AD (0333 800 8099, arcelormittalorbit.com). Stratford tube/ DLR/Overground/rail. **Open** *check website for details.* **Admission** *£12.50; £7.50-£10.50 reductions; £34 family. With slide £17.50; £12.50-£15.50 reductions; £54 family.*

Perhaps the most dramatic structure in the Olympic Park, the Orbit overlooks the Stadium. Designed by sculptor Anish Kapoor and engineer Cecil Balmond, it is red, 374ft (114m) tall and not much loved by locals. The peripheral location – compared to both Shard (*see p94*) and Eye (*see p84*) – meant the view was always interesting rather than must-see, but the addition of a spiral slide by Belgian artist Carsten Höller in 2016 changed the whole nature of the attraction. You can still visit for the view, but most will choose to pay a bit more to fly down the world's longest and tallest tunnel slide – taking a dozen turns around the Orbit in the 40 seconds it takes to zoom through the structure. Note: the slide is for over-sevens only, with a minimum height of 1.3m.

Crystal

Royal Victoria Dock, 1 Siemens Brothers Way, E16 1GB (7055 6400, www.thecrystal. org). Royal Victoria DLR. **Open** *10am-5pm Tue-Sun.* **Admission** *£5; £4 reductions. Tour £10; £6 reductions.*

The Crystal attempts to explain in an engaging fashion how cities work, and how they might meet the challenges of global warming, population growth, ageing and the shortage of key resources, especially water. The two floors of interactives are slick and fun: beat the computer at face recognition, or plan the transport for different cities. There's a good café (open from 8.30am Mon-Fri, 10am Sat, Sun).

Emirates Air Line

North terminal *27 Western Gateway, E16 4FA. Royal Victoria DLR.*

South terminal *Edmund Halley Way, SE10 0FR (www.tfl.gov.uk/modes/emirates-air-line). North Greenwich tube.*

Open *Apr-Sept 7am-9pm Mon-Fri; 8am-9pm Sat; 9am-9pm Sun. Oct-Mar 7am-8pm Mon-Fri; 8am-8pm Sat; 9am-8pm Sun.* **Tickets** *£4.50 single; £2.30 reductions, free under-5s.*

Arguments for a cable car across the Thames as a solution to any of London's many transport problems are, at best, moot, but its value as a tourist thrill is huge. The comfy pods zoom 295ft (90m) up elegant stanchions at a gratifying pace. Suddenly there are brilliant views of the expanses of water that make up the Royal Docks, the ships on the Thames, Docklands and the Thames Barrier. Good fun and good value – but note that the cable car may not run in high winds.

Three Mills Island

Three Mills Lane, E3 3DU (0300 003 0610, www.visitleevalley.org.uk). Bromley-by-Bow tube. **Open** *May-Oct 11am-4pm Sun. Nov-Apr 11am-4pm 1st Sun of mth.* **Admission** *House Mill £3; £1.50 reductions; free under-16s.*

Just south of the Olympic Park, this island on the River Lea takes its name from the three mills that ground flour and gunpowder here. The **House Mill**, built in 1776, is the oldest and largest tidal mill in Britain and can be visited by tour (8980 4626, www. housemill.org.uk). Even when that's closed, the island provides pleasant walks that can feel surprisingly rural – and the new Wild Kingdom children's playground is a joy.

Trinity Buoy Wharf

64 Orchard Place, E14 0JW (7515 7153, www. trinitybuoywharf.com). **Open** *Lighthouse 11am-4pm Sat, Sun (until 5pm in summer).*

Where the River Lea flows into the Thames at Bow Creek, Trinity Buoy Wharf is pure incongruity. Built in the early 1800s, it was a depot and repair yard for shipping buoys, and it was here, in the 1860s, that James Douglass – later designer of the fourth Eddystone Lighthouse – built London's only lighthouse. The lighthouse is the perfect setting for the haunting *Longplayer* sound installation (longplayer.org). Here too, floating on a raft to preserve it, is SS Robin (www.ssrobin.org), a steamship so rare it is included (with the *Cutty Sark, see p280*, and HMS *Belfast, see p96*) in the National Historic Fleet.

In the know
Cable car card entry

Tickets for the Emirates Air Line (*see left*) are cheaper if you use an Oyster card or the contactless card you've been using for public transport, and you'll avoid queuing at the ticket desk.

South London

South London was once best known for its lack of public transport and the late-night cabbies' refrain: 'I don't go south of the river, mate.' Of course, the bus network meant it was always perfectly navigable to those in the know, but the expansion of the Overground network of light rail links (effectively the Tube, but using surface trains) has opened south London up to the uninitiated, with some parts – notably Peckham – rivalling east London for hipster cred. There are superb historic attractions, not least Greenwich and the Royal Botanic Gardens, Kew, both of which are UNESCO World Heritage sites, and Hampton Court Palace, which might as well be. And several of the less prestigious institutions are equally fascinating, with Dulwich Picture Gallery and the Horniman Museum notable. We explore in an arc through south London's key areas, from east to west.

❤ **Don't miss**

1 Maritime Greenwich *p282*
Beautiful buildings, fascinating history.

2 Royal Botanic Gardens, Kew *p292*
A park like no other.

3 Peckham's nightlife *p342*
It's all happening down south.

4 Horniman Museum *p287*
Taxidermy, anthropology and some brilliant jellyfish.

5 Hampton Court Palace *p291*
Ravishing in red brick.

6 Brixton Village *p289*
Contemporary shopping in art deco surroundings.

Royal Observatory & Planetarium *p285*

GREENWICH & AROUND

▶ *North Greenwich tube for Greenwich Peninsula. Cutty Sark DLR or Greenwich DLR/rail for Maritime Greenwich.*

When it was the Millennium Dome, the **O2 Arena** (*see p344*) was universally derided. A couple of decades on, it's a lauded entertainment complex and rather popular landmark. You can get very close to it, too: buy a ticket for **Up at the O2** (www.theo2.co.uk/upattheo2) and you can walk right over the top, safely attached to a security line. The Dome's arrival on the **Greenwich Peninsula** eventually triggered redevelopment of what had been an area of semi-industrial dereliction. Its eastern environs are now a mass of new buildings (www.greenwichpeninsula.co.uk), with a handful of attractions around Peninsula Square: the **Now Gallery** (Peninsula Square, SE10 0ES, nowgallery.co.uk), pricey **Craft London** bar-restaurant (8465 5910, craft-london.co.uk) and the **Peninsula Garden**, designed by Tom Dixon's studio. A rather elegant (but, for public-transport purposes, almost entirely unused) cable car, the **Emirates Air Line** (*see p277*), runs from the east flank of the peninsula right across the Thames. Two miles east in Woolwich is the flood-defying **Thames Barrier**.

The west flank of the peninsula, meanwhile, winds slowly into **Greenwich**, with the riverside walk – opposite the Isle of Dogs and the aggressively bland office blocks of **Canary Wharf** (*see p274*) – affording broad, flat, bracing views and some impressive works of public art: *Slice of Reality*, a rusting ship cut in half by Richard Wilson, sits near Alex Chinneck's 2014 sculpture *A Bullet from a Shooting Star*, a 115-foot (35-metre) electricity pylon turned upside-down.

Riverside Greenwich is an irresistible mixture of maritime, royal and horological history, a combination that earned it recognition as a UNESCO World Heritage Site in 1997 (*see p282*) and, to celebrate the Golden Jubilee, a Royal Borough in 2012. Indeed, royalty has haunted Greenwich since 1300, when Edward I stayed here. Henry VIII was born in Greenwich Palace; the palace was built on land that was later taken over by Wren's Royal Naval Hospital, now the **Old Royal Naval College**. The college is now a very handy first port of call. Its Pepys Building not only contains the **Greenwich Tourist Information Centre** (0870 608 2000, www.visitgreenwich.org.uk), but is also the home of **Discover Greenwich**, which provides a great overview of the area's numerous attractions. Just opposite, shoppers swarm to **Greenwich Market**, a handsome 19th-century building sheltering a mixture of shops and stalls.

Near the DLR stop is Greenwich Pier; every 15 minutes (peak times), the popular and speedy **Thames Clipper boats** (7001 2200, www.thamesclippers.com) shuttle passengers to and from central London. This is where you'll find the **Cutty Sark**, as well as a domed structure that is the entrance to a Victorian pedestrian tunnel that emerges on the far side of the Thames in Island Gardens. The tunnel is rather dingy, due to incomplete repair work, but it's still fun to walk beneath the river.

At the north end of Greenwich Park are the **Queen's House** and **National Maritime Museum**, beyond which it's a ten-minute walk (or shorter shuttle-bus trip) south up the park's dramatically steep slopes to the **Royal Observatory**, offering superb views out over the Royal Naval College to Canary Wharf. At night, the bright green Meridian Line Laser illuminates the path of the Prime Meridian across the London sky.

Sights & museums

Cutty Sark

King William Walk, SE10 9HT (8312 6565, www.rmg.co.uk/cuttysark). Cutty Sark DLR. **Open** *10am-5pm daily.* **Admission** *£13.50; £7-£11.50 reductions; free under-5s.* **Map** *p281 Ab13.*

Built in Scotland in 1869, this tea clipper was the quickest in the business when she was launched in 1870 – renovation after the *Cutty Sark* went up in flames in 2007 was rather slower. But you can visit her once more (by timed tickets) in her permanent berth in a purpose-built dry dock beside the Thames. The ship is now raised three metres off the ground and surrounded by a dramatic glass 'skirt', which allows visitors to admire the hull from underneath for the first time – while sipping a cup of tea from the museum café, should they desire. Critics objected that the glazed canopy obscures the elegant lines of the *Cutty Sark*'s hull – as well as raising fears about the stresses that are being put on the elderly ship – but the visitor experience is much improved, with interactives giving context to a story of reckless, high-speed trade in tea, wine, spirits, beer, coal, jute, wool and castor oil. The sailing clippers were gradually put out of business by steamships: by 1922, the *Cutty Sark* was the last of her breed afloat. The space beneath the ship displays another lost tradition: an exhibit of more than 80 figureheads, including Florence Nightingale, William Wilberforce, Hiawatha and Sir Lancelot.

► *Some of the areas discussed in this chapter are shown on the pull-out map at the back of this guide.*

GREENWICH

Restaurants

1 Goddards at Greenwich *p285*
2 Old Brewery *p285*
3 Parkside Café & Terrace *p285*

Pubs & bars

1 Cutty Sark Tavern *p286*
2 Greenwich Union *p285*, Richard I *p285*

Shops & services

1 Casbah Records *p286*
2 Greenwich Market *p286*
3 Joli Vintage Living *p286*

❤ **Time to eat, drink & shop**

Arcade shopping, south London style
Brixton Village *p289*

Gourmet grub in an unlikely setting
Coal Rooms *p288*,
Smoke & Salt *p291*

'Natural' wine and fine small plates
Naughty Piglets *p290*

Simply superb cooking
Artusi *p287*

Thai street food
Begging Bowl *p288*

Urban sunsets
Frank's Cafe *p288*

♥ Maritime Greenwich

If you're coming to Greenwich, allow yourself two luxuries. First, give yourself a whole day to explore. The Royal Museums Greenwich alone comprise four major attractions – the world's biggest nautical history museum, the **National Maritime Museum** (see p283); tea clipper the **Cutty Sark** (see p280); modest architectural pioneer the **Queen's House** (see p284), and, plonked on the Meridian, the **Royal Observatory** (see p285). On top of that, you'll want time to explore Wren's **Old Royal Naval Hospital** (see p283) and Greenwich Park itself. Second, treat yourself to a boat trip along the Thames to get here (for Thames Clippers, see p407). Seeing the vistas change as you approach this most historic area of London is an unparalleled joy – redolent of the long period when the city was utterly dependent on its river. The Thames was Britain's arterial connection to the world, whether in the form of Tudor explorers setting sail to unknown lands and unimaginable wealth with their monarch's blessing still in their ears, or during the Victorian era, when industrial-scale exploitation of Britain's panoply of colonies meant the river was always choked with vessels and the docks opposite Greenwich on the Isle of Dogs were full of cargo ships and lighters, which carried the cargo to shore.

Inscribed by UNESCO as a World Heritage Site in 1997, Maritime Greenwich should – once you've set foot on land – be approached only one way: through the **Old Royal Naval College**. Walk south between the grand colonnades by Sir Christopher Wren (1632-1723). These were deliberately placed to frame the Queen's House – begun by Inigo Jones (1573-1652) in 1616, the first building in Britain to be designed on Classical principles. You cannot fail to be impressed, perhaps a little daunted, by the ambition of the hospital's late 17th-century architecture.

UNESCO applauded the coherence of the site, the way that its various layers of history played off each other. This continues south into **Greenwich Park**, laid out by André Le Nôtre (1613-1700), who created the gardens at Versailles as the chief gardener of French King Louis XIV. Among the park's ancient trees, a towering slope is topped by the **Royal Observatory** – a collaboration between Wren and the less well-known but extremely significant scientist and polymath, Robert Hooke (1635-1703), which also marks the work of astronomer John Flamsteed (1646-1719), who predicted solar eclipses and laid the groundwork for later advances in navigation.

It was here that the British Empire was born, here that England made the Enlightenment her tool, and here that you can spend happy hours finding out about it all – or just having a boozy picnic on the grass surrounded by extraordinary buildings.

♥ Best Baroque buildings

Christ Church Spitalfields p259
Unforgettable due to Nicholas Hawksmoor's doom-laden spike of a spire.

Monument p235
The least architecturally interesting structure on this list – but it has a fascinating history and wonderful views of the City.

Old Royal Naval College p283
Just for those breathtaking colonnades.

St John's Smith Square p357
Thomas Archer's four corner towers exemplify Baroque inventiveness.

St Paul's Cathedral p224
Wren's masterpiece – and surely the finest Baroque building in the country.

Eltham Palace & Gardens

*Court Yard, SE9 5QE (0370 333 1181, www.english-heritage.org.uk). Eltham or Mottingham rail. **Open** 10am-5pm Mon-Thur, Sun. **Admission** £15; £13.50 reductions; £9 5-15s; £39 family.*

Four miles south of Greenwich, Eltham Palace is a cut-and-shut job: a medieval hall with a fabulous 1930s mansion attached. Henry VIII lived here as a boy, but when millionaire couple Stephen and Virginia Courtauld were looking for a country house within easy reach of London, the derelict palace – its Great Hall was being used as a barn – fitted the bill. They commissioned a state-of-the-art residence filled with mod cons: en suite bathrooms (at a time when only posh hotels offered such luxury); underfloor heating; piped music; and a centralised vacuuming system that hooked up with every room – it occasionally backfired, smothering the maids with dust. You approach the building via the oldest medieval bridge in the country, crossing the moat just like the film stars, explorers, politicians and royalty whom the Courtaulds entertained in their fabulous party palace. The huge, lavish reception rooms, along with Virginia and Stephen's separate bedrooms, bathrooms and sitting rooms, were all opened to the public in 1999, but the latest restoration has spruced up the gardens too: Stephen, a keen gardener, had his prize-winning orchids evacuated to Kew at the start of World War II. In the games room, you're at liberty to play snooker billiards on the original table. There is a children's playground and a restaurant in the glasshouse.

Fan Museum

*12 Crooms Hill, SE10 8ER (8305 1441, www.thefanmuseum.org.uk). Cutty Sark DLR or Greenwich DLR/rail. **Open** 11am-5pm Tue-Sat; noon-5pm Sun. **Admission** £5; £3 reductions; £10 family; free under-7s. **Map** p281 Ab14.*

The world's most important collection of hand-held fans is displayed in a pair of Georgian townhouses. There are about 3,500 fans, including some beauties in the Hélène Alexander collection, but not all are on display at any one time. For details of fan-making workshops and exhibitions, see the website. There's also a lovely orangery serving afternoon tea.

National Maritime Museum

*Park Row, SE10 9NF (8858 4422, information 8312 6565, www.rmg.co.uk/national-maritime-museum). Cutty Sark DLR or Greenwich DLR/rail. **Open** 10am-5pm daily. **Admission** free; donations appreciated.*

*Temporary exhibitions vary; check website for details. **Map** p281 Ab14.*

The world's largest maritime museum contains a huge store of creatively organised maritime art, cartography, models, interactives and regalia. The ground level has galleries covering maritime London, the titanic battle of Dreadnought battleships at Jutland in 1916 and Turner's painting *The Battle of Trafalgar*. You can then weave through to the Sammy Ofer extension, centred on 'Voyagers: Britons and the Sea' – a collection of 200 artefacts, accompanied by an audio-visual installation called the Wave. The Compass Lounge (with free Wi-Fi) allows you to explore the collection using computers, and you'll find the ticket desk, café and shop here, as well as access downstairs to the temporary gallery that is building a reputation for compellingly varied exhibitions (Samuel Pepys, Yinka Shonibare and pioneering American landscape photographer Ansel Adams have all featured) and outside directly into the park.

'The Atlantic: Slavery, Trade, Empires', on Floor 1, recounts the disturbing history of the transport of people and goods between Britain, Africa and the Americas during the 17th to 19th centuries, including a drawing of precisely how slaves were packed into the gunwales of a translatlantic sailing ship, while 'Traders' looks at the East India Company and 'The Great Map' is a large interactive floor map of the oceans.

Floor 2 holds the interactives: 'The Bridge' has a ship simulator, 'All Hands' lets six- to 12-year-olds load cargo (under-eights can enjoy 'Ahoy!' on the ground floor), and you can try your hand as a ship's gunner. But here too is one of the centrepieces of the museum: 'Nelson, Navy, Nation' recalls the seaborne battles of the 18th century, and the glamour and gore of life as a naval officer at the time. The key artefact is Nelson's Trafalgar uniform, bloodstained and with fatal bullet-hole, accompanied by a 3D reconstruction of him, as if laid in his coffin.

In October 2018, the museum opened four new permanent galleries in the East Wing, an area previously closed to the visitors. The 'Endeavour Galleries' contain more than 1,000 objects charting exploration through the ages, with displays on the Pacific and polar regions, Tudor and Stuart sailors, and, enticingly, 'sea things'.

Old Royal Naval College

*2 Cutty Sark Gardens, SE10 9NN (8269 4799, www.ornc.org). Cutty Sark DLR or Greenwich DLR/rail. **Open** 10am-5pm daily. Grounds 8am-11pm daily. **Admission** free. Tours free. **Map** p281 Ab13.*

The block of the Old Royal Naval College nearest to the *Cutty Sark* houses the excellent Visitor Centre. It's full of focused, informative exhibits on architecture and the building techniques of the surrounding buildings, the life of Greenwich pensioners, Tudor royalty and so forth, delivered with a real sense of fun: while grown-ups read about coade stone or scagliola (popular fake-stone building materials), for example, children can build their own chapel with soft bricks or try on a knight's helmet. There's also a well-stocked shop and a Tourist Information Centre.

It's a perfect introduction to the superb collection of buildings that make up the Naval College. Designed by Wren in 1694, with Hawksmoor and Vanbrugh helping to complete the project, it was originally a hospital for the relief and support of seamen and their dependants, with pensioners living here from 1705 to 1869, when the complex became the Royal Naval College. The Navy left in 1998, and the neoclassical buildings now house part of the University of Greenwich and Trinity College of Music. The public are allowed into the impressive rococo chapel, where there are free organ recitals, and the stunningly refurbished **Painted Hall**, which reopened to the public in March 2019. The triumphalist ceiling painting by Sir James Thornhill was created as a tribute to William and Mary and took 19 years to complete (1707-1726). Nelson lay in state in the Painted Hall for three days in 1806, before being taken, in grand river procession, to St Paul's Cathedral for his funeral. Also new from 2019 is the café, shop and Sackler Gallery space.

Queen's House

Queen's House

Romney Road, SE10 9NF (8858 4422, www. rmg.co.uk/queens-house). Cutty Sark DLR or Greenwich DLR/rail. **Open** *10am-5pm daily.* **Admission** *free.* **Map** *p281 Ac14.*

The Queen's House was refurbished in time for its 400th anniversary in 2017, complete with gold-leaf artistry from Turner Prize winner Richard Wright on the ceiling of the Great Hall. Formerly the summer villa of Charles I's queen, Henrietta Maria, the house was completed in 1638 by Inigo Jones, the first Palladian building in the country. As well as the stunning 1635 marble floor, look for Britain's first centrally unsupported spiral staircase (much more beautiful than that makes it sound), fine painted woodwork and ceilings, and the proportions of the Great Hall – it is a perfect cube. The art collection of the National Maritime Museum is held here, with displays including portraits of famous maritime figures, works by Hogarth and Gainsborough, some arresting 20th-century wartime art, and William Hodges' exotic paintings from the voyages of Captain Cook. As part of the refurbishment, Orazio Gentileschi's royal-commissioned painting *Joseph and Potiphar's Wife* is on show here for the first time since 1650.

Ranger's House

Chesterfield Walk, SE10 8QX (8294 2548, www.english-heritage.org.uk). Blackheath rail, Cutty Sark DLR or bus 53. **Open** *Apr-Sept guided tours only. Tours 11am, 2pm Sun-Wed. Oct-Mar closed.* **Tickets** *£7.60; £4.60-£6.80 reductions; free under-5s.* **Map** *p281 Ac15.*

The house of the 'Ranger of Greenwich Park' (a post held by George III's niece, Princess Sophia Matilda, from 1815) now contains the treasure amassed by Julius Wernher, a German who made his considerable fortune trading in South African diamonds. His booty – medieval and Renaissance art, jewellery, bronzes, tapestries, furniture, porcelain, paintings – is displayed through a dozen lovely rooms in this red-brick Georgian villa, built in 1723, the back garden of which hosts the fragrant Greenwich Park rose collection.

Royal Observatory & Planetarium

Blackheath Avenue, Greenwich Park, SE10 8XJ (8312 6565, www.rmg.co.uk/royal-observatory). Cutty Sark DLR or Greenwich DLR/rail. **Open** *10am-5pm daily.* **Admission** *£15; £6.50 child; £20 family; free under-5s.* **Map** *p281 Ac14.*

The northern section of this two-halved attraction chronicles Greenwich's horological connection. Flamsteed House, the observatory built in 1675 on the orders of Charles II, contains the apartments of Sir John Flamsteed and other Astronomers Royal, as well as instruments used in timekeeping since the 14th century. John Harrison's four timekeepers, used to crack the problem of longitude, are here, while the onion dome houses the country's largest (28in) refracting telescope – it was completed in 1893. The courtyard is where tourists gather for their Prime Meridian Line photo-opportunity, and you must pay for entry to this whole section of the attraction.

The south site houses the **Astronomy Centre** (free admission), which is also home to the Peter Harrison Planetarium and the Astronomy & Time Galleries, where daily and weekend star shows cost £5.35-£8. The 120-seat planetarium's architecture cleverly reflects its astronomical position: the semi-submerged cone tilts at 51.5 degrees, the latitude of Greenwich, pointing to the north star, and its reflective disc is aligned with the celestial equator.

Thames Barrier

1 Unity Way, Woolwich, SE18 5NJ (8305 4188, www.environment-agency.gov.uk/thamesbarrier). Woolwich Dockyard rail, or North Greenwich tube then bus 472. **Open** *10.30am-5pm Thur-Sun.* **Admission** *Information Centre £4; £2.50-£3.50 reductions; free under-5s.*

This adjustable dam has been variously called a triumph of modern engineering and the eighth wonder of the world – more prosaically, it's saved London from being flooded approaching 100 times since it was built in 1982 for an eye-watering £535 million. The shiny silver fins, lined up across Woolwich Reach, are an impressive sight. The Barrier is in regular use for maintenance purposes; check the website for a current timetable. To learn more, look around the information centre, where you'll find an account of the 1953 flood that led to the barrier's construction, displays on Thames wildlife and a pleasant café.

Restaurants

On the ground floor of the Sammy Ofer extension of the National Maritime Museum *(see p283)*, the **Parkside Café & Terrace** ❸ offers fine park views, whether you essay solid British eats with cocktails, or cakes and a cuppa.

Goddards at Greenwich £

22 King William Walk, SE10 9HU (8305 9612, www.goddardsatgreenwich.co.uk). Greenwich rail/DLR or Cutty Sark DLR. **Open** *10am-7.30pm Mon-Thur; Sun; 10am-10pm Fri, Sat.* **Map** *p281 Ab14* ❶ *Pie & mash*

A family business since the 1890s, Goddards is a tourist favourite, but that doesn't put the locals off – it's justly one of London's most popular pie shops. The mash and liquor (parsley sauce) are practically perfect, though the pies can be dry and a bit dense. The huge range of fillings now available – steak and ale, lamb and rosemary – rather overshadow the traditional minced beef.

Old Brewery ££

Pepys Building, Old Royal Naval College, SE10 9LW (3437 2222, www.oldbrewerygreenwich.com). Cutty Sark DLR. **Open** *10am-11pm Mon-Sat; 10am-10.30pm Sun. Food served 10am-10pm daily.* **Map** *pp281 Ab13* ❷ *British*

Now run by Young's Brewery, this pub has an enviable location within the grounds of the Old Royal Naval College. You can admire the architecture from the large walled courtyard, or eat decent British pub nosh in the high-ceilinged dining room, decorated with artfully placed bric-a-brac. There are Young's beers, of course, but also craft beers on tap and by the bottle.

Pubs & bars

As well as the **Tasting Rooms**, Meantime also runs a proper pub that's pretty handy for the attractions: the **Greenwich Union** (56 Royal Hill, SE10 8RT, 8692 6258, www.greenwichunion.com); next door, the **Richard I** (8692 2996, www.richardthefirst.co.uk) ❷ is another reliable option.

In the know
River crossings

Connoisseurs of urban infrastructure will enjoy a trip on the workmanlike **Woolwich Ferry**, which carries pedestrians and cars between New Ferry Approach, Woolwich SE18 6DX and Pier Road, Newham, E16 2JJ, every ten minutes daily (free). Next to the ferry pier, the 1,640ft (500m) **Woolwich Foot Tunnel** dives underneath the Thames between Grade II-listed red-brick entrance towers, built in 1912.

Cutty Sark Tavern

*4-6 Ballast Quay, SE10 9PD (8858 3146, www. cuttysarkse10.co.uk). Cutty Sark DLR. **Open** 11.30am-11pm Mon-Sat; noon-10.30pm Sun. Food served noon-10pm Mon-Sat; noon-9pm Sun. **Map** p281 Ac13* ❶

Were it a couple of miles inland, the Cutty Sark would be a charming but unremarkable pub, with better-than-average grub and a decent, if unadventurous, selection of ales and wine. But add the mighty Thames and it becomes three floors of bow-fronted Georgian magic, with the top-level room in particular giving fantastic river views up- and downstream. Secure a window seat, or a table on the cobbled street outside, and imagine yourself in a scene from *Our Mutual Friend*.

Tasting Rooms

*Brewery & Visitor Centre, Lawrence Trading Estate, Blackwall Lane, SE10 0AR (8293 1111, www.meantimebrewing.com/visit/tasting-rooms). North Greenwich tube, then 188 bus/ Maze Hill rail. **Open** noon-8pm Mon, Tue; noon-10pm Wed, Thur; noon-11pm Fri, Sat; noon-6pm Sun.*

In the unimaginable days before every railway arch in the city was a microbrewery (that was 1999, nostalgia fans), Alastair Hook set up Meantime Brewery in Greenwich, with the simple aim of bringing quality beer back to London. After two decades of growth, his beer is available all over the world, but it is still made at a purpose-built brewery in North Greenwich, which has its own brewery tap and kitchen. Every one of the company's beers is available on draught here, from the easy-going London Lager to the Chocolate Porter and fruity Yakima Red. There's beer-friendly grub too, such as ribs, burgers, and fish and chips.

Shops & services

Casbah Records

*320-322 Creek Road, SE10 9SW (8858 1964, www.casbahrecords.co.uk). Cutty Sark DLR. **Open** 11.30am-6pm Mon; 10.30am-6pm Tue-Fri; 10.30am-6.30pm Sat, Sun. **Map** p281 Ab14* ❶ *Music*

After 20 years of trading as a Greenwich Market stall, Casbah Records found a more permanent base. The emphasis is on edgy girl groups, garage, psych and '60s soul, but the store also stocks a variety of classic rock, indie and electronica, along with books, DVDs, prints and vintage comics.

Greenwich Market

*King William Walk, SE10 9HZ (8269 5096, www.greenwichmarketlondon.com). Cutty Sark DLR. **Open** 10am-5.30pm daily. **Map** pp281 Ab14* ❷ *Market*

Greenwich Market can trace its origins to 1737 – although the current covered building dates only to the 19th century. On Thursdays and Fridays, up to 120 stalls are dominated by antiques and classic 20th-century pieces; the weekends are for the craftier end of things. There is also a cluster of shops dedicated to art, fashion and jewellery. If you're flagging, there is plenty of street food.

Joli Vintage Living

*8 Nelson Road, SE10 9JB (3417 5790). Cutty Sark DLR. **Open** 11am-6pm Mon-Fri; 10am-6pm Sat, Sun. **Map** p281 Ab14* ❸ *Vintage*

Just off Church Street, this quirky boutique sells quality retro clothes, chic furniture and eye-popping costume jewellery.

PECKHAM & AROUND

▶ *Peckham Rye or Denmark Hill Overground/rail.*

Over the last few years, Peckham has cemented its position as the capital's trend-setting hotspot. Streets once associated with the sitcom *Only Fools and Horses* are now lined with video arcade bars, cult nightclubs and destination restaurants. With some of the British capital's most reputable arts colleges just a 436 bus ride away, the area has become a breeding ground for south-east London's burgeoning creative scene while staying true to its multicultural roots.

At the heart of the district, Rye Lane is the site of the **Bussey Building** (see *p339*), one of London's finest clubs, the excellent **PeckhamPlex** cinema (see *p327*) and the illustrious car park (of Frank's Cafe fame; *see p288*), now transformed into the multistorey creative space **Peckham Levels** (www.peckhamlevels.org). Within its midst, you'll find bars, restaurants, a music venue and all manner of creative start-ups. Peckham Rye is also the focal point for Britain's largest Nigerian community – this is the beating heart of Little Lagos. It was very different in the late 18th and early 19th centuries: this was then the Oxford Street of south London, with moneyed Victorians flocking in horse-drawn cabs and carriages to department stores Jones & Higgins and Holdron's.

At the northern end, Peckham Square is being redeveloped, with the new **Peckham Platform** gallery (www.peckhamplatform.com) to join Will Allsop's striking, award-winning **Peckham Library** (122 Peckham Hill Street, E15 5JR) in 2020.

Due south of Rye Lane is **Peckham Rye Park**, where as a child, poet-visionary William Blake saw his angels in the 1760s; it's now a prettily laid-out park with well-kept gardens – including a restored Japanese garden created in 1908. To the west, Bellenden Road could be called Peckham Village (it probably already is by the estate agents), with its fancy dining spots, boutiques selling gifts and homewares, and indie grocery shops. Further west is fertile ground for the arts: here you'll find the excellent **South London Gallery**, next door to the **Camberwell College of Arts** (45-65 Peckham Road, 7514 6302, www.arts. ac.uk/camberwell/), where Pink Floyd's Syd Barrett and film director Mike Leigh were once students.

South of Peckham are two worthwhile museums: the **Dulwich Picture Gallery** and the **Horniman Museum**.

Sights & museums

Dulwich Picture Gallery

Gallery Road, Dulwich, SE21 7AD (8693 5254, www.dulwichpicturegallery.org. uk). North Dulwich or West Dulwich rail. **Open** *10am-5pm Tue-Sun. Tours 3pm Sat, Sun.* **Admission** *£9; free-£8 reductions; free under-18s. Special exhibitions vary. Tours free.*

This bijou attraction was designed by Sir John Soane in 1811 as the first purpose-built gallery in the UK but celebrated its bicentenary as a public gallery in 2017. It's a beautiful space that shows off Soane's ingenuity with lighting effects. The gallery displays a small but outstanding collection of work by Old Masters, offering a fine introduction to the Baroque era through works by Rembrandt, Rubens, Poussin and Gainsborough, and the temporary shows are often fantastic. Nice café-restaurant too.

♥ Horniman Museum

100 London Road, Forest Hill, SE23 3PQ (8699 1872, www.horniman.ac.uk). Forest Hill rail. **Open** *10.30am-5.30pm daily.* **Admission** *free; donations appreciated. Temporary exhibitions vary. Aquarium £4; £2 reductions; £10 family; free under-3s.*

The Horniman is an eccentric-looking art nouveau building with extensive gardens. The Natural History Gallery is dominated by an ancient walrus (overstuffed by Victorian taxidermists, who thought they ought to get the wrinkles out of the animal's skin) and ringed by glass cabinets containing pickled animals, stuffed birds and insect models. Other galleries include African Worlds and the Centenary Gallery, which focuses on world cultures. The Music Gallery contains hundreds of instruments: their sounds can be unleashed via touch-screen tables. The museum's popular showpiece Aquarium is a series of tanks and rock pools covering seven distinct aquatic ecosystems.

South London Gallery

65-67 Peckham Road, SE5 8UH (7703 6120, www.southlondongallery.org). Oval tube then bus 436, or Elephant & Castle tube/rail then bus 12, 171. **Open** *11am-6pm Tue, Thur-Sun; 10am-9pm Wed.* **Admission** *free; temporary exhibitions vary.*

In 1891, William Rossiter opened the pioneering South London Fine Art Gallery. A century later, renamed the South London Gallery, it found new renown as the site of the first exhibition of *Everyone I Have Ever Slept With 1963-1995*, Tracy Emin's infamous tent. A beacon for Brit Art in the 1990s, the gallery remains one of London's leading contemporary art venues. A £1.8-million extension swallowed up the three-storey townhouse next door in order to add two extra exhibition spaces, a resident artist's flat and, in an atrium, the Habit Café. In 2018, the SLG also opened the former Peckham Rye Fire Station at 82 Peckham Road as a new contemporary arts space and annexe to the main site.

Restaurants

The food scene in SE15 is so fertile that you can barely stumble out of Peckham Rye station without walking into a fantastic new eaterie. Other recommended spots include **Aside** (56 Goldsmith Road, SE15 5TF, 7358 1760, asidelondon.com, ££) for on-trend pan-European small plates; **Kudu** (119 Queen's Road, SE15 2EZ, 3950 0226, www.kudu-restaurant. com, ££) for ahead-of-the-curve South African small plates, and **Wildflower** (Peckham Levels, 95A Rye Lane, SE15 4ST, wildflowerpeckham.uk, ££) for perfectly pitched vegetarian and vegan dishes.

♥ Artusi ££

161 Bellenden Road, SE15 4DH (3302 8200, artusi.co.uk). Peckham Rye Overground/ rail. **Open** *6-10.30pm Mon; noon-2.30pm, 6-10.30pm Tue-Sat; 12.30-8pm Sun. Italian*

This Peckham restaurant is confidently simple. Chef Jack Beer's menu – only to be found on a chalkboard by the entrance – ranges from safe options such as ricotta and tomato salad, or prosciutto and mortadella, to more adventurous: seared ox heart with olives, perhaps, or pig's head with salsa verde. Precision cooking is evident in mains such as just-cooked whole lemon sole with roasted garlic and monk's beard. It's an unpretentiously low-key place with charming and knowledgeable staff, interesting drinks and excellent food.

💗 Begging Bowl ££
168 Bellenden Road, SE15 4BW (7635 2627, www.thebeggingbowl.co.uk). Peckham Rye Overground/rail. **Open** *6-10pm Mon-Thur; noon-2.30pm, 6-10pm Fri, Sat; noon-3pm, 6-9.30pm Sun.* Thai

Instead of the familiar Thai fare, chef Jane Alty offers street food. Colour-coded by price, and designed for sharing tapas-style, the dishes focus on more unusual ingredients such as a rich but mellow curry featuring firm-fleshed yam bean root. Seasonal Western ingredients are also given some Thai treatment, to produce dishes like trout in sour orange curry, or fennel and chicory with a relish of minced pork, prawn, coconut and yellow bean. The dining room has a contemporary feel, with big windows and colourful, painted reclaimed wood lining one wall, and there's a decent list of wines and cocktails.

💗 Coal Rooms ££
11A Station Way, SE15 4RX (7635 6699, www.coalroomspeckham.com). Peckham Rye Overground. **Open** *6.30am-11pm Mon-Fri; 7.30am-11pm Sat; 8.30am-6pm Sun. Food served noon-3pm, 6-10pm Mon-Fri; 10am-3pm, 6-10pm Sat; noon-5pm Sun.* Global

The old ticket office next door to Peckham Rye station is the Grade II-listed setting for this smoky small-plates joint. Some of the best seats are at the kitchen counter, surrounded by the meaty smells from the robata grill and coal oven behind it. But keep moving and you'll hit an airier, more refined dining room, festooned with Scandi-Japanese furniture and drapey plants. It's ever so cool and reassuringly calm, with none of the brash rowdiness of a lot of Peckham's spots. The menu is a brilliant and varied beast, running the gamut from modern American fare – grits with pickled jalapenos, shrimp with buttermilk – to inspired global fusion dishes, all marked by the kitchen's proclivity for flames. Full-flavoured mutton shoulder, slow-cooked and served with house Wow Wow gravy, is a mound of flesh to rival any in town. Eat it with a side dish of killer roast potatoes covered in a duvet of raclette cheese, stewed onions and beef-fat mayo. The bastardised tiramisu served in a paper coffee cup is a perfect finale.

Persepolis £
28-30 Peckham High Street, SE15 5DT (7693 8007, foratasteofpersia.co.uk). Peckham Rye Overground/rail. **Open** *10.35am-9pm daily.* Persian

This little café inside a Persian delicatessen is a fun place serving fun food – colourful, crowded and charmingly bonkers. A handful of chairs and tables have been shoehorned between shelves stuffed with shisha pipes, embossed glassware, musical instruments,

spices and specialist foodstuffs. They provide the setting for a liberal vegetarian interpretation of Iranian and Levantine dishes. Meze and wraps form the bedrock; seasonally inspired fillings include quince, halloumi and caramelised celeriac.For pud, you'd be mad to miss the turkish delight ice-cream sundae.

Pubs & bars

Four Quarters
187 Rye Lane, SE15 4TP (3754 7622, geocities. fourquartersbar.co.uk). Peckham Rye Overground/rail. **Open** *5.30pm-1am Mon-Wed; 5.30pm-1.30am Thur; 5pm-2am Fri; 1pm-2am Sat; 3.30-11pm Sun.*

A dedicated classic and retro arcade games bar, the Four Quarters is where to go if you want to brush up on your *Street Fighter II* skills or play *Pac Man* until your eyes go square. It's primarily a bar, but also opens as a café in the afternoons. There's a good selection of craft beers to choose from, alongside the usual favourites, and hearty pub food is served. To utilise the stacks of old arcade games, there are regular gaming tournaments, plus one-off events and film screenings.

💗 Frank's Cafe
10th floor, Peckham Levels, 95A Rye Lane, SE15 4TG (7732 5453, boldtendencies.com/ franks-cafe). Peckham Rye Overground. **Open** *May-Sept 5-11.30pm Tue, Wed; 2-11.30pm Thur, Fri; 11am-11.30pm Sat, Sun. Closed Oct-Apr.*

Surely Peckham's worst-kept secret, Frank's Cafe is a summer-only rooftop bar run by the non-profit arts promoter Bold Tendencies and located at the top of a multistorey car park (*see p342*) as part of a season of cultural offerings. An annual fixture since 2009, its concrete-tastic surroundings lend themselves perfectly to urban cocktails at sunset: the view of the London skyline is startlingly good. Frank's is always busy, so arrive early and stick with drinks that are easy to mix in a hurry: the Aperol spritz is deservedly popular.

Ivy House
40 Stuart Road, SE15 3BE (7277 8233, www. ivyhousenunhead.com). Brockley Overground or Nunhead rail. **Open** *noon-11pm Mon-Thur; noon-midnight Fri, Sat; noon-10.30pm Sun.*

In 2012, the owners gave their tenants one week's notice to ship out after selling the Ivy House to developers. Instead of going quietly, the tenants set about raising £1 million to buy the pub and turn it into a cooperative. Nowadays friendly, committed staff welcome locals of all ages for a mates-rates pint of locally brewed ale, carefully sourced pub food (including generous Sunday roasts), and events ranging from live music to yoga classes, knitting circles and kids' dance lessons. It's all housed in a Grade-II listed building, with original beams, wall-to-wall wood panelling, leaded windows and an open fire.

▶ *For more on Peckham's best bars, clubs and arts venues, see p342 A night out in Peckham.*

Shops & services

For fashion, check out **Form SE15** (186 Bellenden Road, SE15 4BW, www.formse15. com) and **D.A.Y.** (143 Bellenden Road, SE15 4DH, www.day-boutique.com).

Review
*131 Bellenden Road, SE15 4QY (www. reviewbookshop.co.uk). Peckham Rye Overground/rail. **Open** 10am-6pm Wed, Fri, Sat; noon-7pm Thur; 11am-5pm Sun. Books*

Review is the brainchild of Roz Simpson, founder of the Peckham Literary Festival (held in the shop each November), and author Evie Wyld. It's a tiny shop that's intelligently curated, with mags and 'zines, as well as other non-book purchases, and it's famously dog-friendly (the website even has a dog-themed reading list). The events programme is particularly strong.

LAMBETH & WANDSWORTH

Vauxhall

▶ *Vauxhall tube/rail.*

Vauxhall's heyday was in the 18th century when the infamous Pleasure Gardens, created back in 1661, reached the height of their popularity: a mingling of wealthy and not-so-wealthy, with everyone getting into trouble on 'lovers' walks'. When the Gardens closed in 1859, the area became reasonably respectable – all that remains is **Spring Garden**, behind popular gay haunt the **Royal Vauxhall Tavern** (aka RVT; *see p335*); there are a number of other, mostly gay clubs nearby with terrifyingly late opening hours. Down on the river is the cream and emerald ziggurat designed by Terry Farrell for the Secret Intelligence Service (formerly MI6).

Brixton

▶ *Brixton tube/rail.*

To the south, Brixton is a lively hub of clubs and music. The town centre has undergone significant redevelopment, with **Windrush Square** completed at the end of Coldharbour Lane in 2010. The square's name is significant: HMT *Windrush* was the boat that brought West Indian immigrants from Jamaica in 1948. They were hardly welcomed, but managed to make Brixton a thriving community. As late as the 1980s, tensions were still strong, as the Clash song 'Guns of Brixton' famously illustrates. The rage of the persecuted black community, still finding itself isolated and under suspicion decades after arriving, is better expressed by dub poet Linton Kwesi Johnson – try 'Sonny's Lettah (Anti-Sus Poem)' for starters. The riots of 1981 and 1985 around Railton Road and Coldharbour Lane left the district scarred for years.

The district's main roads are modern and filled with chain stores, but there's also some attractive architecture – check out the **Ritzy Cinema** (Brixton Oval, Coldharbour Lane, SW2 1JG, 0871 902 5747, www.picturehouses. co.uk), dating to 1911. Brixton's best-known street, **Electric Avenue**, got its name when, in 1880, it became one of the first shopping streets to get electric lights. Now, most visitors come to Brixton to shop, eat and drink at **Brixton Village** and **Market Row** (brixtonmarket.net/brixton-village), two Grade II-listed covered arcades off Electric Avenue and Atlantic Road. Built in the 1920s and '30s, the arcades were home to a Caribbean market from the 1960s onwards but, by the 1990s, many of the units were unoccupied and the old art deco avenues were falling into disrepair. Following regeneration by Lambeth Council, they are now filled with eclectic retailers – from bijou bakeries and vintage boutiques to international eateries and fledgling fashion labels. Another community initiative is **Pop Brixton** (www. popbrixton.org), which operates out of an assortment of shipping containers on Station Road. Pop is home to dozens of local businesses, including restaurants, bars, retailers, street food traders, designers, digital start-ups and social enterprises; it also hosts music and other events year round.

Minutes south of Brixton's hectic centre, flanked by Tulse Hill and Dulwich Road, **Brockwell Park** (www.brockwellpark.com) is one of London's most underrated green spaces. Landscaped in the early 19th century for a wealthy glass-maker, the park contains his Georgian country house – now a café – an open-air swimming pool, bowling green, walled rose garden and miniature railway. Each July, there's an enjoyable country fair.

Battersea

▶ *Battersea Park or Clapham Junction rail.*

Battersea started life as an island in the Thames, but it was reclaimed when the marshes were drained. Huguenots settled here from the 16th century and, prior to the Industrial Revolution, the area was mostly farmland. The river is dominated by Sir Giles Gilbert Scott's four-chimneyed **Battersea Power Station** (www.batterseapowerstation. co.uk), which can be seen close up from all trains leaving Victoria Station. Images of this iconic building have graced album covers (notably Pink Floyd's *Animals*) and films (among them Ian McKellen's *Richard III* and Michael Radford's *1984*), and its instantly recognisable silhouette pops up repeatedly as you move around the capital. Work started on what was to become the largest brick-built structure in Europe in 1929, and the power station was in operation through to the early 1980s. Too impressive to be destroyed, its future continues to be the subject of intense public debate. The current redevelopment masterplan by Uruguayan architect Rafael Vinoly has seen the rebuilding of the weather-damaged chimneys, the construction of (yet more) luxury flats and the provision of a Northern Line tube extension (due to open in 2020). The plans also promise a new 1,500-capacity event space and a panoramic viewing platform in the north-west tower.

Overlooking the river, a little further west, **Battersea Park** (www.batterseapark.org) has beautiful lakes (one with a fine Barbara Hepworth sculpture); the Russell Page Garden, designed for the 1951 Festival of Britain; a Peace Pagoda built by a Buddhist sect in 1985 to commemorate Hiroshima Day; the **Pump House Gallery** (3959 0021, pumphousegallery.org.uk), and the charming **Children's Zoo** (7924 5826, www. batterseaparkzoo.co.uk), which features the usual rabbits, sheep and chickens alongside more exotic creatures, such as meerkats, lemurs and monkeys. The park extends to the Thames; from the wide and lovely riverside walk you can see both the elaborate Albert Bridge and the simpler Battersea Bridge, rebuilt between 1886 and 1890 by sewer engineer Joseph Bazalgette.

Sights & museums

Black Cultural Archives

Windrush Square, SW2 1EF (3757 8500, www. blackculturalarchives.org) Brixton tube/rail. **Open** *10am-6pm Tue-Sat. Reading Room 10am-4pm Wed-Fri.* **Admission** *free.*

Gathered over a quarter of a century, the Black Cultural Archives found a permanent home in the Grade II-listed Raleigh Hall on Brixton's Windrush Square in 2014. The only heritage centre in the country dedicated to collecting, preserving and celebrating the histories of black Britons, this long overdue cultural centre runs a busy programme of events and exhibitions, showcasing how people of African and Caribbean origin have shaped UK history.

Restaurants

Both **Brixton Village** and **Pop Brixton** have numerous food options – from naughty street food to more salubrious international dishes.

Franco Manca £

Unit 4, Market Row, Electric Lane, SW9 8LD (7738 3021, www.francomanca.co.uk). Brixton tube/rail. **Open** *noon-5pm Mon; noon-11pm Tue-Fri; 11.30am-11pm Sat; 11.30am-10.30pm Sun. Pizza*

With its top-notch, UK-sourced (when possible) ingredients, speedy and friendly service, and rapid turnover, the original Brixton branch of Franco Manca remains, for our money, the best pizza joint in London. Here, you can sate a craving for genuine, Neapolitan-style pizza, with a flavourful slow-rise sourdough crust and a variety of traditional and innovative toppings.

Nanban £-££

426 Coldharbour Lane, SW9 8LF (7346 0098, www.nanban.co.uk). Brixton tube/rail. **Open** *5-11pm Mon; noon-3.30pm, 5-11pm Tue-Thur; noon-3pm, 5pm-1am Fri; noon-1am Sat; noon-10pm Sun. Japanese*

Run by former MasterChef winner Tim Anderson, Nanban serves up Japanese soul food. Sure, it's not the cosiest spot, with its bright lighting and hard backless stools, but the staff are lovely and the cooking is comfort food with Asian flavours. Try chicken *karaage*, with its crunchy chilli-and-salt flour coating, or *horumon yaki*, a sweet and savoury pig tripe stir-fried with crunchy rice and sprouts. The absolute must-try, however, is the curry goat *tsukemen*, with its meltingly tender meat and intense flavours.

♥ Naughty Piglets ££

28 Brixton Water Lane, SW2 1PE (7274 7796, www.naughtypiglets.co.uk). Brixton tube/ rail. **Open** *6-10pm Mon-Thur; noon-2.20pm, 6-10pm Fri, Sat. Contemporary European*

Run by husband-and-wife team Joe Sharatt and Margaux Aubry, Naughty Piglets is a 'natural' wine bar with a perfectly matched small-plate menu. Left to ferment naturally with little intervention, the wines are distinctly different in character (tasting something like a dry cider) and

Pop Brixton p289

Open 4.30pm-midnight Mon-Thur;
4.30pm-1am Fri; noon-1am Sat; noon-11pm
Sun. Food served 5-10pm Mon-Fri; noon-
10pm Sat; noon-8pm Sun.

The most exciting feature of this pub is the
lengthy bar with its endless fonts: seven cask
ales, 14 keg beers and ciders. It's a friendly
place, devoted to great beer.

Shops & services

The arcades of **Brixton Village** and
Market Row (*see p289*) are perfect for
relaxed shopping. There's also a variety
of market stalls on Electric Avenue,
Pope's Road and Station Road; see www.
brixtonmarket.net for details.

Bookmongers
*439 Coldharbour Lane, SW9 8LN (7738 4225,
www.bookmongers.com). Brixton tube/rail.
Open 10.30am-6.30pm Mon-Sat; 11am-4pm
Sun. Books*

This Brixton institution is everything you
could want from a second-hand bookshop.
Run by American-born Patrick Kelly, who
opened the shop more than 20 years ago,
it's developed a devoted following. Its stock
is inspiring and well-organised, if slightly
overflowing, and the resident dog adds to
the charm.

go particularly well with steamed mussels
or clams. As well as seafood, the brief
blackboard menu includes French classics
such as fatty duck rillettes or more unusual
options like barbecue Korean pork belly.

❤ Smoke & Salt ££
*Pop Brixton, 49 Brixton Station Road, SW9
8PQ (07421 327556, www.smokeandsalt.com).
Brixton tube/rail. **Open** 6-10pm Mon-Thur;
noon-3pm, 6-10pm Fri; noon-3pm, 5-10pm
Sat. Modern European*

Yes, it's a bit of a squish, with only 20-odd
seats, but the faux marble, dark woods and
moody lighting make this shipping container
slick enough for a Saturday night date. Then
there's the food. Aaron Webster and Remi
Williams serve up the kind of modernist
small plates designed to make you happy.
Our top picks include buttery-soft nuggets
of octopus and rounds of salsify over a thin
chowder-esque base, served in a large clam
shell with accents of blood orange. And, a fat,
fluffy flatbread, with parsnip baked into its
centre, served with wafer-thin parsnip swords
held in a 'burnt yeast cream' and gently
pickled slivers of garlic and apple, studded
with golden raisins. Like Smoke & Salt's other
showstoppers, these dishes are somehow
both homely and stunning. Combine
this food with pitch-perfect service and
ludicrously low prices, and it's no wonder that
S&S is one of Brixton's most prized assets.

SOUTH-WEST LONDON

Affluent and assured, the London Borough
of Richmond in the south-west is blessed
with plenty of green spaces, including the
unexpectedly wild **WWT Reserve** in Barnes,
expansive **Richmond Park** (royalparks.
org.uk) and the unmissable **Royal Botanic
Gardens** at Kew (*see p292*). The Thames
is particularly attractive here too, with
semi-rural stretches through parkland and
meadows. There's picturesque riverfront
architecture at **Richmond**, not to mention
several historic palaces to explore, most
notably **Hampton Court**.

❤ Hampton Court Palace
*East Molesey, Surrey, KT8 9AU (0844 482
7777, www.hrp.org.uk). Hampton Court
rail, or riverboat from Westminster or
Richmond to Hampton Court Pier (Apr-Oct).
Palace Apr-Oct 10am-6pm daily. Nov-Mar
10am-4.30pm daily. **Grounds** dawn-dusk
daily. **Admission** £22.70; £11.35-£18.10
reductions; £40.40-£56.80 family; free
under-5s. Maze only £4.40; £2.70 reductions.*

This spectacular palace, once owned by
Henry VIII, is just a half-hour journey from
central London – but will take you back 500

Pubs & bars

Crown & Anchor
*246 Brixton Road, SW9 6AQ (7737 0060,
www.crownandanchorbrixton.co.uk).
Stockwell tube or Brixton tube/rail.*

❤ Royal Botanic Gardens, Kew

Kew, Richmond, Surrey, TW9 3AB (8332 5655, www.kew.org). Kew Gardens tube/ Overground, Kew Bridge rail or riverboat to Kew Pier. **Open** *10am-4.15pm daily.* **Admission** *£17; £5-£15 reductions; free under-4s.*

Kew's lush, landscaped beauty represents the pinnacle of our national gardening obsession. From the early 1700s until 1840, when the gardens were given to the nation, these were the grounds for two fine royal residences – the White House and Richmond Lodge. Early resident Queen Caroline, wife of George II, was very fond of exotic plants brought back by botanists voyaging to far-flung parts of the world, and these formed the basis for the collection. Then, in 1759, the renowned 'Capability' Brown was employed by George III to improve on the work of his predecessors here, William Kent and Charles Bridgeman. Thus began the shape of the extraordinary garden that today attracts hundreds of thousands of visitors each year – and was made a UNESCO World Heritage Site in 2003. Covering half a square mile, Kew feels surprisingly big – you'll want to pick up a map at the ticket office as well as following the handy signs.

Head straight for the 19th-century greenhouses, filled to the roof with plants – some of which have been here as long as the enormous glass structures themselves. The **Temperate House**, the largest Victorian glasshouse in the world, is home to some of the world's rarest and most threatened plants. It reopened in May 2018 after a five-year refurbishment programme, which saw some 69,000 items cleaned or replaced. The sultry **Palm House** has tropical palms, bamboo, tamarind, fig and mango trees, as well as fragrant hibiscus and frangipani.

Also worth seeking out are the **Princess of Wales Conservatory**, divided into ten climate zones, and the lovely, quiet indoor pond of the **Waterlily House** (closed in winter). At the southern end of the gardens, there's a **Chinese Pagoda** dating from 1762.

Kew doesn't just do history. There's art, too, with sculptures like Henry Moore's *Reclining Mother and Child* in stunning settings that change with the light of each season, and the exquisite Victorian botanical drawings found in the **Marianne North Gallery**.

The **Treetop Walkway** is a hugely popular addition to the gardens, allowing visitors to take a completely different kind of woodland walk – 60ft (18m) up in the leaf canopy. Another is *The Hive*, a 55ft (17m), 40-tonne installation by Wolfgang Buttress set in a wildflower meadow. First erected at the 2015 Milan Expo, it's a massive lattice within which visitors can stand, lie or sit as thousands of LEDs flicker and an orchestral arrangement plays, triggered by the activity of bees in a nearby hive.

❤More great gardens

Chelsea Physic Garden *p137*
London's finest secret garden.

Chiswick House Gardens *p304*
William Kent's 'natural' approach to landscape in the 18th century was revolutionary.

Garden Museum *p83*
Reopened in 2017.

Hampstead Heath *p247*
The whole heath is lovely, but the Pergola and Hill Gardens, overlooking the West Heath, especially so.

Hampton Court Palace *p291*
Versailles on Thames.

Temperate House

years through history. It was built in 1514 by Cardinal Wolsey, the high-flying Lord Chancellor, but Henry liked it so much he seized it for himself in 1528. For the next 200 years it was a focal point of English history: Elizabeth I was imprisoned in a tower by her jealous and fearful elder sister Mary I; Shakespeare gave his first performance to James I in 1603; and, after the Civil War, Oliver Cromwell was so besotted by the building he ditched his puritanical principles and moved in to enjoy its luxuries.

Centuries later, the rosy walls of the palace still dazzle. Its vast size can be daunting, so it's a good idea to take advantage of the guided tours. If you do decide to go it alone, start with Henry VIII's State Apartments, which include the Great Hall, noted for its beautiful stained-glass windows and elaborate religious tapestries; in the Haunted Gallery, the ghost of Catherine Howard – Henry's fifth wife, executed for adultery in 1542 – can reputedly be heard shrieking. The King's Apartments, added in 1689 by Wren, are notable for a splendid mural of Alexander the Great, painted by Antonio Verrio. The Queen's Apartments and Georgian Rooms feature similarly elaborate paintings, chandeliers and tapestries, while the Cumberland Art Gallery – in beautifully restored Georgian rooms – shows works from the Royal Collection by Holbein, Rembrandt and Caravaggio. The Tudor Kitchens are great fun, with their giant cauldrons, fake pies and blood-spattered walls.

More extraordinary sights await outside, where the exquisitely landscaped gardens offer topiary, Thames views, a reconstruction of a 16th-century heraldic garden and the famous Hampton Court maze.

Strawberry Hill
268 Waldegrave Road, Twickenham, Middx, TW1 4ST (8744 1241, www. strawberryhillhouse.org.uk). Richmond tube/ Overground/rail then bus R68, or Strawberry Hill rail. House hours vary; check website for details. Garden 10am-5.30pm daily. Tours 10am Wed; 10.30am Sat. Admission House £12.50; £6.25 reductions; free under-16s. Garden and tours free.

Thames Path

Stretching from Teddington Lock in the south-west to the Thames Barrier (see p285), this National Trail takes in both the north and south banks of the river as it flows through London. The complete distance is 79.5 miles (128km), broken down into four sections. For further details and maps, see tfl.gov.uk/modes/walking/thames-path.

Antiquarian Horace Walpole, who created the Gothic novel with his book *The Castle of Otranto*, had already laid the groundwork for the Gothic Revival of Victorian times as early as the 1700s. Pre-booked tickets, at 20-minute intervals, allow you to explore the crepuscular nooks and crannies of his 'play-thing house', this 'little Gothic castle', including – since 2015 – the study in which he wrote *Otranto*.

Twickenham Rugby Stadium
Whitton Road, Twickenham, Middx, TW2 7BA (8892 8877, www.englandrugby. com/twickenham/world-rugby-museum). Hounslow East tube then bus 281, or Twickenham rail. Open Museum 10am-5pm Tue-Sat; 11am-5pm Sun. Times of tours vary. Admission £20; £12-15 reductions; free under-5s.

Parts of Twickenham Stadium, the home of English rugby union, are currently under redevelopment, though it hasn't affected matches. You can still take a guided tour, too, poking around the England dressing room, the players' tunnel and the Royal Box. The World Rugby Museum has memorabilia charting the game's development from the late 19th century and a scrum machine.

Wimbledon Lawn Tennis Museum
Museum Building, All England Lawn Tennis Club, Church Road, Wimbledon, SW19 5AE (8946 6131, www.wimbledon.com/museum). Southfields tube. Open 10am-5pm daily; ticket holders only during championships. Admission (incl tour) £25; £15-£21 reductions; free under-5s.

Highlights at this popular museum on the history of tennis include a 200° cinema screen that allows you to find out what it's like to play on Centre Court, and a recreation of a 1980s men's dressing room, complete with a 'ghost' of John McEnroe. Visitors can also enjoy a behind-the-scenes tour.

WWT Wetland Centre
Queen Elizabeth's Walk, Barnes, SW13 9WT (8409 4400, www.wwt.org.uk). Hammersmith tube then bus 283, Barnes rail. Open Mar-Oct 9.30am-5.30pm daily. Nov-Feb 9.30am-4.30pm daily. Admission £12.26; £6.75-£9.17 reductions; free under-4s.

The 43-acre Wetland Centre is only four miles from central London, but feels a world away. Quiet ponds, rushes, rustling reeds and wildflower gardens all teem with bird life – some 150 species. There are over 300 varieties of butterfly, 20 types of dragonfly and four species of bat. You can explore water-recycling in the Rain Garden or try the interactive section: pilot a submerged camera around a pond, learn the life-cycle of a dragonfly or make waves in a digital pool.

West London

For a fading cadre of right-wing politicians and a certain kind of celeb, Notting Hill is still the coolest address in town, with Portobello Market surrounded by some of the most expensive addresses in west London. As in so many parts of the capital, any patina of funkiness is down to previous generations of residents – poor working class and immigrants mostly – who made the place in their own image. The huge Notting Hill Carnival gives the best flavour of this community. More high-end, elegant housing is found to the south in Holland Park and Kensington, where there are said to be more millionaires per square mile than in any other part of Europe. Apart from rubbernecking the rich, visitors should come here for the ambitious Design Museum and delightful park. Further afield, you'll find the surprising wealth of sights around Chiswick – and, an arch on the far horizon, Wembley.

❤ **Don't miss**

1 Notting Hill Carnival *p299*
The biggest street party in Europe.

2 Design Museum *p302*
A classic reborn in stunning listed premises.

3 Portobello Road Market *p300*
Big, busy and lots of fun.

4 Holland Park *p302*
One of London's finest parks.

5 Leighton House *p302*
An eccentric Victorian gem.

WEST LONDON

DESIGNER

NOTTING HILL

▶ *Ladbroke Grove, Notting Hill Gate or Westbourne Park tube.*

Long-since supplanted in the urban cool stakes by areas of east and south London, **Notting Hill** still trades on the lingering street cred of its fast-disappearing black and working-class communities. There are attractive leafy avenues south of Notting Hill Gate, while, to the north, Pembridge Road leads to the boutique-filled streets of Westbourne Grove and Ledbury Road.

Most visitors flock to **Portobello Road** for its renowned market; there are actually several markets, with stalls along the length of Portobello Road, under the Westway (the elevated section of the M40 motorway) and north to **Golborne Road**.

Blenheim Crescent has a couple of independent booksellers, but the Travel Bookshop (nos.13-15), on which the movie *Notting Hill* focused its attention, has gone.

Golborne Road is the heartland of London's North African community. Here, too, is a fine Portuguese café-deli, the **Lisboa Pâtisserie** (no.57, 8968 5242). At the north-eastern end of Portobello Road stands **Trellick Tower**, an architecturally significant, like-it-or-loathe-it piece of Ernö Goldfinger modernism.

Stretching north from Holland Park Avenue to Harrow Road, **Ladbroke Grove** is the main road on the route of the **Notting Hill Carnival** (*see p299*). The **Museum of Brands** is just to the west, and **Kensal Green Cemetery** is at its northern tip.

Sights & museums

Kensal Green Cemetery

Harrow Road, Kensal Green, W10 4RA (8969 0152, www.kensalgreencemetery.com). Kensal Green tube/Overground. **Open** *Apr-Sept 9am-6pm Mon-Sat; 10am-6pm Sun. Oct-Mar 9am-5pm Mon-Sat; 10am-5pm Sun.* **Tours** *(meet at the Anglican chapel) Mar-Oct 2pm Sun. Nov-Feb 2pm 1st & 3rd Sun of mth.* **Admission** *free. Tours £7; £5 reductions. No cards.*

Behind a neoclassical gate is a green oasis of the dead. It's the resting place of the Duke of Sussex, sixth son of George III, and his sister, Princess Sophia; also buried here are Wilkie Collins, Anthony Trollope and William Makepeace Thackeray.

❤ **Time to eat**

Modern European masters
108 Garage *p298*, Ledbury *p298*

Start the day like a Dane
Snaps & Rye *p300*

Sushi without soy
Yashin *p303*

Vegetarian eats that don't dress down
Farmacy *p298*

❤ **Time to shop**

Come for the atmosphere – not for bargains
Portobello Road Market *p300*

Like what you saw? Buy it from the shop!
Design Museum *p302*

Next year's fashion, today
Couverture & the Garbstore *p300*

Record store that's the pulse of west London
Honest Jon's *p300*

Portobello Road

NOTTING HILL & HOLLAND PARK

Restaurants

1. 108 Garage *p298*
2. Farmacy *p298*
3. Ledbury *p298*
4. Muffin Man Tea Room *p303*
5. The Shed *p303*
6. Snaps & Rye *p300*
7. Yashin *p303*

Pubs & bars

1. Portobello Star *p300*

Shops & services

1. Couverture & the Garbstore *p300*
2. Honest Jon's *p300*
3. Lutyens & Rubinstein *p300*
4. Portobello Road Market *p300*

Farmacy

Museum of Brands, Packaging & Advertising

111-117 Lancaster Road, W11 1QT (7243 9611, www.museumofbrands.com). Notting Hill Gate tube. **Open** *10am-6pm Tue-Sat; 11am-5pm Sun.* **Admission** *£9; £5-£7 reductions; £24 family; free under-7s.* **Map** *p297 A6.*

In 2015, the Museum of Brands found itself in a glam new home: it's still in Notting Hill, but now has extra space for its seemingly endless collection of wrappers, posters, toys, boxes and general collectibles. The main part of the display is the 'time tunnel', a winding corridor of dark cabinets stuffed with colourful curios arranged chronologically. With the arrival of each new decade an information panel helps to put the changing designs and new fashions into context. A separate gallery functions as a sort of shrine to a few favourite brands: one cabinet holds every iteration of can and bottle produced by Guinness; another is packed with Kellogg's cereal boxes. We'd prefer a bit more analysis of the social trends that created all these designs – but we were delighted to see the 'Time Out 50 Years, 50 Covers' exhibition in 2018-19.

Restaurants

❤ 108 Garage ££

108 Golborne Road, W10 5PS (8969 3769, www.108garage.com). Ladbroke Grove tube. **Open** *6-10pm Tue, Wed; noon-2pm, 6-10pm Thur; noon-2pm, 6-10.30pm Fri; noon-2.30pm, 6-10.30pm Sat.* **Map** *p297 A5* ❶ *Modern European*

This garage conversion is a rather lovely spot, its dining room a handsome mix of dark mid-century furniture, bare bricks,

corrugated iron and great washes of copper. The food is meticulous, from the near-liquid chicken-liver parfait to the lightly seared veal sweetbread atop charred cabbage. Best of all are the desserts: sweet potato ice-cream on a bed of popcorn and zingy sheep's yoghurt; or dense chocolate *crémeux* with artichoke ice-cream perched on a mound of toasted wild rice.

❤ Farmacy ££

74 Westbourne Grove, W2 5SH (7221 0705, www.farmacylondon.com). Bayswater or Royal Oak tube. **Open** *9am-5pm, 6-10pm Mon-Fri; 9am-4pm, 6-10pm Sat; 9am-4pm, 6-9.30pm Sun.* **Map** *p297 C7* ❷ *Vegetarian*

Farmacy (as in health from the farm, geddit?) is free from most things – dairy, refined sugars, meat, additives and chemical nasties – but fortunately, it's not lacking in taste. From the food coming out of the kitchen to the ultra-sleek decor, it's smart, but relaxed and friendly. The menu is 'clean indulgence', which means that it has lots of naughty-sounding but actually super-healthy things to choose from: mushroom tagliatelle made with spelt flour; a nut-based burger loaded with avocado pickle; zingy lemon cheesecake. The weekend High Tea menu is a plant-based, treat-filled extravagance (*see p45*).

❤ Ledbury £££

127 Ledbury Road, W11 2AQ (7792 9090, www.theledbury.com). Westbourne Park tube. **Open** *6.30-9.45pm Mon, Tue; noon-2pm, 6.30-9.45pm Wed-Sun.* **Map** *p297 B6* ❸ *Modern European*

Few haute establishments have the hospitable hum of the Ledbury, and even fewer boast two Michelin stars. But this former pub remains top-tier for gustatory

💜 Notting Hill Carnival

Notting Hill, W10 & W11 (www. thelondonnottinghillcarnival.com). Bayswater tube or Paddington tube/rail (local stations are subject to restrictions). **Date** *late Aug bank hol Sun & Mon.*

Given that an estimated two million people attended in 2018, Notting Hill Carnival undoubtedly deserves its reputation as Europe's biggest street festival. The annual event is a vivid and thrilling spectacle that celebrates and showcases London's rich, varied and magnificent multicultural past and present. And for any party lovers, the Carnival weekend is a vital date in the calendar.

The Carnival has been taking place in west London since 1966 as a celebration of the capital's Caribbean communities, their culture and traditions. It is usually held over the bank holiday weekend at the end of

August and features a parade and fantastic live music, including reggae, dub and salsa. There are also 37 static sound systems, soca floats, steel bands and a whole lot of delicious Caribbean food. The main parade begins on Great Western Road, moving its way along Chepstow Road, before leading on to Westbourne Grove. It then travels down Ladbroke Grove.

The sheer size and excitement of Carnival can be overwhelming, especially if you're unsure exactly what's going on, or if you have children in tow. Try to visit on Sunday's 'Family Day', which is a little quieter than Monday's party, and arrive early to beat the crowds. Pack snacks and water to avoid long queues and bear in mind that your mobile signal may be patchy due to the sheer number of people. Check tfl.com to keep up to date with transport provision to and from the Carnival.

Batala Samba at Notting Hill Carnival

good times. British ingredients – smoked eel, Cumbrian lamb – line up alongside delicacies such as Tokyo turnips, Bresse chicken and black truffle, but it's chef Brett Graham's clever contemporary treatment of them that sets the place apart. Ledbury signatures are consistently thrilling – particularly the flame-grilled mackerel with pickled cucumber, celtic mustard and shiso; and, well, all the desserts.

❤ Snaps & Rye £
93 Golborne Road, W10 5NL (8964 3004, snapsandrye.com). Westbourne Park tube. **Open** *9am-5pm Tue, Wed; 9am-11pm Thur-Sat; 9.30am-5pm Sun. Food served 9am-3pm Tue, Wed; 9am-3pm, 6.30-9pm Thur-Sat; 9.30am-3pm Sun.* **Map** *p297 A5* ❻ *Danish*

Snaps (alcohol infusions) & Rye (the accompanying food) embodies all that's best about Scandinavian design: simple and functional, but every detail designed or chosen with aesthetic pleasure in mind. The owners have also taken great pains to make their food, prepared by British chef Tania Steytler, as good as it can possibly be. While Denmark's famous open-faced sandwiches (*smørrebrød*) are simple in concept, Steytler raises them to great heights through the use of superb ingredients, masterly cooking skills and attention to detail. Other options are meatballs, herring, cured salmon and apple cake. Feeling the cold but don't fancy snaps? Try *cocio*, a Nordic hot chocolate.

Pubs & bars
Portobello Star
171 Portobello Road, W11 2DY (7229 8220, www.portobellostarbar.co.uk). Ladbroke Grove or Notting Hill Gate tube. **Open** *noon-11.30pm Mon-Thur, Sun; 11am-12.30am Fri; 10am-12.30am Sat.* **Map** *p297 A7* ❶

This 'cocktail tavern' deftly blends discerning bar and traditional boozer. The well-stocked bar is manned by friendly staff thoroughly educated in the art of adult refreshment. Mixologist Jake Burger's impeccable, approachable directory of drinks is the last word on sophisticated intoxication.

Shops & services
❤ Couverture & the Garbstore
188 Kensington Park Road, W11 2ES (7229 2178, www.couvertureandthegarbstore.com). Ladbroke Grove tube. **Open** *10am-6pm Mon-Sat; noon-5pm Sun.* **Map** *p297 A7* ❶ *Fashion/homewares*

Cult shop Couverture & the Garbstore sticks it to the Man with an under-the-radar collection of independent labels and up-and-coming

designer fashion ('when it sells out, you're out of luck' is the theme). On the lower level of this slick three-storey boutique is designer Ian Paley's menswear label, the Garbstore. The ground and upper levels house Emily Dyson's much-admired lifestyle concept Couverture, where you'll find an enticing array of homewares and beautiful women's and children's fashion.

❤ Honest Jon's
278 Portobello Road, W10 5TE (8969 9822, www.honestjons.com). Ladbroke Grove tube. **Open** *10am-6pm Mon-Sat; 11am-5pm Sun.* **Map** *p297 A6* ❷ *Music*

Honest Jon's found its way to Notting Hill in 1979, where it is as much a cultural edifice – the shop's owner helped James Lavelle to set up Mo'Wax records – as a music shop. Here you'll find jazz, hip hop, soul, broken beat, reggae and Brazilian music, as well as the label's own brilliant compilations – the first volumes of the *London is the Place for Me* series, detailing calypso, Afro-jazz and highlife in the post-war years, were a revelation.

Lutyens & Rubinstein
21 Kensington Park Road, W11 2EU (7229 1010, www.lutyensrubinstein.co.uk). Ladbroke Grove tube. **Open** *10am-6pm Mon, Sat; 10am-6.30pm Tue-Fri; 11am-5pm Sun.* **Map** *p297 A7* ❸ *Books*

Lutyens & Rubinstein sells a beautifully arranged selection of literary fiction and general non-fiction. The core stock was put together by the owners canvassing hundreds of readers on the books they'd most like to find in a bookshop; thus every book stocked is sold because somebody has recommended it. The result is an appealing alternative to the homogenous chain bookshops, with some unusual titles available. As well as books, the shop stocks a small range of stationery, greetings cards, paperweights, local honey and literary-inspired scents from CB I Hate Perfume.

❤ Portobello Road Market
Portobello Road, W10 (www.portobelloroad. co.uk). Ladbroke Grove or Notting Hill Gate tube. **Open** *9am-6pm Mon-Wed; 9am-1pm Thur; 9am-7pm Fri, Sat.* **Map** *p297 B7* ❹ *Market*

In the know
Cash in

If you're coming to **Portobello Road Market**, be sure to bring plenty of cash: the few cashpoints nearby attract preposterous queues, and not all traders accept cards.

Portobello Road Market

Best known for antiques and collectibles, the markets around Portobello Road now encompass everything from fashion to food. Antiques start at the Notting Hill end, with more than 2,000 specialist antiques dealers squeezed tightly into any available space, and bargain-hunters jostling with camera-laden tourists to the soundtrack of live jazz. There are food stalls to sustain you as you push on to explore the fashion market under the Westway flyover. Best visited on a less-frantic Friday morning, it's here you'll find fashionistas and trendy teens delving through troves of prized vintage, boutique fashion and retro memorabilia. And don't stop there: continue up to Golborne Road for bargains away from the masses, helped by the presence of eccentric second-hand interiors stalls.

KENSINGTON & HOLLAND PARK

▶ *High Street Kensington or Holland Park tube.*

Running south from Notting Hill Gate, **Kensington Church Street** has many antiques shops selling furniture so fine you would probably never dare use it. **St Mary Abbots** (smanews.weebly.com), at the junction of Church Street and High Street, is a Victorian neo-Gothic church. It was built – on the site of the 12th-century original – by Sir George Gilbert Scott between 1869 and 1872. Past worshippers have included Isaac Newton and William Wilberforce. As well as beautiful stained-glass windows, it has London's tallest spire (278 feet, 85 metres).

Across the road, in a striking art deco building, is organic-food superstore **Whole Foods Market** (63-97 Kensington High Street, W8 5SE, 7368 4500, www.wholefoodmarket.com). The **High Street**, a smart but rarely exhilarating shopping drag, runs west from the corner of Kensington Gardens (*see p132*). To the north and south of it are an array of handsome squares, lined with grand 19th-century houses, many of which still serve as single-family homes for the wealthy. South down Derry Street is **Kensington Square**, which has a mighty concentration of blue plaques. The writer William Thackeray lived at no.16 and the painter Edward Burne-Jones at no.41; at no.18, John Stuart Mill's maid made her bid for 'person from Porlock' status by using Carlyle's sole manuscript of *The French Revolution* to light the fire. The houses, though much altered, date from the development of the square in 1685, and were surrounded by fields until 1840.

Further west is one of London's finest green spaces: **Holland Park**, with the fabulous **Design Museum** at its southern edge. Also to the south of the park are a couple of historic houses: **18 Stafford Terrace** and, extensively refurbished **Leighton House**.

Sights & museums

18 Stafford Terrace

18 Stafford Terrace, W8 7BH (tours 7602 3316 Mon-Fri, 7938 1295 Sat, Sun, www.rbkc.gov.uk). High Street Kensington tube. Open Oct-June 2-5.30pm Wed, Sat, Sun. Tours (pre-booked only) 11am Wed, Sat, Sun. Closed end July-Sept. Admission £7; £5 reductions; free under-5s. Tours £10; £8 reductions. Map p297 B10.

The home of cartoonist Edward Linley Sambourne was built in the 1870s and has

Holland Park

almost all of its original fittings and furniture. On Saturdays, tours are led by an actor in period costume.

♥ Design Museum

224-238 Kensington High Street, W8 6AG (3862 5900, designmuseum.org). High Street Kensington tube. **Open** *10am-6pm (last admission 5pm) daily.* **Admission** *free; temporary exhibitions vary.* **Map** *p297 B10.*

In late 2016, the Design Museum finally moved to the grand space its ambition deserves. Dating to 1962, the Grade II*-listed former Commonwealth Institute building on Kensington High Street is itself a classic piece of modern architecture, with a pioneering hyperboloid roof (effectively a series of vertical arches) made of copper-clad concrete. There's plenty of room for temporary exhibitions (three at a time, plus a showcase for designers in residence), the archive, a library, two shops, a ground-floor café and impressive mezzanine restaurant, as well as the permanent collection.

Called 'Designer Maker User', the collection traces the development of 20th- and 21st-century design, starting with a supremely detailed timeline at the entrance. Thereafter there are plenty of artefacts to satisfy visitors who are just looking for a bit of fuzzy hey-wow tech nostalgia – Sony Walkmans, Xbox controllers and early iPhones. The ticketed temporary exhibitions are always worth a look: some focus on particular designers, including Cartier and Camper; some explore broader themes, such as cycling or recycling; and some do a bit of both, as at the necessarily loose but always compelling annual Designs of the Year awards exhibition.

♥ Holland Park

Ilchester Place, W8 6LU (7361 3003, www. rbkc.gov.uk/leisure-and-culture/parks/ holland-park). Holland Park/Kensington High Street tube. **Open** *7.30am-30mins before dusk daily.* **Map** *p297 B10.*

Holland Park, whose 55 acres add up to one of London's finest green spaces, was formerly the grounds of Jacobean mansion Holland House, named after its second owner, the Earl of Holland, whose wife was the first person in England to successfully grow dahlias. In the 19th century, Holland House was a hub of political and literary activity, visited by Disraeli and Lord Byron among others, but it was largely destroyed by the Blitz during World War II – though enough of it remains to have been Grade I-listed and for a fancy-pants youth hostel, **Safestay Holland Park** (7870 9629, www.safestay.com/ss-london-holland-park.html), to move in. These days, dahlias are still grown, but there are also the Japanese-style Kyoto Gardens with their koi carp and bridge at the foot of a waterfall. Holland Walk, along the park's eastern edge, is one of the most pleasant paths in central London, and there's a fine café. In summer, open-air theatre and opera are staged (*see p313*).

♥ Leighton House

12 Holland Park Road, W14 8LZ (7602 3316, www.rbkc.gov.uk). High Street Kensington tube. **Open** *10am-5.30pm Mon, Wed-Sun. Tours 3pm Wed, Sat.* **Admission** *£9; £7 reductions. Tours free.* **Map** *p297 B10.*

In the 1860s, artist Frederic Leighton commissioned a showpiece house. He ensured that, behind the sternly Victorian red-brick façade, it was full of treasures from all over the world, as well as his own works and those of his contemporaries. The house is decorated in high style: magnificent downstairs reception rooms designed for lavish entertaining; a dramatic staircase leading to a light-filled studio that takes up most of the first floor; and, above all, the Arab Hall, which showcases Leighton's huge collection of 16th-century Middle Eastern tiles. The only private space in the whole house is a tiny single bedroom – there are even theatrically Moorish-style screens allowing you to observe the downstairs without being seen.

Restaurants

Just around the corner from Kensington High Street tube, **Muffin Man Tea Room** (12 Wrights Lane, W8 6TA, 7937 6652, www. themuffinmanteashop.co.uk ❹) is an old-school English tearoom where you can relax with a cuppa and a cake or pastry.

Shed £££

122 Palace Gardens Terrace, W8 4RT (7229 4024, www.theshed-restaurant.com). Notting Hill Gate tube. **Open** *6-11pm Mon; noon-3pm, 6-11pm Tue-Fri; noon-4.40pm, 6-11pm Sat.* **Map** *p297 C8* ❺ *British*

From a distance, with its white wooden cladding and high pitched roof, this restaurant does look suspiciously like a shed. Add some piggy portraits, bits of tractor, and charming staff in check shirts and it's a fitting setting for the food, which goes beyond the usual hackneyed take on British. Plates are small and meant for sharing, with delights such as hake with samphire, capers and a slick of red pepper sauce or spatchcock quail with cucumber, poppy seed and barbecue sauce. It's a menu of delicious things that are inventive without becoming tricksy.

❤ Yashin £££

1A Argyll Road, W8 7DB (7938 1536, www. yashinsushi.com). High Street Kensington tube. **Open** *noon-3pm, 6-11pm daily; last order 1hr before closing.* **Map** *p297 C10* ❼ *Sushi*

The centrepiece sushi counter gives the game away: set on the dark green tiles behind the team of *itamae* (sushi chefs), a neon sign reads 'without soy sauce'. This is how the chefs ask you to eat your artfully crafted sushi. In place of a dunking, each piece is finished with its own flavourings or even a quick blast from a blowtorch.

FULHAM

▶ *Fulham Broadway or West Brompton tube.*

Travel west along Fulham Road from Chelsea to reach the gates of **Brompton Cemetery**, whose peace and quiet are regularly disturbed at its southern end by neighbouring **Stamford Bridge** (*see p136*), ground of Chelsea FC. **Craven Cottage**, home to Championship side Fulham FC, is a more historic ground, however: the red-brick entrance and ticket gates (built in 1905) are a lovely example of the work of prime football stadium designer Archibald Leitch, who had to incorporate the Cottage into his design – it's grand for a Cottage, but a wonderfully eccentric part of the fabric of the club. Craven Cottage is at the northern end of the park that contains **Fulham Palace**.

Sights & museums

Brompton Cemetery

Fulham Road, SW10 9UG (brompton-cemetery.org.uk). Earl's Court or Fulham Broadway tube. **Open** *dusk-dawn daily.*

One of the 'magnificent seven' Victorian cemeteries that ring the capital, Brompton is full of magnificent monuments (28 of them sufficiently impressive to gain heritage listing status), including suffragette Emmeline Pankhurst and, his grave marked by a lion, 'Gentleman' John Jackson, who taught Lord Byron to box. It's a truly beautiful place.

Fulham Palace

Bishop's Avenue, off Fulham Palace Road, SW6 6EA (7736 3233, www.fulhampalace. org). Putney Bridge tube. **Open** *Summer 12.30-4.30pm Mon-Thur; noon-5pm Sun. Winter 12.30-3.30pm Mon-Thur; noon-4pm Sun. Walled garden Summer 10.15am-4.15pm daily. Winter 10.15am-3.45pm daily. Botanical gardens dawn-dusk daily. Tours £8; free under 12s.* **Admission** *free.*

Fulham Palace was the episcopal retreat of the Bishops of London. The present building was built in Tudor times, with

In the know
Musical heritage

The atmospheric **Troubadour** (263-267 Old Brompton Road, 7341 6333, www. troubadourlondon.com) is a tiny venue with an impressive pedigree – a young Bob Dylan, in his Greenwich Village folk phase, played in the basement when this was a coffeehouse, as did Hendrix and Joni Mitchell.

Boozy Tours

Tipples by the Thames

Fuller's (Griffin Brewery, Chiswick Lane South, W4 2QB, www.fullers.co.uk, tasting tours £20) is the last of London's great breweries in operation. The family-owned business was sold to Asahi in early 2019, but you can still take a look behind the scenes to find out how cutting-edge tech combined with time-honoured tradition kept Fullers in business for over 170 years. Tours (several daily, Mon-Sat) last 90 minutes and culminate in a tasting of the famous ales. If you'd rather skip the tour, there's also a Tasting Hour (6pm Thur, Fri, £15) where you can sample ales, craft beers and ciders.

Not far away, **Sipsmith** (The Distillery, 83 Cranbrook Road, W4 2LJ, 8747 0753, sipsmith.com, tasting tours £25) was the first of the new wave of London gin distilleries, planting its copper stills in west London in 2009. There are tours on most evenings: you'll get a little history of gin in London, followed by a tour and a tasting. For £85, you also get a three-course dinner and a bottle of London Dry to take away with you.

---

later significant Georgian and Victorian additions. It would be more accurate to call it a manor house than a palace, but it gives a fine glimpse into the changing lifestyles and architecture of nearly 500 years, from the Tudor hall to the Victorian chapel; try out the echo in the courtyard. There are regular guided tours of the palace and grounds, and of the gardens. The grounds offer some lovely spots to take a picnic, or indulge in a classy cake from the Drawing Room café; the walled garden is a particular delight. There's also access to a glorious stretch of riverside.

CHISWICK

▶ *Turnham Green tube or Chiswick rail.*

Once a sleepy, semi-rural suburb, Chiswick is now one of London's swankier postcodes, its residents including broadcasters, actors, advertising bods and a smattering of rock 'n' roll royalty. Visitors, however, should come here rather for the surprising concentration of sightseeing attractions. Chiswick Mall is a beautiful residential road that runs along the river from Hammersmith, and includes **Kelmscott House** (26 Upper Mall, 8741 3735, williammorrissociety.org), once home to pioneering socialist William Morris but now a private house, with a small museum in the coach house and basement; it opens to the public 2-5pm on Thursdays and Saturdays. Further west along the riverbank, you'll find **Emery Walker's House** (7 Hammersmith Terrace, W6 9TS, 8741 4104, www.emerywalker.org.uk, tours only), another Arts and Crafts pioneer, whose house has been beautifully restored. Nearby, at no.3, note the blue plaque for Edward Johnston: he devised the font that bears his name and was used across London's public transport from 1916 until it was reworked in 1979 – in a nice touch, the plaque uses his font rather than the standard English Heritage one. From here, it's a short walk to London's last industrial-scale brewery, **Fuller's** (*see above* Boozy Tours), and **Hogarth's House**, while the **London Museum of Water & Steam** and **Musical Museum** are only a bus ride away. It's possible to return to the river path west of Chiswick House; the wonderful **Royal Botanic Gardens** (*see p292*) are just over Kew Bridge.

Sights & museums

Chiswick House & Gardens

Burlington Lane, W4 2RP (3141 3352, www.chgt.org.uk). Turnham Green tube or Chiswick rail. House Apr-Oct 10am-5pm Mon, Wed-Sun. Gardens 7am-dusk daily. Conservatory 10am-4pm Tue-Sun. Admission £7.50, £5.50 reductions. Gardens and conservatory free.

Richard Boyle, the third Earl of Burlington, designed this romantic Palladian villa in 1725. The house was a showpiece, in which the Earl could display his fine collection of paintings (many of which remain), for the entertainment of the artistic and philosophical luminaries of his day. The house is lovely – and nowadays enhanced by a startlingly modern but thoroughly appropriate café – but the gardens are absolutely gorgeous, a place to stroll in regal tranquillity.

WEST LONDON

Hogarth's House

*Hogarth Lane, Great West Road, W4 2QN (8994 6757, www.hounslow.info). Turnham Green tube or Chiswick rail. **Open** noon-5pm Tue-Sun. **Admission** free.*

Hogarth's House was, from 1749 until his death, the country retreat of 18th-century artist and social commentator William Hogarth (1697-1764). Craving somewhere to escape the noise of central London (his previous home was in what is now Leicester Square), he bought the house when this was still very much a rural area. The house has been superbly restored and is now a museum dedicated to Hogarth's life, displaying works such as *Gin Lane*, *Marriage A-la-Mode* and a copy of *The Four Stages of Cruelty*. Hogarth is buried in the nearby church of St Nicholas, past the horrible roundabout to the river.

London Museum of Water & Steam

*Green Dragon Lane, Brentford, TW8 0EN (8568 4757, waterandsteam.org.uk). Kew Bridge rail. **Open** 10am-4pm Wed-Sun. **Admission** £12.50; £5.50-£11 reductions.*

This Grade I-listed pumping station was built in 1838, the first to drive clean water into people's homes, 24 hours a day – at an affordable price. The museum it now houses combines the remarkable working remains of the building's Victorian industrial heyday – nine machines (five still in their original locations), including the 90-inch (2.3m) steam-powered Cornish Engine – with the story of how London's water has been cleaned up since the 17th century. You can also see the waterwheel and the James Kay rotative engine in use – now powered by that new-fangled electricity stuff. For the museum's prime attraction, visit at the weekend (or on bank holidays), when the ancient engines are fired up and whir into action, along with a puttering narrow-gauge railway and steam-powered fire engine.

Musical Museum

*399 High Street, Brentford, TW8 0DU (8560 8108, www.musicalmuseum.co.uk). Gunnersbury tube or Kew Bridge Overground. **Open** 10.30am-5pm Tue, Fri-Sun. Tours & musical demonstrations 11.30am, 1.30pm, 3.30pm Fri-Sun. **Admission** £11, £5-£9 reductions. Tickets allow unlimited entry for 12mths; under-16s must be accompanied by an adult.*

A converted church contains one of the world's foremost collections of automatic musical instruments, the legacy of the desire to record and reproduce music before the invention of the microphone. Here you'll find tiny clockwork music boxes, reproducing pianos and spooky orchestrions, as well as 30,000 historic musical rolls. There are sophisticated pianolas, cranky barrel organs, violin players

and the self-playing Mighty Wurlitzer, as well as a 230-seat concert hall and orchestra pit from which a Wurlitzer console rises as they used to in 1930s cinemas. The museum coffee shop overlooks the river, and there are fun dance, film and music events, as well as temporary exhibitions.

WEMBLEY

As London extends westwards, attractions necessarily become more widely spread. Footie fans will want to make the pilgrimage to England's home of football, **Wembley Stadium**, with the **Wembley Arena** music venue (*see p350*) beside it.

Wembley Stadium

*Empire Way, Wembley, HA9 0WS (0844 980 8001, www.wembleystadium.com). Wembley Park tube. **Open** Tours 10am-4pm daily, except public holidays & during major events at the stadium. **Admission** Tours £22, £14 reductions.*

Wembley has been hosting the nation's biggest sporting spectacles since 1923, but it was as the home of England's World Cup Final win over West Germany in 1966 that its legendary status was secured. The old twin towers have long gone, with today's 90,000-seat stadium completely rebuilt before reopening in 2007. The arch that now spans the width of the stadium can be seen from as far away as Richmond Park. If you're not coming to see a sports event or a big concert, you can take the 75-minute Wembley Tour. Knowledgeable and impressively enthusiastic guides allow you to pause and soak up the stadium magic, take a few selfies and imagine yourself caught up in Cup Final fever.

The tour includes the England changing rooms, the players' tunnel and the chance to sit in the England manager's hot-seat used during press conferences. You can also climb the 107 steps up to where the winners collect their medals and get your hands on a replica of the FA Cup. There are also exhibits, like the Jules Rimet Trophy and a flag used in the London 1948 Olympic Games.

WEST LONDON

Experience

Events	308
Film	320
LGBT	328
Nightlife	336
Performing Arts	352

Follies, National Theatre *p360*

Events

Your guide to what's happening when

Forget about British reserve. Festivals and events play increasingly elaborate variations on the age-old themes of parading and dancing, nowadays with ever-larger sprinklings of arts and culture. Some are traditional, some innovative, from the splendid ritual of Changing the Guard to the outdoor spectacle of the Greenwich & Docklands International Festival. Weather plays a part in the timing, with a concentration of things to do in the warmer – and sometimes drier – months of summer, but the city's calendar is busy for most of the year.

► *For a sense of seasonal London and advice on when to visit, see p28.*

Field Day *p313*

All year round

For London's glorious military pageantry, *see opposite* Changing the Guard.

Ceremony of the Keys

Tower of London, Tower Hill, the City, EC3N 4AB (3166 6000, www.hrp.org.uk/tower-of-london/whats-on/ceremony-of-the-keys). Tower Hill tube or Tower Gateway DLR. **Date** *9.30pm daily (advance bookings only).*

Join the Yeoman Warders after-hours at the Tower of London as they ritually lock the fortress's entrances in this 700-year-old ceremony. You enter the Tower at 9.30pm and it's all over just after 10pm, but places are hotly sought after – apply at least 12-18 months in advance; full details are available on the website.

Gun Salutes

Green Park, Mayfair & St James's, W1; Tower of London, the City, EC3. **Dates** *6 Feb (Accession Day); 21 Apr & a Sat in June (Queen's birthdays); 2 June (Coronation Day); 10 June (Duke of Edinburgh's birthday); a Sat in June (Trooping the Colour, see p311); State Opening of Parliament (see p313); Lord Mayor's Show (see p317); Remembrance Sunday (see p317); also for state visits.*

There are gun salutes on many state occasions – see the list of dates given above for a complete breakdown of when the cannons roar. A cavalry charge features in the 41-gun salutes mounted by the King's Troop Royal Horse Artillery in Hyde Park at noon (opposite the Dorchester Hotel), whereas, on the other side of town, the Honourable Artillery Company ditches the ponies and piles on the firepower with 62-gun salutes (1pm at the Tower of London). If the dates happen to fall on a Sunday, the salute is held on the following Monday.

Spring

League (EFL) Cup Final

Wembley Stadium, Stadium Way, Wembley, Middlesex, HA9 0WS (cup.efl.com). Wembley Park tube. **Date** *early Mar.*

Less prestigious than the FA Cup, the League Cup is a knockout football competition with a 50-year history – but widely regarded as the annual trophy that's 'better than nothing'. Still, the winners do get to play in the UEFA Europa League.

London Beer Week

drinkup.london/beerweek. **Date** *Mar.*

A city-wide celebration of all things hop. Along with the bevy of participating bars and pubs, there's also a host of beer-pairing dinners, brewery tours – with a rickshaw service laid on to zip between them – and meet-the-maker talks.

WoW: Women of the World

Southbank Centre, Belvedere Road, South Bank, SE1 8XX (3879 9555, www. southbankcentre.co.uk/whats-on/festivals-series/women-of-the-world). **Date** *Mar.*

A festival championing everything that is great about women and girls. Through discussion, debate, performances and activism, female achievements are celebrated and the obstacles that prevent women from achieving their full potential are explored.

Kew Orchid Festival

Kew Gardens, Kew, Surrey, TW9 3AE (8332 5655, www.kew.org). Kew Gardens tube/ Overground, Kew Bridge Overground/rail or riverboat to Kew Pier. **Admission** *£14.90; £12.50 reductions; £4.50 under-17s; cheaper online.* **Date** *early Mar-May.*

The dreary days of February are brightened up by this annual display of orchids in the

---

❤ **Best events**

BBC Proms *p315*
Classical music bonanza.

Changing the Guard
p311
Pomp and ceremony.

London Frieze Art Fair
p317
Arty parky happenings.

London Marathon *p312*
The biggest fundraiser
on earth.

Lord Mayor's Show *p317*
The City on parade.

Notting Hill Carnival
p299
Europe's biggest street party.

Pride London *p314*
Out and about.

Lift 2018 *p313*

Changing the Guard

London is a past master when it comes to military pomp

On alternate days from 10.45am – or daily from 10.15am from April to July – one of the five Foot Guards regiments lines up in scarlet coats and tall bearskin hats in the forecourt of Wellington Barracks; at exactly 11.27am (10.57am April-July),the soldiers start to march to **Buckingham Palace**, joined by their regimental band, to relieve the sentries there in a 45-minute ceremony for **Changing the Guard**. The Guards regiments are the Grenadier, Coldstream, Scots, Irish and Welsh. (For details, visit www.royal.gov.uk/RoyalEventsandCeremonies/ChangingtheGuard/Overview.aspx: do check in advance for weather cancellations or last-minute changes of schedule.)

Not far away, at **Horse Guards Parade** in Whitehall, the Household Cavalry regiments – the Life Guards and Blues and Royals – mount the guard daily at 11am (10am on Sunday). Although this ceremony isn't as famous as the one at Buckingham Palace, it's more visitor-friendly: the crowds aren't as thick as they are at the palace. After the old and new guard have stared each other out in the centre of the parade ground, you can nip through to the Whitehall side to catch the departing old guard perform their dismount choreography: a synchronised, firm slap of approbation to the neck of each horse before the gloved troopers swing off.

As well as these near-daily ceremonies, London sees other, less frequent parades on a far grander scale. The most famous is **Trooping the Colour**, which is staged to mark the Queen's official birthday on the Saturday closest to 13 June (her real birthday is in April). At 10.45am, the Queen rides in a carriage from Buckingham Palace to Horse Guards Parade to watch the soldiers, before heading back to Buckingham Palace for a midday RAF flypast and the impressive gun salute from Green Park.

Also at Horse Guards, for two successive evenings in June, a pageant of military music and precision marching begins at 8pm when the Queen (or another royal) takes the salute of the 300-strong drummers, pipers and musicians of the Massed Bands of the Household Division. This is known as **Beating Retreat** (www.householddivision.org.uk/beating-retreat, tickets 7839 5323).

London Marathon

Princess of Wales conservatory. Visit later in spring to see up to five million flowers carpeting the grounds.

St Patrick's Day Parade & Festival
Piccadilly to Trafalgar Square (7983 4000, www.london.gov.uk/events). Date mid Mar.

Join the London Irish out in force for this annual parade through central London, which is followed by toe-tapping tunes in Trafalgar Square. Held on the Sunday closest to 17 March.

BFI Flare: London LGBT Film Festival
7928 3232, www.bfi.org.uk/flare. Date late Mar.

Highlighting the importance of the city's LGBT communities, the rebranded Lesbian & Gay Film Festival is the UK's third-largest film festival, cramming in a superb range of international films over the best part of a fortnight.

Oxford & Cambridge Boat Race
River Thames, from Putney to Mortlake (www.theboatrace.org). Putney Bridge tube, or Barnes Bridge, Mortlake or Putney rail. Date Apr.

In the know
Goat Race

On the same day as the Oxford and Cambridge rivals row it out on the Thames (see above), a hairier, more haphazard competition is taking place on the other side of town. The event at Spitalfields City Farm (see p259) sees two goats, one named 'Oxford', the other 'Cambridge', going horn to horn to be crowned King Billy. Tickets are £15 and proceeds go to the farm. See Facebook @thegoatrace for more details.

Blue-clad Oxbridge students (dark blue for Oxford, light blue for Cambridge) race each other in a pair of rowing eights, as they have done since 1829, but now watched by tens of millions worldwide. Experience the excitement from the riverbank – along with 250,000 other fans.

❤ London Marathon
Greenwich Park to the Mall via the Isle of Dogs, Victoria Embankment & St James's Park (7902 0200, www. virginmoneylondonmarathon.com). Blackheath & Maze Hill rail (start), or Charing Cross tube/rail (end). Date mid Apr.

One of the world's elite long-distance races, the London Marathon is also one of the world's largest fundraising events – nearly 80% of participants run for charity, so zany costumes abound among the 40,000 starters. Held on a Sunday.

FA Cup Final
Wembley Stadium, Stadium Way, Wembley, Middlesex, HA9 0WS (0800 169 2007 Wembley Stadium, www.thefa.com/ thefacup). Wembley Park tube or Wembley Stadium rail. Date mid May.

The oldest domestic knockout tournament is an annual highlight for many international football fans. For all that the competition – which began in 1871 – has lost a little lustre for the top teams, who all fear being defeated by lowly opposition, it retains the capacity to surprise.

Covent Garden May Fayre & Puppet Festival
Garden of St Paul's Covent Garden, Bedford Street, Covent Garden, WC2E 9ED (7836 5221, actorschurch.org). Covent Garden tube. Date 2nd Sun in May.

All-day puppet mayhem (12.30-5.30pm) devoted to celebrating Mr Punch at the scene of his first recorded sighting in England in 1662. Mr P takes to the church's pulpit at noon. Held on a Sunday.

Chelsea Flower Show
Royal Hospital, Royal Hospital Road, Chelsea, SW3 4SR (01483 479000, www.rhs. org.uk/shows-events). Sloane Square tube. **Date** *mid May.*

Elbow through the huge crowds to admire perfect blooms, or get ideas for your own plot. Entire gardens are laid out for the show, and tents are filled with the colours and scents of countless varietals. The first two days are reserved for Royal Horticultural Society members and tickets for the open days can be hard to come by.

▶ *The show closes at 5.30pm on the final day, but the display plants are sold off from around 4pm.*

State Opening of Parliament
Palace of Westminster, SW1A 0AA (7219 4272, www.parliament.uk). Westminster tube. **Date** *May/June.*

Pomp and ceremony attend the Queen's official reopening of Parliament after its recess, an event that marks the formal beginning of the parliamentary year. She arrives (at about 11.15am) and departs in the State Coach, accompanied by troopers of the Household Cavalry.

Summer

All Points East
Victoria Park, Hackney, E3 5TB (www. allpointseastfestival.com). Bethnal Green or Mile End tube, or Cambridge Heath Overground. **Admission** *Mon-Thur free with some ticketed events. Fri-Sun from £59.95.* **Date** *late May-early June.*

An eclectic ten-day festival takes over Victoria Park. Four days of community-driven entertainment (comedy, film screenings, street food and more) are sandwiched between two weekends of serious music, with 2019 headliners including Christine and the Queens, The Chemical Brothers, Bon Iver and Bring Me the Horizon.

Field Day
Meridian Water, Enfield, N18 3BW (www. fielddayfestivals.com). Tottenham Hale tube/Overground. **Date** *June.*

One of the best music festivals in London, with a leftfield booking policy. Acts range from weird pop and indie rock to underground dance producers and folk musicians.

London Festival of Architecture
www.londonfestivalofarchitecture.org. **Date** *June.*

An entertaining mix of talks, discussions, walks, screenings and other events, always gathered under a punchy theme.

LIFT (London International Festival of Theatre)
7968 6800, www.liftfestival.com. **Date** *June.*

Biennial festival that sees hundreds of artists sharing performances from across the globe in a month-long celebration. The next instalment is in 2020.

Camden Rocks Festival
camdenrocksfestival.com. **Date** *June.*

This one-day festival brings a slavering horde of rock and metal bands to venues all over Camden.

Bushstock
Shepherd's Bush (www.bushstock.co.uk). **Date** *June.*

A multi-venue music festival run by independent record label Communion Presents, focusing on new and emerging talent.

Opera Holland Park
Holland Park, W8 6LU (3846 6222, www. operahollandpark.com). **Date** *June-Aug.*

A canopied outdoor theatre hosts a season of opera, including works aimed at children.

Open Garden Squares Weekend
7839 3969, www.opensquares.org. **Date** *mid June.*

Secret – and merely exclusive – gardens are thrown open to the public for this horticultural shindig. You can visit roof gardens, children-only gardens and prison gardens, as well as a changing selection of those tempting oases railed off in the middle of the city's finest squares. Some charge an entrance fee and must be booked in advance. Tickets available online.

Fever-Tree Tennis Championships
Queens Club, Palliser Road, West Kensington, W14 9EQ (7386 3400, www.queensclub.co.uk). Barons Court tube. **Date** *mid June.*

The pros tend to treat this week-long grass-court tournament as a summer warm-up session for the world-famous Wimbledon Tennis Championships.

Carnaval del Pueblo

Greenwich & Docklands International Festival

*8305 1818, festival.org. **Date** late June/ early July.*

This annual week of outdoor arts, theatre, dance and family entertainment is spectacular. Events take place at the Old Royal Naval College and other sites, including Canary Wharf and Mile End Park.

♥ Pride London

*0844 344 5428, www.prideinlondon.org. **Date** late June/early July.*

This historic celebration of the LGBT community (taking place since 1972, initially in support of the Stonewall rioters) now welcomes a million revellers to a week of events, culminating in a celebratory parade held on Saturday.

Wimbledon Tennis Championships

*All England Lawn Tennis Club, Church Road, Wimbledon, SW19 5AE (8944 1066, www.wimbledon.com). Southfields tube or Wimbledon tube/rail. **Date** late June-mid July.*

Getting into Wimbledon requires considerable forethought, as well as luck. Seats on the show courts are distributed by a ballot, which closes the previous year. Enthusiasts can queue on the day for ground tickets (several thousand released daily), which allow access to the outer courts and atmospheric Henman Hill, where you can watch all the action on a big screen. You can also turn up at the resale kiosk at 3pm and pay reduced rates for seats vacated by spectators who've left early; you may even get rare tickets for Centre Court.

Wireless Festival

*Finsbury Park, N4 2DE (0333 321 9999, www.wirelessfestival.co.uk). Manor House tube or Finsbury Park tube/rail. **Date** early July.*

Three nights of rock and dance acts, with headliners including the likes of The Weeknd and Skepta.

Hampton Court Palace Garden Festival

*Hampton Court Palace, East Molesey, KT8 9AU (0844 995 9664, www.rhs.org.uk/ shows-events/rhs-hampton-court-palace-garden-festival). **Date** early July.*

A spectacular setting featuring world-class gardens, as well as marquees showcasing work by some of the country's leading designers and nurseries.

Summer Streets

*Regent Street, W1 (www.regentstreetonline. com/events/summer-streets). Oxford Circus or Piccadilly Circus tube. **Date** every Sun in July.*

Enjoy the rare spectacle of a traffic-free road in Zone 1 as Regent Street's classy curve is pedestrianised for a street party. The festivities take on a different theme each week, with free entry, installations, demonstrations and activities to get stuck into. A highlight is the Garden Party: the street is lined with grass and a bandstand hosts a live brass band.

Lovebox

*Gunnersbury Park, W3 8LQ (0333 321 9999, loveboxfestival.com). Acton Town tube. **Date** mid July.*

Expect some of the best names that the London nightlife scene has to offer – plus some international big-hitters (Blondie, Sly Stone) – over two days in myriad themed stages, tents and arenas.

Somerset House Summer Series

*Somerset House, the Strand, WC2R 1LA (7845 4600, www.somersethouse.org.uk/ whats-on/summer-series-somerset-house). Temple tube. **Date** mid July.*

Somerset House welcomes an array of big and generally pretty mainstream acts for roughly ten days of open-air gigs, as well as movie screenings.

British Summer Time Festival

*Parade Ground, Hyde Park, W2 2UH (www. bst-hydepark.com). Marble Arch, Lancaster Gate, Hyde Park Corner, or Knightsbridge tube. **Date** July.*

This ten-day event in Hyde Park plays host to some of the planet's biggest musical stars, with an upmarket festival vibe that takes in small stages, theatre and comedy, food and drink.

♥ BBC Proms
*Royal Albert Hall, Kensington Gore, South Kensington, SW7 2AP (7589 8212, www.bbc.co.uk/proms, tickets www. royalalberthall.com). South Kensington tube. **Date** mid July-mid Sept.*

The Proms overshadows all other classical-music festivals in the city, with around 70 concerts, covering everything from early-music recitals to orchestral world premières, and from boundary-pushing debut performances to reverent career retrospectives. BBC Radio 3 plays recordings of the concerts.

RideLondon
*7902 0212, www.prudentialridelondon. co.uk. **Date** early Aug.*

This cycling festival encourages around 100,000 people to don branded fluorescent vests and ride an eight-mile traffic-free circuit from Buckingham Palace to the Tower. Competitive races also form part of the weekend's festivities.

Carnaval del Pueblo
*Burgess Park, Southwark, SE5 7QH (www. carnavaldelpueblo.com). Elephant & Castle tube/rail. **Date** early Aug.*

This vibrant outdoor parade and festival is more than just a loud-and-proud day out for Latin American Londoners: with a procession from Elephant Road to Burgess Park, it attracts people from all walks of life (as many as 60,000, most years) looking to inject a little Latin spirit into the weekend.

Camden Fringe
*camdenfringe.org. **Date** Aug.*

An eclectic bunch of new, experimental and short shows, staged by everyone from experienced performers to newcomers.

Meltdown
*Southbank Centre, Belvedere Road, South Bank, SE1 8XX (7960 4200, www. southbankcentre.co.uk). **Date** mid Aug.*

The Southbank Centre invites a guest artist – in 2018, Robert Smith of the Cure followed the likes of English-Tamil rapper M.I.A, David Bowie, Patti Smith and Ornette Coleman – to curate a fortnight of gigs, films and whatever other events appeal to them.

London Mela
*Southall Park, Uxbridge Road, Southall, UB1 3BT (www.londonmela.org). Southall Overground. **Date** late Aug.*

Thousands flock to this exuberant celebration of Asian culture, dubbed the Asian Glastonbury. You'll find urban, classical and experimental music, circus, dance, comedy, children's events and food.

♥ Notting Hill Carnival
*Notting Hill, W10 & W11 (www. thelondonnottinghillcarnival.com). Ladbroke Grove, Notting Hill Gate or Westbourne Park tube. **Date** late Aug.*

See p299.

South West Four
*Clapham Common, Clapham, SW4 (www. southwestfour.com). Clapham Common or Clapham South tube, or Clapham High Street Overground. **Date** late Aug.*

London's key dance-music festival, held over the August bank holiday weekend.

Autumn

Tour of Britain
*www.tourofbritain.co.uk. **Date** early Sept.*

Join spectators on the streets of the capital for a stage of British cycling's biggest outdoor event.

London African Music Festival
*7328 9613, www.joyfulnoise.co.uk. **Date** Sept.*

A wonderfully eclectic affair, held over a fortnight in September. Recent performers have included Osibisa (from Ghana), Modou Toure (Senegal) and Hanisha Solomon (Ethiopia).

Totally Thames Festival
*Between Westminster Bridge & Tower Bridge (7928 8998, www.totallythames.org). Blackfriars or Waterloo tube/rail. **Date** Sept.*

A giant party along the Thames, this month of events is London's largest free arts festival. It's a family-friendly mix of carnival, pyrotechnics, art installations and live music alongside craft and food stalls. Events include the Great River Race – a 22-mile marathon for all manner of traditional rowed and paddled boats. The festival is brought to an end with a lantern procession and fireworks.

In the know
Find out more

The free weekly *Time Out* magazine has highlights of festivals and events, while our website, www.timeout.com/london, has comprehensive listings. Events can be cancelled and dates may change with little notice, so do check before making plans.

London Design Festival

Victoria & Albert Museum, South Kensington, SW7 2RL, & other locations (www.londondesignfestival.com). **Date** *mid Sept.*

This festival is the ultimate chance to discover design and craft in the capital at its very best. The V&A serves as the festival hub and is filled with eye-popping installations, but there are other events and exhibitions at dozens of locations throughout the capital, with landmark projects commissioned for major public spaces.

Open House London

3006 7008, www.open-city.org.uk. **Date** *mid Sept.*

An opportunity to snoop around other people's property, for one weekend only. Taking part are more than 800 palaces, private homes, corporate skyscrapers, pumping stations and bomb-proof bunkers, many of which are normally closed to the public.

London Fashion Week

Somerset House, the Strand, WC2R 1LA & other locations (www.londonfashionweek. co.uk). Temple tube. **Date** *mid Sept.*

Extraordinary biannual outbreak of fashionable happenings across London (it returns each February). Although mainly focused on Somerset House, events see gaggles of paparazzi and informal catwalks in the most unlikely places.

Bonfire Night fireworks over Albert Bridge

OnBlackheath

Blackheath, SE3 0UA (www.onblackheath. com). Blackheath or Lewisham Overground. **Date** *mid Sept.*

A music and food festival for all the family with a generation-spanning line-up that included Squeeze, Paloma Faith, Billy Bragg and De La Soul among the 2018 headliners.

London Literature Festival

Southbank Centre, Belvedere Road, South Bank, SE1 8XX (3879 9555, www. southbankcentre.co.uk /whats-on/festivals-series/london-literature-festival). Waterloo tube/rail. **Date** *mid Sept-mid Oct.*

The London Literature Festival combines superstar writers with stars from other fields: architects, comedians, sculptors and cultural theorists, examining anything from queer literature to migration.

Great River Race

River Thames, from Millwall Docks, Docklands, to Ham House, Richmond, Surrey (8398 8141, www.greatriverrace. co.uk). **Date** *mid Sept.*

Much more interesting than the Boat Race (*see p312*), the Great River Race sees an exotic array of around 300 traditional rowing boats (including skiffs, canoes, dragon boats and Cornish gigs) from around the globe racing in the 'river marathon'. Hungerford Bridge, the Millennium Bridge and Tower Bridge are all good viewpoints.

Pearly Kings and Queens Harvest Festival

Guildhall Yard, The City, EC2V (www. pearlysociety.co.uk). Bank tube. **Date** *Sept.*

A proper Cockney knees-up with Pearly Kings and Queens, decked in their pearl-button 'smother suits', leading a parade to St Mary-le-Bow church. Expect traditional English entertainment, including maypole dancing, Morris dancers and a marching band.

October Plenty and Apple Day

Southwark, SE1 (www.thelionspart.co.uk/ octoberplenty). **Date** *Oct.*

An autumn harvest festival mixing ancient seasonal customs with contemporary celebrations. Starting with dancing outside Shakespeare's Globe (*see p88*), a procession heads across to Borough Market (*see p93*) for Apple Day activities.

Otherworld

weareculture24.org.uk/otherworld. **Date** *a Fri, Sat in Sept.*

Launched in 2019 to replace the Museums at Night initiative, this two-night festival aims to open up the capital's world-class museums, galleries and historic houses to a new younger audience, with a night-time series of specialist talks, unusual events and one-off exhibitions. Participating venues are organised into five circuits in different areas across the capital, and a single wristband gives entry to all venues.

London Cocktail Week

Old Truman Brewery, Brick Lane, E1 6QL, & other venues (drinkup.london). **Tickets** *£10 digital pass.* **Date** *Oct.*

Download a festival pass and get £6 drinks from the capital's best bars, mixologists and drinks vendors. The pass is valid at 300 bars and pop-up parties across London and also for the Cocktail Village in the Old Truman Brewery, giving you the chance to try some of the finest tipples the capital has to offer.

Dance Umbrella

7407 9380, www.danceumbrella.co.uk. **Date** *Oct.*

A leading international dance festival, featuring a range of events (many free) in unusual spaces.

London Film Festival

www.bfi.org.uk/lff. **Date** *mid Oct.*

The most prestigious of the capital's film fests – in fact, the key film festival in the country. Over 200 new British and international features are screened each year, mainly at the BFI Southbank and Leicester Square's Vue West End, and there's always a smattering of red-carpet events for the celebrity-crazed.

♥ London Frieze Art Fair

Regent's Park, NW1 (3372 6111, friezelondon. seetickets.com). Regent's Park tube. **Date** *mid Oct.*

The biggest contemporary carnival in London's art calendar occupies a purpose-built venue at the south end of Regent's Park, where some 1,000 artists are displayed over the four-day festival. Highlights include the daily-changing Projects; debates and discussions as part of the Talks strand; and Live, showing performance-based installations.

Diwali

Trafalgar Square, WC2N 5DN (7983 4000, www.diwaliinlondon.com). Charing Cross tube/rail. **Date** *Oct/Nov.*

A celebration of the annual Festival of Light by Hindu, Jain and Sikh communities.

London to Brighton Veteran Car Run

Departs Serpentine Road, Hyde Park, W2 2UH (01483 524433, www.veterancarrun. com). Hyde Park Corner tube. **Date** *early Nov.*

The London to Brighton Veteran Car Run is not so much a race as a sedate procession southwards by around 500 pre-1905 cars. The first pair trundles off at sunrise (around 7-8.30am), but you can catch them a little later crossing Westminster Bridge, or view them on a closed-off Regent's Street the day before the event (11am-3pm).

Bonfire Night

Date *5 Nov & around.*

Britain's best-loved excuse for setting off fireworks: the celebration of Guy Fawkes's failure to blow up the Houses of Parliament in 1605. Check the dedicated page at www. timeout.com for a list of public displays right across town – several are put on for free, and many charge only a nominal entry fee.

♥ Lord Mayor's Show

7606 3030, www.lordmayorsshow.org. **Date** *early Nov.*

This big show marks the traditional presentation of the new Lord Mayor for approval by the monarch's justices. The Lord Mayor is a City officer, elected each year by the livery companies and with no real power outside the City of London; don't confuse him with the Mayor of London, currently Sadiq Khan (*see p32*).The Lord Mayor leaves Mansion House in a fabulous gold coach at 11am, along with a colourful procession of floats and marchers. At 5.15pm, there's a fireworks display on the river.

Remembrance Sunday Ceremony

Cenotaph, Whitehall, Westminster, SW1A 2ET. Charing Cross tube/rail. **Date** *early Nov.*

Held on the second Sunday in November, the Sunday nearest to 11 November – the day World War I ended – this solemn commemoration honours those who died fighting in the World Wars and later conflicts. The Queen, the prime minister and other dignitaries lay poppy wreaths at the Cenotaph. A two-minute silence at 11am is followed by a service of remembrance.

London Jazz Festival

efglondonjazzfestival.org.uk. **Date** *mid Nov.*

Covering most bases, from trad to free improv, this is the biggest London jazz festival of the year, lasting the best part of a fortnight.

Winter

Of the big stores, **Fortnum & Mason** (*see p119*) still creates enchantingly old-fashioned Christmas windows. Otherwise, though, skip the commercialised lights on Oxford and Regent streets and head, instead, for smaller shopping areas such as St Christopher's Place, Bond Street, Marylebone High Street and Covent Garden. It's traditional to sing carols beneath a giant Christmas tree in **Trafalgar Square** – an annual gift from Norway in gratitude for Britain's support during World War II – but you can also join in a mammoth singalong at the **Royal Albert Hall** (*see p356*), enjoy the starry choral Christmas Festival at **St John Smith Square** (*see p357*) or an evocative carol service at one of London's historic churches. **Kew Gardens** (*see p292*) puts on a magical display of Christmas lights in its grounds, and **Somerset House** installs an ice rink in the courtyard (*see p190*).

▶ *Timeout.com/london has details of these and plenty of other festive events in the run-up to Christmas.*

Spitalfields Music Festival
7377 1362, www.spitalfieldsmusic.org. uk. **Date** *Dec.*

A series of multi-genre music events, featuring world-class artists, in some of the most extraordinary venues and spaces in East London, ranging from resplendent churches to urban warehouses and vibrant outdoor markets. Also runs one-off events throughout the year.

Great Christmas Pudding Race
Covent Garden Piazza, WC2H 7AR (www. xmaspuddingrace.org.uk). Covent Garden tube. **Date** *Dec.*

This fancy-dress race – during which contestants attempt to keep a pud balanced on a plate while negotiating foam slaloms and other inflatable hazards – is a fundraiser for Cancer Research UK.

New Year's Eve celebrations
Date *31 Dec.*

The focus of London's public celebrations has officially moved from overcrowded Trafalgar Square to the full-on fireworks display launched from the London Eye and rafts on the Thames. You have to get there early for a good view. Those with stamina can take in the New Year's Day Parade in central London the next day (lnydp.com).

London International Mime Festival
www.mimelondon.com/festival. **Date** *Jan/Feb.*

Theatrical magic in many forms, from haunting visual theatre to puppetry for adults.

Vault Festival
The Vaults, Leake Street, Waterloo, SE1 7NN (8050 9241, vaultfestival.com). Waterloo tube/rail. **Tickets** *£9-£12.* **Date** *Jan-Mar.*

A sprawling, crypt-like space near Waterloo Station is the hub for this eight-week fringe festival, featuring some of London's most exciting new and grassroots theatre, cabaret and comedy. There's a packed line-up of immersive experiences, pop-ups, parties, and bags of underground atmosphere.

Great Spitalfields Pancake Race
Old Truman Brewery, 91 Brick Lane, Spitalfields, E1 6QL (8800 6665, www. alternativearts.co.uk). **Date** *Shrove Tue.*

This very silly fundraiser for the London Air Ambulance sees teams of four in fancy dress grab their crêpes and run through the cobbled streets of Spitalfields in the hope of winning a specially engraved frying pan.

Chinese New Year Festival
Around Gerrard Street, Chinatown, W1 & Leicester Square, WC2 (7851 6686, www. lccauk.com). Leicester Square or Piccadilly Circus tube. **Date** *Feb.*

Celebrate the Chinese New Year in style with festivities that engulf Chinatown and Leicester Square. Lion dancers gyrate alongside a host of acts in the grand parade to Trafalgar Square.

London Fashion Week
Date *mid/late Feb.*

See p316 London Fashion Week.

Six Nations Tournament
Twickenham Stadium, 200 Whitton Road, Middlesex, TW2 7BA (www.sixnationsrugby. com). **Date**s *Feb-Mar.*

This major rugby union tournament for the northern hemisphere teams sees England take on Wales, Scotland, Ireland, France and Italy, with England's home fixtures played at the club's headquarters at Twickenham. Book a long way ahead.

Film

There are no limits to London's screen time

Londoners still have a feel for the romance of film that out-of-town multiplexes will never satisfy. Perhaps that's why there's such a lively and varied range of screenings in the capital. Giant picture palaces hosting red-carpet premières attended by A-list actors? Check out the Odeon Leicester Square. Cheap-as-chips repertory cinema? The Prince Charles is right around the corner. Refurbished art deco gems? Try the gorgeous, historic Phoenix or the Rio in Dalston. A world-class film festival? Happens every autumn. Outdoor screenings in remarkable settings, ciné clubs, film seasons devoted to every genre and national cinema under the sun? Yes, yes and yes. So get some popcorn and sit yourself down.

Electric Portobello *p324*

Where to go

Leicester Square has the biggest first-run cinemas and stages most of the big-budget premières – but it also has the biggest prices. By contrast, the independents provide a cheaper night out and they often show films that wouldn't come within a million miles of a red carpet.

Outside the mainstream, the British Film Institute's flagship venue gets top billing. **BFI Southbank** screens seasons exploring and celebrating various genres of cinema and TV. It also has a brilliant bar. After the BFI, the **Curzon** group is the favoured choice for most cineastes, but London has a growing number of arthouse cinemas – and in increasingly unlikely places, such as Kensal Green (**Lexi**) and Crouch End (**ArtHouse**).

There's a vogue for hosting screenings in unusual venues. These include dedicated spaces like the Tanks, a multimedia space in the basement of **Tate Modern** extension (*see p89*), and ad hoc ones in places that are attractions in their own right – even St Paul's Cathedral has got in on the act.

Several luxury hotels have excellent screening facilities: most of the Firmdale mini-chain have screening rooms – the **Covent Garden Hotel** (*see p399*) is a long-term industry favourite – and the Curzon at the **Mondrian** (*see p399*) is a great little cinema, inexpensive for its South Bank location.

Outdoor screenings pop up right across the capital in summer: these are listed on *p326*. And film lovers have two key options when it comes to exhibitions: the **London Film Museum** (*see p182*) is the one for fans of memorabilia, with its display of cars from

---

♥ Best cinemas

BFI IMAX *p322*
An eye-bogglingly big screen makes this the best for blockbusters.

Everyman Belsize Park *p324*
A lovely little luxury cinema.

PeckhamPlex *p327*
Rough-and-ready bargain.

Picturehouse Central *p323*
Central and simply gorgeous.

Prince Charles *p323*
For celluloid silliness, see a singalong screening here.

Rio Cinema *p327*
London's best independent cinema.

In the know
Now screening

Consult listings of the weekly highlights (as well as interviews with the stars) each Tuesday in the free *Time Out* magazine or visit www.timeout.com/film for full details of what's on and performance times; note that the programmes change on a Friday.

the Bond movies, but serious film buffs should book a tour of the **Cinema Museum** (The Master's House, 2 Dugard Way, SE11 4TH, 7840 2200, www.cinemamuseum.org. uk, £10, £7 reductions), where cinema seats and signs, stills and posters, projectors and other machinery tell cinema's history from the 1890s.

Giant screens & multiplex cinemas

♥ BFI IMAX
1 Charlie Chaplin Walk, South Bank, SE1 8XR (0330 333 7878, www.bfi.org.uk/ imax). Waterloo tube/rail. **Tickets** *£17.25-£23; £13.50-£17.50 reductions.* **Screens** *1.* **Map** *p80 N9.*

London's – indeed, the UK's – biggest cinema screen at 5,800sq ft (539sq m), the BFI IMAX is in the centre of a busy roundabout next to Waterloo station. As well as the massive screen, you get superlative sound quality and seats arranged at such a vertiginous angle there's no chance of a head blocking your view. It's not cheap – just over £20 for a premium seat – but if you like your blockbusters vast and noisy, there's really nothing else like it in town.

Cineworld at the O2
The O2, Peninsula Square, Greenwich, SE10 0DX (0330 333 4444, www.cineworld.co.uk). North Greenwich tube. **Tickets** *£12.60; £9.60-£10.10 reductions. Extra for 3D, D-BOX, IMAX.* **Screens** *11.*

People don't just come to the O2 Arena (*see p344*) for gigs: this 11-screen multiplex from the Cineworld chain supersizes everything, from the jaw-dropping dimensions of the Sky Superscreen – the widest in Europe – down to the jam-packed programme.

Cineworld Leicester Square
5-6 Leicester Square, WC2H 7NA (0330 333 4444, www.cineworld.co.uk). Leicester Square tube. **Tickets** *£14.50; £12.50 reductions. Extra for IMAX, Superscreen & 4DX.* **Screens** *9.* **Map** *p165 L8.*

One of London's oldest cinemas (formerly known as the Empire, it opened as a theatre in 1884, then as a cinema after World War II), it was until recently home to London's biggest non-IMAX cinema screen (that's now at the O2 Cineworld). Its massive main auditorium is these days separated into a full IMAX screen with Laser, a huge Superscreen and impressive 4DX experience, with seven smaller screens tucked away elsewhere in the building. The programme is mainstream and prices reflect the central location.

Odeon Leicester Square
24-26 Leicester Square, WC2H 7JY (0333 006 7777, www.odeon.co.uk). Leicester Square tube. **Tickets** *£10.75-£20.75; £10-£12.50 reductions.* **Screens** *5.* **Map** *p165 L8.*

London's number-one destination for red carpet premières was fully refurbished in 2017. Not only do you get blockbuster bangs in the ultra-modern 800-seat auditorium with Dolby Screen; you get them in splendour: there are some gorgeous 1930s art deco features, and it's one of the few remaining cinemas to retain its circle – from which the view (at extra cost) is pretty spectacular.

♥ Picturehouse Central
Trocadero, Shaftesbury Avenue, Piccadilly, W1D 7DH (0871 902 5747, www.picturehouses.com). Piccadilly Circus tube. **Tickets** *£13.50-£16.50; £7.50-£11.50 reductions.* **Screens** *7.* **Map** *p165 L8.*

On the corner of Shaftesbury Avenue, this central London cinema is an absolute gem. It's the antidote to Piccadilly Circus's rage-inducing pavements, with three floors of beautifully designed space. Before you even get anywhere near the plush screening rooms, a hundred hanging lightbulbs lead you up a grand terracotta-tiled staircase past a mural inspired by a century of cinema. A climb up another level will take you to a members-only bar with a roof terrace that looks out over the busy streets of central London.

♥ Prince Charles
7 Leicester Place, off Leicester Square, WC2H 7BY (7494 3654, www.princecharlescinema. com). Leicester Square tube. **Tickets** *£8.50-£12.50.* **Screens** *2.* **Map** *p165 L8.*

This is the only time you'll spend in a cinema when no one's going to shush you. Singalong screenings at the Prince Charles are all about audience participation: whether your movie is *Frozen*, *Rocky Horror* or *The Sound of Music*. You can even settle in for a marathon all-night pyjama party. Having started life screening porn, the Prince Charles is central London's wildcard cinema, providing a fantastic blend of new-ish blockbusters and arthouse titles, with heaps of horror, sci-fi and teen-flick all-nighters, double bills and short seasons. It's comfy, cheap and cheerful.

Arthouse & neighbourhood cinemas
There are plenty of central London arthouses, but several of the most atmospheric are in the suburbs.

ArtHouse Crouch End
159A Tottenham Lane, Crouch End, N8 9BT (8245 3099, www.arthousecrouchend.co.uk). Bus 41, 91, N41, N91,W3. **Tickets** *£7-£11; £5-7 reductions.* **Screens** *2.*

Regularly voted London's best cinema by *Time Out* readers, this two-screen independent in a former Salvation Army Hall opened its doors in 2014 and quickly became a favourite with locals. The ArtHouse prides itself on being not just a cinema but also a venue offering music, comedy and theatre. Its programme leans towards independent and foreign movies, and there's a welcoming foyer bar and café.

Barbican
Silk Street, the City, EC2Y 8DS (7638 8891, www.barbican.org.uk). Barbican tube or Moorgate tube/rail. **Tickets** *£12; £6 Mon; £5-11 reductions.* **Screens** *3.* **Map** *p212 Q6.*

After a top-to-toe refurb, the Barbican Centre cinemas – perhaps the key rival to BFI Southbank – are better than ever. Screen One, inside the main Barbican complex, is a 280-seat auditorium screening the best new blockbusters and high-end arthouse films, while the two smaller screens around the corner on Beech Street have been kitted out with plush, comfy chairs and a friendly, welcoming café-bar serving coffee, cakes, beer, wine and pizza. The programme also includes plenty of festival screenings and classics, many of which are chosen specifically to tie in with art and music events happening elsewhere in the Barbican complex.

BFI Southbank
South Bank, SE1 8XT (7928 3232 tickets, www.bfi.org.uk). Embankment tube or Waterloo tube/rail. **Tickets** *£8.80-£13.75; £8.80-£11.25 reductions.* **Screens** *4.* **Map** *p80 N9.*

A fraction to the east of the Royal Festival Hall complex (*see p82* and alongside the National Theatre (*see p360*), the BFI's success is still built on its core function: thought-provoking seasons giving film fans

FILM

the chance to enjoy rare and significant British and foreign films. It's a terrific place to enjoy movies of all stripes and nations, enhanced by excellent director and actor Q&A events. The two bar-cafés are also of good quality, with the riverside one especially popular – and not only with cinema-goers.

Ciné Lumière

Institut Français, 17 Queensberry Place, South Kensington, SW7 2DT (7871 3515, www.institut-francais.org.uk). South Kensington tube. **Tickets** *£7-£12; £5-£10 reductions.* **Screens** *1.* **Map** *p124 E11.*

The Ciné Lumière in South Kensington is the cinema of the French Cultural Institute and offers a good mix of new releases (focusing on foreign, independent and, of course, French films) and retrospective seasons. It regularly hosts French filmmakers too. The venue itself is welcoming and well equipped, up a marble staircase from a grand lobby area and café-restaurant.

Curzon

Mayfair *38 Curzon Street, W1J 7TY. Green Park or Hyde Park Corner tube.* **Screens** *2.* **Map** *p142 J9.*

Bloomsbury *The Brunswick Centre, WC1N 1AW. Russell Square tube.* **Screens** *6.* **Map** *p194 M5.*

Soho *99 Shaftesbury Avenue, W1D 5DY. Leicester Square tube.* **Screens** *3.* **Map** *p165 L7.*

Victoria *58 Victoria Street, SW1E 6QW. Victoria tube/rail.* **Screens** *5.* **Map** *p102 K11.*

Tickets *0330 500 1331, www. curzoncinemas.com. £12-£16.50; £8-£14 reductions.*

Curzon's key venues are well established, but recent years have seen vigorous expansion. The perennially hip Soho outpost is the coolest, with its buzzing café and decent basement bar, but there's '70s splendour at the Grade II-listed Mayfair outpost, location of occasional premières and a venue so classy it's the only cinema where we've been told off by a fellow movie-goer for eating popcorn too loudly. The Curzon Bloomsbury

has six screens, one of which is – winningly – dedicated to documentaries. Curzon is also responsible for the programming for the Ham Yard hotel (1 Ham Yard, W1D 7DT), just off Piccadilly, and Mondrian at Sea Containers (see p399).

Electric

Portobello *191 Portobello Road, Notting Hill, W11 2ED (7908 9696, www. electriccinema.co.uk). Ladbroke Grove or Notting Hill Gate tube.* **Tickets** *£17.50-£22.50; £8-£10 reductions.* **Screens** *1.* **Map** *p297 A7.*

Shoreditch *64-66 Redchurch Street, E2 7DP (3350 3490, www.electriccinema. co.uk/shoreditch). Shoreditch High Street Overground or Old Street tube/rail.* **Tickets** *£8-£19; £4-£10 reductions.* **Screens** *1.* **Map** *p256 S4.*

Once a past-it fleapit, the Electric Portobello was a pioneer of the 'boutique' cinema trend: a luscious destination with leather seats and sofas, footstools and a bar inside the auditorium, a place where you can sip fine wines with your celluloid pleasures. There are even six date-perfect, luxurious, velvet-lined double beds in the venue. The Electric also has a snug little screen in the East End. Formerly the Aubin, the Electric Shoreditch also exudes class: again, there are leather armchairs and footstools, but we like the cosy cashmere blankets and chic little tables to hold your drinks.

♥ Everyman Cinemas

Everyman Belsize Park *203 Haverstock Hill, NW3 4QG.* **Tickets** *£15.95-£18.75; £13-£16.75 reductions.* **Screens** *1.*

Everyman Hampstead *5 Hollybush Vale, NW3 6TX. Hampstead tube.* **Tickets** *£13.50-£20; £11-£16 reductions.* **Screens** *2.*

Screen on the Green *83 Upper Street, Islington, N1 0NP. Angel tube.* **Tickets** *£16.20-£19; £11.20-£15.55 reductions.* **Screens** *1.*

Tickets *0872 436 9060, www. everymancinema.com.*

Do you like the smell of expensive leather? Everyman has half a dozen venues across London, each with plush seats, posh food and carpets you could lick without getting a stomach bug. It all started with the Everyman Hampstead, which has a glamorous bar and two-seaters in its 'screening lounges', complete with footstools and wine coolers, but the Belsize Park is our favourite – a flagship for the luxe-ing of the chain, it has good food and drink, and seats so comfy you might find yourself nodding off. It was one of three former Screen cinemas, of which Screen on the Green retains its name. It's another beauty, having lost seats to make space for the more comfortable kind, gained a bar and a stage for gigs, but kept its classic neon sign.

Genesis Cinema Whitechapel
93-95 Mile End Road, Stepney, E1 4UJ (7780 2000, www.genesiscinema.co.uk). Whitechapel tube/Overground or Stepney Green tube. **Tickets** *£5.50-£10.50; £5.50-£8.50 reductions.* **Screens** *6.* **Map** *p256 W6.*

Not only is the Genesis cheap, it's also beautifully renovated – by guys who design film sets for a living (try knocking on the bricks on the mezzanine). The end result is a perfect local cinema, with proper old East End ladies drinking coffee in the café next to cool kids on their laptops. There's a bar upstairs, where snacks include crodoughs from 100-year-old Rinkoffs bakery. For a date, book seats in the Studio 5 boutique screening room, which has armchairs.

Hackney Picturehouse
270 Mare Street, Hackney, E8 1HE (0871 902 5747, www.picturehouses.com). Hackney Central or London Fields Overground. **Tickets** *£7.50-£13.50; £5.50-£7.70 reductions.* **Screens** *4.*

FILM

It's impossible to imagine Hackney without this branch of the Picturehouse chain. The buzzy ground-floor bar/café serves good burgers, and bang-on programming mixes top-of-the-range mainstream with artier films – for the former, book Screen 1, with its beast of a screen, big sound and steep incline for uninterrupted viewing. On the top floor, the Hackney Attic is home to music quizzes, open-mic nights and other live events.

Lexi
Pinkham Lighthouse, 194B Chamberlayne Road, Kensal Rise, NW10 3JU (0871 704 2069, thelexicinema.co.uk). Kensal Green tube or Kensal Rise Overground. **Tickets** *£7-11.50; £5-£8.50 reductions.* **Screens** *1.*

Rio Cinema *p327*

Festivals & Summer Screenings

A calendar full of cinema

FILM

The best-known open-air screenings are those held each summer in the lovely neoclassical courtyard of **Somerset House** (www.somersethouse.org.uk/film; see *p190*). Book well ahead – and bring your own picnic and cushions. There are plenty of other alfresco opportunities, however. **Free Film Festivals** (www.freefilmfestivals.org) puts on free outdoor screenings in interesting public spaces, mainly in south-east London, while **Pop Up Screens** (www.popupscreens. co.uk) shows popular films in parks in west London. From May to September, the **Rooftop Film Club** (7635 6655, www.rooftopfilmclub. com) offers a different spin on outdoor films, screening movies in the rooftop garden of the **Queen of Hoxton** (1-5 Curtain Road, EC2A 3JX) or on top of the Bussey Building (*see p339*) and **Roof East** (Roof East, floors 7-8, Stratford multistorey carpark, Great Eastern Way, Stratford, E15 1XE).

There's also a film festival in the capital on pretty much any given week during the year, but the **London Film Festival** in October (www. lff.org.uk) is far and away the most prestigious. Nearly 200 new British and international features are screened, mainly at the BFI Southbank and Leicester Square's Vue West End. It's preceded by the leftfield **Raindance Festival** (www.raindance.org), with a terrific shorts programme. The other highlight of autumn is the **Portobello Film Festival** (www. portobellofilmfestival.com) in early September. It offers an eclectic programme of free

screenings. Short films hog the limelight each January at the **London Short Film Festival** (shortfilms.org.uk). In September, check out the **Open City London Documentary Festival** (www.opencitylondon.com).

March is a busy month. There's the **Human Rights Watch International Film Festival** (www.hrw.org/iff) and the **London International Animation Festival** (www.liaf. org.uk), screening 300 or more animated shorts. Towards the end of the month are the lesbian, gay and transgender screenings of **BFI Flare** (www.bfi.org.uk/llgff), the UK's third-largest film festival. June or July sees the **East End Film Festival** (www.eastendfilmfestival. com) explore its fondness for films starring London. But by now you're way back into the alfresco season...

In a category all of its own is the hugely popular **Secret Cinema** (www.secretcinema. org). Its 'we're not going to tell you what the film is' schtick is a bit tired (everybody works it out in advance, of course), but its events are the apotheosis of event cinema. Effectively building a huge film set and hiring a raft of bit-part actors for each costumed screening – an entire town square was built for *Back to the Future*, but organisers normally 'just' take over a hotel or warehouse – they invite viewers to dress appropriately and learn songs or bits of dialogue, so that they become participants in the film. Secret Cinema is an expensive night out, but boy is it good fun.

Somerset House

One of London's friendliest cinemas, the Lexi is run mostly by enthusiastic local volunteers, with every penny of profits going to charity. You might see anything from recent blockbusters to arthouse and foreign films, with the programme filled out by special events, Q&As and classic-movie seasons (a run of Truffaut oldies was accompanied by cheese and wine tastings). The chairs are comfy, the sound system is great and the bar is cosy. The Lexi team is also responsible for the peripatetic outdoor cinema screen Nomad (www.whereisthenomad.com).

♥ PeckhamPlex
95A Rye Lane, Peckham, SE15 4ST (0844 567 2742, www.peckhamplex.london). Peckham Rye rail. **Tickets** *£4.99-£5.99.* **Screens** *6.*

South London film fans talk of the PeckhamPlex with misty-eyed fondness. Opening in a former supermarket in 1994, it ain't fancy, and you'd struggle to describe the decor in entirely favourable terms, but this rough-around-the-edges institution has character and charm. However, the only thing you really need to know it is that tickets are just £4.99 – or £5.99 if you want to see a film in 3D – all day, every day of the week. That's it: no nonsense, no frills, no faff. The programme focuses on the latest big releases, as well as the odd smaller film too.

Phoenix
52 High Road, East Finchley, N2 9PJ (8444 6789, www.phoenixcinema.co.uk). East Finchley tube. **Tickets** *£7-£12; £5-£8.50 reductions.* **Screens** *1.*

This gorgeous single-screen venue can fairly claim to be London's oldest continuously operating cinema: it was completed in 1910 and opened in 1912. Since 1985, it has been run as a charitable trust. The programme mixes independent and foreign films, and the auditorium is one of the most beautiful places to watch a film in London. This is also a great place to catch directors introducing their work, late-night films and special events.

Regent Street Cinema
University of Westminster, 309 Regent Street, W1B 2UW (7911 5050, www. regentstreetcinema.com). Oxford Circus tube. **Tickets** *£12; £8-£11 reductions.* **Screens** *1.* **Map** *p142 J6.*

This historic beauty is barely a minute's walk north of Oxford Circus. The hall dates to 1848, but the cinema's real claim to fame is that the Lumière brothers demonstrated their pioneering moving-film camera and what they'd shot with it here in 1896 – effectively the first movie screening in Britain. The reborn cinema is state-of-the-art, but can also show work on original 16mm and 35mm formats. The programme covers classics, director retrospectives, double bills, documentaries, world cinema and even kids' films.

♥ Rio Cinema
107 Kingsland High Street, Dalston, E8 2PB (7241 9410, www.riocinema.org.uk). Dalston Kingsland Overground. **Tickets** *£7-£11.50; £6-£9.50 reductions.* **Screens** *1.*

Another great deco survivor, restored to its original sleek lines, this is east London's finest independent. Alongside mainstream releases, the Rio is well known for its programme of Turkish and Kurdish films and documentaries.

Ritzy Picturehouse
Brixton Oval, Coldharbour Lane, Brixton, SW2 1JG (0871 902 5747, www.picturehouses. com). Brixton tube/rail. **Tickets** *£7.70-£14.50; £5.70-£13.50 reductions.* **Screens** *5.*

The Ritzy is a Brixton institution, much loved for its friendly staff and anti-multiplex atmosphere. One of south London's oldest picture palaces (it originally opened in 1911), today the Ritzy has still got a little of that grandeur. Its five screens are all comfortable and reasonably sized, while the programme strikes the perfect balance between major blockbusters and independent films, plus late-night shows and classics. Upstairs at the Ritzy hosts an array of club nights and stand-up shows. There's another popular Picturehouse not far away in Clapham (76 Venn St, SW4 0AT).

FILM

LGBT

London's queer life

Acceptance of queer lifestyles in London feels broader than ever. In fact, many clubs – in Dalston, particularly – no longer bother much about sexual orientation. The attitude is that anyone on the LGBTQ spectrum, plus allies, are welcome as long as they're respectful and ready to have a good time. In recent years the closure of some key LGBT venues has caused plenty of soul-searching. Has Grindr killed the gay bar? Is it rising rents? Noise complaints from intolerant neighbours? But at the same time, several new queer spots have launched with tremendous success, re-energising the scene and proving that gay London isn't about to fade away any time soon. London's headline homo event remains Pride, but it's surrounded throughout the year by smaller, more DIY goings-on and a major LGBT film festival.

18 SPECIAL SERVICE
OXFORD CIRCUS

＃ ACCEPTANCE MATTERS

A ROUTE 2 HIRE -
ROUTEMASTER BUS HIRE

403 CLT

Pride *p314*

Out and about

Roughly speaking, London's gay scene is split into three key zones: **Soho**, **Vauxhall** and **Dalston**. Each of these has its own character, with Soho the most mainstream; Vauxhall is the most decadent, and Dalston the most outré.

Centred on **Old Compton Street**, the Soho scene continues to attract the crowds, with pretty boys sipping espresso martinis at pavement café tables as unfeasibly tanned chaps in muscle vests stroll past. But London's historic gay heartland isn't quite as gay as it once was: a few years back, the cabaret community – ever imaginative – was moved to parade coffins through the streets to protest the death of the area's nightlife. Gay Soho has been caught between the rising rents that now stalk central London and a council that, while friendly to the pink pound, is intolerant of nightlife that might upset affluent residents. As a result, the area now has more fancy restaurants than gay bars, though there are still more than enough for a bar crawl. The party also continues down the road at the legendary **Heaven**, home to **G-A-Y**. If your dream has always been to see Madonna or Kylie in a club, here's your chance – the list of singers who've done PAs here is a *Who's Who* of squeal-tastic gay pop icons.

Down south, Vauxhall is also undergoing redevelopment led by the arrival of the US Embassy. It remains vital for three reasons: long-standing alt-cabaret venue **RVT**; utterly enjoyable club night **Horse Meat Disco**, and, for now, the fact that purist hedonists can arrive in London on a Friday evening and dance non-stop here for an entire weekend before flying out of town again. Though you need a high tolerance for throngs of shirtless, sweaty chaps to do so.

The most alternative, creative and vibrant of the capital's queer scenes is in east London, although even here there are regular closures. Still, in **Dalston Superstore**, **VFD** and the **Glory**, you'll rub shoulders with fashion and music movers and shakers (plus assorted straight folk), to soundtracks built by ferociously underground DJs. With so much coolness, it can get a little snooty, but a lot of the bars and clubs round Shoreditch and Dalston are also properly mixed, which makes the area ideal for a night out with straight mates.

Gals-only events remain under-represented, but **SHE Soho** – the city's only full-time drinking den for lesbians – is still going strong. Also worth checking out are Dalston Superstore, home to several regular nights for queer women, and the Glory, which hosts **BOiBOX**, a monthly drag king night, and **Man Up!**, a drag king talent contest. **Butch, Please!**, a monthly night for gay gals at RVT, is also popular.

Stand-alone nights and one-off events pop up all the time (check out timeout. com for the latest), but **Bombshell** at Ku Bar (bombshellclub.com) and queer performance nights **Duckie** (hosted by London's 'Night Czar', Amy Lamé) and **Bar Wotever** at RVT are popular with people from across the LGBT spectrum. Lastly, special mention should go to the **NYC Downlow** (thedownlowradio.com/the-downlow), a travelling homo disco straight out of 1970s New York that you can catch at festivals such as Lovebox (loveboxfestival. com; *see p314*).

Each spring, in **BFI Flare** (www.bfi.org. uk/flare), London also has its own LGBT film festival – the third largest film festival in the country, gay or straight. But the daddy on the queer calendar is **Pride** (*see p314*), which now attracts around 800,000 LGBT people

---

❤ Best LGBT venues

Dalston Superstore *p334*
Fashionable fun in east London's gay party zone.

Friendly Society *p332*
Best gay bar in Soho.

The Glory *p334*
Cornerstone of the east London queer performance scene.

RVT *p335*
Key alt-cabaret venue in Vauxhall.

SHE Soho *p333*
London's only dedicated lesbian venue.

Pride

and their straight friends. No longer billed as a protest, but a celebration, it's one day in June every year when LGBT people from all over the country descend on London for a massive street party. **UK Black Pride** (ukblackpride.org.uk), Europe's largest celebration for African, Asian, Middle Eastern, Latin American and Caribbean-heritage LGBTQ people, takes place during the same June weekend. It's getting bigger and more jubilant every year.

Restaurants & cafés

More or less every café and restaurant in London welcomes gay custom. Certainly nowhere in or around Soho will so much as bat an eyelid at you and your other half having a romantic dinner. Thanks to its two prime locations on Soho's main drag, **Balans** (34 and 60-62 Old Compton Street, www.balans.co.uk) has long been the gay café-restaurant of choice and opens almost all night for those seeking a post-club bite.

▶ *For other drinking and dining options in Soho, see p164.*

Pubs & bars

Unless otherwise stated, the pubs and bars listed here are open to both gay men and lesbians. If you're in east London, it's worth visiting **Dalston Superstore** (*see p334*) during the day for café grub: the food's good (with breakfast quite a trendy scene) and there are Wi-Fi and art displays.

Circa

62 Frith Street, Soho, W1D 3JN (7734 6826, www.circasoho.com). Tottenham Court Road or Leicester Square tube. **Open** *1pm-1am daily.* **Map** *p165 L7.*

Circa is one of Soho's more versatile LGBT spaces. Swing by in the afternoon and you'll find large leather sofas perfect for sinking into for a catch-up with mates. But later on, the dancefloor area at the back fills up as DJs spin club hits and pop remixes until 1am. It's worth noting that Circa attracts a more image-conscious crowd than many Soho drinking spots. This isn't a place where anyone goes in for 'geek chic' or 'normcore': think tight T-shirts and skinny jeans instead.

The Cock Tavern

340 Kennington Road, Vauxhall, SE11 4LD (thecocktavernlondon.com). Kennington tube. **Open** *5pm-midnight Wed, Thur; 5pm-2am Fri, Sat; 5pm-11pm Sun.*

Run by Farika Holden, former landlady of beloved but now defunct east London pub the Nelson's Head, the Cock Tavern is an incredibly welcome addition to London's queer scene. The unique decor reflects the building's Georgian heritage but merges it with its past life as a tiki bar, creating a space both classy and camp. Come on Wednesday night to take advantage of the free jukebox, a treasure trove of gay anthems from Grace Jones to Girls Aloud, or on Sunday night for a raucous pub quiz. On Friday and Saturday nights things heat up as a (mainly gay) crowd seek hit the dancefloor till 2am.

Comptons of Soho

51-53 Old Compton Street, Soho, W1D 6HN (7096 5470, www.comptonsofsoho.co.uk). Picadilly Circus or Leicester Square tube. **Open** *noon-11.30pm Mon-Thur; noon-midnight Fri, Sat; noon-10.30pm Sun.* **Map** *p165 L7.*

Long before Soho became known as London's gay village, long before the likes of Ku Bar and G-A-Y, there was Compton's. Once an old-fashioned gay club with blacked-out windows and sawdust on the floor, the venue now has two floors, clear-glass windows and far nicer toilets. Compton's is still popular with a crowd of beer-drinking, blokey gay men and remains kinda cruisey. But don't let the throng of punters spilling on to the street put you off. The upstairs lounge is a good place for a date or conversation, and the ground floor is a surprisingly inviting bar space.

Duke of Wellington

77 Wardour Street, Soho, W1D 6QB (7439 1274, www.dukeofwellingtonsoho.co.uk). Leicester Square or Piccadilly Circus tube. **Open** *noon-midnight Mon-Sat; noon-11.30pm Sun.* **Map** *p165 L7.*

This traditional two-floor pub attracts a similar (though less cruisey) crowd to Comptons. Downstairs is a decent-sized drinking space with more standing room than seats; upstairs is a cosier lounge bar that can be hired for private events. The ambience is more chilled than many Soho venues, but it fills up quickly on Friday nights and weekends. The Duke of Wellington is well known for its Wednesday pub quiz hosted by a pair of much-loved local drag queens.

Freedom Bar

66 Wardour Street, Soho, W1F 0TA (7734 0071, freedombarsoho.com). Leicester Square or Piccadilly Circus tube. **Open** *4pm-3am Mon-Thur; 2pm-3am Fri, Sat; 2-10.30pm Sun.* **Admission** *free; £5 after 10pm Fri, Sat.* **Map** *p165 L7.*

This glitzy cocktail lounge and DJ bar, spread over two floors, isn't a designated LGBT venue, but because of its location and laissez-faire ambience, anyone on the LGBT spectrum should feel right at home. The glam ground-floor bar attracts a fashion-conscious crowd, who sip cocktails among chandeliers, zebra-print banquettes and Venetian mirrors. A few 'strays' and dolled-up gal pals add colour. The large basement club and performance space hosts weekday cabaret and gets busy with the gay party crowd over the weekend.

❤ Friendly Society
*79 Wardour Street, Soho, W1D 6QB (7434 3805). Leciester Square tube. **Open** 4-11.30pm Mon-Fri; 4pm-midnight Sat; 4-11pm Sun. **Map** p165 L7.*

Friendly Society benefits from the power of surprise: after entering through a bland back-alley doorway, you're greeted at the bottom of the stairs by Soho's most idiosyncratic drinking den. Barbie dolls hang from the ceiling, there's a big fishbowl in the middle and old movies are projected on to a back wall. Although the short cocktail menu has been the same for ever, the staff always seem perplexed when you order one, though that's definitely part of the charm. The crowd here is gay in the broadest sense – anyone with a sense of fun will feel at home, whatever their gender and sexuality. Come here when you fancy dancing to Donna Summer while sipping (relatively) inexpensive prosecco.

G-A-Y Bar
*30 Old Compton Street, Soho, W1D 4UR (7494 2756, www.g-a-y.co.uk). Leicester Square or Tottenham Court Road tube. **Open** noon-midnight daily. **Map** p165 L7.*

Soho's world-famous G-A-Y Bar has everything you'd expect: cheap drink offers, a young crowd and plenty of Britney. The G-A-Y night at Heaven (*see p330*) gets the celebrity cameos, but this popular bar is still a shrine to queer pop idols, with nightly drinks promos every time they play a video from the current diva du jour. There's also a women's bar in the basement, called (delightfully) Girls Go Down – popular with flirty, studenty lesbians, loathed by most older women. G-A-Y bar's plush late-night sibling, **G-A-Y Late**, is round the corner at 5 Goslett Yard.

Halfway to Heaven
*7 Duncannon Street, off Trafalgar Square, WC2N 4JF (7484 0736, www.halfway2heaven. net). Charing Cross tube/rail. **Open** noon-midnight Mon-Thur; noon-2am Fri, Sat; noon-10pm Sun. **Map** p102 M8.*

A traditional gay boozer, situated halfway between Soho and **Heaven** (*see p335*), hence the name. For a change from the usual central London scene, give those lungs an airing at Kevin Walsh's karaoke nights every Thursday. The main floor is cosy and traditional, while the basement is clubbier and cruisier.

King's Arms
*23 Poland Street, Soho, W1F 8QJ (7734 5907, www.kingsarms-soho.co.uk). Tottenham Court Road tube. **Open** noon-11.30pm Mon-Thur; noon-midnight Fri, Sat; 1-10.30pm Sun. **Map** p165 K7.*

This busy bears' pub has been around for ever, and attracts a loyal crowd of stocky, hairy, beardy guys who like a pint, although anyone's welcome. The aesthetic is old-school and cosy: you could be in a country pub, except it's crammed with gay men. There's a DJ on Saturdays and karaoke on Sundays, but the King's Arms often shows live sport too. Located a five-minute stroll from Old Compton Street, it's worth trying if you fancy seeing a different side to Soho.

Ku Bar & Club
*30 Lisle Street, Chinatown, WC2H 7BA (7437 4303, www.ku-bar.co.uk). Leicester Square or Piccadilly Circus tube. **Open** noon-3am Mon-Sat; noon-midnight Sun. **Map** p165 L8.*

Occupying a prominent spot on Soho's fringes, this large LGBT venue is regularly voted London's best. Ku is a little classier than local rival G-A-Y, but it attracts a broadly similar crowd and the young, up-for-it vibe is just as much fun. The ground floor offers a bright and modern bar space with video screens playing chart hits; downstairs is a clubbier room where fresh-faced types of all genders cut a rug to pop and dance remixes. A second **Ku Bar**, on nearby Frith Street, offers a more sedate spin on the same experience.

New Bloomsbury Set
*The Basement, 76 Marchmont Street, Bloomsbury, WC1N 1AG (7383 3084, www. newbloomsburyset.net). Russell Square tube. **Open** 5-11.30pm Mon-Sat; 5-10.30pm Sun. **Map** p194 M5.*

Because it's a brisk 15-minute walk from Soho's gay village, this small but charming basement bar often gets forgotten about. That's a shame, because New Bloomsbury Set has smart decor that nods to the artistic and literary clique it's named after and a fabulous happy hour offering two-for-one cocktails until 7pm daily. As befits its Bloomsbury surroundings, NBS is a little more distinguished than most London LGBT bars and operates an over-21s door policy. It's open from 5pm daily, so it makes sense to pair it with a visit to **Gay's the Word**, London's legendary LGBT bookshop, which is right around the corner (*see p334*).

Queen Adelaide
*483 Hackney Road, Bethnal Green, E2 9ED (thequeenadelaide.com). Cambridge Heath rail. **Open** 5pm-1am Mon-Wed; 5pm-3am Thur-Fri; 2pm-3am Sat; 2pm-1am Sun. **Map** p256 V3.*

Ku Bar & Club

LGBT

The Queen Adelaide rose from the ashes of beloved east London gay pub the George & Dragon, which closed down in 2015. Opened by the same owner just a mile up the same road, it soon had the capital's queer hipsters flocking back. The QA has similarly kitsch decor to the George – look out for the famous horse's head – but it is also a bit of an upgrade: this time, the merriment spreads out over two floors, and there's a 3am licence at the weekends. Let the polysexual party rage on!

Retro Bar

2 George Court, off the Strand, Covent Garden, WC2N 6HH (7839 8760, www. retrobarlondon.co.uk). Charing Cross tube/ rail or Embankment tube. **Open** *noon-11pm Mon-Fri; 2-11pm Sat, Sun.* **Map** *p181 M8.*

Tucked away down an alley off the Strand, the Retro Bar is one of LGBT London's secret pearls. It's a small, gloriously old-fashioned indie bar where anyone on the LGBT spectrum will feel welcome as they drink and listen to Blondie and Bowie blaring out of the jukebox. If the nostalgic tunes don't give you a warm glow, the cosy decor surely will: the walls are filled with iconic photos of everyone from Boy George to Beth Ditto. The quieter upstairs bar is a good date spot, although it's not open every night.

Rupert Street Bar

50 Rupert Street, Soho, W1D 6DR (7494 3059, www.rupert-street.com). Leicester Square or Piccadilly Circus tube. **Open** *noon-11pm Mon-Thur; noon-11.45pm Fri, Sat; noon-10.30pm Sun.* **Map** *p165 L7.*

If your idea of gay life was shaped by TV's *Queer as Folk*, Rupert Street is the bar for you. It's a little bit of Manchester's Canal Street in the heart of Soho. Trapped in the '90s, the decor is all industrial, boiler-room chic, with glass wraparound windows and a large mirror at the back. The staff are beefy and brisk and the clientele is more smartly dressed than average. Popular with the after-work crowd, it gets even busier later on – and also very cruisey.

♥ SHE Soho

23A Old Compton Street, Soho, W1D 5JL (7437 4303, she-soho.com). Leicester Square tube. **Open** *4-11.30pm Mon-Thur; 4pm-midnight Fri, Sat; 4pm-10.30pm Sun.* **Map** *p165 L7.*

Shockingly, this Soho basement bar is London's only exclusively lesbian venue, and it takes this responsibility seriously. Run by the team behind Ku Bar, SHE has a comparable flair for laying on entertainment: as well as club nights, it regularly offers comedy, cabaret, karaoke and quiz evenings. Open Box, a monthly drag king talent contest hosted by scene heroes Adam All and Apple Derrières, is definitely worth popping in your Google Calendar.

Village Soho

81 Wardour Street, Soho, W1D 6QD (7478 0530, www.village-soho.co.uk). Piccadilly Circus or Leicester Square tube. **Open** *5pm-2am Mon-Thur; 5pm-3am Fri, Sat; 5-11.30pm Sun.* **Map** *p165 L7.*

This large bar overlooking Old Compton Street is nearly always busy. Decent drink deals help, but Village also succeeds because of its appealing ambience. Downstairs is a louche L-shaped space with cute corner seating; upstairs is a calmer room that's great for people watching if you can bag a window seat. Though there are often go-go dancers at weekends – a rarity in London – Village doesn't just attract gay men; it's a sexy yet welcoming venue for all members of the LGBT community.

Yard
57 Rupert Street, Soho, W1D 7PL (7437 2652, www.yardbar.co.uk). Leicester Square or Piccadilly Circus tube. **Open** *2-11.30pm Mon, Tue; noon-11.30pm Wed, Thur; noon-midnight Fri, Sat; noon-10.30pm Sun.* **Map** *p165 L7.*

One of the most reliable gay bars in Soho. The downstairs al fresco courtyard boasts sedate lighting, wooden banquettes and a fair bit of flora, giving things an almost bucolic feel. The upstairs loft bar offers views down to all this, with leather sofas offering spots in which to recline. The Yard hosts a variety of visitors, but mostly it's home to a mature gay crowd.

Clubbing

London's club scene is particularly subject to change: venues close, nights end and new soirées start. Check timeout.com for details of what's on when you're here. If you want to stay up all night and next day as well, head to Vauxhall. Popular nights at **Fire** (South Lambeth Road, SW8 1RT, www.fireclub. co.uk) include Orange, a Sunday staple, or there's **Union** (no.66, www.clubunion.co.uk) on the Albert Embankment.

❤ Dalston Superstore
117 Kingland High Street, Dalston, E8 2PB (7254 2273, dalstonsuperstore.com). Dalston Kingsland Overground. **Open** *noon-midnight Mon; noon-2.30am Tue-Thur; noon-3am Fri; 10am-3am Sat; 10am-2.30am Sun.* **Admission** *varies.*

This Kingsland High Street hangout is a bit of a face on the east London party scene. In true Dalston style it's home to all sorts: popular with a large and diverse LGBT crowd, but welcoming to everyone. A café during the day, at night you can expect queues for a hugely impressive roster of guest DJs spinning a typically east London mix of of pop and dance tunes to a floor that's pitch-black and intense. Regular dates, such as Saturday and Sunday's Disco Brunch (soul, disco and funk with all-day breakfast and cocktails), are well worth putting in the diary. Upstairs, alt-cabaret drag stars whip revellers into shape with sharp one-liners.

Eagle London
349 Kennington Lane, Vauxhall, SE11 5QY (7793 0903, www.eaglelondon.com). Vauxhall tube/rail. **Open** *8pm-late Tue-Thur; 9pm-4am Fri, Sat; 8pm-3am Sun.* **Admission** *varies. No cards.*

In recent years this Vauxhall institution has had a facelift to rival Sharon Osbourne's. Out went the licence permitting sexual activity on the premises; in came trendy decor inspired by New York's Meatpacking District. Eagle's large horseshoe bar still attracts many an older, burlier gay gent, but the overall ambience now feels slick and sexy rather than, well, slightly sleazy. On Sunday nights, the dancefloor welcomes a younger and more fashion-conscious crowd for the glorious **Horse Meat Disco**, one of London's very best club nights. It also has a lovely private beer garden with barbecues in the summer.

❤ The Glory
281 Kingsland Road, Dalston, E2 8AS (7684 0794, www.theglory.co). Haggerston Overground. **Open** *5pm-midnight Mon-Thur; 5pm-2am Fri, Sat; 1-11pm Sun.* **Admission** *varies.* **Map** *p256 S3.*

Just 'a clutch bag's throw away from Haggerston station... and one-and-a-half-songs-on-an-iPod's stroll from Shoreditch High Street', this bar and venue was co-opened by drag legend Jonny Woo. On the one hand it's a place you can nip into for a quick after-work drink: the bar staff offer proper cocktails as well as the usual beers, wines and spirits. But on the other, it's a platform for forward-thinking queer entertainment, hosting everything from cabaret to performance to DJ nights. It's a genuinely mixed space where the vibe is less 'anything goes', more 'everything encouraged' and it is perfect for what Woo clearly regards as something of a crusade: to keep gender-

> **In the know**
> ### Gay's the Word
>
> Established in 1979, **Gay's the Word** (66 Marchmont Street, Bloomsbury, WC1N 1AB, 7278 7654, www.gaystheword.co.uk) is a pioneering independent bookshop, the only dedicated LGBT bookshop in the UK and still flushed from its leading role in the superb gays-and-miners movie *Pride*. The stock covers fiction, history and biography, as well as more specialist subjects such as queer studies, sex and relationships, children and parenting. In addition to regular author readings and book signings, there are weekly lesbian and monthly trans discussion groups.

ambiguous and adventurous alternative cabaret thriving. Prepare to be glorious.

Heaven
Under the Arches, Villiers Street, Covent Garden, WC2N 6NG (7930 2020, heavennightclub-london.com). Embankment tube or Charing Cross tube/rail. **Open** *hours vary.* **Admission** *varies. No cards.* **Map** *p181 M8.*

When it opened in 1979, Heaven was revolutionary. London's first gay superclub, it was the birthplace of Hi-NRG and an early adopter of acid house, as well as being a magnet for queer celebrities. Nearly four decades later, Heaven is far from the cutting edge, but still offers the UK's most famous gay night out. On Thursdays it hosts the G-A-Y Porn Idol amateur strip contest, Fridays is filled with '80s and '90s cheese at G-A-Y Camp Attack, and Saturdays are reserved for the main G-A-Y club night, featuring pop star PAs. Tourists and the younger crowd love it, and just about every LGBT Londoner has danced the night away here at least once.

♥ RVT
Royal Vauxhall Tavern, 372 Kennington Lane, Vauxhall, SE11 5HY (7820 1222, www. rvt.org.uk). Vauxhall tube/rail. **Open** *7pm-midnight Mon-Thur; 6.30pm-3am Fri; 9pm-4am Sat; 3pm-1am Sun.* **Admission** *free-£8.*

To paraphrase a famous saying: after a nuclear holocaust, all that will be left are cockroaches, Cher and the Royal Vauxhall Tavern. This pub-cum-legendary queer performance venue has been threatened for years by greedy property developers, but the RVT Future Committee refuses to let it die. People care about this place because it mixes a rich history – the gay Kray used to drink here and Lily Savage got her start behind the bar – with cutting-edge queer club nights like Duckie and Bar Wotever. The fabulously shabby, grade II-listed surroundings don't hurt, either. As Duckie's host (and London's 'Night Czar') Amy Lamé says: 'Everyone's welcome – just don't wear nice shoes.'

Savage
Metropolis, 234 Cambridge Heath Road, Bethnal Green, E2 9NN (www.savagedisco. com). Cambridge Heath Overground. **Open** *10pm-5am Sat.* **Admission** *£6. No cards.* **Map** *p256 V3.*

The restless polysexual party animals Sink The Pink (sinkthepink.co.uk) helm this weekly disco bash at strip club-cum-club space Metropolis, where you can roam around three floors of filthy fun for only a fiver. If you've never been before, prepare for pure

Vegas decor, a dancing pole running through two floors, a wet room and top London DJs (including Horse Meat Disco's Severino and The 2 Bears' Raf Daddy) on rotation, playing deliciously dirty disco, house and party bangers until 5am. Savage stuff indeed.

VFD
66 Stoke Newington Road, Dalston, N16 7XB (7682 0408, www.vfdalston.com). Dalston Junction or Dalston Kingsland Overground. **Open** *times vary.* **Admission** *£5-£6. No cards.*

Formerly (and still commonly) known as Vogue Fabrics, this bijou Dalston basement hosts drag and spoken word events, as well as genre-spanning club nights and parties. Attracting a creative and fashion-conscious LGBT crowd who love to dress up (though no one will really care if you rock up in sneakers and a polo top), VFD has the chutzpah to host club nights with names like Cuntmafia and Sassitude, but never takes itself too seriously. After all, the venue's most famous feature is the massive penis mural in the loos.

WayOut Club
The Minories, 64-73 Minories, EC3N 1JL (07778 157290, www.thewayoutclub. com). Tower Hill tube. **Open** *9pm-3am Sat.* **Admission** *£10; £12 after 11pm.* **Map** *p212 S8.*

London's best-known trans night has changed venues a few times, but it now takes place every Saturday under a railway arch on the fringe of the City. It's open to everyone at the T end of the LGBT spectrum, plus their friends and admirers, and attracts a loyal crowd of friendly regulars. The capital's nightlife has more options for the trans community now than when WayOut began in 1993, but the night endures because it's so warm and inclusive; there's even a changing area for punters who don't want to travel in drag.

XXL
1 Invicta Plaza, South Bank, SE1 9UF (www. xxl-london.com). Southwark tube. **Open** *9pm-3am Wed; 10pm-7am Sat.* **Admission** *£5-15. No cards.* **Map** *p80 P9.*

Held every week in a cavernous space near Blackfriars Bridge, XXL is the UK's biggest bear night. It's a men-only affair, but you don't have to be hench 'n' hairy to have fun: the crowd is friendly and anyone who enjoys whipping his top off on the dancefloor will feel completely at home. XXL regularly attracts up to 2,000 punters, most of whom will be found dancing to house remixes in the main area; others slope off to explore the dark room.

Nightlife

Head out of central London to discover the best of the city after dark

To say London has brilliant and diverse nightlife is an understatement, whether it's clubbing, gigs, cabaret or comedy. These days, though, big is rarely best. Yes, we have one of the world's largest and most influential nightclubs, Fabric, and the awesome large-scale industrial party space Printworks, but it's the smaller spaces that really buzz. In particular, the Bussey Building defines the revival of Peckham, while good clubbing remains easy to find among the party bars along the Kingsland Road strip in Dalston. There's more new music from the edge at places such as XOYO and the Shacklewell Arms, the latter proving that the London cliché of indie bands in sticky dives endures. London also has more than 250 comedy gigs a week and plenty of alt-cabaret.

CLF Art Café at the Bussey Building

CLUBS

In this era of boutique clubbing, London has all the variety you could possibly wish for – you don't even always have to go to a club to have the club experience. Try bowling and boogieing at **Bloomsbury Bowling Lanes** (*see p346*), for example, or dress up for one of the city's burgeoning number of vintage-themed parties. And these days, some of the best events happen in warehouse locations, usually in east or south London – the **Hydra** (the-hydra.net) and **London Warehouse Events** (www.lwe.events) are worth checking out for a fix of big-name electronica. But the days of epoch-defining megaraves are gone, shattered into a thousand microscenes and sound systems that are fleet of foot and quick to respond to the passions of their audience. Upstairs rooms in pubs and the basements of abandoned shops – still especially in east London – are the birthing ground for DJs and promoters who might graduate to more permanent venues, or might vanish without a trace. It's a bewildering scene, but thrilling too.

Where it's at

Shoreditch was the hub of the capital's nightlife scene for a long time. It has, however, become increasingly commercialised in recent years (witness the weekend trails of hen and office parties between Old Street and Spitalfields), despite the groovy work still being done at live

💙 **Best clubs**

CLF Art Café at the Bussey Building *p339*
Crazily diverse programming and all-round good fun.

Dalston Superstore *p334*
Polysexual party at the heart of Dalston.

Fabric *p339*
The superclub that defies the haters.

Printworks *p340*
Big and brilliant.

XOYO *p343*
Keeping Shoreditch clubbing alive.

space and club **XOYO** – the closure of Plastic People in 2015, after 20 years at the cutting edge, felt like the end of an era. Nights at **Book Club**, which range from disco to science drink-and-thinks, show a newer kind of Shoreditch nightlife. The city's cool kids now routinely take the bus north up the Kingsland Road from Shoreditch into Dalston and beyond into Stoke Newington. When you're there, it can be difficult to find the clubs – even more so what's happening in them. Spend a few moments checking *Time Out* magazine (www.timeout.com/clubs) or hunting on Facebook and you'll unearth fabulous happenings at the likes of **Dalston Superstore** (*see p334*) and in any number of shop basements and other informal spaces.

There's more of interest to the south. Peckham has put itself at the heart of London nightlife with the superb **Bussey Building**, while the arrival of the **Printworks** has been justly lauded. Brixton has a multitude of venues, not least sleek **Phonox**. The gay village in Vauxhall is just as welcoming to open-minded, straight-rolling types, with some big line-ups at **Fire** (39 Parry Street, South Lambeth Road, SW8 1RT, 3242 0040, www.firelondon.net) and Horse Meat Disco at **Eagle London** (see p334), while the calendar is even fuller at **Corsica Studios**.

To the north, up in King's Cross, little remains of the former clubbing nexus that was redeveloped into King's Cross Central. There are some good nights at the **Big Chill** (257-259 Pentonville Road, N1 9NL, 7427 2540, bigchillbar.com) and, with its late weekend licence and killer sound system, the **Star of Kings** pub-club (126 York Way, N1 0AX, 7458 4218, starofkings.co.uk). On the way into Islington, the upstairs room at the **Lexington** (see p347) is known for casual nights with a studenty feel. Further north, Camden is still very popular – especially with tourists – but there are credible nights at teeny pub-rave spot the **Lock Tavern** and bourbon-soaked gig haunt the **Blues Kitchen** (see p349). **Koko** (see p344) runs some of the biggest club nights around, including world-famous cheese-fest Guilty Pleasures (guiltypleasures.co.uk).

In central London, though, there's little to detain clubbers: the West End offers bars, pubs and Soho's lively but not especially adventurous gay scene. The best remaining option is the excellent **Blow Up** (www.blowupclub.com) on Friday nights, which celebrated its 25th birthday with a residency in the club under the St Moritz fondue restaurant (161 Wardour Street, Soho, W1F 8WJ, 7734 3324, www.stmoritz-restaurant.co.uk).

Major venues

♥ CLF Art Café at the Bussey Building

133 Rye Lane, Peckham, SE15 4ST (7732 5275, clfartcafe.org). Peckham Rye Overground. **Admission** *varies.*

Spread over multiple floors of Peckham's beloved Bussey Building, the CLF Art Café hosts a varied programme of music, theatre, film, art and comedy events. Late at night, it operates as a fantastic warehouse-style club, with top promoters consistently bringing in some of the best names on the underground and alternative dance scenes, across pretty much any genre you care to name. It also hosts regular nights that offer more accessible

sounds such as the South London Soul Train, a weekly celebration of everything from Motown to house, funk and disco.

Electric Brixton

Town Hall Parade, Brixton, SW2 1RJ (7274 2290, www.electricbrixton.uk.com). Brixton tube/rail. **Open** *Check website for events.* **Admission** *£15-£35.*

The Fridge was a legendary rave paradise in the early '90s, a stomping ground for the rare groove, funky jazz-house and, later, hard dance and psy-trance beats. In 2011, however, the converted cinema underwent a £1-million refit, with new management in place, and was reborn as Electric Brixton, with a mix of club nights focused on everything from reggaeton to disco and house, and live music from some of the UK's hottest up-and-coming artists.

♥ Fabric

77A Charterhouse Street, Clerkenwell, EC1M 6HJ (7336 8898, www.fabriclondon.com). Farringdon tube/rail. **Open** *11pm-6am Fri; 11pm-7am Sat; 11pm-4am Sun.* **Admission** *£21-£27.* **Map** *p212 P6.*

Fabric is the club that most party people come to see in London – no wonder there was a major campaign to keep it open when two drug-related deaths led to Fabric being temporarily shut down in autumn 2016. Located in a former meatpacking warehouse, it has a well-deserved reputation as the capital's biggest and best club. Line-ups across the three rooms are legendary, with the world's most famous DJs bringing the finest low-frequencies and the deepest grooves, as the hip crowds that pack out the dancefloors testify.

Ministry of Sound

103 Gaunt Street, off Newington Causeway, Elephant & Castle, SE1 6DP (7740 8600, www.ministryofsound.com). Elephant & Castle tube/rail. **Open** *10.30pm-6am Fri; 11pm-6am Sat.* **Admission** *£7-£26.* **Map** *p80 P11.*

Ministry of Sound was once the epitome of warehouse cool and is still the UK's best-known clubbing venue. Laid out across four bars, five rooms and three dancefloors, there's lots to explore. Trance night the Gallery has made its home here on Fridays,

In the know
Getting in

The queues for **Fabric** (see above) are also legendary, so blag on to the guestlist or buy tickets in advance to avoid a two-hour wait.

while Saturday nights are for big-name DJ takeovers from the likes of Roger Sanchez and Erick Morillo.

Oval Space

29-32 The Oval, Bethnal Green, E2 9DT (7183 4422, www.ovalspace.co.uk). Bethnal Green tube/Overgound or Cambridge Heath Overground. **Open** *varies.* **Admission** *varies.* **Map** *p256 V3.*

Located at the base of a disused gasworks off Hackney Road, this hangar-style space is one of the most impressive and exciting recent additions to London's nightlife scene. A mix of ace one-off parties and regular events mark Oval Space out. DJs regularly play spacey techno, twisted electronica, alt hip hop and glitchy house, while on-point events include Secretsundaze. If that wasn't enough, Oval Space also has one of the best terrace spaces in town, put to full use for parties during the summer.

❤ Printworks

Surrey Quays Road, Rotherhithe, SE16 7PJ (8498 4934, www.printworkslondon.co.uk). Rotherhithe Overground or Canada Water tube/Overground. **Open/admission** *check website for events.*

This huge 6,000-capacity cultural venue with a DJ focus opened in February 2017. The team now in charge of this massive industrial complex, where newspapers including the *Daily Mail* used to be printed, deliberately

left it as raw as possible – and Londoners have lapped it up. Printworks is now established as one of the city's most vibrant venues; it's a top-class dance space attracting globally renowned nights such as Glitterbox and Amnesia presents Pyramid, which also books cool music acts like Little Dragon and Bugzy Malone.

Club & pub venues

If you're clubbing in Camden, the gig venues **Koko** (*see p344*) and **Camden Assembly** (*see p346*) also host feisty club nights. In addition to the east London venues below, check out gay hangout the **Dalston Superstore** (*see p334*), and the excellent **Village Underground** (*see p348*) and **Shacklewell Arms** (*see p348*).

Book Club

100-106 Leonard Street, Shoreditch, EC2A 4RH (7684 8618, www.wearetbc.com). Old Street tube/rail. **Open** *8.30am-midnight Mon-Wed; 8.30am-2am Thur; 8.30am-3am Sat; 10am-midnight Sun.* **Admission** *free-£20.* **Map** *p256 S5.*

The Book Club aims to fuse lively creative nights, table tennis (there's a ping pong table and regular tournaments) and late-night drinking. You could visit for the drinks alone – cocktails that come with names like Don't Go To Dalston – but the venue crams in a young and laid-back crowd with a packed timetable of things to do, ranging from

Printworks

Nightlife in London is a strange hybrid: at some clubs, you'll dance all night, but at others you're expected just to sit down and open your ears. Run by DJ Cosmo, **Classic Album Sundays** (classicalbumsundays. com) was the first 'listening party' we came across: Cosmo selects a classic album (Kate Bush, Talking Heads, Jimi Hendrix), which you are invited to listen to, in full and without disturbances, played on heavy vinyl through the best audiophile sound system you're ever likely to experience. The same sound system puts on its party hat at psychedelic discos **Journey Through the Light** (www. loftparty.org) and **Beauty and the Beat** (www.houseparty.org.uk). Further interesting variations on the theme include Played Twice at Dalston's audiophile café bar **Brilliant Corners** (brilliantcornerslondon.co.uk): first a classic jazz LP is played (Ornette, Monk, Alice Coltrane) in its entirety, then a high-calibre contemporary jazz band reinterprets the record.

Sheroes, a celebration of a different female pop culture icon each month, to arty think-and-drink workshops, wellbeing events and classic video-game nights.

❤ Corsica Studios

4-5 Elephant Road, Elephant & Castle, SE17 1LB (7703 4760, www.corsicastudios. com). Elephant & Castle tube/rail. **Open** *8pm-3am Mon-Thur, Sun; 8pm-6am Fri, Sat.* **Admission** *free-£15.* **Map** *p80 P11.*

An independent, not-for-profit arts complex, Corsica Studios seeks to breed a culture of creativity. The flexible warehouse space is one of London's most adventurous, supplementing the DJs that play here with bands, poets, painters and lunatic projectionists. Sure, it's rough around the edges, with makeshift bars and toilets, but the events are second to none. The live-music roster has included gigs from Silver Apples, Acoustic Ladyland and Lydia Lunch.

FOLD

Gillian House, Stephenson Street, Canning Town, E16 4SA. Canning Town tube. **Open** *hours vary; check in advance for 24hr openings.* **Admission** *varies.*

When it opened in August 2018, FOLD gave east London's clubbing scene a welcome shot in the arm – due in no small part to its 24-hour licence. Located in a non-residential area between Bow and Canning Town, it's conveniently close to the Jubilee Line and its Night Tube service. The club, which is run by a group of artists, DJs and party people known

as the Shapes Collective, has a 600-capacity dancefloor, an enviable 110db sound system and a strict no-photos policy, meaning you won't be confronted with any embarrassing drunken selfies the morning after. Or any Instagram posers on the dancefloor.

Lock Tavern

35 Chalk Farm Road, Camden, NW1 8AJ (7482 7163, www.lock-tavern.com). Chalk Farm tube. **Open** *5-11pm Mon; noon-11pm Tue, Wed; noon-midnight Thur; noon-1am Fri, Sat; noon-11pm Sun.* **Admission** *free.* **Map** *p241 J1.*

Londoners seethed in August 2018 when this beloved Camden venue was briefly threatened with closure, but it's since been saved by new owners who've said they won't mess with a winning formula. A favourite of artfully distressed rock urchins, it teems with aesthetic niceties inside (cosy black couches and warm wood panels downstairs; open-air terrace on the first floor), but it's the unpredictable after-party vibe that packs in the punters, with big-name DJs regularly providing the tunes.

Notting Hill Arts Club

21 Notting Hill Gate, Notting Hill, W11 3JQ (7460 4459, www.nottinghillartsclub.com). Notting Hill Gate tube. **Open** *hours vary.* **Admission** *free-£8.* **Map** *pull-out C8.*

It's not easy these days to go for a big night out in west London, which is what makes the scruffily chic basement bar at NHAC such a draw. Regular hip hop nights, indie band showcases and events run by local heroes Communion Records are all part of the venue's busy schedule.

Old Queen's Head

44 Essex Road, Islington, N1 8LN (7354 9993, theoldqueenshead.com). Angel tube. **Open** *noon-midnight Mon-Wed, Sun; noon-1am Thur; noon-2am Fri, Sat.* **Admission** *free; £5 Fri after 9pm; £6 Sat after 8pm; other events vary.*

The Old Queen's Head is another place with long queues at the weekends. There are two floors and outside seating front and back, and during the week you can lounge on battered sofas. Weekends are for dancing, minor-league celeb-spotting and chatting up the bar staff, or trying out the private karaoke room. The Old Queen's Head is one of several regular hosts for the Night Shift (see p355).

Phonox

418 Brixton Road, Brixton, SW9 7AY (7095 9411, phonox.co.uk). Brixton tube/rail. **Open** *Fri-Sun; times vary.* **Admission** *£5-£20.*

Phonox has a similar feel to XOYO – no wonder: the team behind the Shoreditch

💙 A night out in Peckham

Described by *Vogue* as 'the Williamsburg of London' and hailed by *Time Out* as London's coolest neighbourhood, Peckham is an incredibly vibrant and exciting nightlife destination, a place where the streets are buzzing almost every night of the week. Hipsters and culture vultures come for everything from theatre to film, and live music to cutting-edge clubbing. Don't let that put you off. Peckham is undeniably trendy, but it's open, fun and friendly, with something for everybody out looking for a good time.

In a strange way, it all began with trams. The threatened demolition of a Victorian warehouse near Peckham Rye to make space for a tram depot kickstarted a campaign to bring creativity to this shabby but lively corner of south-east London. Locals felt Peckham deserved more than a gigantic transport interchange, and did something about it.

Chronic Love Foundation, a collective dedicated to fostering positive global change through the implementation of creative projects, was given the challenge of putting Peckham on the map, and set about the task with relish and imagination. Using the 120-year-old **Bussey Building** as its canvas, CLF organised a rolling programme of cultural events that took in all areas of the arts but had a focus on fun rather than education. Within the gargantuan Bussey, a vibe developed that helped save the warehouse from demolition and it has remained the base of CLF's activities ever since. Once used to manufacture cricket bats, the Bussey now contains arts studios as well as spaces for clubbing (*see p339*), gigs, theatre and cinema; **Rye Wax** (7732 3176, www.ryewax.com), a record shop in the basement, doubles as a clubbing destination after hours. Events are often rooted in the area's Afro-Caribbean community, but even the Royal Court Theatre (*see p362*) has held events in the space.

Across the railway tracks from the Bussey, Peckham's other flagship venue is **Peckham Levels**, a former car park now transformed into a multi-storey creative hub. It houses tropical-themed cocktail bar **Near & Far** (Level 6, 07554 289 251, www.nearandfarbar.com) and more delicious food traders than you can shake a vegan chicken wing at. In the summer months, the top floors are taken over by Bold Tendencies (boldtendencies.com), a non-profit organisation that commissions site-specific sculpture, orchestral music, dance, opera and architecture; it also hosts London's best-loved rooftop bar, **Frank's Café** (*see p288*), an expansive space which is accessed via a now-iconic (and very Instagram-friendly) pink staircase. Franks's gets very busy, but the combination of cocktails, sculptures and fabulous views over south-east London is definitely worth queuing for.

Around the Bussey and the Levels are a selection of smaller avant-garde galleries, music venues, bars and restaurants, not to mention the much-loved **PeckhamPlex** cinema (*see p327*). Night-time hotspots include **Bar Story** (213 Blenheim Grove, SE15 4QL, 7635 6643, barstory.co.uk) for its terrific value happy hour; **Four Quarters South** (*see p288*) for craft beers, cocktails and retro arcade games; **Peckham Springs** (Units 4-5 Dovedale Business Estate 22A Blenheim Grove, SE15 4QN, peckhamsprings.co.uk) for late-night drinking in its own winter garden; and **Copeland Social** (Unit9A&B, Copeland Park, 133 Rye Lane, SE15, 3146 1774, www.copelandsocial.com) for its lively atmosphere and bangin' sound system. These days, only fools fail to recognise the potential of a night out in Peckham.

Frank's Cafe

venue took over what was Plan B to create a sleek, dark dance cavern where there's plenty of space for a boogie. Programming leans very much towards the leftfield side of dance music – don't expect cheesy '80s nights; new resident DJ Esa ensures it's quality,underground house, techno, disco and bass all the way.

❤ XOYO

32-37 Cowper Street, Shoreditch, EC2A 4AP (7608 2878, www.xoyo.co.uk). Old Street tube/rail. **Open** *varies.* **Admission** *varies.* **Map** *p256 R5.*

There's live music during the week at this 800-capacity venue, but XOYO is first and foremost a club. The former printworks is a bare concrete shell, defiantly taking the 'chic' out of 'shabby chic', but the open space means the atmosphere is always buzzing, as the only place to escape immersion in the music is the small smoking courtyard outside. The Victorian loft-style space provides effortlessly cool programming and high-profile DJs, while the longer residencies – a 13-week stint for drum-and-bass legend Andy C in winter 2018-19, for instance – is the best kind of old-school.

ROCK & POP MUSIC

The rest of the country might not like it, but every musician is going to have to come to London: you might find yourself watching a US country star in a tiny basement, an African group under a railway arch or a torch singer in a church – all in one night, if you've got the stamina. While corporations have invested in venues, resulting in positives (improved facilities and sound systems) and negatives (overpriced bars and ugly branded names), there's still rough and ready individuality to be found – as well as the newest sounds – in venues such as **XOYO** (*see above*) and the **Shacklewell Arms**. There's often a huge disparity between door times and stage times; doors may open at 7pm, for instance, but the gigs often don't start until after 9pm. Some venues run club nights after the gigs, which means the show has to be wrapped up by 10.30pm; but at other venues, the main act won't even start until 11pm. If in doubt, call ahead.

Major venues

In addition to the venues listed below, the **Barbican Centre** (*see p354*), the **Southbank Centre** (*see p357*) and the **Royal Albert Hall** (*see p356*) also stage regular non-classical gigs.

Alexandra Palace

Alexandra Palace Way, N22 7AY (8365 2121, www.alexandrapalace.com). Alexandra Palace rail or W3 bus. **Tickets** *vary; check the promoter's website.*

This hilltop landmark, adorned with sculptures and frescoes, opened in 1873 as the People's Palace and was devastated by fire twice – once only 16 days after opening, and the second time in 1980. The layout means bar and toilet provision can be an irritation, but the sound system is beloved of audiophiles: no wonder the Pixies chose it for their first London shows when they reformed, and James Murphy for the last UK appearances of LCD Soundsystem.

❤ EartH

11-17 Stoke Newington Road, Stoke Newington, N16 8BH (information 7422 7505, earthackney.co.uk). Dalston Kingsland rail. **Tickets** *prices vary.*

Launched in September 2018, this self-styled 'multi-arts space for the 21st century' is an ambitious restoration of the formerly derelict Savoy Cinema. Its slightly ungainly name is short for 'Evolutionary Arts Hackney', but so far the programming is trendy and accessible rather than too highfalutin. There are two atmospheric event spaces – the seated upstairs theatre, and downstairs concert hall which is standing only – and they're already proving a popular stop-off for discerning artists. Indie heroes Lambchop and soul siren Andreya Triana played EartH in 2019, while pop queens Little Mix launched their latest album here in late 2018.

Eventim Apollo

45 Queen Caroline Street, Hammersmith, W6 9QH (information 8563 3800, tickets 0844 249 4300, www.eventimapollo.com).

❤ Best music venues

Café Oto *p349*
For esoteric musical happenings.

Corsica Studios *p341*
Inventive, anything-goes gigging.

O2 Arena & IndigO2 *p344*
The place to catch big-ticket, blockbusting legends.

O2 Academy Brixton *p344*
Classic rock venue with great atmosphere.

Union Chapel *p348*
This Gothic church gives every gig a sense of occasion.

*Hammersmith tube. **Box office** In person from 4pm on performance days. By phone 8am-10pm daily. **Tickets** £10-£150.*

This 1930s cinema doubles as a 3,600-capacity all-seater theatre (popular with big comedy acts and children's shows) and a 5,000-capacity standing-room-only gig space, hosting shows by major rock bands and others not quite ready for the O2. The venue scored a sensational coup at the end of 2014 when Kate Bush's 'Before the Dawn' was performed here – her first gig since 1979.

Koko
*1A Camden High Street, Camden, NW1 7JE (information 7388 3222, tickets 0844 477 1000, www.koko.uk.com). Mornington Crescent tube. **Box office** In person noon-5pm Mon-Fri (performance days only). By phone 24hrs daily. **Tickets** £10-£40. **Map** p241 K3.*

Koko has had a hand in the gestation of numerous styles over the decades. As the Music Machine, it hosted a four-night residency with the Clash in 1978; the venue changed its name to Camden Palace in the '80s, whereupon it became home to the emergent New Romantic movement and saw Madonna's UK debut. Later, it was one of the first 'official' venues to host acid-house events. Since a spruce-up in the early noughties, it has hosted acts as diametrically opposed as Joss Stone and Queens of the Stone Age, not to mention one of Prince's electrifying 'secret' gigs in 2014. Nonetheless, the 1,500-capacity hall majors on weekend club nights – Guilty Pleasures and Buttoned Down Disco – and gigs by indie rockers, from the small and cultish to those on the up.

♥ O2 Academy Brixton
*211 Stockwell Road, Brixton, SW9 9SL (information 7771 3000, tickets 0844 477 2000, academymusicgroup.com/o2academybrixton). Brixton tube/rail. **Box office** In person 2hrs before doors on performance days. By phone 24hrs daily. **Tickets** £10-£40.*

Brixton is still the preferred venue for metal, indie and alt-rock bands looking to play their triumphant 'Look, ma, we've made

In the know
Rock 'n' bowl

Also in the O2 enormodome, **Brooklyn Bowl** (7412 8778, london.brooklynbowl.com) provides surprisingly high-quality gigs – as well as Southern-style eats and, yes, bowling alleys.

it!' headline show. Built in the 1920s, this ex-cinema is the city's most atmospheric big venue. The 5,000-capacity art deco gem straddles the chasm between the pomp and volume of a stadium show and the intimate (read: sweaty) atmosphere of a club. Since becoming a full-time music venue in the '80s, it's hosted names from James Brown to the Stones to Springsteen, Dylan, Prince and Madonna, via the Red Hot Chili Peppers and Run DMC with the Beastie Boys. And with its raked dancefloor, everyone's guaranteed a decent view.

♥ O2 Arena & IndigO2
*Peninsula Square, North Greenwich, SE10 0DX (information 8463 2000, tickets 3481 5503, www.theo2.co.uk). North Greenwich tube. **Box office** In person noon-7pm daily. By phone 9am-7pm Mon-Fri; 10am-6pm Sat, Sun. **Tickets** £15-£70.*

The national embarrassment that was the Millennium Dome has been transformed into the city's de facto home of the mega-gig. This 20,000-seater has outstanding sound, unobstructed sightlines and the potential for artists to perform 'in the round'. Shows from even the world's biggest acts (U2, Beyoncé, the reformed Led Zep, the mostly reformed Monty Python) don't feel too far away, and the venue seems to handle music, comedy and even sport (international tennis, boxing, basketball) with equal aplomb.

On the same site, **IndigO2** is the Arena's little sister – but 'little' only by comparison. It has an impressive capacity of 2,350, arranged as part-standing room, part-amphitheatre seating and, sometimes, part-table seating. IndigO2's niche roster of MOR acts is dominated by soul, funk, pop-jazz and old pop acts, but it does also host after-show parties for headliners from the Arena.

O2 Forum Kentish Town
*9-17 Highgate Road, Kentish Town, NW5 1JY (information 7428 4080, tickets 0844 877 2000, www.academymusicgroup.com/o2forumkentishtown). Kentish Town tube/rail. **Box office** In person 90mins before doors open on show days. By phone 24hrs daily. **Tickets** £10-£40.*

Originally constructed as part of a chain of art deco cinemas with a spurious Roman theme (hence the name, the incongruous bas relief battle scenes and imperial eagles flanking the stage), the 2,000-capacity Forum became a music venue back in the early 1980s. Since then, it's been vital to generations of gig-goers, whether they cut their teeth on Ian Dury & the Blockheads, the Pogues, Duran Duran, Killing Joke or the Wu-Tang Clan, all of whom have played memorable shows here.

EartH p343

O2 Shepherd's Bush Empire

*Shepherd's Bush Green, Shepherd's Bush, W12 8TT (information 8354 3300, tickets 0844 477 2000, www.academymusicgroup. com/o2shepherdsbushempire). Shepherd's Bush Market tube or Shepherd's Bush tube/ Overground/rail. **Box office** from 4pm on performance days. By phone 24hrs daily. **Tickets** £10-£40.*

Once a BBC television theatre, the Empire's baroque interior exudes a grown-up glamour few venues can match. The environment lends a gravitas to the chirpiest of performance, as Lily Allen demonstrated in the flush of her fame, so you can imagine the sensation of seeing the likes of David Bowie or Bob Dylan here. It holds 2,000 standing or 1,300 seated, sightlines are good, the sound is decent (with the exception of the alcove behind the stalls bar and the scarily vertiginous top floor), and the roster of shows is quite varied.

Pickle Factory

*13-14 The Oval, Bethnal Green, E2 9DU (www.thepicklefactory.co.uk). Bethnal Green tube/Overground or Cambridge Heath Overground. **Open/admission** check website. **Map** p256 V3.*

This former industrial building is owned by the team that runs Oval Space (*see p340*), which is directly opposite. It actually was a pickle factory, but – having been used for foodie pop-ups and exhibitions – was fully revamped as an intimate live music and club space. The programme is an alternative and esoteric mix of mind-bendingly arty bands and leftfield but thoroughly banging DJ sets from underground heroes.

Roundhouse

*Chalk Farm Road, Camden, NW1 8EH (tickets 0300 678 9222, www.roundhouse. org.uk). Chalk Farm tube. **Box office** In person 9.30am-5pm Mon, Sat, Sun; 9.30am-9pm Tue-Fri. By phone 9am-7pm Mon-Fri; 9am-4pm Sat; 9.30am-4pm Sun. **Tickets** £5-£25. **Map** p241 H1.*

The main auditorium's supporting pillars mean there are some poor sightlines at the Roundhouse, but this one-time railway turntable shed (hence the name), which was used for hippie happenings in the 1960s before becoming a famous rock (and punk) venue in the '70s, has been a fine addition to London's music venues since its reopening in 2006. Expect a mix of arty rock gigs (the briefly re-formed Led Zeppelin played here), dance performances, theatre and multimedia events.

Tickets & planning

Before even arriving in London, your first stop should be www.timeout.com, which lists hundreds of gigs every week, with the key highlights featured in the weekly free magazine every Tuesday. We've included the websites for each venue here: these detail upcoming shows. But check ticket availability before you set out, as venues large and small can sell out weeks in advance. The main exceptions to this rule are pub venues, which normally sell tickets only on the day. Many venues offer tickets online via their websites, but beware: most online box offices are operated by ticket agencies, which add booking fees that can raise the ticket price by as much as 30 per cent. If possible, try to buy tickets in person from the venue.

Scala

275 Pentonville Road, King's Cross, N1 9NL (information 7833 2022, tickets 0844 477 1000, scala.co.uk). King's Cross tube/rail. **Box office** *10am-6pm Mon-Fri.* **Tickets** *free-£25.* **Map** *p194 M4.*

Although the venue has vacillated between use as a picturehouse and concert hall, the Scala's one consistent trait has been its lack of respect for authority: its stint as a cinema was ended after Stanley Kubrick sued it into bankruptcy for showing *A Clockwork Orange*. Nowadays, it's one of the most rewarding venues in which to push your way to the front for those cusp-of-greatness shows by big names in waiting – names as varied as triple-threat Londoner MNEK and online sensation Poppy.

SSE Arena, Wembley

Arena Square, Engineers Way, Wembley, Middlesex, HA9 0DH (information 8782 5500, tickets 0844 815 0815, www.ssearena.co.uk). Wembley Park tube or Wembley Stadium rail. **Box office** *In person (performance days only) 10.30am-4.30pm Mon-Fri; from noon Sat on performance days; from 2pm Sun on performance days. By phone 24hrs daily.* **Tickets** *£20-£230.*

Although it still hosts shows by big names like Culture Club and country queen Kacey Musgraves, thanks to the ongoing success of the O2 Arena (*see p344*), Wembley Arena now feels like London's second-choice mega-venue. While the food and drink could be better, most Londoners have warm memories of at least one enormogig at the 12,500-capacity Arena, be it rock or stand-up comedy.

Club & pub venues

In addition to the venues listed below, several London nightclubs multitask, staging regular gigs: **Corsica Studios** (*see p341*), the **Notting Hill Arts Club** (*see p341*), **Printworks** (*see p340*) and **Electric Brixton** (*see p339*) are notable. **Borderline** is known for country and folk gigs, but does also host indie bands.

100 Club

100 Oxford Street, Soho, W1D 1LL (7636 0933, www.the100club.co.uk). Oxford Circus or Tottenham Court Road tube. **Shows** *times vary.* **Tickets** *£10-£25.* **Map** *p165 K7.*

The 100 Club began life in 1942 hosting the Feldman Club, but over the decades jazz would give way to punk: one historic show, in September 1976, featured the Sex Pistols, the Clash and the Damned. These days the famous, 350-capacity basement room is more of a hub for pub rockers, blues rockers and, in a return to its roots, trad jazzers. The space comes into its own for the odd secret gig by A-list bands such as Primal Scream and Oasis.

Bloomsbury Bowling Lanes

Basement, Tavistock Hotel, Bedford Way, Bloomsbury, WC1H 9EU (7183 1979, www.bloomsburylive.com). Russell Square tube. **Open** *noon-midnight Mon, Tue, Sun; noon-late Wed, Thur; noon-3am Fri, Sat.* **Admission** *free Mon-Thur, Sun; £5-7 Fri, Sat.* **Map** *p194 L5.*

Offering a late-night drink away from Soho (but not too far away), BBL has been putting on bands and DJs for ages – and the range of activities make it a playground for grown-ups. As well as the eight lanes for bowling, there's pool by the hour, table football, karaoke booths and, beside the entrance, a small cinema.

Bush Hall

310 Uxbridge Road, Shepherd's Bush, W12 7LJ (8222 6955, www.bushhallmusic.co.uk). Shepherd's Bush Market tube. **Open** *varies.* **Shows** *from 7pm.* **Tickets** *£6-£40.*

This handsome room has been a dance hall, soup kitchen and snooker club. Now, with original fittings intact, it plays host to major bands performing stripped-down shows and to rising indie rockers, as well as top folk acts.

Camden Assembly

49 Chalk Farm Road, Camden, NW1 8AN (7424 0800, camdenassembly.com). Chalk Farm tube. **Open** *5pm-1am Mon-Wed; 5pm-2am Thur; 5pm-3am Fri; noon-3am Sat; noon-midnight Sun. Shows from 7pm.* **Admission** *free-£15.* **Map** *p241 H1.*

Formerly the Barfly, this 200-capacity corner venue is a Camden institution, with Coldplay, Franz Ferdinand and Bombay Bicycle Club among the many bands who played early London gigs here. It was a popular hangout during the Britpop and grunge years – no doubt due to the loud post-band DJ sets and late licence – and a key player in the fusion of indie guitars and electro into an unholy, danceable row.

Garage

20-22 Highbury Corner, Highbury, N5 1RD (information 7619 6721, tickets 0844 847 1678, thegarage.london). Highbury & Islington tube/Overground/rail. **Box office** *by phone 24hrs daily.* **Tickets** *free-£20.*

This 650-capacity venue books an exciting and surprisingly wide-ranging calendar of indie, pop and art-rock gigs, from ancient punk survivors such as the Pop Group and Sham 69 to rising stars Girli and Alice Chater. Formerly known as Upstairs, the first-floor space (which hosts smaller gigs) has been rebranded as Thousand Island.

Hoxton Square Bar & Kitchen

2-4 Hoxton Square, Shoreditch, N1 6NU (information 7613 0709; tickets 0844 847 2316, www.hoxtonsquarebar.com). Old Street tube/rail or Shoreditch High Street Overground. **Open** *noon-midnight Mon-Wed; noon-1am Thur; noon-2am Fri; 4pm-2am Sat; 4pm-midnight Sun.* **Tickets** *free-£14.50 after 10pm Fri, Sat.* **Map** *p256 S4.*

This 450-capacity venue is more than just a place to be seen: the line-ups are always cutting-edge and fun, frequently offering a band's first London outing. Get there early or be prepared to queue.

Jazz Café

5 Parkway, Camden, NW1 7PG (7485 6834, thejazzcafelondon.com). Camden Town tube. **Live shows & restaurant** *7-10.30pm daily.* **Club nights** *10.30pm-3am Fri, Sat.* **Tickets** *£5-£30.* **Map** *p241 J2.*

In 2020, the Jazz Café will celebrate 30 years in business, having brought some of the most respected names in the jazz and soul world – D'Angelo, Roy Ayers, Bobby Womack – as well as Amy Winehouse and Adele to Camden Town. The programming focuses on funk, soul, R&B and electronic music, but there are also new and rising acts. With a capacity of 440, it's an intimate space, but the two-level layout offers you a choice: get sweaty in the downstairs standing area, or book an upstairs table for a bit of luxury and guaranteed good view.

Lexington

96-98 Pentonville Road, Islington, N1 9JB (7837 5371, www.thelexington.co.uk). Angel tube. **Open** *noon-2am Mon-Wed, Sun; noon-3am Thur; noon-4am Fri, Sat.* **Tickets** *free-£15.* **Map** *pull-out O3.*

Effectively the common room for the music industry's perennial sixth form, this 200-capacity venue has a superb sound system in place for the leftfield indie bands that dominate the programme. It's where the hottest US exports often make their London debut: indie greats such as the Drums and Sleigh Bells have cut their teeth here in front of London's most receptive crowds. Downstairs, there's a lounge bar with a vast array of US beers and bourbons, above-par bar food and a Rough Trade music quiz (every Monday).

Oslo

1A Amhurst Road, Hackney, E8 1LL (3553 4831, www.oslohackney.com). Hackney Central Overground. **Open** *varies.* **Admission** *varies.*

Young and trendy Hackney folk are blended with older live music fans more smoothly than one of the salted caramel martinis they serve in this Victorian railway station. Oslo is a busy, glowingly lit and rather fancy Scandinavian restaurant downstairs, with a more relaxed area for bar food, but head upstairs and you'll find all sorts of musical happenings, including of-the-moment buzz bands and some club nights. The decent-sized stage and proper sound system and lighting rig ensure a roster of good acts – among them Temples.

♥ Best all-rounders

Corsica Studios *p341*
Gigs, club nights and freaky deaky light shows.

EartH *p343*
Hackney's newest and most versatile arts space.

Printworks *p340*
Huge industrial venue with six event spaces.

Soho Theatre *p367*
Not just plays, but cabaret and comedy.

Village Underground *p348*
Arty happenings, musical and otherwise.

Shacklewell Arms

71 Shacklewell Lane, Dalston, E8 2EB (7249 0810, www.shacklewellarms.com). Dalston Kingsland or Dalston Junction Overground. **Open** *5pm-midnight Mon-Thur; 4pm-3am Fri, Sat; 4pm-midnight Sun.* **Admission** *free-£15.*

The Shacklewell Arms is a magnet for leftfield music. While the bands who have played here include the Horrors, Toy and Haim, DJs tend to come from the electronic, lo-fi, chillwave and post-dubstep arenas, all of which genres contrast brilliantly with the quirkily decorated interior – this former Afro-Caribbean hotspot has had its array of tropical-themed murals and signs pointing to 'the dancehall' updated. Thank goodness.

Underworld

174 Camden High Street, Camden, NW1 0NE (7482 1932, www.theunderworldcamden. co.uk). Camden Town tube. **Open** *times vary.* **Admission** *£5-£24.* **Map** *p241 K2.*

A dingy maze of pillars and bars below Camden, this subterranean oddity is an essential for metal and hardcore fans who want their ears bludgeoned by bands with names such as Bitchwax, Skeletonwitch and Decrepit Birth. Tickets are purchased from the World's End pub upstairs.

♥ Union Chapel

Compton Terrace, off Upper Street, Islington, N1 2UN (7226 1686, www.unionchapel.org. uk). Highbury & Islington tube/Overground/ rail. **Open** *varies.* **Tickets** *free-£40.*

Readers of *Time Out* magazine have three times voted Union Chapel their top music venue – and it's easy to see why. The Grade I-listed Victorian Gothic church, which still holds services and also runs a homeless centre, is a wonderfully atmospheric gig venue. It made its name hosting acoustic events and occasional jazz shows, becoming a magnet for thinking bands and their fans. These days, you'll also find classy intimate shows from bigger artists such as Paloma Faith. Watch out for the Daylight Music free afternoon concerts.

♥ Village Underground

54 Holywell Lane, Shoreditch, EC2A 3PQ (7422 7505, www.villageunderground.co.uk). Shoreditch High Street Overground. **Open** *varies.* **Admission** *varies.* **Map** *p256 S5.*

You can't miss Village Underground: four graffiti-covered tube carriages are perched on its roof. These and a series of shipping containers accommodate artists, writers, designers, filmmakers and musicians, while a Victorian warehouse space hosts exhibitions, concerts, plays, live art and club nights.

Windmill

22 Blenheim Gardens, Brixton, SW2 5BZ (8671 0700, windmillbrixton.co.uk). Brixton tube/rail. **Open** *5-11pm Mon-Thur, Sun; 5.30pm-1am Fri, Sat. Shows vary.* **Admission** *free-£12.*

There's a barbecue every Sunday afternoon in summer; a somewhat scary dog lives on the roof, frightening unsuspecting smokers; and an actual windmill stands in the adjacent park. The Windmill is certainly not your average music venue, but it's been revelling in its rough-around-the-edges eccentricity for years, its unprepossessing exterior a cloak for its dedication to new leftfield music. The programming is biased towards alt country, alt folk and alt punk. It's worth a visit just to pick up an 'I Believe in Roof Dog' T-shirt.

JAZZ, COUNTRY, FOLK & BLUES

The international big hitters keep on visiting London, but there's a lively homegrown jazz scene too, inspired by freewheeling attractions at the **Vortex**, **Café Oto** and the unhinged monthly **Boat-Ting Club** nights (www.boat-ting.co.uk); Portico Quartet, Led Bib and Kit Downes Trio each won Mercury Prize nominations at the turn of the decade. In addition to the venues below, the **100 Club** (*see p346*) hosts blues rock and trad groups, **Bush Hall** (*see p346*) is a great setting for leading folk groups, and the **Spice of Life** (6 Moor Street, Soho, W1D 5NA, 7437 7013, www.spiceoflifesoho. com) has solid mainstream jazz. In Hoxton, **Charlie Wright's International Bar** (Courtyard Theatre, 40 Pitfield Street, N1 6EU, www.charliewrightsproductions.com) usually has a fine jazz programme. The **Jazz Café** (*see p347*) lives up to its name from time to time; there's a lot of very good jazz at the excellent **Kings Place** (*see p392*); and both the **Barbican** (*see p354*) and the **Southbank Centre** (*see p357*) host dozens of big names. For the admirable **London Jazz Festival**, *see p317*.

606 Club

90 Lots Road, Chelsea, SW10 0QD (7352 5953, www.606club.co.uk). Imperial Wharf Overground or bus 11, 211. **Open** *7-11.30pm Mon-Thur; 8pm-12.30am Sat; 12.30-3.30pm, 7-11.30pm Sun. Shows vary.* **Admission** *(non-members) £10-£14.*

Since 1976 Steve Rubie has run this club, which relocated to this 150-capacity space in 1987. Alongside its Brit-dominated bills, expect informal jams featuring musos who've come here to wind down from gigs elsewhere.

Ronnie Scott's p350

There's no entrance fee as such; bands are funded from a music charge added to your bill at the end of the night.

Blues Kitchen

111-113 Camden High Street, Camden, NW1 7JN (7387 5277, theblueskitchen.com). Camden Town or Mornington Crescent tube. **Open** *noon-midnight Mon, Tue; noon-1am Wed, Thur; noon-2.30am Fri; 10am-3am Sat; 10am-1am Sun.* **Admission** *varies.* **Map** *p241 K2.*

The Blues Kitchen combines credible live music of the earthier variety (roots, blues, rockabilly) with a rather smart interior. The food is spicy New Orleans fare and there's a huge range of American bourbon for sippin'. It's a pleasant Sunday afternoon hangout as well as a late-opening gig venue. Outposts in Shoreditch (134-146 Curtain Road, EC2A 3AR, 7729 7216) and Brixton (40 Acre Lane, SW2 5SP, 7274 0591) have a similar vibe.

Borderline

Orange Yard, off Manette Street, Soho, W1D 4JB (information 3871 7777, tickets 0844 847 1678, borderline.london). **Tottenham Court Road tube.** **Shows** *7pm-midnight;* **Club nights** *7pm-4am.* **Admission** *£3-£20.* **Map** *p165 L7.*

The best venue in the West End? Surely. Reopening after a revamp in spring 2017, the Borderline is a 300-capacity dive bar and juke joint, perfectly placed on the fringe of Soho. It has long been a favoured stop-off for touring American bands of the country and blues varieties, though you'll also find a range of indie acts and singer-songwriters going through their repertoire. Be warned: it can get very cramped, but that's all to the good for intimacy and atmosphere.

♥ Café Oto

18-22 Ashwin Street, Dalston, E8 3DL (www.cafeoto.co.uk). Dalston Kingsland or Dalston Junction Overground. **Café** *8.30am-5pm Mon-Fri; 9.30am-5pm Sat; 10.30am-5pm Sun.* **Shows** *8pm; open until 12.30am on show nights.* **Admission** *free-£20.*

This 150-capacity café and music venue can't easily be categorised, though its website offers the tidy definition that it specialises in 'creative new music that exists outside of the mainstream'. That means Japanese noise rockers ('Oto' is Japanese for 'sound'), electronica pioneers, improvisors (the Sun Ra Arkestra has had a couple of residencies), noiseniks and artists from the stranger ends of the rock, folk and classical spectrums.

Cecil Sharp House

2 Regent's Park Road, Camden, NW1 7AY (7485 2206, www.cecilsharphouse. org). Camden Town tube. **Open** *varies.* **Map** *p241 J2.*

Headquarters of the British Folk Dance and Song Society, Cecil Sharp House is a great place to visit, even when there isn't any music playing: there's a folk-arts education centre and archive open during the day. Perhaps that sounds a bit worthy? In fact, the Kennedy Hall performance space – with its comfortably sprung floor – is blessed with a well-informed and enthusiastic team of bookers who ensure all angles of trad music are well represented without being preserved in aspic. Events range from Scottish ceilidhs to alt folk.

Green Note

*106 Parkway, Camden, NW1 7AN (7485 9899, www.greennote.co.uk). Camden Town tube. **Open** 7-11pm Mon-Thur; 7pm-midnight Fri-Sun. Shows 8.30-11pm daily. **Admission** £5-£15. **Map** p241 J2.*

A stone's throw from Regent's Park, this cosy little venue and vegetarian café-bar hosts singer-songwriters, folkies and blues musicians, with a handful of big names in among the listings.

Pizza Express Jazz Club

*10 Dean Street, Soho, W1D 3RW (7439 4962, www.pizzaexpresslive.com). Tottenham Court Road tube. **Open** 6.30-10.30pm Mon-Thur; 6pm-midnight Fri, Sat; 6.30-10pm Sun. **Admission** £15-£25. **Map** p165 L7.*

The upstairs restaurant (7437 9595) is jazz-free, but the 120-capacity basement is one of the best mainstream jazz venues in town. Singers such as Kurt Elling and Lea DeLaria join instrumentalists from home and abroad on the nightly bills.

Ronnie Scott's

*47 Frith Street, Soho, W1D 4HT (7439 0747, www.ronniescotts.co.uk). Leicester Square or Tottenham Court Road tube. **Open** 6pm-3am Mon-Sat; noon-4pm, 6.30pm-midnight Sun. **Admission** free-£50. **Map** p165 L7.*

Opened (on a different site) by the British saxophonist Ronnie Scott in 1959, this jazz institution was the setting for Jimi Hendrix's final UK performance, among many other distinctions. It continues to attract jazz heavyweights – from well-established talents such as Chick Corea to hotly tipped purists such as Kurt Elling to futuristic mavericks such as Robert Glasper. Perch by the rear bar, or get table service at the crammed side-seating or at the more spacious (but noisier) central tables in front of the stage.

Vortex Jazz Club

*11 Gillett Square, Dalston, N16 8AZ (7254 4097, www.vortexjazz.co.uk). Dalston Kingsland or Dalston Junction Overground. **Open** 8pm-midnight daily. **Admission** £5-£18.*

One of the few venues in the city you could visit on spec and be guaranteed to hear something interesting. Along with the nearby Café Oto, the Vortex is one of London's most lovingly curated venues. Jazz is the order of the day, but the Vortex serves it up in kaleidoscopic variety. For the less daring, there's a regular calendar of big band, piano trio, vocal, free improv, world music and folk-oriented sounds, as well as some poetry gigs. The Vortex hosts its own strand of the London Jazz Festival (*see p317*) and various other forward-thinking events.

> **In the know**
> **Booze and tunes**
>
> Also at Gillett Square, the **Servant Jazz Quarters** cocktail dive (10A Bradbury Street, N16 8JN, 7684 8411, servantjazzquarters. com) serves cocktails and programmes gigs – even, sometimes, jazz.

COMEDY & CABARET

While the big stadiums – especially the **O2 Arena** and **SSE Arena, Wembley** – host the massive shows, it's the circuit of pubs and smaller clubs that defines London's comedy scene. In addition to its stellar programme of plays and cabaret, the **Soho Theatre** (*see p367*) has become one of the best places to see comics breaking free from abbreviated club-circuit sets to present more substantial solo gigs. Usually programming hour-long shows rather than the multi-act bills common elsewhere, it's currently the best venue in London for interesting, innovative and downright funny comedy. Another multi-tasking venue is the **Union Chapel** (*see p348*), whose monthly Live at the Chapel night provides line-ups of big guns (Noel Fielding and Stewart Lee, for example) supported by comics who are headliners in their own right, plus a terrific live band.

To see the best cabaret, head to the always interesting **Bethnal Green Working Men's Club** or the even more alternative **RVT** (*see p335*) and the **Glory** (*see p330*). **Proud Embankment** (8 Victoria Embankment, Waterloo, www.proudembankment.com) launched in 2018 as a glamorous cabaret and party venue. Many of the best nights, however, are one-off parties in a range of formal and informal venues.

For the week's best line-ups – whether comedy or cabaret – have a look at the free *Time Out* magazine on Tuesday; for comprehensive listings, see www.timeout.com.

99 Club Leicester Square

*Ruby Blue, 1 Leicester Place, Leicester Square, WC2H 7BP (07760 488119, www.99clubcomedy.com). Leicester Square tube. **Open** 7.30-10.45pm Tue-Sat. **Admission** £7-£17. **Map** p165 L8.*

The general rule when you get a flyer as you walk through Leicester Square is to stick it in the nearest recycling bin – but make an exception for this one. The 99 Club offers quality line-ups five nights a week and tickets are remarkably good value (but expect a hike in prices around Christmas).

Angel Comedy

*Camden Head, 2 Camden Walk, Islington, N1 8DY (www.angelcomedy.co.uk). Angel tube. **Shows** 8pm daily. **Admission** free; donations appreciated. **Map** pull-out P3.*

One of the best comedy nights in London – and certainly the best free night. That means long queues tend to form outside, with the promoters having to turn folk away every weekend. On Fridays and Saturdays, you can catch rising stars and a few professional comics performing their funniest sets, and weekdays feature either new-material spots, improv troupes or solo shows. But the night's biggest sell is the inclusive, welcoming atmosphere – despite being free, punters come for the comedy rather than a cheap night out. Donations are encouraged at the end of the night.

Bethnal Green Working Men's Club

*42-44 Pollard Row, Bethnal Green, E2 6NB (7739 7170, www.workersplaytime. net). Bethnal Green tube. **Open** varies. **Admission** free-£10. **Map** p256 U4.*

Sticky red carpet and broken lampshades perfectly suit the programme of quirky lounge, retro rock 'n' roll and fancy-dress burlesque parties here. You might get to watch a spandex-lovin' dance duo or get hip with burlesque starlets on a 1960s dancefloor. The mood is friendly, the playlist upbeat and the air full of artful, playful mischief.

CellarDoor

*Zero Aldwych, Aldwych, Covent Garden, WC2D 0HS (7240 8848, www.cellardoor. biz). Covent Garden tube. **Open** varies. **Admission** varies. **Map** p181 N8.*

Some staggeringly clever design means that although there's room for just 60 in this subterranean converted Victorian loo, CellarDoor never feels claustrophobic. Musical-theatre cabaret crooners and drag queens are the order of the day, giving this sleek establishment a vintage feel. Nearly all shows are free and often great fun – the incredibly glamorous Vicious Delicious even hosts burlesque lessons here on Saturdays.

Comedy Store

1A Oxendon Street, Soho, SW1Y 4EE (7024 2060, www.thecomedystore.co.uk/london). Leicester Square or Piccadilly Circus tube.

In the know
Laughs in the museum

The people behind **Leicester Square Theatre** (*see below*) also run the **Museum of Comedy** (*see p197*), which has its own performance space for stand-up and comedy-themed plays.

*Open times vary. **Admission** £5-£23.50. **Map** p165 L8.*

The Comedy Store is still the daddy of all the laff clubs. Seemingly as old as London itself (it actually started in 1979, above a strip club), the Store has been instrumental in the growth of alternative comedy, and still to this day hosts stunning shows most nights of the week. The live room was created specifically for stand-up and it shows, with 400 chairs hugging the stage to keep each show intimate. Veteran improvisers the Comedy Store Players perform every Wednesday and Sunday. Don't miss the raucous King Gong new-act night on the last Monday of the month.

Leicester Square Theatre

*6 Leicester Place, Leicester Square, WC2H 7BX (7734 2222, www. leicestersquaretheatre.com). Leicester Square tube. **Open** times vary. **Admission** £5-£50. **Map** p165 L8.*

Not strictly a comedy venue (it hosts music and theatre too), the Leicester Square Theatre's basement space is nonetheless home to enjoyable regular comedy nights and Edinburgh Fringe previews, while the 400-seat main house is a favourite room for big names (Stewart Lee, Jerry Sadowitz and Doug Stanhope often play long runs).

Up the Creek

*302 Creek Road, Greenwich, SE10 9SW (8858 4581, www.up-the-creek.com). Cutty Sark DLR. **Open** 7.30-11pm Wed, Thur; 8-11pm Fri; 7-11pm Sat, Sun. After-party 11pm-2am Fri, Sat. **Admission** £8-£10 Fri; £12-£14 Sat; £4-£7 Sun. After-party £5. **Map** p281 Aa14.*

Set up by the late and legendary alt-comedian Malcolm Hardee in the 1990s, this purpose-built comedy club is still one of the capital's best. The atmosphere is lively: it's less of a bearpit than it used to be, but the locals aren't afraid to torment comics – if a punter thinks of something funnier than what's being said on stage, they will shout it out. The Sunday Special (www.sundayspecial.co.uk) has a more relaxed vibe, cheap tickets and often features arena-filling names testing new material.

NIGHTLIFE

Performing Arts

From high-brow halls to basement dives, this city likes nothing better than putting on a show

Home to Shakespeare, Handel and Pinter (among others), London's theatres and concert halls were iconic centuries before Broadway had been conceived, and they remain some of the world's best and most famous performing arts venues. The city's great stages are a journey through the ages: there are plenty of grand old theatres – the Royal Opera House, the Old Vic, Theatre Royal Drury Lane, Theatre Royal Haymarket – that date back to Victorian times or earlier; the West End features a hodgepodge of ornate but slightly cramped theatres from the Edwardian era, while the National Theatre, Southbank Centre and Barbican are some of the world's most famous brutalist buildings. Away from the limelight, there are numerous venues in old pub back rooms and under railways arches playing host to everything from obscure musical revivals to pop-up operas.

Carmen, Royal Opera *p359*

Young dancer by Enzo Plazzotta, Covent Garden

Artistically, recent years have seen a subtle but sure drift towards artistic directors with a more avant-garde sensibility: witness Vicky Featherstone at the Royal Court, or Daniel Kramer at the ENO. Top ticket prices have soared, but at the bottom end, prices are at their cheapest in years, with theatres determined to be seen as accessible to all. The West End has been bolstered by a string of hit home-grown plays, many of which have gone on to conquer Broadway, notably JK Rowling's *Harry Potter and the Cursed Child*. It's two-way traffic, though, with London more-or-less dependent on New York for a supply of hit musicals; Lin-Manuel Miranda's *Hamilton* being the prime example.

CLASSICAL MUSIC & OPERA

London's classical scene has never looked or sounded more current, with the **Southbank Centre**, the **Barbican Centre** and **Kings Place** all working with strong programmes. Even the once-stuffy **Royal Opera House** has democratised both its building and its programme, following three years of renovations. And despite recent troubled times at **English National Opera**, the company has commissioned and produced top-class work from British composers, such as Ryan Wigglesworth's *The Winter's Tale* (2017) and Iain Bell's *Jack the Ripper: The Women of Whitechapel* (2019).

Tickets and information

Tickets for most classical and opera events are available direct from the venues, online or by phone. It's always advisable to book ahead. Several venues, such as the Barbican Centre and Southbank Centre, operate standby schemes, offering unsold tickets at cut-rate prices just before the show. They also have reduced-price tickets for under-26s.

Classical venues

Barbican Hall in the **Barbican Centre** is the home of the London Symphony Orchestra and boasts the best, albeit flat, orchestral acoustic in the capital; next best is the uneven acoustic of the **Royal Festival Hall**. The BBC Proms take place at the **Royal Albert Hall**, which is suitable for large orchestras and solo pianists, but not for medium-sized bands or Baroque music. Other colossi include **St Paul's Cathedral**, which hosts LSO concerts: it's a gorgeous venue, but – with a delay of over nine seconds and a transept rather than an auditorium – far from ideal.

The city is much better served at the smaller end of the scale. **Wigmore Hall** is the pre-eminent chamber venue and the only one (along with the Royal Opera House) to hold its own internationally; although a runner-up can be found at **Kings Place**. Meanwhile, **Cadogan Hall**, a former church, is the right size for Baroque music, though is curiously home to the mighty Royal Philharmonic Orchestra. The **Milton Court Concert Hall** at the Barbican is a 600-seat auditorium with a bright response, and the **Queen Elizabeth Hall** and **Purcell Room** at the Southbank Centre now have warmer acoustics thanks to refurbishment in 2017.

In addition to the major venues you can hear what tomorrow's classical music might sound like at the city's music schools, which stage regular concerts by pupils and visiting professionals. Check the websites of the **Royal College of Music** (7591 4300, www.rcm.ac.uk), the **Royal Academy of Music** (7873 7373, www.ram.ac.uk), the **Guildhall School of Music & Drama** (7628 2571, www.gsmd.ac.uk) and **Trinity Laban Conservatoire of Music & Dance** (8305 4444, www.trinitylaban.ac.uk). There's also a trend for top-class classical and contemporary classical music in relaxed – for which read 'alcohol friendly' – settings (*see right* Pub Classics).

Barbican Centre

Silk Street, the City, EC2Y 8DS (information 7638 4141, tickets 7638 8891, www.barbican.org.uk). Barbican tube or Moorgate tube/rail. **Box office** *10am-8pm Mon-Sat; 11am-8pm Sun.* **Tickets** *£10-£70.* **Map** *p212 Q6.*

Europe's largest multi-arts centre is famously tricky to navigate, so allow a little extra time to get to your seat. The programming remains as rich as ever, and the London Symphony Orchestra, with Sir Simon Rattle as music director, remains in residence. The BBC Symphony Orchestra also performs an annual series of concerts, including the weekend composer portrait Total Immersion, and

Pub Classics

Classical music, but without the frosty penguin suits

The vibrancy of London's classical music scene can hardly be doubted, but when you find yourself among reverent octogenarians at some London venues, you may feel you have to be on your best behaviour. Not so at the Orchestra of the Age of Enlightenment's popular series of **Night Shift** concerts (www.oae.co.uk/thenightshift), at which you'll see a far younger audience, perhaps belting out drinking songs by Purcell – with lyrics not fit for publication in a family guidebook. The idea is to gather a small group of performers in the relaxed setting of a pub – the **Old Queen's Head** (see p341) and **George Tavern** (373 Commercial Road, Stepney, E1 0LA, 7790 7335, www.thegeorgetavern.co.uk) are regular hosts – to perform canonical composers such as Mozart, Haydn and Handel. There's no shying away from difficult pieces: the professional and seriously talented performers trust that the combination of their skill and enthusiasm with the familiar setting will win new audiences to the classical music they love.

Arguably the pioneer of this informal classical scene is one Gabriel Prokofiev, grandson of the Russian composer. He founded **Nonclassical** (www.nonclassical.co.uk), which promotes new classical, electronic and experimental music in a combination of 'proper' classical venues (**Kings Place**, *see p346*), clubs (**XOYO**, *see p343*; **Village Underground**, *see p348*) and, yes, pubs: **The Victoria** (451 Queensbridge Road, Dalston, E8 3AS) is its flagship venue.

If you like it urban, check out contemporary music venue **Café Oto** (*see p349*), where Kammer Klang hosts a monthly cutting-edge classical night. Keep an eye out too for the summer concerts from **Multi-Story Orchestra** (www.multi-story.org.uk), keeping it real as part of the Bold Tendencies season at **Peckham Levels** (*see p342*).

there's a laudable amount of contemporary classical music. Beyond classical, programming falls into a wide range of genres from Sufi music to New York rock legends.

Cadogan Hall

5 Sloane Terrace, off Sloane Street, Chelsea, SW1X 9DQ (7730 4500, www.cadoganhall.com). Sloane Square tube. **Box office** *Non-performance days 10am-6pm Mon-Sat. Performance days 10am-8pm Mon-Sat; noon-6pm Sun.* **Tickets** *£15-£50.* **Map** *p124 H11.*

Jazz groups and rock bands have been attracted by the acoustics in this renovated former Christian Science church, but the programming at the austere yet comfortable 950-seat hall is dominated by classical. The Royal Philharmonic is resident; other orchestras also perform, and there's regular chamber music.

Kings Place

90 York Way, King's Cross, N1 9AG (7520 1490, www.kingsplace.co.uk). King's Cross-St Pancras tube/rail. **Box office** *noon-8pm Mon, Wed-Sat; noon-5pm Tue; noon-7pm Sun.* **Tickets** *free-£50.* **Map** *p194 M3.*

Once a lone pioneer in the revival of King's Cross, Kings Place suddenly finds itself part of the King's Cross Central cultural hub. Beneath seven office floors and a ground-floor restaurant-bar (with prized seats on the canal basin outside), the 415-seat main hall is a beauty, dominated by wood carved from a single, 500-year-old oak tree and ringed by invisible rubber pads that kill unwanted noise that might interfere with the immaculate acoustics. There's also a versatile second hall and a number of smaller rooms for workshops and lectures. The programming is tremendous and includes curated weeks featuring composers as wide-ranging as atonalist Arnold Schoenberg and jazzer Kit Downes. Other strands include chamber music and experimental classical, and there are spoken-word events too.

LSO St Luke's

UBS & LSO Music Education Centre, 161 Old Street, the City, EC1V 9NG (information 7490 3939, tickets 7638 8891, lso.co.uk/lso-st-lukes). Old Street tube/rail. **Box office** *(at the Barbican Centre) 10am-8pm Mon-Sat; 11am-8pm Sun.* **Tickets** *free-£40.* **Map** *p212 Q5.*

Built by Nicholas Hawksmoor in the 18th century, this Grade I-listed church was beautifully converted into a performance and rehearsal space by the LSO several years ago. The orchestra occasionally welcomes

A Capital Home for Classical Music

Will London finally get a music venue to match its cultural clout?

The need for a new, acoustically excellent venue for classical music in London was first brought to the public's attention by the announcement in 2015 that Sir Simon Rattle was to become musical director of the London Symphony Orchestra in 2017. The news came at the end of his sold-out Berlin Philharmonic concert series at the Barbican and Royal Festival Hall, which created a buzz of the rare kind that spreads even beyond classical music circles. Rattle had ruffled feathers by commenting that the acoustics of the Barbican Hall were merely 'serviceable' and pointing out that, due to size constraints and want of an organ, its stage could only accommodate 80 per cent of the orchestral repertoire. Rattle was right that neither the Barbican nor the Royal Festival Hall are a match for Berlin's Philharmonie or even Birmingham's Symphony Hall (built to accommodate Rattle and his sharply honed CBSO in 1991), but in an age of reduced funding for the arts, a brand new concert hall seemed a tall order.

Then, in 2017, the City of London Corporation announced that it would support the creation of a new world-class Centre for Music as a home for the London Symphony Orchestra and as a key element of its grander ambitions to create a 'Cultural Mile' in the City to rival the artistic powerhouses on the South Bank. The first designs for the 2,000-seater concert hall were revealed to the public in January 2019. The ziggurat building, designed by New York architects Diller Scofidio + Renfro, will sit on the current site of the Museum of London (which is moving to Smithfield; *see p227*), but will transform the unprepossessing roundabout to incorporate a pedestrian plaza and a southern entrance into the Barbican. As well as the concert hall, the centre will have four floors of commercial space, a restaurant and a more intimate top-floor venue for jazz and other performances. It is intended that the estimated cost of £288 million will all come from private donations.

the public for open rehearsals (book ahead); the more formal side of the programme takes in global sounds alongside classical music, including lunchtime concerts every Thursday that are broadcast on BBC Radio 3.

▶ *Intrigued by St Luke's obelisk spire? Hawksmoor also designed the brutal spike of Christ Church Spitalfields (see p259) and the mini-ziggurat atop St George's Bloomsbury (see p200).*

Milton Court
*1 Milton Street, the City, EC2Y 9BH (7628 2571, www.gsmd.ac.uk). Barbican tube or Moorgate tube/rail. **Box office** 10am-8pm Mon-Sat; 11am-8pm Sun. **Tickets** see website for details. **Map** p212 Q6.*

Located a stone's throw from the main external entrance to the Barbican, Milton Court is part of the Guildhall School of Music & Drama. Its main space is a 608-seat concert hall used by both the conservatoire and the

Barbican for performances of classical and contemporary music. Check the Barbican website for details of upcoming events.

Royal Albert Hall
*Kensington Gore, South Kensington, SW7 2AP (7589 8212, www.royalalberthall.com). South Kensington tube or bus 9, 10, 52, 360, 452. **Box office** 9am-9pm daily. **Tickets** £15-£275. **Map** p124 E10.*

In constant use since opening in 1871, with boxing matches, motor shows and Allen Ginsberg's 1965 International Poetry Incarnation among the headline events, the Royal Albert Hall continues to host a very broad programme. The classical side is dominated by the superb BBC Proms (*see p315*), which runs every night for two months in summer and sees a huge array of orchestras and other ensembles battling the difficult acoustics. It's well worth catching a concert that features the thunderous Grand Organ.

St James's Piccadilly
*197 Piccadilly, Piccadilly, W1J 9LL (7381 0441, www.sjp.org.uk). Piccadilly Circus tube. **Box office** 10am-5pm Mon-Sat; 10am-6pm performance days. **Tickets** free-£28. **Map** p142 K8.*

This community-spirited Wren church holds free 50-minute lunchtime recitals (1.10pm Mon, Wed, Fri; suggested donation £3.50) and

In the know
Pipe up

If the 9,999 pipes of the Royal Albert Hall's Grand Organ were laid end to end they would reach nine miles. The largest pipe is over 2ft in diameter and weighs nearly a tonne; the smallest is as wide as a drinking straw.

Royal Albert Hall

offers regular evening concerts covering a variety of musical styles.

St John's Smith Square

Smith Square, Westminster, SW1P 3HA (7222 1061, www.sjss.org.uk). Westminster tube. **Box office** *Non-performance days 10am-5pm Mon-Sat. Performance days 10am-6pm Mon-Fri.* **Tickets** *free-£28.* **Map** *p102 L11.*

St John's is a curiously shaped 18th-century church – it is said that the four-turret design was the result of Queen Anne's demand that architect Thomas Archer make it look like a footstool that she had kicked over – which hosts concerts most nights, as well as Thursday lunchtime recitals. Everything from symphony orchestras to solo recitals make the most of its good acoustics. Down in the crypt are two bars for interval drinks and the Footstool Restaurant.

St Martin-in-the-Fields

Trafalgar Square, Westminster, WC2N 4JH (7766 1100, www.stmartin-in-the-fields.org). Charing Cross tube/rail. **Box office** *In person 10am-5.30pm Mon, Tue; 10am-9pm Wed; 10am-10.30pm Thur-Sat. By phone 10am-5pm Mon-Sat.* **Tickets** *free-£30.* **Map** *p102 M8.*

One of the capital's most amiable venues, St Martin's hosts populist performances of the likes of Bach, Mozart and Vivaldi by candlelight, jazz in the crypt's improved café and lunchtime recitals (1pm Mon, Tue, Fri) from young musicians. There's a fine atmosphere in the beautifully restored interior. For more on the church, *see p104.*

Southbank Centre

Belvedere Road, South Bank, SE1 8XX (3879 9555, www.southbankcentre. co.uk). Embankment tube or Waterloo tube/rail. **Box office** *In person 10am-8pm daily. By phone 9am-8pm daily.* **Tickets** *£7-£75.* **Map** *p80 N9.*

The centrepiece of the cluster of cultural venues collectively known as the Southbank Centre is the 2,500-seat **Royal Festival Hall**, which was renovated acoustically and externally to the tune of £90 million back in 2007; the neighbouring 900-seat **Queen Elizabeth Hall** and attached 365-seat **Purcell Room** have also been given some TLC and reopened in 2018. All three programme a wide variety of events – spoken word, jazz, rock and pop gigs – but classical is very well represented. The RFH has four resident orchestras (the London Philharmonic and Philharmonia Orchestras, the London

Sinfonietta and the Orchestra of the Age of Enlightenment), and hosts music from medieval motets to Messiaen via Beethoven and Elgar. Beneath this main hall, facing the foyer bar, a stage puts on hundreds of free concerts each year.

Wigmore Hall

36 Wigmore Street, Marylebone, W1U 2BP (information 7258 8200, tickets 7935 2141, www.wigmore-hall.org.uk). Bond Street tube. **Box office** *Non-performance days 10am-7pm Mon-Sat; 10am-2pm Sun. Performance days 10am-7pm daily.* **Tickets** *free-£35.* **Map** *p142 J6.*

Built in 1901 as the display hall for Bechstein pianos, this world-renowned, 550-seat concert venue has perfect acoustics for the 460 concerts that take place each year. Music from the classical and romantic periods are mainstays, usually performed by major classical stars to an intense audience, but under artistic director John Gilhooly there has been a broadening in the remit: more Baroque and jazz (with heavyweights like Brad Mehldau), including late-night gigs. Monday lunchtime recitals are broadcast live on BBC Radio 3.

▶ *The nearby Steinway showroom (44 Marylebone Lane, Marylebone, W1U 2DB, 7487 3391, steinway.co.uk/latest-news/concert-schedule) hosts regular recitals.*

Opera venues

In addition to the two big venues listed below, look out for performances at **Cadogan Hall** (*see p355*); summer's **Opera Holland Park** (*see p313*); sporadic appearances by **English Touring Opera** (englishtouringopera.org.uk); and much promising work, often directed by big names, at the city's music schools. The **Linbury**, downstairs at the Royal Opera House, is good for more experimental work. A small but lively fringe opera scene has sprung up, with **Hampstead Garden Opera** (www.hgo.org.uk) now operating from Jackson's Lane theatre (269A Archway Road, N6 5AA, 8341 4421); **Pop-Up Opera** (www.popupopera.co.uk) tours taking in weird and wonderful venues; **OperaUpClose** (www.operaupclose.com) occasionally caught up west at the Soho Theatre (*see p367*); **Charles Court Opera** (www.charlescourtopera.com) doing fine operetta in various small theatres; and the annual **Tête à Tête** (www.tete-a-tete.org.uk), which claims to be 'the world's largest festival of new opera', (it programmes 80 performances over three weeks), now settled in King's Cross.

Coliseum

Coliseum

St Martin's Lane, Covent Garden, WC2N 4ES (7845 9300, www.eno.org). Leicester Square tube or Charing Cross tube/rail. **Box office** *Non-performance days 10am-6pm Mon-Sat. Performance days 10am-8pm Mon-Sat.* **Tickets** *£12-£155.* **Map** *p181 M8.*

It's been a tough few years for the **English National Opera** (ENO). Notionally the hipper and more accessible of London's two principal opera companies (with all works performed in English), it has seriously struggled with its finances, partly as a result of a reduction in subsidy while trying to lower ticket prices. Still, there's plenty of reasons to think things are looking up: in 2017 it was taken out of special funding measures, suggesting that its willingness to open the doors of the London Coliseum – London's biggest theatre – to musicals has paid off. Typically there's now an ENO-produced revival with a starry cast running for a few weeks in the spring, and an outside production in the summer. These run during dark periods, rather than replacing the usual programming, which has remained largely exemplary despite the money woes. Appointed to the artistic directorship in 2017, American Daniel Kramer has kept the ship steady, with a mix of non-traditional takes on the canon and more overtly challenging works. Keeping the prices down has remained a priority, and plans have been announced to diversify the opera's overwhelmingly white chorus.

► *The £20 Secret Seat offer allows you to book an unallocated seat online – the secret lies in its location in the auditorium. Wherever it turns out to be, your seat will always be worth at least £30.*

Royal Opera House

Bow Street, Covent Garden, WC2E 9DD (7304 4000, www.roh.org.uk). Covent Garden tube. **Box office** *10am-8pm Mon-Sat.* **Tickets** *£4-£200.* **Map** *p181 M7.*

Home to both the Royal Opera and the Royal Ballet, the ROH was restored to the ranks of the world's great opera houses thanks to a massive turn-of-the-century refurb. But it went even further with the recent £27-million 'Open Up' redevelopment, which aimed to combat opera's eternally stuffy image by inviting the public to hang out in the building's enhanced public spaces and to enjoy free taster performances. Although it's not had the money worries of its near neighbour the English National Opera, it undeniably has a much more cautious programme. Under the youthful head of opera, Oliver Mears, there were only five new productions in its 2018-19 season, among a slew of safe bets. Still, it pretty much does what you expect a nation's flagship opera company to do: famous shows, big name performers and an admirable focus on opening up the building to new audiences. There's more intimate, experimental work on offer in the basement **Linbury Theatre**.

► *It's not just singing at the Opera House: the Royal Ballet is also based here; see p369.*

Katye Kabanova, Royal Opera

THEATRE

For many people, 'theatre' in London means musicals – and musicals in London are booming, with audiences up eight per cent year on year in 2018. Of late, homegrown musicals have been rather overtaken by Broadway imports: Lin-Manuel Miranda's visionary rap musical *Hamilton* opened at the tail end of 2017 in the lavishly restored Victoria Palace Theatre to a storm of acclaim, while US musicals *Come from Away*, *9 to 5*, *Waitress*, *On Your Feet* and *Dear Evan Hansen* are all on the schedule for 2019, an almost unprecedented influx.

But to the discerning theatregoer the real story lies away from the West End: new plays are what the Brits do best, most of them crafted in London's numerous subsidised theatres, the **National Theatre** (*see p360*) being the most prominent. The sector itself has experienced considerable change of late: once almost entirely run by white men, theatres that have historically aspired towards diversity, but rarely actually achieved it, have been shaken up by high-profile appointments like Kwame Kwei-Armah at the **Young Vic** or Lynette Linton at the **Bush Theatre**. The **Old Vic** has transformed itself under heavyweight director Matthew Warchus, with an eclectic and busy programme that finds room for plenty of big names, but with a much more diverse and experimental line-up than in years past.

On a smaller scale, Off-West End houses such as the **Young Vic** and the **Almeida** continue to produce some of London's most exciting, best-value theatre – much of which moves on to the West End. The **Donmar Warehouse** traditionally lures high-profile film stars to perform at its tiny Earlham Street home, while the **Barbican Centre** (*see p354*) programmes visually exciting and physically expressive work from around the world.

Theatre districts

In strictly geographical terms, the **West End** refers to London's traditional theatre district, a busy area bounded by Shaftesbury Avenue, Drury Lane, the Strand and the Haymarket. Most major musicals and big-money dramas run here, alongside transfers of successful smaller-scale shows. However, the 'West End' appellation is now routinely applied to major theatres elsewhere in town, including a couple of big commercial theatres next to Victoria, the Old Vic (near Waterloo), plus subsidised venues such as the Barbican (in the City), the National Theatre (on the South Bank), the Royal

Court (Sloane Square) and Shakespeare's Globe (Bankside).

Off-West End denotes theatres with smaller budgets and smaller capacities. These venues, many of them sponsored or subsidised, push the creative envelope with new writing, often brought to life by the best young acting and directing talent. The Almeida and Donmar Warehouse offer elegantly produced shows with the odd big star, while the likes of the Bush and Theatre Royal Stratford East bring bold new writing to less central boroughs.

The fringe

The best places to catch next-generation talent include Battersea's **Theatre 503** (503 Battersea Park Road, SW11 3BW, 7978 7040, theatre503.com), above the Latchmere pub. The theatre above the **Finborough** (118 Finborough Road, SW10 9ED, 01223 357851, www.finboroughtheatre.co.uk), a pub in Earl's Court, attracts national critics with its small but perfectly formed revivals of forgotten classics. Other venues worth investigating include the **Yard**, a 130-seat venue near the Olympic Park, made from recycled materials and playing to a house of local hipsters; the **Southwark Playhouse** (77-85 Newington Causeway, Southwark, SE1 6BD, 7407 0234, www.southwarkplayhouse. co.uk); and the **Menier Chocolate Factory** (53 Southwark Street, Southwark, SE1 1RU, 7378 1713, www.menierchocolatefactory. com), which, like the **Union Theatre** (Old Union Arches, 229 Union Street, Southwark, SE1 0LR, 7261 9876, www.uniontheatre.biz), has a knack for programming musicals that thrive up-close.

Buying tickets

If there's a specific show you want to see, aim to book ahead, especially if there's a risk of it selling out. If possible, always try to use the theatre or show's own website, which should minimise the sorts of booking fees that come with agents such as **Ticketmaster** (0333 321 9999, www.ticketmaster.co.uk). Shop around: different agencies offer different prices and discounts.

If you're more flexible about your choice of show or are happy to queue, consider buying from the **tkts** booth (the Lodge, Leicester Square, Soho, WC2H 7DE, www.tkts.co.uk), which sells tickets for big shows at much-reduced rates, either on the day or up to a week in advance. It opens at 10am (11am on Sundays); you can check which shows are available on the website. Before buying, be sure you're at the correct booth, in a stand-alone building on the south side of Leicester Square – the square is ringed with other

Top 20

🖤 National Theatre

*South Bank, SE1 9PX (7452 3000, www. nationaltheatre.org.uk). Embankment or Southwark tube, or Waterloo tube/ rail. **Box office** In person 9.30am-11pm Mon-Sat. By phone 9.30am-8pm Mon-Sat. **Tickets** £15-£52. **Map** p80 N9.*

A still-startling jewel of brutalist design, the National is surely the world's greatest theatre. Nobody would say it gets everything right, but it is worthy of a pilgrimage for anybody remotely interested in the arts. Having passed its 50th anniversary in 2013, the National completed a major programme of expansion and upgrades, which resulted in new restaurants, a new bar, a new main entrance on the riverside and the revamping of the old Cottesloe Theatre into the larger and more high-tech Dorfman. It then waved goodbye to its hugely appreciated artistic director, Nicholas Hytner, who had been in the post since 2003. It was the end of a certain sort of golden age: Hytner rescued the NT from the doldrums, launching endless hit transfers to the West End, got Travelex to sponsor tickets to bring down the prices, and adroitly balanced the programme to mix big, crowd-pleasing stuff by Shakespeare and household names like Alan Bennett with some startling new work and some properly obscure rediscoveries. His landmark successes – Alan Bennett's

The History Boys and War Horse, both of which went on to become successful movies – showed that the state-subsidised home of British theatre could turn out quality drama at a profit, furnishing an array of West End hits.

Successor Rufus Norris has had a slightly more difficult time of it. In the first few months of his tenure, the high-powered chief executive, Tessa Ross departed; big West End money-spinners War Horse and The Curious Incident of the Dog in the Night-Time closed, and the theatre's Arts Council subsidy fell. The press were also unkind, criticising Norris for everything from staging work that was too weird to putting on too much new writing.

Since then, attitudes have mellowed, and Norris has proved that he is able to programme more avant-garde new work, while still pulling in big-name actors and directors. Alongside top-notch Shakespeare, reworked foreign classics and British revivals are agenda-setting productions that attract a slightly younger audience: witness Ivo Van Hove's reworking of classic '70s film Network starring Breaking Bad's Bryan Cranston in 2017, or Martin Crimp's controversially explicit When We Have Sufficiently Tortured Each Other, directed by Katie Mitchell and starring Cate Blanchett in 2019. Arguably the biggest hit, however, has been the marvellous big-budget revival of Steven Sondheim's Follies, directed by Dominic Cooke, which had its second run in spring 2019.

The NT's next big headache will be to find a new backer for its £15 ticket promotions, when Travelex's sponsorship concludes at the end of 2019. In the mean time, the Friday Rush initiative continues (see below), as do the free River Stage performances held outside the National Theatre during the summer. Despite all the changes to the building and the personnel, in many ways the real story of the theatre over the last decade has taken place off-site. Its NT Live programme of live screenings of plays to cinemas has brought the National's repertoire into every town in the country. It's an astonishing, game-changing achievement that we're probably still digesting. There are concerns about what it means for regional and touring theatre, but at the moment the NT is 'national' in a way it never truly was before.

In the know
Friday Rush

At 1pm each Friday, a small number of £20 tickets for the next week's performances in the Olivier, Lyttelton and Dorfman are released for purchase online.

ticket brokers, where the seats are worse and the prices higher.

Many West End theatres hold back a selection of day-seats for each performance, available at a knock-down price to the first customers there in person when the box office opens (usually 10am – but get there much earlier for anything sold out or popular).

Some theatres elect to distribute their day-seats by other means: the phone app **TodayTix** is growing in popularity as a means of dissemination, while *Hamilton* allocates seats by daily lottery.

Watch out, too, for cut-price Travelex tickets and the Friday Rush at the **National** (*see p361*), for 'groundling' tickets (standing) at the **Globe** (*see p363*) and for 'Secret Seats' at the **Coliseum** (*see p358*).

Major theatres

The **Barbican Centre** (*see p354*) continues to cherry-pick exciting and eclectic theatre companies from around the globe. Watch out, too, for imaginatively leftfield family-friendly theatre and installations during the school holidays.

Old Vic

The Cut, Waterloo, SE1 8NB (0844 871 7628, www.oldvictheatre.com). Southwark tube or Waterloo tube/rail. **Box office** *In person Non-performance days Mon-Fri 10am-6pm. Performance days 10am-7pm Mon-Sat. By phone 9am-7.30pm Mon-Fri; 9am-2pm Sat; 9.30am-2pm Sun.* **Tickets** *£10-£90.* **Map** *p80 O10.*

Matthew Warchus is a seriously heavyweight director with a bold, eclectic approach to serious programming. His USP is new

musical work: his brilliant *Groundhog Day* had its tryout run at the Vic in 2016 before heading off to conquer Broadway, and Conor McPherson's universally acclaimed *Girl from the North Country* (2017), based around the music and lyrics of Bob Dylan, transferred to the West End before heading to New York in 2018.

Open Air Theatre

Inner Circle, Regent's Park, Marylebone, NW1 4NR (0333 400 3562, www. openairtheatre.com). Baker Street tube. **Box office** *Non-performance days 11am-6pm daily. Performance days 11am-8pm daily. By phone 9am-9pm daily.* **Tickets** *£18-£60.* **Map** *pull out map H4.*

This stunning alfresco theatre made its name as a house of Shakespeare, but under current artistic director Timothy Sheader musicals are much more the thing – its gritty revival of *Jesus Christ Superstar* was a big hit – combined with the odd bleak American drama and, yes, occasional Shakespeare still.

▶ *If you don't want to bring a picnic, book one at the venue, which can be pre-ordered with reserved seating (£49.50 for two people). Alternatively, good-value, tasty food can be bought at the Garden Café.*

Royal Court Theatre

Sloane Square, Chelsea, SW1W 8AS (7565 5000, royalcourttheatre.com). Sloane Square tube. **Box office** *10am-6pm Mon-Sat.* **Tickets** *£12-£40.* **Map** *p124 H12.*

From John Osborne's *Look Back in Anger*, staged in the theatre's opening year of 1956, to the more recent likes of Jez Butterworth, Simon Stephens and debbie tucker green, the emphasis at the Royal Court has always been on new voices in British and international

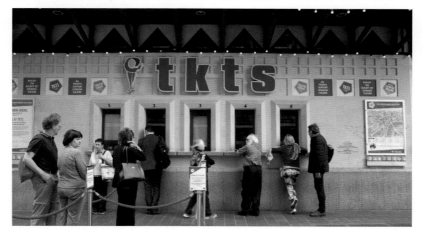

💚 Shakespeare's Globe

21 New Globe Walk, Bankside, SE1 9DT (information 7902 1400, tickets 7401 9919, www.shakespearesglobe.com). Southwark tube or London Bridge tube/rail. **Box office** *10am-6pm daily & before events.* **Tickets** *£15-£100.* **Map** *p80 P8.*

Back in the 1990s, Sam Wanamaker – an American actor and director – dreamt a big dream: why not recreate the theatre where Shakespeare first staged many of his plays, using the original methods and materials? The amazing thing is that in 1997 this flight of fancy became, with a great deal of hard work and determination, a fabulously entertaining reality. Concessions were made along the way – the theatre is some 750 feet (229 metres) from the site of the original – but Wanamaker's conception resulted in an extraordinarily historically accurate facsimile, perched on the bank of the Thames, where Shakespeare is still performed in a theatre as close to the original Globe as could be imagined. But this is far from being a museum exhibit; the Globe is one of the best theatres in the UK and is also one of the most affordable, with tickets for the open-air, standing-room pit costing just £5 each.

After successful tenures as artistic director by Mark Rylance and Dominic Dromgoole, Emma Rice's time in the post was marked by popular success but clashes

PERFORMING ARTS

In the know
The real deal

The site of the original Globe is marked by a partial ring of stones in the ground on the south side of Park Street, should hardcore Shakespeare fans wish to seek it out. For guided tours of the Globe, *see p88*.

with a tradition-loving board who hated her extensive use of electric light and sound. She duly departed in 2018 after just two years at the top to be replaced by Michelle Terry, an acclaimed actor with a scholarly interest in Shakespeare. Terry has eschewed direction in favour of an actor-manager role and has committed the Globe to gender-, colour- and disability-blind casting, which has resulted in some intriguing productions of plays such as *As You Like it* and *Dr Faustus*.

Open April to October, the open-air main space is stunning, but the Globe's indoor Jacobean theatre, the **Sam Wanamaker Playhouse** (completed in 2014), is arguably even more atmospheric. The 340-seat space is made entirely out of wood, exquisitely decorated and lit by candles, just as the Blackfriars theatre that Shakespeare and his King's Men troupe moved to in 1609 would have been. It has a more eclectic programme than the outdoor space and comes into its own during the winter months.

Harry Potter and the Cursed Child

theatre. Since Vicky Featherstone took over as artistic director (the first woman in the role) in 2013, the shows have got artier, though there's still room for established names, including the legendary Caryl Churchill. Expect to find punchy, socially engaged new work by first-time and international playwrights upstairs, and bigger, state-of-the-nation works by household names downstairs.

Royal Shakespeare Company
01789 331111, www.rsc.org.uk. **Box office** *By phone 10am-6pm Mon-Sat.* **Tickets** *£12-£70.*

Britain's most famous theatre company hasn't had an official London base since it quit the Barbican in 2002 and it doesn't seem to be in a hurry to find itself one, with its temporary venue of choice being... the Barbican. Its only permanent London showing is the musical *Matilda (see p365)*, still packing 'em in the best part of a decade after it opened, but each year there's a season of stellar Shakespeare in the capital: the likes of Simon Russell Beale in *The Tempest* or a tetralogy of the Roman plays.

Long-runners & musicals

It's a perilous task predicting which West End shows will run and which will close: homegrown musicals, in particular, have not performed well in recent years. The obvious exceptions are two very different tales of oppressed but gifted children (*Matilda* and *Harry Potter and the Cursed Child*), which pretty much represent the pinnacle of British commercial theatre in their own way: the former a sassy, inventive musical take on Dahl from comic Tim Minchin and the RSC; the latter the visually stunning, two-part, eighth adventure for JK Rowling's wizard Harry Potter by super-producer

Sonia Friedman. Other home-grown successes are *Everybody's Talking About Jamie* (www.everybodystalkingaboutjamie. co.uk), the tale of a wannabe teenage drag queen, and *Tina* (www.tinathemusical.com), which tells the life story of Tina Turner. But, these aside, it seems you have to have been a hit on Broadway first in order to make it big in London: Andrew Lloyd Webber's *School of Rock* (uk.schoolofrockthemusical. com) received his best reviews since the '80s but only after cracking Broadway first. And stateside hits *Come From Away* (comefromaway.co.uk), *Waitress* (waitressthemusical.co.uk) and *Dear Evan Hansen* (dearevanhansen.com/london/) all received their West End premieres in 2019, following on the heels of all-conquering *Hamilton*, which has been here since 2017.

Other long-running musicals that are worthy of your time are the hilarious and irreverent *Book of Mormon*, high-camp *Mamma Mia!* (mamma-mia. com), perennially popular *Wicked* (wickedthemusical.co.uk) and Disney's *The Lion King* (thelionking.co.uk) – slightly patchy but buoyed by the odd jaw-dropping visual sequence. *Les Misérables* continues its indefatigable run, unbroken since the 1980s, with *Phantom of the Opera* at Her Majesty's Theatre (thephantomoftheopera. com) not far behind it.

And it's not just successful musicals that hang about: there are also wild cards like *The Play that Goes Wrong*, a lo-fi fringe comedy that's now been resident in the West End for years, and the creaky but genuinely unsettling *The Woman in Black* (www.thewomaninblack.com), which has been around for even longer. But you'd have to set the time-machine dial 30 years further into history to catch the première of the weary but never-bowed *Mousetrap* (www.the-mousetrap.co.uk), the Agatha Christie drawing-room whodunnit that has been running continuously in the West End since 1952.

The Book of Mormon
Prince of Wales Theatre, Coventry Street, Soho, W1D 6AS (0844 482 5110, www. bookofmormonlondon.com). Piccadilly Circus tube. **Box office** *10am-8pm Mon-Sat.* **Tickets** *£20-£150.* **Map** *p165 L8.*

South Park creators Trey Parker and Matt Stone's smash musical about the absurdities of Mormonism is not as shocking as you might expect. There's lots of swearing and close-to-the-bone jokes, but beneath it all, this is a big-hearted affair that pays note-perfect homage to the spirit and sounds of Broadway's golden age. And it's very, very funny.

Hamilton

Victoria Palace Theatre, 126 Victoria Street, Victoria, SW1E 5EA (0844 248 5138, www. hamiltonmusical.com/london). Victoria tube. **Box office** *10am-5.30pm Mon-Wed, Fri; 10am-12.30pm, 3-5.15pm Thur, Sat.* **Tickets** *£37.50-£190.* **Map** *p102 J11.*

From the moment it opened in November 2017, Lin-Manuel Miranda's Broadway-devouring rap musical about Alexander Hamilton, the first secretary of the US Treasury, has dominated the West End. Much has been made of its diverse casting and sociological import, but the fact is that 'Hamilton' is, first and foremost, a ferociously enjoyable show. Miranda – who wrote everything – understands what mainstream audiences like about musical theatre and hip hop, and he has managed to craft a brilliant hybrid that combines big emotions and big melodies with funny, technically virtuoso storytelling. The best musical of our generation.

Harry Potter and the Cursed Child

Palace Theatre, 113 Shaftesbury Avenue, Soho, W1D 5AY (0844 412 4656, www. harrypottertheplay.com/uk). Leicester Square tube. **Box office** *In person 10am-6pm Mon-Sat.* **Tickets** *£15-£65 (1 part); £30-£130 (both parts).* **Map** *p165 L7.*

The final adventure in JK Rowling's Harry Potter series isn't a book or a film, but a monumentally ambitious two-part London stage play, written by Jack Thorne in collaboration with Rowling. John Tiffany's production is phenomenal, as close as you'll ever get to physically stepping into Harry's magical world – small wonder it won a record *nine* Olivier Awards in 2017. Of course, it's sold

out till the last trumpet blows, but you don't need magic to get in – there's a weekly online sale at 1pm on Fridays (the Friday Forty) and the returns queue is worth a shot.

Matilda the Musical

Cambridge Theatre, 32-34 Earlham Street, Covent Garden, WC2H 9HU (020 7087 7745, www.matildathemusical.com). Covent Garden tube or Charing Cross tube/rail. **Box office** *In person 10am-7.30pm Mon-Sat; 10am-3pm Sun.* **Tickets** *£20-£122.50.* **Map** *p181 M7.*

Adapted from Roald Dahl's riotous children's novel, with songs by superstar Aussie comedian Tim Minchin, this RSC transfer received rapturous reviews on its first outing in Stratford-upon-Avon and has been going strong ever since, winning multiple Olivier awards.

Les Misérables

Queen's Theatre, 51 Shaftesbury Avenue, Soho, W1D 6BA (0844 482 5151, www.lesmis. com). Leicester Square or Piccadilly Circus tube. **Box office** *In person 10am-7.45pm Mon-Sat. By phone 10am-8pm Mon-Sat.* **Tickets** *£12.50-£97.25.* **Map** *p165 L8.*

The RSC's version of Boublil and Schönberg's musical first came to the London stage in 1985. Having recently had its score reworked and gently nudged out of the '80s – and receiving a massive commercial shot in the arm from the successful 2012 film version – it looks like it's going to stick around for a good while longer. It's not the freshest show in town, but the voices remain lush, the revolutionary sets are film-fabulous, and the lyrics and score (based on Victor Hugo's novel) will be considerably less trivial than whatever's on next door.

The Play that Goes Wrong

Duchess Theatre, 3-5 Catherine Street, Covent Garden, WC2B 5LA (0330 333 4810, www.theplaythatgoeswrong. com). Charing Cross tube/rail. **Tickets** *£20-£65.* **Map** *p181 N7.*

Is it a classic British comedy in the lineage of *Fawlty Towers*? Or a low-budget rip-off of Michael Frayn's immortal backstage farce *Noises Off*? Maybe a little of both, but, whatever the case, it's impossible not to be delighted by the success of this play, which began life at the tiny Old Red Lion theatre pub and has now been sitting pretty in the West End since 2014. It even has its own seasonal spin-off, *Peter Pan Goes Wrong*.

Off-West End theatres

Almeida

Almeida Street, Islington, N1 1TA (information 7288 4900, tickets 7359 4404, www.almeida.co.uk). Angel tube or Highbury & Islington tube/rail. **Box office** *10am-7.30pm Mon-Sat.* **Tickets** *£10-£38.*

Since Rupert Goold took over as artistic director in 2013, the Almeida has been reinvented from something rather chintzy to London's hippest theatre, the leftfield programming doing nothing to staunch a seemingly endless stream of acclaimed shows that headed into the West End: *King Charles III, Oresteia, Hamlet, Mary Stuart* and *Summer and Smoke* are all recent transfer hits. The secrets of the Almeida's success are many: Goold's sheer audacity ranks up there, while associate director Robert Icke is probably the most exciting director of his generation. A dud is incredibly rare here: if you can bag a ticket, you should go.

Battersea Arts Centre (BAC)

Lavender Hill, Battersea, SW11 5TN (7223 2223, www.bac.org.uk). Clapham Common tube, Clapham Junction rail/Overground or bus 77, 77A, 345. **Box office** *In person 10am-6pm Mon-Sat. By phone 10am-10pm Mon-Sat.* **Tickets** *£5-£25; pay what you can.*

Housed in the old Battersea Town Hall, the forward-thinking BAC hit the headlines for the wrong reasons in 2015, when it suffered a major fire. The main performance space, the Grand Hall, reopened after restoration in 2018, with a line-up of shows that continues to promote quirky, fun and physical theatre from young companies and from more-established names pursuing new directions.

Bridge Theatre

3 Potters Fields Park, Bermondsey, SE1 2SG (tickets 0333 320 0051, bridgetheatre.co.uk). London Bridge tube/rail. **Box office** *9am-9pm daily.* **Tickets** *£15-£90.* **Map** *p80 S9.*

In 2017 Sir Nicholas Hytner (of National Theatre fame; *see p360*) and Nick Starr opened the new 900-seat Bridge Theatre close to Tower Bridge. It was the first commercial theatre of its size to open in London for decades, and it provides the comfortable seats, plentiful loos, delicious food and, above all, proper new writing that the West End so conspicuously lacks. It is yet to stage a really outstanding transfer-worthy production, but its aim to commission and produce new work attracts big-name playwrights and actors, including Alan Bennett, Martin McDonagh, Rory Kinnear and Simon Russell Beale.

Donmar Warehouse

41 Earlham Street, Covent Garden, WC2H 9LX (3282 3808, www.donmarwarehouse. com). Covent Garden or Leicester Square tube. **Box office** *10am-6pm Mon-Sat.* **Tickets** *£7.50-£35.* **Map** *p181 M7.*

It may be central London's smallest major theatre, but the Donmar's influence outstrips its size many times over. Following on from Sam Mendes and Michael Grandage, boss Josie Rourke made it her mission to steer the Donmar away from boutique productions of classics with big-name celebrities – though those are still here – and aim for a livelier, younger programme that is orientated more towards new writing. Michael Longhurst takes over as artistic director in 2019.

Gate Theatre

Prince Albert, 11 Pembridge Road, Notting Hill Gate, W11 3HQ (7229 0706, www. gatetheatre.co.uk). Notting Hill Gate tube. **Box office** *By phone 10am-6pm Mon-Fri.* **Tickets** *£10-£20.* **Map** *p297 B8.*

A doll's house of a theatre (it has only 70 seats), with rickety wooden chairs, the Gate is the only producing theatre in London dedicated to international work.

Kiln Theatre

269 Kilburn High Road, Kilburn, NW6 7JR (information 7372 6611, tickets 7328 1000, kilntheatre.com). Kilburn tube. **Box office** *In person from 10am Mon-Sat; 1hr before performance Sun. By phone 10am-8pm Mon-Sat; 2-8pm Sun.* **Tickets** *£9-£29.*

A vibrant one-stop-shop for culture in north London, the venue formerly known as the Tricycle underwent an ambitious refurbishment in 2017 and was controversially rebranded as the Kiln Theatre on reopening in 2018. The name is a homage to its home in Kilburn and a signal of its aim to be a crucible for new work that'll get the local community excited. The current artistic director is Indhu Rubasingham, who's steered the venue through its recent transformation. Late 2018 saw an ambitious (and not altogether successful) adaptation of Zadie Smith's hit novel *White Teeth*.

Lyric Hammersmith

Lyric Square, King Street, Hammersmith, W6 0QL (8741 6850, www.lyric.co.uk). Hammersmith tube. **Box office** *9am-6pm Mon-Sat.* **Tickets** *£10-£40.*

The real heart of the Lyric lies with experimental and avant-garde work, as epitomised by outgoing artistic director Sean Holmes. The two-storey extension to the hybrid modern/Victorian theatre adds drama, dance and recording studios, a new café and bar, and even a cinema. Holmes brought writers back into the building plus neglected modern classics and new plays alongside the cutting-edge physical and devised work. His replacement is Rachel O'Riordan.

Park Theatre

Clifton Terrace, Finsbury Park, N4 3JP (7870 6876, www.parktheatre.co.uk). Finsbury Park tube/rail. **Box office** *In person 3-8pm Mon-Wed, Fri; noon-8pm Thur, Sat; also from the café. By phone 10am-6pm Mon-Sat.* **Tickets** *£12.50-£26.50.*

Opened in 2013 in a former office building, this non-subsidised venue offers a busy off-West End programme across two spaces (a 200-seat main house and 90-seat studio), with a pleasant bar-café on the ground floor in which to chew over what you've seen. The shows are a mixed bag, but the theatre has certainly won some influential followers, including Ian McKellan who performed a special one-man fundraiser show for the theatre in the summer of 2017.

Soho Theatre

21 Dean Street, Soho, W1D 3NE (7478 0100, www.sohotheatre.com). Tottenham Court Road tube. **Box office** *9am-9pm Mon-Sat.* **Tickets** *£9-£35.* **Map** *p165 L7.*

Since it opened in 2000, the Soho Theatre has built a terrific reputation – with excellence across three inter-related genres: cabaret, comedy and, yes, theatre. It attracts a younger, hipper crowd than most London spaces, and brings on aspiring writers and youth theatre companies. After a few years finding its feet, it has settled in as a producer of some of the best work to go to the Edinburgh Fringe, and has scored a notable success by launching the career of *Fleabag* creator Phoebe Waller-Bridge. In many ways the biggest draw is comedy: British and international talent has included Russell Brand, Michael McIntyre, Kristen Schaal and Doug Stanhope. The hard lines, low stage

and packed table seating favour comedy over cabaret in the theatre's basement space, but the Soho consistently books outstanding talent from the international cabaret circuit for the room, from Meow Meow and Caroline Nin to London's own David Hoyle, Bourgeois & Maurice and the Tiger Lillies.

Theatre Royal Stratford East

Gerry Raffles Square, Stratford, E15 1BN (8534 0310, www.stratfordeast.com). Stratford tube/Overground/rail/DLR. **Box office** *In person & by phone 10am-6pm Mon-Sat.* **Tickets** *£8-£26.*

In the '50s and '60s Theatre Royal Stratford East was arguably the most influential theatre in London, thanks to the presence of the visionary Joan Littlewood and her Theatre Workshop. These days its output tends to send fewer shockwaves. This is a community theatre, with many shows written, directed and performed by black or Asian artists. However, the arrival of artistic director Nadia Fall has caused a stir. She's scrapped the venue's popular Caribbean café, cut its focus on musical theatre development, and programmed an ambitious set of shows that aim to get audiences in from across the city.

Wilton's Music Hall

1 Graces Alley, off Ensign Street, Whitechapel, E1 8JB (7702 2789, www.wiltons.org.uk). Aldgate East or Tower Hill tube. **Box office** *11am-6pm Mon-Fri.* **Tickets** *£6-£25.*

One of London's last surviving examples of the giant music halls that flourished in the mid 19th century, Wilton's once entertained the masses with acts ranging from Chinese performing monkeys to acrobats, and from contortionists to opera singers. It was here that the can-can first scandalised London. Roughly 150 years later, Wilton's is Grade II*-listed but again operating as a theatre, offering an atmospheric stage for everything from immersive theatre to situation-specific performances of Bach, cinema screenings and magic shows. There's major ongoing restoration, but the programme remains as packed as ever – and the bar is lively.

The Yard

Unit 2A, Queen's Yard, White Post Lane, Hackney, E9 5EN (3111 0570, www.theyardtheatre.co.uk). **Box office** *times vary; see the website for details.* **Tickets** *prices vary.*

Made from recycled materials, and sporting a great, ever-changing bar and kitchen, the Hackney Wick venue is not only a fantastic place to hang out, but a great place to catch leftfield talent before anybody else does. It's even scored a transfer to the National in 2015 with zero-hours contracts drama *Beyond Caring.*

Young Vic

66 The Cut, Waterloo, SE1 8LZ (7922 2922, www.youngvic.org). Waterloo tube/ rail. **Box office** *10am-6pm Mon-Sat.* **Tickets** *£10-£57.* **Map** *p80 O9.*

As the name suggests, this Vic has more youthful bravura than its older sister up the road, and draws a younger crowd, who pack out the open-air balcony and its restaurant and bar on the weekends. They come to see classics with a modern edge, new writing with an international flavour and collaborations with leading companies. Recent winners have included Matthew Lopez's haunting, ambitious *The Inheritance* about the post-AIDS generation, which transferred to the West End in 2018. That year also saw the homecoming of Kwame Kwei-Armah as artistic director. He hit the ground running with a large-scale revival of Danai Gurira's off-West End success *The Convert* and the promise of a collaboration with Idris Elba (of *Luther* fame) later in 2019.

Puppet & children's theatres

Little Angel Theatre

14 Dagmar Passage, Cross Street, Islington, N1 2DN (7226 1787, littleangeltheatre. com). **Box office** *10am-5pm Mon-Fri; 10am-4pm Sat, Sun (from 9am when there is a morning performance).* **Tickets** *£13, £5-£11 reductions.*

Tucked away in the back streets of Islington, Little Angel Theatre is a hub of passionate puppeteering activity. Established by South African John Wright in 1961, the Little Angel

Little Angel Theatre

is London's only permanent puppet theatre and stages diverse productions devised here or by visiting companies. In a quaint twist that reveals the artifice behind the magic, the compact 100-seat theatre shares its space with the workshop where the marionettes are carved and developed. There's a Saturday Puppet Club and workshops and events to inspire the next generation of puppeteers. The shows are very much geared up for audiences of children, so expect to share the auditorium with chatty young'uns.

Polka Theatre

240 The Broadway, Wimbledon, SW19 1SB (8543 4888, polkatheatre.com). South Wimbledon tube. **Box office** *In person 9.30am-4.30pm Wed-Fri; 10am-4.30pm Sat, Sun. By phone 9.30am-5.30pm Mon-Fri; 10am-4.30pm Sat, Sun.* **Tickets** *£12.50-£19.50.*

Since its launch in 1979, this exceptional children's theatre has earned its place in generations of hearts. As well as staging in-house productions, the theatre runs workshops and storytelling sessions for families and schools – look out for literature events featuring children's authors such as Jacqueline Wilson.

Puppet Theatre Barge

Opposite 35 Blomfield Road, Little Venice, W9 2PF (7249 6876, www.puppetbarge. com). Warwick Avenue tube. **Box office** *10am-6pm daily (later during evening performances).* **Tickets** *£13; £9-£10 reductions.* **Map** *pull-out D5.*

This intimate waterborne stage is the setting for quality puppet shows that put a modern twist on traditional tales, such as *Mr Rabbit Meets Brer Santa Claus* and *The Flight of Babuscha Baboon*. The barge is moored here between October and July; shows themselves are held afternoons on Saturday and Sunday, and daily during school holidays, plus some matinées. During the summer (end July-Sept), the barge also holds performances in Richmond (opposite 85 Petersham Road, TW10 6UT).

Unicorn Theatre

147 Tooley Street, Bankside, SE1 2HZ (7645 0560, www.unicorntheatre.com). London Bridge tube/rail. **Box office** *9.30am-6pm Mon-Sat.* **Tickets** *£10-£26; £8-£18 reductions.* **Map** *p80 S9.*

This light, bright building, with a huge white unicorn in the foyer, has two performance spaces. Its small ensemble company performs in all shows and focuses on an outreach programme for local children and schools.

Don Quixote, Royal Ballet

Romeo & Juliet, Royal Ballet

DANCE

London is the home of two long-established classical dance companies. The **Royal Ballet**, resident at the Royal Opera House, is a company of global stature, which managed to lure star Russian ballerina Natalia Osipova into its ranks. Contemporary premières have included Christopher Wheeldon's *The Winter's Tale* and Liam Scarlett's *Frankenstein*, while Wayne McGregor continues to choreograph extraordinary contemporary ballet. The Royal's (friendly) rival is **English National Ballet**, a touring company that performs most often at the Coliseum (*see p358*) and, for the regular *Swan Lake* 'in the round', at the **Royal Albert Hall**, but has expanded into venues more suitable to contemporary dance such as the **Barbican** (*see p354*) and **Sadler's Wells**. The ENB's busy artistic director, Tamara Rojo – also a principal dancer with the company – has breathed real vigour into the ENB, but caused controversy a few years back when bemoaning the lack of a work ethic among local dancers. On the contemporary side, choreographers Akram Khan, Hofesh Shechter and Lloyd Newson of DV8 Physical Theatre went further, suggesting that British ballet schools were failing to produce suitably rigorous dancers, creating a paucity of performers for their challenging work, a claim the schools naturally denied.

Major venues

The **Coliseum** (see *p358*) is home to the English National Ballet, but you'll also see performances there from the likes of the Peter Schaufuss Ballet and visiting Russian companies. The **Barbican** (*see p354*) attracts and nurtures experimental dance, especially in its perfectly intimate Pit Theatre, while London's other major multi-arts centre, the **Southbank Centre** (*see p357*) programmes everything from international contemporary dance and hip hop to South Asian dance at its cluster of venues.

Royal Opera House
For listings, see p359.

For the full ballet experience, nothing beats the Royal Opera House, home of the Royal Ballet. The current incarnation of the building is an appropriately grand space in which to see dreamy ballerinas including Marianela Nuñez and Lauren Cuthbertson. There's edgier fare in the Linbury Studio Theatre. Royal Ballet in Rehearsal sessions offer a rare – and thrillingly close-up – glimpse behind the scenes. The 90-minute sessions are held in the Clore Studio Upstairs, with a capacity of 175. This is ballet at its most stripped-down: no sets, no exquisite costumes and no grand stage. Instead, there's just the piano, the squeak of shoes on the scuffed grey floor, and the intense concentration of the dancers.

Sadler's Wells Theatre

Rosebery Avenue, Finsbury, EC1R 4TN (7863 8000, www.sadlerswells.com). Angel tube. **Box office** *10am-8pm Mon-Sat.* **Tickets** *£12-£72.* **Map** *pull-out O4.*

Built in 1998 on the site of a 17th-century theatre of the same name, this dazzling complex is home to impressive local and international performances of contemporary dance in all its guises. The Lilian Baylis Studio offers smaller-scale new works and works in progress; the Peacock Theatre (on Portugal Street in Holborn) operates as a satellite venue.

Smaller venues

Greenwich Dance

Charlton House, Charlton Road, Greenwich, SE7 8RE (8293 9741, www.greenwichdance. org.uk). **Open** *9am-9pm Mon-Wed; 9am-5pm Thur, Fri; 9am-3pm Sat.* **Tickets** *see website for details.*

Founded in 1993, Greenwich Dance hosts workshops, classes, performances and festivals within its new home at Charlton House and at various venues around the borough of Greenwich.

The Place

17 Duke's Road, Bloomsbury, WC1H 9PY (7121 1100, www.theplace.org.uk). Euston tube/Overground/rail. **Box office** *10.30am-5.30pm Mon-Sat. Performance days 10.30am-7pm.* **Tickets** *£10-£17; £7-£13 reductions.* **Map** *p194 L4.*

For genuinely emerging dance, look to the Place, which is home to the London Contemporary Dance School and the Richard Alston Dance Company. The theatre is behind the biennial Place Prize for choreography (next in 2020), which rewards the best in British contemporary dance, as well as regular seasons showcasing new work, among them Resolution! (Jan/Feb) and Spring Loaded (Apr/May).

Trinity Laban Conservatoire

Laban Theatre, Creekside, Deptford, SE8 3DZ (8305 9400, tickets 8463 0100, www. trinitylaban. ac.uk). Deptford DLR or Greenwich DLR/rail. **Open** *10am-5.30pm Mon-Fri.* **Tickets** *free-£17.50.*

Founded in Manchester by innovative and influential movement theoretician Rudolf Laban (1879-1958), the Laban Centre joined forces in 2005 with Trinity College of Music to create the first ever UK conservatoire for music and dance. The centre was designed by Herzog & de Meuron of Tate Modern fame and features an impressive curving, multicoloured glass frontage. The striking premises include a 300-seat auditorium and are home to Transitions Dance Company.

Sadler's Wells Theatre

THE PHANTOM OF THE OPERA

020 7087 7762 | thephantomoftheopera.com
HER MAJESTY'S THEATRE
HAYMARKET, LONDON SW1Y 4QL

LONDON'S MUSICAL MASTERPIECES

Les Misérables

lesmis.com | 0844 482 5151
Calls cost 7p per minute plus your phone company's access charge
QUEEN'S THEATRE, Shaftesbury Avenue, London W1D 6BA

Understand

| History | 374 |
| Architecture | 386 |

St Paul's Cathedral *p224*

History

The making of modern London

Over the 2,000 years since London began life as a small trading station by a marshy river, the city has faced plague and invasion, fire and war, religious turbulence and financial turmoil, all borne by Londoners with a characteristic upbeat pessimism until the frenzy of commerce can begin again. In the City, Wren churches – built from the ruins of the Great Fire – have walls still blackened by the German incendiary bombs dropped during the Blitz, and shrapnel scars around Cleopatra's Needle remain from a World War I biplane raid. A fragment of glass, embedded in a wall at the Old Bailey, tells of a 1973 IRA terrorist attack, while 52 austere steel columns in Hyde Park commemorate those killed by suicide bombers in 2005. Concrete barriers on major bridges are the legacy of further fatal terrorist attacks in 2017, while the burnt-out remains of Grenfell Tower in west London are, to some, shorthand for government austerity policies and the housing crisis. Evidence of strife is everywhere in this city, yet the true Londoner will cheerfully insist there's worse to come. Just don't bet against them handling it with aplomb.

General Strike outside the Bank of England, 1926

Latin lessons

The city's origins are hardly grand. Celtic tribes lived in scattered communities along the banks of the Thames before the Romans arrived in Britain – creating what archaeologists describe as a 'ritual landscape': a dispersed region of sacred monuments – but there's no evidence of a settlement that we might recognise as the seed of the future metropolis before the invasion of the Emperor Claudius in AD 43. During his conquest, the Romans forded the Thames at its shallowest point (probably near today's London Bridge) and, later, built a timber bridge there. A settlement developed on the north side of this crossing.

Over the next two centuries, the Romans built roads, towns and forts in the area. Progress was halted in AD 61 when Boudicca, the widow of an East Anglian chieftain, rebelled against the imperial forces who had seized her land, flogged her and raped her daughters. She led the Iceni in a revolt, destroying the Roman colony at Colchester before marching on London. The Romans were massacred and their settlement razed.

After order was restored, London was rebuilt; around AD 200, a two-mile-long, 18-foot-high wall was put up around it. Chunks of the wall survive today; the early names of the original gates – Ludgate, Bishopsgate, Newgate and Aldgate – are preserved on the map of the modern city, with the street known as London Wall tracing part of its original course. But by the fourth century, racked by invasions and internal strife, the Roman Empire was in decline. In 410, the troops were withdrawn, and London became a ghost town.

Into the dark

During the fifth and sixth centuries, history gives way to legend. The Saxons crossed the North Sea; apparently avoiding the ruins of London, they built farmsteads and trading posts outside the city walls. Pope Gregory sent Augustine to convert the English to Christianity in 596; Mellitus, one of his missionaries, was appointed the first Bishop of London, founding a cathedral dedicated to St Paul inside the old city walls in 604.

From this period, the history of London is one of expansion. Writing in 731, monk and writer the Venerable Bede described 'Lundenwic' as 'the mart of many nations resorting to it by land and sea'. Only recently have archaeologists found traces of this Anglo-Saxon market around Covent Garden and the Strand. Yet the city faced a new danger during the ninth century: the Vikings. The city was ransacked in 841 and again in 851, when Danish raiders returned with 350 ships. It was not until 886 that King Alfred of Wessex – Alfred the Great – regained the city, re-establishing London as a major trading centre, and refounding it within its old walls.

Throughout the tenth century the city prospered. Churches were built, parishes established and markets set up. However, the 11th century brought more harassment from the Vikings, and the English were forced to accept a Danish king, Cnut (Canute, 1016-35), during whose reign London replaced Winchester as the capital of England.

The country reverted to English control in 1042 under Edward the Confessor, who devoted himself to building England's grandest church two miles west of the

Astronomical clock Hampton Court Palace p291

City on an island in the river marshes at Thorney: 'the West Minster' (Westminster Abbey). Just a week after the consecration, he died. London now had two hubs: Westminster, centre of the royal court, government and law; and the City of London, centre of commerce. On Edward's death, foreigners took over. Duke William of Normandy was crowned king on Christmas Day 1066, having defeated Edward's brother-in-law Harold at the Battle of Hastings. The pragmatic Norman resolved to win over the City merchants by negotiation rather than force, and in 1067 granted the burgesses and the Bishop of London a charter – still available to researchers in the London Metropolitan Archives – that acknowledged their rights and independence in return for taxes. He also ordered strongholds to be built at the city wall 'against the fickleness of the vast and fierce population', including the White Tower (the tallest building in the Tower of London) and the now-lost Baynard's Castle.

Parliament and rights

In 1295, the Model Parliament, held at Westminster Hall by Edward I and attended by barons, clergy and representatives of knights and burgesses, agreed the principles of English government. The first step towards establishing personal rights and political liberty, not to mention curbing the power of the king, had already been taken in 1215 when King John put his seal to Magna Carta. Then, in the 14th century, subsequent assemblies gave rise to the House of Lords and the House of Commons. During the 12th and 13th centuries, the king and his court travelled the kingdom, but the Palace of Westminster was now the permanent seat of law and government; noblemen and bishops began to build palatial houses along the Strand from the City to Westminster, with gardens stretching down to the river.

Relations between the monarch and the City were never easy. Londoners guarded their privileges, and resisted attempts by kings to squeeze money out of them to finance wars and construction projects. Subsequent kings were forced to turn to Jewish and Lombard moneylenders, but the City merchants were intolerant of foreigners too.

The self-regulation privileges granted to the City merchants under Norman kings were extended by the monarchs who followed – in return for finance. In 1191, the City of London was recognised by Richard I as a self-governing community; six years later, it won control of the Thames. In 1215 King John confirmed the city's right 'to elect every year a mayor', a position of authority

with power over the sheriff and the Bishop of London. A month later, the mayor's seal joined those of the rebel barons on Magna Carta.

Over the next two centuries, the power and influence of the trade and craft guilds (later known as the City Livery Companies) increased as dealings with Europe grew. The City's markets drew produce from miles around: livestock at Smithfield, fish at Billingsgate, poultry at Leadenhall. The street markets ('cheaps') around Westcheap (now Cheapside) and Eastcheap were crammed with a variety of goods. The population within the city walls grew from about 18,000 in 1100 to well over 50,000 in the 1340s.

Wake up and smell the issue

Lack of hygiene became a serious problem. Water was provided in cisterns, but the supply, more or less direct from the Thames, was limited and polluted. The street of Houndsditch was so named because Londoners threw their dead animals into the furrow there; in the streets around Smithfield (the Shambles), butchers dumped entrails into the gutters. These conditions helped to foster the greatest catastrophe of the Middle Ages: the Black Death of 1348 and 1349, which killed about 30 per cent of England's population. The plague came to London from Europe – probably carried by rats on ships, although research in 2015 suggested gerbils may have been to blame – and the plague was to recur in London several times during the next three centuries.

Disease left the harvest short-handed, causing unrest among the peasants whose labour was in such demand. Then a poll tax of a shilling a head was imposed. It was all too much: the Peasants' Revolt began in 1381. Thousands marched to Blackheath, south-east London, led by Jack Straw from Essex and Wat Tyler from Kent; the Archbishop of Canterbury was murdered and hundreds of prisoners were set free. After meeting the Essexmen near Mile End, the 14-year-old Richard II rode out to the rioters at Smithfield and spoke with Tyler. During their discussion, Tyler was fatally stabbed by the Lord Mayor; the revolt collapsed and the ringleaders were hanged. But no more poll taxes were imposed.

Roses, wives and Royal Docks

Its growth spurred by the 'discovery' of America and the opening of ocean routes to Africa and the Orient, London became one of Europe's largest cities under the Tudors (1485-1603). The first Tudor monarch, Henry

Elizabeth I
(Nicholas Hilliard, c1573-1575)

sailed to the New World. As trade grew, so did London: it was home to 200,000 people in 1600, many living in overcrowded conditions. The most complete picture of Tudor London is given in John Stow's *Survey of London* (1598), a fascinating first-hand account by a Londoner whose monument stands in the church of St Andrew Undershaft.

These were the glory days of English drama. The Rose (1587) and the Globe (1599, now recreated; *see p363*) theatres were erected at Bankside, providing homes for the works of popular playwrights William Shakespeare and Christopher Marlowe. Deemed 'a naughty place' by royal proclamation, 16th-century Bankside was a vibrant mix of entertainment and 'sport' (bear-baiting, cock-fighting), drinking and whoring – all within easy reach of the City, which had outlawed theatres in 1575.

In 1605, two years after the Tudor dynasty ended with Elizabeth's death, her Stuart successor, James I, narrowly escaped assassination on 5 November. Guy Fawkes had been found underneath the Palace of Westminster, at midnight on 4 November, with 36 barrels of gunpowder. Commemorated with fireworks each year as Bonfire Night, the Gunpowder Plot had been hatched in protest at the failure to improve conditions for the persecuted Catholics, but only resulted in an intensification of anti-papist sentiment. James I is more positively remembered for hiring Inigo Jones to design court masques (musical dramas) and London's first influential examples of the classical Renaissance architectural style: the Queen's House (1616; *see p388*), the Banqueting House (1619; *see p388*) and St Paul's Covent Garden (1631; *see p388*).

VII, had ended the Wars of the Roses by might, defeating Richard III at the Battle of Bosworth and, by policy, marrying Elizabeth of York, a daughter of his rivals. By the time his son took the throne, the Tudor dynasty was firmly established. But progress under Henry VIII was not without its hiccups. His first marriage, to Catherine of Aragon, failed to produce an heir, so in 1527 he determined the union should be annulled. When the Pope refused to co-operate, Henry defied the Catholic Church, demanding to be recognised as Supreme Head of the Church in England and ordering the execution of anyone who opposed the plan (including Sir Thomas More, his otherwise loyal chancellor). The subsequent dissolution of the monasteries transformed the face of the medieval city.

When not transforming the politico-religious landscape, Henry found time to develop a professional navy, founding the Royal Dockyards at Woolwich in 1512. He also established palaces at Hampton Court and Whitehall, and built a residence at St James's Palace. Much of the land he annexed for hunting became today's Royal Parks, among them Greenwich, Hyde and Regent's parks.

Renaissance means rebirth

Elizabeth I's reign (1558-1603) saw the founding of the Royal Exchange in 1566, which enabled London to emerge as Europe's commercial hub. Merchant venturers and the first joint-stock companies established new trading enterprises, as pioneering seafarers Francis Drake, Walter Raleigh and Richard Hawkins

Royalists and Roundheads

Charles I succeeded his father in 1625, but gradually fell out of favour with the City of London and an increasingly independent-minded Parliament over taxation. The country slid into civil war (1642-49), the supporters of Parliament (the Roundheads, led by Puritan Oliver Cromwell) opposing the supporters of the king (the Royalists).

Both sides knew that control of the country's major city and port was vital for victory, and London's sympathies were with the Parliamentarians. In 1642, 24,000 citizens assembled at Turnham Green to face Charles's army, but the king withdrew. The move proved fatal: Charles never threatened the capital again, and was eventually found guilty of treason. Taken to the Banqueting House in Whitehall on 30 January 1649, he declared himself a 'martyr of the people' and was beheaded.

A commemorative wreath is still laid at the site of the execution on the last Sunday in January each year.

For the next decade, the country was ruled as a Commonwealth by Cromwell. But his son Richard's subsequent rule was brief: partly due to the Puritans closing theatres and banning Christmas (a Catholic superstition), the Restoration of the exiled Charles II in 1660 was greeted with great rejoicing. The Stuart king had Cromwell exhumed from Westminster Abbey, and his body was hung in chains at Tyburn (near modern-day Marble Arch). His severed head was displayed on a pole outside the abbey until 1685.

Plague, fire and revolution

The year 1665 saw the most serious outbreak of plague since the Black Death, killing nearly 100,000. Then, on 2 September 1666, a further disaster. The fire that spread from a carelessly tended oven in Thomas Farriner's baking shop on Pudding Lane raged for three days and consumed four-fifths of the City.

The Great Fire at least allowed planners the chance to rebuild London as a modern city. Many blueprints were considered, but Londoners were so impatient to get on with business that the City was reconstructed largely on its medieval street plan (albeit in brick and stone rather than wood). The prolific Sir Christopher Wren oversaw work on 51 of the 54 rebuilt churches. Among them was his masterpiece: the new St Paul's, completed in 1710 and effectively the world's first Protestant cathedral.

In the wake of the Great Fire, many well-to-do City dwellers moved to new residential developments west of the old quarters: the West End. In the City, the Royal Exchange was rebuilt, but merchants increasingly used the new coffee houses to exchange news. With the expansion of the joint-stock companies and the chance to invest capital, the City emerged as a centre not of manufacturing but of finance. Economic instability was common: the 1720 financial disaster known as the South Sea Bubble ruined Sir Isaac Newton.

Anti-Catholic feeling still ran high. The accession in 1685 of Catholic James II aroused such fears of a return to papistry that a Dutch Protestant, William of Orange, was invited to take the throne with his wife, Mary Stuart (James's daughter). James fled to France in 1688 in what became known (by its beneficiaries) as the 'Glorious Revolution'. It was during William's reign that the Bank of England was founded, initially to finance the king's religious wars with France.

Gin Lane (William Hogarth, 1751)

Creation of the prime minister

In 1714, the throne passed to George, the Hanover-born great-grandson of James I. The German-speaking king (he never learned English) became the first of four Georges in the Hanoverian line.

During George I's reign (1714-27), and for several years after, Sir Robert Walpole's Whig party monopolised Parliament. Their opponents, the Tories, supported the Stuarts and had opposed the exclusion of the Catholic James II. On the king's behalf, Walpole chaired a group of ministers (the forerunner of today's Cabinet), becoming, in effect, Britain's first prime minister. Walpole was presented with 10 Downing Street (built by Sir George Downing) as a residence; it remains the official prime ministerial home.

During the 18th century, London grew with astonishing speed. New squares and terraced streets spread across Soho, Bloomsbury, Mayfair and Marylebone, as wealthy landowners and speculative developers cashed in on the new demand for leasehold properties. South London also became more accessible with the opening of the first new bridges for centuries: Westminster Bridge (opened 1750) and Blackfriars Bridge (completed 1769) joined London Bridge, previously the city's only Thames crossing.

Gin-soaked poor, nasty rich

In London's older districts, people were living in terrible squalor. Some of the most notorious slums were located around Fleet Street and St Giles's (north of Covent Garden), only a short distance from fashionable residences. To make matters worse, gin ('mother's ruin') was readily available at low prices; many poor Londoners drank excessive amounts in an attempt to escape the horrors of daily life. The well-off seemed complacent, amusing themselves at the popular Ranelagh and Vauxhall pleasure gardens or with trips to mock the patients at the Bedlam lunatic asylum. Public executions at Tyburn were popular events in the social calendar; it's said that 200,000 people gathered to see the execution (after he had escaped from prison four times) of the folk-hero thief Jack Sheppard in 1724.

The outrageous imbalance in the distribution of wealth encouraged crime, and there were daring daytime robberies in the West End. Reformers were few, though there were exceptions. Henry Fielding, author of the picaresque novel *Tom Jones*, was also an enlightened magistrate at Bow Street Court (now destined to become a hotel). In 1751, he and his blind half-brother John set up a volunteer force of 'thief-takers' to back up the ineffective efforts of the parish constables and watchmen who were, until then, the city's only law-keepers. This crime-busting group of proto-cops, known as the Bow Street Runners, were the earliest incarnation of today's Metropolitan Police (established in 1829).

Meanwhile, five major new hospitals were founded by private philanthropists. St Thomas's and St Bartholomew's were long-established monastic institutions for the care of the sick, but Westminster (1720), Guy's (1725), St George's (1734), the London (1740) and the Middlesex (1745) went on to become world-famous teaching hospitals. Thomas Coram's Foundling Hospital (*see p197*) was another remarkable achievement.

Great Exhibition of 1851

Industry and capital growth

It wasn't just the indigenous population of London that was on the rise. Country folk, whose common land had been replaced by sheep enclosures, were faced with a choice between starvation wages or unemployment, and so drifted into the towns. Just outside the old city walls, the East End drew many poor immigrant labourers to build the docks towards the end of the 18th century. London's total population had grown to one million by 1801, the largest of any city in Europe. By 1837, when Queen Victoria came to the throne, five more bridges and the capital's first passenger railway (from Greenwich to London Bridge) gave hints of huge expansion.

As well as being the administrative and financial capital of the British Empire, London was its chief port and the world's largest manufacturing centre. On the one hand, it had splendid buildings, fine shops, theatres and museums; on the other, it was a city of poverty, pollution and disease. Residential areas were polarised into districts of fine terraces maintained by squads of servants, and overcrowded, insanitary slums.

The growth of the metropolis in the century before Victoria came to the throne had been spectacular, but during her reign (1837-1901), thousands more acres were covered with roads, houses and railway lines. If you visit a street within five miles of central London, its houses are likely to be mostly Victorian. By the end of the 19th century, the city's population had swelled to more than six million, an incredible growth of five million in just 100 years, making London the world's most populous city.

Despite the social problems of the Victorian era, memorably described by Dickens, by the turn of the century steps were being taken to improve conditions for the majority of Londoners. The Metropolitan Board of Works installed an efficient sewerage system, street lighting and better roads. The worst slums were replaced by low-cost housing schemes funded by philanthropists such as the American George Peabody, whose Peabody Donation Fund continues to provide subsidised housing. The London County Council (created in 1888) also helped to house the poor.

The Victorian expansion would not have been possible without an efficient public-transport network with which to speed workers into and out of the city from the new suburbs. The horse-drawn bus appeared on London's streets in 1829, but it was the opening of the first passenger railway seven years later that heralded

The Archaeology of Crossrail

Huge tunnels under London have revolutionised our understanding of its history

There was a great deal of controversy in autumn 2018 when the Crossrail project – originally set to part-open that December – was delayed by at least nine months. Whenever Crossrail eventually opens, it won't just leave London with a new high-speed underground railway. It'll also have been one of the largest archaeological digs ever seen in an urban centre. When completed, the line will connect Heathrow and Canary Wharf, with branches that drift into the suburbs, but the bulk of the engineering challenge has been in central London, where new tunnels connecting east and west London have been driven beneath the city at depths of up to 130 feet (40 metres). For an archaeologist – more than 100 of them have worked on Crossrail sites – that scale of excavation is paradise. Since work began in 2009, they've found more than 10,000 items on 40 different sites, with objects spanning 55 million years of London's history. These include everything from prehistoric animal bones to plague pits.

The Crossrail project – which will be called the Elizabeth Line when it opens, although Londoners have shown few signs of adopting the official name – has given archaeologists an unprecedented opportunity to slice down and across London, allowing them to make numerous points of comparison at different excavations. While most ordinary people are fascinated by the magnificent ephemera that have turned up – a Tudor bowling ball,

medieval ice skates – for the archaeologists the discoveries work together to provide important historical information. The remains of a woolly mammoth jawbone found under Canary Wharf have helped determine the date of their extinction in northern Europe, while DNA testing on teeth taken from skeletons found in a mass grave in the 17th-century Bedlam cemetery near Liverpool Street station confirmed the identity of the bacteria behind London's Great Plague. Human remains have particular value as they allow osteologists to determine things like the diet, life expectancy and lifestyle of everyday Londoners.

Liverpool Street was a particularly rich area. As well as bronze medallions, archaeologists also discovered a graveyard and three Roman-era skeletons that had been decapitated, with the heads laid between their legs – nobody can explain why. Less grisly have been the finds at Tottenham Court Road, where excavations at an old Crosse & Blackwell factory uncovered a treasure trove of 13,000 jam jars. For almost 100 years these had lain undiscovered beneath what became the Astoria theatre.

And Crossrail will leave its own archaeological legacy beneath London. Two of the tunnel boring machines used on the project, Phyllis and Ada, were too large to be extracted from the ground. They've been left buried beneath Farringdon for future archaeologists to discover.

the commuters of the future. The first underground line between Paddington and Farringdon was an instant success, attracting 30,000 travellers on its opening day in 1863. The world's first electric track in a deep tunnel – the 'Tube' – opened in 1890 between the City and Stockwell, later becoming part of the Northern line.

The Crystal Palace

If any single event symbolised this period of industry, science, discovery and invention, it was the Great Exhibition of 1851. Prince Albert, the Queen's Consort, helped to organise the triumphant showcase, for which the Crystal Palace, a vast building of iron and glass, was erected in Hyde Park. It looked like a giant greenhouse; hardly surprising as it was designed not by a professional architect but by the Duke of Devonshire's gardener, Joseph Paxton. Condemned by art critic John Ruskin as the model of dehumanisation in design, the Palace came to be presented as the

prototype of modern architecture. During the five months it was open, the Exhibition drew six million visitors. The profits were used by the Prince Consort to establish a permanent centre for the study of the applied arts and sciences; the enterprise survives today in the South Kensington museums of natural history (*see p390*), science (*see p392*), and decorative and applied arts (the V&A; *see p128*), and in three colleges (of art, music and science). After the Exhibition closed, the Crystal Palace was moved to Sydenham and was used as an exhibition centre until it burned down in 1936.

Zeppelins attack from the skies

London entered the 20th century as the capital of the largest empire in history. Its wealth and power were there for all to see in grandstanding monuments such as Tower Bridge (*see p237*) and the Midland Grand Hotel at St Pancras Station (*see p204*), both of which married the retro stylings of

High Gothic with modern iron and steel technology. During the brief reign of Edward VII (1901-10), London regained some of the gaiety and glamour it had lacked in the later years of Victoria's reign. Parisian chic came to London with the opening of the Ritz; Regent Street's Café Royal hit the heights as a meeting place for artists and writers; gentlemen's clubs proliferated; and 'luxury catering for the little man' was provided at the new Lyons Corner Houses (the Coventry Street branch held 4,500 people).

Road transport, too, was revolutionised in this period. By 1911, horse-drawn buses were abandoned, replaced by motor cars, which put-putted around the city's streets, and the motor bus, introduced in 1904. Disruption came in the form of devastating air raids during World War I (1914-18). Around 650 people lost their lives in Zeppelin raids, but the greater impact was psychological – the mighty city and its populace had experienced helplessness.

Change, crisis and sheer entertainment

Political change happened quickly after the war. Women over 30 who met property qualifications were awarded the vote in 1918, and David Lloyd George's government averted revolution in 1918-19 by promising 'homes for heroes' (the returning soldiers). It didn't deliver, and in 1924 the Labour Party, led by Ramsay MacDonald, formed its first government.

A live-for-today attitude prevailed in the Roaring '20s among the young upper classes, who flitted from parties in Mayfair to dances at the Ritz. But this meant little to the mass of Londoners, who were suffering in the post-war slump. Civil disturbances, brought on by the high cost of living and rising unemployment, resulted in the nationwide General Strike of 1926, when the working classes downed tools en masse in support of striking miners. Prime Minister Stanley Baldwin encouraged volunteers to take over the public services, and the streets teemed with army-escorted food convoys, aristocrats running soup kitchens and students driving buses. After nine days of chaos, the strike was finally called off.

The economic situation only worsened in the early 1930s following the New York Stock Exchange crash of 1929. By 1931, more than three million Britons were jobless. During these years, the London County Council (LCC) began to have a greater impact on the city, clearing slums and building new houses, creating parks and taking control of public services. All the while, London's population increased, peaking at nearly 8.7 million in 1939 – it would be spring 2015 before the city's population exceeded that number. To accommodate the influx, the suburbs expanded, particularly to the north-west with the extension of the Metropolitan line to an area that became known as 'Metroland'. Gabled houses sprang up in their thousands.

At least Londoners were able to entertain themselves with film and radio. Not long after London's first radio broadcast was

St Paul's Cathedral during the Blitz, 29 December 1940

beamed from the roof of Marconi House in the Strand in 1922, families were gathering around huge Bakelite wireless sets to hear the BBC (the British Broadcasting Company; from 1927, the British Broadcasting Corporation). TV broadcasts started on 26 August 1936, when the first telecast went out from Alexandra Palace, but few Londoners could afford televisions until the 1950s.

Blitzkrieg

Abroad, events had taken on a frightening impetus. Neville Chamberlain's policy of appeasement towards Hitler's Germany collapsed when the Germans invaded Poland. Britain duly declared war on 3 September 1939. The government implemented precautionary measures against air raids, including the evacuation of 600,000 children and pregnant mothers, but the expected bombing raids didn't happen during the autumn and winter of 1939-40 (the so-called 'Phoney War'). Then, in September 1940, hundreds of German bombers dumped explosives on east London and the docks, destroying entire streets and killing or injuring more than 2,000 in what was merely an opening salvo. The Blitz had begun. Raids on London continued for 57 consecutive nights, then intermittently for a further six months. Londoners reacted with stoicism, famously asserting 'business as usual'. After a final raid on 10 May 1941, the Nazis had left a third of the City and the East End in ruins.

From 1942 onwards, the tide began to turn, but Londoners had a new terror to face: the V1 or 'doodlebug'. Dozens of these deadly, explosive-packed, pilotless planes descended on the city in 1944, causing widespread destruction. Later in the year, the more powerful V2 rocket was launched. The last fell on 27 March 1945 in Orpington, Kent, around six weeks before Victory in Europe was declared on 8 May 1945.

'Never had it so good'

World War II left Britain almost as shattered as Germany. Soon after VE Day, a general election was held and Winston Churchill was defeated by the Labour Party under Clement Attlee. The new government established the National Health Service in 1948, and began a massive nationalisation programme that included public transport, electricity, gas, postal and telephone services. For most people, however, life remained regimented and austere. In war-ravaged London, local authorities struggled with a critical shortage of housing. Prefabricated bungalows provided a temporary solution for some (60 years later, six prefabs on the Excalibur estate in Catford, south-east London, were given protection as buildings of historic interest), but the huge new high-rise housing estates eventually proved unpopular with their residents.

There were bright spots. London hosted the Olympic Games in 1948; three years later came the Festival of Britain, resulting in the full redevelopment of the riverside site into the South Bank (now Southbank) Centre. As the 1950s progressed, prosperity returned, leading Prime Minister Harold Macmillan in 1957 to proclaim that 'most of our people have never had it so good'. However, Londoners were leaving. The population dropped by half a million in the late 1950s, causing a labour shortage that prompted huge recruitment drives in Britain's former colonies. London Transport and the National Health Service were both particularly active in encouraging West Indians to emigrate to Britain. Unfortunately, as the Notting Hill race riots of 1958 illustrated, the welcome these new immigrants received was rarely friendly. Still, there were several areas of tolerance: Soho, for instance, which became famous for its mix of cultures and the café and club life they brought with them.

The swinging '60s

By the mid 1960s, London had started to swing. The innovative fashions of Mary Quant and others broke the stranglehold Paris had on couture: boutiques blossomed along the King's Road, while Biba set the pace in Kensington. Carnaby Street became a byword for hipness as the city basked in its new-found reputation as music and fashion capital of the world – made official, it seemed, when *Time* magazine devoted its front cover to 'swinging London' in 1966. The year of student unrest in Europe, 1968, saw the first issue of *Time Out* hit the streets in August; it was a fold-up sheet, sold for one shilling. The decade ended with the Rolling Stones playing a free gig in Hyde Park that drew around 500,000 people.

Then the bubble burst. Many Londoners remember the 1970s as a decade of economic strife when the IRA began its bombing campaign on mainland Britain. After the Conservatives won the general election in 1979, Margaret Thatcher instituted an economic policy that cut public services and widened the gap between rich and poor. Riots in Brixton (1981) and Tottenham (1985) were linked to unemployment and heavy-handed policing, keenly felt in London's black communities. The Greater London Council (GLC), led by Ken Livingstone, mounted vigorous opposition to the government with a series of populist measures, but it was abolished in 1986. After the closure of the London Docks in the early '80s, the regeneration of the rebranded 'Docklands' kicked off the ongoing and controversial redevelopment/regeneration/gentrification (delete according to your tastes and politics) of east London.

Things can only get better?

In May 1997, the British electorate ousted the Tories and gave Tony Blair's Labour Party the first of three election victories. Blair left London with two significant legacies. First, the government commissioned the Millennium Dome, whose turn-of-the-century celebrations it hoped would be a 21st-century rival to the Great Exhibition of 1851. Instead, the Dome ate £1 billion and became a national joke. However, as Labour's fortunes declined, the Dome's saw an upturn. As the O2 Arena, it has hosted gigs by the likes of Prince, Lady Gaga and the reformed Led Zeppelin. Second, following a referendum, Labour instituted the Greater London Authority (GLA), the 25-member London Assembly and the London mayoralty. Thus 2000 saw Ken Livingstone return to power as London's first directly elected mayor. He was re-elected in 2004, a thumbs-up for policies that included a traffic congestion charge. Summer 2005 brought elation, as London won the bid to host the 2012 Olympic Games, and devastation the very next day, as bombs on tube trains and a bus killed 52 people and injured 700.

Aided by support from the suburbs, which felt neglected by Livingstone, thatch-haired Tory Boris Johnson became mayor in 2008 with a healthy majority and, again, in 2012 by a slimmer margin. His early policies, such as banning alcohol on London transport, scrapping the western extension of the Congestion Charge, as well as introducing a bike-rental scheme and developing an updated Routemaster bus, were popular. The latter was launched as self-financing through revenue and private sponsorship but was instead regularly topped up with money from Transport for London's already stretched public transport budget (*see p76* Routemasters).

The riots and looting of August 2011, whose flashpoint was again in Tottenham, brought issues of youth unemployment, alienation and policing to the fore. The 2012 Olympics and Paralympics were an unbridled success, yet the promised 'legacy' of improvements at a local level in some of London's poorest areas remains frustratingly elusive – a problem underlined in 2017 by the terrifying fire at Grenfell Tower, a council block in the borough of Kensington & Chelsea where, according to official figures, 72 residents perished.

Johnson declined to run again for mayor in 2016 and, instead, a toxic election campaign pitched Labour's Sadiq Khan, a civil rights lawyer and bus driver's son from Tooting, against the millionaire ecologist Zac Goldsmith. On 6 May 2016, Khan was sworn in as the third Mayor of London with a stonking majority. Then, in June, he suddenly became the anti-Brexit mayor of a broadly anti-Brexit city in a country that had voted to leave the European Union.

Uncertainty around the UK's future relationship with the EU continues to cause jitters, not only for London's construction, banking and hospitality industries, but also for non-UK EU citizens living in the capital – approximately one in ten Londoners. No one seems quite sure what the post-Brexit future will bring. Change, at the largest scale, is part of London's DNA – and it looks as though the city will be getting a bellyful over the coming years.

▶ *For analysis of the most pressing issues facing the capital, see p30 London Today.*

Millennium Dome

Key Events

London's history in brief

43 The Romans invade; the settlement of Londinium is founded on the remains of an ancient ritual landscape.

61 Boudicca burns Londinium; the city is rebuilt and made provincial capital.

200 A city wall is built.

410 Roman troops evacuate Britain.

c600 Saxon London is built to the west.

604 Mellitus is consecrated bishop of London.

841 The Norse raid for the first time.

c871 The Danes occupy London.

886 Alfred the Great takes London.

1042 Edward the Confessor builds a palace and 'West Minster' upstream.

1066 William I crowned in Westminster Abbey.

1078 The Tower of London is begun.

1123 St Bart's Hospital is founded.

1197 Henry Fitzalwin is the first mayor.

1215 The mayor signs Magna Carta.

1240 First Parliament at Westminster.

1290 Jews are expelled from London.

1348 The Black Death arrives.

1381 The Peasants' Revolt.

1397 Richard Whittington is Lord Mayor.

1476 William Caxton sets up the first printing press at Westminster.

1534 Henry VIII cuts England off from the Catholic Church.

1555 Martyrs burned at Smithfield.

1565 Sir Thomas Gresham proposes the Royal Exchange.

1572 First known map of London.

1599 The Globe Theatre opens.

1605 Guy Fawkes's plot to blow up James I fails.

1642 The start of the Civil War.

1649 Charles I is executed; Cromwell establishes the Commonwealth.

1665 Outbreak of the Great Plague.

1666 The Great Fire.

1675 Building starts on the new St Paul's Cathedral.

1694 The Bank of England is set up.

1766 The city wall is demolished.

1773 The Stock Exchange is founded.

1824 The National Gallery opens.

1836 The first passenger railway is inaugurated; Charles Dickens publishes *The Pickwick Papers*, his first novel.

1851 The Great Exhibition takes place.

1858 The Great Stink: pollution in the Thames reaches hideous levels.

1863 The Metropolitan Line opens as the world's first underground railway.

1866 London's last major cholera outbreak; the Sanitation Act is passed.

1868 The last public execution is held at Newgate prison (now the Old Bailey).

1884 Greenwich Mean Time is established as a global standard.

1888 Jack the Ripper prowls the East End; London County Council is created.

1890 The Housing Act enables the LCC to clear the slums; the first electric underground railway opens.

1897 Motorised buses are introduced.

1908 London hosts the Olympic Games for the first time.

1915 Zeppelins begin three years of bombing raids on London.

1940 The Blitz begins.

1948 London again hosts the Olympics.

1951 The Festival of Britain is held.

1952 The last 'pea-souper' smog.

1953 Queen Elizabeth II is crowned.

1981 Riots in Brixton.

1982 The last London docks close.

1986 The Greater London Council is abolished.

1992 One Canada Square tower opens on Canary Wharf.

2000 Ken Livingstone becomes London's first directly elected mayor; Tate Modern and the London Eye bring tourism to the South Bank.

2005 Suicide bombers kill 52 on public transport.

2008 Boris Johnson becomes mayor.

2010 Hung parliament leads to new Conservative-Lib Dem coalition.

2011 Austerity cuts by the Conservative-Lib Dem coalition lead to riots and looting around the city.

2012 London becomes only the second city to host the Olympic Games for a third time.

2015 The population of Greater London reaches 8.7m, the largest number in its history.

2016 Labour's Sadiq Khan elected mayor; the UK votes for Brexit despite most of London voting to remain.

2017 Civilians are killed by terrorist attacks at Westminster Bridge, Borough Market and Finsbury Park Mosque. A huge fire kills 72 residents of Grenfell Tower in west London.

Architecture

A wonderful jumble of world-class buildings

For all the derisive newspaper lists of London's worst new buildings, the best modern architecture is swiftly appreciated here: witness the monumental Switch House extension to Tate Modern, for instance. Even hated buildings are liable to become classics eventually: the brutalist National Theatre and Barbican were pilloried for years, but now enjoy huge Instagram followings.

If you swap Insta snaps for hastily printed coffee-house pamphlets, there's not much difference between now and the 17th century, when Wren's magnificent St Paul's Cathedral was objected to because it looked too Roman Catholic for austere Anglican sensibilities.

The truth is that London's defining characteristic is its aesthetically unhappy mix of buildings, a mess of historic bits and modern bobs that gives the city a unique capacity to surprise and delight. Don't come here for grand Renaissance vistas, then, but you can expect snatches of pure inspiration.

Ancient streets, new city

Modern London sprang into being from the ashes left after the Great Fire of 1666, which destroyed four-fifths of the City of London, burning 13,200 houses and 89 churches. The devastation was explicitly commemorated by Sir Christopher Wren's 202-foot **Monument** (see p235), but many of the finest buildings in the City stand testament to his talent as the architect of the great remodelling, and to the work of his successors.

London had been a densely populated place largely of wood, and fire control was primitive. It was only after the three-day inferno that the authorities insisted on a few basic regulations. Brick and stone became the construction materials of choice, and key streets were widened to act as firebreaks. Yet, despite grand, Classical proposals from several architects (Wren among them), London reshaped itself around its old street pattern, and some structures that survived

St Bride's

the Fire still stand as reminders of earlier building styles. Chief of these are the City's fragments of **Roman wall** – Tower Hill tube station and the grounds of the Museum of London (see p227) have good examples – and the central Norman keep at the **Tower of London** (see p234) – the oldest building in the city that remains fully intact. The Tower was begun soon after William's 1066 conquest and extended over the next 300 years; the Navy saved it from the Great Fire by blowing up surrounding houses before the inferno could reach it.

Another longstanding building, **Westminster Abbey** (see p108) was begun in 1245 when the site lay far outside London's walls; it was completed in 1745 by Nicholas Hawksmoor's distinctive west towers. The abbey is the most French of England's Gothic churches, but the chapel – begun by Henry VII – is pure Tudor. Centuries later, the American writer Washington Irving gushed: 'Stone seems, by the winning labour of the chisel, to have been robbed of its weight and density, suspended aloft, as if by magic.'

A late flowering

The European Renaissance came late to Britain, making its London debut with Inigo Jones's 1622 **Banqueting House** (see p108). The sumptuously decorated ceiling, added in 1635 by Rubens, celebrated the Stuart monarchy's Divine Right to rule, although 14 years later King Charles I provided a greater spectacle as he was led from the room and beheaded on a stage outside. Tourists also have Jones to thank for **St Paul's Covent Garden** (see p184), and the precise little **Queen's House** (see p284) in Greenwich, extensively renovated for its 400th anniversary in 2017. Jones mastered the art of piazzas (notably at Covent Garden), porticoes and pilasters, changing British architecture forever. His work influenced succeeding generations of architects, introducing a habit of venerating the past that it would take 300 years to kick.

Nothing cheers a builder like a natural disaster, and one can only guess at the relish with which Wren and co began rebuilding after the Fire. They brandished Classicism like a new broom: the pointed arches of English Gothic were rounded off, Corinthian columns made an appearance and church spires became as complex, frothy and multi-layered as a wedding cake – as the tour guides never tire of explaining as they point up to the lovely spire of **St Bride's** (see p222) on Fleet Street.

Wren blazed the trail with his daring plans for **St Paul's Cathedral** (see p224), spending an enormous (for the time) £500 on just the oak model of his proposal. But the scheme, incorporating a Catholic dome rather than a Protestant steeple, was too Roman for the establishment and the design was rejected. Wren quickly produced a redesign and gained planning permission by incorporating a spire, only to set about a series of mischievous U-turns to give us the building, domed and heavily suggestive of an ancient temple, that survives to this day.

Wren's work was continued by Nicholas Hawksmoor and James Gibbs, who benefited from an Act of Parliament that in 1710 decreed 50 extra churches should be built using the money raised by a tax on coal. Gibbs became busy around Trafalgar Square with the steepled Roman temple of **St Martin-in-the-Fields** (see p106), as well as the Baroque **St Mary-le-Strand** (see p189) and the tower of **St Clement Danes** (see p189). His work was well received, but the more experimental Hawksmoor had a rougher ride. Not everyone admired his stylistic innovations, including a penchant for occult and masonic symbolism; even fewer approved of his financial planning, or lack of it: **St George's Bloomsbury** (see p200) cost three times its £10,000 budget and took 15 years to build. Nonetheless, Hawksmoor designed, in whole or in part, eight new places of worship. Like Wren, Hawksmoor loved the Classical temple, a style at odds with the Act's insistence on spires. **St Mary Woolnoth** (see p230) and, in east London, **St George-in-the-East** and **St Anne Limehouse**, are all unorthodox resolutions of this contradiction, but the 'spire' of St George's Bloomsbury is barmiest. Aping the Mausoleum of Halicarnassus, Hawksmoor created a peculiar stepped pyramid design, plopped a giant statue of George I in a toga on top and then added unicorns and lions. Hawksmoor's ruinous overspends were one reason why just a dozen of the proposed 50 churches were built.

After action, reaction: one of a large family of Scottish architects, Robert Adam found himself at the forefront of a movement that came to see Italian Baroque as a corruption of the real thing, with architectural exuberance dropped in favour of a simpler interpretation of ancient forms. The best surviving work of Robert and his brothers James, John and William can be found in London's great suburban houses, including **Kenwood House** (see p248), but the project for which they're most famous no longer stands: the cripplingly expensive Adelphi housing estate. Almost all of the complex was pulled down in the 1930s and replaced by an office block, apart from the **Royal Society of Arts** building, just off the Strand on John Adam Street.

Soane and Nash

Just as the first residents were moving into the Adelphi in the early 1770s, a young unknown called John Soane was embarking on a domestic commission in Ireland. It was never completed, but Soane eventually returned to London and went on to build the **Bank of England** and **Dulwich Picture Gallery** (see p287). The Bank was demolished between the wars, leaving only the perimeter walls of Soane's masterpiece, but his gracious Stock Office has been reconstructed in the Bank's **museum** (see p231). A further glimpse of what the bankers might have enjoyed can be gleaned from his own house, the quirkily marvellous and recently extended **Sir John Soane's Museum** (see p216), an exquisite architectural experiment.

A near-contemporary of Soane's, John Nash was a less talented architect, but his contributions – among them the inner courtyard of **Buckingham Palace** (see p114), the **Theatre Royal Haymarket** and **Regent Street** (see p152) – have comparable influence in the look of contemporary London to those of Wren. Regent Street began as a proposal to link the West End to the planned park further north, as well as a device to separate the toffs of Mayfair from the riff-raff of Soho; in Nash's own words, a 'complete separation between the Streets occupied by the Nobility and Gentry, and the narrow Streets and meaner houses occupied by mechanics and the trading part of the community'.

By the 1830s, the Classical form of building had been established in England for some 200 years, but this didn't prevent a handful of upstarts from pressing for change. In 1834, the **Houses of Parliament** (see p107) burned down, leading to the construction of Sir Charles Barry's Gothic masterpiece. Barry sought out Augustus Welby Northmore Pugin. Working alongside Barry, if not always in agreement with him (of Barry's symmetrical layout, Pugin famously remarked, 'All Grecian, sir. Tudor details on a Classic body'), Pugin created a Victorian fantasy that would later be condemned as the Disneyfication of history.

Getting Gothic

This was the beginning of the Gothic Revival, a move to replace what was considered to be foreign and pagan with something that was native and Christian. Architects would often decide that buildings weren't Gothic enough; as with the 15th-century Great Hall at the **Guildhall** (see p231), which gained its corner turrets and central spire only in 1862. The argument

Natural History Museum

between Classicists and Goths erupted in 1857, when the government hired Sir George Gilbert Scott, a leading light of the Gothic movement, to design a new home for the **Foreign Office**. Scott's design incensed anti-Goth Lord Palmerston, then prime minister, whose diktats prevailed. But Scott exacted his revenge by building an office in which everyone hated working, and by going on to construct wonderful Gothic edifices all over town, among them the **Albert Memorial** (*see p124*) and what is now the **Renaissance St Pancras** hotel, which still forms the front of **St Pancras station** (*see p204*). Completed in 1873, after the Midland Railway commissioned Scott to build a London terminus that would dwarf its rival next door at King's Cross, St Pancras was an opportunity for Scott to show his mastery of the Gothic form. His asymmetrical castle obliterated views of the train shed behind, itself an engineering marvel completed earlier by William Barlow.

Other charming, imposing neo-Gothic buildings around the city include the **Royal Courts of Justice** (*see p222*), the **Natural History Museum** (*see p126*) and **Tower Bridge** (*see p237*). Under the influence of the Arts and Crafts movement, medievalism morphed into such mock Tudor buildings as the wonderful half-timbered **Liberty** department store (*see p155*).

Being modern

World War I and the coming of modernism led to a spirit of renewal and a starker aesthetic. **Freemasons' Hall** (*see p182*) and the BBC's **Broadcasting House** (*see p145*) are good examples of the pared-down style of the 1920s and '30s, but perhaps the finest example of between-the-wars modernism can be found at **London Zoo** (*see p245*). Built by Russian émigré Bertold Lubetkin and the Tecton group, the spiral ramps of the former Penguin Pool were a showcase for the possibilities of concrete. The material was also put to good use on the London Underground, enabling the quick, cheap building of cavernous spaces with sleek lines and curves: the collaboration between London Underground supremo Frank Pick and architect Charles Holden created design masterpieces such as **Southgate** and **Arnos Grove** stations at the north end of the Piccadilly Line, and **Chiswick Park station** to the west on the District Line, as well as the transport headquarters at **55 Broadway** – which featured sculptures by modern masters Jacob Epstein, Eric Gill and Henry Moore. Even local government offices were built with care and skill: see for yourself at the likes of the **Town Hall Hotel**, formerly Bethnal Green Town Hall (www. townhallhotel.com). Further innovations were employed on the gorgeous **Daily**

Architectural Showcase

Get the inside view on the city's built environment

Both the **Architectural Association** (36 Bedford Square, Bloomsbury, WC1B 3ES, 7887 4000, www.aaschool.ac.uk, closed Sun) and the appropriately handsome **Royal Institute of British Architects** (66 Portland Place, Marylebone, W1B 1AD, 7580 5533, www.architecture.com, closed Sun) have terrific exhibitions on different aspects of architecture, but for a focused look at London's architectural future, get off the tube at Goodge Street and visit **New London Architecture** (26 Store Street, Bloomsbury, WC1E 7BT, 7636 4044, www. newlondonarchitecture.org, closed Sun). It's been hosting inventive temporary exhibitions for a decade now, but the centrepiece exhibit is permanent: a 39-foot-long scale model of the city, with all major developments with planning permission indicated, gives real insight into the city's recent and future architecture. Exhibitions at the new **City Centre** (80 Basinghall Street, the City, EC2V 5AR, 7600 8362, www.thecitycentre.london, closed Sun) are more narrowly focused on the many developments in the City; it has a good model too (open 10am-5pm Fri, Sat).

In addition, Open City's **Open House London** (see p316) festival is a key date in the architecture calendar each year. It does a brilliant job of getting locals engaged with their city by giving public access to amazing buildings of all epochs.

Express building (121-128 Fleet Street), built in 1931 using the pioneering 'curtain wall' construction, its radical black Vitrolite and glass façade hung on an internal frame.

The bombs of World War II left large areas of London ruined, providing another opportunity for builders to cash in. Lamentably, the city was little improved by the rebuild; in many cases, it was left worse off. The destruction left the capital with a dire housing shortage, so architects were given a chance to demonstrate the grim efficiency with which they could house large numbers of families in tower blocks. There were post-war successes, however, including the **Royal Festival Hall** (see p82) on the South Bank. The sole survivor of the 1951 Festival of Britain, the RFH was built to celebrate the end of the war and the centenary of the Great Exhibition, held in 1851 and responsible for the foundation in South Kensington of the Natural History Museum, the Science Museum and the V&A. Next to the RFH, the recently renovated **Hayward Gallery** is an exemplar of the 1960s vogue for brutalist architecture, a style that is more thoroughly explored at the recently renovated **Barbican** (see p227) and Denys Lasdun's National Theatre. Widely loathed since construction, London's concrete monoliths have since gained a cult following, with various books and Instagram feeds celebrating their divisive beauty.

Here come the Starchitects

The 1970s and '80s offered a pair of alternatives to concrete: postmodernism and high-tech. The former is represented by César Pelli's blandly monumental **One Canada Square** (see p274) in Docklands, an oversized obelisk that's perhaps the archetypal expression of late '80s architecture – and whose impact is hard to imagine now it stands in a copse of inferior office blocks. Richard Rogers's high-tech **Lloyd's of London** building (see p232) is much more widely admired. A clever combination of commercial and industrial aesthetics that adds up to one of the most significant British buildings since the war, it was mocked on completion in 1986 but, having been thoroughly rehabilitated, is now in danger of being choked by surrounding skyscrapers: Rogers' 48-storey **122 Leadenhall** ('the Cheesegrater') stands just opposite, with the bland **22 Bishopsgate**, the City's new tallest building at 912 feet (278 metres) and 62 storeys, behind that.

Apart from Rogers, the city's most visible contemporary architect has been Norman Foster, whose **City Hall** and **30 St Mary Axe** (universally known as 'the Gherkin', for obvious reasons; see p233) caught up with Big Ben and black taxis as movie shorthand for 'Welcome to London!' – only to be overtaken in 2012 by the giant glass spike of Renzo Piano's **Shard** (see p94), facing the City across the Thames. Foster's prolific practice set new standards with the exercise in complexity that is the £100-million Great Court at the **British Museum** (see p198). Most recently, he has overseen the construction of the new **Bloomberg London** building in the City at a cost of £1 billion, which houses a third-century Roman temple as well as a 21st-century business HQ.

Much new architecture is to be found cunningly inserted into old buildings. Herzog & de Meuron's fabulous transformation of a Bankside power station into **Tate Modern** (see p89) is the most famous example – the firm repeated its success, perhaps even bettered it, with the ambitious new Switch House extension, a vast quasi-pyramid that unfolds itself upwards like self-assembled origami. The views from the top are breathtaking – much to the chagrin of dwellers in the luxury flats opposite, who took legal action against the gallery for invasion of privacy.

Zaha Hadid died in spring 2016, but her swooping, sinuous architecture has finally made itself felt in her adopted city: her stunning Aquatics Centre was opened in the Olympic Park in 2011, followed by the **Serpentine Sackler Gallery** (see p133) in 2013 and the new Winton Gallery, the dedicated maths section of the **Science Museum** (see p127), in 2016.

Arts and local colour

Architecture hasn't all been about headline projects and eye-troubling commercial developments. The late Will Alsop's multicoloured **Peckham Library** (122 Peckham Hill Street) helped to redefine community architecture in 2000, and architects have continued to play a major role in redefining public libraries. David Adjaye subsequently designed the **Idea Stores** (www.ideastore.co.uk) in Poplar (1 Vesey Path, East India Dock Road) and Whitechapel (321 Whitechapel Road), with a crisp, softened industrial aesthetic that is a world away from the familiar Victorian library, while in 2011, Piers Gough's upside-down pyramid, **Canada Water Library** (21 Surrey Quays Road), provided a focus for a rather incoherent district in south-east London. The subtle Robbrecht en Daem expansion of **Whitechapel Gallery** (see p263) into the stylistically very different former library next door reversed this process, giving a new democratic openness to a pair of landmark Victorian buildings, while Caruso St John finally won itself a Stirling Prize in 2016 for a brilliant conversion of early 20th-century scenery-painting warehouses into Damien Hirst's vast **Newport Street Gallery** (see p85).

The end of the megabuilds?

In the north of London, the transformation of King's Cross incorporates the reopened St Pancras International station; a refurbished **King's Cross station** with an arresting new roof; the new-build office/concert venue **Kings Place** (see p355); and Central Saint Martins art college, in a redeveloped Victorian granary on the fine **Granary Square**, with its restaurants, geometric, choreographed fountains and terracing down to the canal. As well as the

brand new **Coal Drops Yard**, a shopping and leisure precinct designed by next-gen starchitect Thomas Heatherwick, the 67-acre redevelopment of King's Cross will eventually also comprise 1,900 new homes, serviced by 20 new streets and another four squares, in a part of London that was given its own new postcode: N1C.

Just as impressive – and also with its own postcode, E20, cannily borrowed from the fictional London borough in long-running BBC TV soap opera *EastEnders* – is the **Olympic Park** (see p276). Having fulfilled its function as the heavily policed major venue for the 2012 Olympics and Paralympics, its slow conversion into a public amenity began (its 'legacy', to use the jargon). Taxpayers had reason to expect rather a lot from a project for which the original £2.4-billion budget was increased to an eye-watering £9.3 billion. The shortfall in promised affordable housing on the site remains controversial, but otherwise the results are pretty impressive: from a superb park, with excellent playgrounds, to the beautiful wood-clad Velodrome, Hadid's Aquatics Centre and the red spirals of the Anish Kapoor-designed **ArcelorMittal Orbit** – whose latest bid for local affection was the installation of a giant slide (see p277). The reopening of the Olympic Stadium as West Ham's football ground for the 2016/17 season brought the process to a turbulent end, with poor results on the pitch and talk of unfair financial settlements off it.

The future of the future

When London's population breached the 8.7-million mark in 2015 – it's the city's highest population in history – it seemed clear what architects would be doing for the foreseeable future: housing and planning for housing. Since the country voted for Brexit, despite London mostly voting to remain, things haven't been quite so certain. Will London's population continue to grow so quickly if the UK closes itself to EU migration? Possibly: an impressive proportion of newcomers to London are actually from elsewhere in the UK. But will Brexit also have a chastening effect on the loathed luxury sector of the housing market, which successive London mayors have used to subsidise affordable housing? And what about the city's construction industry, which employs a disproportionate number of EU citizens? In the face of all this uncertainty, plus government reforms to stamp duty, London's property market has started to experience its first signs of stalling.

For now, the megabuilds continue getting the green light: Vauxhall and the long-postponed **Battersea Power Station** (see

Zaha Hadid's Aquatics Centre in the Olympic Park

p290) is one; the regeneration of Tottenham (where the 2011 riots began) focused on Spurs' new football stadium another. But plummeting values on the Earls Court redevelopment in west London, the collapse of a private-public development partnership in Haringey and the failure of many high-end properties to sell at all suggest the lights could be about to change.

There has been a change of tone from the city's political leadership as well. Boris Johnson's mayoralty was synonymous with vanity projects, from the underused Emirates Air Line cable car to the unfeasible 'Boris Island' airport in the Thames estuary. Johnson's final folly, the Garden Bridge, ran out of time and was cancelled by his successor Sadiq Khan – but not before £46 million of public money had been spent without any construction work taking place. Khan has also scrapped the recalibrated definition of 'affordable' used by his predecessor and increased the proportion of new homes priced within reach of the average Londoner. But despite the literally hundreds of new skyscraper projects planned across the city, overall house-building is still nowhere near what London needs to contain its increasing population, and many new housing developments that make it past local planners tend to be functional conservative, neo-Georgian affairs in biscuity brick.

Planners have been pointing east to the 'Thames Gateway' ever since the Docklands were first redeveloped in the 1980s. Now that possibility is underpinned by the unsteady progress of the colossally ambitious **Crossrail** project (*see p381* The Archaeology of Crossrail). The new railway has already wormed its way under key areas of the city, including Oxford Street, connecting London's outlying suburbs to the east and west with the city centre. It is an extraordinary feat of civil engineering, with each new station given an architectural treatment inspired by local history – and it has had an equally extraordinary ripple effect on nearby property values.

Those same planners, however, are also beginning to reach a consensus that London must be allowed to expand outwards on to the sacred 'Green Belt' – a girdle of protected land that is, they argue, less the bucolic fantasy its name conjures than an agglomeration of golf courses, minor industry and low-density suburban dwellings. Khan has explicitly and repeatedly ruled out any such manoeuvre, instead proposing to densify the outer suburbs while increasing the overall amount of green space across town. Meanwhile, long-standing anti-development groups known as NIMBYs ('Not In My Back Yard') are now rivalled by organisations like the London YIMBYs, who advocate for more local construction to solve the city's housing crisis. The battle is on for London's architectural soul – and the ferocity with which it is being fought suggests the city's crazy mixture of new and old is set to continue well into the 21st century.

Plan

Accommodation	396
Getting Around	404
Resources A-Z	410
Further Reference	419
Index	422

Accommodation

London continues to be a magnet for international hoteliers as well as their guests. Whether Brexit cools their ardour remains to be seen, but so far the pace of deluxe openings has hardly slowed, with a host of major new establishments opening their doors in Bloomsbury, the City and Bankside in 2018 and 2019.

The price of rooms in London is pretty shocking, but it's not all top-dollar activity. The pioneering Hoxton has an even better sister-hotel – the Hoxton Holborn – and the excellent Dutch citizenM chain is expanding its properties over here. Qbic and the Z hotels are other favourites for visitors on a budget.

Staying in London

There are some ridiculously good deals offered online for 'London rooms', sometimes even 'central London rooms' or 'well-connected London rooms'. Always do your research on the location before you part with any money. Greater London is pretty huge and few people have a vision of their holiday that involves spending an hour on public transport to get to the heart of things. That said, there's no need to focus exclusively on the West End, fun though a stay bang in the middle of London is – it's a privilege only a tiny percentage of Londoners get to share, after all. Get somewhere to stay on the South Bank and you certainly won't regret it, but the City – the original walled square mile(ish) of London – is a superb concentration of major sights furnished with plenty of business hotels. They may not be the funkiest places, but there are deals to be had, particularly at weekends. East London retains some of its art-and-fashion

In the know
Price categories

Our price categories are based on hotels' standard prices (not including seasonal offers or discounts) for one night in a double room with en suite shower/bath.

Luxury	£350+
Expensive	£250-£350
Moderate	£130-£250
Budget	up to £130

COME LIE WITH US

coolness and is much better served by hotels than it was even a couple of years ago. You'll be delighted you found somewhere thereabouts if you're planning on some hard nights of clubbing. Or, if you can afford it, a stay in one of the grand old Mayfair hotels is a holiday without even having to step out of the door.

Money matters

In London, the average price of a double room for the night seems to be settling somewhere around £150, at the lower end of our 'Moderate' category (*see p396*). But these categories are just a guide. A hotel's rates can vary widely, both top to bottom and over the course of the year. As a rule, it's best to book as far ahead as possible, and always try the hotel's own website first: many offer special online deals throughout the year; pretty much every business hotel will offer steep reductions for a Sunday night stay.

Be aware that a few hotels – particularly at the top of the price range – don't include VAT (a 20 per cent sales tax) in the rates they quote. And watch out for added extras. If you're bringing a car (which we recommend you don't – London isn't a good city for drivers), always check with the hotel before you arrive: few central hotels offer parking, and those that do charge steeply for it.

It's also worth looking at hotel booking websites: uk.hotels.com is often good. And, if you are staying for longer than a weekend, or you fancy staying in one of the thriving neighbourhoods outside central London, then the myriad rental rooms and apartments offered by www.airbnb.co.uk and homeaway.co.uk are worth a look. For a more curated selection, check out www.plumguide.com, which cherry picks the top one per cent of holiday rental properties in the capital.

Great Northern Hotel, designed by Lewis Cubitt, was the city's first railway hotel, opened in 1854, part of the Victorian railway explosion.

Antony Gormley-designed ROOM: a striking Cubist-influenced sculpture outside the front entrance to the Beaumont Hotel.

One of the big openings of 2017, The Ned occupies a former bank building in the City.

Luxury

Other recommended options include the timeless and classy **Langham** (1C Portland Place, Regent Street, W1B 1JA, 7636 1000, www.langhamhotels.com/en/the-langham/london) and the perfectly placed **Covent Garden Hotel** (10 Monmouth Street, Covent Garden, WC2H 9HB, 7806 1000, www.firmdalehotels.com).

The Beaumont

Brown Hart Gardens, Mayfair, W1K 6TF (7499 1001, www.thebeaumont.com). Bond Street tube. **Map** *p142 H7.*

Oddly, the Grade II-listed façade is the least impressive part of this hotel, set in the vast 1926 garage where Selfridges shoppers used to get their jalopies tuned up. It is in the painstakingly rebuilt interiors that this art deco fantasia sings. There's smooth service and a lovely private bar/drawing room off the foyer. The staff gets the marriage of glamorous formality and approachability just right, and the owners' personal travel bugbears have created some really thoughtful touches, from the sliding screens that isolate beds from bathrooms to the free soft drinks, movies and shoeshines.

Towering over the handsome square in front of the Beaumont is the Antony Gormley-designed ROOM: on the outside it's a striking Cubist-influenced sculpture; on the inside it's a two-storey suite in immaculate art deco style, leading through to a low-lit, almost womb-like bedroom right inside the sculpture.

Claridge's

55 Brook Street, Mayfair, W1K 4HR (7629 8860, www.claridges.co.uk). Bond Street tube. **Map** *p142 J7.*

Claridge's is sheer class and pure atmosphere and, with its signature art deco redesign, still simply dazzling. Photographs of past guests, including Churchill and sundry royals, grace the grand foyer, as does an absurdly over-the-top Dale Chihuly chandelier. Without departing too far from the traditional, Claridge's

has managed to keep its restaurants actively fashionable, and A-listers can gather for champers in the discreet bar. The rooms divide evenly between deco and Victorian style, with period touches such as deco toilet flushes in swanky marble bathrooms. Bedside panels control the mod-con facilities at the touch of a button. If money's no object, opt for a David Linley suite, in duck-egg blue and white, or lilac and silver.

The Dorchester

53 Park Lane, Mayfair, W1K 1QA (7629 8888, www.thedorchester.com). Hyde Park Corner tube. **Map** *p142 H8.*

A Park Lane fixture since 1931, the Dorchester's interior may be thoroughly, opulently classical, but the hotel is cutting-edge in attitude, providing an unrivalled level of personal service. With the grandest lobby in town, amazing views of Hyde Park, state-of-the-art mod cons and a magnificent spa, it's small wonder the hotel continues to welcome movie stars (the lineage stretches from Elizabeth Taylor to Tom Cruise) and political leaders (Eisenhower planned the D-Day landings here). It's said to have the deepest baths in London. You're not likely to be eating out, either: the Dorchester employs 90 full-time chefs at the the Grill, Alain Ducasse and the wonderfully atmospheric China Tang. There's even an angelic tearoom in the spa: the Spatisserie.

A few years ago, the Dorchester opened an entirely new hotel, **45 Park Lane** (7493 4545, www.dorchestercollection.com/en/london/45-park-lane), in the former Playboy Club premises, almost opposite the entrance to its predecessor.

The Mandrake

20-21 Newman Street, Fitzrovia, W1T 1PG (3146 7770, www.themandrake.com). Tottenham Court Road tube. **Map** *p194 K6.* Inspired by the plant it's named after and converted from a RIBA-winning building in Fitzrovia, this OTT hotel was an instant hit with

the fashion crowd when it opened in 2017. And no wonder: its dark, intimate and opulent styling is a feast for the senses: there are sumptuous and quirky elements, including a carefully curated private art collection throughout. The 30-plus bedrooms, set over four floors, are little works of art in their own right, featuring bespoke chandeliers, vintage furniture and contemporary trappings. They surround a beautiful hidden courtyard, dripping with jasmine and passion flower. Dining comes courtesy of Serge et le Phoque, an outpost of a hip French restaurant in Hong Kong.

The Ned

27 Poultry, the City, EC2R 8AJ (3828 2000, www.thened.com). Bank tube. **Map** *p212 Q7.*

This five-star hotel and members' club is a collaboration between the Soho House Group and the Sydell Group (a US business behind the NoMad in New York). Together they have lovingly refurbished the Grade I-listed former Midland Bank building in the City to the tune of £200 million to create a seriously swanky spot that has moneyed hipsters swooning. The vast and opulent ground-floor banking hall hosts ten bars and restaurants (*see p224* for our picks). Above are 250 bedrooms and a members' area called Ned's Club that comprises a rooftop pool, gym, spa, hammam and late-night lounge bar. Phew! The accommodation ranges from fairly modest 'Cosy' rooms and 'Crash pads' to more luxurious 'Heritage' rooms that feature French-polished walnut panelling, four-poster beds and other nods to 1920s' opulence. It's worth noting that not all members' areas are open to guests in the cheaper rooms. And the name? The original building was designed by Sir Edwin Lutyens, known to his friends as 'Ned'.

Sea Containers London

20 Upper Ground, South Bank, SE1 9PD (3747 1000, www.seacontainerslondon.com). Blackfriars tube. **Map** *p80 O8.*

Location's everything here: this hotel is right on the Thames, with the views on the bank side of the building among the best in London – low enough to feel part of the city, high enough to feel exclusive. The rooms are nicely furnished by Tom Dixon in a kind of postmodern deco style, minimalist without leaving you feeling the sharp edges. Public spaces are terrific and playfully ship-themed (not least the prow that encases the reception desks) and there are plenty of areas for meetings. The ground-floor cocktail bar, Lyaness (previously the world-famous Dandelyan), is still run by master mixologist Ryan Chetiyawardana, so expect the unexpected. There's a less accomplished restaurant on the ground floor, as well as a blingier bar in a glass cube on the roof (the 12th Knot, closed Mon, Sun) and a cosy Curzon cinema.

Shangri-La at the Shard

31 St Thomas Street, Southwark, SE1 9QU (7234 8000, www. shangri-la.com/london). London Bridge tube/rail. Map p80 R9.
The Shangri-La is unusual in many ways. The hotel proper starts on floor 35 with a spacious foyer and restaurant: the ground floor is just a pre-reception and security bag scanner before the uncannily smooth and swift lift. The building's pyramid shape means every room is different, with most floor space and hence the poshest suites on 36 and 37, not at the top. And the rooms are priced by view: the most expensive look north, offering 180° Thames vistas. Those views are amazing, as you'd expect: absorbing as dusk falls and the city lights come on, especially from the lobby and restaurant. The Skypool, fitness room and bar feel a bit remote, way up on floor 52. The decor is cosmopolitan Asian neutral, with some unimpressive bits of design offset by imaginative touches (binoculars for you to enjoy the view, torches to ease jetlagged room navigation in bedside drawers). Staff members are multicultural and friendly, cheerfully solving problems and seeming rather pleased to be here.

Zetter Townhouse (49-50 St John's Square, EC1V 4JJ, 7324 4567, www.thezettertownhouse. com/clerkenwell) is a great option in Clerkenwell.

Boundary London

2-4 Boundary Street, Shoreditch, E2 7DD (7729 1051, boundary. london). Liverpool Street tube/rail or Shoreditch High Street Overground. Map p256 S5.
Design mogul Sir Terence Conran's Boundary Project warehouse conversion was a labour of love. Its restaurants – which include Albion, Tratra, a French restaurant by best-selling cookery book writer Stéphane Reynaud, and a rooftop bar – are high quality but relaxed places, and all 17 bedrooms are beautifully designed. Each has a handmade bed, but all are otherwise individually furnished with classic pieces and original art. The five studios, lofts and suites range in style from the bright and sea-salt fresh Beach to modern Chinoiserie by Sir David Tang, while the remaining bedrooms (the slightly larger corner bedrooms have windows along both external walls) are themed by design style: Mies van der Rohe, Eames, Shaker. There's also a charming Heath Robinson room, decorated with the cartoonist's sketches of hilariously complex machines.

The Curtain

45 Curtain Road, Shoreditch, EC2A 4PJ (3146 4545, thecurtain. com). Old Street tube/rail. Shoreditch High Street Overground. Map p256 S5.
Curtain's cool Manhattan-style surroundings are perfectly placed a stroll away from both Brick Lane and Hoxton Square. Red brick and glass predominate, creating a warehouse-meets-luxury feel. Overnighters won't want to miss the in-house Red Rooster restaurant (top-notch, Obama-approved, Southern-fried everything) before nipping down to the basement club (Skepta's been) or taking in the rooftop pool and terrace. Bedrooms have quality furnishings, gorgeous bathrooms (with rain showers) and fully stocked minibars.

Great Northern Hotel

King's Cross St Pancras Station, Pancras Road, King's Cross, N1C 4TB (3388 0800, gnhlondon.com). King's Cross tube/rail. Map p194 M3.
Designed by Lewis Cubitt, the city's first railway hotel opened in 1854, part of the Victorian railway explosion. It has had plenty of rough times since then, not least the 12 years it was dark, but almost £40 million of renovation has recreated the place as a classic. The furniture is by artisans and, in many cases, bespoke: witness the Couchette rooms, each with a double bed snugly fitted into the window to playfully echo sleeper carriages; the neatly upholstered bedside cabinets; or the ceiling lights raised and lowered by fabulously steampunk pulleys. You're not expected to suffer the privations of a Victorian traveller, though: fast Wi-Fi, film and music libraries on the large TV, Egyptian cotton sheets and walk-in showers are all standard. There's no room service but each floor has a simply charming pantry, full of jars of vintage sweets, a stand of fresh cakes, tea and coffee, newspapers and books – even a USB printer. There's also Plum + Spilt Milk, a grand restaurant with a quiet bar, on the first floor, while the busy ground-floor GNH Bar has direct access to King's Cross station.

London Edition

10 Berners Street, Fitzrovia, W1T 3NP (7781 0000, www. editionhotels.com/london). Oxford Circus or Tottenham Court Road tube. Map p194 K6.
The London Edition makes a big impact as you walk into its grand hall of a lobby, complete with double-height rococo ceilings, floor-to-ceiling windows and marble pillars. And there's more to the space: it's the setting for the lobby bar, with an eclectic mix of comfortable, snazzy seating – sofas with faux-fur throws and wing-backed chairs – plus a snooker table, a blackened steel bar, a real fire and a colossal silver egg-shaped object hanging where you might expect a chandelier. Off on one side is the equally opulent Berners Tavern (*see p207*), where

Jason Atherton is executive chef. With banquette seating and many paintings, it has the vibe of a grand café and a brasserie-style menu to match. Hidden away at the back of the public area is the clubby, wood-panelled Punch Room bar, where the speciality is – you've guessed it – punch. Bedrooms are a contrast: akin to lodges or dachas, with matte oak floors, wood-panelled walls and more faux-fur throws tossed on luxurious beds. Larger rooms come with sofas, some have large furnished terraces, and all have rainforest showers, Le Labo toiletries (with the hotel's woody signature scent) and iPod docks.

Rookery
12 Peter's Lane, Cowcross Street, Clerkenwell, EC1M 6DS (7336 0931, www.rookeryhotel.com). Farringdon tube/rail. Map p212 P6.
The Rookery has long been something of a celebrity hideaway deep in the heart of Clerkenwell. Its front door is satisfyingly hard to find; when Fabric (see p339) devotees are about the front rooms can be noisy, but the place is otherwise creakily calm as a country manor. Once inside, guests enjoy an atmospheric warren of rooms, each individually decorated in the style of a Georgian townhouse: huge clawfoot baths, elegant four-posters, antique desks, old paintings and brass shower fittings. While the decor is dialled to 18th-century glamour, modernity is definitely not forgotten. There's an honesty bar in the bright and airy drawing room at the back, which opens on to a sweet little patio. The ground-floor suite has its own hallway, a cosy boudoir and a subterranean bathroom with a double-ended cast-iron bath.

W London Leicester Square
10 Wardour Street, Leicester Square, W1D 6QF (7758 1000, www.wlondon.co.uk). Leicester Square tube. Map p165 L8.
Where the old Swiss Centre used to be in the north-west corner of Leicester Square is the UK's first W Hotel, the entire building veiled in translucent glass that is lit in different colours through the day. (The presence of M&M World downstairs dials the wow-factor down a little, but it's the thought that counts.) The brand made its name with hip hotels around the world that offer glamorous bars, upmarket food and functional but spacious rooms. The London W is no exception: the Perception bar is a large nightclub/bar space with possibly the largest glitterball in town; while the W lounge offers classy cocktails and a Sunday brunch party. There's also a branch of the deathlessly popular concept restaurant Burger & Lobster. The rooms – across ten storeys – are well equipped, with their own munchie boxes. FIT (the hotel's state-of-the-art fitness facility), placed next to the pale and serene Away Spa on the sixth floor, offers fine views over Soho. Oh, and there's a private 3D cinema.

Moderate

Hoxton Holborn
199-206 High Holborn, Holborn, WC1V 7BD (7661 3000, thehoxton. com). Holborn tube. Map p181 M6.
Shoebox, Snug, Cosy and Roomy. That's the choice you get when you stay at the Hoxton's trendy Holborn outpost, but who cares about room size when you're just about as close to the centre of London as it's possible to be. In truth, following the template set by the original Hoxton hotel in east London, the rooms are so well designed you barely notice their size. Clever use of mirrors helps to enlarge the space, reflecting the room's dark walls, soft lighting and casually hip vibe. Add to that a snazzy TV and a lovely walk-in shower. The West End's bars and restaurants are right on your doorstep but the hotel bar, decked out in 1970s furniture, does a mean negroni to get you started.

K West
Richmond Way, Shepherd's Bush, W14 0AX (8008 6600, www.k-west.co.uk). Shepherd's Bush tube/ Overground.
Behind the sleek glass façade of this former BBC building – where Bob Marley once played – is a thoroughly modern hotel with a sense of fun. An in-house DJ spins until the early hours at weekends, there's a super-swish spa and each airy, sizeable room comes with its very own smart tablet and, even more helpfully, smart phones that

Hoxton Holborn

come with unlimited data browsing so you can go off into London and explore the city. Service is wonderfully attentive, rooms are clean and smart and it's great value for money.

La Suite West

41-51 Inverness Terrace, Bayswater, W2 3JN (7313 8484, www.lasuitewest.com). Bayswater or Queensway tube. **Map** *pull-out map D7.*

A typical row of west London townhouses on the outside, La Suite has been transformed on the inside by designer Anouska Hempel, with sleek lines and a black and white palette. A discreet side entrance leads into a long, minimalist reception area with an open fire and a zen-like feel. An Asian influence persists in the rooms, with slatted sliding screens for windows, wardrobe and bathrooms helping to make good use of space (which is limited in the cheaper rooms). Thoughtfully designed white marble bathrooms, with rainforest shower and bath, give a feeling of luxury despite not being huge. The large terrace running along the front of the building, with trees planted for an arbour-like effect, is a big summer asset for drinks, lunch or dinner, and the vegan restaurant is an unusual take on hotel dining. All in all, clever design, a friendly vibe and

– importantly – keen pricing make for a great hotel for this price range. Highly recommended.

The Pilgrm

25 London Street, Paddington, W2 1HH (thepilgrm.com). Paddington tube/rail. **Map** *fold-out map E7.*

Hate checking in? You'll love the Pilgrm. With this affordable (by London standards) 73-room hotel, Jason Catifeoglou – formerly of the Zetter group – has done away with reception, minibars and phones to create a hotel that has a personal feel and features super-fast Wi-Fi, Marshall speakers, 24-hour pantries and natural toiletries. (Plastics begone, we're using soap on a rope!) He has sensitively retained and restored original Victorian fixtures and fittings while adding interesting reclaimed ones to create a unique space that's a real winner. Head chef Sara Lewis (formerly of Grain Store) works wonders in the Lounge.

Sanctum Soho

20 Warwick Street, Soho, W1B 5NF (7292 6100, www.sanctumsoho.com). Oxford Circus or Piccadilly Circus tube. **Map** *p165 K8.*

In a former MI5 research building, Sanctum is Soho-club cool with its dark colours, bling room handles and deco lamps, sexed up

with a handful of rotating beds and a no-questions-asked policy. The rooms follow one of four colour schemes, broadly deco or powder-puff boudoir in style, with plenty of mirrors and an unspeakable number of TV channels. The residents-only, 24hr-means-24hr bar is small but funky, opening on to a two-level terrace outside, which is topped off with a multi-person jacuzzi. The fun continues with a guitar-tuning service at reception, a smoothly run and darkly handsome bar-restaurant, louche art in each room and a screening room for hire downstairs.

Shoreditch House

Ebor Street, Shoreditch, E1 6AW (7739 5040, www.sohohouse.com/ houses/shoreditch-house). Shoreditch High Street Overground. **Map** *p256 S5.*

One of several accommodation offerings from the Soho House members' club, Shoreditch House might even be the best, perfectly catching the local atmosphere with its unfussy, slightly retro design. The rooms feel a bit like urban beach huts, with pastel-coloured tongue-and-groove shutters and swing doors to the en suite showers. They feel fresh, bright and comfortable, even though they're furnished with little more than a bed, an old-fashioned phone and DAB radio,

Qbic London City Hotel

and a big, solid dresser (minibar, hairdryer and treats within, flatscreen TV on top). Guests get access to the fine eating, drinking and fitness facilities (yes, there is a gym, but more importantly an excellent rooftop pool) in the members' club next door. Everything's put together with a light touch, from the 'Borrow Me' bookshelf by the lifts (jelly beans, umbrellas, boardgames) to the room grades: Tiny (from just £125), Small or Small+ (with little rooftop balconies from which to survey the grey horizon).

Zetter Hotel

St John's Square, 86-88 Clerkenwell Road, EC1M 5RJ (7324 4567, www.thezetter.com). Farringdon tube/rail. **Map** *p212 P5.*

Zetter is a fun, laid-back, modern hotel with some interesting design notes. There's a refreshing lack of attitude and a forward-looking approach, with friendly staff and firm eco-credentials (such as free Brompton bikes for guests' use). The rooms, stacked up on five galleried storeys around an impressive atrium, look into an intimate and recently refreshed bar area. They are smoothly functional, but cosied up with choice home comforts such as hot-water bottles and old Penguin paperbacks, as well as having walk-in showers with REN smellies. The downstairs is home to Club Zetter, while the fabulous sister-hotel **Zetter Townhouse**, in a historic building just across the square, has a fantastic cocktail bar with a hip vintage feel (*see p219*).

Budget

citizenM London Bankside

20 Lavington Street, Southwark, SE1 0NZ (3519 1680, www.citizenm.com). Southwark tube. **Map** *p124 P8.*

This casually stylish new build is a superbly well-designed – and well-located – addition to London's affordably chic hotels. The ground floor is a slick yet cosy café-bar and reception area: self-check-in, but with staff on hand to help and, where better rooms are available, offer upgrades. Guests

are invited to use this area as their 'living room' and – thanks to the neat design – do so. The rooms themselves are tiny but well thought through: there are blackout blinds, drench showers with removable sideheads, storage under the bed and free movies. The rooms are also fun: those blinds are automatic, controlled – as are the movies, air-con and funky coloured lighting – from a touch-sensitive tablet. **Other locations** 6 Holywell Lane, Shoreditch, EC2A 3ET; 40 Trinity Square, Tower Hill, EC3N 4DJ.

Dictionary Hostel

10-20 Kingsland Road, Shoreditch, E2 8DA (7613 2784, thedictionaryhostel.com/en). Old Street tube/rail or Shoreditch High Street Overground. **Map** *p256 S4.*

Club kids, you've found your home: right at the axis of Kingsland Road and Old Street and so walking – or crawling – distance from Hoxton's best dance spots. There's a bar downstairs, Translate, and also a laundrette, a café, a cute, plant-covered interior courtyard and an intimate roof terrace. There are dorm beds and private rooms starting at £17 (with TVs, kettle and coffee). Jam-jar lighting, swings in the dorms and fairy-lit communal areas are quirky touches, which make for an enjoyable stay. Breakfast is free and includes the highly prized bagels from nearby Brick Lane.

Luxury Inn

156 Tottenham Road, De Beauvoir, N1 4DY (7683 3056, www.theluxuryinn.com). Dalston Junction rail.

If you're after modern amenities in a contemporary setting, which still retains a certain historical charm, then head to this family-run bed and breakfast, set in a converted factory in the conservation area of De Beauvoir, between Islington and Dalston. Its four en suite rooms surround a stylish loft space. With a self-service breakfast in a shared dining room-lounge area, free run of the kitchen, and a lush courtyard garden you can really make yourself at home.

Qbic London City Hotel

42 Adler Street, Whitechapel, E1 1EE (3021 3300, www.qbichotels.com). Aldgate East or Whitechapel tube. **Map** *p256 T7.*

The Dutch invasion of stylish budget hotels continues with this Brick Lane offering, created by the incredibly rapid fit-out of a former office building using modular 'Cubi' bedrooms. The hotel also works with local cycling charity Bikeworks and with Food Cycle, which provides free soup every afternoon. The rooms are sold at four levels – starting at £69 a night for no view, and increasing in price if you want to see the Whitechapel Road, the inner courtyard or Altab Ali Park. Prices are pegged by keeping down the numbers of staff, which means self check-in and no cash accepted – even vending machines are card only. Still, the essentials are covered: TVs in each room, Wi-Fi throughout, free snack breakfast (or £13 for a continental) in the natty social space downstairs. The location is gritty but great: minutes from Brick Lane.

Z Hotel Soho

17 Moor Street, Soho, W1D 5AP (3551 3701, www.thezhotels.com/soho). Leicester Square tube. **Map** *p165 L7.*

For the money, the Z is an absolute bargain. First, the location is superb: it really means Soho, not a short bus-ride away – the breakfast room/bar exits on to Old Compton Street. Then there's the hotel itself, which is surprisingly chic – especially the unexpected interior courtyard, with open 'corridors' stacked above it, and room to sit and drink or smoke at the bottom – and very cheerfully run, down to free wine and nibbles of an evening. The rooms are quite handsome, and have everything you need, from a little desk to free Wi-Fi, but not much more. Including space: expect beds (perhaps a little short for anyone over 6ft tall) to take up most of the room. A great little hotel – in both senses – and, we're pleased to report, part of a chain that's expanding. **Other locations** throughout the city; see the website for details.

Getting Around

ARRIVING & LEAVING

By air

Gatwick Airport *0844 892 0322, www.gatwickairport.com. About 30 miles south of London, off the M23.*

Of the three rail services that link Gatwick to central London, the quickest is the **Gatwick Express** (0345 850 1530, www.gatwickexpress.com) to Victoria; it takes 30mins and runs every 15mins 5am-11.30pm daily. Tickets cost £19.90 single or £37.80 for an open return. Under-16s pay £9.95 for a single and £18.35 for returns; under-5s go free. Online prices are cheaper.

Southern (0345 127 2920, www.southernrailway.com) also runs a rail service between Gatwick and Victoria, with trains every 5-10mins (hourly 2-4am and every 15-30mins midnight-2am, 4-6am). It takes about 35mins, and costs from £15 for a single, £16.30 for a day return (after 9.30am) and £32.40 for an open period return. Under-16s get half-price tickets; under-5s go free. Book online and save 10%.

Thameslink Great Northern (www.thameslinkrailway.com) costs from £16.20 single and from £32.40 for an open return.

For transfers by coach, **National Express** (0871 781 8171, www.nationalexpress.com) runs daily services to Victoria from both terminals, £8 single, £16 return, taking 85mins.

A **taxi** to the centre costs from £90 and takes a bit over an hour.

Heathrow Airport *0844 335 1801, www.heathrowairport.com. About 15 miles west of London, off the M4.*

The **Heathrow Express** train (0845 600 1515, www.heathrowexpress.co.uk) runs to Paddington every 15mins (5.12am-11.42pm daily) and takes 15-20mins. Tickets cost £22-£25 single and £37 return (more if you buy on board); under-15s travel at half-price; under-2s free. Many airlines have check-in desks at Paddington Station.

The journey by tube is longer but cheaper. The 50-60min **Piccadilly line** ride into central London costs £6 one way (half price 11-15s; free under-10s). Trains run every few minutes from 5.10am to 11.45pm daily (5.40am-11.15pm Sun). Fares using Oyster cards are cheaper (£3.10-£5.10).

TfL Rail (0343 222 1234, tfl.gov.uk) trains also run to central London (same fares as the tube). This service is due to become integrated with the new Elizabeth Line when it opens in late 2019 (see p407 Crossrail).

National Express (0871 781 8171, www.nationalexpress.com) runs daily coach services to London Victoria (35-60mins, 4.20am-10.05pm daily), leaving Heathrow Central bus terminal every 20-30mins. It's £8 for a single (£4 under-16s) or £16 (£8 under-16s) for a return.

A **taxi** into town will cost £45-£70 and take 30-60mins.

London City Airport *7646 0088, www.londoncityairport.com. About 9 miles east of central London.*

The **Docklands Light Railway** (DLR) includes a stop for London City Airport and runs every 8-15mins. The journey to Bank station in the City takes around 20mins, and trains run 5.37am-12.17am Mon-Sat, 7.07am-11.17pm Sun. Tickets cost £4.90; £2.40 11-15s. A **taxi** costs around £40 to central London.

Luton Airport *01582 405100, www.london-luton.co.uk. About 30 miles north of London, J10 off the M1.*

It's a short shuttle bus ride from the airport to Luton Airport Parkway station. From here, the **Thameslink Great Northern** rail service (see left) calls at many stations; journey time is 35-45mins. Trains leave every 15mins or so and cost from £16.90 one-way and £18.90 return. Trains between Luton and St Pancras run at least hourly all night.

By coach, the Luton to Victoria journey takes 60-90mins. **Green Line** (0844 801 7261, www.greenline.co.uk) runs a 24hr service. A single is £11 and returns cost £17; under-15s £7.50 single, £12 return; under-5s free.

A **taxi** to London costs from £80.

Stansted Airport *0808 169 7031, www.stanstedairport.com. About 35 miles north-east of London, J8 off the M11.*

The **Stansted Express** train, www.stanstedexpress.com) runs to and from Liverpool Street Station; the journey time is 40-45mins. Trains leave every 15mins, and tickets cost £22.50 single, £39 return; under-16s travel half-price, under-5s free.

Several companies run coaches to central London. The **National Express** service (0871 781 8171, www.nationalexpress.com) from Stansted to Victoria takes 1hr 45mins. Coaches run roughly every 20mins (24hrs daily), more at peak times. A single is £10 (£5 for under-16s), an open return is £20 (£10 for under-16s).

A **taxi** into the centre of London costs from £60.

By coach

Coaches run by **National Express** (0871 781 8171, www.nationalexpress.com), the biggest coach company in the UK, arrive at **Victoria Coach Station** (164 Buckingham Palace Road, SW1W 9TP, 0343 222 1234, tfl.gov.uk), a good 10min walk from Victoria tube station. This is also the destination for coaches to and from Europe.

By rail

Trains from mainland Europe run by **Eurostar** (0343 218 6186, www.eurostar.com) arrive at **St Pancras International** (Pancras Road, Euston Road, N1C 4QP, 7843 7688, www.stpancras.com).

PUBLIC TRANSPORT

Details on timetables and other travel information are provided by **Transport for London** (0343 222 1234, tfl.gov.uk). Complaints or comments on most forms of public transport can also be taken up with **London Travel Watch** (3176 2999, www.londontravelwatch.org.uk).

▶ *For the TfL map of Tube, Overground and rail services, see p430.*

Travel Information Centres
These offer help with the tube, buses and DLR; they can be found in the locations detailed below. Call 0343 222 1234 for more information.

Euston *opposite Platform 8.* **Open** *8am-6pm Mon-Sat; 8.30am-6pm Sun.*
Gatwick Airport *North Terminal arrivals hall & South Terminal arrivals hall.* **Open** *9.15am-4pm daily.*
Heathrow Airport *Terminals 2 & 3 underground station concourse.* **Open** *7.30am-8.30pm daily.*
King's Cross *Western Ticket Hall, near St Pancras.* **Open** *8am-6pm Mon-Sat; 8.30am-6pm Sun.*
Liverpool Street tube **Open** *8am-6pm Mon-Sat; 9am-6pm Sun.*

Piccadilly Circus tube **Open** *9.30am-4pm daily.*
Victoria (main station) *opposite Platform 8.* **Open** *8am-6pm daily.*

Fares & tickets

Tube and DLR fares are based on a system of six zones, stretching 12 miles out from the centre of London. A flat cash fare of £4.90 per journey applies across zones 1-3 on the tube, and £6 for zones 1-6; customers save up to £2.50 per journey with a pre-pay Oyster card or by paying with a contactless debit or credit card. Anyone caught without a ticket, Oyster or contactless card is subject to an £80 on-the-spot fine (reduced to £40 if you pay within three weeks).

Using the system

It is best to use either your contactless credit/debit card (*see right*) or to get an Oyster card (*see below*). The latter can be obtained from tfl.gov.uk/tickets, by calling 0343 222 1234, at tube stations, Travel Information Centres, some rail stations and newsagents.

To enter and exit the tube using an Oyster (or contactless) card, simply touch it to the yellow reader, which will open the gates. Make sure you also touch the card to the reader when you exit the tube, or you'll be charged a higher fare when you next use your card to enter a station. On certain lines, you'll see a pink 'validator' – touch this reader in addition to the yellow entry/exit readers and on some routes it will reduce your fare.

Alternatively, paper single or day tickets can be bought from self-service ticket machines. TfL is in the process of closing all Underground ticket offices; carry a charged-up Oyster card to avoid being stranded. If you are using a paper ticket, enter by placing it in the slot with the black magnetic strip facing down, then pull it out of the top to open the gates. Exiting is done in much the same way; however, if you have a single journey ticket, it will be retained by the gate as you leave.

Oyster cards

A pre-paid smart card, Oyster is a far cheaper way of getting around on public transport than buying paper tickets. You can charge up standard Oyster cards at tube stations, Information Centres (*see left*), some rail stations and newsagents. There is a £5 refundable deposit payable on each card. You can get your pay-as-you-go credit (up to £10) and your deposit refunded at a tube station ticket machine. Young visitor cards are also available for children.

Visitor Oyster cards are available from Gatwick Express outlets, National Express coaches, Superbreak, www.visitbritainshop.com, Oxford Tube coach service and on Eurostar services. The only difference between Visitor Oysters and 'normal' Oysters is that they come pre-loaded with money.

Oyster now has day capping of £7 if you're travelling between zones 1-2 off peak, £10.10 between zones 1-4 off peak, and £12.80 between zones 1-6 off peak – it thus works out cheaper than a Day Travelcard (*see p407*).

Contactless payment

If you have a credit or debit card with the contactless symbol ⟿ you can use it instead of getting an Oyster card – and you will pay the same fare. Just place it on the yellow or pink readers in exactly the same way as you would an Oyster. If you use public transport every day for a week during your stay, it's likely to be marginally cheaper even than Oyster: usage is capped at the level of a weekly – not daily – Travelcard.

Day Travelcards

If you're only using the tube, DLR and buses, using Oyster to pay-as-you-go will always be cheaper than an equivalent Day Travelcard. However, if you're also using certain National Rail services, Oyster may not be accepted: opt, instead, for a Day Travelcard, a standard ticket with a coded stripe that allows travel across all networks.

Anytime Day Travelcards

can be used all day. They cost £13.10 for zones 1-2 (£6.50 child), £18.60 for zones 1-6 (£9.30 child). Tickets are valid for journeys begun by 4.30am the next day. The cheaper **Off-Peak Day Travelcard** allows travel after 9.30am Mon-Fri and all day at weekends and public holidays. It costs £12.80 (£6.50 child) for zones 1-6.

Children

Under-5s travel free on buses without the need to provide any proof of identity. Five-to 10-year-olds can also travel free, but need to obtain a 5-10 Zip Oyster photocard. For details, visit tfl.gov.uk/tickets or call 0343 222 1234.

An 11-15 Zip Oyster photocard is needed by 11- to 15-year-olds to pay as they go with reduced fares on the tube/DLR and to buy 7-day, monthly or longer period Travelcards.

Photocards

Photocards are not required for 7-Day Travelcards or Bus Passes, adult-rate Travelcards or Bus Passes charged on an Oyster card. For details of how to obtain 5-10, 11-15 or 16+ Oyster photocards, see tfl.gov.uk/tickets or call 0343 222 1234. There is a non-refundable £10 administration fee for each ID card.

London Underground

Delays are fairly common, with lines or sections of lines frequently closed at weekends for engineering work. Trains are hot and crowded in rush hour (7.30-9.30am and 4.30-6.30pm Mon-Fri) – avoid the rush by travelling after 9.30am and you'll also pay less for your fare. The 12 colour-coded lines that together comprise the underground rail system – also known as 'the Tube' – remain the quickest way to get around, carrying some 3.5 million passengers every weekday. Comments or complaints are dealt with by **TfL Customer Services** on 0343 222 1234 (8am-8pm daily).

Timetables

Tube trains run daily from around 5.30am (except Sunday, when they start an hour or so later, and Christmas Day, when there's no service). You shouldn't have to wait more than 10mins for a train; during peak times, services should run every 2-3mins. Times of last trains vary; they're usually around 12.30am (11.30pm on Sun). The Night Tube, offering a limited 24hr service, runs Fri and Sat nights on some lines (*see below*). Tubes also run all night on New Year's Eve. Otherwise, you're limited to night buses (*see p407*).

Fares

The single fare for adults across the network is £4.90 for journeys within zones 1-3; £6 for zones 1-6; £7.40 for zones 1-7; £8.50 for zones 1-9. Using Oyster pay-as-you-go or a contactless card, journeys within zone 1 cost £2.40; zones 1-3 costs £2.80 (off peak)/£3.30 (peak); zones 1-6 costs £3.10 (off peak)/ £5.10 (peak). The single fare for children aged 5-15 is 75p (off peak)/85p (peak) for any journey in zones 1-6. Peak hours are 6.30-9.30am, 4-7pm Mon-Fri. Under-5s travel free.

Night Tube

It seems extraordinary that London – the proud city of infrastructure innovations that ran the world's first urban underground railway in 1863 – lacked an all-night tube service until August 2016. Now almost all of the Central, Northern and Piccadilly lines, and the entire Jubilee and Victoria lines, have services through Friday/Saturday and Saturday/Sunday. They are fast, frequent (roughly every 10mins) and, well, pretty much like using the daytime tube. The fares are off-peak and you can continue to use your Day Travelcard (or capped pay-as-you-go card) until 4.30am in the morning after the day covered by that card (or pay-as-you-go cap). If you're lucky enough to be staying near a Night Tube station, you'll bless it; questions about how efficiently the Night Tube will replace the detailed coverage of the routinely derided night bus (*see p407*) network remain, for

now, a subject for nerds, night-workers and transport gurus.

Overground

The Overground (0343 222 1234) is a patchwork of different rail services, some tracing a complex orbital route roughly following the boundary of zones 2 and 3 (the orange-and-white line on the tube map). For those planning to visit areas of London with poor Underground coverage – notably (and perhaps not coincidentally) some of the buzzier bits of east and south London – the Overground is a valuable friend. The Night Tube now runs Overground services as well as Underground services, with a very useful link between New Cross Gate and Highbury & Islington, where it connects to the Victoria line.

Fares

Fares are the same as the tube.

National Rail services

Independently run commuter services co-ordinated by **National Rail** (03457 48 49 50, www.nationalrail.co.uk) leave from the city's main rail stations. Visitors heading to south London, or to more remote destinations such as Hampton Court Palace, use these services.

Fares

Travelcards are valid on these services within the right zones, but not all routes accept Oyster pay-as-you-go or contactless payments.

Docklands Light Railway

The mostly elevated DLR trains (0343 222 1234, tfl. gov.uk/modes/dlr) run from Bank station (where they connect with the Central, Northern and Waterloo & City lines) or Tower Gateway, close to Tower Hill tube (Circle and District lines). At Westferry station, the line splits east and south via Island Gardens to Greenwich and Lewisham; a change at Poplar or Canning Town can take you north to Stratford. The easterly branch forks after Canning Town to either Beckton or Woolwich Arsenal. Trains run 5.30am-12.40am daily, and there are lots of good views of Docklands to be enjoyed.

Fares

Fares are the same as the tube.

Crossrail

The dauntingly massive infrastructure project known as Crossrail (www.crossrail.co.uk) has been burrowing under central London since 2009 and is due finally to open to passengers in late 2019. London's 12th tube line will be known as the Elizabeth Line and will whisk sleeper-town residents into central London from east and west at great speed. The underground section of the line has stops at Paddington, Bond Street, Tottenham Court Road, Farringdon, Liverpool Street, Whitechapel, Canary Wharf, Customs House and Woolwich. *See p381.*

Buses

Buses are now cash-free, so you must have a ticket, valid pass or, better, an Oyster card or contactless payment card (for both, *see p405*) before boarding any bus. You can buy a ticket from machines in tube and rail stations. Inspectors patrol buses at random; if you don't have a ticket, card or pass, you may be fined £80 (£40 if you pay within 21 days).

All buses are now low-floor vehicles that are accessible to wheelchair-users and passengers with buggies. The only exception is Heritage route 15 (heritageroutes.weebly.com), which is served by the historic and world-famous open-platform Routemaster buses.

Fares

Using Oyster pay-as-you-go costs £1.50 a trip; your total daily payment, regardless of how many journeys you take, will be capped at £4.50. Under-16s travel for free (using an Under-11 or 11-15 Oyster photocard, as appropriate; *see p405*). You can take a second bus journey for free if you board within an hour of touching in on your first bus. Be aware that you can't pay your fare on London buses in cash. You'll need a charged Oyster card, valid travel card or contactless debit or credit card ready when you board.

Night buses

Many bus routes operate 24hrs a day, seven days a week. There are also some special night buses with an 'N' prefix, which run from about 11pm to 6am – they're used by a sometimes exhilarating combination of nightshift workers and partiers, in different proportions depending on the time of night. Most night services run every 15-30mins, but busier routes run every 10mins or so. Fares are the same as for daytime buses; Bus Passes and Travelcards can be used at no extra fare until 4.30am of the morning after they expire, with Oyster day-capping in effect until then too.

Green Line buses

These serve the suburbs within 40 miles of London (0344 801 7261, www.greenline.co.uk); services run 24hrs a day.

Water transport

Most river services operate every 20-60mins between 10.30am and 5pm, and may run more often and later in summer. For commuters, **Thames Clippers** (www.thamesclippers.com) runs a service between Embankment

Pier and Royal Arsenal Woolwich Pier (limited period, otherwise to North Greenwich); stops include Blackfriars, Bankside, London Bridge, Canary Wharf and Greenwich. A standard day roamer ticket (valid 9am-9pm) costs £19.50, £9.75 for a child (5-15s), while a single from Embankment to Greenwich is £8.40, £4.20 under-16s, or £5.60 for Oyster cardholders. Book online for reductions.

Westminster Passenger Service Association (7930 2062, www.wpsa.co.uk) runs a daily service from Westminster Pier to Kew, Richmond and Hampton Court from April to October. At around £15 for a single, it's not cheap, but it is a lovely way to see the city, and there are discounts of 33%-50% for Travelcard holders.

Thames River Services (7930 4097, www.thamesriverservices.co.uk) operates from the same pier, with trips to Greenwich and Tower Pier, and the Thames Barrier from May to Oct. A trip to Greenwich costs £12.75. Travelcard holders get a third off. Book online for reductions.

TAXIS & MINICABS

Black cabs

The licensed London taxi, aka 'black cab' (although they now come in many colours), is a much-loved feature of London life. Drivers must pass a test called 'the Knowledge' to prove they know every street within a 6-mile radias of Charing Cross, and the shortest route to it.

If a taxi's orange 'For Hire' sign is lit, it can be hailed. If a taxi stops, the cabbie must take you to your destination if it's within seven miles. Fares rise after 8pm on weekdays and at weekends.

You can book black cabs using the very handy free mytaxi app, or from **Radio Taxis** (7272 0272) and **Dial-a-Cab** (7253 5000; cards only). Complaints about black cabs should be made via Transport for London (0343 222 4000, tfl.gov.uk). Note the cab's badge number, which should be displayed in the rear of the cab and on its back bumper.

Minicabs

Minicabs (saloon cars) are generally cheaper than black cabs, but can be less reliable. The police and TfL regularly warn against the use of any but licensed firms (look for a disc in the front and rear windows), so be sure to avoid drivers who illegally tout for business in the street: if they're unlicensed they might well be uninsured and may be dangerous. When you book a cab, ask the price; when your car arrives, confirm the price with the driver before getting in.

If you text **HOME** to 60835 ('60TFL'), Transport for London will reply with the numbers of the two nearest licensed minicab operators and the number for **Radio Taxis**, which provides licensed black taxis in London (it costs 35p plus standard call rate).

You can also use the **Uber** app to hail – and pay for – a minicab. After being banned from operating in London by TfL, Uber has been given a temporary reprieve until the end of 2019. It's extremely unpopular with black cab drivers, who regard use of the app as a kind of metering, but extremely popular as a cheap and efficient way of getting home.

DRIVING

London's roads are often clogged with traffic and roadworks, and parking (*see right*) is a nightmare: walking or using public transport is almost always the better option. If you hire a car, you can use any valid licence from outside the EU for up to a year after arrival. Speed limits in the city are generally 20 or 30mph.

Congestion charge

Drivers coming into central London between 7am and 6pm Monday to Friday have to pay £11.50, a fee known as the congestion charge. The congestion charge zone is bordered by Marylebone, Euston and King's Cross (N), Old Street roundabout (NE), Aldgate (E), Tower Bridge Road (SE), Elephant & Castle (S), Vauxhall, Victoria (SW), Park Lane and Edgware Road (W). You'll know when you're about to drive into the charging zone from the red 'C' signs on the road. Enter the postcode of your destination at tfl.gov.uk/modes/congestioncharging to discover if it's in the charging zone.

Passes can be bought from some newsagents, garages and NCP car parks; you can also pay online at tfl.gov.uk/modes/congestion charging, by phone on 0343 222 2222 or by SMS. You can pay any time during the day; payments are also accepted until midnight on the next charging day, although the fee is £14 if you pay then. You only pay once per day, no matter how many times you go in and out of the zone. Expect a fine of £160 for non-payment (reduced to £80 if you pay within 14 days).

Breakdown services

AA (*Automobile Association*) 0800 085 2721 *information*, 0800 887766 *breakdown, www.theaa.com.*

ETA (*Environmental Transport Association*) 0333 000 1234, *www.eta.co.uk.*

RAC (*Royal Automobile Club*) 0330 159 1111 *information, 0333 2000 999 breakdown, www.rac.co.uk.*

Parking

Central London is scattered with parking meters, but finding an unoccupied one is usually difficult. Meters cost upwards of £1 for 15mins, and in some areas they are limited to 2hrs; if you're going to spend a lot of time driving in particular areas, find out whether there's an app for that location that allows easy payment – sometimes even permitting remote top-up payments. Parking on a single or double yellow line, a red line or in residents' parking areas during the day is illegal, and you may be fined, clamped or towed.

However, in the evening (from 6pm or 7pm in much of central London) and at various times at weekends, parking on single yellow lines is legal and free. If you find a clear spot on a single yellow line during the evening, look for a sign giving the local regulations. Meters also become free at certain times during evenings and weekends. Parking on double yellow lines and red routes is always illegal.

Use an app like **AppyParking** to help you find the nearest free car parking; otherwise, there are many **NCP** car parks (www.ncp.co.uk), open 24hrs a day.

Clamping & vehicle removal

The immobilising of illegally parked vehicles with a clamp is common in London. You'll have to stump up a release fee (£70) and show a valid licence. The payment centre will de-clamp your car within four hours. If you don't remove your car at once, it may get clamped again, so wait by your vehicle.

If your car has disappeared, it's either been stolen or, if it was parked illegally, towed to a car pound by the local authorities. A release fee of £200 is levied for removal, plus upwards of £40 per day from the first midnight after removal. You'll also probably get a parking ticket, typically £130 (reduced by 50% if paid within 14 days). Contact **Trace Information Service** (0845 206 8602, trace.london).

CYCLING

There has been a lot of talk about improving provision for cyclists in London and impressive sums of transport budget set aside for the purpose. Certain notorious junctions have been improved and work progresses on the 'superhighways' – segregated north–south and east–west cycling routes through the centre of town – but it will be a good while before their success can be judged. Nonetheless, no one needs to be scared of London's streets – some 180 million journeys are made each year by bike, almost all of them safely.

Ride calmly, assertively and obeying the rules of the road, and always avoid getting caught on the inside of a left-turning bus or lorry. TfL's 'Cycle safety tips' are at tfl.gov.uk/modes/cycling. Serious cyclists can contact the **London Cycling Campaign** (7234 9310, www.lcc.org.uk).

TfL also runs a handy **cycle hire scheme** Santander Cycles (0343 222 6666, tfl.gov.uk/modes/cycling/santander-cycles), with more than 750 docking stations and 11,000 bikes in operation. Nicknamed 'Boris Bikes' after the former mayor, Boris Johnson, who introduced them, the cycles – distinguished by their red Santander sponsorship branding – are picked up from and returned to a string of 24hr bicycle stations. To hire a bike, go to a docking station, touch the 'Hire a cycle' icon and insert a credit or debit card. The machine will print out a five-digit access code, which you then tap into the docking point of a bike, releasing the cycle, and away you go. A £2 fee buys 24hr access to the bikes; the first 30 minutes are free.

WALKING

By far the best and most enjoyable way to see London is on foot, but the city's street layout is ancient and therefore complicated. We've included a foldout map of central London at the back of this book, as well as maps in the appropriate Explore chapters; the standard *Geographers' London A-Z* or Collins' *London Street Atlas* are useful supplements if you don't like to navigate by smartphone. There's route advice at tfl.gov.uk/modes/walking (the map of walking times between stations, which can be downloaded from content.tfl.gov.uk/walking-tube-map.pdf, is particularly useful for showing the on-the-ground proximity of various central tube stations) or download the Go Jauntly walking app. Look out too for the yellow-topped 'Legible London' information posts as you stroll around (tfl.gov.uk/microsites/legible-london) – they're basically maps oriented to the direction you're heading, rather than with north at the top. Remember: no matter how well you know our city, going for a walk will reveal further secrets.

Resources A-Z

Travel Advice

For up-to-date information on travel to a specific country – including the latest on safety and security, health issues, local laws and customs – contact your home country government's department of foreign affairs. Most have websites with useful advice for would-be travellers

Australia
www.smartraveller.gov.au

Canada
www.voyage.gc.ca

New Zealand
www.safetravel.govt.nz

Republic of Ireland
www.dfa.ie

UK
www.fco.gov.uk/travel

USA
www.state.gov/travel

ACCIDENT & EMERGENCY

In the event of a serious accident, fire or other incident, call 999 – free from any phone, including payphones – and ask for an ambulance, the fire service or police. If no one is in immediate danger, call 101.

Emergency departments

Listed below are most of the central London hospitals that have Accident & Emergency (A&E) departments that are open 24 hours daily.

Charing Cross Hospital *Fulham Palace Road, Hammersmith, W6 8RF (3311 1234, www.imperial.nhs. uk). Hammersmith tube.*

Chelsea & Westminster Hospital *369 Fulham Road, Chelsea, SW10 9NH (3315 8000, www.chelwest.nhs.uk). South Kensington tube.*

Royal Free Hospital *Pond Street, Hampstead, NW3 2QG (7794 0500, www.royalfree.nhs.uk). Belsize Park tube or Hampstead Heath Overground.*

Royal London Hospital *Whitechapel Road, Whitechapel, E1 1BB (7377 7000, www.bartshealth.nhs.uk). Whitechapel tube/Overground.*

St Mary's Hospital *Praed Street, Paddington, W2 1NY (3312 6666, www.imperial.nhs. uk). Paddington tube/rail.* **Map** *pull-out E6.*

St Thomas' Hospital *Westminster Bridge Road, South Bank, SE1 7EH (7188 7188, www. guysandstthomas.nhs.uk). Westminster tube or Waterloo tube/rail.* **Map** *p80 M10.*

University College Hospital *235 Euston Road, Fitzrovia, NW1 2BU (3456 7890, www.uclh.nhs.uk). Euston Square or Warren Street tube.* **Map** *p194 K5*

ADDRESSES

London postcodes are less helpful than they could be for locating addresses. The first element starts with a compass point – N, E, SE, SW, W and NW, plus the smaller EC (East Central) and WC (West Central). However, the number that follows relates not to geography (unless it's a 1, which indicates central) but to alphabetical order. So N2 is way out in the boondocks (East Finchley), while W2 covers the very central Bayswater district.

AGE RESTRICTIONS

Buying/drinking alcohol 18
Driving 17
Sex 16
Smoking 18

CUSTOMS

▶ *Post-Brexit customs arrangements had not been finalised by the time this guide went to press; for the most up-to-date information, see www.gov.uk.*

Currently, citizens entering the UK from outside the EU must adhere to duty-free import limits:

• 200 cigarettes or 100 cigarillos or 50 cigars or 250g of tobacco
• 4 litres still table wine plus either 1 litre spirits or strong liqueurs (above 22% abv) or 2 litres fortified wine (under 22% abv), sparkling wine or other liqueurs
• other goods to the value of no more than £390

The import of meat, poultry, fruit, plants, flowers and protected animals is restricted or forbidden. There are currently no restrictions on the import or export of currency if travelling from another EU country. If you are travelling from outside the EU, amounts over €10,000 must be declared on arrival.

People over the age of 17 arriving from an EU country are able to import unlimited goods for their own personal use, if bought tax-paid (so not duty-free).

DISABLED

As a city that evolved long before the needs of disabled people were considered, London is difficult for wheelchair users, though access and facilities are slowly improving. All the capital's bus fleet is now low-floor for easier wheelchair access; there are no steps for any of the city's trams, though these are not widespread; and all DLR stations have either lifts or ramp access. However, steps and escalators to the Tube and above-ground trains mean these are often of only limited use to wheelchair users, and even stations with lifts can be a real headache to navigate (King's Cross is but one example). A blue symbol on the tube map (see pp430-431) indicates stations with step-free access. The **Step-free Tube Guide** map is free; call 0343 222 1234 or download it from tfl.gov.uk/accessguides.

Most major attractions and hotels offer good accessibility, though provisions for the hearing- and sight-disabled are patchier. Enquire about facilities in advance.

Access in London is an invaluable reference book for disabled travellers. It's available for a £10 donation (sterling cheque, cash US dollars or via PayPal to gordon_couch@yahoo.com) from **Access Project** (39 Bradley Gardens, W13 8HE, www.accessinlondon.org).

Artsline *www.artsline.org.uk.* Information on disabled access to arts and culture.

Can Be Done *Equity House, 128-136 High Street, Edgware, HA8 7EL (8907 2400, www.canbedone. co.uk). Edgware tube/rail. **Open** 9.30am-5pm Mon-Fri.* Disabled-adapted holidays and tours in London, around the UK and worldwide.

Disability Rights UK *Plexal, 14 East Bay Lane, Here East, Queen Elizabeth Olympic Park, Stratford, E20 3BS (0330 995 0400, www.disabilityrightsuk. org). Hackney Wick or Stratford International rail. **Open** 9am-8pm Mon-Fri; 10am-2pm Sat.* A national organisation for disabled voluntary groups, publishing books and offering advice, links to other organisations for help and courses.

Tourism for All *0845 124 9971, www.tourismforall.org.uk. **Open** Helpline 9am-5pm Mon-Fri.* Information for older people and people with disabilities in relation to accessible accommodation and other tourism services.

Wheelchair Travel & Access Mini Buses *1 Johnston Green, Guildford, Surrey, GU2 9XS (01483 237668, www.wheelchair-travel.co.uk).*

Hires out converted vehicles (a driver is optional), plus cars with hand controls and wheelchair-adapted vehicles.

DRUGS

Illegal drug use remains higher in London than the UK as a whole, though it's becoming less visible on the streets and in clubs. Despite fierce debate, cannabis has been reclassified from Class C to Class B (where it rejoins amphetamines), but possession of a small amount might attract no more than a warning for a first offence. More serious Class B and A drugs (ecstasy, LSD, heroin, cocaine and the like) carry stiffer penalties, with a maximum of seven years in prison for possession plus a fine.

ELECTRICITY

The UK uses the European standard 220-240V, 50-cycle AC voltage. British plugs have three pins, so travellers with two-pin European appliances should bring an adaptor.

Anyone using US appliances, which run off 110-120V, 60-cycle, will need to bring or buy a voltage converter.

EMBASSIES & CONSULATES

Australian High Commission *Australia House, the Strand, Holborn, WC2B 4LA (7379 4334, www.uk.embassy.gov.au). Holborn or Temple tube. **Open** 9am-5pm Mon-Fri. **Map** p181 N7.*

Canadian High Commission *Canada House, Trafalgar Square, Westminster, SW1Y 5BJ (7004 6000, www.canada.org.uk). Charing Cross tube/rail. **Open** 8am-4pm Mon-Fri. **Map** p102 L8.*

Embassy of Ireland *17 Grosvenor Place, Belgravia, SW1X 7HR (7235 2171, 7373 4339 passports & visas, www.dfa.ie/irish-embassy/great-britain). Hyde Park Corner tube. **Open** 9.30am-12.30pm, 2.30-4.30pm Mon-Fri. **Map** p124 H10.*

New Zealand High Commission *New Zealand House, 80 Haymarket, St James's, SW1Y 4TQ (7930 8422, www.mfat.govt. nz/en/embassies). Piccadilly Circus tube. **Open** 9am-4pm Mon-Fri. **Map** p102 L8.*

US Embassy *33 Nine Elms Lane, Wandsworth, SW11 7US (7499 9000, uk.usembassy. gov). Vauxhall tube/rail. **Open** 8am-5.30pm Mon-Fri.*

Climate

Average temperatures and monthly rainfall in London

	Temp High (°C/°F)	Temp Low (°C/°F)	Rainfall (mm/in)
January	6 / 43	2 / 36	54 / 2.1
February	7 / 44	2 / 36	40 / 1.6
March	10 / 50	3 / 37	37 / 1.5
April	13 / 55	6 / 43	37 / 1.5
May	17 / 63	8 / 46	46 / 1.8
June	20 / 68	12 / 54	45 / 1.8
July	22 / 72	14 / 57	57 / 2.2
August	21 / 70	13 / 55	59 / 2.3
September	19 / 66	11 / 52	49 / 1.9
October	14 / 57	8 / 46	57 / 2.2
November	10 / 50	5 / 41	64 / 2.5
December	7 / 44	4 / 39	48 / 1.9

HEALTH

British citizens or those working in the UK can go to any general practitioner (GP). People ordinarily resident in the UK, including overseas students, are also permitted to register with a National Health Service (NHS) doctor. If you fall outside these categories, you will have to pay to see a GP. Your hotel concierge should be able to recommend one.

A pharmacist may dispense medicines on receipt of a prescription from a GP. NHS prescriptions cost £8.80; under-16s, those on benefits and over-60s are exempt from charges. Contraception is free for all. If you're not eligible to see an NHS doctor, you'll be charged cost price for any medicines prescribed.

Free emergency medical treatment under the NHS currently is available to:
• EU nationals and those of Iceland, Norway and Liechtenstein; all may also be entitled to state-provided treatment for non-emergency conditions with an EHIC (European Health Insurance Card). For post-Brexit arrangements, see www.gov.uk
• nationals of New Zealand, Russia, most former USSR states and the former Yugoslavia
• residents (irrespective of their nationality) of Anguilla, Australia, Barbados, the British Virgin Islands, the Falkland Islands, the Isle of Man, Montserrat, Poland, Romania, St Helena and the Turks & Caicos Islands
• anyone who has been in the UK for the previous 12 months, or who has come to the UK to take up permanent residence
• students and trainees whose courses require more than 12 weeks in employment in the first year
• refugees and others who have sought refuge in the UK
• people with HIV/AIDS at a special STD treatment clinic

The NHS does not charge for the following services:
• treatment in A&E departments
• emergency ambulance transport to a hospital
• diagnosis and treatment of certain communicable diseases
• family-planning services
• compulsory psychiatric treatment.

Contraception & abortion

Family-planning advice, contraceptive supplies and abortions are free to British citizens on the NHS, and to EU residents and foreign nationals living in Britain. Visit www.fpa.org.uk for your local Family Planning Association. The 'morning after' pill (around £25), effective up to 72 hours after intercourse, is available over the counter at pharmacies.

British Pregnancy Advisory Service *03457 304 030, www.bpas.org. **Open** Helpline 24hrs daily.*
Callers are referred to their nearest clinic for treatment.

Brook Advisory Centre *0808 802 1234, www.brook.org.uk. **Open** Helpline 9am-5pm Mon-Fri.*
Information on sexual health, contraception and abortion, plus free pregnancy tests for under-25s.

Marie Stopes House *Family Planning Clinic/Well Woman Centre, 108 Whitfield Street, Fitzrovia, W1T 5BE (0345 300 8090, www.mariestopes.org.uk). Warren Street tube. **Open** Clinic 8am-4pm Mon-Fri. Helpline 24hrs daily. **Map** p194 K5.*
Contraceptive advice, emergency contraception, pregnancy testing, an abortion service, cervical and health screening, and gynaecological services. Fees may apply.

Dentists

Dental care is free for resident students, under-18s and people on benefits. All others must pay. To find an NHS dentist, contact the local Health Authority or a Citizens' Advice Bureau (*see p413*).

Dental Emergency Care Service *Guy's Hospital, floors 17-28, Tower Wing, Great Maze Pond, London Bridge,* SE1 9RT (7188 8006, www.guysandstthomas.nhs.uk/our-services/dental). London Bridge tube/rail. **Open** 9am-12.30pm, 1.30-3pm Mon-Fri. **Map** p80 Q9.*
Queues start forming at 8am; arrive by 10am if you're to be seen at all.

Hospitals

For a list of hospitals with Accident & Emergency departments, *see p410*; for other hospitals, check www.yell.com.

Pharmacies

Also called 'chemists' in the UK. Branches of Boots (www.boots.com) and larger supermarkets will have a pharmacy. Most keep shop hours (9am-6pm Mon-Sat, usually shorter hours Sun) but the Boots store at 44-46 Regent Street, Mayfair, W1B 5RA (7734 6126), opens until 11pm Mon-Thur, until midnight Fri, Sat, until 7pm Sun.

STDs, HIV & AIDS

NHS Genito-Urinary Clinics (such as the Mortimer Market Centre for Sexual Health) are affiliated with major hospitals. They provide free, confidential STD testing and treatment, as well as treating other problems such as thrush and cystitis. They also offer counselling about HIV and other STDs, and can conduct blood tests.

The NHS website (www.nhs.uk) also has information, including clinic locations. For helplines, *see p413*; for abortion and contraception, *see p412*.

Mortimer Market Centre for Sexual Health *Mortimer Market, Capper Street, off Tottenham Court Road, Fitzrovia, WC1E 6JB (3317 5252, www.sexualhealth.cnwl.nhs.uk). Goodge Street or Warren Street tube. **Open** 8am-7pm Mon-Thur; 8am-3pm Sat; 9am-3pm Sun. **Map** p194 K5.*

Terrence Higgins Trust *314-320 Gray's Inn Road, King's Cross, WC1X 8DP (0808 802 1221, www.tht.org.uk). King's Cross St Pancras tube/rail. **Open** 9.30am-5.30pm Mon-Fri.*

Helpline 10am-8pm Mon-Fri.
Map *p212 N4.*
Advice for those with HIV/AIDS, their relatives, lovers and friends.

HELPLINES

Helplines dealing with sexual health issues are listed above, under STDs, HIV & AIDS.

Alcoholics Anonymous *0800 917 7650, www.alcoholics-anonymous.org.uk.* **Open** *10am-10pm daily.*

Citizens' Advice Bureaux *03444 111 444 , www.citizensadvice.org. uk.* **Open** *9am-5pm Mon-Fri.* The council-run Citizens' Advice Bureaux offer free legal, financial and personal advice. See the website for the address of your nearest office.

Missing People *116 000 freephone, www.missingpeople. org.uk.* **Open** *24hrs daily.* Information on anyone who is reported missing.

NHS Direct *111, www.nhsdirect. nhs.uk.* **Open** *24hrs daily.* A free, first-stop service for medical advice on all subjects.

Rape Crisis *0808 802 9999, www. rapecrisis.org.uk.* **Open** *noon-2.30pm, 7-9.30pm daily.* Information and support.

Samaritans *freephone 116 123, www.samaritans.org.* **Open** *24hrs daily.* General helpline for those under emotional stress.

Victim Support *0808 168 9111, www.victimsupport.org.uk.* **Open** *24hrs daily.* Emotional and practical support for victims of crime.

ID

Passports and photographic driver's licences are acceptable forms of ID.

INTERNET

Most hotels have free high-speed internet (though some of the more expensive ones still charge a fee) and establishments all over town, especially cafés, have wireless access, usually free. Even the Tube is now on Wi-Fi – although you can only use it while you're in certain stations: see tfl.gov.uk/campaign/station-wifi.

LEFT LUGGAGE

Airports

Gatwick Airport *01293 569 900.*

Heathrow Airport *8759 3344.*

London City Airport *7646 0088.*

Luton Airport *01582 809174.*

Stansted Airport *0330 223 0893.*

Rail & bus stations

London stations tend to have left-luggage desks rather than lockers. Call 0845 748 4950 for details or check www. networkrail.co.uk.

Charing Cross *7930 5444.* **Open** *7am-11pm daily.*

Euston *7387 1499.* **Open** *7am-11pm daily.*

King's Cross *7837 4334.* **Open** *7am-11pm daily.*

Paddington *7262 0344.* **Open** *7am-11pm daily.*

Victoria *7963 0957.* **Open** *7am-midnight daily.*

LEGAL HELP

Those in difficulties can visit a **Citizens' Advice Bureau** (*see p413*) or contact the **Law Centres Federation** (*see below*). Try the **Legal Aid Agency** (0300 200 2020, www.gov.uk/government/organisations/legal-aid-agency) for information. If you're arrested, you should call your embassy (*see p411*).

Law Centres Federation *3637 1330, www.lawcentres.org.uk.* **Open** *11am-5.30pm Mon-Fri.* Free legal help for people who can't afford a lawyer and live or work in the immediate area; this office connects you with the nearest centre.

LGBT

For information on gay and lesbian life in London, *see pp413-335.* The phone lines that we list below provide general help and information for gay and lesbian people; for HIV and AIDS services, *see p412.*

London Friend *86 Caledonian Road, King's Cross, N1 9DN (7833 1674, londonfriend.org.uk).* **Open** *10am-6pm Mon-Fri.*

London Lesbian & Gay Switchboard *0300 330 0630, switchboard.lgbt.* **Open** *10am-10pm daily.*

LOST PROPERTY

Always inform the police if you lose anything, if only to validate insurance claims. Only dial 999 if violence has occurred; use 101 for non-emergencies. Report lost passports both to the police and to your embassy (*see p411*).

Airports

For items left on a plane, contact the relevant airline. Otherwise, phone the following:

Gatwick Airport *01293 223 457.*

Heathrow Airport *3761 1800.*

London City Airport *7646 0000.*

Luton Airport *01582 809174.*

Stansted Airport *0330 024 0099.*

Public transport

Transport for London *Lost Property Office, 200 Baker Street, Marylebone, NW1 5RZ (0343 222 1234, tfl.gov.uk/help-and-contact/lost-property).* *Baker Street tube.* **Open** *8.30am-4pm Mon-Fri.* **Map** *p142 H5.* Allow two to ten working days from the time of loss. If you lose something on a bus, call 0343 222 1234 and ask for the numbers of the depots at either end of the route. For tube losses, pick up a lost-property form from any station. There is a fee to cover costs.

Taxis

The Transport for London office (*see p405*) deals with property found in registered black cabs. Allow two to ten days from the time of loss. For items lost in a minicab or Über, contact the relevant company.

MEDIA

Magazines & newspapers

Time Out remains London's only quality listings magazine – and it's free. If you want to know what's going on and whether it's any good, this is the place to look. It's widely available in central London every Tuesday. Head to the website www.timeout.com/london for regular updates and more comprehensive listings. The capital's main daily paper (also free) is the sensationalist *Evening Standard*, published Monday to Friday. In the mornings, in Tube station dispensers and discarded in the carriages, you'll find *Metro*, a free *Standard* spin-off.

Radio

The stations below are broadcast on standard wavebands as well as digital, where they are joined by interesting additional channels (notably the BBC's genre-busting music channel 6 Music).

Absolute *105.8 FM.*
Laddish rock.

BBC London *94.9 FM.*
All things to do with the capital.

BBC Radio 1 *98.8 FM.*
Youth-oriented pop, indie and dance.

BBC Radio 2 *89.1 FM.*
Bland during the day; better after dark.

BBC Radio 3 *91.3 FM.*
Classical music dominates, but there's also discussion, world music and arts.

BBC Radio 4 *93.5 FM, 198 LW.*
The BBC's main speech station is led by news agenda-setter *Today* (6-9am Mon-Fri, 7-9am Sat).

BBC Radio 5 *Live 693, 909 AM.*
Rolling news and sport. Avoid the morning phone-ins, but Test Match Special cricket commentary is a British institution.

BBC World Service *648 AM.*
Some repeats, some new shows, transmitted globally.

Capital *FM 95.8 FM.*
Pop and chat.

Classic FM 100.9 FM.
Easy-listening classical.

Heart FM *106.2 FM.*
Capital FM for grown-ups.

Kiss *100 FM.*
Dance music.

LBC *97.3 FM.*
Phone-ins and talk.

Magic *105.4 FM.*
Familiar pop.

Resonance *104.4 FM.*
Arts radio – an inventively oddball mix.

Smooth *102.2 FM.*
Aural wallpaper.

XFM *104.9 FM.*
Alternative-ish rock.

Television

With a multiplicity of formats, there are plenty of pay-TV options, but binge-watching quality drama via on-demand services is the current obsession. The five main free-to-air networks are as follows:

BBC One
The Corporation's mass-market station. Relies too much on soaps, game shows and lifestyle TV, but has high-quality offerings too, not least the excellent news coverage. The BBC runs no commercials.

BBC Two
A reasonably intelligent cultural cross-section, but now upstaged by BBC Four.

ITV
Weekday mass-appeal shows, with ITV2 producing similar fare.

Channel 4
Successful US imports, more or less unwatchable home-grown entertainment, some great documentaries and quality news.

Channel Five
From high culture to lowbrow filth. An unholy mix.

Satellite, digital and cable channels include the following:

BBC Four
Highbrow stuff, including fine documentaries and dramas.

BBC News
Rolling news.

BBC Parliament
Live debates.

CBBC, CBeebies
Children's programmes – the latter for toddlers.

Discovery Channel
Science and nature documentaries.

E4, More4, Film4
Channel 4's entertainment and movie channels.

5USA
US comedy and drama, plus Australian soaps.

ITV2, ITV3, ITV4
US shows on 2, British reruns on 3 and 4.

Sky News
Rolling news.

Sky One
Sky's version of ITV.

Sky Sports
Four channels.

MONEY

Britain's currency is the pound sterling (£). One pound equals 100 pence (p). Coins are copper (1p, 2p), silver (round: 5p, 10p; seven-sided: 20p, 50p), or dual metal with a silver-coloured centre and a gold-coloured edge (12-sided £1; round £2). Polymer notes are blue (£5) or orange (£10); paper notes are purple (£20) or red (£50). All paper notes will be replaced with polymer in the next couple of years. You can exchange foreign currency at banks, bureaux de change and post offices; there's no commission charge at the last of these (for addresses of the most central, *see p415*). Many large stores also accept euros (€), notwithstanding Brexit.

Western Union *0808 234 9168, www.westernunion.co.uk.*
The old standby for sending and receiving money.

Banks & ATMs

ATMs can be found inside and outside banks, in some shops and in larger stations. Machines in many commercial premises levy a charge for each withdrawal, usually £1.50. If you're visiting from outside the UK, your card should work via one of the debit networks, but check charges in advance. ATMs also allow you to make withdrawals on your credit card if you know your PIN; you'll be charged interest plus, usually, a currency-exchange fee. Generally, getting cash with a card is the cheapest form of currency exchange but there are hidden charges, so do your research.

Credit cards, especially Visa and MasterCard, are accepted in most shops (except small corner shops) and restaurants (except caffs). However, American Express and Diners Club tend to be accepted only at more expensive outlets. You will usually have to have a PIN number to make a purchase.

No commission is charged for cashing sterling travellers' cheques if you go to one of the banks affiliated with the issuing company. You do have to pay to cash travellers' cheques in foreign currencies, and to change cash. You will always need to produce ID when you want to cash travellers' cheques.

Bureaux de change

You'll be charged for cashing travellers' cheques or buying and selling foreign currency at bureaux de change. Major stations have bureaux, and there are many in tourist areas and on major shopping streets. Most open 8am-10pm.

Covent Garden FX *30A Jubilee Market Hall, Covent Garden, WC2E 8BE (7240 9921, www. coventgardenfx.com). Covent Garden tube.* **Open** *9.30am-6pm Mon-Fri; 10am-5pm Sat; 10am-3pm Sun.* **Map** *p181 M8.*

Thomas Exchange *5 Market Place, W1W 8AE (7637 7336, www.tefx.co.uk). Oxford Circus tube.* **Open** *9am-6pm Mon-Fri; 10am-5pm Sat, Sun.* **Map** *p142 K7.*

Lost/stolen credit cards

Report lost or stolen credit cards both to the police and to the 24-hour phone lines listed below.

American Express *01273 696 933, www.americanexpress.com.*

Diners Club *0800 862 0935, www.dinersclub.co.uk.*

MasterCard *0800 964767, www. mastercard.com.*

Visa *0800 891725, www. visa.co.uk.*

Tax

With the exception of food, books, newspapers and a few other items, purchases in the UK are subject to Value Added Tax (VAT), aka sales tax. The rate is currently set at 20%. VAT is included in all prices quoted by mainstream shops, although it may not be included in hotel rates.

Foreign visitors may be able to claim back the VAT paid on most goods that are taken out of the EU (European Union) as part of a scheme generally called 'Tax Free Shopping'. To be able to claim a refund, you must be a non-EU visitor to the UK, or a UK resident emigrating from the EU. When you buy the goods, the retailer will ask to see your passport, and will then ask you to fill in a simple refund form. You need to have one of these forms to make your claim; till receipts alone will not do. If you're leaving the UK direct for outside the EU, you must show your goods and refund form to UK customs at the airport/port from which you're leaving. If you're leaving the EU via another EU country, you must show your goods and refund form to customs staff of that country.

After customs have certified your form, get your refund by posting the form to the retailer from which you bought the goods or to a commercial refund company, or by taking your form to a refund booth to get immediate payment. Customs are not responsible for making the refund: when you buy the goods, ask the retailer how the refund is paid.

▶ *For tax free shopping arrangements after Brexit, see www.gov.uk.*

OPENING HOURS

Government offices close on bank (public) holidays (*see p416*), but big shops often remain open, with only Christmas Day sacrosanct. Most attractions remain open on the other public holidays.

Banks *9am-4.30pm (some close at 3.30pm, some 5.30pm) Mon-Fri; some also Sat mornings.*

Businesses *9am-5pm Mon-Fri.*

Post offices *9am-5.30pm Mon-Fri; 9am-noon Sat.*

Pubs & bars *11am-11pm Mon-Sat; noon-10.30pm Sun; many pubs and bars, particularly in central London, stay open later.*

Shops *10am-6pm Mon-Sat, some to 8pm. Many also open on Sun, usually 11am-5pm or noon-6pm.*

POLICE

For emergencies, call 999. The non-emergency number is 101. London's police are used to helping visitors. If you've been robbed, assaulted or a victim of crime, go to your nearest police station. (We've listed a handful in central London; look under 'Police' in Directory Enquiries, *see p415*.)

If you have a complaint, ensure that you take the offending officer's identifying number (it should be displayed on his or her epaulette). The Independent Police Complaints Commission website, www.ipcc.gov.uk, has details of how to complain to the relevant police force.

Belgravia Police Station *202-206 Buckingham Palace Road, Pimlico, SW1W 9SX. Victoria tube/rail.* **Map** *p102 J12.*

Charing Cross Police Station *Agar Street, Covent Garden, WC2N 4JP. Charing Cross tube/rail.* **Map** *p181 M8.*

Holborn Police Station *10 Lambs Conduit Street, Bloomsbury, WC1N 3NR. Holborn tube.* **Map** *p194 N6.*

Islington Police Station *2 Tolpuddle Street, Islington, N1 0YY. Angel tube.* **Map** *pull-out O3.*

Kensington Police Station *72-74 Earls Court Road, W8 6EQ. High Street Kensington tube.*

West End Central Police Station *27 Savile Row, Mayfair, W1S 2EX. Oxford Circus tube.* **Map** *p142 K8.*

POSTAL SERVICES

The UK has a reliable postal service. Royal Mail customer services are on 0345 774 0740.

Post offices are usually open 9am-5.30pm during the week and 9am-noon on Saturdays, although some post offices shut for lunch and smaller offices may close for one or more afternoons each week. Some central post offices are listed below; for others, check the Royal Mail website www.royalmail.com.

You can buy individual stamps at post offices, and books of six or 12 first- or second-class stamps at newsagents and supermarkets that display the appropriate red sign. A first-class stamp for a regular letter costs 67p; second-class stamps are 58p. It costs £1.25 to send a letter or postcard abroad. For details of other rates, see the Royal Mail website.

Post offices

An exception to the usual opening hours (*see above*) is the Lower Regent Street post office (11 Lower Regent Street, SW1Y 4LR, 0345 611 2970), which opens 8am-6.30pm Mon-Fri; 9am-5.30pm Sat; noon-4pm Sun. Listed below are the other main central London offices. For general enquiries, call 0845 611 2970 or consult www.postoffice.co.uk.

Baker Street *no.111, Marylebone, W1U 6SG. Baker Street tube.* **Map** *p142 H6.*

Great Portland Street *nos.54-56, Fitzrovia, W1W 7NE. Oxford Circus tube.* **Map** *p194 K6.*

High Holborn *no.181, Holborn, WC1V 7RL. Holborn tube.* **Map** *p181 M7.*

Poste restante

If you want to receive mail while you're away, you can have it sent to Lower Regent Street Post Office (*see above*), where it will be kept for a month. Your name and 'Poste Restante' must be clearly marked on the letter. You'll need ID to collect it.

PUBLIC HOLIDAYS

On public holidays (bank holidays), many shops remain open, but public-transport services generally run to a Sunday timetable. On Christmas Day, almost everything, including public transport, closes down.

Good Friday *Fri 10 Apr 2020, Fri 2 Apr 2021*

Easter Monday *Mon 13 Apr 2020, Mon 5 Apr 2021*

May Day Holiday *Mon 4 May 2020, Mon 3 May 2021*

Spring Bank Holiday *Mon 27 May 2019, Mon 25 May 2020, Mon 31 May 2021*

Summer Bank Holiday *Mon 26 Aug 2019, Mon 31 Aug 2020*

Christmas Day *Wed 25 Dec 2019, Fri 25 Dec 2020*

Boxing Day *Thur 26 Dec 2019, Mon 28 Dec 2020*

New Year's Day *Wed 1 Jan 2020, Fri 1 Jan 2021*

RELIGION

Times of services may vary, particularly at festivals and holy days; phone to check.

Anglican & Baptist

Bloomsbury Central Baptist Church *235 Shaftesbury Avenue, Covent Garden, WC2H 8EP (7240 0544, www.bloomsbury.org.uk). Tottenham Court Road tube.* **Services & meetings** *11am, 6pm Sun.* **Map** *p181 M7.*

St Paul's Cathedral *For listings, see p388.* **Services** *7.30am, 8am, 12.30pm, 5pm Mon-Sat; 8am, 10.15am, 11.30am, 3.15pm, 6pm Sun.* **Map** *p212 P7.*

Westminster Abbey *For listings, see p102.* **Services** *7.30am, 8am, 12.30pm, 5pm Mon-Sat; 8am, 10am, 11.15am, 3pm, 5.45pm, 6.30pm Sun.* **Map** *p102 L10.*

Buddhist

Buddhapadipa Thai Temple *14 Calonne Road, Wimbledon, SW19 5HJ (8946 1357, www.watbuddhapadipa.org).*

Wimbledon tube/rail then bus 93. **Open** *Grounds Spring, summer 9.30am-6pm daily. Autumn, winter 9am-5pm daily. Temple weekends or by appointment. Meditation retreat 7-9.30pm Tue, Thur; 4-6.30pm Sat.*

London Buddhist Centre *51 Roman Road, Bethnal Green, E2 0HU (8981 1225, www.lbc.org.uk). Bethnal Green tube.* **Open** *10am-5pm Mon-Sat.*

Catholic

Brompton Oratory *For listings, see p134.* **Services** *7am, 8am (Latin mass), 10am, 12.30pm, 6pm (Latin mass) Mon-Fri; 7am, 8am (Latin mass), 10am, 6pm Sat; 8am, 9am (Latin mass), 10am, 11am, 12.30pm, 4.30pm, 7pm Sun.* **Map** *p124 F11.*

Westminster Cathedral *For listings, see p111.* **Services** *7am, 8am, 10.30am (Latin mass), 12.30pm, 1.05pm, 5pm (Vespers), 5.30pm Mon-Fri; 8am, 9am, 10.30am, 12.30pm, 6pm Sat; 8am, 9am, 10.30am, noon, 5.30pm, 7pm Sun.* **Map** *p102 K11.*

Islamic

East London Mosque *82-92 Whitechapel Road, Whitechapel, E1 1JQ (7650 3000, www.eastlondonmosque.org.uk). Aldgate East tube.* **Services** *times vary; check website for details.* **Map** *p256 U6.*

Islamic Cultural Centre & London Central Mosque *146 Park Road, Marylebone, NW8 7RG (7724 3363, www.iccuk.org). Baker Street tube or bus 13, 113, 274.* **Services** *times vary; check website for details.*

Jewish

Liberal Jewish Synagogue *28 St John's Wood Road, St John's Wood, NW8 7HA (7286 5181, ljs.org). St John's Wood tube.* **Services** *6.45pm Fri; 11am Sat.* **Map** *pull-out F4.*

West Central Liberal Synagogue *The Montagu Centre, 21 Maple Street, Fitzrovia, W1T 4BE (7636 7627, www.wcls.org.uk). Warren Street tube.* **Services**

times vary; check website for details. **Map** _p194 K5._

Methodist & Quaker

Methodist Central Hall _Storey's Gate, Westminster, SW1H 9NH (7654 3809, www.methodist-central-hall.org.uk). St James's Park tube._ **Services** _12.45pm Wed; 11am, 5.30pm Sun._ **Map** _p102 L10._

Religious Society of Friends (Quakers) _173-177 Euston Road, Bloomsbury, NW1 2BJ (7663 1000, www.quaker.org.uk). Euston tube/ Overground/rail._ **Meetings** _11am daily; 6.30-9pm Mon; 6.30pm Thur; 11am Sun._ **Map** _p194 L4._

SAFETY & SECURITY

Notwithstanding the terrorist outrages of 2017, you're much more likely to get hurt in a car accident than as a result of criminal activity, but pickpockets do haunt busy shopping areas and transport nodes as they do in all cities.

Use common sense and follow some basic rules. Keep wallets and purses out of sight, and handbags securely closed. Never leave bags or coats unattended, beside, under or on the back of a chair – even if they aren't stolen, they could trigger a bomb alert. Don't put bags on the floor near the door of a public toilet. Don't take short cuts through dark alleys and car parks. Keep your passport, cash and credit cards in separate places. Don't carry a wallet in your back pocket. And always be aware of your surroundings.

SMOKING

A ban on smoking in all enclosed public spaces, including pubs, bars, clubs, restaurants, hotel foyers and shops, as well as on public transport, was introduced in 2007. Smokers now face a penalty fee of £50 or a maximum fee of £200 if they are prosecuted for smoking in a smoke-free area. Many bars and clubs offer smoking gardens or terraces for smokers.

TELEPHONES

Dialling & codes

London's dialling code is 020; standard landlines have eight digits after that. You don't need to dial the 020 from within the area, so we have not given it in this book.

If you're calling from outside the UK, dial your international access code, then the UK code, 44, then the full London number, omitting the first 0 from the code. For example, to make a call to 020 7813 3000 from the US, dial 011 44 20 7813 3000. To dial abroad from the UK, first dial 00, then the relevant country code from the list below. For more international dialling codes, check the phone book or see countrycode.org/uk.

Australia _61_

Canada _1_

New Zealand _64_

Republic of Ireland _353_

South Africa _27_

USA _1_

Mobile phones

Mobile phones in the UK operate on the 900 MHz and 1800 MHz GSM frequencies common throughout most of Europe. If you're travelling to the UK from Europe, your phone should be compatible; if you're travelling from the US, it may not be. Either way, check your phone is set for international roaming, and that your service provider at home has a reciprocal arrangement with a UK provider.

The simplest option may be to buy a 'pay-as-you-go' phone (about £10-£200); there's no monthly fee – you top up talk time using a card. Check before buying whether it can make and receive international calls.

Operator services

Call 100 for the operator if you have difficulty in dialling; for an alarm call; to make a credit card call; for information about the cost of a call; and for help with international person-to-person calls. Dial 155 for the international operator if you need to reverse the charges (call collect) or if you can't dial direct; this service is very expensive.

Directory Enquiries

This service is now provided by various six-digit 118 numbers. They're pretty pricey to call: dial (free) 0800 953 0720 for a rundown of options and prices. A better option is to check numbers online at www.yell.com or www.ukphonebook.com.

TIME

London operates on Greenwich Mean Time (GMT), five hours ahead of the US's Eastern Standard Time. In spring the UK puts its clocks forward by one hour to British Summer Time. In autumn, the clocks go back to GMT.

TIPPING

In Britain, it's accepted that you tip in taxis, minicabs, restaurants (some waiting staff rely heavily on tips), hotels, hairdressers and some bars (not pubs). Around 10% is normal, but some restaurants add as much as 15%. Always check whether service has been included in your bill: some restaurants include an automatic service charge, but also give the opportunity for a gratuity when paying with a card.

TOILETS

Pubs and restaurants generally reserve the use of their toilets for customers. However, all mainline rail stations and a few tube stations – Piccadilly Circus, for one – have public toilets (you may be charged a small fee: have some coins handy for the entrance gate). Department stores usually have loos that you can use free of charge, and museums (most no longer charge an entry fee) generally have good facilities. At night, options are much worse. The coin-operated toilet booths around the city may be your only option.

TOURIST INFORMATION

In addition to the tourist information centres listed below, travel information centres at King's Cross, Euston, Liverpool Street and Victoria stations, and at Piccadilly Circus tube station (*see p405*) sell tickets for travel and London attractions.

City of London Information Centre *St Paul's Churchyard, City, EC4M 8BX (7332 3456, www.cityoflondon.gov.uk).* **Open** *9.30am-5.30pm Mon-Sat; 10am-4pm Sun.* **Map** *p212 P7.*

Greenwich Tourist Information Centre *Old Royal Naval College, 2 Cutty Sark Gardens, Greenwich, SE10 9LW (0870 608 2000, www. visitgreenwich.org.uk). Cutty Sark DLR.* **Open** *10am-5pm daily.*

Holborn Information Kiosk *89-94 Kingsway, outside Holborn tube, WC2B 6AA (no phone).* **Open** *8am-6pm Mon-Fri.* **Map** *p212 M6.*

Twickenham Visitor Information Centre *Civic Centre, 44 York Street, Twickenham, Middx, TW1 3BZ (8891 1441, www.visitrichmond.co.uk). Twickenham rail.* **Open** *9am-5.15pm Mon-Thur; 9am-5pm Fri.*

WEIGHTS & MEASURES

The UK is moving slowly and reluctantly towards full metrication. Distances are still measured in miles but all goods are officially sold in metric quantities, with no legal requirement for the imperial equivalent to be given. Nonetheless, imperial measurements are still more commonly used, so we use them in this guide.

Below are listed some useful conversions, first into the metric equivalents from the imperial measurements, then from the metric units back to imperial:

1 inch (in) = 2.54 centimetres (cm)
1 yard (yd) = 0.91 metres (m)
1 mile = 1.6 kilometres (km)
1 ounce (oz) = 28.35 grams (g)
1 pound (lb) = 0.45 kilograms (kg)
1 UK pint = 0.57 litres (l)
1 US pint = 0.8 UK pints or 0.46 litres
1 centimetre (cm) = 0.39 inches (in)
1 metre (m) = 1.094 yards (yd)
1 kilometre (km) = 0.62 miles
1 gram (g) = 0.035 ounces (oz)
1 kilogram (kg) = 2.2 pounds (lb)
1 litre (l) = 1.76 UK pints or 2.2 US pints

Further Reference

BOOKS

Fiction

Peter Ackroyd *Hawksmoor*
Adventures of an occultist
architect modelled on Wren's
counterpart.

Martin Amis *London Fields*
Darts and drinking way out east.

Ned Beauman *Glow* Bright
young novelist takes on
the rave scene in noughties
south London.

Anthony Burgess *Dead Man
in Deptford* Fictionalised
biography of Marlowe.

Norman Collins *London
Belongs to Me* Witty saga of '30s
Kennington.

Sir Arthur Conan Doyle
*The Complete Sherlock
Holmes* Reassuring sleuthing
shenanigans.

Joseph Conrad *The Secret
Agent* Anarchism in seedy Soho.

Charles Dickens *Bleak
House* The Victorian master's
finest London-centric novel.

Anthony Frewin *London
Blues* Kubrick assistant
explores the 1960s Soho porn-
movie industry.

Jeremy Gavron *An Acre of
Common Ground* Best of
the noughties glut of Brick
Lane fiction.

George the Poet *Search
Party* Buzzy debut from the
council estate-born, Cambridge-
educated poet.

Graham Greene *The End of
the Affair* A tale of adultery,
Catholicism and the Blitz.

Patrick Hamilton *Twenty
Thousand Streets Under the
Sky* Dashed dreams at the bar
of the Midnight Bell in Fitzrovia.

Neil Hanson *The Dreadful
Judgement* Embers of the
Great Fire.

Melissa Harrison *Clay
East* European immigrant and
latch-key kid seek redemption
amid the urban nature of
south London.

Alan Hollinghurst *The
Swimming Pool Library* Gay life
in the former cruising hotspot
Russell Square.

BS Johnson *Christie Malry's
Own Double Entry* A London
clerk plots revenge on...
everybody.

Doris Lessing *The Golden
Notebook* Nobel winner's
feminist classic, set mainly
in London.

Colin MacInnes *City of Spades;
Absolute Beginners* Coffee 'n'
jazz, Soho 'n' Notting Hill.

Michael Moorcock *Mother
London* A roomful of
psychiatric patients live a love
letter to London.

Alan Moore *From Hell* Dark
and epic graphic novel on
the Ripper.

Nick Papadimitriou *Scarp*
Hallucinatory explorations
of the high ground north
of London.

Derek Raymond *I Was
Dora Suarez* The blackest
London noir.

Nicholas Royle *The Matter
of the Heart; The Director's
Cut* Abandoned buildings
and secrets.

Iain Sinclair *White
Chappell/Scarlet Tracings*
Psychogeographer in chief
combines the Ripper and dodgy
book dealers.

Sarah Waters *The Night
Watch* World War II on the
Home Front.

Virginia Woolf *Mrs Dalloway*
A kind of London *Ulysses*.

Non-fiction

Peter Ackroyd *London: The
Biography* Loving and wilfully
idiosyncratic history of the city.

Nicholas Barton *The Lost
Rivers of London* A classic study.

**David Bownes, Oliver Green &
Sam Mullins**
Underground Illustrated
celebration of 150 years of the
Tube, which opened in 1863.

**James Cheshire & Oliver
Uberti** *The Information
Capital* Fabulous infographics
about all aspects of London life.

Mark Daly *Unseen London* Fine
behind-the-scenes pics of
the city.

Paul Du Noyer *In the
City* London in song.

**Henry Eliot and Mat Lloyd-
Rose** *Curiocity: In Pursuit of
London* Endlessly brilliant
compilation of genuinely
fascinating trivia.

Sarah Hartley *Mrs P's
Journey* Biography of the
woman who created the A–Z
street atlas.

Leo Hollis *The Stones of
London* A superb take on the
city's history – through 12 of its
key buildings.

Lucy Inglis *Georgian London* Charming history of the period.

Simon Inglis *Played in London* Comprehensive and riveting account of London's sporting heritage.

Lee Jackson *Dirty Old London* Gripping tale of how the Victorians fought to clean up the Big Smoke.

Edward Jones & Christopher Woodward *A Guide to the Architecture of London*

Ben Judah *This is London* Migrants speak in a self-consciously dystopic portrait of the modern city.

Jenny Landreth *The Great Trees of London* Ancient trees in famous and unlikely city locations.

David Lawrence (ed) *Omnibus* Social history of the London bus.

Jenny Linford *London Cookbook* Unsung producers and chefs share their food secrets.

Jack London *The People of the Abyss* Poverty in the East End.

Anna Minton *Ground Control* Important questions about Canary Wharf-style developments – updated to cover the Olympic Park.

HV Morton *In Search of London* A sparky tour of post-Blitz London.

Iain Nairn *Nairn's London* Opinionated architecture critic's bracing take on the city in 1966.

George Orwell *Down and Out in Paris and London* Waitering, begging and starving.

Samuel Pepys *Diaries* Plagues, fires and bordellos.

Cathy Phillips (ed) *London through a Lens; Londoners through a Lens* Captivating photographs of the city from the Getty archive.

Roy Porter *London: A Social History* An all-encompassing work.

Sukhdev Sandhu *Night Haunts* London and Londoners after dark.

Iain Sinclair *Lights Out for the Territory* Time-warp visionary crosses London.

Craig Taylor *Londoners: The Days and Nights of London Now* A superb and revealing collection of interviews with modern Londoners.

Richard Trench & Ellis Hillman *London under London* Tunnels, lost rivers, disused tube stations and military bunkers.

Peter Watts *Up in Smoke: The Failed Dreams of Battersea Power Station* Multiple failings of the redevelopers of a London icon.

Ben Weinreb & Christopher Hibbert (eds) *The London Encyclopaedia* Indispensable brick of a book.

Jerry White *London in the 18th Century; London in the 19th Century; London in the 20th Century* How London became a global city.

FILMS

28 Days Later *dir Danny Boyle, 2002* Post-apocalyptic London, with bravura opening sequence.

Blow-Up *dir Michelangelo Antonioni, 1966* Unintentionally hysterical portrayal of Swinging London.

Death Line *dir Gary Sherman, 1972* Lost Victorian cannibal race is discovered in Russell Square tube station.

Dirty Pretty Things *dir Stephen Frears, 2002* Body-organ smuggling.

Fires Were Started *dir Humphrey Jennings, 1943* War propaganda about the London Fire Brigade.

How We Used to Live *dir Paul Kelly, 2013* Rare post-war footage, with Saint Etienne soundtrack.

Hyena *dir Gerard Johnson, 2015* London-set crime flick.

The Krays *dir Peter Medak, 1990* The life and times of the East End gangsters.

The Ladykillers *dir Alexander Mackendrick, 1951* Classic Ealing comedy.

Happy-Go-Lucky *dir Mike Leigh, 2008* Day and night with a north London optimist.

Lock, Stock & Two Smoking Barrels *dir Guy Ritchie, 1998* Cheeky London faux-gangster flick.

London *dir Patrick Keiller, 1994* Arthouse documentary tracing London's lost stories.

London: The Modern Babylon *dir Julien Temple, 2012* Rousing montage portrait, driven by music, of London from the birth of cinema.

The Long Good Friday *dir John MacKenzie, 1989* Classic London gangster flick.

The National Gallery *dir Frederick Wiseman, 2015* Inquisitive documentary on the employees and paintings of the historic gallery.

Oliver! *dir Carol Reed, 1968* Fun musical Dickens adaptation.

Paddington *dir Paul King, 2014* The immigrant Peruvian bear gets his own movie.

Passport to Pimlico *dir Henry Cornelius, 1949* Ealing comedy classic.

Peeping Tom *dir Michael Powell, 1960* Creepy serial-killer flick.

Performance *dir Nicolas Roeg & Donald Cammell, 1970* Cult movie to end all cult movies.

Sex & Drugs & Rock & Roll *dir Mat Whitecross, 2009* Delirious biopic of Ian Dury.

Skyfall *dir Sam Mendes, 2012* See the SIS building blown up and Bond nearly run over by the Tube.

Withnail & I *dir Bruce Robinson, 1987* Classic Camden lowlife comedy.

Wonderland *dir Michael Winterbottom, 1999* Love, loss and deprivation in Soho.

MUSIC

Billy Bragg *Must I Paint You a Picture? The Essential Billy Bragg* The bard of Barking's greatest hits.

Blur *Parklife* Key Britpop album.

Burial *Untrue* Pioneering dubstep album – still the benchmark.

Chas & Dave *Don't Give a Monkey's* Cockney singalong.

The Clash *London Calling* Era-defining punk classic.

Dizzee Rascal *Boy in Da Corner* Rough-cut sounds and inventive lyrics from a Bow council estate.

Hot Chip *The Warning* Wonky electro-pop.

Ian Dury *New Boots & Panties!!* Cheekily essential listening from the Essex pub maestro.

The Jam *This is the Modern World* Weller at his fiercest and finest.

Kate Tempest *Everybody Down* Young Brockley-born street poet's debut album.

The Kinks *Something Else* 'Waterloo Sunset' and all.

Linton Kwesi Johnson *Dread, Beat an' Blood; Forces of Victory; Bass Culture* Angry reggae from the man Brixton calls 'the Poet'.

Little Simz *Stillness in Wonderland* London-born Nigerian rapper's concept album.

Madness *Ultimate Madness* The Nutty Boys' wonderful best.

Melt Yourself Down *Melt Yourself Down* Wigged-out psych-jazz-funk supergroup.

MIA *Arular* Agit-pop raver's debut album – and still her best.

Public Service Broadcasting *Inform–Educate–Entertain* Narration from documentaries set to music – shouldn't work, but it does.

Saint Etienne *Tales from Turnpike House* Kitchen-sink opera by London-loving indie dance band.

Skepta *Konnichiwa* Tottenham grime star's 2016 Mercury Prize winner.

Squeeze *Greatest Hits* Lovable south London geezer pop.

The Streets *Original Pirate Material* Pirate radio urban meets Madness on Mike Skinner's debut.

WEBSITES

www.bbc.co.uk/london News, travel, weather, sport.

www.britishpathe.com Archive newsreel footage, from spaghetti-eating contests to pre-war Soho.

bugwomanlondon.com North London nature obsessive.

catsmeatshop.blogspot.co.uk Expert on Victorian hygiene explains urine deflectors and the like.

diamondgeezer.blogspot.com One of London's key bloggers.

www.filmlondon.org.uk London's cinema organisation – with mapped location tours.

greatwen.com Engaged, fun and often thought-provoking blog by one of our contributors

www.hidden-london.com Undiscovered gems – and a neat pronunciation guide to place names.

www.london.gov.uk The official website for the Greater London Assembly, the city's government.

londonist.com News, culture and things to do.

londonreconnections. blogspot.com Heaven for transport geeks: everything from rolling stock plans to major infrastructure work.

www.londonremembers. com Definitive site for London memorials.

mappinglondon.co.uk Great-looking site with the best maps – and ways of mapping – the city.

spitalfieldslife.com Lovely London blog: focused, charming, informative and very human.

www.timeout.com/ london Eating, drinking, features and events listings – a vital resource.

www.tfl.gov.uk Information, journey planners and maps from Transport for London, the city's central travel organisation.

APPS

Appy Parking *(free)* Extremely helpful: shows you vacant parking spaces across London.

City Mapper *(free)* Simply the greatest London journey planner, smoothly integrating multimodal transport – tube, rail, bus and bike – with estimated times and much more.

City Toilet Finder *(free)* Where's the nearest free public loo in the City?

Hailo *(free)* Calls a black cab, tells you how long it will be, and deducts the meter fare from your account.

London: A City Through Time *(£13.99)* Expensive for an app – but you get the superb London Encyclopaedia (clumsily typeset, but perfectly legible), plus interactives.

StreetMuseum *(free)* Brilliant Museum of London app – archive shots geolocated to where you're standing, with informative captions.

Time Out London *(free)* Our indispensable guide to the week's happenings in the capital.

Uber *(free)* Hails a minicab, with fare quotes – the cab is paid for through the app (prices rise, airline-style, with demand), so no cash is needed.

William Blake's London *(free)* Geolocate your way round the poet-artist's London with this Tate app.

Index

2 Willow Road 247
5USA 414
10 Greek Street 164
18 Stafford Terrace 301
19 Princelet Street 258
22 Bishopsgate 232, 391
30 St Mary Axe 391
40 Well Walk 247
45 Park Lane 399
55 Broadway 390
69 Colebrooke Row 251
99 Club Leicester Square 350
100 Club 346, 348
108 Garage 298
122 Leadenhall 391
606 Club 348
& Other Stories 156

A

Abbey Road Studios 245
Abney Park Cemetery 271
abortion 412
accident & emergency 410
Accommodation 396–403
price categories 396
addresses 410
Adventure Balloons 76
afternoon tea 45
age restrictions 410
airports 404, 413
Albam 174
Albert Memorial 126, 390
Alcoholics Anonymous
helpline 413
Aldwych 189
Alexander Fleming
Laboratory Museum 147
Alexander McQueen 160
Alexandra Palace 343
Alfie's Antique Market 151
Algerian Coffee Stores 168
All Hallows by the Tower
233, 235
Allpress Espresso Bar 265
All Saints 206
All Souls Church 145
All Star Lanes 201
Almeida 366
American Football: NFL 316
Amy 330
Anchor Bankside 90
Anchor & Hope 87
And Did Those Feet 76
Angel 145
Angela Flanders 269
Angel Comedy 351
Anspach & Hobsday 99
Apple Day festival 316
Apple Store 187
apps 421
Apsley House 120
aquariums 85, 287
Aquascutum 273
Arancini Brothers Factory 242
ArcelorMittal Orbit 276, 277, 392
Architecture 386–393
Aria 252
Arnos Grove station 390
Arsenal Museum 250
arthouse cinemas 323
ArtHouse Crouch End cinema 323
Arthur Beale 187
Artsline 411
Artusi 287

Aside 287
Astronomy Centre 285
Atika 260
ATMs 414
Axel Arigato 171

B

Bad Egg 229
Baiwei 176
Baker Street 147
Balans 331
Baltic 87
Bank 229
Bank of England 229, 389
Bank of England Museum
229, 231
banks 414
Bankside 88
Bankside Gallery 88
Banqueting House 108, 388
Bao 172
Bar Américain 174
The Barbary 185
Barbican 226, 227, 229, 348, 391
Barbican Art Gallery 227
Barbican Centre 343, 354
Barbican cinema 323
Bar Boulud 135
Bar Hercules 164
Bar Italia 164
Bar Kick 219
Barn the Spoon 66
Barrafina 167, 185, 205
Barrica 209
bars. See pubs & bars
Bar Story 342
Bar Termini 168
Barts Pathology Museum 228
Battersea 290
Battersea Arts Centre (BAC) 366
Battersea Park 290
Battersea Park Zoo 290
Battersea Pie 185
Battersea Power Station 290, 392
B Bakery's Afternoon Tea
Bus 45
BBC Broadcasting House 145
BBC Proms 315
Beatles Store 147
Beaufort Bar 191
The Beaumont 399
Bedford Square 196
beer 57, 99
Begging Bowl 288
Belgrave Square 134
Belgravia 134
Benjamin Franklin House 190
Benjamin Pollock's Toy
Shop 187
Bentley's Oyster Bar &
Grill 154
Bermondsey 'Beer Mile' 99
Bermondsey Square Antiques
Market 98
Berners Tavern 207
Berry Bros & Rudd 160
Berwick Street 169, 170
Bethnal Green 268
Bethnal Green Working
Men's Club 350, 351
Bevis Marks Synagogue 233
BFI Flare: London LGBT Film

Festival 312, 326, 330
BFI IMAX 322
BFI Southbank 323
Big Ben 107, 108
Big Bus Company 76
Big Chill 339
Billingsgate Market 232
Bistrotheque 269
Black Box 273
black cabs 407
Black Cultural Archives 290
Black Death 379
Blackfriar 221, 222
Blackfriars Bridge 88, 221
Blackout II 187
Black Rock 229
Black Taxi Tours 76
Blade Rubber Stamps 201
Bleecker 112
Blenheim Crescent 296
Blind Pig 174
Blitz, the 383
Bloomberg London 391
Bloomsbury 196
Bloomsbury Bowling Lanes
201, 338, 346
Bloomsbury Central Baptist
Church 416
**Bloomsbury & King's Cross
192–209**
Bloomsbury Square 196
Blow Up 339
Bluebird 136
Blue Posts 169
Blues Kitchen 240, 339, 349
Boat-Ting Club 348
Bocca di Lupo 169
Boisdale of Belgravia 112
Bonfire Night 317
Book Club 338, 340
The Book of Mormon 364
Booking Office 205
Bookmongers 291
books 419
bookshops 68
Borderline 346, 349
Boris Bikes 76
Borough 90
Borough Market 93
Bounce Old Street 267
Boundary London 400
Boutique 1 139
bowling 201
Bow Street Magistrates
Court 182
Boxpark 267
Bradley's Spanish Bar 209
Brasserie Zédel 172
Brat 264
Bread Street Kitchen 224
Breaker's Yard 271
Brew By Numbers 99
Brewer Street 172
Brick Lane 258
Brick Lane Beigel Bake 259
Bridge Theatre 366
British Library 203
British Museum 15, 198, 391
British Pregnancy Advisory
Service 412
British Summer Time Festival 314
Brixton 289
Brixton Village 289, 291
Brixton Windmill 289
Broadcasting House 390

Broadway Market 271, 273
Brockwell Park 289
Brompton Cemetery 136, 303
Brompton Oratory 134, 416
Brook Advisory Centre 412
Brook Street 157
Browns 160
Brown's Hotel 45
Brunswick Centre 196
Buckingham Palace 114, 311, 389
Buck Street Market 244
Buddhapadipa Thai Temple 416
The Bull 249
Bull & Last 248
Bunhill Fields 227
Bun House 167
Burberry 156
Burberry factory outlet 273
bureaux de change 415
Burgh House 247
Burlington Arcade 160
Busaba Eathai 145
buses 407
Bush Hall 346, 348
Bushstock festival 313
Bussey Building (CLF Art
Cafe) 339

C

cable car 276, 277
Cadenhead's Whisky Shop &
Tasting Room 151
Cadogan Hall 355
Café Kick 219
Café Oto 271, 348, 349
cafés 59
Café Sou 224
Camberwell College of
Arts 287
Camden 240, 339
Camden Arts Centre 247
Camden Assembly 240, 340, 346
Camden Fringe festival 315
Camden Lock Market 244
Camden Market 240, 244
Camden Rocks Festival 313
Camisa 166
Camley Street Natural Park 204
Canada Water Library 392
Canal Museum 204
Canary Wharf 274
Can Be Done 411
Caravan King's Cross 205
Carlyle's House 137
Carnaby Street 172, 174
Carnaval del Pueblo 315
Cartoon Museum 207
Casa Pastor 205
Casbah Records 286
Cask 111
Cass Art 252
Casse-Croûte 96
Cecil Court 177
Cecil Sharp House 349
CellarDoor 351
Cenotaph 106
Centre of the Cell 263
Ceremony of the Keys 310
Ceviche 164

Changing the Guard 116, 311
Charing Cross Hospital 410

Charles Dickens Museum 196
Charlie Wright's International Bar 266, 348
The Cheese Bar 242
Cheesegrater 232
Chelsea 122, 136
Chelsea Arts Club 136
Chelsea Centenary Museum 137
Chelsea Farmers' Market 136
Chelsea FC 136
Chelsea Flower Show 313
Chelsea Old Church 136
Chelsea Physic Garden 137
Chelsea & Westminster Hospital 410
Chicken Shop 242
Chick'n'Sours 185
children
    travel 406
Chiltern Firehouse 149
Chiltern Street 147
Chinatown 175
Chinese New Year Festival 318
Chiswell Street Dining Rooms 229
Chiswick 304
Chiswick House & Gardens 304
Chiswick Park station 390
Christchurch Gardens 111
Christ Church Spitalfields 259
Christie's 112
Churchill War Rooms 110
Church Street 271
Ciné Lumière 324
Cinema Museum 184, 322
cinemas 320, 322
Cineworld at the O2 322
Circa 331
citizenM London Bankside 403
Citizens' Advice Bureaux 413
The City 210–237
City Càphê 232
City Cruises 76
City Hall 94, 391
City of London Information Centre 75, 214, 418
City of London Police Museum 230
City Social Bar 237
Clarence House 116
Claridge's 45, 399
classical music venues 354
Claude Bosi at Bibendum 131
Cleopatra's Needle 189
Clerkenwell 216
CLF Art Café at the Bussey Building 339
climate 411
Clink Prison Museum 90
Clissold Park 271
Clove Club 264
clubbing
    LGBT 334
    nightlife 340
The Coach 217
coaches 405
Coach & Horses 168
Coal Drops Yard 203
Coal Rooms 288
Coburg Bar 159
cocktails 57
Cock Tavern 272
Coco de Mer 188
coffee 59
Colbert 138
Coliseum 358

Collaborative Store 151
Columbia Road Market 270
Comedy Store 351
Common Greenway Café 276
Comptons of Soho 331
congestion charge 408
The Connaught Bar 159
Conran Shop 131
contraception 412
A Conversation with Oscar Wilde 189
Cooke, F 273
Copeland Social 342
Copita 169
Coram's Fields 197
Cork Street 157
Corsica Studios 339, 341, 346
County Hall 82
Courtauld Gallery 190
Couverture & the Garbstore 300
Covent Garden 178, 180
    shopping 67
Covent Garden Hotel 399
Covent Garden May Fayre & Puppet Festival 312
Covent Garden Piazza 180
Covent Garden & the Strand 178–191
craft beer 57
Craft Beer Company 252
Craft London 280
Cromwell, Oliver 378
Cross Keys 187
Crossrail 381, 407
Crown & Anchor 291
Crown Tavern 216
Crystal 276, 277
Cub 264
cuisine. *See* food
Curtain Theatre 264
Curzon cinemas 324
customs 410
Cutty Sark 280
Cutty Sark Tavern 286
cycling 409

D
Daily Express building 220, 390
Dalston 271
Dalston Eastern Curve Garden 271
Dalston Jazz Bar 271
Dalston Superstore 330, 334, 338
dance 347
Dance Umbrella 317
Daquise 131
Darwin Brasserie 237
Daunt Books 151
D.A.Y. 289
Dean Street 167
Delaunay 191
Dennis Severs' House 259
Dental Emergency Care Service 412
dentists 412
Department of Coffee & Social Affairs 216
department stores 65
Design Museum 302
dialling codes 417
Diamond 232
Diana, Princess of Wales Memorial Playground 133
Dictionary Hostel 403
Dinerama 48
Dingwalls 240
Directory Enquiries 417
Disability Rights UK 411
disabled resources 410
Discover Children's Story

Centre 276
Dishoom 185, 205
Diwali 317
Docklands 274
Docklands Light Railway 406
Donmar Warehouse 366
Doodle Bar 98
The Dorchester 399
Dover Street Market 119
Downing Street 106
Draft House 237
Drake's 160
Draper's Arms 250
Draughts Café 252
DR Harris 119
Drinking 54–61
driving 408
Dr Johnson's House 221
drugs 411
Dublin Castle 240
Duck & Waffle 237
Duke of Wellington 331
Duke of York Square 136
Dukes Bar 119
Dulwich Picture Gallery 287, 389

E
Eagle 216, 218
Eagle London 334
Earl of Essex 252
EartH 343
East End Film Festival 326
East London 254–277
East London Mosque 262, 416
East London Tech City 263
Eating 40–53
Edgware Road 147
Eleanor Cross 189
Electric Avenue 289
Electric Ballroom 240
Electric Brixton 339
Electric cinema 324
electricity 411
Elephant & Castle 88
Elizabeth I 378
Elizabeth II 114
Elliot's 92
Eltham Palace & Gardens 283
Ely Place 214
Embankment 189
Embankment Galleries 190
embassies & consulates 411
Ember Yard 169
Emery Walker's House 304
Emirates Air Line 276, 277
Emirates Stadium 250
Engineer 246
English National Opera 358
E Pellicci 269
Espresso Bar 244
Estorick Collection of Modern Italian Art 250
Ethos 207
Eventim Apollo 343
Events 308–319
Every Cloud 273
Everyman Cinemas 324
Exmouth Market 216, 218
Experimental Cocktail Club 177

F
Fabric 226, 339
FA Cup Final 312
family itinerary 27
Fan Museum 283
Faraday Museum 159
Farmacy 298
Farringdon 216
Fashion & Textile Museum

96
Fawkes, Guy 378
Fenchurch Restaurant 237
Fenton House 247
Fernandez & Wells 191
ferries 407
festivals. *See also* Events
    film 326
Field Day 313
Fischer's 149
Fitzrovia 206
Fitzroy Square 206
Fleet Street 220
Florence Nightingale Museum 83
Floris 119
food. *See also* Eating
    British 43
    brunch 46
    global 43
    tapas 46
    vegan/vegetarian 44
Foreign Office 390
Form SE15 289
Fortnum & Mason 119
Forum 240
Foster, Norman 391
Foundling Museum 197
Fourpure 99
Four Quarters 288
Foyles 166
Francis Crick Institute 204
Franco Manca 290
Frank's Cafe 288
Freedom Bar 331
Free Film Festivals 326
Freemasons' Hall 182, 390
French House 168
Frenchie 186
Freud Museum 247
Friendly Society 332
Frieze Art Fair, London 317
fringe 360
Frith Street 164
Fulham 303
Fulham Palace 303
Fuller's 304
Further Reference 419

G
Gabriel's Wharf 82
Gallery Mess 138
Gallery of Everything 151
Garage 347
Garden Museum 83
Gate Theatre 366
G-A-Y 330
G-A-Y Bar 332
gay London. *See* LGBT
Geffrye Museum 264
Gelupo 169
Genesis Cinema Whitechapel 325
George Tavern 355
George, The 91
German Gymnasium 205
Getting Around 404–409
Getting Started 72–77
Gherkin 233
Gibson Hall 233
gin 58
Globe Theatre 15, 88
Glory 330, 334, 350
Goat Race 312
Goddards at Greenwich 285
Golden Heart 258
Golden Hinde 91
Golden Square 172
Gŏng 98
Good Egg 272
Goodhood Store 267
Gosh! 171

Granary Square 392
Grant Museum of Zoology 197
Grapes 275
Grays Antique Market 161
Gray's Inn 214
Grays in the Mews 161
Great Christmas Pudding Race 318
Great Fire of London 379
Great Northern Hotel 400
Great Queen Street 186
Great River Race 316
Great Spitalfields Pancake Race 318
Greek Street 164
Green Note 350
Green Park 120
Greenwich 18, 280
Greenwich Dance 370
Greenwich & Docklands International Festival 314
Greenwich Market 286
Greenwich Peninsula 280
Greenwich Tourist Information Centre 75, 280, 418
Greenwich Union 285
Grosvenor Square 157
Groucho Club 167
Guards Museum 116
Guildhall 230, 231, 389
Guildhall Art Gallery 230, 231
Guildhall Library 230
Gunpowder 259
Gun Salutes 310
Gymkhana 159

H
Hackney 271
Hackney Central 271
Hackney Empire 271
Hackney Museum 271
Hackney Picturehouse 271, 325
Hackney Walk 273
Hackney Wick 271
Hadid, Zaha 134, 392
Halfway to Heaven 332
Hamilton 365
Hamleys 156
Hampstead 246
Hampstead Heath 246
Hampstead Heath Swimming Ponds 247
Hampstead Scientific Society Observatory 247
Hampton Court Palace 291
Hampton Court Palace Garden Festival 314
Handel & Hendrix in London 158
Happiness Forgets 267
Harley Street 145
Harrods 135
Harry Potter and the Cursed Child 365
Harry Potter Shop 202
Harvey Nichols 135
Harwood Arms 139
Hatton Garden 214
Hawksmoor, Nicholas 388
Hawksmoor Seven Dials 186
Hay's Galleria 94
Hayward Gallery 84, 391
Heal's 209
health 412
   emergencies 410
Heaven 330, 335
helplines 413
Henry VIII 378
Herman Ze German 167
Heron Tower 232
Highbury Fields 250

Highgate 249
Highgate Cemetery 249
Highgate Wood 249
Hill Garden & Pergola 247
History 374–385
HMS Belfast 96
Hogarth's House 305
Holborn 214
Holborn Information Kiosk 75, 418
Holland Park 301, 302
Holly Bush 247, 248
Holmes, Sherlock 149
Homeslice 207
Honest Jon's 300
Honey & Co 207
Hook Camden Town 243
Hoppers 164
Horniman Museum 287
Horse Guards Parade 311
Horse Meat Disco 330, 334
hospitals 412
Hostem 265
hotels 396
Hour Glass 131
Household Cavalry Museum 116
House of Hackney 268
House of Illustration 204
Houses of Parliament 107, 389
Hoxton 263
Hoxton Holborn 401
Hoxton Square Bar & Kitchen 347
Hoxton Street Monster Supplies 268
Human Rights Watch International Film Festival 326
Hunterian Museum 214
Hutong 97
Hyde Park 132
Hyde Park Corner 120
Hydra 338

I
ICA 116
Icco 207
ID 413
Idea Stores 392
Ikoyi 118
Imperial War Museum 86
Inner Temple 220
Institute of Contemporary Arts 116
internet 413
Islamic Cultural Centre & London Central Mosque 416
Island Gardens 274
Isle of Dogs 274
Islington 249
   shopping 67
Islington Museum 216
Itadaki Zen 46
Itineraries 22–29
Iveagh Bequest 248
Ivy House 288
Ivy Market Grill 186

J
Jacey Withers 269
James I 378
James J Fox 119
James Smith & Sons 188
Jamme Masjid Mosque 258
Japan Centre 177
Jason's Trip Canal Boats 76
Jazz Café 240, 347, 348
J Crew 156
Jermyn Street 119
Jerusalem Tavern 219
Jewel Tower 110
Jewish Museum 240
Jidori 272

John, Bell and Croyden 151
John Sandoe 139
John Wesley's House 227
Joli Vintage Living 286
Jones Dairy 269
Jones, Inigo 388
J Sheekey Atlantic Bar 187
Jubilee Gardens 82
Jugged Hare 229
juice bars 59

K
Kanada-Ya 186
Kapoor, Anish 392
K Bar 131
Keats House 247, 248
Kelmscott House 304
Kensal Green Cemetery 296
Kensington 301
Kensington Church Street 301
Kensington Gardens 132
Kensington Palace 133
Kentish Town 240
Kenwood House 248, 389
Kerb 48, 205
Kernel 99
Kerridge's Bar & Grill 106
Kew Gardens 17, 292, 310
Khan, Sadiq 32
Kiln Theatre 366
Kingly Court 175
King's Arms 332
King's Cross 292
King's Cross station 392
Kings Place 348, 355, 392
King's Road 136
The Kitchens 259
Kitty Fisher's 159
KJ's Laundry 152
Klaus Haapaniemi & Co 265
Knightsbridge 134
Koba 208
Koko 339, 340, 344
Kricket 172
Kristina Records 273
Ku Bar & Club 332
Kudu 287
K West 401

L
Labour & Wait 265
Ladies & Gentlemen 243
Lady Ottoline 201
Lamb 201
Lambeth 86
Lambeth Bridge 82
Lambeth Palace 82
Lamb Tavern 232
Langham 399
Langham Hotel 145
Langham Place 145
Lansdowne 246
Lantana 208
La Suite West 402
Lauderdale House 249
Leadenhall Market 232
League (EFL) Cup Final 310
Leather Lane 214
Lea Valley 276
Ledbury 298
left luggage 413
legal help 413
Leicester Square 175, 176
Leicester Square Theatre 351
Leighton House 302
Lemonia 246
Les Misérables 365
Lewis Leathers 209
Lexi cinema 325
Lexington 339, 347
LGBT 328–335, 413
LGBT bookshop 334
Liberal Jewish Synagogue 416

Liberty 19, 155, 390
Liberty Drives 133
Libreria 261
licensing laws 60
LIFT (London International Festival of Theatre) 313
Lima London 208
Lincoln's Inn Fields 214
Lisboa Pâtisserie 296
Little Angel Theatre 368
Lloyd's of London 232, 391
LN-CC 273
Lock & Co Hatters 120
Lock Tavern 243, 339, 341
London African Music Festival 315
London Beer Week 310
London Bicycle Tour Company 76
London Bridge 94
London Buddhist Centre 416
London Canal Museum 204
London Central Mosque 244
London City Airport 276
London Cocktail Week 317
London Design Festival 316
London Dungeon 84
London Edition 400
London Eye 84
London Fashion Week 316, 318
London Festival of Architecture 313
London Fields 271
London Film Festival 317, 326
London Film Museum 182, 322
London Helicopter 76
London International Animation Festival 326
London International Mime Festival 318
London Jazz Festival 317, 348
London Kayak Tours 76
London Literature Festival 316
London Marathon 312
London Mela 315
London Mithraeum Bloomberg Space 229, 231
London Museum of Water & Steam 305
London Pass 75
London Pavilion 154
London Review Bookshop 201
London Short Film Festival 326
London Silver Vaults 214
London Stone 230
London to Brighton Veteran Car Run 317
London Today 30–39
London Transport Museum 20, 183
London Transport Museum Depot 182
London Warehouse Events 338
London Waterbus Company 242
London Zoo 390
Look Mum No Hands 218
Lord Mayor's Show 317
Lord's Tour & MCC Museum 245
lost property 413
   airports 413
lost/stolen credit cards 415
Lovebox 314
LSO St Luke's 355
Lutyens & Rubinstein 300
Luxury Inn 403

Lyaness 86, 400
Lyle's 266
The Lyric 170
Lyric Hammersmith 367

M
MAC Carnaby 175
Machine-A 171
Madame Tussauds 148
Madhubon Sweet Centre 259
Magna Carta 377
Maison Bertaux 166
Maltby Street 98
Mansion House 229
M Manze 94
Marble Arch 145
Marie Stopes House 412
Maritime Greenwich 282
Maritime Museum 283
Market Row 202
markets 66. See also shops & services
Mark's Bar 174
Marksman 270
Marx Memorial Library 216
Marylebone 147
  shopping 67
Marylebone High Street 147
Marylebone Lane 147
Mary Stuart 379
Matches Fashion 273
Matilda the Musical 365
Maureen Paley Gallery 268
Mayfair 157
Mayor of Scaredy Cat Town 260
media 414
Medlar 139
Meltdown festival 315
Mercantile London 261
Methodist Central Hall 417
Michael, George 249
Middle Temple 220
Mildred's 46
Milk and Honey 174
Millbank 111
Millennium Bridge 88, 223
Millennium Dome 280. See also O2 Arena
minicabs 408
Ministry of Sound 339
Missing People helpline 413
mobile phones 417
mocktails 58
Modern Pantry 218
Modern Society 265
Mona Lisa 139
money 414
Monki 175
Monologue London 265
Monty's Deli 266
Monument 232, 235, 388
More London 94
Morito 219
Moro 219
Morris, William 274
Mortimer Market Centre for Sexual Health 412
Mr Fogg's Residence 45, 159
Mudchute Park & Farm 274
Muffin Man Tea Room 303
Multi-Storey Orchestra 355
Museum of Brands 298
Museum of Comedy 197
Museum of Immigration and Diversity 258

Museum of London 215, 226, 227
Museum of London Docklands 274
Museum of Methodism 227
Museum of the Order of St John 216, 217

Museum of St Bartholomew's Hospital 228
museums. See sights & museums
museum shops 68
Museum Tavern 201
music 421
Musical Museum 305
musicals 364

N
Nanban 290
Narrow 275
Nash, John 389
National Army Museum 138
National Dining Rooms 106
National Gallery 105
National Maritime Museum 283
National Portrait Gallery 105
National Rail 406
National Theatre 16, 82, 360
Natural History Museum 126, 390
Naughty Piglets 290
Neal's Yard Dairy 188
Near & Far 342
The Ned 399
Needoo Grill 259, 263
Nelson's Column 104
Nelson's Head 269
New Bloomsbury Set 332
Newport Street Gallery 85, 392
newspapers 414
New Year's Day Parade 318
New Year's Eve celebrations 318
NHS Direct helpline 413
NHS treatment 412
Nigel Cabourn Army Gym 188
Nightlife 336–351
Peckham 342
Night Tube 406
No.1 Poultry 229
North London 238–253
Notting Hill 296
Notting Hill Arts Club 341, 346
Notting Hill Carnival 294, 299, 315
Notting Hill Gate 296
Novelty Automation 197
Now Gallery 280

O
O2 Academy Brixton 344
O2 Arena 344, 350
O2 Forum Kentish Town 344
O2 Shepherd's Bush Empire 345
October Plenty festival 316
Odeon Leicester Square 323
off-West End theatres 366
Oklava 266
Old Bailey 224
Old Blue Last 267
Old Brewery 285
Old Compton Street 166, 330
Old Curiosity Shop 214
Ye Olde Cheshire Cheese 221
Ye Olde Mitre 214, 216

Old Operating Theatre, Museum & Herb Garret 91
Old Queen's Head 251, 341
Old Royal Naval College 283
Oldroyd 250
Old Spitalfields Market 258, 261

Old Truman Brewery 258
Old Vic 362
Olympic Park 276, 392
Olympic Stadium 276
OnBlackheath festival 316
One Canada Square 274, 391
One New Change 223, 226
Open Air Theatre 244, 362
Open City London Documentary Festival 326
Open Garden Squares Weekend 313
Open House London 316
opening hours 64, 415
Opera Holland Park 313
opera venues 358
Order of St John 216
Original London Sightseeing Tour 76
Original London Walks 76
Oriole 229
Oslo 347
Otherworld 316
Ottolenghi 250
outdoor cinema 326
Oval Space 340
Overground trains 406
Owl & Pussycat 265
Oxford & Cambridge Boat Race 312
Oxford Street 144
Oxford Street, Marylebone & Mayfair 140–161
Oxo Tower Restaurant 86
Oxo Tower Wharf 82
Oyster cards 76, 405

P
Paddington Station 147
Padella 92
Painted Lady 265
Palace of Westminster 108
Palace Theatre 175
Pall Mall 112
Palomar 176
Parasol Unit 264
parking 408
Parkside Café & Terrace 285
Park Theatre 367
Parliament Square 106
Partizan 99
El Pastór 92
Paternoster Square 223
Paul Smith 161
Pearly Kings and Queens Harvest Festival 316
Peckham 286
Peckham Levels 286, 342
Peckham Library 286, 392
PeckhamPlex 327
Peckham Springs 342
Peninsula Garden 280
Pentreath & Hall 202
Performing Arts 352–371
Persephone Books 202
Persepolis 288
Peter Pan 132
Petrie Museum of Egyptian Archaeology 200
Petticoat Lane Market 258
P Franco 272
pharmacies 412
Phoenix cinema 327
Phonox 339, 341
Photographers' Gallery 172
Piccadilly 157
Piccadilly Circus 152
Pickle Factory 345
Picturehouse Central 323
The Pilgrm 402
Pineapple 243
Pizarro Restaurant 98
Pizza East 242

Pizza Express Jazz Club 350
The Place 370
Planetarium. See Royal Observatory
Platform 9¾ 202
playground 132, 133
The Play that Goes Wrong 366
police 415
Pollock's Toy Museum 207
Polpo Soho 172
Pop Brixton 289
Pop Up Screens 326
Portland 208
Portland Place 145
Portobello Film Festival 326
Portobello Road Market 300
Portobello Star 300
Port of London HQ 235
Postal Museum & Mail Rail 217
postal services 416
Postcard Teas 161
poste restante 416
Postman's Park 226, 228
post offices 416
price categories
  hotels 396
  restaurants 42
Prick 66
Pride London festival 314, 330
Pride of Spitalfields 258
Primrose Hill 244
Prince Charles cinema 176, 323
Princess Diana Memorial Fountain 132
Princess Louise 216
Pringle 273
Printworks 339, 340
Prism 152
Prospect of Whitby 274
Providores & Tapa Room 150
Prufrock Coffee 216
pub classical 355
public holidays 416
public transport 405, 413
pubs & bars 54–61, 56
  Bethnal Green 270
  Bloomsbury 201
  Borough 93
  Camden & around 243
  Chinatown 177
  Clerkenwell 219
  Covent Garden 187
  Dalston & Hackney 272
  Docklands 275
  Farringdon 219
  Fitzrovia 209
  Fleet Street 222
  Greenwich 285
  Hampstead 248
  Highgate 249
  Holborn 216
  Islington 251
  King's Cross & St Pancras 205
  LGBT 331
  London Bridge to Tower Bridge 98
  Marylebone & Baker Street 151
  Mayfair 159
  Millbank 111
  Monument 235
  North of St Paul's 229
  Notting Hill 300
  Old Compton Street 168
  outdoor 59
  Peckham 288
  Shoreditch & Hoxton 266
  South Bank 86

South Kensington 131
Spitalfields & Brick Lane 260
St James's 119
Strand, Embankment & Aldwych 191
Temple 222
Tower of London 237
Trafalgar Square 110
Vauxhall & Brixton 291
Victoria 112
Wardour Street 170
Waterloo & Lambeth 88
West Soho 174
Pump House Gallery 290
puppet & children's theatres 368
Purl 151

Q

Qbic London City Hotel 403
Queen Adelaide 332
Queen Elizabeth Olympic Park 276
Queen Mary's Garden 244
Queen of Hoxton cinema 326
Queen's House 284, 388
Queen Sonia 365
Quo Vadis 168

R

Rabbit 139
radio 414
Ragged School Museum 269
Raindance Festival 326
Ranger's House 284
Rape Crisis helpline 413
Rasa 271
Rasa W1 159
Raven Row 264
record shops 68
Redchurch Street 18, 265
Red House 304
Red Lion 110
Regency Café 112
Regent's Canal 240, 242
Regent's Park 244
Regent Street 152, 154, 389
Regent Street Cinema 327
religion 416
Religious Society of Friends (Quakers) 417
Remembrance Sunday Ceremony 317
Renaissance St Pancras 390
Resources A-Z 410–418
restaurants
    Bank 232
    Bankside 90, 92
    Bethnal Green 269
    Bloomsbury 201
    Camden & around 242
    cheap 50
    Chelsea 138
    Chinatown 176
    Clerkenwell 217
    Covent Garden 185
    Dalston & Hackney 272
    Docklands 275
    Farringdon 217
    Fitzrovia 207
    Greenwich 285
    high end 50
    Holborn 216
    Hyde Park & Kensington Gardens 134
    Islington 250
    Kensington & Holland Park 303
    King's Cross & St Pancras 205
    Knightsbridge 134

LGBT 331
London Bridge to Tower Bridge 96
Marylebone & Baker Street 149
Mayfair 159
Monument 237
North of St Paul's 229
Notting Hill 298
Old Compton Street 167
Oxford Street 145
Peckham 287
Piccadilly Circus & Regent Street 154
Regent's Park & around 246
Shoreditch & Hoxton 264
Soho Square & around 164
South Bank 86
South Kensington 131
Spitalfields & Brick Lane 259
St James's 118
St Paul's Cathedral 224
Strand, Embankment & Aldwych 191
Tower of London 237
Vauxhall & Brixton 290
Victoria 112
walk-in 43
Wardour Street 169
Waterloo & Lambeth 87
West Soho 172
Whitechapel 263
Restaurant Story 98
Retro Bar 333
Reuters building 220
Revealing the Charterhouse 217
Review 289
Richard I 285
RideLondon 315
Rigby & Peller 161
Rio Cinema 327
Ritz 120
Ritzy Cinema 289
Ritzy Picturehouse 327
Roald Dahl Museum & Story Centre 148
Rochelle Canteen 266
Roka 209
Roman wall 388
Ronnie Scott's 350
Rookery 401
Roti Chai 146
Rough Trade East 262
Roundhouse 240, 345
Routemaster buses 76
Royal Academy of Arts 158
Royal Academy of Music 147
Royal Albert Hall 126, 343, 356
Royal Ballet 369
Royal Botanic Gardens, Kew 17, 292, 304
Royal China 134
Royal College of Art 126
Royal College of Music 126
Royal Courts of Justice 220, 222, 390
Royal Court Theatre 362
Royal Docks 276
Royal Exchange 229, 232
Royal Festival Hall 82, 391
Royal Free Hospital 410
Royal Hospital Chelsea 138
Royal Institution 159
Royal London Hospital 410
Royal London Hospital Archives & Museum 263
Royal Mews 114
Royal Oak 93
Royal Observatory & Planetarium 285

Royal Opera House 184, 359, 369
Royal Shakespeare Company 364
Royal Society of Arts 389
Royal Victoria Dock 274
Rupert Street Bar 333
Russell Square 196
RVT 330, 335, 350
Rye Wax 342

S

Saatchi Gallery 138
Sadler's Wells Theatre 370
Safestay Holland Park 302
safety 417
Sager + Wilde Paradise Row 270
St Anne Limehouse 389
St Bride's 388
St Clement Danes 189, 389
St George-in-the-East 389
St George's Bloomsbury 200, 389
St James's Park 19
St James's Piccadilly 356
St John-at-Hampstead Church 247
St John's Smith Square 357
St John's Wood 244
St Luke's 136
St Martin-in-the-Fields 357, 389
St Mary Abbots 301
St Mary-le-Strand 189, 389
St Mary's Hospital 410
St Mary Woolnoth 389
St Nicholas 305
St Pancras 202
St Pancras Gardens 204
St Pancras International 204, 390
St Pancras Old Church 204
St Patrick's Day Parade & Festival 312
St Paul's Cathedral 16, 388, 416
St Paul's Covent Garden 184, 388
St Thomas' Hospital 410
St Alban 231
St Andrew Undershaft 233
St Bartholomew-the-Great 226, 228
St Bartholomew's Hospital 226
St Botolph's-without-Aldgate 233, 236
St Bride's 220, 222
St Clement 230
St Dunstan-in-the-West 220
St Edmund the King 230
St Ethelburga Centre for Reconciliation & Peace 236
St Etheldreda 214
St George's Church 157
St Giles Cripplegate 227
St Helen's Bishopsgate 233, 236
St James Garlickhythe 223
St James's 112
St James's Café 118
St James's Palace 112
St James's Park 112
St James's Piccadilly 116

St James's Roman Catholic Church 147
St John (restaurant) 216, 219
St Katharine Cree 233
St Katharine Docks 235
St Lawrence Jewry 231

St Lawrence Jewry Memorial Fountain 223
St Magnus the Martyr 232, 236
St Margaret Lothbury 230
St Margaret Pattens 232
St Margaret's 110
St Martin-in-the-Fields 106
St Mary Abchurch 230
St Mary Aldermary 223
St Marylebone Church 147
St Mary-le-Bow 223
St Mary Woolnoth 230
St Michael Cornhill 230
St Michael Paternoster Royal 230
St Olave 233
St Paul's Cathedral 223, 224
St Peter-upon-Cornhill 230
St Stephen Walbrook 229
St Vedast-alias-Foster 226
Sake no Hana 118
Salut! 250
Samaritans helpline 413
Sam Wanamaker Playhouse 89
Sanctum Soho 402
Satan's Whiskers 270
Savage 335
Savile Row 157
Savoy Hotel 189
Scala 346
Science Museum 127, 392
Scottish Stores 205
Sea Containers London 86, 399
Sea Life London Aquarium 85
Secret Cinema 326
security 417
Sefton 67
Selfridges 146
Senate House 196
Serpentine 132
Serpentine Gallery 133
Serpentine Sackler Gallery 133, 392
sexual health clinics 412
Shacklewell Arms 340, 343, 347
Shaftesbury Avenue 175
Shaftesbury Memorial 152
Shakespeare's Globe 15, 88, 363
Shangri-La at the Shard 400
The Shard 14, 94, 391
The Shed 303
J Sheekey 186
Shepherd Market 157
Sherlock Holmes Museum 148
SHE Soho 333
The Shop at Bluebird 188
Shopping 62–69
shopping districts 67
shops & services 135
    Bank 232
    Bethnal Green 270
    Bloomsbury 201
    Borough 93
    Camden & around 244
    Chelsea 139
    Chinatown 177
    Covent Garden 187
    Dalston & Hackney 273
    Fitzrovia 207
    Greenwich 286
    Islington 252
    King's Cross & St Pancras 206
    London Bridge to Tower Bridge 98
    Marylebone & Baker Street 151

Mayfair 160
Notting Hill 300
Old Compton Street 168
Oxford Street 146
Peckham 289
Piccadilly Circus & Regent Street 156
Shoreditch & Hoxton 267
Soho Square & around 166
South Kensington 131
Spitalfields & Brick Lane 260
St James's 119
St Paul's 226
Vauxhall & Brixton 291
Wardour Street & around 170
West Soho 174
Shoreditch 263, 338
shopping 67
Shoreditch House 402
Shoryu Ramen 176
Shrek's Adventure! 86
Shuang Shuang 177
sights & museums
Bank 231
Bankside 88, 91
Bethnal Green 269
Bloomsbury 196
Camden & around 240
Chelsea 137
Chiswick 304
Clerkenwell 216
Covent Garden 182
Dalston & Hackney 271
Docklands 274
Earl's Court & Fulham 303
Farringdon 216
Fitzrovia 206
Fleet Street 221
Green Park & Hyde Park Corner 120
Greenwich 280
Hampstead 247
Highgate 249
Holborn 214
Hyde Park & Kensington Gardens 133
Islington 250
Kensington & Holland Park 301
King's Cross & St Pancras 203
Knightsbridge 134
London Bridge to Tower Bridge 96
Marylebone & Baker Street 147
Mayfair 158
Monument 235
North of St Paul's 227
Notting Hill 296
Olympic Park & Lea Valley 277
Oxford Street 145
Peckham 287
Piccadilly Circus & Regent Street 154
Regent's Park 245
Shoreditch & Hoxton 264
South Bank 83
South Kensington 126
Spitalfields & Brick Lane 259
St James's 114
St Paul's 224

Strand, Embankment & Aldwych 190
Temple 221
Tower of London 235
Trafalgar Square 105, 108
Vauxhall & Brixton 290
Victoria 111

Waterloo & Lambeth 86
West Soho 172
Whitechapel 263
Singapore Garden 246
Sir John Soane's Museum 214, 215, 389
Six Nations Tournament 318
Skoob 202
Sky Garden 232, 236
Skylon 84
Sky Pod Bar 237
Sloane Square 136
Small Car Big City 76
Smithfield Market 226
Smokehouse 251
Smoke & Salt 291
Smokestak 260
smoking 417
Smoking Goat 266
Smythson 161
Snaps & Rye 300
Soane, John 389
Social Eating House 174
Soho 162
LGBT scene 330
shopping 67
Soho House 167
Soho & Leicester Square 162–177
Soho Square 164
Soho Theatre 350, 367
Somerset House 190
Somerset House outdoor cinema 326
Somerset House Summer Series 314
Som Saa 260
Sông Quê 264
Sounds of the Universe 171
South Bank & Bankside 78–99
Southbank Centre 82, 343, 348, 357
Southgate station 390
South Kensington & Chelsea 122–139
South London 278–293
South London Gallery 287
South Molton Street 157
Southwark Cathedral 91
South West Four festival 315
Spa Terminus 98
Speakers' Corner 132
Spencer House 118
Spice of Life 348
Spiritland 206
Spitalfields 258
Spitalfields City Farm 259
Spitalfields Music Festival 318
Spring Garden 289
SSE Arena, Wembley 346, 350
Stables Market 244
Stafford Terrace 301
Stamford Bridge 136, 303
Star of Kings 339
State Opening of Parliament 313
STDs 412
Stella McCartney 161
Stephen's Tavern 110
Stoke Newington 271
The Strand 178, 189
Strawberry Hill 293
Street Feast 48
street food 48
streetlamps 118
Summer Streets 314
Sunspel 265
Supreme 171
Supreme Court 110
Sushisamba 237
Sutton House 271
Swan at Shakespeare's Globe 90

Sweetings 226
Swift 168

T
Tamada 246
Tandoor Chop House 187
Tasting Rooms 286
Tate Britain 19, 113
Tate Modern 89, 391
Tate-to-Tate boat 89
Tatty Devine 262
tax 415
taxis 407, 413
black cabs 407
minicabs 408
Uber 408
Tayyabs 259, 263
Telegraph building 220
telephones 417
television 414
Temper 170
Temple 220
Temple Bar 223
Temple Church 220, 222
Temple of Seitan 46
Ten Bells 258
tennis
Fever-Tree Championships 313
Wimbledon Championships 314
Terrence Higgins Trust 412
Terroirs 187
terrorist attacks 106
Thames Barrier 285
Thames Barrier Park 276
Thames Clipper 280
Thames Path 293
Thames RIB Experience 76
theatre 359
theatre Districts 359
Theatre Royal 182
Theatre Royal Haymarket 389
Theatre Royal Stratford East 367
Three Mills Island 276, 277
Ticketmaster 360
time 417
Tipperary 221
tipping 417
tkts 360
toilets 417
Top 20 12–21
Topshop/Topman 146
Totally Thames Festival 315
Tourism for All 411
tourist information centres 418
Tour of Britain 315
tours 76
Tower 42 232
Tower Bridge 94, 235, 390
Tower Bridge Exhibition 237
Tower House 263
Tower of London 17, 233, 234, 388
Town Hall Hotel 390
Town of Ramsgate 274
Trafalgar Square 104
trains 406
transport 404
children 406
fares 406
Transport for London 413
travel advice 410
travelcards 405
travel information centres 75, 405
Trellick Tower 296
Trinity Buoy Wharf 276, 277
Trinity House 263
Trinity Laban Conservatoire 370
Trinity Square Gardens 235
Trooping the Colour 311

Troubadour 303
Trullo 251
tube, see Underground 406
twentytwentyone 252
Twickenham Rugby Stadium 293
Twickenham Visitor Information Centre 418
Twinings 222
Twist 150
Two Temple Place 220, 222
Tyburn 145

U
UK Black Pride 331
Underground trains 406
Underworld 240, 347
Union Chapel 250, 348, 350
Universal Works 170
University College Hospital 410
University of London 196
Unseen Tours 76
Up at the O2 280
Up the Creek 351

V
V&A Museum of Childhood 269
VAT 415
Vauxhall 289
LGBT scene 330
Vauxhall Cross 111
Vauxhall Tavern 289
vegan and vegetarian restaurants 44
VFD 335
Victim Support helpline 413
Victoria 111, 380
Victoria & Albert Museum 12, 128
Victoria Beckham 161
Victoria Miro 264
Victoria Park 271
Victoria Tower Gardens 111
View Tube 276
Viktor Wynd Museum of Curiosities 269
Village Soho 333
Village Underground 340, 348
Vintage Showroom 188
Vortex Jazz Club 271, 348, 350

W
Wahaca 185
WAH Nails 171
Walker's Quay 242
Walkie Talkie 232
walking 409
Wallace Collection 148
Wapping 274
Wardour Street 169
Warner Brothers Studios London 202
Waterloo 86
Waterloo Bridge 82
Waterloo Tap 86
Waterlow Park 249
Waterstones Piccadilly 120
water transport 407
Way Out Club 335
weather 411
websites 421
We Built This City 175
weekend itinerary 22

weights & measures 418
Wellcome Collection 200
Wellington Arch 121
Wembley 305
Wembley Stadium 305
West Central Liberal Synagogue 416

Western Union 414
West London 294–305
Westminster 100
Westminster Abbey 108, 388, 416
Westminster & St James's 100–121
Westminster Arms 110
Westminster Bridge 82
Westminster Cathedral 111, 416
wheelchair access 410
Wheelchair Travel & Access Mini Buses 411
Whitechapel 262
Whitechapel Bell Foundry 262

Whitechapel Gallery 262, 263, 392
Whitechapel Road 259
White Cube art gallery 94
Whitehall 106
Whole Foods Market 301
Wigmore Hall 358
Wildflower 287
wild swimming 274
William Morris Gallery 274, 304
Wilton's Music Hall 367
Wimbledon Lawn Tennis Museum 293
Wimpole Street 145
Windmill 348
wine 58

Wireless Festival 314
W London Leicester Square 401
Wolseley 118
Woolwich Ferry 285
Woolwich Foot Tunnel 285
Word on the Water 272
World's End 136, 240
WoW: Women of the World 310
Wren, Christopher 379, 388
WWT Wetland Centre 293

X
XOYO 338, 343
Xu 177
XXL 335

Y
The Yard 367
Yard 334
Yashin 303
Yauatcha 170
YMC 175
Young Vic 86, 368

Z
Zabludowicz Collection 240
Zetter Hotel 403
Zetter Townhouse 400
Z Hotel Soho 403
Zoilo 150
zoo
ZSL London Zoo 245
ZTH Cocktail Lounge 219

Picture credits

2 (bottom) GagliardiImages/Shutterstock.com; 2 (top), 295 Gareth Gardner/Design Museum; 3 © Plastiques Photography, courtesy Science Museum Group; 5, 18 (middle), 279, 284 © National Maritime Museum, Greenwich, London; 6 S.Borisov/Shutterstock.com; 13 (top) Kerb Food; 13 (bottom) photocritical/Shutterstock.com; 14 (top) Alexey Fedorenko/Shutterstock.com; 14 (bottom) Hutong; 15 (top), 104 Claudio Divizia/Shutterstock.com; 15 (bottom) CLS Digital Arts/Shutterstock.com; 16 (top) Graham W Lacdao; 16 (middle) Ralf Neumann/Shutterstock.com; 16 (bottom) asiastock/Shutterstock.com; 17 (top) Historic Royal Palaces; 17 (middle) VASYL LEIBIUK/Shutterstock.com; 17 (bottom) © RBG Kew; 18 (top) Dean and Chapter of Westminster Abbey; 18 (bottom), 301 (top) Christian Mueller/Shutterstock.com; 19 (top), 141, 155 Liberty London, libertylondon.com; 19 (bottom) irisphoto1/Shutterstock.com; 20 (top) CLF Art Café; 20 (bottom) Conran Design; 22 Salvador Maniquiz/Shutterstock.com; 23 (top) Dave Goodman/Shutterstock.com; 23 (bottom) Mike Smallcombe; 24 (top), 74, 144, 291 Willy Barton/Shutterstock.com; 24 (bottom) Brynley Davies; 25 (top) © V&A. Alan Williams Photography; 25 (bottom) simona flamigini/Shutterstock.com; 26 (top), 275 Graphical_Bank/Shutterstock.com; 26 (bottom) August_0802/Shutterstock.com; 27 (top), 276 Phillip Maguire/Shutterstock.com; 27 (botttom) Georgethefourth/Shutterstock.com; 28 (top), 158, 221, 388 chrisdorney/Shutterstock.com ; 28 (middle), 166 ChameleonsEye/Shutterstock.com; 28 (bottom) Raymond Gubbay Ltd/RGB Kew; 31 GMIsserlis/Shutterstock.com; 32 keith Larby/Shutterstock.com; 33 R A Mukerjea/Shutterstock.com; 34 Ben Gingell/Shutterstock.com; 36 Lenscap Photography/Shutterstock.com; 37 Ink Drop/Shutterstock.com; 41 Social Eating House; 42 Andy Parsons/Time Out; 44 (top) Caitlin Isola; 44 (bottom) © Per-Anders Jorgensen; 45 Mr Fogg's ;46, 79, 92 Helen Cathcart/El Pastór; 48 debora palazzo/Savage Salads; 49 Savage Salads; 49 (right) Club Mexicana; 50, 93 (bottom), 163 Alena.Kravchenko/Shutterstock.com; 51 Roka; 52 Time Out; 55 Bar Américain; 56 (top) Alys Tomlinson/Time Out; 56 (bottom) jean.cuomo/Shutterstock.com; 57, 168, 251 Addie Chinn; 58 (top), 321 Rob Greig/Time Out; 58 (bottom) Oliver Dixon; 59 Sipsmith Distillery; 60 Dave Carr-Smith; 63, 179 The Shop at Bluebird; 64, 68 Ed Marshall/Time Out; 65 (top), 137, 198, 265 Britta Jaschinski/Time Out; 65 (bottom) Kevin Lake/We Built This City; 66 (top) Paolo Paradiso/Shutterstock.com; 66 (bottom), 270 ElenaChaykinaPhotography/Shutterstock.com; 67 DrimaFilm/Shutterstock.com; 70 f11photo/Shutterstock.com; 73 Neil Lang/Shutterstock.com; 82, 90 Philip Bird LRPS CPAGB/Shutterstock.com; 83 Morley von Sternberg; 84, 199 (bottom) FotoGraphic/Shutterstock.com; 85 alachan/Shutterstock.com; 87 Pajor Pawel/Shutterstock.com; 88 Pres Panayotov/Shutterstock.com; 89 A.B.G./Shutterstock.com; 91 Marius_Comanescu/Shutterstock.com; 93 (top), 121, 239, 242, 248, 262, 409 I Wei Huang/Shutterstock.com; 95, 146, 184 Tony Baggett/Shutterstock.com; 96 Melanie Major/Shutterstock.com; 99 Matt Hickman/Anspach & Hobday; 101, 105, 189, 408 Bikeworldtravel/Shutterstock.com; 107 Offcaania/Shutterstock.com; 109, 114, 132 cowardlion/Shutterstock.com; 113, 129 (bottom), 258 Kiev.Victor/Shutterstock.com; 117 Uellue/Shutterstock.com; 123 khankanen/Shutterstock.com; 127 elRoce/Shutterstock.com; 129 (top), 152, 365 Chrispictures/Shutterstock.com; 130 Jody Kingzett; 133 Ron Ellis/Shutterstock.com; 135 Ioan Florin Cnejevici; 149 Anton_Ivanov/Shutterstock.com; 150 © The Wallace Collection; 156 Benjamin B/Shutterstock.com; 167 Stephen Morris; 170, 208 Ming Tang-Evans/Time Out; 176 chaloemsak seesaikam/Shutterstock.com; 180 Christian Bertrand/Shutterstock.com; 182 Thomas Hauschildt/Shutterstock.com; 183 Heike Bohnstengel/Time Out ; 190 Mabelwhite/Shutterstock.com; 191, 358 Cedric Weber/Shutterstock.com; 193 Ben Gilbert/Wellcome Collection; 199 (top) FenlioQ/Shutterstock.com; 200 Michael Bowles/Wellcome Collection; 203 Hufton + Crow/John Sturrock; 205 AC Manley/Shutterstock.com; 211 ZGPhotography/Shutterstock.com; 215, 349 Jonathan Perugia/Time Out ; 218 Miles Willis; 223 antb/Shutterstock.com; 224 PitK/Shutterstock.com; 225 Luciano Mortula - LGM/Shutterstock.com; 230 Pavel Rumme/Shutterstock.com; 233 peresanz/Shutterstock.com; 234 Historic Royal Palaces/Royal Armouries; 235 Historic Royal Palaces/James Linsell-Clark; 243 Jennifer Balcombe; 245 marcela novotna/Shutterstock.com; 246 BBA Photography/Shutterstock.com; 255 Sven Hansche/Shutterstock.com; 260 Iwan Baan/Libreria; 261 DrimaFilm/Shutterstock.com; 267 Alistair Hall/www.wemadethis.co.uk; 268 House of Hackney; 282, 316, 393 BBA Photography/Shutterstock.com; 292 Kornelija Cakarun/Shutterstock.com; 296 Richie Chan/Shutterstock.com; 299 Ms Jane Campbell/Shutterstock.com; 301 (bottom) Bruno Mameli/Shutterstock.com; 302 Kit Leong/Shutterstock.com; 306 Johan Persson; 309 Giles Smith; 310 Historic Royal Palaces/Richard Lea-Hair; 311 stoyanh/Shutterstock.com; 312 Mr Pics/Shutterstock.com; 314 Pres Panayotov/Shutterstock.com; 325 Alastair Philip Wiper; 326 Peter Macdiarmid/Somerset House; 327 Adam Lee Davies; 329 Kath Watson/Shutterstock.com; 330, 364 John Gomez/Shutterstock.com; 333 charliebard.com; 337, 340 © Photography by Jake Davis (fb.com/hungryvisuals); 338 South London Soul Train; 342 Bold Tendencies; 345 Caro Gomes Pak; 345 Luke Hayes; 353 © ROH/Bill Cooper; 354 a-image/Shutterstock.com; 357 (top) Chris Christodoulou; 357 (bottom) David Iliff; 359 © ROH 2019/Clive Barda; 360, 361 (left) National Theatre; 361 (right) Franklyn Rodgers; 362 Thinglass/Shutterstock.com; 363 Gimas/Shutterstock.com; 368 Ellie Kurtz; 369 (top) © ROH/Johan Persson; 369 (bottom) Alice Pennefather; 370 Philip Vile; 372 Lois GoBe/Shutterstock.com; 375, 380, 382 Everett Historical/Shutterstock.com; 376 Alexey Fedorenko/Shutterstock.com; 378 Everett - Art/Shutterstock.com; 379 Vincent Brault/Ens de Lyon William Hogarth [Public domain], via Wikimedia Commons; 384, 406 mikecphoto/Shutterstock.com; 387 The-Walker/Shutterstock.com; 390 ileana_bt/Shutterstock.com; 394 sematadesign/Shutterstock.com; 396 The Beaumont; 398 (top) Great Northern Hotel; 398 (bottom) Willy Barton/Shutterstock.com; 401 Hoxton Holborn; 402 Qbic London City Hotel; 407 Chris Jenner/Shutterstock.com; 418 Andriy Blokhin/Shutterstock.com

Credits

Crimson credits

Editor Sophie Blacksell Jones
Contributors Sonya Barber, Megan Carnegie, Katie Dailey, Kitty Drake, Nicola Gibbs, Thomas Howells, Nick Levine, Andrzej Lukowski, James Manning, Ellie Walker-Arnott
Proofreader Ros Sales
Layouts Emilie Crabb, Patrick Dawson
Cartography Gail Armstrong

Series Editor Sophie Blacksell Jones
Production Manager Kate Michell
Design Mytton Williams

Chairman David Lester
Managing Director Andy Riddle

Advertising Media Sales House
Marketing Lyndsey Mayhew-Dehaney
Sales Lyndsey Mayhew-Dehaney

Acknowledgements

The editor would like to thank the staff at Time Out London, especially Gail Tolley, James Manning and Ellie Walker-Arnott, and all contributors to previous editions of *Time Out London* whose work forms the basis of this guide.

Photography credits

Front cover dynasoar/iStockphoto
Back cover left: Lois GoBe/Shutterstock.com; centre: Richie Chan/Shutterstock.com; right: Willy Barton/Shutterstock.com.
Interior photography credits, *see p428*

Publishing information

London City Guide 25th edition
© TIME OUT ENGLAND LIMITED 2019
May 2019

ISBN 978 1 780592 67 1
CIP DATA: A catalogue record for this book is available from the British Library

Published by Crimson Publishing
21d Charles Street, Bath, BA1 1HX (01225 584 950, www.crimsonpublishing.co.uk) on behalf of Time Out England.

Distributed by Grantham Book Services
Distributed in the US and Canada by Publishers Group West (1-510-809-3700)

Printed by Replika Press, India

London Transport Map

TRANSPORT
FOR LONDON

UNDERGROUND

EVERY JOURNEY MATTERS

ail updates
:/emailupdates

@TfLTravelAlerts

urney, please check before you travel

Version A TfL 12.2018

Correct at time of going to print

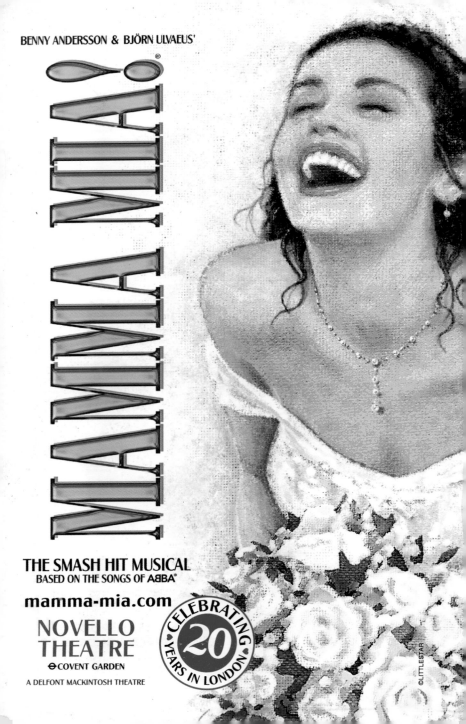